PRICE AND PRODUCTIVITY MEASUREMENT

Volume 6 - Index Number Theory

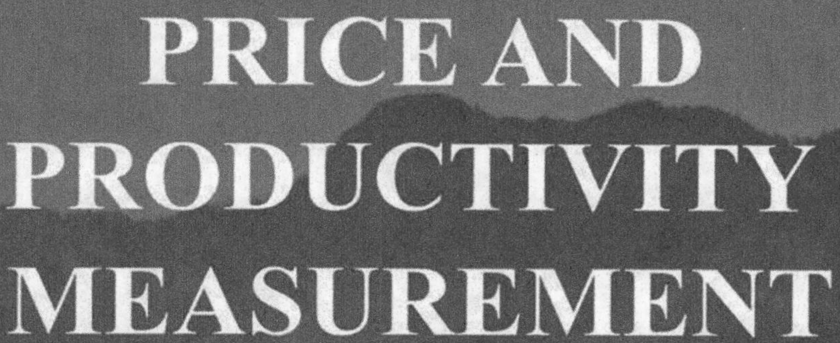

Volume Editors
W. Erwin Diewert, Bert M. Balk, Dennis Fixler,
Kevin J. Fox, Alice O. Nakamura

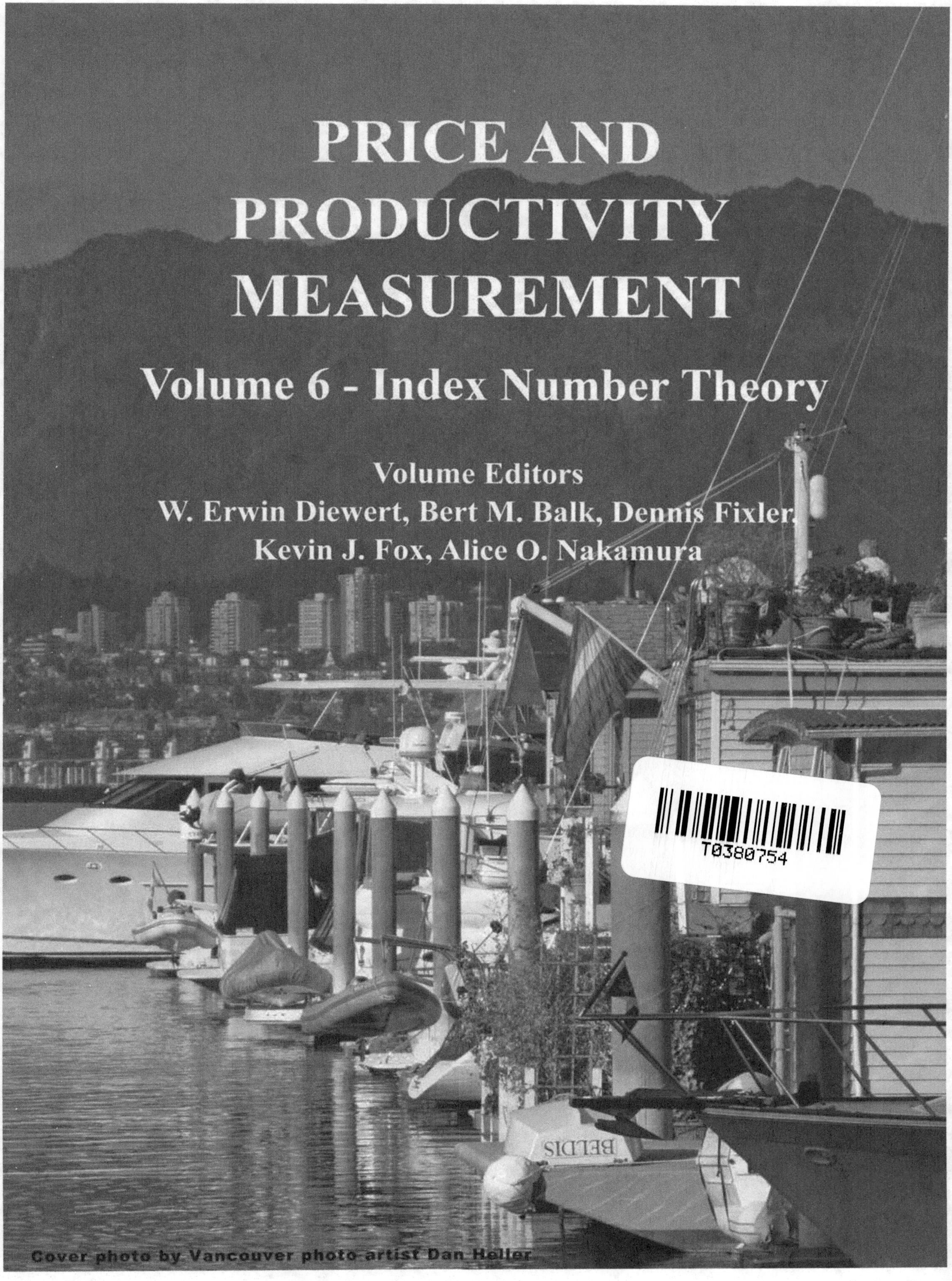

T0380754

Cover photo by Vancouver photo artist Dan Heller

Order this book online at www.trafford.com
or email orders@trafford.com

Most Trafford titles are also available at major online book retailers.

© Copyright 2012 Alice Nakamura.
All rights reserved. No part of this publication may be reproduced, stored in a retrieval system, or transmitted, in any form or by any means, electronic, mechanical, photocopying, recording, or otherwise, without the written prior permission of the author.

Printed in the United States of America.

ISBN: 978-1-4251-7780-5 (sc)

Trafford rev. 02/05/2012

www.trafford.com

North America & international
toll-free: 1 888 232 4444 (USA & Canada)
phone: 250 383 6864 • fax: 812 355 4082

PRICE AND PRODUCTIVITY MEASUREMENT: Volume 6 -- Index Number Theory

W. Erwin Diewert, Bert M. Balk, Dennis Fixler, Kevin J. Fox and Alice O. Nakamura (editors)

1. INTRODUCTION TO INDEX NUMBER THEORY FOR PRICE AND PRODUCTIVITY MEASUREMENT
Bert M. Balk, W. Erwin Diewert and Alice O Nakamura — 1-10

PART I Productivity Measures and Decompositions

2. MEASURING MULTI-FACTOR PRODUCTIVITY WHEN RATES OF RETURN ARE EXOGENOUS
Paul Schreyer — 13-40

3. ON MEASURING THE CONTRIBUTION OF ENTERING AND EXITING FIRMS TO AGGREGATE PRODUCTIVITY GROWTH
W. Erwin Diewert and Kevin J. Fox — 41-66

4. ON THE TANG AND WANG DECOMPOSITION OF LABOUR PRODUCTIVITY GROWTH INTO SECTORAL EFFECTS
W. Erwin Diewert — 67-76

5. EXACT INDUSTRY CONTRIBUTIONS TO LABOR PRODUCTIVITY CHANGE
Marshall Reinsdorf and Robert Yuskavage — 77-102

6. LABOR PRODUCTIVITY: AVERAGE VS. MARGINAL
Ulrich Kohli — 103-132

7. MEASURING PRODUCTIVITY CHANGE WITHOUT NEOCLASSICAL ASSUMPTIONS: A CONCEPTUAL ANALYSIS
Bert M. Balk — 133-184

PART II Index Number Formulas

8. THE LOWE CONSUMER PRICE INDEX AND ITS SUBSTITUTION BIAS
Bert M. Balk and W. Erwin Diewert — 187-196

9. LOWE INDICES
T. Peter Hill — 197-216

10. DIRECT AND CHAINED INDICES: A REVIEW OF TWO PARADIGMS
Bert M. Balk — 217-234

11. ON THE STOCHASTIC APPROACH TO INDEX NUMBERS
W. Erwin Diewert — 235-262

12. ALTERNATIVE APPROACHES TO INDEX NUMBER THEORY
W. Erwin Diewert and Robert J. Hill — 263-278

13. CHAIN AND VOLUME AGGREGATES FOR THE NATIONAL ACCOUNTS
Andrew Baldwin — 279-316

14. INEXACT INDEX NUMBERS AND ECONOMIC MONOTONICITY VIOLATIONS: THE GDP IMPLICIT PRICE DEFLATOR
Ulrich Kohli — 317-328

15. ECONOMIC MONOTONICITY OF PRICE INDEX FORMULAS
Ludwig von Auer — 329-332

16. AXIOMATIC AND ECONOMIC APPROACHES TO ELEMENTARY PRICE INDEXES
W. Erwin Diewert — 333-360

Citation for volume: **W.E. Diewert, B.M. Balk, D. Fixler, K.J. Fox and A.O. Nakamura (2011),**
***PRICE AND PRODUCTIVITY MEASUREMENT: Volume 6 -- Index Number Theory*. Trafford Press.**

Chapter 1
INTRODUCTION TO INDEX NUMBER THEORY FOR PRICE AND PRODUCTIVITY MEASUREMENT

Bert M. Balk, W. Erwin Diewert and Alice O. Nakamura[1]

Formal index number theory is not needed for measurement when the definition of a measure is obvious and its properties are apparent. However, there is a need to choose among many seemingly appropriate ways that have been proposed to meet important economic measurement needs such as assessing the rates of inflation and productivity growth for a nation and the determinants of changes over time or differences in the standard of living. The papers in this volume attempt to meet needs for theory in price and productivity measurement.

The papers fall in two groups. Part I papers deal with alternative productivity measures and decompositions of productivity growth. Part II papers focus on the properties of alternative index number formulas for price and productivity measurement. This volume is intended for specialists, in contrast to most of the other volumes in this Price and Productivity Measurement series (the "Vancouver Volumes") that should be accessible also for non specialists. The papers have been ordered within each of the two parts of this volume to assist students and others trying to attain a specialist level of understanding in mastering key terms.

PART I Productivity Measures and Decompositions

In **chapter 2, Paul Schreyer** of the Organization for Economic Co-operation and Development (OECD) explains that different ways of specifying computable measures of multifactor productivity (MFP) embed different assumptions about the technology and competition on output markets. The author focuses especially on assumptions often invoked in the absence of direct information about the prices and volumes of capital services.

Schreyer develops a very general model which provides a decomposition of traditional Total Factor Productivity or Multifactor Productivity growth (which he calls Apparent Multifactor Productivity, or AMFP, growth) into economic explanatory factors; see his equation (17c). The explanatory factors include:

- Possible nonconstant returns to scale;
- Technical progress (a shift in the production or cost function);
- Possible monopolistic pricing of products, and
- Possible omitted inputs.

---

[1] Bert Balk is with the Rotterdam School of Management, Erasmus University, and Statistics Netherlands, and can be reached at email bbalk@rsm.nl. Erwin Diewert is with the Department of Economics at the University of British Columbia. He can be reached at diewert@econ.ubc.ca. Alice Nakamura is with the University of Alberta School of Business and can be reached at alice.nakamura@ualberta.ca.

Citation: **B.M. Balk, W.E. Diewert and A.O Nakamura (2011),**
"Introduction to Index Number Theory for Price and Productivity Measurement," chapter 1, pp. 1-10 in
W.E. Diewert, B.M. Balk, D. Fixler, K.J. Fox and A.O. Nakamura,
***PRICE AND PRODUCTIVITY MEASUREMENT: Volume 6 -- Index Number Theory*. Trafford Press.**

© Alice Nakamura, 2011. Permission to link to, or copy or reprint, these materials is granted without restriction, including for use in commercial textbooks, with due credit to the authors and editors.

Schreyer's decomposition of apparent productivity growth into explanatory factors generalizes the analysis of Denny, Fuss and Waverman (1981), which developed a similar methodology that included the first three factors listed above but not the fourth.[2] Schreyer goes on to make additional assumptions that will allow statistical agencies to implement his general productivity formula. Schreyer lists five sets of assumptions and develops alternative empirical productivity growth estimates for Canada, France, Japan, and the United States. Empirically, the different assumptions are found to matter. The problem of deciding which set of assumptions is "best" has still not been solved in the literature but Schreyer's chapter should be required reading for statistical agencies contemplating the implementation of a multifactor productivity measure.

Different investigators have chosen different methods for measuring the contributions to industry productivity growth of entering and exiting firms. In **chapter 3**, **W. Erwin Diewert** of the University of British Columbia and **Kevin J. Fox** of the University of New South Wales propose a new formula for decomposing industry productivity growth into terms that reflect the productivity growth of individual production units that operate in both the base and comparison time periods (the "continuing firms") as well as the impacts on industry productivity growth of firm entry and exit. This formula is initially developed for the simplistic case in which each production unit produces a single homogeneous output and uses a single homogeneous input. Diewert and Fox then take up the problems involved in combining many outputs and many inputs into aggregates. There are some significant index number problems. There is no problem in using normal index number theory to construct output and input aggregates for each *continuing* firm present for both periods under consideration. However, this approach does not work with entering and exiting firms, since there is no natural base or current period observation to use as a standard of comparison for the single period data for these firms. The authors address this problem (which has not been widely recognized in the literature) by applying multilateral index number theory. In this approach, the data for each firm in each period is regarded as if it pertained to a "country" and various multilateral methods are applied. They illustrate their methodology using an artificial data set.

In **chapter 4**, **W. Erwin Diewert** of the University of British Columbia first focuses on a decomposition derived by Tang and Wang (2004) of economy wide labour productivity into sectoral contributions. Diewert reworks the Tang-Wang result so as to provide a more transparent and simple decomposition. He also explores another decomposition approach due to Gini which is a generalization of the Fisher ideal index number methodology to aggregates that are products of three factors: (i) growth in the labour productivity of individual sectors, (ii) changes in sectoral real output prices, and (iii) changes in the allocation of labour across sectors.

Policy makers are also interested in estimates of the contributions to aggregate productivity growth of particular industries. **Marshall Reinsdorf** and **Robert Yuskavage** of the U.S. Bureau of Economic Analysis (BEA) explain in **chapter 5** that the lack of an additive formula for industry contributions to real output growth means that formulas for industry contributions to aggregate productivity growth also generally add up to incorrect totals. The authors observe that the unavailability of exact formulas for industry contributions to aggregate productivity growth has led to reliance on approximate decomposition formulas. They show, however, that the approximate formulas examined can work well. In addition to its

[2] Schreyer's analysis is also related to Balk (2011a), Diewert and Fox (2008), and Diewert et al. (2011). These last authors do not consider the case where assets are missing and so Schreyer's framework is more general.

methodological contributions, this paper makes an empirical contribution to the literature on the industry sources of the post-1995 rebound in productivity growth. Reinsdorf and Yuskavage note that interest in investigating industry sources of productivity change has been further heightened by the availability for the United States, since June 2004, of data on industry gross output, intermediate inputs and value added resulting from the integration of the GDP-by-industry accounts and the annual I-O accounts. Using these data, the authors find that information technology (IT) producing industries directly account for far less of the post-1995 *speedup* in productivity growth than the wholesale and retail trade industries.

In **chapter 6**, **Ulrich Kohli**, who was chief economist of the Swiss National Bank when this chapter was written and is now with the University of Geneva, points out that most headline productivity measures refer to the *average* product of labor. Kohli notes, however, that a more relevant measure might be the *marginal* product. Nevertheless, as long as the income share of labor remains essentially constant, the two measures give very similar results. In the case of the United States, Kohli observes, the share of labor has been quite steady over 1971-2001 and the paths of both measures have been similar. The stability of the labor share explains why the Cobb-Douglas production function fits U.S. data well. Yet Kohli shows that a more thorough look at the evidence reveals that the historical constancy is the outcome of opposing forces.

Kohli expands the model by adopting the GDP function framework. Using a functional form more flexible than the Cobb-Douglas, he finds on the one hand that the Hicksian elasticity of complementarity between labor and capital has been significantly greater than one. Thus capital deepening has tended to increase the share of labor and raise its marginal product by relatively more than its average product. On the other hand, he finds that technological change has had an offsetting effect. An improvement in the terms of trade and a depreciation of the home currency are also shown to have impacts on average labor productivity. This paper seeks to analytically disentangle these effects and proposes a measurement methodology which is then applied to produce a multiplicative decomposition of the average and marginal U.S. labor productivity over the past three decades. Both econometric and index number methods are used.

In **chapter 7**, **Bert M. Balk** of the Rotterdam School of Management, Erasmus University, and Statistics Netherlands argues that official statistics agencies should adopt a definition for productivity growth that does not embed strong assumptions that are not supported by empirical evidence such as a constant returns to scale technology, competitive input and output markets, optimizing behaviour, and perfect foresight. Instead, Balk urges that total factor productivity growth (which official statistics agencies measure as MFP growth) should be defined as an output quantity index divided by an input quantity index.[3] Balk also provides an alternative framework for measuring productivity growth that is based on a difference approach to index number theory as opposed to the usual ratio approach. Balk shows that this alternative approach has some advantages over the traditional approach. The difference approach to index number theory was originally developed by Montgomery (1937) and Diewert (2005) but has not attracted much attention in the index number literature. However, Balk shows that the difference approach to measuring productivity change has a significant advantage over the traditional ratio approach in that it is invariant to whether output is measured as gross output or real value added.

The paper systematically considers the measurement of productivity change using a KLEMS framework and illustrates how the analysis can be conducted without imposing

[3] Diewert and Nakamura (2007) also advocate this definition of total factor productivity growth.

neoclassical assumptions. The paper also provides a rigorous discussion of the issues relating to the measurement of the cost of capital. When it comes to the explanation of productivity change, Balk explains that there are two main directions. The first is disaggregation: the explanation of productivity change at an aggregate level (economy, sector, industry) by productivity change at lower levels (firm, plant) and other factors subsumed under the heading of re-allocation (expansion, contraction, entry, and exit of production units). The second direction is concerned with the decomposition of productivity change into factors such as technological change, scale effects, input- and output-mix effects, and random chance. "And here come the neoclassical assumptions," writes Balk, "at the end of the day rather than at its beginning."

Balk's contribution also has three valuable appendices. Appendix A gives the reader a brief overview of the axiomatic approach to bilateral index number theory (a ratio approach) and also the axiomatic approach to indicators[4] (a difference approach to the aggregation of prices and quantities). For additional material on the axiomatic approach to bilateral index number theory, see Diewert (1992b); on the axiomatic approach to indicators, see Diewert (2005), and Diewert and Mizobuchi (2009); and on both approaches, see Balk (2008). Appendix B in Balk's contribution shows how value added ratios can be decomposed into price and quantity components. Finally appendix C provides a comprehensive discussion of possible methods for decomposing time series depreciation into revaluation and depreciation or deterioration terms.

PART II Index Number Formulas

Many official statistical agencies state that they use a Laspeyres price index as a conceptual target for their consumer price index. However, in **chapter 8, Bert M. Balk** of the Rotterdam School of Management, Erasmus University, and Statistics Netherlands, and **W. Erwin Diewert** of the University of British Columbia note that the headline inflation figure for the Netherlands, for example, in 2007 was obtained as the percentage change between a current month and the corresponding month of the prior year, with 2006 serving as the reference year for the quantity weights. This is *not* a Laspeyres index; they call this a "Lowe index" since the English economist, Joseph Lowe, suggested this type of index in 1823. More specifically, they define a Lowe index to be a fixed basket index where the commodity basket corresponds to household consumption patterns in a base year and this basket is priced out using current month prices in the numerator and base month prices in the denominator of the index. Thus there are two separate bases for this index: a base year for the quantity basket and a base month for the prices. The base year always proceeds the base month. Most CPIs are actually Lowe indexes.

Suppose households had preferences defined over the commodities in the annual basket given by the utility function, $f(q)$ say, where q is a consumption vector. Let the base year consumption vector be q^b. Then a Konüs true cost of living index comparing the cost of achieving utility level $u^q \equiv f(q^b)$ at the month t prices, p^t, to the cost of achieving the same utility level at the base month prices, p^0, is equal to the cost ratio, $C(u^b, p^t) / C(u^b, p^0)$, where $C(u, p)$ is the minimum cost of achieving the utility level u when the household faces the prices p. This true cost of living index can be compared to the corresponding Lowe index,

[4] Diewert (1992a) introduced the term "indicator" into the economics literature as a term to describe the difference counterpart to a bilateral index number formula.

$p^t \cdot q^b / p^0 \cdot q^b$, and the bias in this Lowe index can be estimated. The authors derive first and second order approximations to the substitution bias of a Lowe index. They then make assumptions about price trends and substitution elasticities and develop approximations to the bias in a Lowe index relative to the corresponding true cost of living index.

In **chapter 9**, **T. Peter Hill**, the editor of the international *Consumer Price Index Manual: Theory and Practice* (ILO et al. 2004) explains that this Manual and a 2003 working paper by Balk and Diewert (published as chapter 8 in this volume) are where the term "Lowe Index" was introduced. For a *Lowe price index*, Hill explains, the quantity weights are fixed and predetermined but need not pertain to either time period for which prices are being compared. Hill also introduces the concept of a *Lowe quantity index* in which the price weights are fixed, but need not pertain to either time period for which quantities are being compared. Hill discusses the fact that there are many ways in which the reference quantities or prices might be specified for a Lowe index. His results make it clear that the importance of the Balk-Diewert chapter 8 paper is rooted in the fact that in naming the Lowe index, they also defined a class of indexes, the members of which have valuable properties in common. For example, Lowe indexes are transitive and have additive decompositions, and can be expressed as ratios of Laspeyres indexes. They can also be viewed as chain indexes that link through some other period, country or group of countries. Two classes of indexes used in international comparisons that, in fact, are Lowe indexes are the average quantity methods and the average price methods. Hill reminds the reader, however, that these are not described as "Lowe" PPPs or indexes in earlier literature because the term was only introduced in 2003. Hill also argues that, in the case of temporal price or quantity indexes where the link is some past period, its relevance necessarily diminishes as it recedes into the past. Hill thus favours frequent updating of the reference prices in Lowe quantity indexes and of the reference quantity baskets in Lowe price indexes.

A recurrent theme when measuring aggregate price and quantity change between more than two periods is the choice between the computation of direct or chained index numbers. The impression one gets from the literature is that chained index numbers are closer to the truth than direct index numbers. **Bert M. Balk** of the Rotterdam School of Management, Erasmus University, and Statistics Netherlands rigorously explores this issue in **chapter 10**.

Balk notes that statistical agencies, until the recent past, favoured the use of fixed base or direct indexes, usually of the Paasche or Laspeyres variety (or perhaps of the Lowe type), but now opinion has shifted to the use of chained indexes, at least for annual data. Balk notes that the 2004 CPI Manual recommends the use of chained indexes provided that the prices and quantities of adjacent periods are *more similar* than the prices and quantities of more distant periods. In this circumstance, chaining will tend to reduce the spread between Paasche and Laspeyres indexes and indeed of superlative indexes as well.[5] Balk reviews the arguments for and against chaining as opposed to the use of direct indexes[6] and then he goes on to show mathematically, that it is impossible to reconcile the two approaches.

[5] For an introduction to the use of similarity measures to determine a path for chaining indexes, see section 10 of the Diewert and Fox contribution to this volume (chapter 3), which in turn draws on the work of Robert Hill.

[6] Some of the problems associated with the use of fixed base indexes for measuring price and quantity change for adjacent periods within the sample period are discussed by Balk in section 2 but it should be noted that some of these problems were already anticipated by Hill (1988).

In section 5 of this chapter, Balk relates the question "to chain or not to chain" to the modern theory of revealed preference developed by Afriat, Diewert and Varian. Balk develops criteria that may be helpful in answering the basic question as to whether one should use chained indexes or not. Of particular interest is Balk's section 5.3, where he develops a theory for the cost of living index that is an extension of his earlier theory for Konüs type cost of living indexes when preferences change between the two periods in the comparison.[7]

In section 6, Balk reviews Divisia's continuous time approach to index number theory and notes that this approach provides some justification for the use of chained index numbers over their direct counterparts since "chained index numbers also use the available data for the intermediate periods and map out a segmented path that coincides with the true one at the observation points." In section 7, Balk concludes that chaining is probably preferable to the use of direct indexes provided that quantities (and prices) do not exhibit "cyclical behaviour"; i.e., they do not "bounce" up and down as over time.[8] Balk also provides a useful appendix which looks (somewhat critically) at the index number program proposed by Claude Hillinger in 2002.

In **chapter 11**, **W. Erwin Diewert** of the University of British Columbia provides a selective review of the stochastic approach to index numbers, from its inception in the 1800s through a recent resurrection of interest. This paper was written in 1995 and has been much cited, including by other Vancouver Volume papers. Thus it is included in this volume to aide readers in checking this reference and because it ties in well with material in other papers in this volume.

Diewert explains that the two main competing approaches to index number theory are the test approach and the economic approach. In the test approach, the vectors of prices and quantities for the two periods being compared are regarded as independent variables. In contrast, in the economic approach, the prices are regarded as independent variables but the quantities are viewed as solutions to economic maximization or minimization problems. Diewert goes on to explain that the economic approach to index number theory concentrates on finding functional forms for price indexes that are *exact* for flexible unit cost functions, and on finding functional forms for quantity indexes that are *exact* for flexible linearly homogeneous utility functions. Index number formulas that are exact for flexible functional forms are called *superlative*.

Diewert notes that the traditional test and economic approaches to index number theory do not provide estimates of reliability for index number formulas: a shortcoming that proponents feel the stochastic approach can overcome. Basically, the early proponents of the stochastic approach to index number theory (Jevons and Edgeworth) looked at the price relatives or ratios for commodity i for periods 0 and t, p_{it}/p_{i0} for $i = 1,\ldots,N$, and made the assumption that the price relatives have a common mean. This line of reasoning leads to the arithmetic mean index, called the Carli index and written as $P_C \equiv \sum_{i=1}^{N}(1/N)(p_{it}/p_{i0})$, as an estimator of the common trend in prices and an advantage of this estimator (over the economic and test approaches) is that a measure of precision can be attached to it. Edgeworth did not argue for this specification of the problem of measuring the trend in prices: rather he argued it would be more appropriate to

[7] See Balk (1989) for this earlier theory.

[8] This is consistent with Peter Hill's (1988) earlier advice on this topic. The term "price bouncing behavior" was introduced by Szulc (1983), who showed that bad things can happen with chained index numbers if there is price bouncing behavior. For a more recent study that attempts to deal with the chain drift problem with sub-annual data, see Ivancic, Diewert and Fox (2010), who apply multilateral comparison methods to eliminate chain drift.

assume that the logarithms of the price ratios have a common mean, which leads to the Jevons index, $P_J \equiv \prod_{i=1}^{N} (p_{it} / p_{i0})^{1/N}$, as the estimator of the common trend in prices. Diewert reviews these approaches in section 2-4, and in 6 he reviews the more recent approaches. He argues that the more recent approaches are flawed due to their assumptions about the variances of the price relative components.

In the later sections of his paper, Diewert turns from being negative on the stochastic approach to being somewhat positive. Thus in section 5, he reformulates a stochastic model due to Edgeworth (which Irving Fisher thought was totally impractical) and shows that it can be estimated. The essence of this neo-Edgeworthian approach is that the variance for each of the N commodity classes is empirically determined. Thus an empirically determined parameter replaces the assumption that the error variances are known up to a multiplicative constant. In section 7, Diewert changes the focus from an econometric model (with assumptions about error variances) to *descriptive statistics*. He sets up his descriptive statistics framework along the lines suggested by the following quotation from the chapter: "A more direct approach to the reliability of a price index, $P(p^s, p^t, q^s, q^t)$, is to simply look at the variability of the individual price relatives, p_{it} / p_{is}, around the index number "average" value, $P(p^s, p^t, q^s, q^t)$." Diewert goes on to suggest several alternative measures of the variability of individual price relatives. The approach of Theil (1967; 136-137) to the Törnqvist-Theil index number formula is an example of this descriptive statistics approach. It can also be seen that Diewert's work in section 7 of the present paper is a precursor to his work on similarity indexes; see Diewert (2009).

As said, this chapter was written in 1995 and there are many further developments associated with the stochastic approach to index numbers. The models have become more complex than the original straightforward approaches proposed by Jevons and Edgeworth. For an up to date, excellent review of these later developments, see Clements et al. (2006).[9]

In **chapter 12**, **W. Erwin Diewert** of the University of British Columbia and **Robert J. Hill** of the University of Graz, Austria and also the University of New South Wales reconsider the fundamental concepts of true and exact indexes, as these concepts are defined in the index number literature. The authors explain that these concepts form the bedrock of the economic approach to index number theory. They review these concepts. In brief, a *true index* is the underlying target; it is a formal statement of the measurement objective. An empirically calculable index is *exact* when, under certain conditions, it exactly equals the true index. Van Veelen and van der Weide (2008) recently introduced alternative definitions of true indexes. These combine the existing literature's identification of a true index, such as the Allen (1949) quantity index or the Konüs cost of living index, with some of Afriat's (1981) ideas for checking whether a given set of data are actually consistent with the maximizing or minimizing hypotheses underlying the definitions of the '"true" indexes. Diewert and Hill conclude that it would be preferable for those authors to come up with a new term to describe their concept.

In **chapter 13**, **Andrew Baldwin** of Statistics Canada endorses the 1993 System of National Accounts (SNA93) recommendation for chain linking, but not its support for chain Fisher aggregates, nor, as a second-best solution, chain Laspeyres aggregates. Baldwin argues it is feasible and desirable to calculate chain fixed price aggregates that are not vulnerable to chain

9 See also the summary in Balk (2008, section 1.8).

drift. According to Baldwin, these aggregates can be calculated as direct series for the most recent period so that they are additive over commodities, industries or regions, in contrast to their chain Fisher counterparts. The Edgeworth-Marshall formula is what Baldwin recommends. He notes that it respects the property of transactions equality (i.e., the importance of a transaction in the formula does not depend on the period in which it occurs). Also, it does not discard commodities from a volume aggregate if the price goes to zero from a positive price or *vice versa*, nor does it discard commodities from a price index if the quantity goes to zero from a positive quantity or *vice versa*. Baldwin feels it is unfortunate that the index number theory literature has focused on two formulas -- the Laspeyres and the Fisher -- neither of which is well-suited, in his view, for the calculation of chain aggregates.[10]

Ulrich Kohli who was chief economist of the Swiss National Bank when this chapter was written and is now with the University of Geneva reports in **chapter 14** that several countries have switched – or are about to switch – to chained price and quantity indexes for their national accounts. In particular, the United States and Canada have adopted the chained Fisher indexes, whereas the United Kingdom, Switzerland, Australia and New Zealand have opted for chained Laspeyres indexes for real GDP, and chained Paasche for the implicit price deflator. Yet Kohli notes that the vast majority of countries, including most OECD members, still have not embraced chaining. In these countries the GDP implicit price deflator is still computed as a *direct* (or fixed-base) Paasche price index. Changes in the price level over consecutive periods are measured by the change in the direct Paasche index, a use for which Kohli feels this index is ill suited. Using the economic approach to index numbers, Kohli shows that because of this failure, the price index can register a drop between consecutive periods *even though none of the disaggregate prices has fallen, and some have actually increased.* He notes that a similar result holds for the direct Fisher index. In his view (and our view as well), this provides a powerful argument in favor of chaining, at least for annual data subject to smooth trends. Kohli gives strong arguments against the use of direct indexes in addition to the arguments that were suggested in the earlier work of Hill (1988) and in chapter 10 by Balk in this volume.

Kohli argues that the fact that the direct Paasche GDP deflator is not monotonically increasing in prices makes it a poor indicator of inflation, since it might point at a price increase when prices are actually falling, and *vice versa*. Yet it is widely used in the literature. According to Kohli, there are other reasons why the use of the direct Paasche GDP deflator as a measure of the price level should be avoided, independently of whether chaining takes place or not. GDP price deflators incorporate terms-of-trade changes, which are fundamentally a real – not a price – phenomenon. The problem with the standard procedure becomes apparent if import prices fall, for instance. This will increase the GDP price deflator (since import prices enter the calculation of the GDP deflator with a negative weight), even though this shock is clearly not inflationary.

Ludwig von Auer in **chapter 15** follows up on Kohli's chapter 14. He extends Kohli's results to show that a run of direct Laspeyres indexes can also violate a monotonicity property if there are more than two periods in the run of time periods. This extension provides a more symmetric definition of the basic monotonicity test used by Kohli. The net impact of von Auer's paper is to reinforce the case for using chained indexes when we have annual data.

[10] However, the reader is reminded of Balk's appendix in his chapter 10 where he finds some problems with the use of the Edgeworth-Marshall index number formula.

In **chapter 16**, **W. Erwin Diewert** of the University of British Columbia considers problems involved in collecting and aggregating price and quantity information at the lowest level of aggregation. This chapter was originally written in 1995 and, like chapter 11 above, it was not updated. However, it proved to be an important source on elementary indexes for the 2004 Consumer Price Index Manual. Diewert develops an axiomatic approach for finding an appropriate functional form for an elementary level price index. The axiomatic properties of the Carli (arithmetic average of price relatives), Jevons (geometric average of the price relatives), and Dutot (ratio of average prices) elementary indexes are obtained and the Jevons index emerges as the winner. Finally, Diewert also discusses the problem of price and quantity aggregation at the very first stage of aggregation when individual transactions over a time period must be aggregated into price and quantity aggregates that can be inserted into a bilateral index number formula. It turns out that unit value prices and total quantities transacted (over a set of transactions involving a "homogeneous" commodity) emerge as reasonable aggregates at this first stage of aggregation. Finally, the paper catalogues sources of bias in consumer price indexes and makes rough guesses as to the likely magnitude of the biases. Diewert's rough guesses proved to be very similar to the Boskin Commission's guestimates of biases.

References (including full references for all chapter titles)

Afriat, S.N. (1981), "On the Constructability of Consistent Price Indices between Periods Simultaneously," in *Essays in the Theory and Measurement of Consumer Behaviour in Honour of Sir Richard Stone*, ed. Angus S. Deaton, pp. 133-161, Cambridge University Press.

Allen, R.G.D. (1949), "The Economic Theory of Index Numbers", *Economica* 16, 197-203.

Baldwin, A. (2011), "Chain and Volume Aggregates for the System of National Accounts," chapter 13, pp. 279-316 in W.E. Diewert, B.M. Balk, D. Fixler, K.J. Fox, and A.O. Nakamura (eds.), *Price and Productivity Measurement: Volume 6 -- Index Number Theory*, Trafford Press.

Balk, B.M (1989), "Changing Consumer Preferences and the Cost of Living Index: Theory and Nonparametric Expressions", *Journal of Economics* 50:2, 157-169.

Balk, B.M. (2008), *Price and Quantity Index Numbers; Models for Measuring Aggregate Change and Difference*, Cambridge University Press.

Balk, B.M. (2011a), "Measuring Productivity Change without Neoclassical Assumptions: A Conceptual Analysis," chapter 7, pp. 133-184 in W.E. Diewert, B.M. Balk, D. Fixler, K.J. Fox, and A.O. Nakamura (eds.), *Price and Productivity Measurement: Volume 6 -- Index Number Theory*, Trafford Press.

Balk, B.M. (2011b), "Direct and Chained Indices: A Review of Two Paradigms," chapter 10, pp. 217-234 in W.E. Diewert, B.M. Balk, D. Fixler, K.J. Fox, and A.O. Nakamura (eds.), *Price and Productivity Measurement: Volume 6 -- Index Number Theory*, Trafford Press.

Balk, B.M. and W.E. Diewert (2011), "The Lowe Consumer Price Index and Its Substitution Bias," chapter 8, pp. 187-196 in W.E. Diewert, B.M. Balk, D. Fixler, K.J. Fox, and A.O. Nakamura (eds.), Price and Productivity Measurement: Volume 6 -- Index Number Theory, Trafford Press.

Clements, K.W., H.Y. Izan and E.A. Selvanathan (2006), "Stochastic Index Numbers: A Review", *International Statistical Review* 74, 235-270.

Denny, M., M. Fuss and L. Waverman (1981), "The Measurement and Interpretation of Total Factor Productivity in Regulated Industries, with an Application to Canadian Telecommunications", in *Productivity Measurement in Regulated Industries*, T.G. Cowing and R.E. Stevenson (eds.), Academic Press.

Diewert, W.E. (1992a), "Exact and Superlative Welfare Change Indicators", *Economic Inquiry* 30, 565-582.

Diewert, W.E. (1992b), "Fisher Ideal Output, Input and Productivity Indexes Revisited", *Journal of Productivity Analysis* 3, 211-248.

Diewert, W.E. (2005), "Index Number Theory Using Differences Instead of Ratios", *The American Journal of Economics and Sociology* 64:1, 311-360.

Diewert, W.E. (2009), "Similarity Indexes and Criteria for Spatial Linking", in *Purchasing Power Parities of Currencies: Recent Advances in Methods and Applications*, D.S. Prasada Rao (ed.), Edward Elgar.

Diewert, W.E. (2011a), "On the Tang and Wang Decomposition of Labour Productivity Growth into Sectoral Effects," chapter 4, pp. 67-76 in W.E. Diewert, B.M. Balk, D. Fixler, K.J. Fox, and A.O. Nakamura (eds.), *Price and Productivity Measurement: Volume 6 -- Index Number Theory*, Trafford Press.

Diewert, W.E. (2011b), "On the Stochastic Approach to Index Numbers," chapter 11, pp. 235-262 in W.E. Diewert, B.M. Balk, D. Fixler, K.J. Fox, and A.O. Nakamura (eds.), *Price and Productivity Measurement: Volume 6 -- Index Number Theory*, Trafford Press.

Diewert, W.E. (2011c), "Axiomatic and Economic Approaches to Elementary Price Indexes," chapter 16, pp. 333-360 in W.E. Diewert, B.M. Balk, D. Fixler, K.J. Fox, and A.O. Nakamura (eds.), *Price and Productivity Measurement: Volume 6 -- Index Number Theory*, Trafford Press.

Diewert, W.E. and K.J. Fox (2008), "On the Estimation of Returns to Scale, Technical Progress and Monopolistic Markups", *Journal of Econometrics* 145, 173-194.

Diewert, W.E. and K.J. Fox (2011), "On Measuring the Contribution of Entering and Exiting Firms to Aggregate Productivity Growth," chapter 3, pp. 41-66 in W.E. Diewert, B.M. Balk, D. Fixler, K.J. Fox, and A.O. Nakamura (eds.), *Price and Productivity Measurement: Volume 6 -- Index Number Theory*, Trafford Press.

Diewert, W.E. and R.J. Hill (2011), "Alternative Approaches to Index Number Theory," chapter 12, pp. 163-178 in W.E. Diewert, B.M. Balk, D. Fixler, K.J. Fox, and A.O. Nakamura (eds.), *Price and Productivity Measurement: Volume 6 -- Index Number Theory*, Trafford Press.

Diewert, W.E. and H. Mizobuchi (2009), "Exact and Superlative Price and Quantity Indicators", *Macroeconomic Dynamics* 13 (Supplement 2), 335-380.

Diewert, W.E., T. Nakajima, A. Nakamura, E. Nakamura and M. Nakamura (2011), "Returns to Scale: Concept, Estimation and Analysis of Japan's Turbulent 1964-1988 Economy," *Canadian Journal of Economics* 44 (2), 451-485.

Diewert, W.E. and A.O. Nakamura (2007), "The Measurement of Productivity for Nations," in *Handbook of Econometrics*, Volume 6A , J.J. Heckman and E.E. Leamer (eds.), Elsevier.

Hill, T.P. (1988), "Recent Developments in Index Number Theory and Practice," *OECD Economic Studies* 10, 123-148.

Hill, T.P. (2011), "Lowe Indices," chapter 9, pp. 197-216 in W.E. Diewert, B.M. Balk, D. Fixler, K.J. Fox, and A.O. Nakamura (eds.), *Price and Productivity Measurement: Volume 6 -- Index Number Theory*, Trafford Press.

Hillinger, C. (2002), "Consistent Aggregation and Chaining of Price and Quantity Measures," *Journal of Economic and Social Measurement* 28, 1-20.

ILO, IMF, OECD, UNECE, Eurostat and the World Bank (2004), "Consumer Price Index Manual: Theory and Practice," Geneva. http://www.ilo.org/public/english/bureau/stat/guides/cpi/index.htm

Ivancic, L., W.E. Diewert and K.J. Fox (2010), "Scanner Data, Time Aggregation and the Construction of Price Indexes," *Journal of Econometrics*, forthcoming.

Kohli, U. (2011a), "Labor Productivity: Average vs. Marginal," chapter 6, pp. 103-132 in W.E. Diewert, B.M. Balk, D. Fixler, K.J. Fox, and A.O. Nakamura (eds.), *Price and Productivity Measurement: Volume 6 -- Index Number Theory*, Trafford Press.

Kohli, U. (2011b), "Inexact Index Numbers and Economic Monotonicity Violations: The GDP Implicit Price Deflator," chapter 14, pp. 317-328 in W.E. Diewert, B.M. Balk, D. Fixler, K.J. Fox, and A.O. Nakamura (eds.), *Price and Productivity Measurement: Volume 6 -- Index Number Theory*, Trafford Press.

Montgomery, J.K. (1937), *The Mathematical Problem of the Price Index*, Orchard House, P.S. King & Son.

Reinsdorf, M. and R. Yuskavage (2011), "Exact Industry Contributions to Labor Productivity Change," chapter 5, pp. 77-102 in W.E. Diewert, B.M. Balk, D. Fixler, K.J. Fox, and A.O. Nakamura (eds.), *Price and Productivity Measurement: Volume 6 -- Index Number Theory*, Trafford Press.

Schreyer, P. (2011), "Measuring Multi-Factor Productivity When Rates of Return Are Exogenous," chapter 2, pp. 13-40 in W.E. Diewert, B.M. Balk, D. Fixler, K.J. Fox, and A.O. Nakamura (eds.), *Price and Productivity Measurement: Volume 6 -- Index Number Theory*, Trafford Press.

Szulc, B.J. (1983), "Linking Price Index Numbers," in *Price Level Measurement*, W.E. Diewert and C. Montmarquette (eds.), Statistics Canada.

Tang, J. and W. Wang (2004), "Sources of Aggregate Labour Productivity Growth in Canada and the United States", *Canadian Journal of Economics* 37, 421-444.

Theil, H. (1967), *Economics and Information Theory*, North-Holland.

van Veelen, M. and R. van der Weide (2008), "A Note on Different Approaches to Index Number Theory", *American Economic Review* 98 (4), 1722-1730.

von Auer, L. (2011), "Economic Monotonicity of Price Index Formulas," chapter 15, pp. 329-332 in W.E. Diewert, B.M. Balk, D. Fixler, K.J. Fox, and A.O. Nakamura (eds.), *Price and Productivity Measurement: Volume 6 -- Index Number Theory*, Trafford Press.

PART I Productivity Measures and Decompositions

CHAPTER 2

MEASURING MULTI-FACTOR PRODUCTIVITY WHEN RATES OF RETURN ARE EXOGENOUS

Paul Schreyer[1]

1. Introduction: Gross Operating Surplus and the Remuneration of Capital

Official statistics do not normally provide direct observations on the price and volume of capital services. What is available from the national accounts is a residual measure of gross operating surplus (GOS): a measure often interpreted as profits from normal business activity, including mixed income which is the income of self-employed persons. Thus, the national accounts provide the researcher with data according to the following accounting identity:

$$(1) \qquad P \cdot Q = wL + GOS$$

where $P \cdot Q$ is the sum of current-price output in the economy, $P = [P_1, P_2, ... P_M]$ denotes the vector of prices and $Q = [Q_1, Q_2, ... Q_M]$ denotes the vector of quantities of output. To simplify notation, we use $P \cdot Q \equiv \sum_{i=1}^{M} P_i Q_i$ for the inner product between P and Q. Note, however, that normally the quantities in Q are not directly measured. Output is defined and measured as value-added, and prices are defined and measured at basic prices, i.e., they exclude all product taxes but include subsidies on products. The term wL is the remuneration of labour, with wage component w and volume component L, with the value and price components measured directly. For simplicity, it will be assumed here that mixed income is either zero or is split up between the labour and the GOS components. Thus, the two sides of (1) represent the total production and the total income sides of the national accounts.

The national accounts provide no guidance as to the factors of production that are remunerated through GOS. Fixed assets certainly are among these factors, but there could be others too. The business literature has discussions about the importance of intangible assets, and there are good reasons to argue that such assets account at least for part of GOS. While this may appear a minor point, it calls into question an assumption often made by analysts of productivity and growth, namely that GOS exactly represents the remuneration of the fixed assets recognised in the System of National Accounts (SNA), or the value of the services of these.

---

[1] The contact information for the author is: Paul Schreyer, OECD Statistics Directorate, Paul.Schreyer@OECD.org. Opinions expressed in this paper are those of the author and do not necessarily reflect views of the OECD or its Member countries. The author thanks Erwin Diewert, Chuck Hulten and Alice Nakamura for helpful comments. Special thanks go also to Mathilde Mas (University of Valencia and IVIE) for useful discussions on the subject.

Citation: **Paul Schreyer (2011), "Measuring Multi-Factor Productivity when Rates of Return Are Exogenous," chapter 2, pp. 13-40 in**
W.E. Diewert, B.M. Balk, D. Fixler, K.J. Fox and A.O. Nakamura,
***PRICE AND PRODUCTIVITY MEASUREMENT: Volume 6 -- Index Number Theory.* Trafford Press.**

© Alice Nakamura, 2011. Permission to link to, or copy or reprint, these materials is granted without restriction, including for use in commercial textbooks, with due credit to the authors and editors.

Let $u^* = [u_1^*, u_2^*, ... u_N^*]$ denote a vector of user costs for N types of capital services and let $K = [K_1, K_2, ..., K_N]$ denote the corresponding vector of the quantities of capital service flows. The assumption typically made is:

$$(2) \qquad u^* \cdot K = GOS,$$

where $u^* \cdot K$ denotes the inner product of the price and quantity vectors: i.e., where $u^* \cdot K \equiv \sum_{i=1}^{N} u_i^* K_i$. In other words, it is assumed that remuneration of capital services exactly exhausts gross operating surplus. Empirically, the equality $u^* \cdot K = GOS$ is obtained by choosing what is thought to be an appropriate value for the net rate of return on assets, which is part of the user costs.[2] With this formulation, the rate of return is assumed to adjust *endogenously*. This setup is consistent with competitive behaviour on product and factor markets and a production process that exhibits constant returns to scale. Under these conditions, (1) can be restated as

$$(3) \qquad P \cdot Q = wL + u^* \cdot K,$$

since these conditions ensure that the gross operating surplus corresponds exactly to the remuneration of the assets included in K; hence if only fixed assets are assumed to be in K, this is equivalent to assuming that GOS corresponds to the remuneration of fixed assets. Note that this setup also depends on the following being true:

- the set of assets $[K_1, K_2, ... K_N]$ is complete; i.e., all assets are observed by the official statisticians who compile the national accounts and there are only the stated fixed assets;
- the ex-post rate of return on each asset (implicitly observed by the national accountants as part of GOS) equals its ex-ante rate of return, which is the economically relevant part in the user cost of capital services;
- there are no residual profits (or losses) such as might arise in the presence of market power, or with non-constant returns to scale, or owing to the availability of publicly available or any other uncounted or miscounted capital assets.

Several questions arise when some of the above conditions do not hold. For example, when there is independent information about the rates of return to capital services, there is no guarantee that the sum of labour remuneration and the observed capital remuneration will equal measured total value added at current prices. How should multi-factor productivity (MFP) be conceptually defined, computed and interpreted? How should growth accounting exercises be carried out? How should measures of technical change be defined and evaluated? These are the questions explored in this paper. In the rest of this paper, a preference is expressed for a simple

---

[2] In a simple continuous-time formulation, the user cost or rental price of an asset (Jorgenson and Griliches, 1967) is given by $u^i = q^i(r + \delta^i - d\ln q^i / dt)$ where $q^i(t)$ is the purchase price of a new asset of type i, $r(t)$ is the net rate of return, δ^i is a rate of depreciation, and $d\ln q/dt$ is the rate of change of q^i.

MFP measure that is consistent with index number traditions. Such a measure cannot be interpreted as capturing only, or all, technical change.[3]

2. Why GOS May Differ from Remuneration of Capital

This paper generalizes the formulation of the income-production relationship (3) by allowing for and utilizing independent measures of capital remuneration, $u = [u_1, u_2, ... u_N]$ that may not satisfy condition (2). Under these circumstances, equation (3) is replaced by

$$(4) \qquad P \cdot Q - wL = GOS = u \cdot K + M,$$

where the term M denotes the difference obtained by subtracting from current-price output both the remuneration of assets included in K,[4] $u \cdot K$, and the value of the labour input; i.e., it is the observed current price output minus observed factor payments. $C \equiv wL + u \cdot K$ is used as shorthand for observed factor payments. Hence gross operating surplus can be split into a component that reflects observable factor remuneration plus a residual M with several possible interpretations. In principle, there is no restriction on the sign of M. However, if the sign were negative over an extended period of time, this would imply sustained losses. Since this seems economically implausible, in what follows, the non-negativity of M is assumed.[5]

Four possible reasons for nonzero values of M are considered in this paper.

Models of short-run disequilibrium over the business cycle provide a first possible theoretical justification for the existence of nonzero values of M.[6]

A second possibility is that M reflects the existence of pure profits as a consequence of the presence of decreasing returns to scale combined with marginal cost pricing for outputs, or of increasing returns to scale and a positive mark-up over marginal costs. If returns to scale are the key source of non-zero values of M, then the size of M will depend on the degree of competition in output markets: free market entry and competition would be expected to drive mark-ups and prices to a level where total revenues just cover total costs, implying M = 0.

The Lucas-Romer model of endogenous growth (Romer, 1990) provides a third possible justification for non-zero M values. According to this model, at the firm level, returns to scale are constant, but at the aggregate level there are increasing returns to scale due to externalities.

A fourth possibility is that M reflects the existence of unobserved inputs and hence reflects a measurement problem. This situation could arise if not all of the capital inputs that give rise to operating surplus are recognised in the national accounts. In contrast to the second

---

[3] Aspects of the interpretation and derivations that follow build on Jorgenson and Griliches (1967), Fuss and McFadden (eds.) (1978), Diewert and Nakamura (2007) and Harper et al. (1989).

[4] As the context makes clear, the symbol M is also used sometimes to denote the number of output goods.

[5] In the empirical part of the paper, M is positive for the four countries reviewed (Canada, France, Japan, United States) for most years over 1980-2002. If M were negative over an extended period of time, this would cast doubt on the measures for the remuneration of capital, and in particular on the choice of the exogenous rates of return.

[6] These include models of time-varying capacity utilisation of the sort investigated by Berndt and Fuss (1986) and Hulten (1986). The cyclicality of productivity measures and the relation of these to technical change are dealt with by Basu and Kimball (1997). They find strong effects of variable capacity utilisation on measures of productivity.

interpretation, in this case we would expect M to remain positive even in the longer run because true total costs are higher than what the observed assets would justify and M would cover these.[7]

3. Production Technology and Producer Behaviour

We let Z(t) denote a feasible set of inputs and outputs in period t. We further assume that there is a total cost function TC that shows the minimum costs of production, given a vector Q of quantities $[Q_1, Q_2, ... Q_M]$ for the M outputs and given a corresponding set of input prices. Inputs comprise labour L, N types of observed capital services $K_1, K_2, ... K_N$ and one unobserved asset D. The corresponding prices are the wage rate, w, the user costs of capital, $u = [u_1, u_2, ... u_M]$, and the price of the unobserved input D, ϕ. The total cost function is defined as:

$$(5) \qquad TC[Q, w, u, \phi, t] = \min_{L,K,D} \{wL + u \cdot K + \phi D : (Q, L, K, D) \text{ belongs to } Z(t)\}.$$

The cost function is linearly homogenous in input prices and non-decreasing, but not necessarily linearly homogenous in the vector of outputs $[Q_1, ... Q_M]$. Thus, there is no assumption of constant returns to scale. However, producers are assumed to minimise total cost, so that actual costs equal minimum costs ($wL + u \cdot K + \phi D = TC(Q, w, u, \phi, t)$). Furthermore, producers are assumed to face competitive factor markets so that Shephard's (1970) conditions for optimality for factor inputs apply:

$$(6a) \qquad L = \left(\frac{\partial TC}{\partial w}\right);$$

$$(6b) \qquad K_i = \left(\frac{\partial TC}{\partial u_i}\right), \quad i = 1, \ldots, N;$$

$$(6c) \qquad D = \left(\frac{\partial TC}{\partial \phi}\right).$$

On the output side, imperfect product markets are allowed for with the sole stipulation that output prices are proportional to marginal costs. No explicit assumption is made about the kind of imperfect competition that prevails or concerning whether producers are profit maximising or not. All that is needed is a relationship between prices and marginal costs so that if the price of output i is P_i and if $1 \le 1/\mu_i$ is a product-specific, time-varying mark-up factor, producer behaviour on the output side is described by

$$(7) \qquad P_i \mu_i = \partial TC / \partial Q_i \quad i = 1, ..., M.$$

Next, we follow the literature (e.g., Panzar 1989) and define the local elasticity of cost with respect to scale as

[7] Non-observed inputs and their link to measured MFP growth and technical change have been investigated by Basu et al. (2003). They introduce unobserved intangible organisational capital that they take as complementary to observed investment in information technology. Unlike the present model, however, theirs is a general equilibrium setting that tries to account not only for the unobserved intangible inputs but also for their unobserved production.

$$(8) \qquad \varepsilon \equiv \sum_{i=1}^{M} \frac{\partial \ln TC}{\partial \ln Q_i}.$$

Hence, $\varepsilon > 0$ indicates the percentage change in total cost for a given percentage change in all outputs. The inverse of this parameter can readily be interpreted as a measure of local returns to scale for the production unit. For instance, $\varepsilon > 1$ implies that a one percent rise in the quantity of each of the outputs increases total costs by more than one percent, which is tantamount to a situation of decreasing returns to scale. Similarly, $\varepsilon < 1$ and $\varepsilon = 1$ correspond to increasing and constant returns to scale, respectively.[8]

Given (7), the measure of the cost elasticity defined in (8) can be further transformed:

$$\begin{aligned} \varepsilon &\equiv \sum_{i=1}^{M} \frac{\partial \ln TC}{\partial \ln Q_i} = \sum_{i=1}^{M} \frac{P_i Q_i \mu_i}{TC} \\ (9) \qquad &= \sum_{i=1}^{M} \frac{P_i Q_i \mu_i}{P \cdot Q} \frac{P \cdot Q}{TC} \\ &= \mu \frac{P \cdot Q}{TC} \quad \text{where } \mu \equiv \sum_{i=1}^{M} \frac{P_i Q_i}{P \cdot Q} \mu_i. \end{aligned}$$

In (9), μ is the economy-wide inverted average mark-up factor – a weighted average of industry-specific mark-ups with simple output shares as weights. Expression (9) can be rearranged as

$$(10) \qquad P \cdot Q = (\varepsilon / \mu) TC.$$

Thus, the value of total output revenues equals total costs, adjusted by a mark-up factor $1/\mu$ and ε, the parameter for the scale elasticity.

The equalities in (9) can now be combined with the national accounts information mentioned earlier. In particular, it was pointed out that gross operating surplus is defined as the difference between the value of output and labour income: $GOS = P \cdot Q - wL$. Using the result $P \cdot Q = (\varepsilon / \mu) TC$ in (10), from (4), one obtains

$$(11) \qquad GOS = TC(\varepsilon / \mu) - wL.$$

Recall that the difference between GOS and observed capital income has been labelled M: $M = GOS - u \cdot K$. Using the expression (11) for GOS and taking into account the definition of TC now allows us to derive a relation for M that can readily be interpreted:

[8] As we operate with a multi-product cost function, a distinction needs to be made between general economies of scale and product-specific economies of scale. The former – treated here – deals with changes in costs when all outputs are changed by the same proportion. The latter deals with changes in costs as one particular output is increased while holding all other outputs constant. For the latter form of economies of scale, see Panzar (1989).

$$M = GOS - u \cdot K = PQ - wL - u \cdot K \quad \text{from (4)}$$

$$= \left(\frac{\varepsilon}{\mu}\right) TC - wL - u \cdot K \quad \text{from (10)}$$

(12a) $$= \left(\frac{\varepsilon}{\mu}\right) TC - TC + (TC - wL - u \cdot K) = \left(\frac{\varepsilon}{\mu}\right) TC - TC + \phi D \quad \text{using (5)}$$

$$= \left(\frac{\varepsilon}{\mu} - 1\right) TC + \phi D$$

or alternatively

(12b) $$M = P \cdot Q\left(1 - \frac{\mu}{\varepsilon} + \frac{\phi D}{P \cdot Q}\right) \quad \text{using (10).}$$

Expressions (12a) and (12b) show how the difference M between GOS from the national accounts and the sum of payments to observed factors reflects mark-ups and returns to scale (captured by ε/μ) and the influence of unobserved capital inputs (captured by ϕD). The expressions in (12) will be instrumental for the discussion in the following sections.

4. Technical Change

In an environment of constant returns to scale, Hicks-neutral technical change can be defined either as a shift of the production function over time (an output-based measure) or as a shift of the cost function over time (an input-based measure). Here producer behaviour has been described by way of a cost function, so we shall use the input-based approach to derive measures of technical change. One important advantage of the cost-based measure is that no assumptions about profit or revenue maximisation need to be made for the output markets.

If there were an assumption of constant returns to scale, and competitive markets, the choice of the input-based productivity measure would simply be a matter of convenience, with no consequences for results. However, for the moment we have imposed no such a-priori condition, and the input-based measure will in general be different from the output-based measure, as will be shown in section 5.2.5.

Technical change is measured here as a downward shift over time of the total cost function. To derive an analytical expression, TC is differentiated totally and technical change is then defined as the negative of the partial derivative of the cost function with respect to time:

(13) $$-\frac{\partial TC}{\partial t}\frac{1}{TC} = -\frac{\partial \ln TC}{\partial t} = \sum_{i=1}^{M} \frac{\partial \ln TC}{\partial \ln Q_i}\frac{d \ln Q_i}{dt} - \left(\frac{d \ln TC}{dt} - \frac{\partial \ln TC}{\partial \ln w}\frac{d \ln w}{dt} - \sum_{i=1}^{N} \frac{\partial \ln TC}{\partial \ln u_i}\frac{d \ln u_i}{dt} - \frac{\partial \ln TC}{\partial \ln \phi}\frac{d \ln \phi}{dt}\right).$$

To interpret (13), consider its parts in turn. On the right-hand side, first there is a Divisia-type output quantity change index, $\sum_{i=1}^{N}\frac{\partial \ln TC}{\partial \ln Q_i}\frac{d\ln Q_i}{dt}$, that aggregates the growth rates of the quantities of individual outputs. To find a computable expression for the growth rate of output, use (7) and (9) to obtain:

$$\sum_{i=1}^{M}\frac{\partial \ln TC}{\partial \ln Q_i}\frac{d\ln Q_i}{dt}=\sum_{i=1}^{M}\frac{\partial TC}{\partial Q_i}\frac{Q_i}{TC}\frac{d\ln Q_i}{dt}=\sum_{i=1}^{M}P_i\mu_i\frac{Q_i}{TC}\frac{d\ln Q_i}{dt}$$

(14a)
$$=\sum_{i=1}^{M}\frac{P_iQ_i}{P\cdot Q}\mu_i\frac{P\cdot Q}{TC}\frac{d\ln Q_i}{dt}=\frac{P\cdot Q}{TC}\sum_{i=1}^{M}\frac{P_iQ_i}{P\cdot Q}\mu_i\frac{d\ln Q_i}{dt}$$

$$=\varepsilon\sum_{i=1}^{M}\frac{P_iQ_i\mu_i}{P\cdot Q\mu}\frac{d\ln Q_i}{dt}.$$

Thus, the output aggregate resembles a traditional output aggregate with revenue shares as weights, but the latter are now corrected for the relative mark-ups μ_i/μ and the scale factor ε.

Moving on to the terms in brackets on the right hand side of (13), it can be seen that these measure the difference in the growth rate of total costs and the growth rates of the various types of input prices. In fact, $\left(\frac{\partial \ln TC}{\partial \ln w}\frac{d\ln w}{dt}+\sum_{i=1}^{N}\frac{\partial \ln TC}{\partial \ln u_i}\frac{d\ln u_i}{dt}+\frac{\partial \ln TC}{\partial \ln \phi}\frac{d\ln \phi}{dt}\right)$ is a Divisia index of input prices. This is apparent by invoking the optimality conditions for factor inputs (6a)-(6c) and then inserting them into the above expression which now becomes $\left(\frac{wL}{TC}\frac{d\ln w}{dt}+\sum_{i=1}^{N}\frac{u_iK_i}{TC}\frac{d\ln u_i}{dt}+\frac{\phi D}{TC}\frac{d\ln \phi}{dt}\right)$. Moreover, by construction, the difference between the Divisia index of total costs and the Divisia index of input prices is the Divisia index of input quantities. The term in brackets on the right hand side of (13) can be rewritten as

(14b)
$$\left(\frac{d\ln TC}{dt}-\frac{\partial \ln TC}{\partial w}\frac{d\ln w}{dt}-\sum_{i=1}^{N}\frac{\partial \ln TC}{\partial \ln u_i}\frac{d\ln u_i}{dt}-\frac{\partial \ln TC}{\partial \ln \phi}\frac{d\ln \phi}{dt}\right)$$

$$=\left(\frac{wL}{TC}\frac{d\ln L}{dt}+\sum_{i=1}^{N}\frac{u_iK_i}{TC}\frac{d\ln K_i}{dt}+\frac{\phi D}{TC}\frac{d\ln D}{dt}\right).$$

Hence, the theoretical index (13) becomes:

(15a)
$$-\frac{\partial \ln TC}{\partial t}=\varepsilon\sum_{i=1}^{M}\left(\frac{P_iQ_i}{P\cdot Q}\frac{\mu_i}{\mu}\right)\frac{d\ln Q_i}{dt}-\left(\frac{wL}{TC}\frac{d\ln L}{dt}+\sum_{i=1}^{N}\frac{u_iK_i}{TC}\frac{d\ln K_i}{dt}+\frac{\phi D}{TC}\frac{d\ln D}{dt}\right).$$

Turned around, the 'growth accounting' form of (15a) is:

(15b)
$$\varepsilon\sum_{i=1}^{M}\left(\frac{P_iQ_i}{P\cdot Q}\frac{\mu_i}{\mu}\right)\frac{d\ln Q_i}{dt}=\left(\frac{wL}{TC}\frac{d\ln L}{dt}+\sum_{i=1}^{N}\frac{u_iK_i}{TC}\frac{d\ln K_i}{dt}+\frac{\phi D}{TC}\frac{d\ln D}{dt}\right)-\frac{\partial \ln TC}{\partial t}.$$

Expression (15b) delivers an explicit formula for the change in aggregate inputs and outputs. If there were no unobserved factor D, and if mark-up factors and the local scale elasticity were known, (15b) could readily be implemented. However, with an unobserved factor D, things are more complicated. We start with a proposal for a computable MFP measure and follow with a discussion of its interpretation.

5. Deriving Computable Measures

There are essentially three strategies for the implementation of expression (15b): (i) to introduce additional, and typically restrictive, hypotheses about the size or nature of the unknown variables until an expression emerges that is both computable and that offers a (seemingly) clear interpretation of productivity growth; (ii) to stay away from invoking additional hypotheses, and define a computable measure of productivity growth while allowing for the fact that it may reflect more than pure technology shifts; or (iii) impose the assumptions needed to apply econometric methods to estimate or correct for the unknown factor and construct estimates of the conceptually correct aggregates of outputs, inputs and productivity.

We discard the third possibility simply because it is not a practical way for statistical offices when they have to compute and publish periodic and easily reproducible statistical series. We do, however, acknowledge that this econometric option may be an important one for more research-oriented, one-off projects. As such it may also deliver useful insights concerning the empirical importance of the unobserved factor. Similarly, to assess some of the choices among non-parametric methods as described below, econometric studies (such as Paquet and Robidoux, 2001 or Oliveira-Martins et al., 1996) can be very useful.

5.1 Apparent Multi-Factor Productivity

We first follow avenue (ii) and propose a measure of 'apparent multi-factor productivity'. Then, in the following subsection we consider strategy (i).

For the purpose at hand, let there be an aggregator X that combines the quantities of the *observable* inputs K and L. Specifically, define

(16) $$\frac{d\ln X}{dt} \equiv \sum_{i=1}^{N} \frac{u_i K_i}{C} \frac{d\ln K_i}{dt} + \frac{wL}{C} \frac{d\ln L}{dt}$$

as a Divisia quantity index of observable inputs, noting that the weights correspond to the shares of each input in total *observable* inputs, as $C \equiv wL + u \cdot K$. Next, define the rate of apparent multi-factor productivity growth (AMFP) as the difference between a Divisia quantity index of output and the quantity index of observable inputs as specified above in (16):

(17a) $$\text{AMFP} \equiv \frac{d\ln Q}{dt} - \frac{d\ln X}{dt}.$$

The Divisia output index in (17a) is a 'traditional' one, i.e., an average of rates of change for individual outputs, each weighted by its revenue share: $\frac{d\ln Q}{dt} \equiv \sum_{i=1}^{M} \left(\frac{P_i Q_i}{P \cdot Q} \right) \frac{d\ln Q_i}{dt}$. Note that this Divisia output index differs from the more general output growth index identified in (15). The growth accounting equation that corresponds to (17a) is:

(17b) $$\frac{d\ln Q}{dt} = \sum_{i=1}^{N} \frac{u_i K_i}{C} \frac{d\ln K_i}{dt} + \frac{wL}{C} \frac{d\ln L}{dt} + \text{AMFP}$$

where, in conjunction with (15b), it can be shown that:

$$\text{(17c)} \qquad AMFP = -\frac{\partial \ln TC}{\partial t} + \sum_{i=1}^{M} \frac{P_i Q_i}{P \cdot Q}\left(1 - \frac{\varepsilon \mu_i}{\mu}\right)\frac{d \ln Q_i}{dt} + \frac{\phi D}{TC}\left(\frac{d \ln D}{dt} - \frac{d \ln X}{dt}\right).$$

According to (17b), the direct growth contribution of observed capital inputs and labour is given by the rate of change in these variables weighted by their respective average shares in observed costs C. The productivity term AMFP reflects the three factors shown in (17c): pure technical change or the shift of the cost function, a term that captures the effects of mark-ups and non-constant returns, and a term that captures the effects of the non-observed variable D. Consider the following special cases:

- If there is no unobserved input (D=0), the third term in (17c) disappears and AMFP captures technical change plus a term that reflects the non-constant returns and mark-ups – a result similar to the one developed by Denny, Fuss and Waverman (1981). AMFP will exactly correspond to technical change if there are constant returns to scale ($\varepsilon = 1$) and if the same mark-up factor applies throughout the economy ($\mu_i = \mu$).
- If the volume change of the unobserved input equals the volume change of observed inputs, the third term disappears also and AMFP reflects only technical change and the effects of non-constant returns and mark-ups.

We conclude that, whatever the exact nature of the unobserved factor D, the AMFP computation will capture 'pure' technical change, the growth contributions of unobserved assets and scale effects, and also the distribution of mark-ups. With the exception of the mark-ups that can be a consequence of market power, these effects are technology-related and could be considered analytically meaningful expressions of productivity growth. These effects are now path independent – they vary with the levels and growth rates of observed and non-observed inputs, and the latter depend in turn on prices of inputs and outputs as well as on mark-up size.

The contribution of productivity change to output growth is given by AMFP. Clearly, the interpretation of AMFP has to be kept in mind: it reflects the combined effects of technical change, of non-observed inputs, of non-constant returns to scale and of deviations from perfect competition in product markets. In other words, AMFP is a true 'residual' or a non-theoretic productivity measure. But for many practical purposes, it will fulfil its role as a multi-faceted measure of productivity growth.[9] We note in passing that AMFP could also serve as a useful measure of productivity growth when technical change is of a more general nature, and not necessarily Hicks-neutral.

If one wants to extend the analysis, an additional analytical step could be taken to decompose AMFP into its technical change component and other effects. However, this requires invoking parametric methods of estimation if one does not want to impose competitive behaviour on output product markets.

[9] As can be seen from the list of assets in our empirical implementation, one important asset that is left out is land, which is not considered a produced asset by the national accounts. This asset presumably does not grow much so the last term in (17c) is likely to be negative in OECD countries, pointing to a downward bias of AMFP as a measure of technical change.

5.2 Invoking Additional Assumptions

This subsection follows the approach (i) outlined at the start of the section: additional hypotheses are invoked to deal with the possible presence of unobserved inputs, non-constant returns to scale and mark-ups. Each set of hypotheses is designed so as to lead to a 'correct' measure of MFP in the sense that it reflects Hicks neutral technical change *if the hypotheses hold.* In addition, consideration is given to how, under the assumed circumstances, the pragmatic AMFP measure would fare. It is of interest, for example, whether its use would imply an upward or downward bias for measuring technical change and when the values would coincide with those for the conventional MFP measure.

5.2.1 Assuming no unobserved input, common mark-up factors and CRS

If one assumes that there are no unobserved inputs (D = 0), and a common mark-up factor in the different output markets ($\mu_i = \mu$), the only possibility to explain a difference between total costs of observed measures and GOS are the combined effects of a positive mark-up and non-constant returns. In this case, the mark-up/returns to scale ratio is given by $\frac{\mu}{\varepsilon} = 1 - \frac{M}{P \cdot Q}$, so it is determined by the ratio $M / P \cdot Q$ where M corresponds to the difference between non-labour income (GOS) and the sum of observed capital costs and where $P \cdot Q$ is the sum of revenues. If empirical information exists on the average mark-up factor, μ, it can be used to determine ε. Alternatively, information may exist on the average degree of returns to scale in the economy. If not, an additional assumption has to be invoked – typically that of constant returns to scale ($\varepsilon = 1$). Having defined away D, one finds that total costs equal observed costs, or TC = C.

In this case, the growth accounting equation (15b) can be expressed as

(18a) $$\sum_{i=1}^{M} \left(\frac{P_i Q_i}{P \cdot Q} \right) \frac{d \ln Q_i}{dt} - \left(\frac{wL}{C} \frac{d \ln L}{dt} + \sum_{i=1}^{N} \frac{u_i K_i}{C} \frac{d \ln K_i}{dt} \right) = MFP1, \text{ with}$$

(18b) $$MFP1 = -\frac{\partial \ln TC1}{\partial t}.$$

Here, TC1 is the modified cost function that applies under the conditions D = 0, $\mu_i = \mu$ and $\varepsilon = 1$. Expression (18b) indicates that MFP1 correctly traces technical change provided the assumptions D = 0, $\mu_i = \mu$ and $\varepsilon = 1$ are accurate. Under the stated assumptions, it is easy to see that $MFP1 = \frac{d \ln Q}{dt} - \frac{d \ln X}{dt}$, where this is the definition of AMFP given in (17a). Thus, if the assumptions above hold, the true productivity measure MFP1 given in (18b) coincides with the result obtained from applying an AMFP measure.

5.2.2 Assuming proportionality of D and K, absence of mark-up factors and CRS

A second possibility is to allow for an unobserved factor (D > 0) but to impose marginal cost pricing (hence $\mu_i = 1$ for $i = 1, \ldots, M$) and constant returns to scale. This is equivalent to assuming fully competitive output markets, and means that (10) implies that $P \cdot Q = TC$. With this setup, it follows that the entire difference between GOS and the sum of observed payments to capital is identified with payments to the unobserved input: $M = \phi D$. To evaluate (15b) for this situation, an additional assumption is needed. One possibility would be to assume that the rate of change of the unobserved input D equals that of the observed capital inputs: $\frac{d\ln D}{dt} = \frac{d\ln K}{dt}$, where $\frac{d\ln K}{dt} \equiv \sum_{i=1}^{N} \frac{u_i K_i}{u \cdot K} \frac{d\ln K_i}{dt}$ is a Divisia quantity index of observed fixed assets. Under these conditions, the growth accounting equation (15b) can be written as

$$\sum_{i=1}^{M} \frac{P_i Q_i}{P \cdot Q} \frac{d\ln Q_i}{dt} = \frac{wL}{P \cdot Q} \frac{d\ln L}{dt} + \frac{u \cdot K}{P \cdot Q} \frac{d\ln K}{dt} + \frac{M}{P \cdot Q} \frac{d\ln D}{dt} + MFP2$$

(19a)

$$= \frac{wL}{P \cdot Q} \frac{d\ln L}{dt} + \left(\frac{u \cdot K}{P \cdot Q} + \frac{M}{P \cdot Q} \right) \frac{d\ln K}{dt} + MFP2, \text{with}$$

(19b) $$MFP2 = -\frac{\partial \ln TC2}{\partial t}.$$

Now MFP2 given in (19b) traces the shift of the cost function TC2 correctly as long as the assumptions hold. The measured growth contribution of the observed capital inputs merits further discussion. It is easily verified that $\left(\frac{wL}{P \cdot Q} + \frac{u \cdot K}{P \cdot Q} + \frac{M}{P \cdot Q} \right) = 1$ so that the weight that now attaches to the observed capital inputs, $\left(\frac{u \cdot K}{P \cdot Q} + \frac{M}{P \cdot Q} \right) = \frac{GOS}{P \cdot Q}$, equals the share of GOS in total production, which in turn is the complement to the labour share in total income. Thus, the income of the unobserved factor D is distributed across the observed capital inputs, and (19a) can be rewritten as:

(19c) $$\frac{d\ln Q}{dt} = \left(\frac{wL}{P \cdot Q} \frac{d\ln L}{dt} + \frac{GOS}{P \cdot Q} \frac{d\ln K}{dt} \right) + MFP2,$$

using the expression for $(d\ln Q/dt)$ in the paragraph that follows equation (17a). Equation (19c) bears a strong resemblance to a model with endogenous net rates of return as described below in section 5.2.3. In both cases, the overall rate of growth of capital services, $d\ln K/dt$, enters with the same weight – one minus the labour share in total income. Of course, in the endogenous model, the growth rate of observed capital services, $d\ln K^*/dt$, will in general be different from $d\ln K/dt$ in the present case since each asset's user cost term is based on an endogenous rather than an exogenous rate of return. Nonetheless, as will be apparent from the empirical section, the two MFP measures trace each other quite closely, at least for the four countries examined and for the time period used in the empirical part of this paper.

Suppose the above assumptions are true but an AMFP measure is applied. What would be the resulting bias with regard to the 'true' MFP2 measure? After some manipulations, it can be shown that

(20) $$AMFP = MFP2 + \frac{M}{PQ} \left(\frac{d\ln K}{dt} - \frac{d\ln X}{dt} \right).$$

Thus, AMFP will overstate MFP2 if the growth rate of observed capital assets – and by assumption the growth rate of the unobserved asset – exceeds the growth rate of all observed inputs. In the empirical examples presented in section 6, this is the case and AMFP turns out to be consistently higher than MFP2.

5.2.3 Defining away mark-ups and unobserved inputs and assuming CRS

These are the assumptions invoked when MFP computations rely on endogenous rates of return: output markets are taken as competitive ($\mu_i = 1;\ i = 1,\dots,M$), there are no unobserved factors (D = 0) and there are constant returns to scale. The endogenous approach goes back to Christensen and Jorgenson (1969), and has been applied in many subsequent studies of productivity growth, including many carried out by national statistical offices (e.g., BLS 2003). This is the most widely-used methodology but also the one that requires the most restrictive set of assumptions: the assumptions needed to justify the use of endogenous rates of return[10]. In addition to the above assumptions, there must be perfect anticipation of asset price changes and depreciation. This implies that $P\cdot Q = wL + u^{*}\cdot K$. The growth accounting model (15b) becomes

(21a) $$\sum_{i=1}^{M}\left(\frac{P_iQ_i}{P\cdot Q}\right)\frac{d\ln Q_i}{dt} = \left(\frac{wL}{P\cdot Q}\frac{d\ln L}{dt} + \sum_{i=1}^{N}\frac{u_i^{*}K_i}{P\cdot Q}\frac{d\ln K_i}{dt}\right) + MFP3,\ \text{where}$$

(21b) $$MFP3 = -\frac{\partial \ln TC3}{\partial t},$$

and where TC3 denotes a cost function with observed inputs only. If the additional restrictions hold, measured productivity change corresponds to the shift of a cost function TC3 with CRS and only observed inputs. As alluded to above, there is similarity with (19c) because (21a) can be re-written as

(22) $$\frac{d\ln Q}{dt} = \left(\frac{wL}{P\cdot Q}\frac{d\ln L}{dt} + \frac{GOS}{P\cdot Q}\frac{d\ln K^{*}}{dt}\right) + MFP3\ \text{where}\ \frac{d\ln K^{*}}{dt} \equiv \sum_{i=1}^{N}\frac{u_i^{*}K_i}{u^{*}\cdot K}\frac{d\ln K_i}{dt},$$

so that the contribution of capital assets is the product of the rate of growth of observed capital services and the share of GOS in total output or cost.

If the above assumptions are correct, and if an endogenous rate of return is used, the evaluation of AMFP* would yield the correct result since $AMFP^{*} = -\frac{\partial \ln TC3}{\partial t} = MFP3$ in this case. We have marked AMFP* with an asterisk here to draw attention to the fact that AMFP is based on a capital measure that reflects endogenous rates of return. If AMFP is computed on the basis of exogenous rates, it would clearly differ from MFP3. This is also borne out in the empirical example below. However, no a-priori statement can be made as to the sign of this difference.

5.2.4 Assuming no mark-ups, no unobserved input and decreasing returns to scale: an input-based measure

This constitutes yet another possibility for dealing with the difference between revenues and observed factor payments: the unobserved factor is defined away (D = 0) as well as mark-ups of prices over marginal costs ($\mu_i = 1;\ i = 1,\dots M$), but the production technology is assumed

[10] The endogenous rate of return is computed by choosing that net rate of return that just equalizes the sum of user costs of observed assets with non-labour income (GOS for simplicity). Using the same notation for user costs as in footnote 2, this means that $GOS = \sum_{i=1}^{N} q^{i}(r^{*}+\delta^{i} - d\ln q^{i}/dt)K^{i}$.

to exhibit decreasing returns to scale ($\varepsilon > 1$). Then, the entire difference between GOS and observed asset rental payments is ascribed to the effects of marginal cost pricing under decreasing returns to scale: $M = (\varepsilon - 1)TC$ and TC = C. Under these circumstances, the returns to scale parameter can be computed as $\varepsilon = M/TC + 1$. Given a value for ε, (15b) can be rewritten as

$$\text{(23a)} \qquad \varepsilon \sum_{i=1}^{M} \left(\frac{P_i Q_i}{P \cdot Q} \right) \frac{d\ln Q_i}{dt} = \left(\frac{wL}{TC} \frac{d\ln L}{dt} + \sum_{i=1}^{N} \frac{u_i K_i}{TC} \frac{d\ln K_i}{dt} \right) + MFP4, \text{ where}$$

$$\text{(23b)} \qquad MFP4 = -\frac{\partial \ln TC4}{\partial t}$$

and where TC4 is a cost function with decreasing returns to scale and with observed factor inputs only. Some more discussion is useful here. First, because all costs are observed, TC = C and (23a) can be written as

$$\text{(23c)} \qquad \varepsilon \frac{d\ln Q}{dt} = \frac{d\ln X}{dt} + MFP4.$$

We note in passing that the same growth accounting equation and/or productivity measure MFP4 could have been derived from a model with a constant returns to scale cost function for observed and unobserved inputs, but with the added assumption that the quantity of the unobserved input is positive and fixed.[11] The unobserved input then acts as the additional cost factor that is equivalent to a decreasing returns to scale technology.

If the assumptions above are correct, how does MFP4 relate to AMFP? It is easily established that under these circumstances, $AMFP = MFP4 - (\varepsilon - 1)\frac{d\ln Q}{dt}$. If returns to scale are decreasing ($\varepsilon > 1$), and if the quantity of output increases ($d\ln Q / dt > 0$), AMFP will be smaller than MFP4, since AMFP captures both the effects of pure technical change and non-constant returns. This is borne out in the empirical section 6.

5.2.5 Assuming no mark-ups, no unobserved input and decreasing returns to scale: an output-based measure

It is well known that a production technology with non-constant returns to scale gives rise to several productivity measures (see, for example, Balk 1998). In particular there are differences between output-based measures of technology such as the shift of a production function or of a revenue function over time and input-based measures of technology such as the shift of a cost function or of an input distance function over time. In the sections above, the analysis has been based on a cost function, i.e., an input-based measure. To introduce an alternative and output-based measure of technical change, we shall consider a revenue function and its shift over time. As in section 5.2.4, we assume that there is no unobserved input and that there are no mark-ups. As a consequence, the value of M is entirely determined by the decreasing returns to scale and total costs equal observed costs (since $M = (\varepsilon - 1)TC$ where TC = C).

---

[11] The idea is based on Diewert and Nakamura (2007) who introduce an unknown variable into a cost function to deal with decreasing returns to scale.

To derive the output-based productivity measure, consider the revenue function[12] R, defined so as to show maximum revenues given a vector of inputs and a vector of output prices:

$$(24) \qquad R(P,L,K,t) = \max_{Q}\{P \cdot Q : (Q,L,K) \text{ belongs to } Z(t)\}.$$

Diewert (1983) first used a revenue function to define a theoretical productivity index, albeit in discrete time. We follow his approach and define the continuous-time equivalent as the partial derivative of the revenue function with respect to time: total differentiation of R yields the following output-based measure of technical change:

$$(25) \qquad \frac{\partial \ln R}{\partial t} = \frac{d\ln R}{dt} - \sum_{i=1}^{M} \frac{\partial \ln R}{\partial \ln P_i}\frac{d\ln P_i}{dt} - \frac{\partial \ln R}{\partial \ln L}\frac{d\ln L}{dt} - \sum_{i=1}^{N} \frac{\partial \ln R}{\partial \ln K_i}\frac{d\ln K_i}{dt}.$$

To derive a computable measure of the output-based productivity measure, an additional assumption has to be introduced: revenue-maximising behaviour on the part of producers. Then, observed revenues equal maximum revenues: $P \cdot Q = R$. If in addition firms are price takers, one gets $Q_i = \partial R / \partial P_i$. It is then straightforward to obtain a computable expression for the elasticity of revenues with respect to output prices:

$$(26) \qquad \frac{\partial \ln R}{\partial \ln P_i} = \frac{P_i Q_i}{R} = \frac{P_i Q_i}{P \cdot Q}.$$

Note that the assumptions of revenue maximisation and price taking on output markets were not necessary for the derivation of the input-based measure in section 5.2.4. Thus, the output-based productivity statistic requires different assumptions than the input-based statistic.

Now define the Divisia decomposition of total revenues into a price and a quantity index:

$$(27) \qquad \frac{d\ln R}{dt} = \sum_{i=1}^{M} \frac{P_i Q_i}{P \cdot Q}\frac{d\ln P_i}{dt} + \sum_{i=1}^{M} \frac{P_i Q_i}{P \cdot Q}\frac{d\ln Q_i}{dt}.$$

The first two expressions on the right hand side of (25) are equivalent to a Divisia quantity index of outputs: $\frac{d\ln R}{dt} - \sum_{i=1}^{M} \frac{P_i Q_i}{P \cdot Q}\frac{d\ln P_i}{dt} = \sum_{i=1}^{M} \frac{P_i Q_i}{P \cdot Q}\frac{d\ln Q_i}{dt} \equiv \frac{d\ln Q}{dt}$.

To find computable expressions for the input elasticities of the revenue function, we invoke the profit-maximising behaviour of producers. This implies that they solve a maximisation problem of the kind $\max_{L,K}\{R(P,L,K,t) - wL - u \cdot K\}$. The first order conditions for a maximum are $\partial R / \partial L = w$ and $\partial R / \partial K_i = u_i$ (i=1,...N). Consequently, $\partial \ln R / \partial \ln L = wL / R$ and $\partial \ln R / \partial \ln K_i = u_i K_i / R$ (i=1,...N). Then, the third and fourth expression on the right-hand side of (25) can be rewritten as

[12] The concept of a revenue function is due to Samuelson (1953-54).

$$\frac{\partial \ln R}{\partial \ln L}\frac{d\ln L}{dt}+\sum_{i=1}^{N}\frac{\partial \ln R}{\partial \ln K_i}\frac{d\ln K_i}{dt}=\frac{wL}{R}\frac{d\ln L}{dt}+\sum_{i=1}^{N}\frac{u_iK_i}{R}\frac{d\ln K_i}{dt}$$

(28)
$$=\frac{C}{R}\left(\frac{wL}{C}\frac{d\ln L}{dt}+\sum_{i=1}^{N}\frac{u_iK_i}{C}\frac{d\ln K_i}{dt}\right).$$
$$=\frac{C}{R}\frac{d\ln X}{dt}.$$

But $C/R = TC/P\cdot Q = 1/\varepsilon$ and the final computable expression for the output side-based productivity measure in (25) is

(29)
$$\frac{\partial \ln R}{\partial t}=\frac{d\ln Q}{dt}-\frac{1}{\varepsilon}\frac{d\ln X}{dt}=MFP5.$$

The link to AMFP is readily established: it can be shown that

(30)
$$MFP5=\frac{d\ln Q}{dt}-\frac{d\ln X}{dt}-\left(\frac{1}{\varepsilon}-1\right)\frac{d\ln X}{dt}=AMFP+\left(1-\frac{1}{\varepsilon}\right)\frac{d\ln X}{dt}.$$

Thus, MFP5 will exceed AMFP if the quantity index of inputs grows at a positive rate as can be observed in the country examples in section 6.

5.2.6 *A note on increasing returns to scale*

There is no reason to believe that returns to scale may not be locally increasing; hence this case must be treated as well. Suppose that $\varepsilon<1$. Unless the case of M < 0 is allowed, implying continuing losses for producers, increasing returns to scale must go together with positive mark-ups over marginal costs. Thus, in order to have M > 0 under increasing returns to scale, μ_i must be positive, but also less than unity for at least one product.

Then, $M = P\cdot Q(1-\mu/\varepsilon)$ if we assume that there is no unobserved input (D = 0). Under these assumptions, the growth accounting and productivity equation (15b) takes the form:

(31)
$$\frac{\varepsilon}{\mu}\sum_{i=1}^{M}\frac{P_iQ_i}{P\cdot Q}\mu_i\frac{d\ln Q_i}{dt}=\frac{d\ln X}{dt}+MFP6.$$

While (31) is a valid measure for the shift in a cost function, TC6, given increasing returns to scale and without unobserved inputs, it is apparent that with the observable information on prices, quantities and factor remuneration (31) still cannot be computed. Although ε/μ is known, there is not enough information to deduce values for product-specific mark-up factors μ_i. Extraneous information about mark-ups is required to compute MFP6. While such information sometimes is available, this cannot be expected on an ongoing, timely and comprehensive basis. For example, Oliveira-Martins et al. (1996) estimated mark-up ratios for 14 OECD countries by industry and report estimates of the typically positive mark-ups. But one-off studies are quickly outdated. Also, industry-level mark-up estimates are frequently confined to manufacturing industries, leaving uncovered important areas of the service sector. Overall, it would not seem practical for a statistical office to rely on mark-up estimates for purposes of productivity statistics. For the same reason, we are not in a position to compute empirical results for MFP6.

6. Empirical Implementation

After the theoretical derivations in section 5, we shall now move on to empirical considerations. Several questions arise. One concerns index numbers: how should the continuous-time formulae be translated into discrete index number formulae to accommodate the fact that data observations come in discrete form? A second question relates to how exactly some of the variables should be measured, in particular capital services and user costs of capital. Finally, we wish to compare the various productivity measures to get a sense of the importance of choices of assumptions.

6.1 Choice of Index Number Formulae

Concerning the index number issue, our approach has been one of approximating the continuous-time Divisia indices in the theoretical part of the paper by Törnqvist-type indices for the present empirical part. We are aware of the methodological shortcomings of this procedure: this discrete approximation is essentially an arbitrary choice,[13] not rigorously backed up by theory. A more thorough procedure would have been to start out with discrete formulations for the cost and revenue functions and then derive the appropriate index number formulae together with the productivity measure.[14] However, we feel that the theoretical advantages of a full derivation in discrete time are outweighed by the algebraic complications that such an approach brings along with including all the interaction terms which would add little to the message delivered in the present paper while making the exposition much less readable.

For the purpose at hand then, we chose the following Törnqvist-type approximations to the above Divisia-type formulations of the various productivity indices:

(32a) $$\frac{d\ln Q}{dt} \approx \sum_{i=1}^{M} \frac{1}{2}\left(\frac{P_i^t Q_i^t}{P^t \cdot Q^t} + \frac{P_i^{t-1} Q_i^{t-1}}{P^{t-1} \cdot Q^{t-1}}\right) \ln\left(\frac{Q_i^t}{Q_i^{t-1}}\right) \equiv \ln\left(\frac{Q^t}{Q^{t-1}}\right)$$

(32b)
$$\frac{d\ln X}{dt} \approx \frac{1}{2}\left(\frac{w^t L^t}{C^t} + \frac{w^{t-1} L^{t-1}}{C^{t-1}}\right) \ln\left(\frac{L^t}{L^{t-1}}\right) + \sum_{i=1}^{N} \frac{1}{2}\left(\frac{u_i^t K_i^t}{C^t} + \frac{u_i^{t-1} K_i^{t-1}}{C^{t-1}}\right) \ln\left(\frac{K_i^t}{K_i^{t-1}}\right) \equiv \ln\left(\frac{X^t}{X^{t-1}}\right)$$

(32c) $$AMFP^{t/t-1} = \ln\left(\frac{Q^t}{Q^{t-1}}\right) - \ln\left(\frac{X^t}{X^{t-1}}\right)$$

(32d) $$MFP1^{t/t-1} = AMFP^{t/t-1}$$

---

[13] That nearly all common index number formulae can be considered as discrete approximations to the Divisia index has already been shown by Frisch (1936). For a more recent statement, see Diewert (1980) or Balk (2005).

[14] Examples are provided by Balk (1998, section 3.7).

(32e)
$$MFP2^{t/t-1} = \ln\left(\frac{Q^t}{Q^{t-1}}\right) - \frac{1}{2}\left(\frac{w^t L^t}{P^t \cdot Q^t} + \frac{w^{t-1} L^{t-1}}{P^{t-1} \cdot Q^{t-1}}\right)\ln\left(\frac{L^t}{L^{t-1}}\right) - \sum_{i=1}^{N} \frac{1}{2}\left(\frac{u_i^t K_i^t + M^t}{P^t \cdot Q^t} + \frac{u_i^{t-1} K_i^{t-1} + M^{t-1}}{P^{t-1} \cdot Q^{t-1}}\right)\ln\left(\frac{K_i^t}{K_i^{t-1}}\right)$$

(32f)
$$MFP3^{t/t-1} = \ln\left(\frac{Q^t}{Q^{t-1}}\right) - \frac{1}{2}\left(\frac{w^t L^t}{P^t \cdot Q^t} + \frac{w^{t-1} L^{t-1}}{P^{t-1} \cdot Q^{t-1}}\right)\ln\left(\frac{L^t}{L^{t-1}}\right) - \sum_{i=1}^{N} \frac{1}{2}\left(\frac{u_i^{*t} K_i^t}{P^t \cdot Q^t} + \frac{u_i^{*t-1} K_i^{t-1}}{P^{t-1} \cdot Q^{t-1}}\right)\ln\left(\frac{K_i^t}{K_i^{t-1}}\right)$$

(32g)
$$MFP4^{t/t-1} = \frac{1}{2}\left(\varepsilon^t + \varepsilon^{t-1}\right)\ln\left(\frac{Q^t}{Q^{t-1}}\right) - \ln\left(\frac{X^t}{X^{t-1}}\right)$$

(32h)
$$MFP5^{t/t-1} = \ln\left(\frac{Q^t}{Q^{t-1}}\right) - \frac{1}{2}\left(\frac{1}{\varepsilon^t} + \frac{1}{\varepsilon^{t-1}}\right)\ln\left(\frac{X^t}{X^{t-1}}\right).$$

6.2 Measuring Outputs and Inputs

The empirical productivity measures developed in the present paper all relate to the total economy. This reflects data constraints rather than a preferred choice which would have been to limit computations to the corporate or business sector. Neither capital input measures nor hours worked are easily available in such a sectoral breakdown and calculations remain at the aggregate level, in line with the data available from the *OECD Productivity Database*.[15]

6.2.1 Outputs

Value-added has been measured at basic prices, i.e., excluding taxes on products but including product subsidies, because this valuation constitutes the economically relevant variable from a producer perspective. Time series on value-added and net indirect taxes were taken from the *OECD Annual National Accounts*.

A second adjustment to aggregate value-added is also required to maintain consistency between input and output data: capital input in the *OECD Productivity Database* is limited to non-residential, fixed assets in scope and consequently, the value-added produced with residential assets should be excluded from productivity calculations. Thus, total value-added is corrected for the production of owner-occupiers.[16] Note that both adjustments (valuation of output at basic prices and exclusion of the production of owner-occupiers of dwellings) have immediate consequence for the size of the endogenous rate of return as computed in MFP3 and for the weights that attach to capital and labour in MFP2. AMFP, on the other hand, is influenced

[15] www.oecd.org/statistics/productivity.

[16] The need for this exclusion and possible consequences for the measurement of the endogenous rates of return were pointed out to me by Mathilde Mas (University of Valencia).

by these adjustments only to the extent that they bear on the volume growth rate of output. Moreover, current-price value-added does not enter the AMFP computation because labour and capital weights are determined independently of the output measure. This is a distinct advantage in the presence of the AMFP approach.[17]

6.2.2 *Inputs*

Labour input is measured as total hours worked in the economy – a difficult task, especially at the international level. Even so, this remains an imperfect measure: no account is taken of differences in the value of hours of persons with different skill and experience levels. A more appropriate index of labour input would weight different types of hours worked by their corresponding shares in overall compensation. The most important measurement issues are described in a note available on the site of the *OECD Productivity Database*.

Capital inputs are derived with the perpetual inventory method. The estimation of capital service flows starts with identifying those assets that correspond to the breakdown currently available from the OECD/Eurostat National Accounts questionnaire, augmented by information on information and communication technology assets. Only non-residential gross fixed capital formation is considered for seven types of assets or products: Products of agriculture, metal products and machinery (IT hardware; communications equipment; other); transport equipment; non-residential construction; other products (software; other).

Investment. For each type of asset, a time series of current-price investment expenditure and the corresponding price indices are assembled starting with 1960. For many countries, this involves a certain amount of estimation, in particular for the period 1960-80. Such estimates are typically based on national accounts data prior to the introduction of SNA93, or on relationships between different types of assets that are established for recent periods and projected backwards. For purposes of exposition of the methodology, the current price investment series for asset type i in year t are denoted by IN_t^i (i=1,2, ..., 7) and the corresponding price index is denoted by $q_{t,0}^i$. Price indices are normalised to the reference year 1995 where $q_{t,0}^i = 1$.

Price indices should be constant quality deflators that reflect price changes for a given investment good. This is particularly important for those items that have seen rapid quality change such as information and communication technology (ICT) assets. For instance, observed price changes of 'computer boxes' had to be quality-adjusted to permit comparison of different vintages. Schreyer (2000) used a set of 'harmonised' ICT deflators to control for some of the differences in methodology.[18] We follow this approach and assume that the ratios between ICT and non-ICT asset prices evolve in a similar manner across countries, using the United States as the benchmark. Although no claim is made that the 'harmonised' deflator is necessarily the

[17] For example, the available OECD national accounts data do not allow us to single out the production of the owner-occupied dwellings industry – only the parent aggregate with real estate, renting and business activities is available. For purposes of the present computations, an assumption had to be made that the production of owner-occupiers accounts for one third of the entire industry. Obviously, this introduces a potential bias in those computations that depend on this adjustment.

[18] Wyckoff (1995) was one of the first to point out that the large differences that could be observed between computer price indices in OECD countries were likely much more a reflection of differences in statistical methodology than true differences in price changes. In particular, those countries that employ hedonic methods to construct ICT deflators tend to register a larger drop in ICT prices than countries that do not.

correct price index for a given country, the possible error due to using a harmonised price index is smaller than the bias arising from comparing capital services based on national deflators[19].

Productive stocks. Given price and volume series for investment goods, for each of the (supposedly) homogenous asset types, a productive stock S_t^i has been constructed as follows:

(33) $$S_t^i = \sum_{\tau=1}^{T^i} (IN_{t-\tau}^i / q_{t-\tau,0}^i) h_\tau^i F_\tau^i , \quad i=1, \ldots, 7.$$

In this expression, the productive stock of asset i at the beginning of period t is the sum over all past investments for this asset, where current price investment in past periods, $IN_{t-\tau}^i$ has been deflated with the purchase price index of new capital goods, $q_{t-\tau,0}^i$. T^i represents the maximum service life of asset type i. Because past vintages of capital goods are less efficient than new ones, an age efficiency function h_τ^i has been applied. It describes the efficiency time profile of an asset, conditional on its survival and is defined as a hyperbolic function of the form used by the United States Bureau of Labor Statistics (BLS 1983), $h_\tau^i = (T^i - \tau)/(T^i - \beta\tau)$.

Capital goods of the same type purchased in the same year do not generally retire at the same moment. More likely, there is a retirement distribution around a mean service life. In the present calculations, a normal distribution with a standard deviation of 25 percent of the average service life is chosen to represent the probability of retirement. The distribution was truncated at an assumed maximum service life of 1.5 times the average service life. The parameter F_τ^i is the cumulative value of this distribution, describing the probability of survival over a cohort's life span. The following average service lives are assumed for the different assets: 7 years for IT equipment; 15 years for communications equipment, other equipment and transport equipment; 60 years for non-residential structures; 3 years for software; and 7 years for the remaining products. The parameter β in the age-efficiency function was set to 0.8. Service lives and parameter values were specified following BLS practices.

User costs of capital. In a fully functioning asset market, the purchase price of an asset will equal the discounted flow of the value of services that the asset is expected to generate in the future. This equilibrium condition is used to derive the rental price or user cost expression for assets. Let $q_{t,0}^i$ denote the purchase price in year t of a new (zero-year old) asset of type i, and let $u_{t+\tau,\tau}^i$ be the rental price that this asset is expected to fetch in period $t+\tau$ (first subscript to the right) when the asset will be of age τ (second subscript to the right). With r as the nominal discount rate valid at time t, the asset market equilibrium condition for a new asset (age zero) is:

(34a) $$q_{t,0}^i = \sum_{\tau=0}^{\infty} u_{t+\tau+1,\tau}^i (1+r)^{-(\tau+1)} .$$

[19] See Schreyer et al. (2003) for details. There is a difficulty with the harmonised deflator that should be noted. From an accounting perspective, adjusting the price index for investment goods for any country implies an adjustment of the volume index of output. In most cases, such an adjustment would increase the measured rate of volume output change. At the same time, effects on the economy-wide rate of GDP growth appear to be relatively small (see Schreyer (2002) for a discussion).

This formulation implies that rentals are paid at the end of each period. To solve this expression for the rental price, the price for a one year old asset in period t+1 is computed as $q^i_{t+1,1} = \sum_{\tau=0}^{\infty} u^i_{t+\tau+2,\tau+1}(1+r)^{-(\tau+1)}$ and then subtracted from the expression above to obtain $u^i_{t+1,0} = q^i_{t,0}(1+r) - q^i_{t+1,1}$ or $u^i_{t,0} = q^i_{t-1,0}(1+r) - q^i_{t,1}$ which can be transformed into

(34b) $$u^i_{t,0} = q^i_{t-1,0}(r + d^i_{t,0} - \zeta^i_{t,0} + d^i_{t,0}\zeta^i_{t,0}).$$

This is the user cost formulation[20] applied in the present paper, where the rate of depreciation of asset i has been defined as $d^i_{t,s} \equiv 1 - q^i_{t,s+1}/q^i_{t,s}$ and the rate of price change of the same asset is given by $\zeta^i_t \equiv q^i_{t,s}/q^i_{t-1,s} - 1$. Note that the different variables in the user cost equation are expectations because they invoke knowledge about price changes in future periods.

These expectations govern the rental price. The System of National Accounts that capital stock data should tie into is based on ex-post prices, observed in the context of actual transactions. Would the use of user cost expressions such as those discussed above be in contradiction with the principles of national accounts?

The answer is 'no'. The presence of expectations does not make the user cost term less 'real': transactions are concluded at this price, even if with hindsight (ex post) the expectations underlying the transactions may turn out to be wrong. This is most apparent when one thinks of a case where capital goods are rented: the observed rental price characterises the transaction and is the relevant market price, typically dependent on expectations on the side of the lessor and the lessee. Nobody would challenge using such observed prices in the national accounts. If rental prices are not observable, values have to be imputed, and the expression above indicates how this can be done on the basis of economic theory. Imputations are numerous in the national accounts, and in this sense, the imputation of user costs would not constitute an exception.

Thus, it is not the presence of an expected variable as such that is at issue. The real issue from a capital and productivity measurement viewpoint is whether the realised, but unobserved, marginal productivity of fixed assets is better approximated by an ex-ante or an ex-post measure of user costs.[21] On this matter, Berndt (1990) points out that: "…if one wants to use a measure of capital to calculate actual multifactor productivity growth, then theory tells us quite clearly that we should weight the various traditionally measured capital inputs by their realised marginal products, not their expected marginal products. This means that in choosing capital service price weights, one should employ shadow values or ex post rates of return, and not the ex ante rates of return that are appropriate in the investment context."

While we concur with Berndt's statement that for purposes of productivity measurement, realised marginal products are the appropriate weights, this does not mean that ex post rates of return are always the preferred approximation to realised marginal productivity. Suppose that a

---

[20] Jorgenson and Yun (2001) show how tax considerations enter the user cost of capital and how they affect measured economic performance. This is one of the projects for expansion of the OECD Productivity Database. At present, however, these parameters are not considered in our set of user costs and capital measures.

[21] The distinction between ex-ante and ex-post user costs has been discussed by Berndt and Fuss (1986), Harper et al. (1989), Diewert (2001), Berndt (1990) in his discussion of Hulten (1990) and Hill and Hill (2003).

capital asset is rented by a producer at a given, pre-agreed rental price to be paid by the end of the period. The lessee of the asset will use it in his production process as planned regardless of the ex-post rental price. Therefore, the marginal productivity of the asset in the production process would best be approximated by the ex-ante rental price that is the price at which the rental transaction actually took place.

Take another case of an owner/producer and suppose that there has been investment at the beginning of the period in line with the ex-ante user cost. Now let there be a change in market conditions that leads to a modification of expectations and of user costs. If capital is fully flexible and can be adjusted continuously, it will be adjusted in line with the new user cost term. But the user cost term is governed by expectations, even though the expectations may have changed. It is only when capital cannot be adjusted that the ex-post user cost term would furnish the preferred approximation to the realised marginal productivity of an asset. This is the case that Berndt (1990) and Berndt and Fuss (1986) have in mind and it relies on quasi-fixity of capital in the production process. Thus, there is no general conclusion that ex-post user cost measures should always be preferred to ex-ante ones for measuring and aggregating capital input.

There is another conceptual difficulty with ex post user costs: the computation of the realised rates of return is commonly done by choosing a rate of return so that the ensuing user cost and total value of capital services just exhausts the measured gross operating surplus available from the national accounts. This computation relies, however, on the assumption that there is only one ex-post rate of return that applies to all assets. While equalisation of rates of return across assets is a natural assumption in an ex-ante context, it is much harder to justify in an ex-post context, especially given states of disequilibrium. Essentially it amounts to imposing an equilibrium condition to implement an (ex-post) measure that was specifically chosen on the grounds that it captures the nature of a situation of disequilibrium.

Diewert (2001) also points out that while the ex-post measure (of the nominal rate of return) is widely used in empirical research, it is subject to measurement error and it may not reflect the economic conditions facing producers at the beginning of the period.

A practical argument against the use of an ex-post rate is that its calculation requires information on the level of the productive capital stock at current prices (or alternatively on the wealth stock at current prices). However, levels of capital stocks tend to be less reliable statistics than their rates of change, especially when long historical investment series have to be estimated. This problem does not arise when user costs and nominal rates of return are of an ex-ante nature and therefore are exogenous variables. On the other hand, ex-post rates of return are of interest as such, and straightforward to compute. In sum then, there is no clear conclusion on this matter. In the present work, preference is given to an ex-ante approach, mainly because it allows us to develop capital service measures independently from measures of labour compensation, gross operating surplus and mixed income in the national accounts.

Exogenous net rate of return. To compute the net rate of return, following a suggestion of Diewert (2001), the starting point is the constant value for the expected real interest rate rr. The constant real rate is computed by taking a series of annual observed nominal rates (an unweighted average of interest rates with different maturities[22]) and deflating them by the

[22] These are the average bank rate, the bank rate on prime loans, long-term government bond yields, short-term government bond yields, the interest rate on a 90 day bank fixed deposit, and the treasury bill rate.

consumer price index. The resulting series of real interest rates is averaged over the period (1980-2000) to yield a constant value for rr. The expected nominal interest rate for every year is then computed as $r_t = (1+rr)(1+p_t)-1$ where p is the expected value of an overall deflator, the consumer price index.

To obtain a measure for p, the expected overall inflation, we construct a 5-year centered moving average of the rate of change of the consumer price index $p_t = \sum_{s=-2}^{+2} CPI_{t-s}$, where CPI_t is the annual percentage change of the consumer price index. This equals the expected rate of overall price change and, by implication, the nominal net rate of return.

Expected asset price changes, another element in the user cost equation, are derived as a smoothed series of actual asset price changes: a 5-year centered moving average filter is used.

Depreciation rates have been computed using the definition given above, $d_{t,0}^i \equiv 1 - q_{t,1}^i / q_{t,0}^i$. So, the rate of depreciation for a new asset equals one minus the ratio of the market price for a year old asset over the market price for a new asset. The market price for a new asset can be observed directly, but the price for a one-year old asset must be computed using the asset market equilibrium condition (34), the age-efficiency function h and the discount rate.

6.3 Results

Tables 1-4 summarise empirical results for Canada, France, the United States and Japan. They show the rates of change of output (GDP) and labour input as well as the volume changes of capital services alternatively based on exogenous and endogenous rates of return as well as the various MFP measures. The first observation is that moving from an endogenous to an exogenous rate of return leads to a rise in the observed measure of capital input – at least in the case of the countries considered and for the period at hand. Also, labour and capital shares turn out to be quite different when based on total costs rather than total revenue.

The second panel in each table reviews results for the five alternative MFP measures presented in the text above. It is immediately apparent that the different options – each associated with a particular set of assumptions about market structures or production technology – can lead to considerable variation in the resulting MFP measures, France being a noticeable exception. Unless a-priori knowledge about technology and market structure are available, it will be difficult to choose between the different options. Also, every different MFP measure implies a different message about the relative contribution of capital services to output growth. For all four countries examined, measured productivity growth turns out to be slowest when based on endogenous rate models (MFP3) or when assuming proportionality between capital input and an unobserved factor (MFP2). The output-based productivity measure that allows for decreasing returns to scale (MFP5) is generally the fastest-growing item in each country, followed by the input-based productivity measure with decreasing returns to scale (MFP4).

However, a simple geometric average of the five specific MFP measures yields a time series that is very close to the simple AMFP measure. In the absence of a-priori information on mark-ups, returns to scale, or unobserved assets, the choice of a measure that is close to the average of the different options may be a reasonable one. This is one of our conclusions.

Table 1. Canada

Basic series

	Output	Hours worked		Capital services			
				Exogenous RoR		Endogenous RoR	
	Volume index	Cost share	Volume index	Cost share	Volume index	Revenue share	Volume index
1985	100.0	71.70%	100.0	28.30%	100.0	33.30%	100.0
1986	102.4	72.69%	102.9	27.31%	105.0	32.28%	105.8
1987	106.7	73.54%	106.4	26.46%	110.6	32.41%	112.1
1988	112.0	73.69%	110.7	26.31%	116.9	32.07%	119.2
1989	114.9	71.39%	112.9	28.61%	123.1	31.36%	126.5
1990	115.1	70.34%	112.6	29.66%	128.7	30.49%	133.1
1991	112.6	69.61%	109.2	30.39%	133.7	28.71%	139.1
1992	113.6	73.23%	108.0	26.77%	138.3	28.19%	144.5
1993	116.3	72.76%	110.1	27.24%	142.7	28.52%	149.7
1994	121.8	75.35%	113.3	24.65%	147.6	30.91%	155.4
1995	125.2	74.38%	114.6	25.62%	152.9	32.32%	161.2
1996	127.3	76.10%	116.8	23.90%	158.6	32.16%	167.3
1997	132.7	74.31%	118.5	25.69%	166.5	32.65%	175.5
1998	138.1	74.22%	121.5	25.78%	175.3	31.48%	184.6
1999	145.8	73.00%	125.4	27.00%	184.9	32.94%	194.5
2000	153.5	74.31%	128.4	25.69%	194.3	34.56%	204.3
2001	156.4	72.66%	128.4	27.34%	202.9	..	204.3
2002	161.6	72.29%	130.3	27.71%	209.7	..	204.3
85-90	2.81%	72.23%	2.37%	27.77%	5.05%	31.98%	5.71%
90-95	1.70%	72.61%	0.35%	27.39%	3.45%	29.86%	3.84%
95-00	4.07%	74.38%	2.28%	25.62%	4.80%	32.69%	4.73%
95-02	3.64%	73.91%	1.84%	26.09%	4.51%	32.69%	3.38%

Productivity measures

	MFP1 =AMFP	MFP2	MFP3	MFP4	MFP5	Average
1985	100.0	100.0	100.0	100.0	100.0	100.0
1986	99.0	98.9	98.6	99.2	99.2	99.0
1987	99.2	99.1	98.6	99.8	99.8	99.3
1988	99.7	99.4	98.8	100.6	100.6	99.8
1989	99.3	98.9	98.1	100.4	100.4	99.4
1990	98.4	97.9	96.9	99.5	99.5	98.5
1991	97.3	96.9	95.7	98.4	98.4	97.3
1992	98.0	97.5	96.2	99.1	99.0	98.0
1993	98.1	97.6	96.2	99.2	99.2	98.0
1994	99.7	99.2	97.7	101.1	101.0	99.7
1995	100.7	100.1	98.4	102.4	102.2	100.8
1996	100.0	99.2	97.6	101.9	101.7	100.0
1997	101.9	100.8	99.2	104.3	103.8	102.0
1998	102.7	101.5	99.9	105.5	105.0	102.9
1999	104.5	103.1	101.5	107.9	107.1	104.8
2000	106.7	105.1	103.5	110.7	109.7	107.1
2001	107.5	..	..	110.7	..	109.1
2002	108.8	..	..	108.5	..	108.7
85-90	-0.31%	-0.42%	-0.63%	-0.09%	-0.10%	-0.31%
90-95	0.46%	0.43%	0.32%	0.58%	0.53%	0.46%
95-00	1.15%	0.97%	0.99%	1.56%	1.42%	1.22%
95-02	1.10%	..	..	0.82%	..	1.08%

Source: OECD Productivity Database May 2004.

Table 2. France

Basic series

	Output	Hours worked		Capital services			
				Exogenous RoR		Endogenous RoR	
	Volume index	Cost share	Volume index	Cost share	Volume index	Revenue share	Volume index
1985	100.0	69.53%	100.0	30.47%	100.0	24.32%	100.0
1986	102.4	70.42%	99.8	29.58%	102.7	26.56%	102.8
1987	105.0	71.36%	100.3	28.64%	105.7	27.46%	105.9
1988	109.8	71.48%	101.3	28.52%	109.4	28.88%	109.6
1989	114.4	70.06%	101.9	29.94%	113.7	30.06%	113.9
1990	117.4	69.81%	102.8	30.19%	118.4	29.80%	118.6
1991	118.6	69.11%	102.4	30.89%	122.7	29.94%	123.0
1992	120.4	68.10%	101.8	31.90%	126.5	30.39%	126.9
1993	119.3	68.26%	99.7	31.74%	129.4	30.59%	129.9
1994	121.8	67.91%	99.5	32.09%	132.3	31.64%	132.7
1995	123.8	68.67%	98.8	31.33%	135.0	31.89%	135.4
1996	125.2	68.86%	99.5	31.14%	137.7	31.71%	138.2
1997	127.5	69.50%	99.5	30.50%	140.5	32.30%	141.0
1998	131.9	70.50%	100.3	29.50%	144.0	33.09%	144.4
1999	136.1	71.89%	101.9	28.11%	148.5	32.87%	148.6
2000	141.3	71.12%	101.3	28.88%	153.6	33.21%	153.5
2001	144.2	68.83%	101.5	31.17%	158.5	33.00%	158.3
2002	146.0	69.40%	101.1	30.60%	161.7	32.38%	161.5
85-90	3.21%	70.44%	0.56%	29.56%	3.37%	27.85%	3.42%
90-95	1.06%	68.64%	-0.79%	31.36%	2.62%	30.71%	2.64%
95-00	2.64%	70.09%	0.50%	29.91%	2.59%	32.51%	2.50%
95-02	2.36%	69.85%	0.33%	30.15%	2.59%	32.56%	2.52%

Productivity measures

	MFP1 =AMFP	MFP2	MFP3	MFP4	MFP5	Average
1985	100.0	100.0	100.0	100.0	100.0	100.0
1986	101.8	101.9	101.9	101.6	101.7	101.8
1987	103.1	103.3	103.2	102.9	103.0	103.1
1988	106.0	106.2	106.2	105.7	105.9	106.0
1989	108.8	109.0	108.9	108.5	108.7	108.8
1990	109.6	109.8	109.7	109.3	109.5	109.6
1991	109.8	110.0	109.9	109.5	109.7	109.8
1992	110.8	111.1	111.0	110.5	110.7	110.8
1993	110.5	110.9	110.8	110.3	110.4	110.6
1994	112.2	112.6	112.5	111.9	112.1	112.3
1995	113.9	114.3	114.1	113.6	113.8	113.9
1996	113.9	114.3	114.2	113.6	113.8	114.0
1997	115.3	115.7	115.6	115.0	115.2	115.4
1998	117.7	118.1	118.0	117.6	117.7	117.8
1999	119.1	119.4	119.3	119.2	119.2	119.2
2000	122.9	122.9	123.0	123.3	123.1	123.1
2001	124.2	124.1	124.1	124.7	124.4	124.3
2002	125.2	125.1	125.1	125.8	125.4	125.3
85-90	1.83%	1.86%	1.85%	1.78%	1.81%	1.83%
90-95	0.77%	0.80%	0.80%	0.77%	0.77%	0.78%
95-00	1.53%	1.46%	1.49%	1.65%	1.57%	1.54%
95-02	1.35%	1.29%	1.31%	1.46%	1.39%	1.36%

Source: OECD Productivity Database May 2004.

Table 3: Japan

Basic series

	Output	Hours worked		Capital services			
				Exogenous RoR		Endogenous RoR	
	Volume index	Cost share	Volume index	Cost share	Volume index	Revenue share	Volume index
1985	100.0	73.61%	100.0	26.39%	100.0	29.35%	100.0
1986	103.0	75.51%	100.7	24.49%	104.4	29.98%	104.4
1987	106.9	77.02%	101.1	22.98%	109.3	30.28%	109.2
1988	114.1	77.74%	102.0	22.26%	115.2	31.72%	114.8
1989	120.1	77.24%	102.4	22.76%	122.2	32.42%	121.3
1990	126.4	73.80%	102.2	26.20%	129.1	32.60%	128.0
1991	130.6	73.72%	102.6	26.28%	136.4	32.19%	135.1
1992	131.9	72.24%	102.0	27.76%	143.2	32.16%	141.8
1993	132.2	72.20%	99.3	27.80%	149.2	31.81%	147.7
1994	133.7	72.84%	99.0	27.16%	154.4	31.49%	152.9
1995	136.2	72.40%	98.4	27.60%	160.2	31.23%	158.6
1996	140.9	71.80%	99.3	28.20%	167.2	32.28%	165.2
1997	143.5	70.92%	98.8	29.08%	174.4	32.22%	172.0
1998	141.9	69.20%	97.0	30.80%	181.0	31.91%	178.6
1999	142.0	71.00%	94.5	29.00%	187.3	32.11%	184.5
2000	146.0	71.88%	95.0	28.12%	192.9	32.60%	189.5
2001	146.7	69.41%	93.8	30.59%	197.2	32.61%	194.0
2002	146.1	71.57%	92.0	28.43%	198.9	32.80%	195.5
85-90	4.68%	75.82%	0.43%	24.18%	5.11%	31.06%	4.94%
90-95	1.50%	72.87%	-0.75%	27.13%	4.32%	31.91%	4.29%
95-00	1.38%	71.20%	-0.71%	28.80%	3.71%	32.06%	3.56%
95-02	1.00%	71.02%	-0.96%	28.98%	3.08%	32.22%	2.99%

Productivity measures

	MFP1 =AMFP	MFP2	MFP3	MFP4	MFP5	Average
1985	100.0	100.0	100.0	100.0	100.0	100.0
1986	101.3	101.1	101.2	101.5	101.4	101.3
1987	103.7	103.3	103.4	104.3	103.9	103.7
1988	108.6	107.8	108.2	110.1	109.1	108.7
1989	112.5	111.1	111.8	114.8	113.2	112.7
1990	117.0	115.0	115.7	120.1	117.9	117.1
1991	118.9	116.4	117.2	122.4	119.9	118.9
1992	118.9	116.1	116.7	122.6	120.1	118.9
1993	120.2	117.1	117.4	123.9	121.3	119.9
1994	120.6	117.3	117.3	124.4	121.7	120.2
1995	122.3	118.7	118.8	126.2	123.4	121.8
1996	124.2	120.4	120.8	128.5	125.5	123.8
1997	125.3	121.3	121.7	129.8	126.7	124.9
1998	124.2	120.0	120.3	128.5	125.6	123.7
1999	125.2	120.9	121.1	129.6	126.6	124.6
2000	127.3	122.7	122.8	132.0	128.7	126.7
2001	128.1	123.4	123.3	132.9	129.6	127.4
2002	129.1	124.3	123.5	133.8	130.5	128.2
85-90	3.14%	2.79%	2.91%	3.67%	3.29%	3.16%
90-95	0.88%	0.63%	0.54%	0.99%	0.92%	0.79%
95-00	0.80%	0.68%	0.66%	0.89%	0.84%	0.77%
95-02	0.78%	0.66%	0.56%	0.84%	0.79%	0.72%

Source: OECD Productivity Database May 2004.

Table 4: United States

Basic series

	Output	Hours worked		Capital services			
				Exogenous RoR		Endogenous RoR	
	Volume index	Cost share	Volume index	Cost share	Volume index	Revenue share	Volume index
1985	100.0	73.26%	100.0	26.74%	100.0	27.77%	100.0
1986	103.4	73.67%	101.1	26.33%	103.7	27.54%	103.7
1987	106.8	74.09%	104.0	25.91%	107.3	27.42%	107.1
1988	111.3	74.58%	107.1	25.42%	110.7	27.06%	110.5
1989	115.2	73.18%	110.0	26.82%	114.5	28.07%	114.2
1990	117.2	72.79%	110.7	27.21%	118.0	27.51%	117.7
1991	116.6	72.21%	108.9	27.79%	121.0	27.12%	120.7
1992	120.2	73.41%	109.2	26.59%	124.2	27.33%	123.9
1993	123.4	75.19%	112.0	24.81%	127.6	27.55%	127.1
1994	128.4	75.47%	114.8	24.53%	131.4	28.19%	130.7
1995	131.9	76.20%	117.4	23.80%	136.3	28.50%	135.2
1996	136.7	76.16%	119.0	23.84%	142.4	29.37%	140.6
1997	142.8	76.71%	122.3	23.29%	150.2	29.91%	147.3
1998	148.9	76.08%	125.3	23.92%	159.4	28.95%	155.1
1999	155.1	76.76%	127.7	23.24%	169.6	28.59%	163.8
2000	161.0	76.51%	129.4	23.49%	179.5	27.52%	172.4
2001	161.4	74.35%	128.4	25.65%	186.9	27.56%	179.1
2002	165.3	73.32%	127.8	26.68%	192.6	..	..
85-90	3.17%	73.60%	2.03%	26.40%	3.32%	27.56%	3.25%
90-95	2.36%	74.21%	1.18%	25.79%	2.88%	27.70%	2.78%
95-00	3.98%	76.40%	1.95%	23.60%	5.51%	28.81%	4.86%
95-02	3.22%	75.76%	1.21%	24.24%	4.94%	28.63%	..

Productivity measures

	MFP1 =AMFP	MFP2	MFP3	MFP4	MFP5	Average
1985	100.0	100.0	100.0	100.0	100.0	100.0
1986	101.6	101.6	101.5	101.6	101.6	101.6
1987	101.9	101.8	101.7	102.0	102.0	101.9
1988	103.0	103.0	102.8	103.2	103.2	103.0
1989	103.6	103.6	103.5	103.9	103.9	103.7
1990	104.1	104.0	103.8	104.4	104.3	104.1
1991	104.1	104.1	103.7	104.4	104.3	104.1
1992	106.3	106.2	105.9	106.6	106.5	106.3
1993	106.4	106.3	106.0	106.7	106.7	106.4
1994	107.9	107.8	107.6	108.4	108.3	108.0
1995	108.0	107.8	107.9	108.7	108.5	108.2
1996	109.6	109.3	109.6	110.6	110.3	109.9
1997	110.7	110.2	111.0	112.1	111.7	111.1
1998	111.8	111.1	112.4	113.7	113.1	112.4
1999	113.1	112.1	113.7	115.3	114.6	113.7
2000	114.6	113.4	115.1	117.2	116.4	115.3
2001	114.4	113.0	114.4	117.0	116.2	115.0
2002	116.7	..	..	..	..	116.7
85-90	0.80%	0.79%	0.75%	0.86%	0.84%	0.81%
90-95	0.73%	0.72%	0.76%	0.81%	0.79%	0.76%
95-00	1.19%	1.00%	1.30%	1.50%	1.39%	1.28%
95-02	1.11%	..	..	..	..	1.08%

Source: OECD Productivity Database May 2004.

7. Conclusions

This paper examined productivity and growth accounting measures when rates of return to capital inputs are exogenously determined. Several hypotheses about competition on output markets and about technology are invoked, each of which is compatible with exogenous rates of return. The following conclusions emerge.

The endogenous case – widely used in empirical research – imposes quite stringent assumptions: constant returns to scale and fully competitive output markets, no unobserved capital inputs and perfect foresight for producers regarding the expected changes in prices and rates of return and depreciation.

Different hypotheses are consistent with different MFP measures. In the absence of further a-priori information or recourse to parametric techniques, there is no obvious way of discriminating among the different hypotheses and hence making an informed choice among the alternative productivity and growth accounting measures.

This is evidenced for the four countries. In total, five different productivity measures were computed, each consistent with a set of assumptions. Empirically, the differences matter.

The paper suggests a pragmatic way forward: using an 'Apparent' MFP (AMFP) measure that is simply the ratio between a volume index of output and a volume index of the observed inputs. AMFP is not a pure measure of technical change defined as a path-independent shift in the production or cost function. However, AMFP is shown to have the following properties:

- The measure is close to the average of other measures.
- It is easy to explain.
- It can be applied when assumptions about the nature of 'pure' technical change are relaxed allowing, for example, formulations that encompass neutral and biased technical change.
- It relies on input measures that are independent from output measures and whose quality therefore does not vary with the quality and available detail of production or value-added data.

Clearly, the interpretation of AMFP has to be kept in mind: it reflects the combined effects of technical change, of unobserved inputs, of non-constant returns to scale and, indirectly, of deviations from perfect competition in product markets. In other words, AMFP is a true 'residual'. But for many practical purposes, it should prove useful as a multi-faceted measure of productivity growth.

References

Balk, Bert M. (1998), *Industrial Price, Quantity, and Productivity Indices*, Kluwer Academic Publishers.

Balk, Bert M. (2000), "Divisia Price and Quantity Indices: 80 Years After," *Statistica Neerlandica* 59, 119-158.

Basu, Susanto, John G. Fernald, Nicholas Oulton and Sylaja Srinivasan (2003), "The Case of the Missing Productivity Growth: or, does Information Technology Explain why Productivity Accelerated in the United States but not in the United Kingdom?," *NBER Working Paper Series*, Working Paper 10010.

Basu, Susanto and Miles S. Kimball (1997), "Cyclical Productivity with Unobserved Input Variation," *NBER Working Paper Series*, Working Paper No 5915.

Berndt, Ernst R. (1990), Comments on Hulten (1990) in Ernst R. Berndt and Jack Triplett (eds.), *Fifty Years of Economic Measurement*, NBER.

Berndt, Ernst R. and Melvyn A. Fuss (1986), "Productivity Measurement with Adjustments for Variations in Capacity Utilisation and Other Forms of Temporary Equilibria," *Journal of Econometrics* 33, 7-29.

Bureau of Labor Statistics (BLS) (2003), Multi-factor Productivity Measures, available from www.bls.gov/mfp/home.htm.

Bureau of Labor Statistics (BLS) (1983), Trends in Multifactor Productivity, 1948-81, Bulletin 2178.

Christensen, Laurits R. and Dale W. Jorgenson (1969), "The Measurement of U.S. Real Capital Input, 1919-67," *Review of Income and Wealth*, Series 15, No. 4, 293-320.

Denny, Michael, Melvyn Fuss and Leonard Waverman (1981), "The Measurement and Interpretation of Total Factor Productivity in Regulated Industries with an Application to Canadian Telecommunications," in T. Cowing and R. L. Stevenson (eds.), *Productivity Measurement in Regulated Industries*, Academic Press.

Diewert, W. Erwin (1980), "Aggregation Problems in the Measurement of Capital," in Dan Usher (ed.), *The Measurement of Capital*, University of Chicago Press.

Diewert, W. Erwin (1983), "The Theory of the Output Price Index and the Measurement of Real Output Change," in W. E. Diewert and C. Montmarquette (eds.), *Price Level Measurement*, Statistics Canada, Ottawa.

Diewert, W. Erwin (2001), "Measuring the Price and Quantity of Capital Services under Alternative Assumptions," *Department of Economics Working Paper* No 01-24, University of British Columbia.

Diewert, W. Erwin and Alice O. Nakamura (2007), "The Measurement of Aggregate Total Factor Productivity Growth," in J. Heckman and E. Leamer (eds.) *Handbook of Econometrics*, Volume 6, North Holland.

Frisch, Ragnar (1936), "Annual Survey of General Economic Theory: The Problem of Index Numbers," *Econometrica* 4, 1-39.

Fuss, Melvin and Daniel McFadden (eds.) (1978), *Production Economics: A Dual Approach to Theory and Applications*, North Holland, Amsterdam.

Harper, Michael J., Ernst R. Berndt and David O. Wood (1989), "Rates of Return and Capital Aggregation Using Alternative Rental Prices," in Dale W. Jorgenson and Ralph Landau (eds.), *Technology and Capital Formation*, MIT Press.

Hill, Peter and Robert Hill (2003), "Expectations, Capital Gains and Income," *Economic Inquiry* 41, 607-619.

Hsieh, Chang-Tai (2002), "What Explains the Industrial Revolution in East Asia? Evidence from the Factor Markets," *American Economic Review*, Volume 92, Issue 3, 502-526.

Hulten, Charles R. (1986), "Productivity Change, Capacity Utilisation, and the Sources of Efficiency Growth", *Journal of Econometrics* 33, 31-50.

Hulten, Charles (1990), "The Measurement of Capital," in Ernst R. Berndt and Jack Triplett (eds.), *Fifty Years of Economic Measurement*, NBER.

Jorgenson, Dale W. and Kun-Young Yun (2001), *Investment Volume 3, Lifting the Burden: Tax Reform, the Cost of Capital and U.S. Economic Growth*, MIT Press.

Jorgenson, Dale and Zvi Griliches (1967) "The Explanation of Productivity Change," *Review of Economic Studies* 34, 249-83.

Oliveira Martins, Joaquim, Stefano Scarpetta and Dirk Pilat (1996), "Mark-up Ratios in Manufacturing Industries - Estimates for 14 OECD Countries," *OECD Economics Department Working Papers* Nr 162.

Panzar, John C. (1989), "Technological Determinants of Firm and Industry Structure" in Richard Schmalensee and Robert D. Willig (eds.) *Handbook of Industrial Organization*; North Holland.

Paquet, Alain and Benoît Robidoux (2001), "Issues on the Measurement of the Solow Residual and the Testing of its Exogeneity: Evidence from Canada," *Journal of Monetary Economics* 47, 595-612.

Romer, Paul (1990), "Endogenous Technical Change," *Journal of Politica*l Economy 98, 71-102.

Samuelson, Paul A. (1953-54), "Prices of Factors and Goods in General Equilibrium," *Review of Economic Studies* 21, 1-20.

Schreyer, Paul (2000), "The Contribution of Information and Communication Technology to Output Growth: A Study of the G7 Countries," *OECD STI Working Paper.*

Schreyer, Paul (2001), "Information and Communication Technology and the Measurement of Volume Output and Final Demand – A Five Country Study", *Economics of Innovation and New Technology* 10, 339-376.

Schreyer, Paul (2002), "Computer Price Indices and International Growth and Productivity Comparisons," *Review of Income and Wealth*, Series 48, Vol. 1, 15-33.

Schreyer, Paul, Emmanuel Bignon et Julien Dupont (2003), "OECD Capital Services Measures: Methodology and a First Set of Results," *OECD Statistics Working Papers.*

Shephard, Ronald W. (1970), *Theory of Cost and Production Functions*, Princeton University Press.

Wyckoff, Andrew (1995), "The Impact of Computer Prices on International Comparisons of Productivity," *Economics of Innovation and New Technology,* Vol. 3, 277-293.

Chapter 3

ON MEASURING THE CONTRIBUTION OF ENTERING AND EXITING FIRMS TO AGGREGATE PRODUCTIVITY GROWTH

W. Erwin Diewert and Kevin J. Fox[1]

1. Introduction

A recent development in productivity analysis is the increased focus on the impact of firm entry and exit on aggregate levels of productivity growth. Haltiwanger, and Bartelsman and Doms, in their survey papers make the following observations:[2]

> "There are large and persistent differences in productivity across establishments in the same industry... – for total factor productivity [TFP] the ratio of the productivity level for the plant at the 75th percentile to the plant at the 5th percentile in the same industry is 2.4 (this is the average across industries) – the equivalent ratio for labour productivity is 3.5." John Haltiwanger (2000; 9)

> "The ratio of average TFP for plants in the ninth decile of the productivity distribution relative to the average in the second decile was about 2 to 1 in 1972 and about 2.75 to 1 in 1987." Eric J. Bartelsman and Mark Doms (2000; 579)

Thus the recent productivity literature has demonstrated empirically that increases in the productivity of the economy can be obtained by reallocating resources[3] away from low

---

[1] Erwin Diewert can be reached at the Department of Economics, University of British Columbia, Vancouver, B.C., Canada, V6T 1Z1, e-mail: diewert@econ.ubc.ca. Kevin Fox can be reached at the School of Economics, University of New South Wales, Sydney 2052, Australia, e-mail: K.Fox@unsw.edu.au. The authors thank Bert Balk, Alice Nakamura, Mark Roberts and Thai Vinh Nguyen for helpful comments, the University of Valencia for hospitality, and the SSHRC of Canada, the Australian Research Council (DP0559033), the Ministry of Education and Science of Spain (Secretaría de Estado de Universidades e Investigatción, SAB2003-0234) and the School of Economics at the University of New South Wales for financial support. None of the above is responsible for any opinions expressed.

[2] See their papers for many additional references to the literature. Some of the more important references are Baldwin and Gorecki (1991), Baily, Hulten and Campbell (1992), Griliches and Regev (1995), Baldwin (1995), Haltiwanger (1997), Ahn (2001), Foster, Haltiwanger and Krizan (2001), Aw, Chen and Roberts (2001), Fox (2002), Baldwin and Gu (2002), Balk (2003), Bartelsman, Haltiwanger and Scarpetta (2004) and Foster, Haltiwanger and Syverson (2008).

[3] A more precise meaning for the term "reallocating resources" is "changing input shares".

Citation: **W. Erwin Diewert and Kevin J. Fox (2011), "On Measuring the Contribution of Entering and Exiting Firms to Aggregate Productivity Growth, chapter 3, pp. 41-66 in**
W.E. Diewert, B.M. Balk, D. Fixler, K.J. Fox and A.O. Nakamura,
***PRICE AND PRODUCTIVITY MEASUREMENT: Volume 6 -- Index Number Theory*. Trafford Press.**

© Alice Nakamura, 2011. Permission to link to, or copy or reprint, these materials is granted without restriction, including for use in commercial textbooks, with due credit to the authors and editors.

productivity firms in an industry to the higher productivity firms.[4] However, different investigators have chosen different methods for measuring the contributions to industry productivity growth of entering and exiting firms and the issue remains open as to which method is "best". We propose yet another method for accomplishing this decomposition. It differs from existing methods in that it treats time in a symmetric fashion so that the industry productivity difference in levels between two periods reverses sign when the periods are interchanged, as do the various contribution terms.[5] Our proposed productivity decomposition is explained in sections 2 and 3 below, assuming that each firm in the industry produces only one homogeneous output and uses only one homogeneous input. In the literature, it is often assumed there is only one output and one input that each firm produces and uses.

With multiple outputs and inputs, so long as the list of outputs being produced and inputs being used by each firm is constant across firms, then there is no problem in using normal index number theory to construct output and input aggregates for each continuing firm that is present for the two periods under consideration.[6] We turn our attention to the multiple input, multiple output case beginning with section 4. However, this approach does not work with entering and exiting firms, since there is no natural base observation for comparing the single period data for these firms. This problem does not seem to have been widely recognized in the literature, though there are notable exceptions.[7] Hence in the remainder of the paper, we focus on this problem. Our proposed approach is to use *multilateral index number theory* so that each firm's data in each time period is treated as if it were pertaining to a "country." There are many multilateral methods that could be used, and we compare our new method with some of the alternatives.

In section 5 below, we construct an artificial data set involving three continuing firms, one entering firm and one exiting firm. In the remaining sections of the paper, we use various multilateral aggregation methods in order to construct firm output and input aggregates, which we then use in our suggested productivity growth decomposition formula. The multilateral aggregation methods we consider are: the star system (section 6); the GEKS system (section 7); the own share system (section 8); the "spatial" linking method due to Robert Hill (section 9), and a simple deflation of value aggregates method (section 10). Section 11 concludes.

2. Aggregate Productivity Level Measurement in the One Output One Input Case

We begin with a very simple case where firms produce one output with one input so it is very straightforward to measure the productivity of each firm by dividing its output by its input.[8]

[4] This conclusion has also emerged from the extensive literatures on benchmarking and on data envelopment analysis; e.g., see Coelli, Prasada Rao and Battese (1998).

[5] Balk (2003; 29) also emphasized the importance of a symmetric treatment of time. A symmetric decomposition was proposed by Griliches and Regev (1995) and a modification of it was used by Aw, Chen and Roberts (2001).

[6] An economic justification for using a superlative index to accomplish this aggregation can be supplied under some separability assumptions; see Diewert (1976).

[7] Aw, Chen and Roberts (2001) and Aw, Chung and Roberts (2003) recognized the importance of this problem and used a modification of a multilateral method proposed by Caves, Christensen and Diewert (1982). The modification is due to Good (1985) and explained in Good, Nadiri and Sickles (1997). The Caves, Christensen and Diewert method was designed for a single cross section and is not suitable for use in a panel data context with inflation.

[8] We will consider the case of many outputs and many inputs in sections 4-10 below.

We assume that these firms are all in the same industry, producing the same output and using the same input, so that it is very straightforward to measure industry productivity for each period by dividing aggregate industry output by aggregate industry input. *Our measurement problem is to account for the contributions to industry productivity growth of entering and exiting firms.*

In what follows, C denotes the set of continuing production units that are present in periods 0 and 1, X denotes the set of exiting firms that are present in only period 0, and N denotes the set of new firms present in only period 1. Let $y_{Ci}^t > 0$ and $x_{Ci}^t > 0$ denote, respectively, the output and input for continuing firm $i \in C$ during periods t = 0, 1. Let $y_{Xi}^0 > 0$ and $x_{Xi}^0 > 0$ denote the output and input of exiting firm $i \in X$ in period 0. Finally, let $y_{Ni}^1 > 0$ and $x_{Ni}^1 > 0$ denote the output and input of the new firm $i \in N$ in period 1.

The *productivity level* Π_{Ci}^t of a continuing firm $i \in C$ in each period t can be defined as:

$$(1) \quad \Pi_{Ci}^t \equiv y_{Ci}^t / x_{Ci}^t, \quad i \in C, \quad t = 0,1.$$

The productivity levels of each *exiting* firm in period 0 and each *entering* firm in period 1 are defined in a similar fashion, as follows:

$$(2) \quad \Pi_{Xi}^0 \equiv y_{Xi}^0 / x_{Xi}^0, \quad i \in X;$$

$$(3) \quad \Pi_{Ni}^1 \equiv y_{Ni}^1 / x_{Ni}^1, \quad i \in N.$$

Assuming for now that the output and input products are the same for all firms, a natural definition for period 0 *industry productivity* Π^0 is aggregate output divided by aggregate input:[9]

$$(4) \quad \begin{aligned} \Pi^0 &\equiv [\textstyle\sum_{i \in C} y_{Ci}^0 + \sum_{i \in X} y_{Xi}^0]/[\sum_{i \in C} x_{Ci}^0 + \sum_{i \in X} x_{Xi}^0] \\ &= S_C^0 \textstyle\sum_{i \in C} s_{Ci}^0 \Pi_{Ci}^0 + S_X^0 \sum_{i \in X} s_{Xi}^0 \Pi_{Xi}^0, \end{aligned}$$

where the *aggregate input shares* of the continuing and exiting firms in period 0 are:

$$(5) \quad S_C^0 \equiv \textstyle\sum_{i \in C} x_{Ci}^0 / [\sum_{i \in C} x_{Ci}^0 + \sum_{i \in X} x_{Xi}^0];$$

$$(6) \quad S_X^0 \equiv \textstyle\sum_{i \in X} x_{Xi}^0 / [\sum_{i \in C} x_{Ci}^0 + \sum_{i \in X} x_{Xi}^0].$$

The period 0 *micro input share*, s_{Ci}^0, for a *continuing* firm $i \in C$ is defined as follows:

$$(7) \quad s_{Ci}^0 \equiv x_{Ci}^0 / \textstyle\sum_{k \in C} x_{Ck}^0, \quad i \in C.$$

Similarly, the period 0 *micro input share* for *exiting* firm $i \in X$ is:

[9] It is possible to rework our analysis by reversing the role of inputs and outputs so that output shares replace input shares in the decomposition formulae. Then at the end, we can take the reciprocal of the aggregate inverse productivity measure and obtain an alternative productivity decomposition. We owe this suggestion to Bert Balk.

(8) $s_{Xi}^0 \equiv x_{Xi}^0 / \sum_{k\in X} x_{Xk}^0$, $i\in X$.

The period 0 *aggregate productivities for continuing and exiting firms*, Π_C^0, and Π_X^0, can be defined in a similar manner to the definition in (4) of Π^0 for the entire industry as:

(9) $\Pi_C^0 \equiv \sum_{i\in C} y_{Ci}^0 / \sum_{i\in C} x_{Ci}^0 = \sum_{i\in C} s_{Ci}^0 \Pi_{Ci}^0$;

(10) $\Pi_X^0 \equiv \sum_{i\in X} y_{Xi}^0 / \sum_{i\in X} x_{Xi}^0 = \sum_{i\in X} s_{Xi}^0 \Pi_{Xi}^0$.

Substituting of (9) and (10) back into (4) for the aggregate period 0 level of productivity of the industry and using $S_C^0 = 1 - S_X^0$ leads to the following decomposition of period 0 productivity:

(11) $\Pi^0 = S_C^0 \Pi_C^0 + S_X^0 \Pi_X^0$

(12) $\quad = \Pi_C^0 + S_X^0(\Pi_X^0 - \Pi_C^0)$.

In expression (12), the first term, Π_C^0, represents the productivity contribution of continuing firms while the second term, $S_X^0(\Pi_X^0 - \Pi_C^0)$, represents the contribution of exiting firms, relative to continuing firms, to the overall period 0 productivity level. Usually the exiting firm will have lower productivity levels than the continuing firms so that Π_X^0 will be less than Π_C^0. Thus, under normal conditions, the second term on the right-hand side of (12) will make a *negative contribution* to the overall level of period 0 productivity.[10] Substituting (9) and (10) into (12) leads to the following decomposition of the period 0 productivity into the contributions of firms grouped by whether they are continuing or exiting:

(13) $\Pi^0 = \sum_{i\in C} s_{Ci}^0 \Pi_{Ci}^0 + S_X^0 \sum_{i\in X} s_{Xi}^0 (\Pi_{Xi}^0 - \Pi_C^0)$,

where we have also used the fact that $\sum_{i\in X} s_{Xi}^0$ sums to unity.

The above material can be repeated with minor modifications to provide a decomposition of the industry period 1 productivity level Π^1 into its components. Thus, Π^1 is defined as:

$$\begin{aligned}(14)\quad \Pi^1 &\equiv [\sum_{i\in C} y_{Ci}^1 + \sum_{i\in N} y_{Ni}^1]/[\sum_{i\in C} x_{Ci}^1 + \sum_{i\in N} x_{Ni}^1] \\ &= S_C^1 \sum_{i\in C} s_{Ci}^1 \Pi_{Ci}^1 + S_N^1 \sum_{i\in N} s_{Ni}^1 \Pi_{Ni}^1,\end{aligned}$$

where the period 1 aggregate input shares of continuing and new firms, S_C^1 and S_N^1, and individual continuing and new firm shares, s_{Ci}^1 and s_{Ni}^1, are defined as follows:

[10] Olley and Pakes (1996; 1290) have an alternative covariance type decomposition of the overall level of productivity in a given period into firm effects but it is not suitable for our purpose, which is to highlight the differential effects on overall period 0 productivity of the exiting firms compared to the continuing firms.

(15) $S_C^1 \equiv \sum_{i\in C} x_{Ci}^1 / [\sum_{i\in C} x_{Ci}^1 + \sum_{i\in N} x_{Ni}^1]$;

(16) $S_N^1 \equiv \sum_{i\in N} x_{Ni}^1 / [\sum_{i\in C} x_{Ci}^1 + \sum_{i\in N} x_{Ni}^1]$;

(17) $s_{Ci}^1 \equiv x_{Ci}^1 / \sum_{k\in C} x_{Ck}^1$, $i\in C$;

(18) $s_{Ni}^1 \equiv x_{Ni}^1 / \sum_{k\in N} x_{Nk}^1$, $i\in N$.

The period 1 counterparts to Π_C^0 and Π_X^0 in (9) and (10) are the *aggregate period one productivity levels of continuing firms* Π_C^1 and *entering firms* Π_N^1, defined as follows:

(19) $\Pi_C^1 \equiv \sum_{i\in C} y_{Ci}^1 / \sum_{i\in C} x_{Ci}^1 = \sum_{i\in C} s_{Ci}^1 \Pi_{Ci}^1$;

(20) $\Pi_N^1 \equiv \sum_{i\in N} y_{Ni}^1 / \sum_{i\in N} x_{Ni}^1 = \sum_{i\in N} s_{Ni}^1 \Pi_{Ni}^1$.

Substituting (19) and (20) back into definition (14) for the aggregate period 1 level of productivity leads to the following decomposition counterparts of (11) and (12) -- a decomposition of aggregate period 1 productivity into its continuing and new components:

(21) $\Pi^1 = S_C^1 \Pi_C^1 + S_N^1 \Pi_N^1$

(22) $\quad = \Pi_C^1 + S_N^1 (\Pi_N^1 - \Pi_C^1)$,

where (22) follows from (21) using $S_C^1 = 1 - S_N^1$. Thus the aggregate period 1 productivity level Π^1 is equal to the aggregate period 1 productivity level of continuing firms, Π_C^1, plus a second term, $S_N^1(\Pi_N^1 - \Pi_C^1)$, which represents the contribution of the new entrants' productivity levels, Π_N^1, relative to that of the continuing firms, Π_C^1.[11] Substituting (19) and (20) into (22) leads to the following decomposition of the aggregate period 1 productivity level Π^1 into its individual firm contributions:

(23) $\Pi^1 = \sum_{i\in C} s_{Ci}^1 \Pi_{Ci}^1 + S_N^1 \sum_{i\in N} s_{Ni}^1 (\Pi_{Ni}^1 - \Pi_C^1)$.

This completes our discussion of how the levels of productivity in periods 0 and 1 can be decomposed into individual firm contribution effects. In the following section, we study the more difficult problem of decomposing the aggregate productivity change, Π^1 / Π^0, into individual firm growth effects, taking into account that not all firms are present in both periods.

[11] Baldwin (1995) in his study of the Canadian manufacturing sector showed that on average, the productivity level of new entrants is below that of continuing firms. However, he found that for new entrants that survive, they reach the average productivity level of continuing firms in about a decade. For additional empirical evidence on the relative productivity levels of entering and exiting firms, see Bartelsman and Doms (2000; 581). See also Aw, Chen and Roberts (2001) (who also find that the productivity level of new entrants is below that of incumbents) and section 5 of Bartelsman, Haltiwanger and Scarpetta (2004).

3. The Measurement of Productivity Change between Two Periods

It is traditional to define productivity change from period 0 to period 1 as a ratio of the productivity levels in the two periods rather than as a difference. This is because the ratio measure will be independent of the units of measurement while the difference measure will not (unless some normalization is performed). However, in the present context, as we are attempting to calculate the contribution of new and disappearing production units to overall productivity change, it is more convenient to work with the difference concept, at least initially.

Using formula (13) for the period 0 productivity level Π^0 and (23) for the period 1 productivity level Π^1, we obtain the following decomposition of the *productivity difference*:

$$\Pi^1 - \Pi^0 = \sum_{i\in C} s^1_{Ci}\Pi^1_{Ci} - \sum_{i\in C} s^0_{Ci}\Pi^0_{Ci} + S^1_N \sum_{i\in N} s^1_{Ni}(\Pi^1_{Ni} - \Pi^1_C) - S^0_X \sum_{i\in X} s^0_{Xi}(\Pi^0_{Xi} - \Pi^0_C) \tag{24}$$

$$= \Pi^1_C - \Pi^0_C + S^1_N(\Pi^1_N - \Pi^1_C) - S^0_X(\Pi^0_X - \Pi^0_C), \tag{25}$$

where (25) follows from (24) using (12) and (22). Thus the overall industry productivity change, $\Pi^1 - \Pi^0$, is equal to the productivity change of the continuing firms, $\Pi^1_C - \Pi^0_C$, plus a term that reflects the contribution to overall productivity change of new entrants, $S^1_N(\Pi^1_N - \Pi^1_C)$,[12] and a term that reflects the contribution to overall productivity change of exiting firms, $-S^0_X(\Pi^0_X - \Pi^0_C)$.[13] Note that the reference productivity levels that the productivity levels of the entering and exiting firms are compared with, Π^1_C and Π^0_C respectively, are *different* in general, so even if the average productivity levels of entering and exiting firms are the *same* (so that Π^1_N equals Π^0_X), the contributions to overall industry productivity *growth* of entering and exiting firms can still be nonzero if $\Pi^1_N \neq \Pi^1_C$ or $\Pi^0_X \neq \Pi^0_C$.[14]

---

[12] This term is positive if and only if the average level of productivity of the new entrants in period 1, Π^1_N, is *greater* than the average productivity level of continuing firms in period 1, Π^1_C.

[13] This term is positive if and only if the average level of productivity of the firms who exit in period 0, Π^0_X, is *less* than the average productivity level of continuing firms in period 0, Π^0_C.

[14] Haltiwanger (1997) (2000; 10) argues that if the productivity levels of entering and exiting firms or establishments are exactly the same, then the sum of the contribution terms of entering and exiting firms should be zero. However, our perspective is different: we want to measure the differential effects on productivity *growth* of entering and exiting firms and so what counts in our framework are the productivity levels of entering firms relative to continuing firms in period 1 and the productivity levels of exiting firms relative to continuing firms in period 0. Thus if continuing firms show productivity growth over the two periods, then if the entering and exiting firms have the same productivity levels, the effects of entry and exit will be to decrease productivity growth compared to the continuing firms. Balk (2003; 28) follows the example of Haltiwanger (1997) in choosing a common reference level of productivity to compare the productivity levels of entering and exiting firms but Balk chooses the arithmetic average

The first two terms on the right-hand side of (24) give the aggregate effects of the changes in productivity levels of the continuing firms. It is useful to further decompose this aggregate change in the productivity levels of continuing firms into two sets of components: the first set of terms measures the productivity change of each continuing production unit, $\Pi_{Ci}^1 - \Pi_{Ci}^0$, and the second set reflects the shifts in the share of resources used by each continuing production unit, $s_{Ci}^1 - s_{Ci}^0$. As Balk (2003; 26) notes, there are two natural decompositions for the difference in the productivity levels of the continuing firms, (27) and (29) below, that are the difference counterparts to the decomposition of a value ratio into the product of a Laspeyres (or Paasche) price index times a Paasche (or Laspeyres) quantity index:

$$(26) \quad \Pi_C^1 - \Pi_C^0 = \sum_{i\in C} s_{Ci}^1 \Pi_{Ci}^1 - \sum_{i\in C} s_{Ci}^0 \Pi_{Ci}^0$$

$$(27) \quad = \sum_{i\in C} s_{Ci}^0 (\Pi_{Ci}^1 - \Pi_{Ci}^0) + \sum_{i\in C} \Pi_{Ci}^1 (s_{Ci}^1 - s_{Ci}^0);$$

$$(28) \quad \Pi_C^1 - \Pi_C^0 = \sum_{i\in C} s_{Ci}^1 \Pi_{Ci}^1 - \sum_{i\in C} s_{Ci}^0 \Pi_{Ci}^0$$

$$(29) \quad = \sum_{i\in C} s_{Ci}^1 (\Pi_{Ci}^1 - \Pi_{Ci}^0) + \sum_{i\in C} \Pi_{Ci}^0 (s_{Ci}^1 - s_{Ci}^0).$$

We now note a severe disadvantage associated with either (27) [15] or (29): *these decompositions are not invariant with respect to the treatment of time*. If we reverse the roles of periods 0 and 1, we would like the decomposition of the aggregate productivity difference for continuing firms, $\Pi_C^0 - \Pi_C^1 = \sum_{i\in C} s_{Ci}^0 \Pi_{Ci}^0 - \sum_{i\in C} s_{Ci}^1 \Pi_{Ci}^1$ (an aggregate productivity difference that involves the individual productivity differences $\Pi_{Ci}^0 - \Pi_{Ci}^1$ and share differences $s_{Ci}^0 - s_{Ci}^1$) to satisfy a symmetry or invariance property, but unfortunately it does not. [16] A solution to this problem is to take the arithmetic average of (26) and (28), leading to a *Bennet* (1920) *type decomposition of the productivity change of continuing firms*:

$$(30) \quad \Pi_C^1 - \Pi_C^0 = \sum_{i\in C} (1/2)(s_{Ci}^0 + s_{Ci}^1)(\Pi_{Ci}^1 - \Pi_{Ci}^0) + \sum_{i\in C} (1/2)(\Pi_{Ci}^0 + \Pi_{Ci}^1)(s_{Ci}^1 - s_{Ci}^0).$$

The use of this decomposition for continuing firms dates back to Griliches and Regev (1995; 185). [17] Balk (2003; 29) also endorsed the use of this symmetric decomposition. [18] We endorse it since it is symmetric and can also be given a strong axiomatic justification. [19]

---

of the industry productivity levels in periods 0 and 1 (which is at least a symmetric choice) whereas Haltiwanger chooses the industry productivity level of period 0 (which is not a symmetric choice). In any case, our approach seems to be different from other approaches suggested in the literature.

[15] The decomposition defined by (26) is the one used by Baily, Hulten and Campbell (1992; 193) for continuing firms except that they used *logs* of the TFP levels Π_{Ci}^t instead of the levels themselves.

[16] We want the difference decomposition to satisfy a differences counterpart to the index number time reversal test.

[17] Griliches and Regev (1995; 185) also have a symmetric treatment of the industry difference in total factor productivity (TFP) levels, but firms that exit and enter during the two periods being compared are treated as one firm and they make a direct comparison of the change in productivity of all entering and exiting firms on this basis. There are problems in interpretation if there happen to be no entering (or exiting) firms in the sample or more generally, if there are big differences in the shares of entering and exiting firms. Aw, Chen and Roberts (2001; 73) also use this symmetric methodology, except they work with logs of TFP.

Substitution of (30) into (24) gives our final "best" decomposition of the aggregate productivity difference $\Pi^1 - \Pi^0$ into micro firm effects:

$$\begin{aligned}(31)\quad \Pi^1 - \Pi^0 = {} & \textstyle\sum_{i\in C}(1/2)(s^0_{Ci} + s^1_{Ci})(\Pi^1_{Ci} - \Pi^0_{Ci}) + \sum_{i\in C}(1/2)(\Pi^0_{Ci} + \Pi^1_{Ci})(s^1_{Ci} - s^0_{Ci}) \\ & \textstyle + S^1_N \sum_{i\in N} s^1_{Ni}(\Pi^1_{Ni} - \Pi^1_C) - S^0_X \sum_{i\in X} s^0_{Xi}(\Pi^0_{Xi} - \Pi^0_C).\end{aligned}$$

The first set of terms on the right hand side of (31), $\sum_{i\in C}(1/2)(s^0_{Ci} + s^1_{Ci})(\Pi^1_{Ci} - \Pi^0_{Ci})$, gives the contribution of the productivity growth of each continuing firm to the aggregate productivity difference between periods 0 and 1, $\Pi^1 - \Pi^0$. The second set of terms, $\sum_{i\in C}(1/2)(\Pi^0_{Ci} + \Pi^1_{Ci})(s^1_{Ci} - s^0_{Ci})$, gives the contribution of the effects of the reallocation of resources between continuing firms. The third set of terms, $S^1_N \sum_{i\in N} s^1_{Ni}(\Pi^1_{Ni} - \Pi^1_C)$, gives the contribution of each entering firm to productivity growth. The final set of terms, $-S^0_X \sum_{i\in X} s^0_{Xi}(\Pi^0_{Xi} - \Pi^0_C)$, gives the contribution of each exiting firm.

Note that the decomposition in (31) is symmetric: if we reverse the role of periods 0 and 1, then the new aggregate productivity difference will equal the negative of the original productivity difference and each individual firm contribution term on the new right hand side will equal the negative of the original firm contribution effect. The only decomposition we are aware of in the literature that has this time reversal property is due to Balk (2003; 28). His decomposition differs from what we propose in that he compares the productivity levels of entering and exiting firms to the arithmetic average of the industry productivity levels in periods 0 and 1 instead of to the average productivity level of continuing firms in period 1 for entering firms, and continuing firms in period 0 for exiting firms as we do.

We now make a final adjustment to (31) in order to achieve invariance to changes in the units of measurement of output and input: we divide both sides of (31) by the base period productivity level Π^0.[20] With this adjustment, (31) becomes the following TFPG expression:

$$\begin{aligned}(32)\quad [\Pi^1/\Pi^0] - 1 = {} & \textstyle[\sum_{i\in C}(1/2)(s^0_{Ci} + s^1_{Ci})(\Pi^1_{Ci} - \Pi^0_{Ci}) + \sum_{i\in C}(1/2)(\Pi^0_{Ci} + \Pi^1_{Ci})(s^1_{Ci} - s^0_{Ci}) \\ & \textstyle + S^1_N \sum_{i\in N} s^1_{Ni}(\Pi^1_{Ni} - \Pi^1_C) - S^0_X \sum_{i\in X} s^0_{Xi}(\Pi^0_{Xi} - \Pi^0_C)]/\Pi^0.\end{aligned}$$

In the following sections, we illustrate the aggregate productivity decomposition (32) using an artificial data set. *Note that (32) is only valid for an industry that produces a single output and*

[18] "In view of its symmetry it should be the preferred one." Bert M. Balk (2003; 29).

[19] Diewert (2005) showed that the Bennet decomposition of a difference of the form $\sum_i p^1_i q^1_i - \sum_i p^0_i q^0_i$ into a sum of terms reflecting price change and a sum of terms reflecting quantity change can be given an axiomatic justification that is analogous to the axiomatic justification for the use of the Fisher (1922) ideal index in index number theory. The adaptation of this axiomatic theory to provide a decomposition of $\sum_i p^1_i s^1_i - \sum_i p^0_i s^0_i$ is straightforward.

[20] Instead of dividing by Π^0, we could divide by the logarithmic mean of Π^0 and Π^1. The left hand side of the resulting counterpart to (32) reduces to $\ln(\Pi^0/\Pi^1)$, which is completely symmetric in the data whereas the left hand side of (32) is not. We owe this suggestion to Bert Balk.

uses a single input. However, in practice, firms in an industry produce many outputs and use many inputs. Hence, before decomposition (32) can be implemented, it is necessary to aggregate the many outputs produced and inputs used by each firm into aggregate firm output and input. This problem is not straightforward because of firms entering and exiting. In the following section, we address this unconventional aggregation problem.[21]

4. How Can the Inputs and Outputs of Entering and Exiting Firms Be Aggregated?

The aggregate productivity decomposition defined by (32) above assumes that each firm produces only one output and uses only one input. However, firms in the same industry typically produce many outputs and utilize many inputs. Thus in order to apply (32), we have to somehow aggregate all of the outputs produced by each firm into an aggregate output that is comparable across firms and across time periods and aggregate all of the inputs utilized by each firm into an aggregate input that is comparable across firms and across time periods. It can be seen that these two aggregation problems are in fact *multilateral aggregation problems*;[22] i.e., the output, or input, vector of each firm in each period must be compared with the corresponding output, or input, vectors of all other firms in the industry over the two time periods involved in the aggregate productivity comparison.[23] In the following sections of this paper, we will illustrate how these firm output and input aggregates can be formed using several methods that have been suggested in the multilateral aggregation literature.

In order to make the comparison of alternative multilateral methods of aggregation more concrete, we will utilize an artificial data set. In the following section, we table our data set and calculate the aggregate productivity of the industry using normal index number methods.

5. Industry Productivity Aggregates Using an Artificial Data Set

We consider an industry over two periods, 0 and 1, that consists of five firms. Each firm f produces varying amounts of the same two outputs and uses varying amounts of the same two inputs. The output vector of firm f in period t is defined as $y_f^t \equiv [y_{f1}^t, y_{f2}^t]$ and the corresponding input vector is defined as $x_f^t \equiv [x_{f1}^t, x_{f2}^t]$ for t = 0,1 and f = 1,2,…,5. Firms 1,2 and 3 are continuing firms, firm 4 is present in period 0 but not 1 (and hence is an exiting firm) and firm 5 is not present in period 0 but is present in period 1 (and hence is an entering firm). Firm 1 is medium sized, firm 2 is tiny and firm 3 is very large. The output price vector of firm f in period t is $p_f^t \equiv [p_{f1}^t, p_{f2}^t]$ and the corresponding input price vector is $w_f^t \equiv [w_{f1}^t, w_{f2}^t]$ for t = 0,1 and f = 1,2,…,5. The firm price and quantity data are listed in table 1.

[21] As noted earlier, Aw, Chen and Roberts (2001) (2003) also addressed this aggregation problem.

[22] Bilateral index number theory compares the price and quantity vectors pertaining to two situations whereas multilateral index number theory attempts to construct price and quantity aggregates when there are more than two situations to be compared. See Balk (1996) (2001) and Diewert (1999) for recent surveys of multilateral methods.

[23] Fox (2002) seems to have been the first to notice that aggregating firm outputs and inputs into aggregate outputs and inputs should be treated as a multilateral aggregation problem in order to avoid paradoxical results.

Table 1. Firm Price and Quantity Data for Periods 0 and 1

	Firm 1		Firm 2		Firm 3		Firm 4		Firm 5	
Output prices										
	p_{11}^t	p_{12}^t	p_{21}^t	p_{22}^t	p_{31}^t	p_{32}^t	p_{41}^t	p_{42}^t	p_{51}^t	p_{52}^t
t=0	1	1	0.8	1.2	0.9	0.8	1.2	1.1	---	---
t=1	15	7	13	8	14	7	---	---	16	8
Output quantities										
	y_{11}^t	y_{12}^t	y_{21}^t	y_{22}^t	y_{31}^t	y_{32}^t	y_{41}^t	y_{42}^t	y_{51}^t	y_{52}^t
t=0	12	8	1	1	50	50	7	9	---	---
t=1	15	8	3	2	60	45	---	---	16	8
Input prices										
	w_{11}^t	w_{12}^t	w_{21}^t	w_{22}^t	w_{31}^t	w_{32}^t	w_{41}^t	w_{42}^t	w_{51}^t	w_{52}^t
t=0	1	1	0.7	0.8	0.9	1.1	1.2	1	---	---
t=1	10	23	13	16	8	26	---	---	14	20
Input quantities										
	x_{11}^t	x_{12}^t	x_{21}^t	x_{22}^t	x_{31}^t	x_{32}^t	x_{41}^t	x_{42}^t	x_{51}^t	x_{52}^t
t=0	10	10	1	1	45	35	13	12	---	---
t=1	8	6	2	2	35	30	---	---	7	6

Thus the period 0 output price vector for firm 1 is $p_1^0 = [1,1]$, the period 1 output price vector for firm 1 is $p_1^1 = [15,7]$ and so on. Note that there has been a great deal of general price level change going from period 0 to 1.[24]

In the following sections, we will look at various methods for forming output and input aggregates for each firm and each period but before we do this, it is useful to compute *total industry supplies* of the two outputs, $y^t \equiv [y_{\bullet 1}^t, y_{\bullet 2}^t]$ for each period t and *total industry demands* for each of the two inputs $x^t \equiv [x_{\bullet 1}^t, x_{\bullet 2}^t]$ for each period t as well as the corresponding *unit value prices*, $p^t \equiv [p_{\bullet 1}^t, p_{\bullet 2}^t]$ and $w^t \equiv [w_{\bullet 1}^t, w_{\bullet 2}^t]$.[25] This information is listed in (33) below:

(33) $p^0 = [0.946, 0.869]$; $p^1 = [14.468, 7.159]$; $w^0 = [0.968, 1.057]$; $w^1 = [9.308, 24.318]$;

$y^0 = [70, 68]$; $y^1 = [94, 63]$; $x^0 = [69, 58]$; $x^1 = [52, 44]$.

[24] In some applications of the literature on the contribution of entry and exit to aggregate productivity growth, the comparison periods are a decade apart and so the period 0 and 1 price levels can differ considerably.

[25] The unit value price of output n in period t is defined as $p_{\bullet n}^t \equiv \Sigma_{f=1}^5 p_{fn}^t y_{fn}^t / \Sigma_{f=1}^5 y_{fn}^t$ for n = 1,2 and t = 0,1. The unit value price of input n in period t is defined as $w_{\bullet n}^t \equiv \Sigma_{f=1}^5 w_{fn}^t x_{fn}^t / \Sigma_{f=1}^5 x_{fn}^t$ for n = 1,2 and t = 0,1.

Note that industry output 1 has increased from 70 to 94 but industry output 2 decreased slightly from 68 to 63. However, both industry input demands dropped markedly; input 1 decreased from 69 to 52 and input 2 decreased from 58 to 45. Thus overall, industry productivity improved markedly going from period 0 to 1.

In order to benchmark the reasonableness of the various productivity decompositions given by (32) above for different multilateral methods to be discussed in the following four sections, it is useful to use the industry data in (33) to construct normal index number estimates of industry total factor productivity growth (TFPG). Following Jorgenson and Griliches (1967) (1972),[26] TFPG can be defined as a quantity index of output growth, $Q(p^0,p^1,q^0,q^1)$, divided by a quantity index of input growth, $Q^*(w^0,w^1,x^0,x^1)$:

(34) $$TFPG \equiv Q(p^0,p^1,q^0,q^1)/Q^*(w^0,w^1,x^0,x^1).$$

In order to implement (34), one needs to choose an index number formula for Q and Q^*. From an axiomatic perspective, the "best" choices seem to be the Fisher (1922) ideal formula[27] or the Törnqvist (1936) Theil (1967) formula.[28] With these two choices of index number formula, the resulting TFP growth rates[29] for the data listed in (33) are as follows:

(35) $$TFPG_F = 1.5553;\ TFPG_T = 1.5573.$$

If we subtract 1 from the above TFPG rates, we obtain industry aggregate counterparts to the left hand side of (32), $[\Pi^1/\Pi^0]-1$. Thus using the Fisher formula, industry productivity improved 55.53% and using the Törnqvist Theil formula, industry productivity improved 55.73%. These productivity growth rates should be kept in mind as we look at alternative multilateral methods for constructing output and input aggregates for each firm in each period so that we can implement the decomposition formula (32). In other words, a multilateral method that leads to an aggregate productivity growth rate $[\Pi^1/\Pi^0]-1$ that is different from the range of .5553 to .5573 is probably not very reliable. We now turn to our first multilateral method.

6. The Star System for Making Multilateral Comparisons

Recall that in the previous section, we defined the firm f and period t output and input vectors as $y_f^t \equiv [y_{f1}^t, y_{f2}^t]$ and $x_f^t \equiv [x_{f1}^t, x_{f2}^t]$ for t = 0,1 and f = 1,2,...,5. However, for t = 0 and f = 5 and also for t = 1 and f = 4, there are no data, since these two firms are entering and exiting respectively. Thus there are actually a total of 8 output and input quantity vectors instead of 10. It will prove to be more convenient to relabel our data so that there are only 8 distinct

[26] For recent surveys on how to measure TFPG, see Balk (2003) and Diewert and Nakamura (2003).

[27] See Diewert (1992). The Fisher output quantity index is defined as $Q_F(p^0,p^1,q^0,q^1) \equiv [p^0q^1p^1q^1/p^0q^0p^1q^0]^{1/2}$ where p·q denotes the inner product of the vectors p and q.

[28] See Diewert (2004). Both of these formulae can be given economic justifications as well; see Diewert (1976).

[29] Actually these rates are 1 plus the total factor productivity growth rates.

output and input quantity vectors. Thus define the output quantity vectors y^1, y^2, y^3 and y^4 as the previously defined vectors y_1^0, y_2^0, y_3^0 and y_4^0 respectively (these are the nonzero period 0 output quantity vectors) and define the vectors y^5, y^6, y^7 and y^8 as the previously defined vectors y_1^1, y_2^1, y_3^1 and y_5^1 respectively (these are the nonzero period 1 output quantity vectors). Similarly, define the output price vectors p^1, p^2, p^3 and p^4 as the previously defined vectors p_1^0, p_2^0, p_3^0 and p_4^0 respectively and define the vectors p^5, p^6, p^7 and p^8 as the previously defined vectors p_1^1, p_2^1, p_3^1 and p_5^1, respectively. Undertake the same reordering of the data for inputs. Now we can apply multilateral methods. In effect, we treat each of the 8 output (or input) price and quantity vectors as if they corresponded to the data for a country.[30]

The first multilateral method we consider is the star system.[31] To implement this, we choose a bilateral index number formula, say the Fisher formula Q_F, and choose one observation as the base (or star), say observation k, and then compute the Fisher quantity aggregate of each observation relative to the base k, $Q_F(p^k, p^1, y^k, y^1)$, $Q_F(p^k, p^2, y^k, y^2), \ldots, Q_F(p^k, p^8, y^k, y^8)$. The resulting sequence of 8 numbers can serve as output aggregates for our 8 observations.

Of course, the problem with the star system aggregates is that it is necessary to asymmetrically choose one observation as the "star" and usually, it is not clear which observation should be chosen.[32] Thus in tables 2 and 3 below, we list each of the 8 output and input aggregates respectively, choosing each observation as the base in turn. In order to make these output and input aggregates comparable, we divide each set of parities by the parity for the first observation. Thus the output and input parities listed in tables 2 and 3 for are the following normalized parities for outputs and inputs, for k = 1,...,8, respectively:[33]

(36) $1,\ Q_F(p^k, p^2, y^k, y^2)/Q_F(p^k, p^1, y^k, y^1), \ldots,\ Q_F(p^k, p^8, y^k, y^8)/Q_F(p^k, p^1, y^k, y^1)$,

(37) $1,\ Q_F(w^k, w^2, x^k, x^2)/Q_F(w^k, w^1, x^k, x^1), \ldots,\ Q_F(w^k, w^8, x^k, x^8)/Q_F(w^k, w^1, x^k, x^1)$.

The input aggregates for observations 1 and 2 are the same regardless of the base. This is due to the use of the Fisher formula and the fact the input vectors for observations 1 and 2 are proportional.[34] If the quantity vectors for the observations being compared are proportional, then the Fisher quantity index will reflect this factor of proportionality.[35] In general, however, the choice of the base observation affects the output and input parities.

---

[30] Note that we need to make two multilateral comparisons: one for outputs and one for inputs.

[31] This terminology is due to Kravis (1984; 10).

[32] In our particular example, a case could be made for choosing either observation 3 or 7; i.e., the observations that correspond to the very large firm. So, there are two choices and again, it is not clear which of these two is better.

[33] Recall that our final decomposition of the industry productivity change defined by (32) does not depend on our rather arbitrary units of measurement for aggregate firm outputs and inputs.

[34] The input vector for firm 1 in period 0 is $x^1 = [10,10]$ and for firm 2 in period 0 is $x^2 = [1,1]$.

[35] Similarly, if the two price vectors are proportional, then the Fisher price index between the two observations will reflect this factor of proportionality. The Fisher formula seems to be the only superlative formula that is consistent with both Hicks' and Leontief's aggregation theorems; see Allen and Diewert (1981).

Table 2. Fisher Star Output Aggregates

Outputs	y_1	y_2	y_3	y_4	y_5	y_6	y_7	y_8
Base=1	1	0.102	4.971	0.794	1.170	0.250	5.203	1.225
Base=2	1	0.102	5.103	0.824	1.199	0.256	5.405	1.247
Base=3	1	0.099	4.971	0.79	1.216	0.256	5.365	1.270
Base=4	1	0.098	4.997	0.794	1.243	0.26	5.482	1.296
Base=5	1	0.100	4.785	0.748	1.17	0.247	5.070	1.232
Base=6	1	0.100	4.857	0.764	1.184	0.25	5.169	1.243
Base=7	1	0.098	4.821	0.754	1.201	0.252	5.203	1.261
Base=8	1	0.100	4.794	0.751	1.163	0.246	5.052	1.225

Table 3. Fisher Star Input Aggregates

Inputs	x_1	x_2	x_3	x_4	x_5	x_6	x_7	x_8
Base=1	1	0.100	3.975	1.252	0.680	0.200	3.183	0.646
Base=2	1	0.100	3.958	1.251	0.677	0.200	3.175	0.644
Base=3	1	0.100	3.975	1.243	0.692	0.201	3.281	0.650
Base=4	1	0.100	4.005	1.252	0.690	0.200	3.229	0.650
Base=5	1	0.100	3.904	1.234	0.680	0.201	3.260	0.644
Base=6	1	0.100	3.949	1.250	0.675	0.200	3.170	0.643
Base=7	1	0.100	3.856	1.235	0.664	0.201	3.183	0.637
Base=8	1	0.100	3.946	1.244	0.682	0.201	3.228	0.646

Now go along each row of table 2 and divide by the corresponding input aggregate listed in the corresponding row of table 3. This determines the productivity level of each observation. These star productivity levels are listed in table 4. There can be considerable variation in the productivity levels for each observation, depending on which observation is chosen as the base in the star system comparison. Thus if we choose the base to equal 1 (firm 1 in period 0), the productivity level of firm 2 in period 0 is 1.021 whereas if we choose the base to equal 7 (firm 3 in period 1), the productivity level of firm 2 in period 0 is 0.980: a 4% variation in productivity.[36]

Aggregate output prices that correspond to the 8 output aggregates that are listed in table 2 for each choice of base observation can be obtained by dividing the value of output produced by each firm in each period by the corresponding output listed for that observation in table 2. Similarly, aggregate input prices that correspond to the 8 input aggregates that are listed in table 3 for each choice of base observation can be obtained by dividing the value of inputs used by each firm in each period by the corresponding input listed for that observation in table 3. Once these aggregate output and input prices have been constructed, then we are in a position to apply the decomposition analysis that was discussed in sections 2 and 3 above.

[36] Ideally, we would like all the entries in each column of table 4 to be identical so that the productivity levels of each firm observation do not depend on the choice of index number base.

Table 4. Fisher Star Productivity Levels

Prod Levels	y_1/x_1	y_2/x_2	y_3/x_3	y_4/x_4	y_5/x_5	y_6/x_6	y_7/x_7	y_8/x_8
Base=1	1	1.021	1.251	0.634	1.721	1.250	1.635	1.897
Base=2	1	1.021	1.289	0.659	1.771	1.279	1.703	1.937
Base=3	1	0.990	1.251	0.636	1.756	1.271	1.635	1.953
Base=4	1	0.982	1.247	0.634	1.802	1.296	1.698	1.993
Base=5	1	0.992	1.226	0.606	1.721	1.226	1.555	1.914
Base=6	1	0.997	1.230	0.612	1.754	1.250	1.630	1.933
Base=7	1	0.980	1.250	0.611	1.809	1.253	1.635	1.981
Base=8	1	1	1.215	0.604	1.706	1.227	1.565	1.897

We define the various terms that occur on the right and left hand sides of the aggregate productivity growth decomposition (32) as follows:

(38) $\Gamma \equiv [\Pi^1/\Pi^0]-1$ (aggregate industry productivity growth);

(39) $\Gamma_{CD} \equiv \sum_{i\in C}(1/2)(s_{Ci}^0+s_{Ci}^1)(\Pi_{Ci}^1-\Pi_{Ci}^0)/\Pi^0$

(the direct productivity growth contribution of continuing firms);

(40) $\Gamma_{CR} \equiv \sum_{i\in C}(1/2)(\Pi_{Ci}^0+\Pi_{Ci}^1)(s_{Ci}^1-s_{Ci}^0)/\Pi^0$ (continuing firm reallocation contribution);

(41) $\Gamma_N \equiv S_N^1\sum_{i\in N}s_{Ni}^1(\Pi_{Ni}^1-\Pi_C^1)/\Pi^0$ (the contribution of entering firms to TFPG);

(42) $\Gamma_X \equiv S_X^0\sum_{i\in X}s_{Xi}^0(\Pi_{Xi}^0-\Pi_C^0)/\Pi^0$ (the contribution of exiting firms to TFPG).

The terms defined by (38)-(42) are listed in table 5 for each choice of base; i.e., we use the data in tables 2-4 above (along with the corresponding prices) in order to construct an aggregate industry productivity growth decomposition for each of the 8 bases.

Table 5. Aggregate Productivity Growth Decompositions for Each Choice of Base

	Γ	Γ_{CD}	Γ_{CR}	Γ_N	Γ_X
Base=1	0.5356	0.4054	-0.0061	0.0337	0.1025
Base=2	0.5496	0.4247	-0.0062	0.0300	0.1010
Base=3	0.5471	0.4128	-0.0063	0.0391	0.1015
Base=4	0.6025	0.4704	-0.0071	0.0374	0.1017
Base=5	0.5174	0.3739	-0.0066	0.0440	0.1061
Base=6	0.5684	0.4311	-0.0070	0.0387	0.1056
Base=7	0.5678	0.4249	-0.0075	0.0425	0.1080
Base=8	0.5296	0.3887	-0.0065	0.0418	0.1056

The choice of base matters. Aggregate productivity growth using observation 5 (data of firm 1 in period 1) as the base leads to estimating industry productivity growth as 51.74% whereas if observation 4 (data of the disappearing firm 4 in period 0) is used as the base, then industry productivity growth is estimated as much larger at 60.25%.[37] In the last 4 columns in table 5, the direct productivity growth of continuing firms accounts for most of the industry productivity growth (between 37.39% and 47.04%), the contribution of the exiting firm is between 10% and 11%, the contribution of the entering firm is between 3.0% and 4.4%, and the reallocation of resources between continuing firms sums to a negligible contribution.

Now, define the three continuing firm terms on the right hand side of (39) as Γ_{CD1}, Γ_{CD2} and Γ_{CD3}: the direct productivity growth contributions of continuing firms 1, 2 and 3 respectively. Define the three terms on the right hand side of (40) as Γ_{CR1}, Γ_{CR2} and Γ_{CR3}: the reallocation contributions of continuing firms 1, 2 and 3 respectively. These terms are listed in table 6. We see that the largest contribution to industry TFP growth is the direct TFP growth of firm 3 (the large firm); it contributes between 24.29% (the index base 5 estimate) and 32.61% (the index base 4 estimate). The next largest contribution comes from the medium sized firm 1. The other contribution terms are all less than 5%.

Some form of averaging of the star decompositions is called for. Our next method takes the geometric averages of the output and input aggregates in tables 2 and 3 and implements (32).

Table 6. Direct and Reallocation Contributions to Aggregate Productivity Growth for Each Continuing Firm and for Each Choice of Base

	Γ_{CD1}	Γ_{CD2}	Γ_{CD3}	Γ_{CR1}	Γ_{CR2}	Γ_{CR3}
Base=1	0.1210	0.0073	0.2771	-0.0372	0.0309	0.0002
Base=2	0.1262	0.0080	0.2905	-0.0381	0.0305	0.0014
Base=3	0.1263	0.0088	0.2777	-0.0396	0.0296	0.0037
Base=4	0.1345	0.0099	0.3261	-0.0367	0.0305	-0.0009
Base=5	0.1234	0.0076	0.2429	-0.0456	0.0298	0.0093
Base=6	0.1289	0.0082	0.2939	-0.0403	0.0312	0.0021
Base=7	0.1372	0.0089	0.2788	-0.0492	0.0304	0.0112
Base=8	0.1216	0.0074	0.2597	-0.0414	0.0305	0.0044

7. The GEKS Method for Making Multilateral Comparisons

The GEKS method dates back to Gini (1931), Eltetö and Köves (1964) and Szulc (1964). As already indicated, this method takes the geometric mean of the star output and input

37 The choice of observations 2, 3, 6 and 7 as the index number base gives rise to industry TFP growth rates that are closest to our target rates of around 55.53% and 55.73%; recall (35) above. Note that the average of the industry productivity growth rates for the large firm observations (3 and 7) is 55.74%.

parities.[38] The GEKS relative output and input aggregates are listed in table 7. Once the output and input aggregates have been constructed, then the GEKS productivity levels can be constructed by dividing each output aggregate by the corresponding input aggregate, as in table 7.

Table 7. GEKS Output and Input Aggregates and Productivity Levels

Outputs	y_1	y_2	y_3	y_4	y_5	y_6	y_7	y_8
	1	0.100	4.911	0.777	1.193	0.252	5.242	1.250
Inputs	x_1	x_2	x_3	x_4	x_5	x_6	x_7	x_8
	1	0.100	3.946	1.245	0.680	0.201	3.213	0.645
Prod Levels	y_1/x_1	y_2/x_2	y_3/x_3	y_4/x_4	y_5/x_5	y_6/x_6	y_7/x_7	y_8/x_8
	1	0.998	1.245	0.624	1.755	1.256	1.631	1.938

Aggregate output prices that correspond to the 8 output aggregates that are listed in table 7 can be obtained by dividing the value of output produced by each firm in each period by the corresponding output listed for that observation in table 7. Similarly, aggregate input prices that correspond to the 8 input aggregates that are listed in table 7 can be obtained by dividing the value of inputs used by each firm in each period by the corresponding input listed for that observation in table 7. Once these aggregate output and input prices have been constructed, then we can repeat the decomposition analysis that was implemented in the previous section.

The productivity growth decomposition terms defined by (38)-(42) are listed in table 8 below. We also list the direct and reallocation contribution terms defined by the individual terms in (39) and (40) for each continuing firm in table 8.

Table 8. The GEKS Aggregate Productivity Growth Decomposition

Γ	Γ_{CD}	Γ_{CR}	Γ_N	Γ_X	
0.5521	0.4162	-0.0066	0.0384	0.1040	
Γ_{CD1}	Γ_{CD2}	Γ_{CD3}	Γ_{CR1}	Γ_{CR2}	Γ_{CR3}
0.1274	0.0083	0.2806	-0.041	0.0304	0.0039

From Table 8, the GEKS aggregate productivity growth Γ is 55.21%, which is reasonably close to our target rates of around 55.53% to 55.73%; recall (35) above. Thus we conclude that the GEKS method for constructing relative output and input levels for each firm in each period is satisfactory, at least for our particular numerical example.

One problem with the (unweighted) GEKS method is that each firm observation is given equal weighting. For example, for small firms, their star parities could be quite different than for large firms. Hence it may not be wise to give these small firms equal weighting in the construction of the output and input aggregates. In the following section, we look at a multilateral method that gives large firms more weight.

[38] The GEKS aggregates can be defined in a number of equivalent ways; see for example, Diewert (1999; 31-37).

8. The Own Share Method for Making Multilateral Comparisons

Recall our discussion in section 6 when we described how the star output aggregates could be constructed using observation k as the base. We noted that the sequence of 8 numbers, $Q_F(p^k,p^1,y^k,y^1)$, $Q_F(p^k,p^2,y^k,y^2)$, …, $Q_F(p^k,p^8,y^k,y^8)$, could serve as comparable output aggregates for our 8 observations. Hence, using observation k as the base, the *share of total output of observation k* is:

$$(43)\quad \begin{aligned} s_k^* &\equiv Q_F(p^k,p^k,y^k,y^k)/[Q_F(p^k,p^1,y^k,y^1)+Q_F(p^k,p^2,y^k,y^2)+\ldots+Q_F(p^k,p^8,y^k,y^8)] \\ &= 1/[Q_F(p^k,p^1,y^k,y^1)+Q_F(p^k,p^2,y^k,y^2)+\ldots+Q_F(p^k,p^8,y^k,y^8)]; \quad k=1,\ldots,8. \end{aligned}$$

The last equation in (43) follows from the fact that the Fisher ideal quantity index satisfies an identity test and hence $Q_F(p^k,p^k,y^k,y^k)$ equals 1. Thus, using the metric of observation k to make the index number comparisons, the share of observation k in "world" output, s_k^*, is defined by (43) for k = 1,2, …, 8. Each observation's *own share* of "world" output is defined by (43). Put another way, if we look at the entries in table 2 above, the numbers listed in the Base=1 row determine the share of observation 1 in total output over the two periods, s_1^*; the numbers listed in the Base=2 row determine the share of observation 2 in total output over the two periods, s_2^*; …; and the numbers listed in the Base=8 row determine the share of observation 8 in total output over the two periods, s_8^*. Thus each row in table 2 determines only one share of "world" output and so the rows that correspond to smaller shares of world output get a smaller influence in the overall multilateral comparison. This means that the own share system does weight the individual star parities according to their economic importance as opposed to the more democratic GEKS method where each star parity has the same importance.

Unfortunately, the own shares s_k^* defined by (43) do not sum up to unity and so we renormalize these "shares" to sum up to unity as follows:[39]

$$(44)\quad y_k \equiv s_k^*/[\textstyle\sum_{j=1}^{8} s_j^*], \quad k=1,\ldots,8.$$

The output aggregates y_k defined by (44) are the *own share output aggregates.*[40] The same procedure can be used to define own share input aggregates. The own share relative output and input aggregates as well as the output to input productivity ratios are listed in table 9. Once these aggregates have been constructed, then the own share productivity levels can be constructed by dividing each output aggregate by the corresponding input aggregate. The resulting 8 productivity levels are listed in the bottom row of table 9.[41]

---

[39] In our empirical example, the s_k^* summed up to 0.99996 so that the differences between the y_k and the s_k^* were negligible. The corresponding input shares summed up to 0.99997.

[40] The own share system was proposed by Diewert (1988; 69). For axiomatic properties see Diewert (1999; 37-39).

[41] Note that the units of measurement for the output and input aggregates are quite different in Tables 7 and 9. This illustrates the importance of providing a productivity growth decomposition that is independent of the units.

Table 9. Own Share Output and Input Aggregates and Productivity Levels

Outputs	y_1	y_2	y_3	y_4	y_5	y_6	y_7	y_8
	0.068	0.007	0.332	0.052	0.082	0.017	0.357	0.085
Inputs	x_1	x_2	x_3	x_4	x_5	x_6	x_7	x_8
	0.091	0.009	0.357	0.113	0.062	0.018	0.293	0.058
Prod Levels	y_1/x_1	y_2/x_2	y_3/x_3	y_4/x_4	y_5/x_5	y_6/x_6	y_7/x_7	y_8/x_8
	0.75	0.742	0.931	0.465	1.322	0.943	1.218	1.462

Aggregate output prices that correspond to the 8 output aggregates listed in table 9 can be obtained by dividing the value of output produced by each firm in each period by the corresponding output listed for that observation in table 9. Similarly, aggregate input prices that correspond to the 8 input aggregates that are listed in table 9 can be obtained by dividing the value of inputs used by each firm in each period by the corresponding input listed for that observation in table 9. Once these aggregate output and input prices have been constructed, then we can repeat the decomposition analysis that was implemented in the previous sections.

The productivity growth decomposition terms defined by (38)-(42) are listed in table 10. Here we also list the direct and reallocation contribution terms, defined by the individual terms in (39) and (40) for each continuing firm. From table 10, the own share aggregate productivity growth Γ is 55.45%, which is close to our target rate of 55.53% to 55.73%; recall (35) above.[42] Thus we conclude that the own share method is very satisfactory, at least for our example.

Table 10. The Own Share Aggregate Productivity Growth Decomposition

Γ	Γ_{CD}	Γ_{CR}	Γ_N	Γ_X	
0.5545	0.4165	-0.0067	0.0403	0.1044	
Γ_{CD1}	Γ_{CD2}	Γ_{CD3}	Γ_{CR1}	Γ_{CR2}	Γ_{CR3}
0.1290	0.0086	0.2789	-0.0423	0.0302	0.0054

9. Hill's Method for Making Multilateral Comparisons

Another method for finding output and input aggregates is based on the following idea: observations which are most similar in their price structures (i.e., their output prices are closest to being proportional across items) should be linked using a bilateral index number formula first. Then the observation outside of the first two observations that has the most similar relative prices to the first two observations should be added, etc. This basic idea has been successfully exploited by Robert Hill at higher levels of aggregation[43] with complete price and expenditure data.

[42] The own share decomposition is very close to the GEKS decomposition in table 8. Diewert (1988; 69) (1999; 38) showed that the own share aggregates and the GEKS aggregates will usually approximate each other closely.

[43] See Robert Hill (1999a) (1999b) (2001) (2004). The basic idea of spatially linking countries with the most similar price and quantity structures dates back to Fisher (1922; 271-272). We apply the idea here to firm observations.

To apply this idea, it is necessary to choose a measure of the degree of *dissimilarity* for the (relative) output prices corresponding to any two observations. There are many measures of relative price dissimilarity that could be chosen.[44] Our pick is the following one that measures the degree of dissimilarity between the output prices of observations j and k ($j,k = 1,\ldots,8$):

$$(45) \quad D(p^j,p^k) \equiv \{\ln[p_1^k / P_F(p^k,p^j,q^k,q^j)p_1^j]\}^2 + \{\ln[p_2^k / P_F(p^k,p^j,q^k,q^j)p_2^j]\}^2,$$

where $P_F(p^k,p^j,q^k,q^j)$ is the Fisher output price index of observation j relative to k.[45] Thus instead of comparing the price of output 1 for observation k, p_1^k, with the price of output 1 for observation j, p_1^j, we multiply p_1^j by the Fisher price index for observation k relative to j, $P_F(p^k,p^j,q^k,q^j)$, which inflates the base prices j by a general inflation factor that makes the prices of k comparable to the inflated j prices. In particular, if the j prices are equal to λ times the k prices, so that $p^j = \lambda p^k$, then the Fisher index that compares the j prices to the k prices will pick up this proportionality factor so that $P_F(p^k,p^j,q^k,q^j) = \lambda$. In this case, the dissimilarity measure defined by (45) will be zero; i.e., we will have $D(p^j,p^k) = 0$. It can also be verified that the dissimilarity measure defined by (45) satisfies the following *symmetry property*:

$$(46) \quad D(p^k,p^j) = D(p^j,p^k) \qquad j,k = 1,\ldots,8.$$

Table 11 lists the Fisher output price indexes $P_F(p^k,p^j,q^k,q^j)$ between pairs of observations.[46]

Table 11. Fisher Output Price Indexes Between Each Pair of Observations

Base k=1	1	0.980	0.855	1.152	12.007	11.000	11.100	13.064
Base k=2	1.021	1	0.850	1.133	11.963	10.969	10.904	13.093
Base k=3	1.170	1.176	1	1.354	13.518	12.570	12.591	14.738
Base k=4	0.868	0.883	0.738	1	9.811	9.190	9.145	10.720
Base k=5	0.083	0.084	0.074	0.102	1	0.927	0.949	1.081
Base k=6	0.091	0.091	0.080	0.109	1.079	1	1.016	1.170
Base k=7	0.090	0.092	0.079	0.109	1.054	0.985	1	1.143
Base k=8	0.077	0.076	0.068	0.093	0.925	0.855	0.875	1

[44] See Diewert (2009) for an axiomatic treatment of the topic.

[45] This dissimilarity measure is essentially equal to that used by Allen and Diewert (1981) except that they used the Törnqvist index $P_T(p^k,p^j,q^k,q^j)$ to adjust for general price level change in place of the Fisher index $P_F(p^k,p^j,q^k,q^j)$ in (45). Diewert (2009) defined a weighted counterpart to (45) which he called the weighted log quadratic index of relative price dissimilarity.

[46] The Fisher (1922) output price index is defined as $P_F(p^0,p^1,q^0,q^1) \equiv [p^1q^0p^1q^1/p^0q^0p^0q^1]^{1/2}$. Row k of table 11 is equal to $P_F(p^k,p^1,q^k,q^1)$, $P_F(p^k,p^2,q^k,q^2)$, … , $P_F(p^k,p^8,q^k,q^8)$.

Note that Fisher output price levels for firms present in period 1 are 9.145 to 14.738 times the levels of prices for firms present in period 0 (see the entries in the northeast corner of Table 11). Table 12 lists the dissimilarity measures $D(p^j, p^k)$ defined by (45): a symmetric matrix.

Table 12. Log Quadratic Output Price Dissimilarity Measures

0	0.08220	0.00705	0.00380	0.34067	0.12932	0.26641	0.28161
0.08220	0	0.13759	0.12365	0.71777	0.40242	0.61510	0.63505
0.00705	0.13759	0	0.00047	0.23304	0.07164	0.17715	0.18557
0.00380	0.12365	0.00047	0	0.24608	0.08182	0.19079	0.19811
0.34067	0.71777	0.23304	0.24608	0	0.04837	0.00305	0.00324
0.12932	0.40242	0.07164	0.08182	0.04837	0	0.02565	0.02722
0.26641	0.61510	0.17715	0.19079	0.00305	0.02565	0	0
0.28161	0.63505	0.18557	0.19811	0.00324	0.02722	0	0

Note that the dissimilarity measure between observations 7 and 8 is 0; this is due to the fact that the output price vectors for these two observations are proportional.

Inspection of table 12 shows that the lowest dissimilarity measures that link the data are: 7-8; 7-5; 7-6; 3-4; 1-4; 1-2 and 3-5. This set of links will enable us to construct output aggregates, $y_1,\ldots,y_8$, which are listed in table 15 below. The same strategy that was used to construct Hill output aggregates can be used to construct input aggregates. The input counterparts to tables 11 and 12 are tables 13 and 14.

Table 13. Fisher Input Price Indexes Between Each Pair of Observations

Base k=1	1	0.750	0.994	1.102	16.029	14.500	16.650	16.884
Base k=2	1.333	1	1.331	1.471	21.474	19.333	22.257	22.570
Base k=3	1.006	0.752	1	1.117	15.842	14.497	16.254	16.867
Base k=4	0.907	0.680	0.895	1	14.338	13.131	14.896	15.214
Base k=5	0.062	0.047	0.063	0.070	1	0.898	1.014	1.056
Base k=6	0.069	0.052	0.069	0.076	1.114	1	1.153	1.169
Base k=7	0.060	0.045	0.062	0.067	0.986	0.867	1	1.028
Base k=8	0.059	0.044	0.059	0.066	0.947	0.855	0.972	1

Fisher input price levels for firms present in period 1 are 13.131 to 22.570 times the levels of prices for firms present in period 0 meaning that input prices grew faster than output prices.

Inspection of table 14 shows that the lowest dissimilarity measures that link the data are: 3-6; 2-3; 1-2; 1-4; 6-8; 5-7 and 5-8. This set of links will enable us to construct Hill input aggregates, $x_1,\ldots,x_8$, which are listed in table 15. The eight Hill productivity levels, $y_1/x_1,\ldots,y_8/x_8$, are also listed in table 15.

Table 14. Log Quadratic Input Price Dissimilarity Measures

0	0.00893	0.02014	0.01669	0.35300	0.02161	0.73589	0.06377
0.00893	0	0.00225	0.04993	0.25127	0.00277	0.58761	0.02507
0.02014	0.00225	0	0.07378	0.20284	0.00002	0.50447	0.01219
0.01669	0.04993	0.07378	0	0.51780	0.07605	0.95664	0.14529
0.35300	0.25127	0.20284	0.5178	0	0.20208	0.06805	0.11723
0.02161	0.00277	0.00002	0.07605	0.20208	0	0.51192	0.01122
0.73589	0.58761	0.50447	0.95664	0.06805	0.51192	0	0.36697
0.06377	0.02507	0.01219	0.14529	0.11723	0.01122	0.36697	0

Table 15. Hill Output and Input Aggregates and Productivity Levels

Outputs	y_1	y_2	y_3	y_4	y_5	y_6	y_7	y_8
	1	0.102	4.997	0.794	1.222	0.256	5.295	1.284
Inputs	x_1	x_2	x_3	x_4	x_5	x_6	x_7	x_8
	1	0.100	3.958	1.252	0.681	0.200	3.263	0.644
Prod Levels	y_1/x_1	y_2/x_2	y_3/x_3	y_4/x_4	y_5/x_5	y_6/x_6	y_7/x_7	y_8/x_8
	1	1.021	1.262	0.634	1.795	1.277	1.623	1.992

Comparing the entries in table 15 with the corresponding GEKS entries in table 7, it can be seen that with the exceptions of observations 1 and 7, the Hill productivity levels tend to be greater than the corresponding GEKS productivity levels.

Aggregate output prices that correspond to the 8 output aggregates that are listed in table 15 can be obtained by dividing the value of output produced by each firm in each period by the corresponding output listed for that observation in table 15. Similarly, aggregate input prices that correspond to the 8 input aggregates that are listed in table 15 can be obtained by dividing the value of inputs used by each firm in each period by the corresponding input listed for that observation in table 15. Once these aggregate output and input prices have been constructed, then we can repeat the decomposition analysis that was implemented in the previous sections.

The productivity growth decomposition terms defined by (38)-(41) are listed in table 16 below. We also list the direct and reallocation contribution terms defined by the individual terms in (39) and (40) for each continuing firm in table 16.

Table 16. The Hill Aggregate Productivity Growth Decomposition

Γ	Γ_{CD}	Γ_{CR}	Γ_N	Γ_X
0.5401	0.3986	-0.0063	0.044	0.1038

Γ_{CD1}	Γ_{CD2}	Γ_{CD3}	Γ_{CR1}	Γ_{CR2}	Γ_{CR3}
0.1318	0.008	0.2588	-0.0428	0.0301	0.0064

From table 16, the Hill aggregate productivity growth Γ is 54.01%, which is not as close to our target rates of around 55.53% to 55.73% compared to the GEKS and own share decompositions of productivity growth. Thus for this particular numerical example, we conclude that the Hill method for constructing relative output and input levels for each firm in each period is satisfactory but not as good at the GEKS and own share estimates.

10. An Approximate Method for Constructing Output and Input Aggregates

The multilateral methods for constructing output and input aggregates that have been discussed in the previous 3 sections are theoretically satisfactory methods. However, they suffer from two major disadvantages:

- They may not be practical for very large data sets; i.e., they are computation intensive.
- Detailed price and quantity information may not be available for each firm; i.e., only information on output revenues and input costs by unit may be available.

Thus in the present section, we assume that we have only information on firm revenues and costs by period and that we also have aggregate intertemporal price indexes for both outputs and inputs available. In particular, we assume that we have the aggregate Fisher output and input price indexes at our disposal. Using the aggregate period 0 and 1 information on the industry's two outputs and inputs listed in section 5 above,[47] the Fisher and Törnqvist output price index numbers for period 1 are 12.283 and 12.239 respectively[48] while the Fisher and Törnqvist input price index numbers for period 1 are 16.035 and 15.998 respectively. We will use the Fisher industry price index values for outputs and inputs for period 1, $P_F(p^0,p^1,q^0,q^1)$ and $P_F{}^*(w^0,w^1,x^0,x^1)$ respectively, to deflate all of the period 1 firm revenues and costs in order to make them at least approximately comparable to the period 0 firm revenues and costs. Recalling the notation that was introduced at the beginning of section 6, for observations 1-4, we define firm aggregate outputs and inputs as firm revenues and costs respectively; i.e., define the *output and input aggregates*, y_1,y_2,y_3,y_4 and x_1,x_2,x_3,x_4 respectively, as follows:

$$(47) \quad y_k \equiv p^k y^k \; ; k = 1,2,3,4 \; ; \quad x_k \equiv w^k x^k \; ; k = 1,2,3,4 \,.$$

For observations 5-8 (the period 1 observations), we define firm aggregate outputs and inputs as Fisher index deflated firm revenues and costs respectively; i.e., define the *output and input aggregates*, y_5,y_6,y_7,y_8 and x_5,x_6,x_7,x_8 respectively, as follows:

$$(48) \quad y_k \equiv p^k y^k / P_F(p^0,p^1,q^0,q^1) \text{ and } x_k \equiv w^k x^k / P_F^*(w^0,w^1,x^0,x^1) \text{ for } k=5,6,7,8.$$

Obviously, the output and input aggregates defined by (47) and (48) are not going to be as accurate as the output and input aggregates defined in the previous 3 sections. However, it is still of some interest to see how close these approximate aggregates are to the previously defined multilateral aggregates. The approximate output and input aggregates are listed in table 17 along with the corresponding plant productivity levels.

[47] See the listing of the industry data in (33) above.

[48] The corresponding index values are 1 in period 0.

Table 17. Approximate Output and Input Aggregates and Productivity Levels

Outputs	y_1	y_2	y_3	y_4	y_5	y_6	y_7	y_8
	20.000	2.000	85.000	18.300	22.877	4.478	94.031	26.052
Inputs	x_1	x_2	x_3	x_4	x_5	x_6	x_7	x_8
	20.000	1.500	79.000	27.600	13.595	3.617	66.105	13.595
Prod Levels	y_1/x_1	y_2/x_2	y_3/x_3	y_4/x_4	y_5/x_5	y_6/x_6	y_7/x_7	y_8/x_8
	1	1.333	1.076	0.663	1.683	1.238	1.422	1.916
GEKS	1	0.998	1.245	0.624	1.755	1.256	1.631	1.938

In order to make the units of measurement for outputs and inputs listed in table 17 comparable to the units listed in the corresponding GEKS table 7, it is necessary to divide the outputs row by 20 and the inputs row by 20. The productivity levels row in table 17 is comparable to the corresponding row in table 7. For easy reference, the GEKS productivity levels are listed as the last row in table 17. It can be seen that there are some rather substantial differences in the GEKS productivity levels compared to the corresponding approximate ones.

As usual, aggregate output prices that correspond to the 8 output aggregates listed in table 17 can be obtained by dividing the value of output produced by each firm in each period by the corresponding output listed for that observation in table 17. Similarly, aggregate input prices that correspond to the 8 input aggregates listed in table 17 can be obtained by dividing the value of inputs used by each firm in each period by the corresponding input listed for that observation in table 17. Once these aggregate output and input prices have been constructed, then we can repeat the decomposition analysis that was implemented in the previous sections.

The productivity growth decomposition terms defined by (38)-(41) are listed in table 18 below. We also list the direct and reallocation contribution terms defined by the individual terms in (39) and (40) for each continuing firm in table 18. For ease of comparison, we list the decompositions for the GEKS, own share and Hill methods in table 18 as well.

Table 18. The Approximate Method Aggregate Productivity Growth Decomposition

	Γ	Γ_{CD}	Γ_{CR}	Γ_N	Γ_X	
Approx Method	0.5553	0.4033	-0.0023	0.0659	0.0885	
GEKS	0.5521	0.4162	-0.0066	0.0384	0.104	
Own Share	0.5545	0.4165	-0.0067	0.0403	0.1044	
Hill	0.5401	0.3986	-0.0063	0.044	0.1038	
	Γ_{CD1}	Γ_{CD2}	Γ_{CD3}	Γ_{CR1}	Γ_{CR2}	Γ_{CR3}
Approx Method	0.1264	-0.0028	0.2798	-0.0491	0.0374	0.0094
GEKS	0.1274	0.0083	0.2806	-0.041	0.0304	0.0039
Own Share	0.129	0.0086	0.2789	-0.0423	0.0302	0.0054
Hill	0.1318	0.008	0.2588	-0.0428	0.0301	0.0064

From table 18, the approximate method aggregate productivity growth Γ is 55.53%, which is exactly equal to our target Fisher rate of 55.53%. This exact equality is not a statistical fluke but is a consequence of the fact that we have used the industry Fisher price indexes to deflate the period 1 value data. Thus our approximate method works extremely well in terms of replicating the industry's aggregate productivity growth. However, the other terms on the right hand side of (32) are not always well predicted by the approximate method. In particular, it leads to a contribution of entry term Γ_N equal to 6.59% whereas the other methods lead to contribution terms in the 3.84 to 4.40% range. Also, the approximate method leads to a contribution of exit term Γ_X equal to 8.85% whereas the other methods lead to contribution terms in the 10.38 to 10.44% range. However, considering the simplicity of the approximate method, we conclude that at least for this example, this method was suitable for constructing output and input aggregates to be used in a productivity growth decomposition such as (32), though, of course, it was not as good as the GEKS and own share methods.

11. Conclusion

This paper proposes a new formula (32) for decomposing industry productivity growth into terms that reflect the productivity growth of individual production units that operate in both the base and comparison periods, and also the reallocation of resources among continuing firms from lower productivity to higher productivity units, as well as entry and exit contribution terms. Unfortunately, this formula and the other formulae presented in the literature are derived under the assumption that each production unit produces a single homogeneous output and uses a single homogeneous input. Most of the paper (sections 4-10) is concerned with the problems involved in aggregating many outputs and many inputs into output and input aggregates. In order to accomplish this aggregation, we suggested the use of multilateral methods and we implemented four multilateral methods on a test data set that is described in section 5 above. For our test data set, we found that the own share method worked best but the GEKS method was very close. The Hill methods and an approximate method that used value aggregates in the base period and deflated value aggregates in the comparison period also worked reasonably well for our data set. The fact that the approximate method worked so well is very encouraging for empirical work in this area, since variants of it are what have been used in empirical applications of productivity decompositions that involve entry and exit.[49]

References

Aw, B.Y., X. Chen and M.J. Roberts (2001), "Firm Level Evidence on Productivity Differentials and Turnover in Taiwanese Manufacturing," *Journal of Development Economics* 66, 51-86.

[49] In our test example, we used the actual "industry" Fisher output and input price indexes as the deflators. In empirical work, the deflators that are available are unlikely to be the exact industry deflators. Also, in real life, it is unlikely that all of the production units in a given industry are producing positive amounts of a common list of outputs and using positive amounts of a common list of inputs, as for our example.

Aw, B.Y., S. Chung and M.J. Roberts (2003), "Productivity, Output and Failure: A Comparison of Taiwanese and Korean Manufacturers," *Economic Journal* 113, F485-F510.

Ahn, S. (2001), "Firm Dynamics and Productivity Growth: A Review of Micro Evidence from OECD Countries," OECD Economics Department Working Paper No. 297, OECD, Paris.

Allen, R.C. and W.E. Diewert (1981), "Direct versus Implicit Superlative Index Number Formulae," *Review of Economics and Statistics* 63, 430-435.

Baily, M.N., C. Hulten, D. Campbell, (1992), "Productivity Dynamics in Manufacturing Establishments," *Brookings Papers on Economic Activity: Microeconomics 1992*, 187-249.

Baldwin, J.R. (1995), *The Dynamics of Industrial Competition: A North American Perspective*, Cambridge: Cambridge University Press.

Baldwin, J.R. and P.K. Gorecki (1991), "Entry, Exit, and Productivity Growth," in: P.A. Geroski and J. Schwalbach (eds.), *Entry and Market Contestability: An International Comparison*, Oxford: Blackwell.

Baldwin, J.R. and W. Gu (2002), "Plant Turnover and Productivity Growth in Canadian Manufacturing," OECD STI Working Paper 2002/1, Paris: OECD. Available at www.statcan.ca/english/studies/prod.htm

Balk, B.M. (1996), "A Comparison of Ten Methods of Multilateral International Price and Volume Comparisons," *Journal of Official Statistics* 12, 199-222.

Balk, B.M. (2001), "Aggregation Methods in International Comparisons: What Have we Learned?," Erasmus Research Institute of Management, Erasmus University Rotterdam, June.

Balk, B.M. (2003), "The Residual: on Monitoring and Benchmarking Firms, Industries and Economies with Respect to Productivity," *Journal of Productivity Analysis* 20, 5-47.

Bartelsman, E.J. and M. Doms (2000), "Understanding Productivity: Lessons from Longitudinal Microdata," *Journal of Economic Literature* 38, 569-595.

Bartelsman, E., J. Haltiwanger and J. Scarpetta (2004), "Microeconomic Evidence of Creative Destruction in Industrial and Developing Countries," unpublished manuscript.

Bennet, T.L. (1920), "The Theory of Measurement of Changes in Cost of Living," *Journal of the Royal Statistical Society* 83, 455-462.

Caves, D.W., L. Christensen, and W.E. Diewert (1982), "Multilateral Comparisons of Output, Input, and Productivity Using Superlative Index Numbers," *Economic Journal* 92 (365): 73-86.

Coelli, T., D.S. Prasada Rao and G. Battese (1998), *An Introduction to Efficiency and Productivity Analysis*, Boston: Kluwer Academic Publishers.

Diewert, W.E. (1976), "Exact and Superlative Index Numbers," *Journal of Econometrics* 4, 115–146.

Diewert, W.E. (1988), "Test Approaches to International Comparisons," pp. 76-86 in *Measurement in Economics*, W. Eichhorn (ed.), Heidelberg: Physica-Verlag.

Diewert, W.E. (1992), "Fisher Ideal Output, Input and Productivity Indexes Revisited," *Journal of Productivity Analysis* 3, 211-248; reprinted as pp. 317-353 in *Essays in Index Number Theory, Volume 1*, W.E. Diewert and A.O. Nakamura (eds.), Amsterdam: North-Holland, 1993.

Diewert, W.E. (1999), "Axiomatic and Economic Approaches to International Comparisons," pp. 13-87 in *International and Interarea Comparisons of Income, Output and Prices*, A. Heston and R.E. Lipsey (eds.), Studies in Income and Wealth Volume 61, NBER, Chicago: The University of Chicago Press.

Diewert, W.E. (2004), "A New Axiomatic Approach to Index Number Theory," Discussion Paper 04-05, Department of Economics, University of British Columbia, Vancouver, B.C., Canada, V6T 1Z1. http://www.econ.ubc.ca/diewert/hmpgdie.htm

Diewert, W.E. (2005), "Index Number Theory Using Differences Rather than Ratios," *American Journal of Economics and Sociology* 64:1, 347-395.

Diewert, W.E. and A.O. Nakamura (2003), "Index Number Concepts, Measures and Decompositions of Productivity Growth," *Journal of Productivity Analysis* 19, 127-159. http://www.econ.ubc.ca/diewert/other.htm

Diewert, W.E. (2009), "Similarity Indexes and Criteria for Spatial Linking", pp in Purchasing Power Parities of Currencies: Recent Advances in Methods and Applications, D.S. Prasada Rao (ed.), Cheltenham, UK: Edward Elgar.

Eltetö, O. and P. Köves (1964), “On a Problem of Index Number Computation Relating to International Comparisons,” *Statisztikai Szemle* 42, 507-518.

Fisher, I. (1922), *The Making of Index Numbers*, Boston: Houghton Mifflin.

Foster, L., J. Haltiwanger and C.J. Krizan (2001), “Aggregate Productivity Growth: Lessons from Microeconomic Evidence,” pp. 303-372 in *New Developments in Productivity Analysis*, C.R. Hulten, E.R. Dean and M.J. Harper (eds.), NBER Studies in Income and Wealth Volume 63, Chicago: University of Chicago Press.

Foster, L., J. Haltiwanger and C. Syverson (2008), “Reallocation, Firm Turnover and Efficiency: Selection on Productivity or Profitability?”, *American Economic Review* 98, 394-425.

Fox, K.J. (2002), “Problems with (Dis)Aggregating Productivity and another Productivity Paradox,” Discussion Paper, School of Economics, University of New South Wales, Sydney.

Gini, C. (1931), “On the Circular Test of Index Numbers,” *Metron* 9:9, 3-24.

Good, D. (1985), *The Effect of Deregulation on the Productive Efficiency and Cost Structure of the Airline Industry*, Ph. D thesis, University of Pennsylvania.

Good, D.H., M.I. Nadiri and R. Sickles (1997), “Index Number and Factor Demand Approaches to the Estimation of Productivity,” pp. 14-80 in H. Pesaran and P. Schmidt (eds.), *Handbook of Applied Econometrics: Microeconometrics*, Volume II, Oxford: Basil Blackwell.

Griliches, Z. and H. Regev (1995), “Firm Productivity in Israeli Industry: 1979-1988,” *Journal of Econometrics* 65, 175-203.

Haltiwanger, J. (1997), “Measuring and Analyzing Aggregate Fluctuations: The Importance of Building from Microeconomic Evidence,” *Federal Reserve Bank of St. Louis Economic Review* 79 (3), 55-77.

Haltiwanger, J. (2000), “Aggregate Growth: What have we Learned from Microeconomic Evidence?,” OECD Economics Department Working Paper No. 267, OECD, Paris.

Hill, R.J. (1999a), “Comparing Price Levels across Countries Using Minimum Spanning Trees,” *Review of Economics and Statistics* 81, 135-142.

Hill, R.J. (1999b), “International Comparisons using Spanning Trees,” pp. 109-120 in *International and Interarea Comparisons of Income, Output and Prices*, A. Heston and R.E. Lipsey (eds.), Studies in Income and Wealth Volume 61, NBER, Chicago: The University of Chicago Press.

Hill, R.J. (2001), “Measuring Inflation and Growth Using Spanning Trees,” *International Economic Review* 42, 167-185.

Hill, R.J. (2004), “Constructing Price Indexes Across Space and Time: The Case of the European Union,” *American Economic Review* 94 (5), 1379-1410.

Jorgenson, D.W. and Z. Griliches (1967), “The Explanation of Productivity Change,” *Review of Economic Studies* 34, 249-283.

Jorgenson, D.W. and Z. Griliches (1972), “Issues in Growth Accounting: A Reply to Edward F. Denison,” *Survey of Current Business* 52, no. 5, part 2, 65-94.

Kravis, I.B. (1984), “Comparative Studies of National Incomes and Prices,” *Journal of Economic Literature* 22, 1-39.

Olley, G.S. and A. Pakes (1996), “The Dynamics of Productivity in the Telecommunications Equipment Industry,” *Econometrica* 64, 1263-1297.

Szulc, B. (1964), “Indices for Multiregional Comparisons,” *Przeglad Statystyczny* 3, 239-254.

Theil, H. (1967), *Economics and Information Theory*, Amsterdam: North-Holland.

Törnqvist, L. (1936), “The Bank of Finland’s Consumption Price Index,” *Bank of Finland Monthly Bulletin* 10: 1-8.

Chapter 4
ON THE TANG AND WANG DECOMPOSITION OF LABOUR PRODUCTIVITY GROWTH INTO SECTORAL EFFECTS

W. Erwin Diewert[1]

1. Introduction

Jianmin Tang and Weimin Wang (2004; 426) provide an interesting decomposition for economy wide labour productivity into sectoral contribution effects. However, the interpretation of the individual terms in their decomposition is not completely clear and so in section 2, we rework their methodology in order to provide a more transparent and simple decomposition. In section 3, we pursue a somewhat different approach due to Gini (1937) which is a generalization of the Fisher (1922) ideal index number methodology to aggregates that are products of three factors rather than two. Overall growth in labour productivity is due to three factors: (i) growth in the labour productivity of individual sectors; (ii) changes in real output prices of the sectors and (iii) changes in the allocation of labour across sectors.

2. The Tang and Wang Methodology Reworked

Let there be N sectors or industries in the economy. Suppose that for period t = 0,1 and for $n = 1,\ldots,N$, the output (or real value added) of sector n is Y_n^t with corresponding price P_n^t and labour input L_n^t. We assume that the labour inputs can be added across sectors and that the economy wide labour input in period t is L^t defined as

$$(1) \qquad L^t \equiv \sum_{n=1}^{N} L_n^t ; \qquad t = 0,1.$$

Labour productivity for industry n in period t, X_n^t, is defined as industry n output divided by industry n labour input; i.e.,

$$(2) \qquad X_n^t \equiv Y_n^t / L_n^t ; \qquad t = 0,1;\ n = 1,\ldots,N.$$

---

[1] W. Erwin Diewert is with the University of British Columbia and can be reached at diewert@econ.ubc.ca. The author thanks Bert Balk and Jianmin Tang for helpful comments on earlier drafts of this note.

Citation: **W. Erwin Diewert (2011), "On the Tang and Wang Decomposition of Labour Productivity Growth into Sectoral Effects," chapter 4, pp. 67-76 in**
W.E. Diewert, B.M. Balk, D. Fixler, K.J. Fox and A.O. Nakamura,
***PRICE AND PRODUCTIVITY MEASUREMENT: Volume 6 -- Index Number Theory.* Trafford Press.**

© Alice Nakamura, 2011. Permission to link to, or copy or reprint, these materials is granted without restriction, including for use in commercial textbooks, with due credit to the authors and editors.

It is not entirely clear how aggregate labour productivity should be defined since the outputs produced by the various industries are measured in heterogeneous, noncomparable units. We need to weight these heterogeneous outputs by their prices, sum the resulting period t values and then divide by a general output price index, say P^t for period t, in order to make the economy wide nominal value of aggregate output comparable in real terms across periods. Thus with an appropriate choice for the aggregate output price index P^t, the period t economy wide labour productivity, X^t, is defined as follows:[2]

$$(3)\qquad X^t \equiv \sum_{n=1}^{N} P_n^t Y_n^t / P^t L^t ; \qquad t = 0,1 .$$

We can simplify the expression for aggregate labour productivity in period 0, X^0, by a judicious choice of units of measurement for each industry output. We will choose to measure each industry's output in terms of the number of units of the industry's output that can be purchased by one dollar in period 0. The effect of these choices for the units of measurement is to set the price of each industry's output equal to unity in period 0; i.e., we have:[3]

$$(4)\qquad P_n^0 \equiv 1 ; \qquad n = 1,\ldots,N .$$

We will also normalize the economy wide price index to equal unity in period 0; i.e., we have:[4]

$$(5)\qquad P^0 \equiv 1 .$$

Using definition (3) for t = 0 along with the normalizations (4) and (5), it can be seen that the period 0 economy wide labour productivity X^0 is equal to the following expression:

$$\begin{aligned}(6)\qquad X^0 &= \sum_{n=1}^{N} Y_n^0 / L^0 \\ &= \sum_{n=1}^{N} X_n^0 L_n^0 / L^0 && \text{using definitions (2)} \\ &= \sum_{n=1}^{N} s_{L,n}^0 X_n^0 ,\end{aligned}$$

where the share of labour used by industry n in period t, s_{Ln}^t, is defined in the obvious way as:

$$(7)\qquad s_{L,n}^t \equiv L_n^t / L^t ; \qquad n = 1,\ldots,N;\ t = 0,1 .$$

Thus aggregate labour productivity for the economy in period 0 is a (labour) share weighted average of the sectoral labour productivities, which is a sensible result.

Using definition (3) for $t = 1$ and the definitions (7) for $t = 1$ leads to the following expression for aggregate labour productivity in period 1:[5]

---

[2] This follows the methodological approach taken by Tang and Wang (2004; 425).

[3] In reality, each industry will be producing many products and so P_n^1 will be say the Fisher (1922) price index for all of the industry n products going from period 0 to 1.

[4] Typically, P^1 will be the Fisher price index going from period 0 to 1 where the period 0 and 1 price and quantity vectors are the period t industry price and quantity vectors, $[P_1^t,\ldots,P_N^t]$ and $[Y_1^t,\ldots,Y_N^t]$ respectively for $t=0,1$.

$$(8)\qquad X^1 \equiv \sum_{n=1}^{N} P_n^1 Y_n^1 / P^1 L^1$$
$$= \sum_{n=1}^{N} [P_n^1 / P^1][Y_n^1 / L_n^1][L_n^1 / L^1]$$
$$= \sum_{n=1}^{N} [P_n^1 / P^1] X_n^1 s_{L,n}^1 \qquad \text{using (2) and (7) for } t = 1$$
$$= \sum_{n=1}^{N} p_n^1 s_{L,n}^1 X_n^1,$$

where the period t industry n real output price, p_n^t, is defined as the industry t output price, P_n^t, divided by the aggregate output price index for t, P^t; i.e., we have the following definitions:[6]

$$(9)\qquad p_n^t \equiv P_n^t / P^t; \qquad n = 1,\ldots,N;\ t = 0,1.$$

Thus economy wide labour productivity in period 1, X^1, is *not* equal to the (labour) share weighted average of the sectoral labour productivities, $\sum_{n=1}^{N} s_{L,n}^1 X_n^1$. Instead, X^1 is equal to $\sum_{n=1}^{N} p_n^1 s_{L,n}^1 X_n^1$, so that the labour productivity of, say, sector n which has experienced a real output price increase (so that p_n^1 is greater than one) gets a weight that is greater than its labour share weighted contribution, $s_{L,n}^1 X_n^1$; in particular, sector n gets the weight $p_n^1 s_{L,n}^1 X_n^1$.

Up to this point, our analysis follows that of Tang and Wang (2004; 425-426) except that Tang and Wang did not bother with the normalizations (4) and (5). However, in what follows, we hopefully provide some additional value added to their analysis.

First, we define the *value added or output share of industry* n *in period* 0, $s_{Y,n}^0$, as:

$$(10)\qquad s_{Y,n}^0 \equiv P_n^0 Y_n^0 / \sum_{i=1}^{N} P_i^0 Y_i^0; \qquad n = 1,\ldots,N$$
$$= Y_n^0 / \sum_{i=1}^{N} Y_i^0 \qquad \text{using the normalizations (4).}$$

Note that the product of the sector n labour share in period 0, $s_{L,n}^0$, with the sector n labour productivity in period 0, X_n^0, equals the following expression:

$$(11)\qquad s_{L,n}^0 X_n^0 = [L_n^0 / L^0][Y_n^0 / L_n^0]; \qquad n = 1,\ldots,N$$
$$= Y_n^0 / L^0.$$

Using (11), we can establish the following equalities:

$$(12)\qquad s_{L,n}^0 X_n^0 / \sum_{i=1}^{N} s_{L,i}^0 X_i^0 = [Y_n^0 / L^0] / \sum_{i=1}^{N} [Y_i^0 / L^0] \qquad n = 1,\ldots,N$$
$$= Y_n^0 / \sum_{i=1}^{N} Y_i^0$$

---

[5] Equation (8) corresponds to equation (2) in Tang and Wang (2004; 426).

[6] These definitions follow those of Tang and Wang (2004; 425).

$$= s^0_{Y,n} \qquad \text{using (10).}$$

Now we are ready to develop an expression for the rate of growth of economy wide labour productivity. Using expressions (6) and (8), we have:

$$(13) \quad X^1/X^0 = \sum_{n=1}^N p^1_n s^1_{L,n} X^1_n / \sum_{n=1}^N s^0_{L,n} X^0_n$$

$$= \sum_{n=1}^N p^1_n [s^1_{L,n}/s^0_{Ln}] [X^1_n/X^0_n] s^0_{L,n} X^0_n / \sum_{n=1}^N s^0_{L,n} X^0_n$$

$$= \sum_{n=1}^N p^1_n [s^1_{L,n}/s^0_{L,n}] [X^1_n/X^0_n] s^0_{Y,n} \qquad \text{using (12)}$$

$$= \sum_{n=1}^N [p^1_n/p^0_n] [s^1_{L,n}/s^0_{L,n}] [X^1_n/X^0_n] s^0_{Y,n} \qquad \text{using (4) and (5).}$$

Thus overall economy wide labour productivity growth, X^1/X^0, is an output share (see the term $s^0_{Y,n}$ in (13) above) weighted average of three growth factors associated with industry n. The three growth factors are:

1. X^1_n/X^0_n, (one plus) the rate of growth in the labour productivity of industry n;
2. $s^1_{L,n}/s^0_{L,n}$, (one plus) the rate of growth in the share of labour being utilized by industry n, and
3. $p^1_n/p^0_n = [P^1_n/P^0_n]/[P^1/P^0]$ which is (one plus) the rate of growth in the real output price of industry n.

Thus in looking at the contribution of industry n to overall (one plus) labour productivity growth, we start with a straightforward share weighted contribution factor, $s^0_{Y,n}[X^1_n/X^0_n]$, which is the period 0 output or value added share of industry n in period 0, $s^0_{Y,n}$, times the industry n (one plus) rate of labour productivity growth, X^1_n/X^0_n. This straightforward contribution factor will be augmented if real output price growth is positive (i.e., if p^1_n/p^0_n is greater than one) and if the share of labour used by industry n is growing (i.e., if $s^1_{L,n}/s^0_{L,n}$ is greater than one). The decomposition of overall labour productivity growth given by the last line of (13) seems to be more intuitively reasonable and simpler than the Tang-Wang decomposition (2004; 426).

3. An Alternative Decomposition due to Gini

Rewrite (13), making use of (4), (5) and (9) as follows:

$$(14) \quad X^1/X^0 = \sum_{n=1}^N p^1_n s^1_{L,n} X^1_n / \sum_{n=1}^N p^0_n s^0_{L,n} X^0_n .$$

Suppose we want to decompose X^1/X^0, the overall change in aggregate productivity, into the product of three effects:

1. One effect that holds constant the sectoral labour shares $s_{L,n}^t$ and the sectoral productivities X_n^1 and just gives us the effects of the changes in the real prices p_n^1;
2. Another effect that holds constant the real prices p_n^1 and the sectoral productivities X_n^t and gives us the effects of the changes in the sectoral labour shares $s_{L,n}^t$, and
3. A final effect that holds constant the individual labour shares $s_{L,n}^t$ and real prices p_n^1 and gives us the effects of the changes in the sectoral productivities X_n^t.

This is a well known problem that has been studied extensively by Balk (2002/3) and Balk and Hoogenboom-Spijker (2003) and by many others. In particular, the generalization of the Fisher (1922) ideal index to an aggregate that is the product of 3 different factors made by Gini (1937; 72) seems to be appropriate for the present situation.

A relatively simple way to derive Gini's formula is as follows. X^1/X^0 is equal to the ratio $\sum_{n=1}^N p_n^1 s_{L,n}^1 X_n^1 / \sum_{n=1}^N p_n^0 s_{L,n}^0 X_n^0$. Let us write this ratio as a product of three similar ratios, where in each of these three ratios, one of the factors in the numerator is set equal to either p_n^1 or $s_{L,n}^1$ or X_n^1 and the same factor in the denominator is set equal to either p_n^0 or s_{Ln}^0 or X_n^0. The remaining factors in the numerator and denominator are constant. There are only 6 ways this can be done and the resulting decompositions are as follows:

$$\text{(15)}\quad \frac{X^1}{X^0} = \left[\frac{\sum_{n=1}^N p_n^1 s_{L,n}^1 X_n^1}{\sum_{n=1}^N p_n^0 s_{L,n}^1 X_n^1}\right]\left[\frac{\sum_{n=1}^N p_n^0 s_{L,n}^1 X_n^1}{\sum_{n=1}^N p_n^0 s_{L,n}^0 X_n^1}\right]\left[\frac{\sum_{n=1}^N p_n^0 s_{L,n}^0 X_n^1}{\sum_{n=1}^N p_n^0 s_{L,n}^0 X_n^0}\right] \equiv P(1)S(1)X(1);$$

$$\text{(16)}\quad \frac{X^1}{X^0} = \left[\frac{\sum_{n=1}^N p_n^1 s_{L,n}^1 X_n^1}{\sum_{n=1}^N p_n^0 s_{L,n}^1 X_n^1}\right]\left[\frac{\sum_{n=1}^N p_n^0 s_{L,n}^1 X_n^0}{\sum_{n=1}^N p_n^0 s_{L,n}^0 X_n^0}\right]\left[\frac{\sum_{n=1}^N p_n^0 s_{L,n}^1 X_n^1}{\sum_{n=1}^N p_n^0 s_{L,n}^1 X_n^0}\right] \equiv P(2)S(2)X(2);$$

$$\text{(17)}\quad \frac{X^1}{X^0} = \left[\frac{\sum_{n=1}^N p_n^1 s_{L,n}^0 X_n^0}{\sum_{n=1}^N p_n^0 s_{L,n}^0 X_n^0}\right]\left[\frac{\sum_{n=1}^N p_n^1 s_{L,n}^1 X_n^0}{\sum_{n=1}^N p_n^1 s_{L,n}^0 X_n^0}\right]\left[\frac{\sum_{n=1}^N p_n^1 s_{L,n}^1 X_n^1}{\sum_{n=1}^N p_n^1 s_{L,n}^1 X_n^0}\right] \equiv P(3)S(3)X(3);$$

$$\text{(18)}\quad \frac{X^1}{X^0} = \left[\frac{\sum_{n=1}^N p_n^1 s_{L,n}^0 X_n^0}{\sum_{n=1}^N p_n^0 s_{L,n}^0 X_n^0}\right]\left[\frac{\sum_{n=1}^N p_n^1 s_{L,n}^1 X_n^1}{\sum_{n=1}^N p_n^1 s_{L,n}^0 X_n^1}\right]\left[\frac{\sum_{n=1}^N p_n^1 s_{L,n}^0 X_n^1}{\sum_{n=1}^N p_n^1 s_{L,n}^0 X_n^0}\right] \equiv P(4)S(4)X(4);$$

$$\text{(19)}\quad \frac{X^1}{X^0} = \left[\frac{\sum_{n=1}^N p_n^1 s_{L,n}^1 X_n^0}{\sum_{n=1}^N p_n^0 s_{L,n}^1 X_n^0}\right]\left[\frac{\sum_{n=1}^N p_n^0 s_{L,n}^1 X_n^0}{\sum_{n=1}^N p_n^0 s_{L,n}^0 X_n^0}\right]\left[\frac{\sum_{n=1}^N p_n^1 s_{L,n}^1 X_n^1}{\sum_{n=1}^N p_n^1 s_{L,n}^1 X_n^0}\right] \equiv P(5)S(5)X(5);$$

$$(20)\quad \frac{X^1}{X^0} = \left[\frac{\sum_{n=1}^{N} p_n^1 s_{L,n}^0 X_n^1}{\sum_{n=1}^{N} p_n^0 s_{L,n}^0 X_n^1}\right]\left[\frac{\sum_{n=1}^{N} p_n^1 s_{L,n}^1 X_n^1}{\sum_{n=1}^{N} p_n^1 s_{L,n}^0 X_n^1}\right]\left[\frac{\sum_{n=1}^{N} p_n^0 s_{L,n}^0 X_n^1}{\sum_{n=1}^{N} p_n^0 s_{L,n}^0 X_n^0}\right] \equiv P(6)S(6)X(6),$$

where P(1) is defined as the price index which is the first term in brackets on the right hand side of (15), S(1) is defined as the share index which is the second term in brackets on the right hand side of (15) and X(1) is the productivity index which is the third term in brackets on the right hand side of (15) and so on for the definitions in (16)-(20). All of the decompositions of the ratio X^1/X^0 are equally valid so it seems sensible to define an overall index of price change, say P, as a symmetric average of the individual price indexes P(1)-P(6) which appeared in (15)-(20). It is also natural to follow the example of Fisher (1922) and Gini (1937; 72) and take geometric means so that the indexes will satisfy the time reversal test and also preserve the exact decomposition of X^1/X^0 into the product of three explanatory factors. Hence letting p^t, s^t and X^t be the N dimensional vectors of the real prices in period t, p_n^t, the labour shares in period t, $s_{L,n}^t$, and the sectoral productivities in period t, X_n^t, respectively, we have the following expression for the *Gini price change contribution factor to overall labour productivity growth*:

$$(21)\quad P(p^0,s^0,X^0,p^1,s^1,X^1) \equiv [P(1)P(2)\ldots P(6)]^{1/6}$$

$$= \left\{\left[\frac{\sum_{n=1}^{N} p_n^1 s_{L,n}^1 X_n^1}{\sum_{n=1}^{N} p_n^0 s_{L,n}^1 X_n^1}\right]^2\left[\frac{\sum_{n=1}^{N} p_n^1 s_{L,n}^0 X_n^0}{\sum_{n=1}^{N} p_n^0 s_{L,n}^0 X_n^0}\right]^2\left[\frac{\sum_{n=1}^{N} p_n^1 s_{L,n}^1 X_n^0}{\sum_{n=1}^{N} p_n^0 s_{L,n}^1 X_n^0}\right]\left[\frac{\sum_{n=1}^{N} p_n^1 s_{L,n}^0 X_n^1}{\sum_{n=1}^{N} p_n^0 s_{L,n}^0 X_n^1}\right]\right\}^{1/6}.$$

In a similar manner, we can derive the following expression for the *Gini labour share change contribution factor to overall labour productivity growth*:

$$(22)\quad S(p^0,s^0,X^0,p^1,s^1,X^1) \equiv [S(1)S(2)\ldots S(6)]^{1/6}$$

$$= \left\{\left[\frac{\sum_{n=1}^{N} p_n^1 s_{L,n}^1 X_n^1}{\sum_{n=1}^{N} p_n^1 s_{L,n}^0 X_n^1}\right]^2\left[\frac{\sum_{n=1}^{N} p_n^0 s_{L,n}^1 X_n^0}{\sum_{n=1}^{N} p_n^0 s_{L,n}^0 X_n^0}\right]^2\left[\frac{\sum_{n=1}^{N} p_n^0 s_{L,n}^1 X_n^1}{\sum_{n=1}^{N} p_n^0 s_{L,n}^0 X_n^1}\right]\left[\frac{\sum_{n=1}^{N} p_n^1 s_{L,n}^1 X_n^0}{\sum_{n=1}^{N} p_n^1 s_{L,n}^0 X_n^0}\right]\right\}^{1/6}.$$

Finally, we can derive the following expression for the *Gini pure productivity change contribution factor to overall labour productivity growth* (which holds constant the effects of changing real output prices and changing sector labour shares):

$$(23)\quad X(p^0,s^0,X^0,p^1,s^1,X^1) \equiv [X(1)X(2)\ldots X(6)]^{1/6}$$

$$= \left\{\left[\frac{\sum_{n=1}^{N} p_n^1 s_{L,n}^1 X_n^1}{\sum_{n=1}^{N} p_n^1 s_{L,n}^1 X_n^0}\right]^2\left[\frac{\sum_{n=1}^{N} p_n^0 s_{L,n}^0 X_n^1}{\sum_{n=1}^{N} p_n^0 s_{L,n}^0 X_n^0}\right]^2\left[\frac{\sum_{n=1}^{N} p_n^1 s_{L,n}^0 X_n^1}{\sum_{n=1}^{N} p_n^1 s_{L,n}^0 X_n^0}\right]\left[\frac{\sum_{n=1}^{N} p_n^0 s_{L,n}^1 X_n^1}{\sum_{n=1}^{N} p_n^0 s_{L,n}^1 X_n^0}\right]\right\}^{1/6}.$$

Balk (2002/3; 210) suggests axioms that index number formulae of the type defined by (21)-(23) should satisfy.[7] It can be verified that the above Gini indexes satisfy all of Balk's suggested tests.

Another interesting aspect of the Gini formulae is that if the labour shares are constant across the two periods, so that $s^0 = s^1$, then the labour share contribution factor $S(p^0,s^0,X^0,p^1,s^1,X^1)$ defined by (22) is unity, the real price change contribution factor $P(p^0,s^0,X^0,p^1,s^1,X^1)$ defined by (21) reduces to the ordinary Fisher price index, P_F, and the pure productivity change contribution factor $X(p^0,s^0,X^0,p^1,s^1,X^1)$ defined by (23) reduces to the ordinary Fisher quantity index Q_F, where P_F and Q_F are defined as follows:

$$(24) \quad P_F(p^0,p^1,X^0,X^1) \equiv [p^1X^0p^1X^1/p^0X^0p^0X^1]^{1/2}$$

$$(25) \quad Q_F(p^0,p^1,X^0,X^1) \equiv [p^0X^1p^1X^1/p^0X^0p^1X^0]^{1/2} .$$

Similarly, if the real prices are constant across the two periods, then the real price change contribution factor $P(p^0,s^0,X^0,p^1,s^1,X^1)$ is unity, the labour share contribution factor $S(p^0,s^0,X^0,p^1,s^1,X^1)$ collapses to the Fisher index $[s^1X^0s^1X^1/s^0X^0s^0X^1]^{1/2}$ and the pure productivity change contribution factor $X(p^0,s^0,X^0,p^1,s^1,X^1)$ reduces to the Fisher quantity index $[s^0X^1s^1X^1/s^0X^0s^1X^0]^{1/2}$ (except that the labour shares s^0 and s^1 play the role of prices in this Fisher type formula).

Each of the contribution factors defined by (21)-(23) has an interpretation as an index of change of prices, labour shares and sectoral labour productivities, holding constant the other two factors. However the interpretation of (21) and (22) is not completely straightforward (as it is in the case of normal index number theory) since shares by definition cannot *all* grow from one period to the next and so the interpretation of (22) as a weighted average of the individual share growth rates, s_n^1/s_n^0, while valid does not seem to be very intuitive. Similarly, the interpretation of (21) as a weighted average of the growth rates of the sectoral real output prices, p_n^1/p_n^0, also seems to lack intuitive appeal since the average of the real prices p_n^t for each period t will necessarily be close to one, and hence, it will not be possible for *all* of the relative prices, p_n^1/p_n^0, to exceed unity under normal conditions. Fortunately, it is possible to reinterpret each of the contribution factors defined by (21) and (22) as indicators of *structural change* as we will now show.

In order to derive these alternative interpretations of (21) and (22), it is first necessary to develop an identity that was used by Bortkiewicz (1923; 374-375) in an index number context. Suppose that we have two N dimensional vectors, $x \equiv [x_1,\ldots,x_N]$ and $y \equiv [y_1,\ldots,y_N]$, and an

[7] Balk (2002/3; 211) also notes with approval the Gini formulae defined by (21)-(23) and gives additional historical references to the literature.

N dimensional vector of positive share weights $s \equiv [s_1,\ldots,s_N]$.[8] We use these shares in order to define the *share weighted averages* of x and y, x^* and y^* respectively, and the *share weighted covariance* between x and y, Cov(x,y;s):

$$(26)\quad x^* \equiv \sum_{n=1}^N s_n x_n\,;\; y^* \equiv \sum_{n=1}^N s_n y_n\,;\text{ and } \mathrm{Cov}(x,y;s) \equiv \sum_{n=1}^N s_n (x_n - x^*)(y_n - y^*).$$

It is straightforward to use the above definitions in order to derive the following identity:

$$(27)\quad \sum_{n=1}^N s_n x_n y_n = \mathrm{Cov}(x,y;s) + x^* y^*.$$

Now consider a generic share index of the type defined by S(1) to S(6) in (15)-(20). We have the following decomposition of such an index, which we label as S:[9]

$$(28)\quad S \equiv \sum_{n=1}^N p_n s_n^1 X_n \Big/ \sum_{n=1}^N p_n s_n^0 X_n$$
$$= \sum_{n=1}^N (s_n^1 / s_n^0) s_n^0 p_n X_n \Big/ \sum_{n=1}^N s_n^0 p_n X_n$$
$$= \sum_{n=1}^N s_n^0 x_n (z_n / z^*) = \sum_{n=1}^N s_n^0 x_n y_n\,,$$

defining $x_n \equiv s_n^1 / s_n^0$; $z_n \equiv p_n X_n$, $z^* \equiv \sum_{n=1}^N s_n^0 z_n$, and $y_n \equiv z_n / z^*$ for $n = 1,\ldots,N$. Note that the s_n^0 share weighted means of the x_n and y_n are both equal to one; i.e., we have:

$$(29)\quad x^* \equiv \sum_{n=1}^N s_n^0 x_n = \sum_{n=1}^N s_n^0 (s_n^1 / s_n^0) = \sum_{n=1}^N s_n^1 = 1\,;$$

$$(30)\quad y^* \equiv \sum_{n=1}^N s_n^0 y_n = \sum_{n=1}^N s_n^0 (z_n / z^*) = z^* / z^* = 1\,.$$

Each z_n is equal to the product of the generic real output price in sector n, p_n, which will typically be close to one, times the generic productivity level of sector n, X_n. Thus z^* is the s_n^0 weighted average of the sector n real price weighted productivity levels, $\sum_{n=1}^N s_n^0 p_n X_n$. And, $y_n = p_n X_n / \sum_{j=1}^N s_j^0 p_j X_j$ is the real price weighted generic productivity level of sector n relative to a s_n^0 weighted average of these same price weighted productivity levels. Applying identity (27) to the last line in (28), we obtain the following decomposition for the generic S:

$$(31)\quad S = \sum_{n=1}^N s_n^0 (x_n - x^*)(y_n - y^*) + x^* y^*$$
$$= \sum_{n=1}^N s_n^0 (x_n - 1)(y_n - 1) + 1 \qquad \text{using (29) and (30)}$$

---

[8] We assume that the shares sum to unity; i.e., $\sum_{n=1}^N s_n = 1$.

[9] The generic sector n real output price p_n will be equal to p_n^0 or p_n^1 and the generic sector n labour productivity level X_n will be equal to X_n^0 or X_n^1.

$$= \text{Cov}(x,y;s^0) + 1.$$

Thus the generic labour share change contribution factor to overall labour productivity growth S defined by the first equation in (28) will be greater than one if and only if the $\text{Cov}(x,y;s^0)$ is positive. Thus if the s^0 share weighted correlation between the $x_n \equiv s_n^1 / s_n^0$ (one plus the rate of change of the sectoral labour shares) and the sectoral real price weighted productivity levels relative to their s^0 share weighted average levels $y_n = p_n X_n / \sum_{j=1}^N s_j^0 p_j X_j$ is positive, then S will be greater than one. Put another way, if the labour shares going from period 0 to 1 change in such a way that higher shares go to higher productivity sectors, then the contribution factor S to overall labour productivity growth will be positive. Thus the Gini labour share contribution factor $S(p^0,s^0,X^0,p^1,s^1,X^1)$ defined by (22) will be greater than one if all 6 of the covariances $\text{Cov}(x,y;s^0)$ of the type defined in (31) are positive for the specific indexes defined by S(1) to S(6). Thus the Gini labour share contribution factor can be interpreted as a measure of structural shifts of labour across industries of varying productivity levels.

Now consider a generic real output price index of the type defined by P(1) to P(6) in (15)-(20). We have the following decomposition of such an index, which we label as P:[10]

$$(32) \quad P \equiv \sum_{n=1}^N p_n^1 s_n X_n / \sum_{n=1}^N p_n^0 s_n X_n$$

$$= \sum_{n=1}^N (p_n^1 / p_n^0) s_n p_n^0 X_n / \sum_{n=1}^N s_n p_n^0 X_n$$

$$= \sum_{n=1}^N s_n x_n (z_n / z^*) = \sum_{n=1}^N s_n x_n y_n$$

defining $x_n \equiv p_n^1 / p_n^0$; $z_n \equiv p_n^0 X_n$; $z^* \equiv \sum_{n=1}^N s_n z_n$, and $y_n \equiv z_n / z^*$ for $n = 1,\ldots,N$. Note that the s_n share weighted mean of the y_n is equal to one but we cannot establish the same equality for the mean of the x_n; i.e., we have:

$$(33) \quad x^* \equiv \sum_{n=1}^N s_n x_n = \sum_{n=1}^N s_n (p_n^1 / p_n^0);$$

$$(34) \quad y^* \equiv \sum_{n=1}^N s_n y_n = \sum_{n=1}^N s_n (z_n / z^*) = 1.$$

Each z_n is equal to the product of the period 0 real output price in sector n, p_n^0, which will typically be close to one, times the generic productivity level of sector n, X_n. Thus z^* is the generic s_n weighted average of these sector n real price weighted productivity levels, $\sum_{n=1}^N s_n \, p_n^0 X_n$. Hence $y_n = p_n^0 X_n / \sum_{j=1}^N s_j p_j X_j$ is the real price weighted generic productivity

[10] The generic sector n labour share s_n will be equal to s_n^0 or s_n^1 and the generic sector n labour productivity level X_n will be equal to X_n^0 or X_n^1.

level of sector n relative to an s_n weighted average of these same price weighted productivity levels. Now apply the identity (27) to the last line in (32) and we obtain the following decomposition for the generic P:

$$\begin{aligned} P &= \sum_{n=1}^{N} s_n (x_n - x^*)(y_n - y^*) + x^* y^* \\ \text{(35)} \quad &= \sum_{n=1}^{N} s_n (x_n - x^*)(y_n - 1) + x^* \qquad \text{using (34)} \\ &= \mathrm{Cov}(x, y; s) + x^* . \end{aligned}$$

The interpretation of (35) is not as straightforward as was the interpretation of (31). The price contribution factor P defined by (32) will be greater than one if the sum of the covariance term $\mathrm{Cov}(x, y; s)$, equal to $\sum_{n=1}^{N} s_n (x_n - x^*)(y_n - 1)$, and the mean real price change x^*, equal to $\sum_{n=1}^{N} s_n (p_n^1 / p_n^0)$, is greater than one. The interpretation of the x^* term is straightforward. P is equal to this straightforward effect (which will generally be close to one) plus the covariance term, $\sum_{n=1}^{N} s_n (x_n - x^*)(y_n - 1)$. Recalling that x_n is equal to (one plus) the rate of growth of the sector n real output price, p_n^1 / p_n^0, and that y_n is the productivity level of sector n relative to an average productivity level, it can be seen that this covariance will be positive if the sectors which have high rates of growth of real output prices are associated with sectors that have high relative productivity levels.

4. Conclusion

The Gini (1937) decomposition of aggregate labour productivity into sectoral contribution factors and associated structural shifts seems promising. In terms of simplicity, our decomposition given by (13) also seems attractive. There seem to be multiple reasonable decompositions. It appears that there is room for additional research for developing the axiomatic approach to the topic, an approach initiated by Balk (2002/3). An economic approach may also be useful for indicating what a "best" decomposition might be.

References

Fisher, I. (1922), *The Making of Index Numbers*, Boston: Houghton-Mifflin.

Balk, B.M. (2002/3), "Ideal Indices and Indicators for Two or More Factors", *Journal of Economic and Social Measurement* 28, 203-217.

Balk, B.M. and E. Hoogenboom-Spijker (2003), "The Measurement and Decomposition of Productivity Change: Exercises on the Netherlands' Manufacturing Industries", Voorburg: Statistics Netherlands.

Bortkiewicz, L. von (1923), "Zweck und Struktur einer Preisindexzahl", *Nordisk Statistisk Tidsskrift* 2, 369-408.

Gini, C. (1937), "Methods of Eliminating the Influence of Several Groups of Factors", *Econometrica* 5, 56-73.

Tang, J. and W. Wang (2004), "Sources of Aggregate Labour Productivity Growth in Canada and the United States", *The Canadian Journal of Economics* 37, 421-444.

Chapter 5
EXACT INDUSTRY CONTRIBUTIONS TO LABOR PRODUCTIVITY CHANGE

Marshall Reinsdorf and Robert Yuskavage[1]

1. Introduction

Industry contributions to aggregate productivity growth have been a topic of great interest in recent years. One reason for this is a desire for insight into the sources of the remarkable speedup of productivity growth in the late 1990s. The U.S. Bureau of Labor Statistics (BLS) estimates that output per hour in the nonfarm business sector grew at an average rate of around 3 percent per year from 1995 to 2003, compared with 1.5 percent per year between 1987 and 1995. Interest in investigating industry sources of productivity change has been further heightened by the availability of new and improved data on industry gross output, intermediate inputs and value added, resulting from the integration of the GDP-by-industry accounts and the annual I-O accounts in data sets released in June 2004. Evidence on industry contributions to productivity change has been used to resolve controversies concerning the economic gains from information technology (IT), the causes of the post-1995 speedup in productivity growth, possible measurement errors in prices or output, and other important questions.[2]

As Nordhaus (2002, p. 213) observes, the use of chain-weighted output measures makes disentangling the contributions of individual components to aggregate productivity growth a complex problem. To account for substitution effects, non-linear chain-weighted index number formulas such as the Fisher index or the Törnqvist index must be used to measure aggregate real output growth. Although in nominal terms, aggregate output is the sum of every industry's value added, with the chain-weighted index number formulas, aggregate real output fails to equal the sum over all industries of each industry's real value added. The lack of an additive formula for industry contributions to real output growth implies that formulas for industry contributions to

---

[1] The authors are both with the U.S. Bureau of Economic Analysis (BEA). Marshall Reinsdorf can be reached at Marshall.Reinsdorf@bea.gov. Robert Yuskavage can be reached at Robert.Yuskavage@bea.gov. The views expressed in this paper are those of the authors and should not be attributed to the BEA. We are grateful to Mike Harper, Ana Aizcorbe and Jack Triplett for helpful comments.

[2] Some recent studies of industry contributions to productivity change are Bosworth and Triplett (2004), Klein et al. (2003), Basu and Fernald (2002), Gullickson and Harper (2002), Nordhaus (2002), Stiroh (2002), Jorgenson (2001), Mc Kinsey Global Institute (2001), ten Raa and Wolff (2001), Jorgenson and Stiroh (2000a, 2000b), Oliner and Sichel (2000), and Corrado and Slifman (1999). The present paper is part of a collaborative project on this topic between the U.S. Bureau of Economic Analysis (BEA) and the Office of Productivity and Technology of the U.S. Bureau of Labor Statistics (BLS).

Citation: **Marshall Reinsdorf and Robert Yuskavage (2011), "Exact Industry Contributions to Labor Productivity Change," chapter 5, pp. 77-102 in W.E. Diewert, B.M. Balk, D. Fixler, K.J. Fox and A.O. Nakamura, *PRICE AND PRODUCTIVITY MEASUREMENT: Volume 6 -- Index Number Theory*. Trafford Press.**

© Alice Nakamura, 2011. Permission to link to, or copy or reprint, these materials is granted without restriction, including for use in commercial textbooks, with due credit to the authors and editors.

aggregate productivity growth also generally add up to incorrect totals, because aggregate productivity is measured as the difference between the log-change in aggregate real output and the log-change in aggregate inputs.

The unavailability of exact formulas for industry contributions to aggregate productivity growth has led to reliance on approximate decomposition formulas. In the appendix we derive the change in real GDP implied by a commonly used Törnqvist approach to industry contributions to productivity change. The resulting expression in equation (A-4) is different enough from ordinary approximations for the change in real GDP to raise questions about the accuracy of those approximations: questions for which we nevertheless produce a reassuring answer in this paper.

In this paper we derive an exactly additive decomposition of aggregate labor productivity growth into industry sources using results from the literature on index number formulas. Included in our decomposition are contributions to aggregate productivity growth due to changes at the industry level in real gross output per hour and in the relative use of intermediate inputs. The sum of the first two of these effects equals the contribution to aggregate productivity of changes in an industry's real value added per hour. A third effect comes from changes in the allocation of labor between industries with different productivity levels. In the productivity literature, this effect has been variously referred to as a "shift effect," a "Denison effect," or a "labor reallocation effect." Bosworth and Triplett (2004) point out that ignoring the labor allocation effect may lead to misleading inferences concerning the proportion of aggregate productivity change attributable to a particular group of industries, such as ones that produce information technology (IT) products. Previous authors have treated the labor reallocation term as a kind of residual that cannot be included in the additive decomposition, but we show how it can be included.

In addition to its methodological contributions, this paper makes an empirical contribution to the literature on the industry sources of the post-1995 rebound in productivity growth. Among its empirical findings are a modest direct contribution of the IT-producing industries to the productivity speedup, large contributions for Wholesale trade and Retail trade, and a negative contribution for the Electric, gas and sanitary services industry, reflecting the increased use of intermediate inputs.

2. Exactly Additive Contributions of Commodities to Change in Fisher Indexes

The two widely used chain-weighted index number formulas are the Fisher index and the Törnqvist index.[3] Here we take the Fisher measure of aggregate productivity growth as the object of investigation. Although the Törnqvist index is easily decomposed into *commodity* contributions to the log-change in the aggregate, for the problem of finding *industry* contributions to change, the Fisher index is actually more tractable. Another advantage of our Fisher approach is that the results can be used to obtain decompositions of productivity growth that are precisely consistent with official measures of real output, which the BEA constructs

[3] Diewert and Nakamura (2003) survey some of the reasons for this.

from Fisher indexes. Furthermore, the Fisher contributions formula has an economic justification that other formulas lack. Finally, we note that the Fisher index has an appealing justification as a measure of aggregate welfare change for a society as a whole. In particular, Pollak (1981) shows that the aggregate Laspeyres price index is an upper bound for the Scitovsky-Laspeyres social cost of living index, which measures the change in the aggregate income that would be required for a social planner to keep every household in a society on its original indifference curve.[4] Diewert (2001, pp. 172-173) observes that the Paasche index is a lower bound for the analogously defined Scitovsky-Paasche social cost of living index and that the Fisher index can therefore be justified as an average of lower and upper bounds for social cost of living indexes based on a pair of relevant Scitovsky contours.[5]

To solve the problem of identifying industry sources of productivity change, we use the formula for additive contributions to the change in a Fisher quantity index that underlies the tables of contributions to change reported in the U.S. National Income and Product Accounts (NIPAs). This formula was discovered by van IJzeren (1952) as part of an argument that the Fisher index had a unique property that could justify its use.[6] It was then forgotten, until its independent rediscovery by Dikhanov (1997).

Van IJzeren considered the problem of finding an average basket for a price index that would be unaffected by an equiproportional change in all quantities and an average price vector for a quantity index that would be unaffected by an equiproportional change in all prices. In doing this, he effectively posited the desirability of the decomposition formula now used by BEA and Statistics Canada, and then showed this property implies the Fisher formula for the index.[7]

Index number formulas that use simple averages of prices or baskets are known as Edgeworth (or Edgeworth-Marshall) indexes. The Edgeworth quantity index, E^Q, uses an average of initial and final prices to value quantity changes:

$$E^Q(\mathbf{p}_t, \mathbf{p}_{t+1}, \mathbf{q}_t, \mathbf{q}_{t+1}) \equiv \frac{\mathbf{q}_{t+1}'(\mathbf{p}_t + \mathbf{p}_{t+1})/2}{\mathbf{q}_t'(\mathbf{p}_t + \mathbf{p}_{t+1})/2}. \tag{1}$$

Similarly, the Edgeworth price index uses as its basket an average of the baskets from the initial and final periods:

[4] This theory concerns commodities that are consumed directly, but, under certain assumptions, it can be extended to the measurement of output that includes investment goods used to produce commodities for consumption in future time periods. In particular, we can treat investments that raise future consumption possibilities as part of consumption for welfare measurement purposes; see Basu and Fernald (2002) and Weitzman (1976).

[5] To justify a Törnqvist index as a measure of aggregate welfare change requires stronger assumptions. Assuming that households have preferences that are homothetic — but not necessarily identical — and they have total expenditures that are constant shares of aggregate total expenditures, the aggregate log Törnqvist index is a weighted average of individual log Törnqvist indexes, which are themselves superlative measures of individual consumers' welfare change. Exactly additive industry contributions to a Törnqvist measure of aggregate productivity growth are available from the authors upon request. For more on the properties of Fisher indexes, see also Diewert (1992).

[6] See Reinsdorf, Diewert and Ehemann (2002), and Balk (2004).

[7] See van IJzeren (1987) for more background. The use of this formula in BEA's National Income and Product Accounts (NIPAs) is discussed in Moulton and Seskin (1999). A related multiplicative decomposition of the change in the Fisher index is presented in Kohli (2011).

$$(2) \qquad E^P(\mathbf{p}_t,\mathbf{p}_{t+1},\mathbf{q}_t,\mathbf{q}_{t+1}) \equiv \frac{\mathbf{p}_{t+1}'(\mathbf{q}_t+\mathbf{q}_{t+1})/2}{\mathbf{p}_t'(\mathbf{q}_t+\mathbf{q}_{t+1})/2}.$$

A high rate of inflation (or the multiplication of all final period prices by any scalar other than 1) will arbitrarily change the weights in the Edgeworth quantity index, and similarly a high rate of real growth will arbitrarily change the weights in the Edgeworth price index. To correct the Edgeworth indexes so that they always give equal weight to relative prices and quantities in both periods, period t prices must be rescaled by a price index I^P before averaging them with prices from period t+1, and period t quantities must be rescaled by a quantity index I^Q before they can be averaged with quantities from period t+1. This gives the pair of simultaneous equations:

$$(3) \qquad I^Q(\mathbf{p}_t,\mathbf{p}_{t+1},\mathbf{q}_t,\mathbf{q}_{t+1};I^P) \equiv \frac{\mathbf{q}_{t+1}'(\mathbf{p}_t I^P+\mathbf{p}_{t+1})/2}{\mathbf{q}_t'(\mathbf{p}_t I^P+\mathbf{p}_{t+1})/2}, \text{ and}$$

$$(4) \qquad I^P(\mathbf{p}_t,\mathbf{p}_{t+1},\mathbf{q}_t,\mathbf{q}_{t+1};I^Q) \equiv \frac{\mathbf{p}_{t+1}'(\mathbf{q}_t I^Q+\mathbf{q}_{t+1})/2}{\mathbf{p}_t'(\mathbf{q}_t I^Q+\mathbf{q}_{t+1})/2}.$$

Van IJzeren shows that the solution to these equations sets I^Q equal the Fisher quantity index, F^Q, and I^P equal the Fisher price index, F^P, where a Fisher index is defined as the geometric mean of a Paasche index and a Laspeyres index.

In addition to van IJzeren's axiomatic justification for the decomposition formula for Fisher indexes given by the right side of equation (3) or equation (4), it has an economic justification. Reinsdorf, Diewert and Ehemann (2002) show that this formula is a second order approximation to a decomposition formula that measures the contribution of each item i to the change in a flexible production function of the form $[\sum_i \sum_j a_{ij} q_i q_j]^{1/2}$, where the coefficients satisfy $a_{ij} = a_{ji}$ The van IJzeren decomposition can, therefore, be expected to provide a good measure of the economic contributions of the various inputs to the change in output.

In the NIPAs, commodity contributions to the change in F_t^Q, the Fisher index for real GDP, are calculated by expressing F_t^Q in the form given by equation (3). In this index, the quantities from period t and the quantities from period t+1 are both valued at a constant set of prices. These constant prices equal inflation-corrected averages of the prices from the periods being compared. Hence, the constant price for the arbitrary commodity c, denoted by p_{ct}^*, equals $(p_{ct}F_t^P + p_{c,t+1})/2$, where F_t^P denotes the Fisher price index calculated from final expenditures on commodities, e_{ct} and $e_{c,t+1}$, and the corresponding price indexes. To adjust the expenditure on commodity c, denoted by e_{ct}, from current-year dollars to the constant price p_{ct}^*, it is multiplied by an average of F_t^P and the price relative for commodity c, $p_{c,t+1}/p_{ct}$; hence,

$$(5) \qquad E_{ct} = e_{ct}\frac{p_{ct}F_t^P + p_{c,t+1}}{2p_{ct}}.$$

Similarly, to adjust the final expenditure $e_{c,t+1}$ to equal the value it would have had at price p^*_{ct}, it is multiplied by an average of the ratio of F^P to commodity c's price relative and 1:

$$(6) \qquad E_{c,t+1} = e_{c,t+1} \frac{p_{ct} F_t^P + p_{c,t+1}}{2p_{c,t+1}}.$$

The Fisher quantity index for GDP then tracks the change in GDP measured using the constant prices p^*_{ct}:

$$(7) \qquad F_t^Q = \frac{\sum_c E_{c,t+1}}{\sum_c E_{ct}}.$$

The contribution to the change in F_t^Q of the arbitrary commodity γ is, then, given by:

$$\frac{E_{\gamma,t+1} - E_{\gamma t}}{\sum_c E_{ct}}.$$

3. Exactly Additive Contributions of Industries to Change in Fisher Indexes

The production approach estimate of GDP is calculated as the sum over all industries of current-year dollar value added v_t. If y_{it} is the gross output of industry i and m_{it} is its use of intermediate inputs, then $v_t = \sum_i v_{it} = \sum_i (y_{it} - m_{it})$. Given consistent data, the production approach estimate of current-year dollar GDP equals the expenditure approach estimate of GDP, defined as $\sum_c e_{ct}$ where e_{ct} is the final demand for commodity c. BEA calculates the Fisher index for the total value added of all industries — the production approach estimate of real GDP — in a way that makes it theoretically equal to the expenditure approach estimate of real GDP.[8]

The same estimate of real GDP can be obtained if the adjustment factors on the right side of equations (5) and (6) are used to convert current-year dollar values of gross output and intermediate inputs into constant dollar values. To convert to constant dollars for decomposing real GDP change between period t and period t+1, measures of gross output and intermediate inputs based on prices from period t are multiplied by the same factor as e_{ct} in equation (5), and measures in prices from period t+1 are multiplied by the same factor as $e_{c,t+1}$ in equation (6). If

[8] See Moyer, Reinsdorf and Yuskavage (2003) and also Yuskavage (1996). These authors used a consistent set of data from the GDP by Industry Accounts, so their estimate of real GDP was the same using either the production approach or the expenditure approach. However, aggregate real output for all industries from the GDP by Industry accounts usually differs from real GDP from the NIPAs because of inconsistencies between deflators in the two sets of accounts. Also, before June 2004, the sum of value added from the GDP-by-Industry Accounts equaled the income side estimate of the GDP, not the expenditure approach estimate. For related productivity measurement issues, see Eldridge (1999).

L_{it}^{YP} represents the Laspeyres price index for the gross output of industry i and P_{it}^{YP} represents the Paasche price index, the constant-price measure of this industry's gross output of industry i in year t, denoted by Y_{it}, is:

$$(8) \qquad Y_{it} = y_{it}[F_t^P + L_{it}^{YP}]/2,$$

and, using this same set of prices to value its output in year t+1 gives a constant-price measure of:

$$(9) \qquad Y_{i,t+1} = y_{i,t+1}[F_t^P / P_{it}^{YP} + 1]/2.$$

The equations for constant-price intermediate inputs, denoted by M_{it} and $M_{i,t+1}$, are analogous to those for constant-price gross output.

Constant-price value added in industry i, V_{it}, is defined as $Y_{it} - M_{it}$, and constant-price GDP, denoted by V_t, is defined as $\sum_i V_{it}$. Moyer, Reinsdorf and Yuskavage (2004, proposition 1) show that V_{t+1}/V_t equals the Fisher index for real GDP. That is,

$$(10) \qquad F_t^Q = \frac{Y_{t+1} - M_{t+1}}{Y_t - M_t}.$$

Industry i's additive contribution to the change in real GDP, C_{it}, can then be calculated as:

$$(11) \qquad C_{it} = \frac{V_{i,t+1} - V_{it}}{V_t},$$

where $\sum_i C_{it} = F_t^Q - 1$.

4. Exactly Additive Industry Contributions to Change in Labor Productivity

4.1 Contributions to the Change in Aggregate Real Value Added per Hour

Some simple measures of industry contributions to productivity change are decompositions of the change in the production approach estimate of real GDP per hour. In a Laspeyres framework, these decompositions provide industry contributions that sum exactly to the change in aggregate productivity because the sum of Laspeyres real value added over all industries equals Laspeyres real GDP. However, the existing methods for calculating industry contributions to real GDP per hour provide only approximate decompositions for Fisher or Törnqvist measures of real GDP and real value added.

Balk (2003, p. 28, equation 51) provides an appealing formula for industry contributions to real GDP per hour based on the Bennet decomposition.[9] Using Fisher indexes for real value

[9] Diewert (2000; 2005) shows that the quantity components of the Bennet decomposition of nominal output change, defined as $\bar{p}_i \Delta q_i + \bar{q}_i \Delta p_i$, have an economic interpretation as an approximation to the contributions to change in production function that implies the Fisher index formula.

added in this formula, which preserves the symmetry properties of the Bennet decomposition, creates a discrepancy between the total over all industries of real value added and the Fisher measure of real GDP. As a result, the industry contributions fail to sum to the total change in GDP per hour.

Adopting the Fisher index for measurement of real output, and letting H_t denote aggregate hours or full-time equivalents (FTEs), the objective of the Bennet decomposition is to calculate industry contributions to aggregate productivity change, measured in dollars of year t per hour, as $F_t^Q v_t / H_{t+1} - v_t / H_t$. Using the constant-price measures of value added in the Bennet decomposition corrects its non-additivity because the industry contributions based on V_{it} and the $V_{i,t+1}$ add up to the Fisher measure of real GDP per hour.[10] Let $\overline{h}_i$ denote the average of H_{it} / H_t and $H_{i,t+1} / H_{t+1}$ and let Δh_i equal $H_{i,t+1} / H_{t+1} - H_{it} / H_t$, where H_{it} / H_t is industry i's share of aggregate labor input in year t. Then industry i has an additive Bennet contribution C_{it}^* to arithmetic change in aggregate labor productivity equal to:

$$C_{it}^* = \frac{v_t}{V_t}\overline{h}_i\left[\frac{V_{i,t+1}}{H_{i,t+1}} - \frac{V_{it}}{H_{it}}\right] + \frac{v_t}{V_t}\Delta h_i\left\{\frac{1}{2}\left[\frac{V_{i,t+1}}{H_{i,t+1}} + \frac{V_{it}}{H_{it}}\right] - \frac{1}{2}\left[\frac{V_{t+1}}{H_{t+1}} + \frac{V_t}{H_t}\right]\right\} \tag{12}$$

The term on the first line of equation (12) represents the direct effect from productivity growth in industry i. The term on the second line of equation (12) represents a labor allocation effect, or shift effect. An increase in the share of aggregate labor allocated to an industry with above-average productivity will raise productivity by an amount that is measured by the expression on the second line of equation (12).

4.2 Contributions to Log-Change in Output

The use in equation (12) of differences in real valued added per hour to measure productivity change has the advantage of simplicity, but it also has some disadvantages. First, this measure can be distorted by substitution induced by changes in the relative price of intermediate inputs; for example, it will tend to rise if the price of intermediate inputs falls even in the absence of any genuine productivity gain.[11] Second, often researchers are interested in comparing multi-year periods of high productivity growth with multi-year periods of low productivity growth but, unlike logarithmic measures of productivity change, the C_{it}^* cannot be averaged over years.

[10] This method also offers the advantage of a unified approach to statistical agencies that publish contributions to change in Fisher indexes as well as contributions to productivity change, such as Statistics Canada.
[11] Capital deepening can cause a similar rise in any kind of measure of labor productivity, but in this case measures of labor productivity that include gains from capital deepening are still of interest.

To avoid such problems, researchers generally use the log-change in gross output per hour as the measure of an industry's labor productivity.[12] Since BEA measures real output growth by a Fisher quantity index, let the log-change in real GDP be the log of the Fisher index F_t^Q, which may be calculated using the price indexes for commodities and the final expenditures on commodities, e_{ct} and $e_{c,t+1}$. The aggregate labor productivity change between year t and year t+1 is then:

$$\text{(13)} \qquad ALP_t = \log F_t^Q - d\log H_t$$

where $d\log H_t \equiv \log(H_{t+1}/H_t)$ is the log-change in hours of labor input.[13]

Identification of the industry sources of aggregate labor productivity change as measured by equation (13) requires formulas for contributions to the log-change in real GDP and in aggregate hours. Equation (12) describes a contribution to a difference; not to a log-change. Yet, as Balk (2003, pp. 41-2) points out, logarithmic means can be used to convert difference measures to log-change measures. If $s_{it} \neq s_{i,t+1}$, the logarithmic mean $m(s_{it}, s_{i,t+1})$ is defined as:

$$\text{(14)} \qquad m(s_{it}, s_{i,t+1}) \equiv (s_{i,t+1} - s_{it}) / \log(s_{i,t+1}/s_{it}).$$

The main index formula that uses logarithmic means is the Sato-Vartia index (see Sato, 1976 and Vartia, 1976).[14] The log Sato-Vartia quantity index is defined as a weighted average of log-changes in quantities, where the weights are normalized to sum to 1 and are proportional to logarithmic means of the expenditure shares s_{it} and $s_{i,t+1}$.

To decompose the log-change in GDP into industry contributions, let w_{it}^Y denote the weight for the gross output of industry i and let w_{it}^M denote the weight for its intermediate inputs. In this case, the Sato-Vartia weights are normalized so that the sum of the gross output weights less the sum of the intermediate input weights w_{it}^M equals 1. The Sato-Vartia weight w_{it}^Y for the log change in industry i's gross output is:

$$\text{(15)} \qquad w_{it}^Y = \frac{m(Y_{it}/V_t, Y_{i,t+1}/V_{t+1})}{\sum_j [m(Y_{jt}/V_t, Y_{j,t+1}/V_{t+1}) - m(M_{jt}/V_t, M_{j,t+1}/V_{t+1})]}.$$

Similarly, the Sato-Vartia weight w_{it}^M for the log change in industry i's intermediate inputs is:

---

[12] Hulten (1978) shows that use of the log-change in industry gross output to calculate industry contributions to total factor productivity growth results in estimates with an economic interpretation as measures of technological change.
[13] A Fisher index of various types of labor input would provide valuable additional information on the effects of changes in the composition of industry labor forces. Unfortunately, data to compute such input indexes are lacking.
[14] Balk (1995) discusses the axiomatic properties of the Sato-Vartia index, including the basket test, and finds that its axiomatic properties are on a par with the Fisher index. Its economic interpretation is discussed in Lau (1979).

(16) $$w_{it}^{M}=\frac{m(M_{it}/V_t, M_{i,t+1}/V_{t+1})}{\sum_j [m(Y_{jt}/V_t, Y_{j,t+1}/V_{t+1})-m(M_{jt}/V_t, M_{j,t+1}/V_{t+1})]}.$$

Proposition 1 shows that the weights defined in (15) and (16) furnish exactly additive contributions by industry to the log change in real GDP.

PROPOSITION 1: Let $\hat{C}_{it}=w_{it}^{Y}\,d\log Y_{it}-w_{it}^{M}\,d\log M_{it}$. Then $\sum_i \hat{C}_{it}=\log F_t^{Q}$.

PROOF:

(17) $$\begin{aligned}&\sum_i w_{it}^{Y}(d\log Y_{it}-\log F^{Q})-\sum_i w_{it}^{M}(d\log M_{it}-\log F^{Q})\\&=\frac{\sum_i (Y_{i,t+1}/V_{t+1}-Y_{it}/V_t)-\sum_i (M_{i,t+1}/V_{t+1}-M_{it}/V_t)}{\sum_j [m(Y_{jt}/V_t, Y_{j,t+1}/V_{t+1})-m(M_{jt}/V_t, M_{j,t+1}/V_{t+1})]}\\&=\frac{\sum_i (Y_{i,t+1}-M_{i,t+1})/V_{t+1}-\sum_i (Y_{it}-M_{it})/V_t}{\sum_j [m(Y_{jt}/V_t, Y_{j,t+1}/V_{t+1})-m(M_{jt}/V_t, M_{j,t+1}/V_{t+1})]}\\&=0\end{aligned}$$

Consequently, $\sum_i w_{it}^{Y}\,d\log Y_{it}-\sum_i w_{it}^{M}\,d\log M_{it}=[\sum_i w_{it}^{Y}-\sum_i w_{it}^{M}](\log F_t^{Q})=\log F_t^{Q}$.

4.3 Exact Industry Contributions to Aggregate Productivity

Following the approach of Stiroh (2002, p. 1572, equation (6)), the weights that permit a decomposition of the log-change in real output can be used to show how industry productivity changes contribute to aggregate productivity change. Let LP_{it}^{Y} denote labor productivity in industry i, defined as the log-change in gross output per hour, or $d\log(Y_{it}/H_{it})$. In addition, define the value-added shares w_{it}^{V} as $w_{it}^{Y}-w_{it}^{M}$. Then a partial decomposition of the log-change in aggregate labor productivity is:

(18) $$\begin{aligned}ALP_t^{V}=&[\sum_i w_{it}^{V}LP_{it}^{Y}]-[\sum_i w_{it}^{M}(d\log M_{it}-d\log Y_{it})]\\&+[\sum_i w_{it}^{V}(d\log H_{it})-d\log H_t].\end{aligned}$$

The first term in equation (18) shows that an industry's direct contribution to aggregate labor productivity is its productivity in producing gross output times its average share of value added $w_{it}^{Y}-w_{it}^{M}$. The second term adjusts the industry's direct contribution to aggregate productivity for the effect of the change in the intermediate inputs required to produce a given amount of gross output. Combined, these terms provide the contribution of an industry's log-change in real value added per employee hour to the log-change in aggregate productivity.

Equation (18) is an incomplete decomposition of aggregate productivity growth because in the last term d log H_t is not expressed as a sum of industry contributions. This term represents an effect from changes in the allocation of hours between industries with different levels of average output per hour. For example, suppose that a high-productivity industry begins to contract out some average-productivity activity it had performed in-house to a low-productivity industry, with a concomitant movement of employees. Aggregate productivity is, of course, unchanged, but productivity (as measured by real value added per hour) rises in both of the affected industries. The negative allocation effect offsets the positive contributions of the rising productivity within the two industries to hold aggregate productivity constant.

We can add an expression that exactly accounts for the contributions of the labor allocation effect to equation (18) using an approach similar to Nordhaus' (2002, pp. 214-5) "Denison effect." Under this approach, the difference between an industry's value added share in the economy and its labor input share in the economy is used to measure the contribution to aggregate output of changes in the relative size of its labor force. For our exact decomposition of the labor reallocation effect, we use labor shares w_{it}^{H} that resemble Sato-Vartia weights:

$$w_{it}^{H} = \frac{m(H_{it}/H_t, H_{i,t+1}/H_{t+1})}{\sum_j m(H_{jt}/H_t, H_{j,t+1}/H_{t+1})}. \tag{19}$$

Equation (19) makes an exact decomposition of the labor reallocation effect possible because the weights w_{it}^{H} add up to 1 and the weighted average $\sum_i w_{it}^{H}(d\log H_{it})$ equals $d\log H_t$, which is the only term in equation (19) not decomposed by industry. The relative amount of labor that is reallocated into industry i equals $d\log H_{it} - d\log H_t$. We assume that reallocated labor always has an opportunity cost equal to the economy's average level of productivity; that is, the labor that is released by an industry has the average level of real value added per hour in the industries where it is redeployed, and the extra labor that is absorbed by an industry would have had the average level of real valued added per hour in its alternative use.[15] Then the marginal effect on aggregate real output of labor reallocation into industry i is $w_{it}^{V*} - w_{it}^{H}$, where w_{it}^{V*} is the log-change in aggregate real output from a 1 log point change in hours in industry i and w_{it}^{H} is the log-change in aggregate real output per hour when the amount of labor representing a 1 log point change in industry i is added to an industry with the average productivity level. Thus, the contribution to the log-change in real output due to reallocation is $(w_{it}^{V*} - w_{it}^{H})(d\log H_{it} - d\log H_t)$, which essentially equals $(w_{it}^{V} - w_{it}^{H})(d\log H_{it} - d\log H_t)$.

Substituting $\sum_i w_{it}^{H}(d\log H_{it})$ for $d\log H_t$ in equation (18) and then subtracting $\sum_i (w_{it}^{V} - w_{it}^{H})(d\log H_t)$, which equals 0, gives:

[15] Note that when the aggregate under investigation excludes important industries, the average level of productivity in the aggregate may differ significantly from the average level of productivity in the economy as a whole. The decomposition of the labor reallocation effect must reflect the average level of productivity in the aggregate under investigation, because the labor reallocation effect for any aggregate reflects only reallocation within that aggregate.

$$\text{(20)}\quad \begin{aligned} ALP_t^V &= \left[\sum_i w_{it}^V LP_{it}^Y\right] - \left[\sum_i w_{it}^M (d\log M_{it} - d\log Y_{it})\right] \\ &\quad + \left[\sum_i (w_{it}^V - w_{it}^H)(d\log H_{it} - d\log H_t)\right]. \end{aligned}$$

In the last term in (20), an industry's contribution to the labor reallocation effect depends on its relative efficiency at using labor, measured by the difference between its share of GDP and its share of labor input, and the growth of its labor input share. An inefficient industry—one with a value added share w_{it}^V below its labor share w_{it}^H—has a positive labor reallocation effect if it releases labor for use in other industries, and a relatively efficient industry has a positive reallocation effect if it absorbs labor released by other industries.

4.4 Comparison with a Decomposition that Uses Real Value Added per Hour

The exact decomposition in equation (20) closely approximates a decomposition that, like the Bennet decomposition in equation (12), uses real value added per hour, albeit in log-change form. In the decomposition of the log-change in real value added per hour, the weights $\bar{h}_i$ in equation (12) are replaced by Sato-Vartia weights based not on industry hours but on industry constant-price value added. Let $w_{it}^{V*} \equiv m(V_{it}/V_t, V_{i,t+1}/V_{t+1}) / \sum_j m(V_{jt}/V_t, V_{j,t+1}/V_{t+1})$, and let the direct measure of the change in real value added per hour in industry i be $LP_{it}^V = d\log V_{it} - d\log H_{it}$. Then the logarithmic decomposition based on industries' value added productivity is:

$$\text{(20')}\quad \begin{aligned} ALP_t^V &= \left[\sum_i w_{it}^H LP_{it}^V\right] + \left[\sum_i (w_{it}^{V*} - w_{it}^H)[d\log(V_{it}/V_t)]\right] \\ &= \left[\sum_i w_{it}^{V*} LP_{it}^V\right] + \left[\sum_i (w_{it}^{V*} - w_{it}^H)[(d\log H_{it}/H_t)]\right]. \end{aligned}$$

In the first line of equation (20′) the weights on industry productivity gains are similar to the $\bar{h}_i$ weights in equation (12), but in the shift effect term on that line, the measure of changes in industry relative size, $d\log(V_{it}/V_t)$, differs from the measure given by Δh_i in equation (12) because it uses industry output; not labor input. An input-based measure of relative size would be more consistent with the intuition that the shift effect comes from changes in allocation of labor from low-productivity to high-productivity industries. Such a measure appears in the second line of equation (20′), but with this version of the shift effect, the weights on the industry productivity changes, w_{it}^{V*}, differ from the $\bar{h}_i$ weights in equation (12) because they are based on industry output. Nevertheless, the pattern of direct contributions implied by the $w_{it}^{V*} LP_{it}^V$ in equation (20′) can be expected to resemble the pattern implied by the first term in equation (12).

The measure of the contribution of industry i's value added productivity to aggregate productivity given by the second line of equation (20′) closely approximates the measure of the contribution of industry i's gross output productivity adjusted for its use of intermediate inputs that appears in equation (20). The value added contribution measure in (20′) equals the gross output contribution measure in (20) times a slope coefficient that approximately equals 1 plus an intercept that approximately equals 0. The slope λ_t equals the ratio of the normalization factors for the Sato-Vartia weights under the two approaches:

$$(21) \qquad \lambda_t \equiv \frac{\sum_j [m(Y_{it}/V_t, Y_{j,t+1}/V) - m(M_{jt}/V_t, M_{j,t+1}/V_{t+1})]}{\sum_j m(V_{jt}/V_t, V_{j,t+1}/V_{t+1})}.$$

The intercept equals $(w_{it}^{V*} - \lambda_t w_{it}^{V})(d\log F_t^Q)$.

4.5 Consistency with Decompositions that Use Domar Weights

Readers familiar with the literature on industry contributions to productivity change may wonder whether the decomposition given by equation (20) is consistent with well-known decompositions that use Domar weights. Domar weights are ratios, such as w_{it}^{Y}, of industry gross output to aggregate value added. Domar weights are required to decompose multifactor productivity growth (see Gullikson and Harper, 1999, p. 51.) The use of w_{it}^{V} as a weight on gross output productivity in the first term of equation (20) may appear inconsistent with the need to use Domar weights. Equation (20) is, however, easily reconciled with the Domar weighting scheme. For this reconciliation, the third term in equation (20) can be disregarded because a reallocation effect is not part of the original Domar (1961) framework.[16] The Domar contribution of an industry to productivity change can be described as the sum of an output change contribution and an input change contribution. The output change contribution $w_{it}^{Y}(d\log Y_{it})$ is the sum of the $w_{it}^{M}(d\log Y_{it})$ part of the second term in (20) and the $w_{it}^{V}(d\log Y_{it})$ part of $w_{it}^{V}LP_{it}^{Y}$ in the first term. The only inputs explicitly considered in this paper are M_{it} and H_{it}, which is consistent with a production model in which V_{it} is identified with the cost of labor inputs in period t. The sum of $w_{it}^{V}(d\log H_{it})$ implicitly included in the first term of equation (20) and $w_{it}^{M}(d\log M_{it})$ from the second term effectively equals the Domar weight times the measure of combined labor and material inputs.

5. Comparison with Törnqvist Contributions to Productivity Change

In contrast to the exact approach to industry contributions to productivity change, an approximate approach based on industry-level Törnqvist indexes has been used for important studies of the sources of productivity change. The Törnqvist contributions to aggregate

[16] A Domar weighted decomposition of translog aggregate multi-factor productivity growth that includes reallocation effects was developed by Jorgenson, Gollop and Fraumeni (1987, p. 66) and used in modified form by Jorgenson, Ho and Stiroh (2002, p. 9.)

productivity change solve neither the problem of decomposing a Törnqvist measure of aggregate productivity change nor the problem of decomposing an aggregate Fisher measure. They fail to solve the Törnqvist decomposition problem because aggregation of Törnqvist measures of industry value added does not yield the measure of real GDP calculated from a Törnqvist index of final uses of commodities.

Let $\bar{v}_i$ denote a simple average of the current-year dollar shares of value added in periods t and t+1 in industry i, let $\overline{m}_i$ denote the average ratio of current-year dollar intermediate inputs to value added in industry i, let F_{it}^{QM} denote the Fisher quantity index for intermediate inputs to industry i, let F_{it}^{QY} denote the Fisher quantity index for gross output in industry i, and let $LP_{it}^{\tilde{Y}}$ denote labor productivity in industry i measured as the difference between $\log F_{it}^{QY}$ and the log-change in hours. (We use Fisher quantity indexes rather than Törnqvist indexes at the industry level because the available industry level indexes are Fisher indexes.) The Törnqvist decomposition formula from Stiroh (2002) is:

$$\begin{aligned} ALP_t^{\tilde{V}} &= [\textstyle\sum_i \bar{v}_{it} LP_{it}^{\tilde{Y}}] - [\textstyle\sum_i \overline{m}_{it} (d\log F_{it}^{QM} - d\log F_{it}^{QY})] \\ &\quad + [\textstyle\sum_i \bar{v}_{it} d\log H_{it} - d\log H_t]. \end{aligned} \tag{22}$$

The Törnqvist index weights in equation (22) differ from the Sato-Vartia index weights in equation (18) because they use simple averages rather then normalized logarithmic means and because they are based on current-year dollar measures of value added and intermediate inputs. An analysis of these differences suggests that their effect will often be small.

To explore the effect of the functional form difference, assume that the industry shares of aggregate value added (i.e. of GDP) are the same in current-year dollars as in constant dollars. Let $\gamma_{it} = |v_{i,t+1} - \bar{v}_{it}| / \bar{v}_{it}$, which is the two-period coefficient of variation of the industry i's value added share. Finally, note that a Taylor series for $\log(1+\gamma_{it})$ minus a Taylor series for $\log(1-\gamma_{it})$ equals $\frac{2}{3}\gamma_{it} + \frac{2}{5}\gamma_{it}^3 + \frac{2}{7}\gamma_{it}^5 + \cdots$. Then,

$$\begin{aligned} m(v_{it}, v_{i,t+1}) &= \bar{v}_{it} 2\gamma_{it} / \log[(1+\gamma_{it})/(1-\gamma_{it})] \\ &= \bar{v}_{it} / (1 + \tfrac{1}{3}\gamma_{it}^2 + \tfrac{1}{5}\gamma_{it}^4 + \tfrac{1}{7}\gamma_{it}^6 + \cdots) \end{aligned} \tag{23}$$

Let $\overline{\gamma_t^2} = \sum_i \bar{v}_{it}\gamma_{it}^2$. Since γ_{it}^4, γ_{it}^6, etc. are very small, a reduction in their coefficients will have almost no effect on the value of the expansion in equation (23). In particular,

$$\bar{v}_{it}(1 - \tfrac{1}{3}\gamma_{it}^2) = \bar{v}_{it} / (1 + \tfrac{1}{3}\gamma_{it}^2 + \tfrac{1}{9}\gamma_{it}^4 + \tfrac{1}{27}\gamma_{it}^6 + \cdots) \approx \bar{v}_{it} / (1 + \tfrac{1}{3}\gamma_{it}^2 + \tfrac{1}{5}\gamma_{it}^4 + \tfrac{1}{7}\gamma_{it}^6 + \cdots) = m(v_{it}, v_{i,t+1}).$$

Therefore, the Sato-Vartia index weight for industry i based on current-year dollar shares, denoted by $\overline{w}_{it}$, approximately equals $\bar{v}_{it}(1 - \frac{1}{3}\gamma_{it}^2)/(1 - \frac{1}{3}\overline{\gamma^2})$. Another version of this approximation simply adjusts the Törnqvist weights by amounts proportional to deviations in the squared coefficients of variation:

$$\text{(24)} \qquad \overline{w}_{it} \approx \overline{v}_{it}[1-\frac{1}{3}(\gamma_{it}^2-\overline{\gamma_t^2})].$$

Equation (24) reveals that the Sato-Vartia index formula differs from the Törnqvist index formula only by incorporating an adjustment to each item weight that is inversely proportional to the excess volatility of its expenditure share. Consequently, industries with volatile shares tend to receive slightly lower weights in the contributions formula based on the Sato-Vartia index than they do in equation (22). However, equation (24) also implies that any differences in weights caused by the use of logarithmic means instead of the simple averages of the Törnqvist index are likely to be small.

Another difference between the exactly additive contributions to productivity change in equation (20) and the Törnqvist contributions in equation (22) is the use of constant-price measures of real change in equation (20) and the use of industry-level Fisher indexes in equation (22). However, $d\log Y_{it}$, the log-change in the constant-price index for gross output in equation (20), can be expected to differ only slightly from $d\log F_{it}^{QY}$ in equation (22), and similarly $d\log F_{it}^{QM} \approx d\log M_{it}$. For example, substituting into equation (3) and simplifying shows that F_{it}^{QY} can be expressed as an average of the Laspeyres and Paasche quantity indexes for gross output in industry i, L_{it}^{QY} and P_{it}^{QY}, with weights proportional to the Laspeyres and Fisher price indexes, L_{it}^{PY} and F_{it}^{PY}.[17] The constant-price measure of gross output change, $d\log Y_{it}$, differs from the Fisher measure only by giving the Laspeyres quantity index a weight proportional to the overall Fisher price index for GDP, F_t^P, instead of the industry-specific index, F_{it}^{PY}. Thus,

$$\text{(25)} \qquad \begin{aligned} d\log Y_{it} - d\log F_{it}^{QY} &= \log\left[\frac{F_t^P}{F_t^P + L_{it}^{PY}} L_{it}^{QY} + \frac{L_{it}^{PY}}{F_t^P + L_{it}^{PY}} P_{it}^{QY}\right] \\ &\quad - \log\left[\frac{F_{it}^{PY}}{F_{it}^{PY} + L_{it}^{PY}} L_{it}^{QY} + \frac{L_{it}^{PY}}{F_{it}^{PY} + L_{it}^{PY}} P_{it}^{QY}\right]. \end{aligned}$$

The difference in weights between the terms of equation (25) generally has a very small effect.

The resemblance of the terms in equation (22) to their counterparts in equation (20) means that the Törnqvist contributions can be expected to approximate the exactly additive contributions closely. Furthermore, it implies that Törnqvist weights can be substituted for the Sato-Vartia weights in the labor reallocation term of equation (20) to obtain approximate contributions to the labor reallocation effect. On the other hand, the formula for the log change in total real GDP implicit in equation (22), which is derived in appendix A as equation (A-4), differs considerably from the direct Fisher measure of this change. This suggests that the total of

[17] Dumagan (2002) discusses this expression for contributions to change in the Fisher index; see his equation (9).

the contributions calculated using the Törnqvist approach could differ from the aggregate change in productivity by a non-trivial amount. We investigate the question of how well (A-4) approximates the log-change in the Fisher quantity index empirically in the next section.

6. Empirical Results

6.1 Differences between Exact Contributions and Törnqvist Contributions

To investigate the differences between exactly additive industry contributions to productivity change and Törnqvist contributions, we use 2003 vintage data for the years from 1987 to 2001 from BEA's GDP-by-Industry accounts. In these accounts in 2003, industry nominal value added was estimated from income data, so that the sum over all industries of value added equals the income-side estimate of GDP. This sum is, therefore, less than the expenditure-side estimate of GDP from the 2003 vintage NIPA data by an amount equal to the statistical discrepancy. For years from 1987 to 1995, the statistical discrepancy averaged 0.36 percent of GDP, but from 1996 to 2001 it averaged about –0.41 percent of GDP. Other things being equal, therefore, output measures based on income side data can be expected to imply larger gains between these periods than output measures based on expenditure data.

We include in our analysis only the industries in the nonfarm private business sector.[18] Some of these industries include nonprofit institutions, many of which are measured in a way that assumes no productivity change; these institutions are important in the health services, educational services, and social services industries, and in membership organizations. We exclude holding and investment companies because of measurement problems and the owner-occupied housing portion of the real estate industry because it has no labor input.[19] These exclusions leave 58 industries in the data set, which account for about 92 percent of the value added of the nonfarm private business sector.

To construct the constant-price measures required for the exact decomposition of industry sources of productivity growth (the V_{it}, Y_{it}, M_{it} and the $V_{i,t+1}$, $Y_{i,t+1}$, $M_{i,t+1}$) we use unpublished data on the Laspeyres and Paasche components of the Fisher indexes in the GDP-by-Industry accounts. In addition, to measure labor inputs we use published data on full-time equivalent employees (FTE's) by detailed industry from the NIPAs.

[18] Although the theoretical discussion treated all of GDP as the aggregate of interest, studies of industry sources of productivity change generally exclude some industries whose productivity is not well measured.

[19] Owner-occupied housing is removed by subtracting its nominal and deflated gross output and intermediate inputs based on data from NIPA tables 8.12 and 8.13. In data released after the 2003 Comprehensive Revision of the NIPAs (after the research for this paper was done), owner-occupied housing was longer part of the real estate sector.

Table 1. Exact and Törnqvist Contributions to Value Added Productivity of FTEs: Average Growth Rates in Percentage Points

Industry	Exactly Additive Value Added Productivity 1987-1995	Törnqvist Value Added Productivity 1987-1995	Exactly Additive Value Added Productivity 1995-2001	Törnqvist Value Added Productivity 1995-2001
Agricultural, forestry and fishing services	-0.0124	-0.0124	-0.0009	-0.0009
Metal mining	0.0052	0.0052	0.0119	0.0120
Coal mining	0.0252	0.0252	0.0149	0.0150
Oil and gas extraction	0.0475	0.0484	-0.0518	-0.0528
Nonmetallic minerals, except fuels	0.0000	0.0000	0.0068	0.0068
Construction	0.0067	0.0067	-0.0554	-0.0553
Lumber and wood products	-0.0208	-0.0208	-0.0089	-0.0089
Furniture and fixtures	0.0029	0.0029	0.0034	0.0034
Stone, clay, and glass products	0.0164	0.0164	-0.0013	-0.0013
Primary metal industries	0.0212	0.0212	0.0197	0.0198
Fabricated metal products	0.0226	0.0226	0.0021	0.0022
Industrial machinery and equipment	**0.1550**	**0.1545**	**0.2283**	**0.2255**
Electronic and other electric equipment	**0.2914**	**0.2878**	**0.3732**	**0.3639**
Motor vehicles and equipment	0.0154	0.0154	0.0187	0.0190
Other transportation equipment	-0.0098	-0.0097	0.0330	0.0331
Instruments and related products	0.0016	0.0018	-0.0176	-0.0172
Miscellaneous manufacturing industries	0.0065	0.0065	0.0151	0.0151
Food and kindred products	0.0493	0.0494	-0.0708	-0.0701
Tobacco products	-0.0048	-0.0049	-0.0369	-0.0369
Textile mill products	0.0153	0.0153	0.0063	0.0063
Apparel and other textile products	0.0145	0.0145	0.0178	0.0178
Paper and allied products	-0.0010	-0.0010	0.0094	0.0095
Printing and publishing	-0.0375	-0.0375	-0.0163	-0.0163
Chemicals and allied products	0.0558	0.0558	0.0357	0.0357
Petroleum and coal products	-0.0039	-0.0035	0.0022	0.0015
Rubber and miscellaneous plastics products	0.0321	0.0321	0.0279	0.0279
Leather and leather products	0.0041	0.0041	-0.0004	-0.0004
Railroad transportation	0.0265	0.0265	0.0127	0.0127
Local and interurban passenger trans	-0.0070	-0.0070	0.0032	0.0032
Trucking and warehousing	0.0439	0.0438	-0.0018	-0.0019
Water transportation	0.0083	0.0083	0.0032	0.0032
Transportation by air	0.0106	0.0105	0.0074	0.0073
Pipelines, except natural gas	-0.0045	-0.0047	0.0041	0.0041
Transportation services	-0.0017	-0.0018	0.0109	0.0109
Telephone and telegraph	0.1362	0.1362	0.1372	0.1367
Radio and television	0.0429	0.0430	-0.0133	-0.0134
Electric, gas, and sanitary services	0.1053	0.1054	-0.0009	-0.0012

Table 1. Continued

Industry	Exactly Additive Value Added Productivity 1987-1995	Törnqvist Value Added Productivity, 1987-1995	Exactly Additive Value Added Productivity, 1995-2001	Törnqvist Value Added Productivity, 1995-2001
Wholesale trade	0.2419	0.2416	0.5484	0.5482
Retail trade	0.1022	0.1022	0.5180	0.5178
Depository institutions	0.0953	0.0952	0.1424	0.1425
Nondepository institutions	0.0105	0.0101	0.0796	0.0797
Security and commodity brokers	0.0636	0.0617	0.2333	0.2375
Insurance carriers	0.0217	0.0217	0.0218	0.0220
Insurance agents, brokers, and services	-0.0430	-0.0429	-0.0021	-0.0021
Real estate w/o owner occ	0.1227	0.1225	0.1156	0.1155
Hotels and other lodging places	0.0070	0.0070	-0.0149	-0.0149
Personal services	-0.0016	-0.0016	-0.0010	0.0010
Business services	0.0153	0.0153	0.0323	0.0330
Auto repair, services, and parking	-0.0107	-0.0107	0.0097	0.0097
Miscellaneous repair services	-0.0025	-0.0025	-0.0166	-0.0165
Motion pictures	-0.0092	-0.0092	0.0031	0.0031
Amusement and recreation services	-0.0029	-0.0029	-0.0123	-0.0123
Health services	-0.1526	-0.1526	-0.0125	-0.0125
Legal services	-0.0085	-0.0085	0.0035	0.0032
Educational services	-0.0028	-0.0028	-0.0141	-0.0141
Social services	-0.0019	-0.0019	-0.0159	-0.0159
Membership organizations	0.0018	0.0018	-0.0445	-0.0445
Other services	-0.0052	-0.0052	0.0865	0.0865
TOTAL	**1.500**	**1.494**	**2.391**	**2.391**
Addendum:				
Total excluding industrial machinery and electronic equipment industries	**1.054**	**1.052**	**1.790**	**1.794**
Total excluding productivity change in 1987-88 from average for the pre-1995 period	**1.215**	**N/A**	**N/A**	**N/A**

Note: Excludes government, farms, owner-occupied housing, investment and holding company offices, and private households. FTE–Full time equivalent employment.

Table 1 shows the contributions of industries' log-changes in real value added per employee hour to the log-change in aggregate real value added per employee hour net of the labor reallocation effect, which is excluded. The exactly additive contributions in table 1 are calculated as the sum of the first two terms in equation (20), and the Törnqvist contributions are calculated as the sum of the corresponding terms in equation (22). Averages for two periods are shown, one from 1987 to 1995, and another for the period from 1995 to 2001. A speedup in productivity growth seems to start in 1995,[20] so a comparison of these two periods provides important evidence on industry contributions to the productivity speedup.

The exactly additive contributions to productivity change in table 1 generally differ from their Törnqvist counterparts by less than 0.001, but a few important industries have more appreciable discrepancies. Most notably, the "industrial machinery and equipment" industry, which contains computers, and the "electronic and other electric equipment" industry, which contains semiconductors, both have slightly higher contributions to productivity growth based on the exact method than they do based on the Törnqvist method. The combined contribution of these two industries in the pre-1995 period is 0.446 percentage points using the exact method and 0.442 using the Törnqvist method; in the post-1995 period their exact contribution is 0.602 and their Törnqvist contribution is 0.589. Their exact contribution to the productivity speedup is therefore 0.156, compared with a Törnqvist contribution of 0.147.

The tendency of the Törnqvist method to imply smaller estimates is evident in the aggregate, as well. For the pre-1995 period, the total over all industries of value added contributions is 1.500 percentage points using the exact method and 1.494 using the Törnqvist method. Since the goal is to decompose the direct measure of aggregate productivity change, the differences between the total of the Törnqvist contributions and the exact total may be interpreted as indicative of downward bias in the Törnqvist contribution formula. The two approaches give the same total for the post-1995 period, so the speedup in aggregate real value added per FTE net of the reallocation effect is lower using the exact method than using the Törnqvist method: 0.891 compared with 0.897. Aggregate output grew sharply between 1987 and 1988, and a negative statistical discrepancy in 1988 made the growth of the income-based measure particularly strong. As a result, the productivity speedup appears larger when the starting point is 1988 rather than when it is 1987; in particular, the value in the bottom row of table 1 implies a speedup of 1.176 percent per year between the period from 1988 to 1995 and the period from 1995 to 2001.

6.2 Estimates of Industry Contributions to the Productivity Speedup

Table 2 shows contributions of important groups of industries — including those that have negative contributions — to the productivity speedup based on comparisons of the period from 1988 to 1995 in table 1 to the period from 1995 to 2001. One of the advantages of the exact industry contributions is that they can be combined into analytically interesting groups of industries, such as IT or ICT industries, with no loss of precision. Furthermore, combining the exact contributions of the individual industries in a group yields a result virtually identical to the one that could be calculated by aggregating these industries in the I-O tables and then calculating the exact contribution of the aggregate.[21]

[20] Output per hour for nonfarm business from BLS grows at an average rate of about 1.5 percent per year from 1987 to 1995, and at 2.4 percent per year from 1995 to 2001. BLS data used to construct multifactor productivity growth in nonfarm business up to 2001 implies that 0.3 percentage points of the speedup in output per hour growth come from faster multifactor productivity growth, and 0.6 percentage points come from growth of ordinary capital and human capital as measured in the "labor composition" adjustment. See http://www.bls.gov/lpc/home.htm#data.

[21] The two results may not be precisely identical because the factor needed to scale the Sato-Vartia weights to add up to 1, which is itself quite near 1, may change when industries are aggregated in the I-O tables.

In the aggregate, the contribution to the productivity speedup of changes in gross output per hour (0.40 percent per year) is smaller than the indirect effect of declining intermediate input utilization (0.49 percent per year). The labor reallocation effect is negative in both periods, but it contributes to the productivity speedup by rising from –0.46 percent per year before 1995 to –0.33 percent per year after 1995.

The largest contribution to the productivity speedup in table 2, of 0.74 percentage points, comes from the combined wholesale and retail trade industries. Productivity gains from improvements in business processes (e.g. a "Wal-Mart effect") facilitated by increased IT use, as well as the substitution of capital for labor, are probably both important reasons for the surge in productivity in the distribution industries. In addition, Bosworth and Triplett (2004) observe that productivity in these industries may benefit in another way from rising quality levels of IT goods; in particular, if the amount of real resources required to sell a box to a retail customer is constant, but we count the box as containing twice as much "computing power" as before, measured productivity in retailing will rise. A preliminary analysis suggests, however, that this effect — which is sometimes viewed as a spurious increase in productivity — is small.

Another industry with a large contribution to the productivity speedup in table 2 is securities and commodity brokers. This industry makes intensive use of IT capital goods, so falling prices for these goods may have enabled it to substitute more capital for labor and intermediate inputs in the later period and to realize gains in multifactor productivity.

The health services industry made an important contribution to the overall speedup because its value added productivity went from a negative growth rate to around 0 in the post-1995 period. Most of this improvement resulted from a large improvement in the growth rate of gross output per hour, which became positive after 1995. Although the pickup in productivity in this industry may be real, its relatively poor performance in the pre-1995 period could partly be due to measurement error, perhaps as a result of quality improvements not captured by its output price index. (In addition, health services contains many nonprofit institutions whose real output is partly measured as a deflated cost of inputs including compensation of employees, resulting in a questionable measure of productivity change.) The productivity speedup may, therefore, partly reflect improvements in measurement techniques in the late 1990s.

The industries that contain computers and semiconductors (industrial machinery and electrical equipment) make relatively large contributions to productivity growth in both periods. This qualitative result is consistent with what previous researchers have found, but table 2 shows a slightly smaller pickup in this contribution than others have found; indeed, less than one-sixth of the productivity speedup (or 0.156 percentage points) is directly attributable to these industries.[22] Within these industries, most of the productivity speedup comes from declining relative use of intermediate inputs; not rising gross output per hour. The relative decline in the real intermediate inputs after 1995 partly reflects a relatively large pickup in the rate of decline of the price deflator for these industries' gross output.

[22] Note that contributions to the level or to the speedup of aggregate productivity must be interpreted carefully because some negative contributions are present. In table 2, as a group the industries with positive contributions can "explain" about 180 percent of the total speedup.

Table 2. Contributions to Aggregate Growth in Real Output per FTE for Nonfarm Private Business: Selected Groups of Industries

Group of Industries	Gross Output Labor Productivity	LESS: Intermediate Input Intensity Effect	EQUALS: Value Added Labor Productivity	PLUS: Labor Reallocation Effect	EQUALS: Contribution to Agg. Labor Productivity
Nonfarm Private Business					
Average, 1995-2001	2.290	-0.101	2.391	-0.326	2.065
LESS: Average, 1988-1995	1.891	0.391	1.500	-0.460	1.040
EQUALS: Speedup	0.399	-0.492	0.891	0.134	1.025
Industries with Positive Contributions to Speedup in Aggregate Productivity Growth					
All 34 Industries with Positive Total Contributions					
Average contribution, 1995-2001	2.225	-0.418	2.643	-0.029	2.614
LESS: Average Contribution, 1988-1995	1.525	0.522	1.003	-0.225	0.778
EQUALS: Contribution to Speedup	0.700	-0.940	1.640	0.196	1.836
Wholesale and Retail Trade					
Average contribution, 1995-2001	0.650	-0.417	1.066	-0.008	1.059
LESS: Average Contribution, 1988-1995	0.384	0.040	0.344	-0.022	0.322
EQUALS: Contribution to Speedup	0.266	-0.456	0.722	0.014	0.736
Security and Commodity Brokers					
Average contribution, 1995-2001	0.132	-0.102	0.233	0.047	0.280
LESS: Average Contribution, 1988-1995	0.080	0.016	0.064	0.008	0.071
EQUALS: Contribution to Speedup	0.052	-0.118	0.170	0.039	0.209
Health Services					
Average contribution, 1995-2001	0.050	0.062	-0.012	0.000	-0.012
LESS: Average Contribution, 1988-1995	-0.044	0.108	-0.153	-0.034	-0.187
EQUALS: Contribution to Speedup	0.094	-0.046	0.140	0.034	0.175
Electronic and other electric equipment					
Average contribution, 1995-2001	0.276	-0.097	0.373	-0.011	0.362
LESS: Average Contribution, 1988-1995	0.250	-0.041	0.291	-0.012	0.280
EQUALS: Contribution to Speedup	0.026	-0.056	0.082	0.000	0.082
Telephone and Telegraph					
Average contribution, 1995-2001	0.204	0.067	0.137	0.039	0.176
LESS: Average Contribution, 1988-1995	0.155	0.019	0.136	-0.035	0.101
EQUALS: Contribution to Speedup	0.049	0.048	0.001	0.074	0.075
Industrial Machinery					
Average contribution, 1995-2001	0.139	-0.090	0.228	-0.001	0.227
LESS: Average Contribution, 1988-1995	0.159	0.004	0.155	-0.002	0.153
EQUALS: Contribution to Speedup	-0.021	-0.094	0.073	0.001	0.074

Table 2. Continued

Group of Industries	Gross Output Labor Productivity	LESS: Intermediate Input Intensity Effect	EQUALS: Value Added Labor Productivity	PLUS: Labor Reallocation Effect	EQUALS: Contribution to Agg. Labor Productivity
All Services except health services					
Average contribution, 1995-2001	0.322	0.304	0.018	-0.201	-0.183
LESS: Average Contribution, 1988-1995	0.148	0.169	-0.071	-0.155	-0.226
EQUALS: Contribution to Speedup	0.174	0.135	0.089	-0.046	0.043
Business Services					
Average contribution, 1995-2001	0.205	0.173	0.032	-0.069	-0.036
LESS: Average Contribution, 1988-1995	0.095	0.079	0.015	-0.057	-0.042
EQUALS: Contribution to Speedup	0.111	0.094	0.017	-0.012	0.005
Industries with Negative Contributions to the Speedup in Aggregate Productivity Growth					
All 24 Industries with Negative Total Contributions					
Average contribution, 1995-2001	0.065	0.317	-0.252	-0.297	-0.549
LESS: Average Contribution, 1988-1995	0.366	-0.131	0.498	-0.236	0.262
EQUALS: Contribution to Speedup	-0.301	0.448	-0.749	-0.062	-0.811
Electric, Gas, and Sanitary Services					
Average contribution, 1995-2001	0.060	0.061	-0.001	-0.068	-0.069
LESS: Average Contribution, 1988-1995	0.094	-0.011	0.105	-0.047	0.058
EQUALS: Contribution to Speedup	-0.033	0.073	-0.106	-0.021	-0.128
Food and Kindred Products					
Average contribution, 1995-2001	0.016	0.087	-0.071	-0.003	-0.073
LESS: Average Contribution, 1988-1995	0.026	-0.023	0.049	-0.002	0.048
EQUALS: Contribution to Speedup	-0.010	0.110	-0.120	-0.001	-0.121
Nondurable Manufacturing					
Average contribution, 1995-2001	0.137	0.162	-0.025	0.002	-0.023
LESS: Average Contribution, 1988-1995	0.137	0.013	0.111	-0.017	0.094
EQUALS: Contribution to Speedup	0.000	0.149	-0.136	0.019	-0.117
Membership organizations					
Average contribution, 1995-2001	-0.031	0.014	-0.045	-0.071	-0.116
LESS: Average Contribution, 1988-1995	0.000	-0.002	0.002	-0.029	-0.028
EQUALS: Contribution to Speedup	-0.030	0.016	-0.046	-0.042	-0.088
Construction					
Average contribution, 1995-2001	-0.097	-0.042	-0.055	-0.018	-0.073
LESS: Average Contribution, 1988-1995	-0.049	-0.056	0.007	0.004	0.011
EQUALS: Contribution to Speedup	-0.048	0.014	-0.062	-0.022	-0.084

Two industries in the service sector round out our group of positive contributors to the productivity speedup. These are telephone and telegraph, and business services. In the high-productivity telephone industry, rapid growth of hours boosted its contribution from the labor reallocation effect from –0.035 in the pre-1995 period to 0.039 in the post-1995 period, and value added per hour also accelerated. In business services, gross output per FTE grew much faster in the post-1995 period, but a rise in use of intermediate inputs appeared to account for most of this gain, leaving only a small contribution to aggregate value added per FTE. Also, a pickup in employment in the low-productivity business services industry reduced its labor reallocation contribution from –0.057 to –0.069. This may reflect an increased tendency for high-productivity industries to contract out activities that have low value added per hour worked. Since industries engaged in such contracting out would show a gain in their value added productivity without making any real improvement in production technology, some of the negative labor reallocation contribution of business services could arguably be attributable to other industries that showed large productivity gains.

Three of the four detailed industries in table 2 with noteworthy negative contributions to the productivity speedup include negative components from the labor reallocation effect. Decelerating growth of employment in the capital-intensive electric, gas and sanitary services industry depressed its labor reallocation contribution from –0.047 to –0.068.

Finally, table 2 shows that increased utilization of intermediate inputs is an important cause of a productivity slowdown in two industries: food and kindred products, and electric, gas and sanitary services.[23] Business services such as payroll processing may be increasing their use of computer power more rapidly than their growth of real output. Estimates of the growth of the intermediate inputs in the food product manufacturing industry may be affected by difficulties in estimating the portion of the output of vertically integrated producers of food products attributable to the farm industry. The growing consumption of organic foods, which are more expensive to farm, may also have contributed to the relatively rapid growth of intermediate inputs. Finally, the electric services may have substituted to cleaner, more expensive fuels, such as lower sulfur coal or natural gas, to comply with environmental standards. Such substitution would likely register as growing use of intermediate inputs. Also, since gas-burning electric plants are less capital intensive than most other kinds of powered plants, it may also result in the substitution of intermediate inputs for capital services.

7. Conclusion

This paper has derived exactly additive formulas for the decomposition of industry sources of a Fisher measure of aggregate labor productivity growth. The Törnqvist formulas for industry contributions to labor productivity change developed by Basu and Fernald (1995 and 1997) and by Stiroh (2002) theoretically approximate the exact contributions. In empirical tests, the Törnqvist formulas exhibit a slight downward bias in measuring aggregate productivity growth, and in measuring the contributions of the IT producing industries to aggregate

---

[23] Basu (1995) was among those who urged a closer look at the role of intermediate inputs more than a decade ago.

productivity growth. Nevertheless, on the whole, the agreement between the Törnqvist formulas and the exact formulas is remarkably close. The results therefore show that the Törnqvist approximations provide acceptable measures of industry contributions to aggregate labor productivity change.

This paper also provides new empirical evidence on industry contributions to labor productivity growth. The IT producing industries directly account for a quarter to two-fifths of aggregate productivity growth, but their direct contribution to the post-1995 productivity speedup in productivity growth is only around one-sixth of the total speedup. In contrast, the wholesale and retail trade industries account for more than half of the speedup.

Appendix: Derivation of Törnqvist Measure of Aggregate Growth

Let $d\log\hat{V}_t d$ denote the change in real GDP implied by the Törnqvist formulas for industry contributions to productivity change. To solve for $d\log\hat{V}_t$, let y_{it} denote current-dollar gross output in industry i, let m_{it} denote current-dollar intermediate inputs, and let v_t denote current-dollar GDP, or the sum over all industries of current-dollar value added. Then, substituting v_{it} for $y_{it}-m_{it}$, the change in aggregate output implied by equation (22) is

$$\text{(A-1)}\quad \begin{aligned} d\log\hat{V}_t &= \sum_i 0.5\left[\frac{y_{i,t+1}}{v_{t+1}}+\frac{y_{it}}{v_t}\right](d\log F_{it}^{QY}) - \sum_i 0.5\left[\frac{m_{i,t+1}}{v_{t+1}}+\frac{m_{it}}{v_t}\right](d\log F_{it}^{QY}) \\ &= \sum_i 0.5\left[\frac{y_{i,t+1}}{v_{t+1}}+\frac{y_{it}}{v_t}\right]\left[d\log F_{it}^{QY} - \frac{m_{i,t+1}/v_{t+1}+m_{it}/v_t}{y_{i,t+1}/v_{t+1}+y_{it}/v_t}(d\log F_{it}^{QM})\right] \\ &= \sum_i 0.5\left[\frac{v_{i,t+1}}{v_{t+1}}+\frac{v_{it}}{v_t}\right]\left[\frac{y_{i,t+1}/v_{t+1}+y_{it}/v_t}{v_{i,t+1}/v_{t+1}+v_{it}/v_t}\right] \\ &\quad \times\left[d\log F_{it}^{QY} - \frac{m_{i,t+1}/v_{t+1}+m_{it}/v_t}{y_{i,t+1}/v_{t+1}+y_{it}/v_t}(d\log F_{it}^{QM})\right] \end{aligned}$$

Using the notation of Stiroh's (2002) equation (5), define $\bar{s}_{Mit}$ as the ratio of average deflated intermediate inputs to average deflated gross outputs:

$$\text{(A-2)}\qquad \bar{s}_{Mit} \equiv \frac{m_{i,t+1}/v_{t+1}+m_{it}/v_t}{y_{i,t+1}/v_{t+1}+y_{it}/v_t}.$$

Also, following Basu and Fernald (1997), define the log change in the arbitrary industry i's real value added as:

$$\text{(A-3)}\qquad d\log\hat{V}_{it} \equiv \frac{d\log F_{it}^{QY} - \bar{s}_{Mit}(d\log F_{it}^{QM})}{1-\bar{s}_{Mit}}.$$

Then the log change in aggregate output implied by the Törnqvist decomposition is:

(A-4) $\quad d\log\hat{V}_t = \sum_i \bar{v}_{it}(d\log\hat{V}_{it})$.

The functional form in equation (A-4) is quite different from the formula for the Fisher quantity index for GDP. This makes an analytical analysis of how well $d\log\hat{V}_t$ approximates $d\log V_t$ difficult, leaving the question to be addressed with empirical evidence.

References

Balk, Bert M. (1995), "Axiomatic Price Theory: A Survey." *International Statistical Review* 63, 69-93.

Balk, Bert M. (2003), "The Residual: On Monitoring and Benchmarking Firms, Industries, and Economies with Respect to Productivity," *Journal of Productivity Analysis* 20, July, 5-47.

Balk, Bert M. (2004), "Decompositions of Fisher Indexes," *Economics Letters* 82, 107-113.

Basu, Susanto (1995), "Intermediate Goods and Business Cycles: Implications for Productivity and Welfare," *American Economic Review* 85, June, 512-531.

Basu, Susanto and John Fernald (1995), "Aggregate productivity and the productivity of aggregates," International Finance Discussion Papers 532, U.S. Board of Governors of the Federal Reserve System.

Basu, Susanto and John Fernald (1997), "Returns to Scale in U.S. Production: Estimates and Implications," *Journal of Political Economy* 105, April, 249-283.

Basu, Susanto and John Fernald (2002), "Aggregate Productivity and Aggregate Technology," *European Economic Review* 46, 963 – 991

Bosworth, Barry and Jack Triplett (2004), "Overview: Industry Productivity Trends," in *Productivity in the U.S. Services Sector: New Sources of Economic Growth*, B. Bosworth and J. Triplett, eds., Brookings Institute Press: Washington.

Corrado, Carol, and Lawrence Slifman (1999), "Decomposition of Productivity and Unit Costs." *American Economic Review, Papers and Proceedings* 89 (2), 328-332.

Diewert, W. Erwin (1992), "Fisher Ideal Output, Input and Productivity Indexes Revisited," *Journal of Productivity Analysis* 3 (2), 211-248.

Diewert, W. Erwin (2000), "Productivity Measurement Using Differences Rather than Ratios: A Note." University of New South Wales working paper.

Diewert, W. Erwin (2001), "The Consumer Price Index and Index Number Purpose," *Journal of Economic and Social Measurement* 27, 167-248.) (see also Discussion Paper No. 00-02, Department of Economics, University of British Columbia, Vancouver, Canada, V6T 1Z1.)

Diewert, W. Erwin (2005), "Index Number Theory Using Differences Rather Than Ratios," *The American Journal of Economics and Sociology* (January), 347-395.

Diewert, Erwin W. and Alice O. Nakamura (2003), "Index Number Concepts, Measures and Decompositions of Productivity Growth," *Journal of Productivity Analysis* 19, April, 127-160.

Dikhanov, Yuri (1997), "The Sensitivity of PPP-Based Income Estimates to Choice of Aggregation Procedures", mimeo, International Economics Department, The World Bank, Washington, DC.

Domar, Evsey D. (1961), "On the Measurement of Technological Change," *EconomicJournal*, December, 709–729.

Dumagan, Jesus C. (2002), "Comparing the Superlative Törnqvist and Fisher Ideal Indexes," *Economics Letters* 76, July, 251-258.

Eldridge, Lucy P. (1999), "How Price Indexes Affect BLS Productivity Measures," *Monthly Labor Review*, February, 35-46.

Gullickson, William and Michael J. Harper (1999), "Possible Measurement Bias in Aggregate Productivity Growth." *Monthly Labor Review*, February, 47-67.

Gullickson, William and Michael J. Harper (2002), "Bias in Aggregate Productivity Trends Revisited," *Monthly Labor Review*, March, 32-40.

Hulten, Charles (1978), "Growth Accounting With Intermediate Inputs." *Review of Economic Studies* 45, 511-518.

Jorgenson, Dale W. (2001), "Information Technology and the U.S. Economy," *American Economic Review* 91, no. 1 (March), 1-32.

Jorgenson, Dale, Frank Gollop, and Barabara Fraumeni (1987), *Productivity and U.S. Economic Growth*, Harvard University Press: Cambridge.

Jorgenson, Dale W., Mun S. Ho, and Kevin J. Stiroh (2002), "Information Technology, Education, and the Sources of Economic Growth across U.S. Industries," presented at a CRIW conference on "Measuring Capital in the New Economy."

Jorgenson, Dale W. and Kevin J. Stiroh (2000a), "Raising the Speed Limit: U.S. Economic Growth in the Information Age." *Brookings Papers on Economic Activity*, no. 1, 125-211.

Jorgenson, Dale W. and Kevin J. Stiroh (2000b), "U.S. Economic Growth at the Industry Level," *American Economic Review* 90 (2) May, 161-167.

Klein, Lawrence R., Cynthia Saltzman, and Vijaya G. Duggal (2003), "Information Technology and Productivity: The Case of the Financial Sector". *Survey of Current Business* 83 (August), 32-37.

Kohli, Ulrich (2011), "A Multiplicative Decomposition of the Fisher Index of Real GDP," THIS VOLUME.

Lau, Lawrence J. (1979), "On Exact Index Numbers." *Review of Economics and Statistics* 61, 73-82.

Levinsohn, James and Petrin, Amil (2003), "On the Micro-Foundations of Productivity Growth," presented at an NBER Productivity Workshop, November.

McKinsey Global Institute (2001), *US Productivity Growth 1995-2000: Understanding the Contribution of Information Technology Relative to Other Factors*. Washington, D.C.: McKinsey Global Institute, October.

Moulton, Brent R. and Eugene P. Seskin (1999), "A Preview of the 1999 Comprehensive Revision of the National Income and Product Accounts Statistical Changes," *Survey of Current Business* 79, October, 6–17.

Moyer, Brian, Marshall Reinsdorf and Robert Yuskavage (2004), "Aggregation Issues in Integrating and Accelerating BEA's Accounts: Improved Methods for Calculating GDP by Industry" in *A New Architecture for the U.S. National Accounts*, D.W. Jorgenson, J.S. Landefeld and W.D. Nordhaus, eds., University of Chicago Press for the Conference on Research in Income and Wealth (CRIW).

Nordhaus, William D. (2002), "Productivity Growth and the New Economy," *Brookings Papers on Economic Activity* 2, 211-264.

Oliner, Stephen D., and Daniel E. Sichel (2000), "The Resurgence of Growth in the Late 1990s: Is Information Technology the Story?" *Journal of Economic Perspectives* 14, Fall, 3-22.

Pollak, Robert A. (1981), "The Social Cost-of-Living Index" *Journal of Public Economics* 15, June, 311-36. Reprinted in Pollak, Robert A. (1989), *The Theory of the Cost-of-Living Index* Oxford Univ. Press, New York, 128-152.

Reinsdorf, Marshall B., W. Erwin Diewert, and Christian Ehemann (2002), "Additive Decompositions for Fisher, Törnqvist and Geometric Mean Indexes," *Journal of Economic and Social Measurement* 28, 51–61.

Sato, Kazuo (1976), "The Ideal Log-Change Index Number," *Review of Economics and Statistics* 58, 223-228.

Stiroh, Kevin J. (2002), "Information Technology and the US Productivity Revival: What Do the Industry Data Say?" *American Economic Review* 92, December, 1559-1576.

ten Raa, Thijs and Edward N. Wolff (2001), "Outsourcing of Services and the Productivity Recovery in U.S. Manufacturing in the 1980s and 1990s," *Journal of Productivity Analysis* 16, Sept., 149-165.

Vartia, Yrjö O. (1976), "Ideal Log-Change Index Numbers," *Scandinavian Journal of Statistics* 3, 121-126.

van IJzeren, J. (1952), "Over de Plausibiliteit van Fisher's Ideale Indices," (On the Plausibility of Fisher's Ideal Indices), Statistische en Econometrische Onderzoekingen (Centraal Bureau voor de Statistiek), Nieuwe Reeks 7, 104–115.

van IJzeren, J. (1987), *Bias in International Index Numbers: A Mathematical Elucidation*, Eindhoven, the Netherlands,.

Weitzman, Martin L. (1976), "On the Welfare Significance of National Product in a Dynamic Economy," *Quarterly Journal of Economics* 90, 156-162.

Yuskavage, Robert E. (1996), "Improved Estimates of Gross Product by Industry, 1959–94" *Survey of Current Business* 76, August, 133-155.

Chapter 6
LABOR PRODUCTIVITY: AVERAGE VS. MARGINAL

Ulrich Kohli[1]

1. Introduction

Most headline productivity measures refer to the *average* product of labor, with productivity growth being typically explained by capital deepening and technological progress. One might argue, however, that from an economic perspective a more relevant measure of the productivity of labor is its *marginal* product. This is certainly true if one is interested in the progression of real wages. It turns out, however, that as long as the income share of labor remains essentially constant through time, the two productivity measures give almost identical results. In the case of the United States, the share of labor *has* been fairly steady over the past thirty years.[2] Moreover, the paths of both measures of labor productivity for the United States have been very similar over the 1971-2001 period.

The stability of the labor share also explains why the Cobb-Douglas production function – which restricts the Hicksian elasticity of complementarity between inputs to be unity and thus forces the input shares to be constant – appears to fit U.S. data reasonably well. Any increase in the relative endowment of capital or any technological change, independently of whether it is labor or capital augmenting, necessarily leaves factor shares unchanged with this specification, and thus is measured to impact on the average and marginal products of labor to exactly the same extent. A more thorough look at the evidence, however, reveals that the historical empirical constancy of U.S. factor shares is *not* a law of nature; it is the outcome of opposing forces.

Using a functional form more flexible than the Cobb-Douglas, we find on the one hand that over the past three decades the Hicksian elasticity of complementarity between labor and capital has been significantly greater than one. Thus capital deepening, other things equal, has lead to an increase in the share of labor and thus raised its marginal product by relatively more than its average product. On the other hand, we find that technological change has had an offsetting effect over 1971-2001. It has basically been labor augmenting, and given the large elasticity of complementarity, has tended to reduce the share of labor and thus to raise its average product relative to its marginal product. This paper seeks to analytically disentangle these effects and proposes a measurement methodology which is then applied to produce a multiplicative decomposition of the average and marginal U.S. labor productivity over the past three decades.

---

[1] When this paper was written, the author was the chief economist, Swiss National Bank. He is now with the University of Geneva and can be reached at Ulrich.Kohli@unige.ch. The author is grateful to W. Erwin Diewert, Alice Nakamura, and Marshall Reinsdorf for their comments on an earlier draft, but has sole responsibility for any errors or omissions.

[2] Between 1971 and 2001, the GDP share of labor in the United States fluctuated over the range of .70 to .74, with an apparent mild downward time trend. See the appendix for a description of the data.

Citation: **Ulrich Kohli (2011), "Labor Productivity: Average vs. Marginal," chapter 6, pp. 103-132 in W.E. Diewert, B.M. Balk, D. Fixler, K.J. Fox and A.O. Nakamura,**
***PRICE AND PRODUCTIVITY MEASUREMENT: Volume 6 -- Index Number Theory.* Trafford Press.**

© Alice Nakamura, 2011. Permission to link to, or copy or reprint, these materials is granted without restriction, including for use in commercial textbooks, with due credit to the authors and editors.

While labor productivity is often the focus of attention, many economists are more interested in *total factor productivity*. Though less intuitive, total factor productivity, as indicated by its name, is more general. It encompasses all factors of production rather than just one of them. It turns out that total factor productivity is an essential component of the average productivity of labor. A third contribution of this paper is to document this important relationship. We present estimates for the United States for the 1971-2001 period that are derived from two different approaches: an econometric approach and one based on index numbers.

A fourth contribution of the paper is to move beyond the rather restrictive two-input, one-output production-function setting. We expand the model by adopting the GDP function framework that allows for many inputs and outputs, including imports and exports. This not only makes it possible to get a better estimate of the elasticity of complementarity between domestic primary inputs, but it also shows that there are additional forces at work including changes in the terms of trade and in the real exchange rate. Complete multiplicative decompositions of both measures of labor productivity and of total factor productivity are provided for this case as well for the United States for the 1971-2001 time period.

2. The Two-Input, One-Output Case

Assume that the aggregate technology can be represented by the following two-input, one-output production function:

(1) $$y_t = y(v_{L,t}, v_{K,t}, t) \, ,$$

where y_t measures the quantity of output, $v_{L,t}$ denotes the input of labor services, and $v_{K,t}$ is the input of capital services, with all three quantities being measured at time t. Note that the production function itself is allowed to shift over time to account for technological change. We assume that the production function is linearly homogeneous, increasing, and concave with respect to the two input quantities.

Under competitive conditions and profit maximization, the following first order conditions must be met:

(2) $$y_L(v_{L,t}, v_{K,t}, t) \equiv \frac{\partial y(v_{L,t}, v_{K,t}, t)}{\partial v_{L,t}} = \frac{w_{L,t}}{p_t}$$

(3) $$y_K(v_{L,t}, v_{K,t}, t) \equiv \frac{\partial y(v_{L,t}, v_{K,t}, t)}{\partial v_{K,t}} = \frac{w_{K,t}}{p_t},$$

where $w_{L,t}$ and $w_{K,t}$ represent the rental prices of labor and capital, and p_t is the price of output. The partial derivative $y_L(\cdot)$ on the left-hand side of (2) is the *marginal* product of labor.

The *average* product of labor ($g_{L,t}$), on the other hand, is simply defined as:

(4) $$g_{L,t} \equiv \frac{y_t}{v_{L,t}} .$$

Using production function (1), we can also write the average product of labor as follows:

$$(5)\qquad g_{L,t} = g_L(v_{L,t}, v_{K,t}, t) \equiv \frac{y(v_{L,t}, v_{K,t}, t)}{v_{L,t}}.$$

An index of *average* labor productivity ($A_{t,t-1}$) can be expressed as one plus the rate of increase in the average product of labor between period t-1 and period t, which is:

$$(6)\qquad A_{t,t-1} \equiv \frac{g_L(v_{L,t}, v_{K,t}, t)}{g_L(v_{L,t-1}, v_{K,t-1}, t-1)}.$$

Similarly, we can define an index of *marginal* labor productivity ($M_{t,t-1}$) as:

$$(7)\qquad M_{t,t-1} \equiv \frac{y_L(v_{L,t}, v_{K,t}, t)}{y_L(v_{L,t-1}, v_{K,t-1}, t-1)}.$$

Note that it follows from the linear homogeneity of the production function that both $g_L(\cdot)$ and $y_L(\cdot)$ are homogeneous of degree zero in $v_{L,t}$ and $v_{K,t}$. The same is therefore true for the two measures of labor productivity, which thus depend only on changes in *relative* factor endowments and on the passage of time.

Next, we define $s_{L,t}$ as the share of labor in total revenues (i.e., GDP):

$$(8)\qquad s_{L,t} \equiv \frac{w_{L,t} v_{L,t}}{p_t y_t}.$$

It follows from (1), (2), (4) and (5) that:

$$(9)\qquad s_{L,t} = s_L(v_{L,t}, v_{K,t}, t) \equiv \frac{y_L(v_{L,t}, v_{K,t}, t)}{g_L(v_{L,t}, v_{K,t}, t)}.$$

Using (9) in (6) and (7), we can rewrite the index of marginal labor productivity growth as

$$(10)\qquad M_{t,t-1} = S_{t,t-1} \cdot A_{t,t-1},$$

where $S_{t,t-1}$ is the labor share index:

$$(11)\qquad S_{t,t-1} \equiv \frac{s_L(v_{L,t}, v_{K,t}, t)}{s_L(v_{L,t-1}, v_{K,t-1}, t-1)}.$$

This index is greater or smaller than one, depending on whether the share of labor has increased or fallen between period t-1 and period t.

3. The Role of the Hicksian Elasticity of Complementarity

According to (10), the growth of the marginal productivity of labor will be higher (lower) than the growth of the average productivity if technological progress and changes in relative factor endowments lead to an increase (decrease) in labor's share over time. Using (9), we find:

$$\frac{\partial s_L(\cdot)}{\partial v_{K,t}} = \frac{g_L(\cdot)\partial y_L(\cdot)/\partial v_{K,t} - y_L(\cdot)\partial g_L(\cdot)/\partial v_{K,t}}{g_L(\cdot)^2}$$

$$(12) \qquad = \frac{v_{L,t}}{y(\cdot)^2}[y_{LK}(\cdot)y(\cdot) - y_L(\cdot)y_K(\cdot)]$$

$$= \frac{s_L(\cdot)s_K(\cdot)}{v_{K,t}}(\psi_{LK} - 1),$$

where $y_{LK}(\cdot) \equiv \partial^2 y(\cdot)/(\partial v_{L,t}\partial v_{K,t})$ and where ψ_{LK} is the Hicksian elasticity of complementarity between labor and capital defined as:[3]

$$(13) \qquad \psi_{LK} \equiv \frac{y_{LK}(\cdot)y(\cdot)}{y_L(\cdot)y_K(\cdot)}.$$

Thus, capital deepening will lead to an increase (decrease) in the share of labor if and only if the elasticity of complementarity is greater (smaller) than one.

Next, to assess the impact of the passage of time, we take the partial derivative of s_L with respect to t, which yields:

$$\frac{\partial s_L(\cdot)}{\partial t} = \frac{g_L(\cdot)\partial y_L(\cdot)/\partial t - y_L(\cdot)\partial g_L(\cdot)/\partial t}{g_L(\cdot)^2}$$

$$(14) \qquad = \frac{v_{L,t}}{y(\cdot)^2}[y_{LT}(\cdot)y(\cdot) - y_L(\cdot)y_T(\cdot)]$$

$$= \frac{s_{L,t}(\cdot)y_T(\cdot)}{y(\cdot)}(\psi_{LT} - 1),$$

where $y_T(\cdot) \equiv \partial y(\cdot)/\partial t$, $y_{LT}(\cdot) \equiv \partial^2 y(\cdot)/(\partial v_{L,t}\partial t)$, and where ψ_{LT} is defined as follows:

$$(15) \qquad \psi_{LT} \equiv \frac{y_{LT}(\cdot)y(\cdot)}{y_L(\cdot)y_T(\cdot)}.$$

The ratio $y_{LT}(\cdot)/y_L(\cdot)$ is the elasticity of the real wage rate with respect to time. The ratio $y(\cdot)/y_T(\cdot)$, on the other hand, is the inverse of the instantaneous rate of technological change (μ_t). Thus, ψ_{LT} will be greater than one if and only if technological change tends to favor labor relative to capital, in the sense that the wage rate increases by relatively more than the return to capital.[4] In that case the share of labor will increase with the passage of time.

---

[3] In the two input case, ψ_{LK} is necessarily positive; that is, the two inputs are necessarily Hicksian complements for each other. Moreover, in the two input case, the Hicksian elasticity of complementarity is then equal to the inverse of the Allen-Uzawa elasticity of substitution (see footnote 12).

[4] In that case, technological change is said to be pro-labor biased. See Kohli (1994) and section 6 below.

4. Disembodied Factor Augmenting Technological Change

To better track the impact of technological change on the share of labor, let us assume for a moment that technological change is disembodied, factor augmenting, and takes place exponentially. We can then rewrite the production function (1) as follows:

$$(16)\qquad y(v_{L,t},v_{K,t},t)=f(v_{L,t}e^{\mu_L t},v_{K,t}e^{\mu_K t})=f(\tilde{v}_{L,t},\tilde{v}_{K,t}),$$

where μ_L and μ_K are the rates of factor-augmenting technological change for labor and capital ($\mu_L \geq 0, \mu_K \geq 0$), and $\tilde{v}_{L,t}$ and $\tilde{v}_{K,t}$ are the quantities of labor and capital measured in terms of efficiency units ($\tilde{v}_{L,t} \equiv v_{L,t}e^{\mu_L t}$, $\tilde{v}_{K,t} \equiv v_{K,t}e^{\mu_K t}$). The marginal product of labor $y_L(\cdot)$ is:

$$(17)\qquad y_L(v_{L,t},v_{K,t},t)=\frac{\partial f(v_{L,t}e^{\mu_L t},v_{K,t}e^{\mu_K t})}{\partial v_{L,t}}=e^{\mu_L t}f_L(\cdot)\ ,$$

where $f_L(\cdot) \equiv \partial f(\cdot)/\partial \tilde{v}_{L,t}$. The average product of labor, on the other hand, is equal to:

$$(18)\qquad g_L(v_{L,t},v_{K,t},t)=\frac{f(v_{L,t}e^{\mu_L t},v_{K,t}e^{\mu_K t})}{v_{L,t}},$$

and the labor share can now be expressed as:

$$(19)\qquad s_L(v_{L,t},v_{K,t},t)=\frac{v_{L,t}e^{\mu_L t}f_L(v_{L,t}e^{\mu_L t},v_{K,t}e^{\mu_K t})}{f(v_{L,t}e^{\mu_L t},v_{K,t}e^{\mu_K t})}.$$

Differentiating expression (19) with respect to time, we get:

$$(20)\qquad \begin{aligned}\frac{\partial s_L(\cdot)}{\partial t}&=\frac{\mu_L\tilde{v}_{L,t}f_L(\cdot)+\tilde{v}_{L,t}(f_{LL}\mu_L\tilde{v}_{L,t}+f_{LK}\mu_K\tilde{v}_{K,t})}{f(\cdot)}\\&\quad-\frac{\tilde{v}_{L,t}f_L(\cdot)(f_L\mu_L\tilde{v}_{L,t}+f_K\mu_K\tilde{v}_{K,t})}{f(\cdot)^2}=s_{L,t}(1-s_{L,t})(\mu_K-\mu_L)(\psi_{LK}-1)\end{aligned}$$

where we have taken into account the restrictions $f_{LL}\tilde{v}_{L,t}+f_{LK}\tilde{v}_{K,t}=0$ and $f_L\tilde{v}_{L,t}+f_K\tilde{v}_{K,t}=f(\cdot)$ that arise from the linear homogeneity of the production function.

Thus, the labor share will increase with the passage of time if $\mu_K > \mu_L$ and $\psi_{LK} > 1$, or, alternatively, if $\mu_K < \mu_L$ and $\psi_{LK} < 1$. If technological change is Harrod-neutral, for instance ($\mu_L > 0$ and $\mu_K = 0$ in that case) and if labor and capital are relatively good complements, then the share of labor will tend to fall over time. The increase in the available amount of labor measured in terms of efficiency units will tend to have a sufficiently large positive impact on the marginal product of capital for the share of capital to increase and the share of labor to fall.

5. The Cobb-Douglas Functional Form

Suppose the production function (1) has the Cobb-Douglas form:

$$(21) \quad y(v_{L,t}, v_{K,t}, t) = e^{\alpha_0} v_{K,t}^{\beta_K} v_{L,t}^{1-\beta_K} e^{\mu t},$$

where $0 < \beta_K < 1$ and μ is the rate of Hicks-neutral technological change. One would normally expect this rate to be positive. This indeed turns out to be the case as indicated by the estimates of (21) reported in table 1, column 1.[5]

Note that the production function (21) could just as well have been written as:

$$(22) \quad y(v_{L,t}, v_{K,t}, t) = e^{\alpha_0} (v_{K,t} e^{\mu_K t})^{\beta_K} v_{L,t}^{1-\beta_K},$$

or as

$$(23) \quad y(v_{L,t}, v_{K,t}, t) = e^{\alpha_0} v_{K,t}^{\beta_K} (v_{L,t} e^{\mu_L t})^{1-\beta_K},$$

where $\mu_K \equiv \mu / \beta_K$ and $\mu_L \equiv \mu/(1-\beta_K)$. What this means is that it is not possible, in the Cobb-Douglas case, to discriminate between the Hicks-neutral, the Solow-neutral, and the Harrod-neutral cases of technological change.

In any case, it is well known that in the Cobb-Douglas case, the marginal product of labor is proportional to its average product:

$$(24) \quad y_L(v_{L,t}, v_{K,t}, t) = (1-\beta_K) \frac{e^{\alpha_0} v_{K,t}^{\beta_K} v_{L,t}^{1-\beta_K} e^{\mu t}}{v_{L,t}} = (1-\beta_K) g_L(v_{L,t}, v_{K,t}, t).$$

It follows from (9) and (24) that $1-\beta_K$ can be interpreted as the share of labor in total income, which is thus invariant by construction in the Cobb-Douglas case:

$$(25) \quad s_{L,t} = 1 - \beta_K.$$

To sum up, in the Cobb-Douglas case, the two measures of labor productivity defined in (6) and (7) must give exactly the same result because $S_{t,t-1}$ is equal to unity in (10).

6. The Translog Functional Form

The Cobb-Douglas function forces the Hicksian elasticity of complementarity to be unity. A more general representation of the technology is given by the translog functional form.[6] Maintaining for the time being the assumption of disembodied, factor-augmenting technological change, we can represent the translog production function as follows:

---

[5] See the appendix for a description of the data. We jointly estimated equations (21) (in logarithmic form) and (25). The estimation method is Zellner's method for seemingly unrelated equations as implemented in TSP, version 4.3A. The value of the logarithm of the likelihood function (LL) is also reported.

[6] See Christensen, Jorgenson and Lau (1973), and Diewert (1974).

(26) $$\ln y_t = \alpha_0 + \beta_K \ln \tilde{v}_{K,t} + (1-\beta_K)\ln \tilde{v}_{L,t} + \frac{1}{2}\phi_{KK}(\ln \tilde{v}_{K,t} - \ln \tilde{v}_{L,t})^2 .$$

Making use of the definitions of $\tilde{v}_{L,t}$ and $\tilde{v}_{K,t}$, we get:

(27) $$\begin{aligned}\ln y_t &= \alpha_0 + \beta_K \ln v_{K,t} + (1-\beta_K)\ln v_{L,t} + \frac{1}{2}\phi_{KK}(\ln v_{K,t} - \ln v_{L,t})^2 \\ &+ \{\mu_L + (\mu_K - \mu_L)[\beta_K + \phi_{KK}(\ln v_{K,t} - \ln v_{L,t})]\}t \\ &+ \frac{1}{2}\phi_{KK}(\mu_K - \mu_L)^2 t^2 .\end{aligned}$$

The labor share is obtained by logarithmic differentiation:

(28) $$s_{L,t} = (1-\beta_K) - \phi_{KK}(\ln v_{K,t} - \ln v_{L,t}) - \phi_{KK}(\mu_K - \mu_L)t .$$

The Hicksian elasticity of complementarity can be obtained as:

(29) $$\psi_{LK} = \frac{-\phi_{KK} + s_{L,t}(1-s_{L,t})}{s_{L,t}(1-s_{L,t})} .$$

ψ_{LK} is greater than one if and only if ϕ_{KK} is negative.[7] In that case the share of labor increases with capital intensity. This matches our result of section 2.

However, it is also apparent from (28) that the form of technological change plays a role. If $\mu_L > \mu_K$ and $\phi_{KK} > 0$, or, alternatively, if $\mu_K > \mu_L$ and $\phi_{KK} < 0$, technological change is pro-labor biased in that the share of labor will increase as the result of the passage of time. In that case, the marginal product of labor will tend to increase more rapidly than the average product.

Parameter estimates for equation (27) are reported in table 1, column 2.[8] These results suggest that $\mu_L > \mu_K$ and $\phi_{KK} < 0$ in the case of the United States. Thus, technological change is labor augmenting, but anti-labor biased.

Function (27) is flexible with respect to the quantities of labor and capital, but not with respect to time.[9] A TP-flexible translog production function formulation is given by:

(30) $$\begin{aligned}\ln y_t &= \alpha_0 + \beta_K \ln v_{K,t} + (1-\beta_K)\ln v_{L,t} + \frac{1}{2}\phi_{KK}(\ln v_{K,t} - \ln v_{L,t})^2 + \\ &\phi_{KT}(\ln v_{K,t} - \ln v_{L,t})t + \beta_T t + \frac{1}{2}\phi_{TT} t^2 .\end{aligned}$$

[7] Note that concavity of the production function requires ψ_{LK} to be positive; that is, the following constraint must hold: $\phi_{KK} < s_{L,t}(1-s_{L,t})$.

[8] Equation (27) was estimated jointly with (28) by nonlinear iterative Zellner as implemented into TSP, version 4.3A; see Berndt, Hall, Hall, and Hausman (1974). The standard errors are computed from the quadratic form of the analytic first-order derivatives. The estimate of ψ_{LK} is reported in table 1 as well.

[9] Here we are using the terminology of Diewert and Wales (1992). They define as TP flexible functional form a function that not only is flexible (i.e. gives a second-order approximation) with respect to input quantities, but that is also flexible with respect to technological progress (i.e. it is quadratic with respect to time).

Table 1. Parameter Estimates

	Equation: (21) Cobb-Douglas production function	(27) Translog production function	(30) TP-flexible translog production function	(76) Translog real value added function
α_0	8.966[a]	8.970[a]	8.971[a]	8.970[a]
α_Q				-0.125
α_E				-0.019[a]
β_K	0.277[a]	0.284[a]	0.285[a]	0.285[a]
γ_{QQ}				0.0109
γ_{QE}				-0.0940[a]
γ_{EE}				0.0997[a]
φ_{KK}		-0.1360[a]	-0.1532[a]	-0.2806[a]
δ_{QK}				0.0679[a]
δ_{EK}				-0.0354
δ_{QT}				-0.0043[a]
δ_{ET}				0.0018[a]
φ_{KT}			0.0017[a]	0.0016[a]
β_T			0.0111[a]	0.0108[a]
φ_{TT}			0.00008	0.00010[a]
μ	0.0098[a]			
μ_K		0.0018		
μ_L		0.0134[a]		
LL	213.63	224.09	226.70	469.78
ψ_{KL}	1.00	1.67	1.75	2.39

Note: A superscript a indicates a coefficient that is significantly different from zero with a 95 percent level of confidence using a two tailed test.

Comparing (27) with (30), one sees that the latter contains one extra parameter. The share of labor is now given by:

$$(31) \quad s_{L,t} = (1-\beta_K) - \phi_{KK}(\ln v_{K,t} - \ln v_{L,t}) - \phi_{KT}\, t .$$

It is immediately obvious that technological change is anti-labor biased in the sense that it leads to a reduction in the share of labor if and only if $\phi_{KT} > 0$. This turns out to be the case as shown by the parameter estimates of (30) reported in table 1, column 3.[10]

[10] These figures were obtained by estimating (30) and (31) jointly, the estimation method again being iterative Zellner.

7. On the Form of Technological Change: a Digression

When it comes to technological progress and the analysis of its impact on labor and capital, one finds many different competing concepts in the literature. The overall picture can therefore become quite confusing. Thus, does technological progress favor labor or capital? Is technological progress labor saving, labor using, labor augmenting, labor rewarding, or labor penalizing? Is it pro- (or anti-) labor biased, or even ultra pro- (or anti-) labor biased? To some extent, these concepts apply to different situations and they are not mutually exclusive. In the production-function context, where the input quantities are taken as exogenous and their marginal products as endogenous, technological change will tend to impact on these marginal products. Technological progress can be said to favor – or reward – labor and/or capital, in so far as it increases the marginal products of labor and/or capital, respectively. Technological progress may favor one more than the other when it favors both. It may also penalize one factor by reducing its marginal product, although, other things equal, a technological improvement must necessarily have a favorable impact on at least one factor.

In the production function context, one can also think of technological change as being factor augmenting; i.e., it can increase the endowment of one or both factors in terms of efficiency units even if the observed quantities have not changed. If technological change is labor augmenting in this sense (i.e. $\mu_L > 0$), it will, other things equal, tend to depress the marginal product of an efficiency unit of labor and enhance the marginal product of capital.[11] Whether the actual marginal product of labor increases or not will ultimately depend on the Hicksian elasticity of complementarity between the two factors. If labor and capital are strong complements, labor might well be penalized and suffer a drop in its wage. Unless labor and capital are indeed rather weak Hicksian complements, the share of labor will tend to decrease. In that sense, technological change can be said to be inherently anti-labor biased. If the share of labor not only falls, but the wage rate declines too, one could think about this as an ultra anti-labor bias.

Appendix table A1 gives an overview of the cases that might occur with just two inputs, and assuming that technological change is disembodied and factor augmenting. For simplicity, we only consider the polar cases of Harrod-, Hicks- and Solow-neutrality, but intermediate situations can obviously arise as well.[12] Based on the estimates of the translog function (27) discussed in section 5 and reported in table 1, column 2, technological change is nearly Harrod-neutral. It is thus labor augmenting. The elasticity of complementarity is greater than one, but less than the inverse of the capital share. The case described in the second column of table A1 is therefore the one that is relevant for the United States over the 1971-2001 period. Although technological change is labor (and capital) rewarding, viewed in a 2-input production function framework it is nevertheless anti-labor (and pro-capital) biased.

[11] The return of labor per unit of efficiency can be defined as $\tilde{w}_{L,t} \equiv w_{L,t} e^{-\mu_L t}$.

[12] The ε_{jT}'s ($j=L,K$) are the semi-elasticities of factor rewards with respect to time; see Diewert and Wales (1987). The κ_j's ($\kappa_j \equiv \varepsilon_{jT} - \mu$) measure the bias; see Kohli (1994) for details. The hats indicate relative changes. The changes in factor rental prices are derived under the assumption that the price of output remains constant.

The terms labor (or capital) using and saving are what are relevant when the technology is described by a cost function instead of a production function.[13] In the aggregate, this would be appropriate in a Keynesian setting, where output and factor rental prices can be viewed as predetermined and where the model yields the demand for labor and capital services. For a given level of output, technological progress will lead to a reduction in the demand for one or both inputs. In that sense, technological progress can be labor and/or capital saving, just like it could be labor or capital using (but not both). In this context, factor rental prices are assumed to be given, but the share of labor can change either way depending on how strongly technological change impacts on labor relative to capital.

If the labor share increases, one might say that technological progress is pro-labor biased, although this outcome is possible whether technological progress is labor using or labor saving. If the labor share falls, technological change would necessarily have to be labor saving, but at the same time, it can be either capital using or capital saving. In this context, we can also think of technological change as modifying the effective rental price of one or both inputs. That is, technological progress could lead to the lowering of the rental price of labor per unit of efficiency. Other things equal, this will favor the demand for labor at the expense of capital in terms of efficiency units, but whether or not the measured demand for labor increases or not depends on the size of the Allen-Uzawa elasticity of substitution between labor and capital. If that elasticity is close to zero, the actual demand for labor might well fall. It is easy to see that the share of labor could in general go in either direction.

Appendix table A2 summarizes the possible outcomes in the cost function setting.[14] Given the empirical results to which we alluded earlier, we can conclude that in the U.S. case, technological change is labor- (and capital-) saving, and anti-labor biased.

In the two input case, there is a simple correspondence between the cost function setting and the production function setting, since the elasticity of substitution is then equal to the inverse of the elasticity of complementarity. This is no longer the case if the number of inputs exceeds two, since the transformation of one type of elasticity into the other requires the inversion of a bordered Hessian matrix.[15] It is no longer true, then, that an elasticity of complementarity between a pair of inputs greater than one necessarily implies that the corresponding elasticity of substitution is less than unity. In fact, the two elasticities need not even have the same sign. This makes any characterization of technological progress without reference to the analytical framework at best ambiguous, and at worst useless.

8. Accounting for Labor Productivity

We now turn to the task of accounting for the changes over time in the average and the marginal products of labor. Using (6) as a starting point, we can define the following index that

---

[13] See Jorgenson and Fraumeni (1981), for instance.

[14] The function $c(\cdot)$'s (j=L,K) is the unit cost function, and σ_{LK} is the Allen-Uzawa elasticity of substitution. The ε_{jT} 's (j=L,K) now designate the semi-elasticities of input demands with respect to time. In deriving these results, we have assumed that output remains constant.

[15] See Kohli (1991).

isolates the impact of changes in factor endowments over consecutive periods of time on the average productivity of labor:

$$(32)\qquad A^{L}_{V,t,t-1} \equiv \frac{g_L(v_{L,t}, v_{K,t}, t-1)}{g_L(v_{L,t-1}, v_{K,t-1}, t-1)}.$$

When defining $A^{L}_{V,t,t-1}$ we have held the technology constant at its initial (period *t*-1) state. $A^{L}_{V,t,t-1}$ thus has the Laspeyres form, so to speak. Alternatively, we could adopt the technology of period *t* as a reference. We would then get the following Paasche-like index:

$$(33)\qquad A^{P}_{V,t,t-1} \equiv \frac{g_L(v_{L,t}, v_{K,t}, t)}{g_L(v_{L,t-1}, v_{K,t-1}, t)}.$$

Since there is no reason *a priori* to prefer either measure (32) or (33), we follow Diewert and Morrison's (1986) example and take the geometric mean of the two indexes. We thus get:

$$(34)\qquad A_{V,t,t-1} \equiv \left\{ \frac{g_L(v_{L,t}, v_{K,t}, t-1)}{g_L(v_{L,t-1}, v_{K,t-1}, t-1)} \cdot \frac{g_L(v_{L,t}, v_{K,t}, t)}{g_L(v_{L,t-1}, v_{K,t-1}, t)} \right\}^{1/2}.$$

Note that if capital deepening takes place, both $A^{L}_{V,t,t-1}$ and $A^{P}_{V,t,t-1}$ will be greater than one, in which case $A_{V,t,t-1}$ must exceed one as well.

Similarly, we can define the following index that isolates the impact of technological change. That is, we compute the index of average labor productivity allowing for the passage of time, but holding factor endowments fixed, first at their level of period *t-1*, and then at the level of period *t*:

$$(35)\qquad A^{L}_{T,t,t-1} \equiv \frac{g_L(v_{L,t-1}, v_{K,t-1}, t)}{g_L(v_{L,t-1}, v_{K,t-1}, t-1)}$$

$$(36)\qquad A^{P}_{T,t,t-1} \equiv \frac{g_L(v_{L,t}, v_{K,t}, t)}{g_L(v_{L,t}, v_{K,t}, t-1)}.$$

Taking the geometric mean of these two indexes, we get:

$$(37)\qquad A_{T,t,t-1} \equiv \left\{ \frac{g_L(v_{L,t-1}, v_{K,t-1}, t)}{g_L(v_{L,t-1}, v_{K,t-1}, t-1)} \cdot \frac{g_L(v_{L,t}, v_{K,t}, t)}{g_L(v_{L,t}, v_{K,t}, t-1)} \right\}^{1/2}.$$

It can easily be seen that $A_{V,t,t-1}$ given in (34) and $A_{T,t,t-1}$ given in (37) together yield a complete decomposition of the index of average labor productivity:

$$(38)\qquad A_{t,t-1} = A_{V,t,t-1} \cdot A_{T,t,t-1}.$$

We can proceed along exactly the same lines with the marginal productivity index. We thus get the two following partial indexes:

$$(39)\qquad M_{V,t,t-1} \equiv \left\{ \frac{y_L(v_{L,t}, v_{K,t}, t-1)}{y_L(v_{L,t-1}, v_{K,t-1}, t-1)} \cdot \frac{y_L(v_{L,t}, v_{K,t}, t)}{y_L(v_{L,t-1}, v_{K,t-1}, t)} \right\}^{1/2}$$

$$(40)\qquad M_{T,t,t-1} \equiv \left\{ \frac{y_L(v_{L,t-1}, v_{K,t-1}, t)}{y_L(v_{L,t-1}, v_{K,t-1}, t-1)} \cdot \frac{y_L(v_{L,t}, v_{K,t}, t)}{y_L(v_{L,t}, v_{K,t}, t-1)} \right\}^{1/2}.$$

Together these two partial indexes provide a complete decomposition of $M_{t,t-1}$:

$$(41)\qquad M_{t,t-1} = M_{V,t,t-1} \cdot M_{T,t,t-1}.$$

An alternative way of tackling the decomposition of $M_{t,t-1}$ would be on the basis of (9). Indeed, since $y_L(\cdot) = s_L(\cdot) g_L(\cdot)$, $M_{V,t,t-1}$ could also be expressed as:

$$(42)\qquad M_{V,t,t-1} = S_{V,t,t-1} \cdot A_{V,t,t-1},$$

where

$$(43)\qquad S_{V,t,t-1} \equiv \left\{ \frac{s_L(v_{L,t}, v_{K,t}, t-1)}{s_L(v_{L,t-1}, v_{K,t-1}, t-1)} \cdot \frac{s_L(v_{L,t}, v_{K,t}, t)}{s_L(v_{L,t-1}, v_{K,t-1}, t)} \right\}^{1/2}$$

measures the contribution of changes in factor endowments on the share of labor. Similarly, it can be seen that:

$$(44)\qquad M_{T,t,t-1} = S_{T,t,t-1} \cdot A_{T,t,t-1},$$

where

$$(45)\qquad S_{T,t,t-1} \equiv \left\{ \frac{s_L(v_{L,t-1}, v_{K,t-1}, t)}{s_L(v_{L,t-1}, v_{K,t-1}, t-1)} \cdot \frac{s_L(v_{L,t}, v_{K,t}, t)}{s_L(v_{L,t}, v_{K,t}, t-1)} \right\}^{1/2}.$$

$S_{T,t,t-1}$ measures the contribution of technological progress to changes in the share of labor; it will be greater than one if technological change is pro-labor biased, and less than one otherwise.

Note that (38) and (41) only hold as long as $A_{t,t-1}$ and $M_{t,t-1}$ are indeed given by (6) and (7). If one uses actual data and if the average product of labor is measured as output per unit of labor and its marginal product is measured by its real wage rate, then one cannot expect expressions such as (38) and (41) to hold exactly, since production function (1) itself is only an approximation of reality, and the same is true for first order condition (2).

Let $AA_{t,t-1}$ and $MM_{t,t-1}$ be the *observed* values of the average and marginal productivities of labor, respectively:

$$(46) \qquad AA_{t,t-1} \equiv \frac{y_t / v_{L,t}}{y_{t-1} / v_{L,t-1}}$$

$$(47) \qquad MM_{t,t-1} \equiv \frac{w_{L,t} / p_t}{w_{L,t-1} / p_{t-1}}.$$

The full decomposition of both indexes is then given by:

$$(48) \qquad AA_{t,t-1} = A_{V,t,t-1} \cdot A_{T,t,t-1} \cdot A_{U,t,t-1}$$

$$(49) \qquad MM_{t,t-1} = M_{V,t,t-1} \cdot M_{T,t,t-1} \cdot M_{U,t,t-1},$$

where $A_{U,t,t-1}$ and $M_{U,t,t-1}$ are error (or unexplained) components defined by:

$$(50) \qquad A_{U,t,t-1} \equiv \frac{AA_{t,t-1}}{A_{t,t-1}}$$

$$(51) \qquad M_{U,t,t-1} \equiv \frac{MM_{t,t-1}}{M_{t,t-1}}.$$

9. Labor Productivity vs. Total Factor Productivity

While labor productivity remains the concept of choice when it comes to the public debate, most economists prefer to think in terms of total factor productivity. The measure of total factor productivity treats all inputs symmetrically. In the production function context, it can be defined as the increase in output that is not explained by increases in input quantities. Put differently, it is the increase in output made possible by technological change, holding all inputs constant. One state-of-the art definition of total factor productivity, $Y_{T,t,t-1}$, is drawn from the work of Diewert and Morrison (1986):[16]

$$(52) \qquad Y_{T,t,t-1} \equiv \left\{ \frac{y(v_{L,t-1}, v_{K,t-1}, t)}{y(v_{L,t-1}, v_{K,t-1}, t-1)} \cdot \frac{y(v_{L,t}, v_{K,t}, t)}{y(v_{L,t}, v_{K,t}, t-1)} \right\}^{1/2}.$$

In view of the definition of $g_L(\cdot)$, clearly $Y_{T,t,t-1}$ as given by (52) is in fact identical to $A_{T,t,t-1}$ as defined by (37). That is, total factor productivity in this model is equal to the contribution of technological change when explaining the average productivity of labor. The average productivity of labor will exceed total factor productivity to the extent that capital deepening occurs ($A_{V,t,t-1} > 1$).

10. Measurement

Consider first the case of the Cobb-Douglas production function. It is straightforward to show that:

[16] It too can be thought of as the geometric average of Laspeyres-like and Paasche-like measures.

$$(53)\quad A_{V,t,t-1} = M_{V,t,t-1} = \left(\frac{v_{K,t}}{v_{L,t}} \bigg/ \frac{v_{K,t-1}}{v_{L,t-1}} \right)^{\beta_K}$$

$$(54)\quad A_{T,t,t-1} = M_{T,t,t-1} = e^{\mu}.$$

It is interesting to note that, since $e^{\mu} = e^{(1-\beta_K)\mu_L} = e^{\beta_K \mu_K}$, it does not matter for (54) to hold whether technological change is Hicks-neutral, Harrod-neutral, or Solow-neutral, or more general form.[17]

Recall that we report in table 1, first column, the parameter estimates of the Cobb-Douglas production function (21). In table 2 we show annual estimates of the decomposition of the average and marginal productivity of labor. The factor endowments and the technological change components are the same in both tables, but the observed values of average and marginal productivity differ, so that the corresponding error terms differ as well. According to table 2, labor productivity has increased by close to 1.3% per annum over the sample period. Technological progress accounted for the bulk of the increase, with a contribution of about one percentage point. Capital deepening added about a quarter of a percentage point on average.

Consider next the translog functional form. Introducing (30) into (34) and (37), we find that:

$$(55)\quad \begin{aligned} \ln A_{V,t,t-1} &= \left(\beta_K + \frac{1}{2}\phi_{KT}(2t-1) \right) \left(\ln \frac{v_{K,t}}{v_{L,t}} - \ln \frac{v_{K,t-1}}{v_{L,t-1}} \right) \\ &+ \frac{1}{2}\phi_{KK} \left[\left(\ln \frac{v_{K,t}}{v_{L,t}} \right)^2 - \left(\ln \frac{v_{K,t-1}}{v_{L,t-1}} \right)^2 \right] \end{aligned}$$

$$(56)\quad \ln A_{T,t,t-1} = \beta_T + \frac{1}{2}\phi_{KT} \left(\ln \frac{v_{K,t}}{v_{L,t}} + \ln \frac{v_{K,t-1}}{v_{L,t-1}} \right) + \frac{1}{2}\phi_{TT}(2t-1).$$

For the marginal productivity indexes, we can apply (42) and (44) after having introduced (31) into (43) and (45) to get:

$$(57)\quad S_{V,t,t-1} \equiv \sqrt{ \frac{1-\beta_K - \phi_{KK} \ln \frac{v_{K,t}}{v_{L,t}} - \phi_{KT}(t-1)}{1-\beta_K - \phi_{KK} \ln \frac{v_{K,t-1}}{v_{L,t-1}} - \phi_{KT}(t-1)} \cdot \frac{1-\beta_K - \phi_{KK} \ln \frac{v_{K,t}}{v_{L,t}} - \phi_{KT} t}{1-\beta_K - \phi_{KK} \ln \frac{v_{K,t-1}}{v_{L,t-1}} - \phi_{KT} t} }$$

$$(58)\quad S_{T,t,t-1} \equiv \sqrt{ \frac{1-\beta_K - \phi_{KK} \ln \frac{v_{K,t-1}}{v_{L,t-1}} - \phi_{KT} t}{1-\beta_K - \phi_{KK} \ln \frac{v_{K,t-1}}{v_{L,t-1}} - \phi_{KT}(t-1)} \cdot \frac{1-\beta_K - \phi_{KK} \ln \frac{v_{K,t}}{v_{L,t}} - \phi_{KT} t}{1-\beta_K - \phi_{KK} \ln \frac{v_{K,t}}{v_{L,t}} - \phi_{KT}(t-1)} }.$$

[17] See (21)–(23) above.

Table 2. Decompositions of the 2-Input Cobb-Douglas Production Function

	Average productivity of labor				Marginal productivity of labor			
Year	$AA_{t,t-1}$ (1)	$A_{V,t,t-1}$ (2)	$A_{T,t,t-1}$ (3)	$A_{U,t,t-1}$ (4)	$MM_{t,t-1}$ (5)	$M_{V,t,t-1}$ (6)	$M_{T,t,t-1}$ (7)	$M_{U,t,t-1}$ (8)
1971	1.0325	1.0082	1.0099	1.0140	1.0210	1.0082	1.0099	1.0028
1972	1.0182	0.9999	1.0099	1.0083	1.0126	0.9999	1.0099	1.0028
1973	1.0186	0.9996	1.0099	1.0091	1.0112	0.9996	1.0099	1.0018
1974	0.9901	1.0071	1.0099	0.9736	1.0108	1.0071	1.0099	0.9939
1975	1.0281	1.0149	1.0099	1.0031	1.0200	1.0149	1.0099	0.9952
1976	1.0214	0.9976	1.0099	1.0138	1.0193	0.9976	1.0099	1.0117
1977	1.0121	0.9989	1.0099	1.0033	1.0042	0.9989	1.0099	0.9955
1978	1.0076	0.9965	1.0099	1.0013	1.0029	0.9965	1.0099	0.9966
1979	1.0020	1.0013	1.0099	0.9910	1.0088	1.0013	1.0099	0.9977
1980	1.0018	1.0087	1.0099	0.9835	1.0203	1.0087	1.0099	1.0016
1981	1.0199	1.0058	1.0099	1.0041	1.0126	1.0058	1.0099	0.9969
1982	1.0064	1.0127	1.0099	0.9841	1.0185	1.0127	1.0099	0.9959
1983	1.0251	1.0010	1.0099	1.0141	1.0120	1.0010	1.0099	1.0011
1984	1.0174	0.9933	1.0099	1.0143	0.9936	0.9933	1.0099	0.9906
1985	1.0107	1.0007	1.0099	1.0001	1.0165	1.0007	1.0099	1.0058
1986	1.0238	1.0051	1.0099	1.0087	1.0405	1.0051	1.0099	1.0251
1987	1.0025	0.9987	1.0099	0.9940	0.9962	0.9987	1.0099	0.9878
1988	1.0125	0.9991	1.0099	1.0036	1.0011	0.9991	1.0099	0.9923
1989	1.0055	0.9987	1.0099	0.9970	1.0070	0.9987	1.0099	0.9985
1990	1.0119	1.0047	1.0099	0.9973	1.0182	1.0047	1.0099	1.0035
1991	1.0156	1.0103	1.0099	0.9954	1.0219	1.0103	1.0099	1.0016
1992	1.0230	1.0027	1.0099	1.0103	1.0278	1.0027	1.0099	1.0150
1993	1.0009	0.9985	1.0099	0.9927	0.9963	0.9985	1.0099	0.9881
1994	1.0050	0.9962	1.0099	0.9990	1.0001	0.9962	1.0099	0.9941
1995	1.0014	0.9992	1.0099	0.9924	0.9908	0.9992	1.0099	0.9819
1996	1.0199	1.0028	1.0099	1.0072	1.0095	1.0028	1.0099	0.9969
1997	1.0112	0.9984	1.0099	1.0029	1.0041	0.9984	1.0099	0.9958
1998	1.0177	1.0014	1.0099	1.0064	1.0261	1.0014	1.0099	1.0147
1999	1.0144	1.0011	1.0099	1.0034	1.0175	1.0011	1.0099	1.0065
2000	1.0236	1.0047	1.0099	1.0089	1.0323	1.0047	1.0099	1.0174
2001	1.0154	1.0104	1.0099	0.9951	1.0246	1.0104	1.0099	1.0042
1971-2001	**1.0134**	**1.0025**	**1.0099**	**1.0010**	**1.0128**	**1.0025**	**1.0099**	**1.0004**

Recall that parameter estimates of the TP-flexible translog production function are reported in table 1, column 3. A decomposition of the average and marginal productivity indexes based on the translog functional form is provided in columns 1-4 and 5-8 of table 3. Remember that $A_{T,t,t-1}$ in table 3 can also be interpreted as a model-based measure of total factor productivity. The decomposition of the average productivity index is similar to the one obtained with the Cobb-Douglas, with total factor productivity accounting for about four fifths of the increase in average labor productivity. The decomposition of the marginal productivity index, on the other hand, shows a somewhat different picture: technological progress accounts for less than two thirds of real wage increases with capital deepening now playing a larger role. The reason has to do with the estimate of the elasticity of complementarity, which is significantly larger than one. We find that by restricting this elasticity to be unity, the Cobb-Douglas functional form leads to an underestimation of the impact of capital deepening on the marginal product of labor.

11. The Average Productivity of Labor: An Index Number Approach

To make the decomposition (55)–(58) operational one needs econometric estimates of the parameters of the translog production function. This is indeed how we were able to construct the figures reported in columns 1-4 and 5-8 of table 3. It turns out, however, that, as long as the true production function is translog, the decomposition of the average productivity of labor can also be obtained on the basis of knowledge of the data alone; that is, without needing to know the individual parameters of the production function.

Table 3. Decompositions for a 2-Input Translog Production Function

	Average productivity of labor				Marginal productivity of labor				Average productivity of labor: index number approach		
	$AA_{t,t-1}$	$A_{V,t,t-1}$	$A_{T,t,t-1}$	$A_{U,t,t-1}$	$MM_{t,t-1}$	$M_{V,t,t-1}$	$M_{T,t,t-1}$	$M_{U,t,t-1}$	$AA_{t,t-1}$	$A_{V,t,t-1}$	$A_{T,t,t-1}$
Year	(1)	(2)	(3)	(4)	(5)	(6)	(7)	(8)	(9)	(10)	(11)
1971	1.0325	1.0081	1.0088	1.0152	1.0210	1.0144	1.0065	1.0000	1.0325	1.0081	1.0243
1972	1.0182	0.9999	1.0089	1.0093	1.0126	0.9999	1.0066	1.0061	1.0182	0.9999	1.0183
1973	1.0186	0.9996	1.0090	1.0100	1.0112	0.9993	1.0066	1.0053	1.0186	0.9996	1.0191
1974	0.9901	1.0070	1.0091	0.9744	1.0108	1.0125	1.0067	0.9917	0.9901	1.0070	0.9833
1975	1.0281	1.0145	1.0092	1.0041	1.0200	1.0260	1.0069	0.9874	1.0281	1.0145	1.0135
1976	1.0214	0.9977	1.0094	1.0142	1.0193	0.9959	1.0070	1.0163	1.0214	0.9977	1.0238
1977	1.0121	0.9989	1.0094	1.0037	1.0042	0.9981	1.0071	0.9991	1.0121	0.9989	1.0132
1978	1.0076	0.9966	1.0095	1.0016	1.0029	0.9939	1.0071	1.0019	1.0076	0.9966	1.0112
1979	1.0020	1.0013	1.0096	0.9913	1.0088	1.0023	1.0072	0.9993	1.0020	1.0013	1.0007
1980	1.0018	1.0087	1.0097	0.9837	1.0203	1.0154	1.0073	0.9975	1.0018	1.0087	0.9934
1981	1.0199	1.0057	1.0098	1.0043	1.0126	1.0102	1.0074	0.9950	1.0199	1.0057	1.0142
1982	1.0064	1.0123	1.0099	0.9843	1.0185	1.0221	1.0076	0.9890	1.0064	1.0123	0.9943
1983	1.0251	1.0010	1.0100	1.0139	1.0120	1.0017	1.0077	1.0026	1.0251	1.0010	1.0241
1984	1.0174	0.9934	1.0101	1.0139	0.9936	0.9884	1.0077	0.9976	1.0174	0.9934	1.0243
1985	1.0107	1.0007	1.0102	0.9998	1.0165	1.0013	1.0078	1.0073	1.0107	1.0007	1.0099
1986	1.0238	1.0051	1.0103	1.0083	1.0405	1.0090	1.0079	1.0232	1.0238	1.0051	1.0186
1987	1.0025	0.9987	1.0104	0.9935	0.9962	0.9977	1.0080	0.9906	1.0025	0.9987	1.0038
1988	1.0125	0.9991	1.0104	1.0030	1.0011	0.9984	1.0080	0.9948	1.0125	0.9991	1.0135
1989	1.0055	0.9987	1.0105	0.9964	1.0070	0.9977	1.0081	1.0012	1.0055	0.9987	1.0069
1990	1.0119	1.0047	1.0106	0.9966	1.0182	1.0084	1.0082	1.0015	1.0119	1.0047	1.0071
1991	1.0156	1.0104	1.0107	0.9946	1.0219	1.0184	1.0083	0.9952	1.0156	1.0104	1.0053
1992	1.0230	1.0027	1.0108	1.0094	1.0278	1.0048	1.0084	1.0143	1.0230	1.0027	1.0203
1993	1.0009	0.9985	1.0109	0.9917	0.9963	0.9973	1.0085	0.9906	1.0009	0.9984	1.0024
1994	1.0050	0.9962	1.0110	0.9979	1.0001	0.9933	1.0086	0.9983	1.0050	0.9962	1.0088
1995	1.0014	0.9992	1.0110	0.9912	0.9908	0.9986	1.0086	0.9837	1.0014	0.9992	1.0021
1996	1.0199	1.0028	1.0111	1.0059	1.0095	1.0050	1.0087	0.9958	1.0199	1.0028	1.0170
1997	1.0112	0.9984	1.0112	1.0016	1.0041	0.9972	1.0088	0.9982	1.0112	0.9984	1.0129
1998	1.0177	1.0014	1.0113	1.0049	1.0261	1.0025	1.0089	1.0146	1.0177	1.0014	1.0162
1999	1.0144	1.0012	1.0114	1.0019	1.0175	1.0020	1.0089	1.0065	1.0144	1.0012	1.0132
2000	1.0236	1.0049	1.0115	1.0071	1.0323	1.0086	1.0090	1.0143	1.0236	1.0049	1.0187
2001	1.0154	1.0107	1.0116	0.9931	1.0246	1.0188	1.0092	0.9965	1.0153	1.0107	1.0048
1971-2001	**1.0134**	**1.0025**	**1.0102**	**1.0006**	**1.0128**	**1.0044**	**1.0078**	**1.0005**	**1.0134**	**1.0025**	**1.0109**

Following Diewert and Morrison (1986), one can show that, as long as the true production function is given by (30), $A_{T,t,t-1}$ defined by (37) – or, equivalently, $Y_{T,t,t-1}$ defined by (52) – can be computed as:

$$(59)\quad A_{T,t,t-1} = \frac{Y_{t,t-1}}{V_{t,t-1}},$$

where $Y_{t,t-1}$ is the index of real GDP:

$$(60)\quad Y_{t,t-1} \equiv \frac{y_t}{y_{t-1}},$$

and $V_{t,t-1}$ is a Törnqvist index of input quantities:

$$(61)\quad V_{t,t-1} \equiv \exp\left[\sum_{i\in\{L,K\}} \frac{1}{2}(s_{i,t} + s_{i,t-1})\ln\frac{v_{i,t}}{v_{i,t-1}}\right],$$

where $s_{K,t}$ $(= 1 - s_{L,t})$ is the income share of capital. Hence the following gives a complete decomposition of real GDP growth:

$$(62)\quad Y_{t,t-1} = Y_{L,t,t-1} \cdot Y_{K,t,t-1} \cdot A_{T,t,t-1},$$

where

$$(63)\quad Y_{L,t,t-1} \equiv \exp\left[\frac{1}{2}(s_{L,t} + s_{L,t-1})\ln\frac{v_{L,t}}{v_{L,t-1}}\right]$$

$$(64)\quad Y_{K,t,t-1} \equiv \exp\left[\frac{1}{2}(s_{K,t} + s_{K,t-1})\ln\frac{v_{K,t}}{v_{K,t-1}}\right].$$

$Y_{L,t,t-1}$ and $Y_{K,t,t-1}$ can be interpreted as the contributions of labor and capital to real GDP growth.

Next, let $L_{t,t-1}$ be the labor input index:

$$(65)\quad L_{t,t-1} \equiv \frac{v_{L,t}}{v_{L,t-1}}.$$

It follows from (46) that:

$$(66)\quad AA_{t,t-1} \equiv \frac{Y_{t,t-1}}{L_{t,t-1}}.$$

Making use of (62) – (64), we get:

$$(67)\quad AA_{t,t-1} = A_{V,t,t-1} \cdot A_{T,t,t-1},$$

where

$$(68)\quad A_{V,t,t-1} \equiv \exp\left[\frac{1}{2}(s_{K,t}+s_{K,t-1})\left(\ln\frac{v_{K,t}}{v_{L,t}}-\ln\frac{v_{K,t-1}}{v_{L,t-1}}\right)\right].$$

We show in columns 9-11 of table 3 the decomposition of the average productivity of labor based on (67). This decomposition does not require knowledge of the parameters of the translog function.[18] This is obviously very convenient. On the other hand, as indicated by (59), the total factor productivity term ($A_{T,t,t-1}$) is obtained as a Solow residual. Hence, unlike what is done in (48), it is not possible to split it up into a secular component and an error term.[19] Note that the estimates shown in columns 9-11 of table 3 are very similar to those shown in columns 1-4 of the table, except obviously for the total factor productivity term that now incorporates the unexplained component.

12. Domestic Real Value Added

A production function framework is limiting since it requires the number of outputs to be one.[20] Moreover, the production function approach makes it impossible to take into account imports and exports. In what follows, we therefore opt for the description of the aggregate technology by a real value added (or real income) function, such as the one proposed by Kohli (2004a) that is based on the GDP function approach to modeling the production sector of an open economy.[21] We assume that the technology has two outputs, domestic (nontraded) goods (*D*) and exports (*X*) and three inputs: labor (*L*), capital (*K*), and imports (*M*). Treating imports as a variable input is equivalent to treating imports as a negative output.

We denote the output quantities (including imports) by y_i and their prices by p_i, $i \in \{D, X, M\}$. Furthermore, we denote the inverse of the terms of trade by q ($q \equiv p_M/p_X$) and the relative price of tradables vs. nontradables by e ($e \equiv p_X/p_D$). Note that for given terms of trade, a change in e can be interpreted as a change in the real exchange rate, an increase in e being equivalent to a real depreciation of the home currency. Let π_t be nominal GDP:

$$(69)\quad \pi_t \equiv p_{D,t}y_{D,t} + p_{X,t}y_{X,t} - p_{M,t}y_{M,t} = p_t y_t .$$

Domestic real value added (z_t) – or real gross domestic income (GDI) – is defined as nominal GDP deflated by the price of domestic output:

$$(70)\quad z_t \equiv \frac{\pi_t}{p_{D,t}} = y_{D,t} + e_t y_{X,t} - e_t q_t y_{M,t} .$$

---

[18] This index number approach essentially boils down to using the observed share of labor (8) instead of the fitted one as given by (31). See Kohli (1990) for a further discussion of the differences between the two approaches.

[19] An index number approach is not feasible for the marginal productivity index because, even if the true production function is translog, the first-order condition is not; as shown by (31), it is linear in logarithms, rather than quadratic.

[20] Alternatively, one must assume that outputs are globally separable from domestic inputs.

[21] See Kohli (1978) and Woodland (1982).

Let T_t be the production possibilities set at time t. We assume that T_t is a convex cone. The aggregate technology can be described by a real valued added function defined as follows:

$$(71) \quad z(q_t, e_t, v_{K,t}, v_{L,t}, t) \equiv \max_{y_D, y_X, y_M} \left\{ \begin{array}{l} y_{D,t} + e_t y_{X,t} - e_t q_t y_{M,t} : \\ (y_{D,t}, y_{X,t}, y_{M,t}, v_{K,t}, v_{L,t}) \in T_t \end{array} \right\}.$$

In this context, the *average* real value added of labor ($h_{L,t}$) can be expressed as:

$$(72) \quad h_{L,t} = h_L(q_t, e_t, v_{K,t}, v_{L,t}, t) \equiv \frac{z(q_t, e_t, v_{K,t}, v_{L,t}, t)}{v_{L,t}},$$

whereas as the *marginal* real value added of labor ($z_{L,t}$) is given by:

$$(73) \quad z_{L,t} = z_L(q_t, e_t, v_{K,t}, v_{L,t}, t) \equiv \frac{\partial z(q_t, e_t, v_{K,t}, v_{L,t}, t)}{\partial v_{L,t}}.$$

The average and marginal productivity indexes are now as follows:

$$(74) \quad A_{t,t-1} \equiv \frac{h_L(q_t, e_t, v_{K,t}, v_{L,t}, t)}{h_L(q_{t-1}, e_{t-1}, v_{K,t-1}, v_{L,t-1}, t-1)}$$

$$(75) \quad M_{t,t-1} \equiv \frac{z_L(q_t, e_t, v_{K,t}, v_{L,t}, t)}{z_L(q_{t-1}, e_{t-1}, v_{K,t-1}, v_{L,t-1}, t-1)}.$$

The translog representation of the real value added function is as follows:

$$(76) \quad \begin{aligned} \ln z_t &= \alpha_0 + \alpha_Q \ln q_t + \alpha_E \ln e_t + \beta_K \ln v_{K,t} + (1-\beta_K) \ln v_{L,t} \\ &+ \frac{1}{2}\gamma_{QQ}(\ln q_t)^2 + \gamma_{QE} \ln q_t \ln e_t + \frac{1}{2}\gamma_{EE}(\ln e_t)^2 \\ &+ \frac{1}{2}\phi_{KK}(\ln v_{K,t} - \ln v_{L,t})^2 + (\delta_{QK} \ln q_t + \delta_{EK} \ln e_t)(\ln v_{K,t} - \ln v_{L,t}) \\ &+ (\delta_{QT} \ln q_t + \delta_{ET} \ln e_t)t + \phi_{KT}(\ln v_{K,t} - \ln v_{L,t})t + \beta_T t + \frac{1}{2}\phi_{TT} t^2. \end{aligned}$$

Logarithmic differentiation yields the following system of equations:[22]

$$(77) \quad \frac{\partial \ln z(\cdot)}{\partial \ln q_t} = -s_{M,t} = \alpha_Q + \gamma_{QQ} \ln q_t + \gamma_{QE} \ln e_t + \delta_{QK}(\ln v_{K,t} - \ln v_{L,t}) + \delta_{QT} t$$

$$(78) \quad \frac{\partial \ln z(\cdot)}{\partial \ln e_t} = s_{B,t} = \alpha_E + \gamma_{QE} \ln q_t + \gamma_{EE} \ln e_t + \delta_{EK}(\ln v_{K,t} - \ln v_{L,t}) + \delta_{ET} t$$

$$(79) \quad \frac{\partial \ln z(\cdot)}{\partial \ln v_{L,t}} = s_{L,t} = 1 - \beta_K - \delta_{QK} \ln q_t - \delta_{EK} \ln e_t - \phi_{KK}(\ln v_{K,t} - \ln v_{L,t}) - \phi_{KT} t$$

---

[22] See Kohli (2004a).

$$(80) \qquad \frac{\partial \ln z(\cdot)}{\partial t} \equiv \mu_t = \beta_T + \delta_{QT} \ln q_t + \delta_{ET} \ln e_t + \phi_{KT} (\ln v_{K,t} - \ln v_{L,t}) + \phi_{TT} \, t,$$

where s_M is the GDP share of imports ($s_M \equiv p_M y_M / \pi$), s_B is the trade balance relative to GDP ($s_B \equiv (p_X y_X - p_M y_M)/\pi$), s_L is, as before, the GDP share of labor, and μ is again the instantaneous rate of technological change.

Parameter estimates, obtained from the joint estimation of equations (76)–(80), are reported in the last column of table 1.[23] It is noteworthy that the labor share now depends on four items. Besides relative factor endowments and the passage of time, the terms of trade and the real exchange rate may influence the share of labor as well now. A deterioration in the terms of trade (an increase in *q*) will tend to lower the share of labor as indicated by the positive estimate of δ_{QK}. Similarly, a real appreciation of the home currency (a fall in *e*) will tend to reduce s_L in view of the negative estimate of δ_{EK}. In both these cases, the marginal product of labor would, *ceteris paribus*, increase less rapidly than its average product.

13. Average Productivity in the Open Economy

Proceeding along the same lines as in section 8, we can define the following index to capture the contribution of changes in the terms of trade to the average productivity of labor:

$$(81) \qquad A_{Q,t,t-1} \equiv \left\{ \frac{h_L(q_t, e_{t-1}, v_{K,t-1}, v_{L,t-1}, t-1)}{h_L(q_{t-1}, e_{t-1}, v_{K,t-1}, v_{L,t-1}, t-1)} \cdot \frac{h_L(q_t, e_t, v_{K,t}, v_{L,t}, t)}{h_L(q_{t-1}, e_t, v_{K,t}, v_{L,t}, t)} \right\}^{1/2}.$$

Similarly, we can identify the contribution of changes in the real exchange rate as:

$$(82) \qquad A_{E,t,t-1} \equiv \left\{ \frac{h_L(q_{t-1}, e_t, v_{K,t-1}, v_{L,t-1}, t-1)}{h_L(q_{t-1}, e_{t-1}, v_{K,t-1}, v_{L,t-1}, t-1)} \cdot \frac{h_L(q_t, e_t, v_{K,t}, v_{L,t}, t)}{h_L(q_t, e_{t-1}, v_{K,t}, v_{L,t}, t)} \right\}^{1/2},$$

the contribution of changes in domestic factor endowments:

$$(83) \qquad A_{V,t,t-1} \equiv \left\{ \frac{h_L(q_{t-1}, e_{t-1}, v_{K,t}, v_{L,t}, t-1)}{h_L(q_{t-1}, e_{t-1}, v_{K,t-1}, v_{L,t-1}, t-1)} \cdot \frac{h_L(q_t, e_t, v_{K,t}, v_{L,t}, t)}{h_L(q_t, e_t, v_{K,t-1}, v_{L,t-1}, t)} \right\}^{1/2},$$

and, finally, the contribution of technological progress:

$$(84) \qquad A_{T,t,t-1} \equiv \left\{ \frac{h_L(q_{t-1}, e_{t-1}, v_{K,t-1}, v_{L,t-1}, t)}{h_L(q_{t-1}, e_{t-1}, v_{K,t-1}, v_{L,t-1}, t-1)} \cdot \frac{h_L(q_t, e_t, v_{K,t}, v_{L,t}, t)}{h_L(q_t, e_t, v_{K,t}, v_{L,t}, t-1)} \right\}^{1/2}.$$

Assuming that the real value added function is given by (76) and that its parameters are known, it is straightforward to compute the values of (81)–(84). Moreover, it can easily be

[23] The estimation method again is the non-linear iterative algorithm for estimating Zellner's seemingly unrelated equations as implemented in TSP.

shown that these four effects together give a complete decomposition of the average productivity of labor as defined by (74):

(85) $$A_{t,t-1} = A_{Q,t,t-1} \cdot A_{E,t,t-1} \cdot A_{V,t,t-1} \cdot A_{T,t,t-1}.$$

Moreover, if we seek to explain the *observed* increase in average labor productivity, we get:

(86) $$AA_{t,t-1} = A_{Q,t,t-1} \cdot A_{E,t,t-1} \cdot A_{V,t,t-1} \cdot A_{T,t,t-1} \cdot A_{U,t,t-1},$$

where $AA_{t,t-1}$ is now defined as:

(87) $$AA_{t,t-1} \equiv \frac{z_t / v_{L,t}}{z_{t-1} / v_{L,t-1}},$$

and $A_{U,t,t-1}$ is the unexplained component of $AA_{t,t-1}$:

(88) $$A_{U,t,t-1} = \frac{AA_{t,t-1}}{A_{t,t-1}}.$$

If the true real value added function is translog it is possible to compute (81)–(84) based on the data alone, without knowledge of the parameters of (76). Indeed, one can show that:[24]

(89) $$A_{Q,t,t-1} = \exp\left[\frac{1}{2}(-s_{M,t} - s_{M,t-1}) \ln \frac{q_t}{q_{t-1}}\right]$$

(90) $$A_{E,t,t-1} = \exp\left[\frac{1}{2}(s_{B,t} + s_{B,t-1}) \ln \frac{e_t}{e_{t-1}}\right]$$

(91) $$A_{V,t,t-1} \equiv \exp\left[\frac{1}{2}(s_{K,t} + s_{K,t-1})\left(\ln \frac{v_{K,t}}{v_{L,t}} - \ln \frac{v_{K,t-1}}{v_{L,t-1}}\right)\right]$$

(92) $$A_{T,t,t-1} \equiv \frac{Y_{t,t-1}}{V_{t,t-1}},$$

so that:

(93) $$AA_{t,t-1} = A_{Q,t,t-1} \cdot A_{E,t,t-1} \cdot A_{V,t,t-1} \cdot A_{T,t,t-1}.$$

A decomposition of the average productivity of labor according to (86) and (93) is reported in columns 1-6 and 7-11 of table 4, respectively.

14. Accounting for Changes in the Share of Labor

In the next section, we will focus on the decomposition of the *marginal* productivity index, but first we will briefly turn our attention to the behavior of the labor share. Indeed, we

[24] See Kohli (2004a).

will follow here essentially the same route as in the production function context; that is, we will exploit the link between the marginal and average productivity measures via a labor share index.

There is one key difference compared to the treatment in section 8, however. A decomposition such as (41), which is exact independently of the underlying functional form, only holds if the number of elements on the right-hand side is two. However, if the underlying functional form is translog, the decomposition is exact even if the number of components is larger; see (85), for instance. But even if the underlying function is translog, as here, the first-order conditions are not. As shown by (77)–(80), the share equations are linear in logarithms. Hence the best we can hope for is a linear approximation of the decomposition of the marginal productivity and labor share indices. With this in mind, we will proceed as in sections 8 and 9.[25]

In the context of the real value-added function, the labor share index can be defined as:

$$(94)\quad S_{t,t-1} \equiv \frac{s_L(q_t, e_t, v_{K,t}, v_{L,t}, t)}{s_L(q_{t-1}, e_{t-1}, v_{K,t-1}, v_{L,t-1}, t-1)},$$

where $s_L(q_t, e_t, v_{K,t}, v_{L,t}, t)$ is given by the right-hand side of (79). This index can easily be calculated once the parameters of the real value-added function are known. The same holds true for the following four indices that identify the contributions of the terms of trade, the real exchange rate, the relative factor endowments and the passage of time:

$$(95)\quad S_{Q,t,t-1} \equiv \left\{ \frac{s_L(q_t, e_{t-1}, v_{K,t-1}, v_{L,t-1}, t-1)}{s_L(q_{t-1}, e_{t-1}, v_{K,t-1}, v_{L,t-1}, t-1)} \cdot \frac{s_L(q_t, e_t, v_{K,t}, v_{L,t}, t)}{s_L(q_{t-1}, e_t, v_{K,t}, v_{L,t}, t)} \right\}^{1/2}$$

$$(96)\quad S_{E,t,t-1} \equiv \left\{ \frac{s_L(q_{t-1}, e_t, v_{K,t-1}, v_{L,t-1}, t-1)}{s_L(q_{t-1}, e_{t-1}, v_{K,t-1}, v_{L,t-1}, t-1)} \cdot \frac{s_L(q_t, e_t, v_{K,t}, v_{L,t}, t)}{s_L(q_t, e_{t-1}, v_{K,t}, v_{L,t}, t)} \right\}^{1/2}$$

$$(97)\quad S_{V,t,t-1} \equiv \left\{ \frac{s_L(q_{t-1}, e_{t-1}, v_{K,t}, v_{L,t}, t-1)}{s_L(q_{t-1}, e_{t-1}, v_{K,t-1}, v_{L,t-1}, t-1)} \cdot \frac{s_L(q_t, e_t, v_{K,t}, v_{L,t}, t)}{s_L(q_t, e_t, v_{K,t-1}, v_{L,t-1}, t)} \right\}^{1/2}$$

$$(98)\quad S_{T,t,t-1} \equiv \left\{ \frac{s_L(q_{t-1}, e_{t-1}, v_{K,t-1}, v_{L,t-1}, t)}{s_L(q_{t-1}, e_{t-1}, v_{K,t-1}, v_{L,t-1}, t-1)} \cdot \frac{s_L(q_t, e_t, v_{K,t}, v_{L,t}, t)}{s_L(q_t, e_t, v_{K,t}, v_{L,t}, t-1)} \right\}^{1/2}.$$

An approximation to $S_{t,t-1}$ is given by the following:[26]

$$(99)\quad S_{t,t-1} \cong S_{Q,t,t-1} \cdot S_{E,t,t-1} \cdot S_{V,t,t-1} \cdot S_{T,t,t-1}.$$

We next define the *observed* labor share index:

$$(100)\quad SS_{t,t-1} \equiv \frac{x_{L,t} w_{L,t} / \pi_t}{x_{L,t-1} w_{L,t-1} / \pi_{t-1}}.$$

---

[25] See Sfreddo (2001) for a further discussion and for three alternative decompositions of the first-order conditions.

[26] See Sfreddo (2001); we have verified that the residual is almost zero.

A complete decomposition of the change in the labor share is hence given by:

$$(101)\quad SS_{t,t-1} \cong S_{Q,t,t-1} \cdot S_{E,t,t-1} \cdot S_{V,t,t-1} \cdot S_{T,t,t-1} \cdot S_{U,t,t-1},$$

where $S_{U,t,t-1}$ is the unexplained component which can be represented as:

$$(102)\quad S_{U,t,t-1} = \frac{SS_{t,t-1}}{S_{t,t-1}}.$$

Table 4. Decompositions for a 2-Input, 3-Output Translog Real Domestic Value Added Function

	Average productivity of labor						Average productivity of labor: index number approach				
Year	$AA_{t,t-1}$ (1)	$A_{Q,t,t-1}$ (2)	$A_{E,t,t-1}$ (3)	$A_{V,t,t-1}$ (4)	$A_{T,t,t-1}$ (5)	$A_{U,t,t-1}$ (6)	$AA_{t,t-1}$ (7)	$A_{Q,t,t-1}$ (8)	$A_{E,t,t-1}$ (9)	$A_{V,t,t-1}$ (10)	$A_{T,t,t-1}$ (11)
1971	1.0310	0.9986	1.0000	1.0081	1.0098	1.0143	1.0310	0.9986	1.0000	1.0079	1.0229
1972	1.0161	0.9979	1.0001	0.9999	1.0097	1.0084	1.0161	0.9979	1.0001	0.9999	1.0162
1973	1.0164	0.9980	0.9997	0.9996	1.0097	1.0093	1.0164	0.9980	0.9998	0.9996	1.0168
1974	0.9792	0.9892	0.9998	1.0071	1.0096	0.9737	0.9792	0.9890	0.9999	1.0070	0.9724
1975	1.0298	1.0016	1.0000	1.0144	1.0097	1.0038	1.0298	1.0016	1.0000	1.0144	1.0151
1976	1.0214	1.0001	1.0000	0.9978	1.0098	1.0136	1.0214	1.0001	0.9999	0.9977	1.0238
1977	1.0083	0.9962	1.0001	0.9989	1.0098	1.0034	1.0083	0.9961	1.0002	0.9989	1.0094
1978	1.0068	0.9991	1.0001	0.9966	1.0097	1.0014	1.0068	0.9991	1.0001	0.9965	1.0104
1979	0.9976	0.9959	0.9999	1.0013	1.0097	0.9908	0.9976	0.9959	0.9997	1.0013	0.9963
1980	0.9894	0.9882	1.0000	1.0089	1.0095	0.9831	0.9894	0.9876	1.0000	1.0085	0.9810
1981	1.0219	1.0018	1.0002	1.0059	1.0094	1.0044	1.0219	1.0019	1.0001	1.0056	1.0163
1982	1.0105	1.0038	1.0008	1.0124	1.0096	0.9841	1.0105	1.0038	1.0003	1.0121	0.9984
1983	1.0295	1.0042	1.0004	1.0009	1.0099	1.0139	1.0295	1.0040	1.0003	1.0009	1.0286
1984	1.0198	1.0018	1.0003	0.9935	1.0101	1.0141	1.0197	1.0018	1.0005	0.9933	1.0267
1985	1.0128	1.0006	1.0007	1.0007	1.0101	1.0007	1.0128	1.0006	1.0015	1.0008	1.0121
1986	1.0233	0.9985	1.0006	1.0050	1.0101	1.0089	1.0233	0.9984	1.0011	1.0051	1.0181
1987	0.9995	0.9968	1.0001	0.9987	1.0101	0.9938	0.9995	0.9967	1.0002	0.9987	1.0007
1988	1.0124	1.0004	0.9997	0.9991	1.0102	1.0031	1.0124	1.0004	0.9995	0.9991	1.0134
1989	1.0052	0.9993	1.0003	0.9987	1.0103	0.9967	1.0052	0.9993	1.0003	0.9987	1.0065
1990	1.0102	0.9978	1.0006	1.0048	1.0103	0.9968	1.0102	0.9979	1.0004	1.0047	1.0054
1991	1.0178	1.0021	1.0004	1.0104	1.0104	0.9945	1.0178	1.0020	1.0002	1.0103	1.0074
1992	1.0227	0.9995	1.0006	1.0027	1.0105	1.0093	1.0227	0.9995	1.0001	1.0027	1.0200
1993	1.0020	1.0010	1.0005	0.9985	1.0106	0.9916	1.0020	1.0010	1.0002	0.9985	1.0036
1994	1.0053	1.0003	1.0002	0.9962	1.0107	0.9981	1.0053	1.0002	1.0001	0.9962	1.0091
1995	1.0009	0.9996	1.0000	0.9992	1.0107	0.9915	1.0009	0.9996	1.0000	0.9992	1.0017
1996	1.0210	1.0007	1.0006	1.0028	1.0108	1.0059	1.0210	1.0007	1.0004	1.0029	1.0180
1997	1.0142	1.0026	1.0006	0.9984	1.0109	1.0016	1.0142	1.0026	1.0004	0.9983	1.0159
1998	1.0223	1.0042	1.0005	1.0014	1.0111	1.0050	1.0223	1.0041	1.0004	1.0014	1.0208
1999	1.0137	0.9988	1.0004	1.0012	1.0112	1.0021	1.0137	0.9988	1.0005	1.0012	1.0126
2000	1.0196	0.9960	1.0002	1.0049	1.0112	1.0072	1.0196	0.9957	1.0003	1.0049	1.0147
2001	1.0195	1.0029	1.0006	1.0106	1.0113	0.9941	1.0195	1.0032	1.0010	1.0105	1.0090
1971-2001	**1.0128**	**0.9993**	**1.0003**	**1.0025**	**1.0102**	**1.0006**	**1.0128**	**0.9992**	**1.0002**	**1.0025**	**1.0104**

Table 5. Decompositions for a 2-Input, 3-Output Translog Real Domestic Value Added Function

	Share of labor						Marginal productivity of labor					
	$SS_{t,t-1}$	$S_{Q,t,t-1}$	$S_{E,t,t-1}$	$S_{V,t,t-1}$	$S_{T,t,t-1}$	$S_{U,t,t-1}$	$MM_{t,t-1}$	$M_{Q,t,t-1}$	$M_{E,t,t-1}$	$M_{V,t,t-1}$	$M_{T,t,t-1}$	$M_{U,t,t-1}$
Year	(1)	(2)	(3)	(4)	(5)	(6)	(7)	(8)	(9)	(10)	(11)	(12)
1971	0.9889	0.9976	0.9991	1.0115	0.9978	0.9831	1.0196	0.9962	0.9992	1.0196	1.0075	0.9971
1972	0.9945	0.9965	0.9994	0.9999	0.9978	1.0008	1.0105	0.9945	0.9995	0.9998	1.0075	1.0092
1973	0.9927	0.9970	1.0036	0.9994	0.9978	0.9949	1.0090	0.9951	1.0033	0.9990	1.0075	1.0042
1974	1.0209	0.9864	1.0056	1.0099	0.9978	1.0213	0.9996	0.9758	1.0055	1.0171	1.0074	0.9945
1975	0.9921	1.0018	1.0006	1.0207	0.9978	0.9719	1.0217	1.0034	1.0006	1.0354	1.0074	0.9756
1976	0.9979	1.0001	0.9988	0.9967	0.9978	1.0044	1.0193	1.0003	0.9988	0.9945	1.0076	1.0181
1977	0.9922	0.9958	0.9987	0.9984	0.9978	1.0014	1.0005	0.9920	0.9988	0.9974	1.0075	1.0049
1978	0.9953	0.9991	0.9995	0.9951	0.9978	1.0039	1.0021	0.9982	0.9995	0.9917	1.0075	1.0053
1979	1.0067	0.9959	1.0015	1.0018	0.9978	1.0098	1.0043	0.9919	1.0014	1.0031	1.0074	1.0006
1980	1.0184	0.9885	0.9998	1.0123	0.9977	1.0202	1.0076	0.9768	0.9999	1.0213	1.0072	1.0030
1981	0.9928	1.0017	0.9992	1.0082	0.9978	0.9861	1.0146	1.0036	0.9994	1.0141	1.0071	0.9904
1982	1.0121	1.0036	0.9975	1.0177	0.9978	0.9956	1.0226	1.0074	0.9982	1.0303	1.0074	0.9798
1983	0.9872	1.0040	0.9986	1.0014	0.9978	0.9855	1.0164	1.0082	0.9990	1.0023	1.0077	0.9992
1984	0.9766	1.0017	0.9988	0.9907	0.9978	0.9875	0.9959	1.0035	0.9991	0.9843	1.0078	1.0013
1985	1.0057	1.0006	0.9973	1.0010	0.9978	1.0091	1.0186	1.0012	0.9980	1.0018	1.0079	1.0098
1986	1.0163	0.9985	0.9982	1.0071	0.9978	1.0147	1.0400	0.9970	0.9988	1.0122	1.0079	1.0238
1987	0.9937	0.9971	0.9997	0.9982	0.9978	1.0010	0.9931	0.9939	0.9998	0.9969	1.0079	0.9947
1988	0.9888	1.0003	1.0009	0.9987	0.9978	0.9911	1.0011	1.0007	1.0006	0.9977	1.0079	0.9942
1989	1.0014	0.9994	0.9990	0.9981	0.9977	1.0072	1.0066	0.9987	0.9994	0.9968	1.0080	1.0038
1990	1.0062	0.9982	0.9984	1.0066	0.9977	1.0053	1.0165	0.9960	0.9990	1.0115	1.0080	1.0021
1991	1.0062	1.0017	0.9990	1.0145	0.9978	0.9932	1.0241	1.0038	0.9994	1.0251	1.0081	0.9878
1992	1.0046	0.9996	0.9987	1.0038	0.9978	1.0048	1.0274	0.9991	0.9992	1.0065	1.0082	1.0141
1993	0.9953	1.0008	0.9989	0.9978	0.9978	1.0000	0.9974	1.0019	0.9994	0.9963	1.0083	0.9916
1994	0.9951	1.0002	0.9996	0.9947	0.9978	1.0029	1.0004	1.0005	0.9997	0.9908	1.0084	1.0011
1995	0.9894	0.9996	1.0001	0.9989	0.9977	0.9930	0.9903	0.9992	1.0000	0.9981	1.0084	0.9846
1996	0.9898	1.0005	0.9985	1.0039	0.9977	0.9892	1.0105	1.0012	0.9990	1.0068	1.0085	0.9950
1997	0.9930	1.0020	0.9984	0.9978	0.9977	0.9971	1.0070	1.0046	0.9990	0.9961	1.0086	0.9987
1998	1.0083	1.0031	0.9985	1.0019	0.9977	1.0070	1.0308	1.0073	0.9990	1.0033	1.0088	1.0120
1999	1.0031	0.9991	0.9988	1.0016	0.9977	1.0058	1.0169	0.9980	0.9993	1.0027	1.0089	1.0079
2000	1.0085	0.9971	0.9995	1.0067	0.9977	1.0075	1.0282	0.9932	0.9997	1.0117	1.0089	1.0147
2001	1.0091	1.0021	0.9987	1.0147	0.9977	0.9960	1.0288	1.0050	0.9992	1.0254	1.0090	0.9901
1971-2001	**0.9994**	**0.9990**	**0.9994**	**1.0035**	**0.9978**	**0.9997**	**1.0122**	**0.9983**	**0.9997**	**1.0060**	**1.0079**	**1.0002**

15. Accounting for Changes in Real Wages

We are now in a position to account for the marginal productivity index and the changes in real wages. Recall that the marginal productivity index is defined by (75). We can also identify the following partial effects:

$$M_{Q,t,t-1} \equiv \left\{ \frac{z_L(q_t, e_{t-1}, v_{K,t-1}, v_{L,t-1}, t-1)}{z_L(q_{t-1}, e_{t-1}, v_{K,t-1}, v_{L,t-1}, t-1)} \cdot \frac{z_L(q_t, e_t, v_{K,t}, v_{L,t}, t)}{z_L(q_{t-1}, e_t, v_{K,t}, v_{L,t}, t)} \right\}^{1/2} \quad (103)$$

$$(104)\quad M_{E,t,t-1} \equiv \left\{ \frac{z_L(q_{t-1}, e_t, v_{K,t-1}, v_{L,t-1}, t-1)}{z_L(q_{t-1}, e_{t-1}, v_{K,t-1}, v_{L,t-1}, t-1)} \cdot \frac{z_L(q_t, e_t, v_{K,t}, v_{L,t}, t)}{z_L(q_t, e_{t-1}, v_{K,t}, v_{L,t}, t)} \right\}^{1/2}$$

$$(105)\quad M_{V,t,t-1} \equiv \left\{ \frac{z_L(q_{t-1}, e_{t-1}, v_{K,t}, v_{L,t}, t-1)}{z_L(q_{t-1}, e_{t-1}, v_{K,t-1}, v_{L,t-1}, t-1)} \cdot \frac{z_L(q_t, e_t, v_{K,t}, v_{L,t}, t)}{z_L(q_t, e_t, v_{K,t-1}, v_{L,t-1}, t)} \right\}^{1/2}$$

$$(106)\quad M_{T,t,t-1} \equiv \left\{ \frac{z_L(q_{t-1}, e_{t-1}, v_{K,t-1}, v_{L,t-1}, t)}{z_L(q_{t-1}, e_{t-1}, v_{K,t-1}, v_{L,t-1}, t-1)} \cdot \frac{z_L(q_t, e_t, v_{K,t}, v_{L,t}, t)}{z_L(q_t, e_t, v_{K,t}, v_{L,t}, t-1)} \right\}^{1/2}.$$

Since $z_L(\cdot) = h_L(\cdot) \cdot s_L(\cdot)$ under profit maximization (as long as the timing of the arguments is the same in all three functions), it immediately follows that:

$$(107)\quad M_{t,t-1} = A_{t,t-1} \cdot S_{t,t-1}$$

$$(108)\quad M_{Q,t,t-1} = A_{Q,t,t-1} \cdot S_{Q,t,t-1}$$

$$(109)\quad M_{E,t,t-1} = A_{E,t,t-1} \cdot S_{E,t,t-1}$$

$$(110)\quad M_{V,t,t-1} = A_{V,t,t-1} \cdot S_{V,t,t-1}$$

$$(111)\quad M_{T,t,t-1} = A_{T,t,t-1} \cdot S_{T,t,t-1}\ .$$

Furthermore, it follows from (85) and (99) that:

$$(112)\quad M_{t,t-1} \cong M_{Q,t,t-1} \cdot M_{E,t,t-1} \cdot M_{V,t,t-1} \cdot M_{T,t,t-1}.$$

We finally consider the *observed* marginal productivity of labor index. It is now as follows:

$$(113)\quad MM_{t,t-1} \equiv \frac{w_{L,t} / p_{D,t}}{w_{L,t-1} / p_{D,t-1}}\ .$$

A complete decomposition of the progression in real wages is therefore given by:

$$(114)\quad MM_{t,t-1} \cong M_{Q,t,t-1} \cdot M_{E,t,t-1} \cdot M_{V,t,t-1} \cdot M_{T,t,t-1} \cdot M_{U,t,t-1},$$

where $M_{U,t,t-1}$ is as usual the unexplained component which can be represented as

$$(115)\quad M_{U,t,t-1} = \frac{MM_{t,t-1}}{M_{t,t-1}}.$$

We show in columns 7-12 of table 5 the decomposition of the marginal productivity of labor based on (114). Real wages increased by just over 1.2% per year over the sample period. This increase is dominated by technological progress, though capital deepening played a role too. In fact, comparing these results with those in columns 1-6 of table 4, we again find that capital deepening has a relatively larger impact on marginal productivity than on average productivity. Terms-of-trade changes have reduced real wages by approximately 0.1% per annum on average.

Changes in the real exchange rate have had a negligible effect on average, although the impact has been noticed in some years such as 1974 when it added about 0.6% to real wages.

16. About Unit Labor Costs

Many economic analysts attach much importance to the development of unit labor costs. An increase in unit labor costs – that is, an increase in nominal wages that is not matched by an increase in average productivity – is often viewed as being a threat to price stability. This concern as to the inflationary consequences of an increase in unit labor costs can be understood if one considers that, in most industries and for the economy as a whole, labor costs are the largest component of total costs. This might explain why increases in unit labor costs are sometimes thought of as being the prime source of inflation, even though a theory of inflation that leaves no place for money may sound suspect. In any case, it may be useful to investigate what role unit labor costs play in the analysis in this paper.

Unit labor costs ($\omega_{L,t}$) can be defined as follows:

$$(116)\quad \omega_{L,t} \equiv \frac{w_{L,t}}{z_t / v_{L,t}}.$$

In view of our earlier definitions, unit labor costs can also be expressed as:

$$(117)\quad \omega_{L,t} = \frac{w_{L,t}}{h_{L,t}} = \frac{z_{L,t} \cdot p_{D,t}}{h_{L,t}} = s_{L,t} \cdot p_{D,t}.$$

In terms of change factors we get:

$$(118)\quad \Omega_{L,t,t-1} = SS_{L,t,t-1} \cdot P_{D,t,t-1},$$

where $\Omega_{L,t,t-1}$ is the unit labor cost index and $P_{D,t,t-1}$ is (one plus) the domestic inflation rate:

$$(119)\quad \Omega_{L,t,t-1} \equiv \frac{\omega_{L,t}}{\omega_{L,t-1}} \text{ and}$$

$$(120)\quad P_{D,t,t-1} \equiv \frac{p_{D,t}}{p_{D,t-1}}.$$

Looking at (118), the link between increases in unit labor costs and inflation is evident. In fact, if the share of labor is constant ($SS_{t,t-1} = 1$ in that case), the correlation is perfect. An increase in unit labor costs, be it as the result of an increase in nominal wages or a reduction in average productivity, would necessarily go hand in hand with an increase in the price of output. Correlation is not causation, however. Nominal wages need not be exogenous, no more than average productivity. It is reasonable to assume both are endogenous for the economy as a whole, and this is how they have been treated in the model developed in this paper. Similarly, as stressed throughout the paper, the share of labor is endogenous too. Rather than viewing changes in unit labor costs as an exogenous factor impacting on prices, it might be more useful to explain the changes in unit labor costs as a function of the factors that we have identified earlier on.

In the context of our model, it is clear from (118) that changes in unit labor costs reflect changes in (i) the share of labor and (ii) the price of output. As to the second item, it could be argued that unit labor costs mirror changes in the general price level, rather than cause them. Regarding the impact of changes in the labor share, we refer the reader to section 13 as summarized in columns 1-6 of table 5. Thus, in the U.S. case, a worsening in the terms of trade and/or a real appreciation of the currency, other things equal, reduce unit labor costs. The same is true for technological change, whereas capital deepening acts to increase unit labor costs. Some of these results may sound counter-intuitive. Thus, an increase in the stock of capital, which, for a given labor endowment, must unambiguously increase output and average labor productivity, might yet increase unit labor costs if the marginal product of labor (i.e. real wages) increases by relatively more. If the Hicksian elasticity of complementarity is greater than one, this will be so.

17. Conclusions

In this paper we try to sort out some ideas linked to productivity and to identify the main components of labor productivity. A distinction is drawn between the marginal and the average productivity of labor. This leads to a focus on the GDP share of labor. This in turn helps to illuminate the main forces at work: technological progress, capital deepening, terms-of-trade changes, and changes in the real exchange rate. These last two factors, though statistically significant, were found to play minor roles. This may be because the United States is a relatively closed economy. It is very possible that changes in the terms of trade and in the real exchange rate play a more important role for labor productivity in more open economies.

Our analysis leads to an emphasis on the role played by the Hicksian elasticity of complementarity. This elasticity is significantly greater than unity. This explains to a large extent why the share of labor has been fairly steady over time, and thus why the marginal and average measures of labor productivity have moved in unison. Capital deepening tends to increase the marginal product of labor, and given the large elasticity of complementarity this tends to increase the share of labor. Technological progress, on the other hand, by being mainly labor augmenting can be thought of as anti-labor biased (although not ultra anti-labor biased). This tends to reduce the share of labor, largely offsetting the impact of capital deepening. The slight deterioration in the terms of trade and the small real appreciation of the U.S. dollar that took place over the sample period have further contributed to containing the increase in the labor share.

This paper documents the relationship between total factor and labor productivity. Even if total factor productivity is the main driving force in the increase in output and average productivity, expression (93) shows that there are other forces at work as well. The growth in U.S. labor productivity since the mid-1990s is often considered as a tribute and testimony to the performance of American workers. However, the headline figures typically relate to the nonfarm business sector only. The farming sector, the government sector and the household sector – close to half the economy – are left out of the calculation. Also, productivity growth can be the outcome of a conjunction of favorable events. Thus, capital deepening will unavoidably increase the average and the marginal productivity of labor. And technological progress will necessarily increase average productivity too, but it may impact either way on real wages, although in the U.S. case, the effect is positive. An improvement in the terms of trade and a depreciation of the home currency also lead to increases in average labor productivity, and, in the U.S. case, the impact on real wages is magnified through the increase in the GDP share of labor.

References

Berndt, E.R., B.H. Hall, R.E. Hall, and J.A. Hausman (1974) "Estimation and Inferences in Nonlinear Structural Models", *Annals of Economic and Social Measurement* 3/4, 653-665.

Christensen, L.R., D.W. Jorgenson, and L.J. Lau (1973), "Transcendental Logarithmic Production Frontiers", *Review of Economics and Statistics* 55, 28-45.

Diewert, W.E. (1974), "Applications of Duality Theory", in Michael D. Intriligator and David A. Kendrick (eds.) *Frontiers of Quantitative Economics*, Vol. 2, North-Holland.

Diewert, W.E. (1976), "Exact and Superlative Index Numbers", *Journal of Econometrics* 4, 115-145.

Diewert, W.E. and C.J. Morrison (1986), "Adjusting Output and Productivity Indexes for Changes in the Terms of Trade", *Economic Journal* 96, 659-679.

Diewert, W.E. and T.J. Wales (1987), "Flexible Functional Forms and Global Curvature Conditions", *Econometrica* 55, 43-68.

Diewert, W.E. and T.J. Wales (1992), "Quadratic Spline Models for Producer's Supply and Demand Functions", *International Economic Review* 33, 705-722.

Jorgenson, D.W. and B.M. Fraumeni (1981), "Relative Prices and Technical Change", in Ernst R. Berndt and Barry C. Fields (eds.) *Modeling and Measuring Natural Resource Substitution*, MIT Press.

Kohli, U. (1978), "A Gross National Product Function and the Derived Demand for Imports and Supply of Exports", *Canadian Journal of Economics* 11, 167-182.

Kohli, U. (1990), "Growth Accounting in the Open Economy: Parametric and Nonparametric Estimates", *Journal of Economic and Social Measurement* 16, 125-136.

Kohli, U. (1991), *Technology, Duality, and Foreign Trade: The GNP Function Approach to Modeling Imports and Exports*, University of Michigan Press.

Kohli, U. (1994), "Technological Biases in U.S. Aggregate Production", *Journal of Productivity Analysis* 5, 5-22.

Kohli, U. (2004a), "Real GDP, Real Domestic Income and Terms-of-Trade Changes", *Journal of International Economics* 62, 83-106.

Kohli, U. (2004b), "An Implicit Törnqvist Index of Real GDP", *Journal of Productivity Analysis* 21, 337-353.

Sfreddo, C. (2001), *Trade, Technology, and Factor Prices: A GDP Function Approach for the European Union*, doctoral thesis, University of Geneva.

United States Department of Commerce, Bureau of Economic Analysis, *http://www.bea.doc.gov*.

United States Department of Labor, Bureau of Labor Statistics, *http://www.bls.gov*.

Woodland, A.D. (1982), *International Trade and Resource Allocation*, North-Holland.

Appendix

A1. Description of the Data

All data are annual for the period 1970 to 2001. We require the prices and quantities of all inputs and outputs. The data for GDP and its components, in nominal and in real terms, are taken from the *Bureau of Economic Analysis* website. Prices are then obtained by deflation. Data on the capital stock, labor compensation, and national income are also retrieved from the *BEA* website. The quantity of capital services is assumed to be proportional to the stock. Capital income is defined as national income minus labor compensation. The quantity of labor services is computed by multiplying the total number of employees on nonfarm payrolls by an index of the average number of weekly hours worked in the nonfarm business sector. Both these series are taken from the *Bureau of Labor Statistics* website. The user costs of labor and capital are then obtained by dividing labor and capital income by the corresponding quantity series. For the purpose of sections 9 and 10, output is expressed as an implicit Törnqvist index of real GDP; see Kohli (2004b) for details. In sections 11 to 15, the price of nontraded goods is computed as a Törnqvist price index of the deflators of consumption, investment and government purchases.

A2. Neutral, Disembodied and Factor-Augmenting Technological Change

The first of the two tables that follow (A1) gives an overview, in a production function setting, of the cases that might occur with just two inputs, and assuming that technological change is disembodied and factor augmenting. For simplicity, we only consider the polar cases of Harrod-, Hicks- and Solow-neutrality, but intermediate situations can obviously arise as well.

The second of the following tables (A2) summarizes the possible outcomes in a cost function setting.

Table A1. Neutral, Disembodied, Factor-Augmenting Technological Change in the 2-Input Case: Production-Function Setting

$$y_t = f(v_{L,t}e^{\mu_L t}, v_{K,t}e^{\mu_K t})$$

$\mu_L > 0, \mu_K = 0$ **Harrod-neutral** *(L-augmenting)*				$\mu_L = \mu_K (\equiv \mu) > 0$ **Hicks-neutral** *(L & K-augmenting)*	$\mu_L = 0, \mu_K > 0$ **Solow-neutral** *(K-augmenting)*			
$\hat{\tilde{w}}_L < 0, \hat{\tilde{w}}_K > 0$				$\hat{\tilde{w}}_L = \hat{\tilde{w}}_K = 0$	$\hat{\tilde{w}}_L > 0, \hat{\tilde{w}}_K < 0$			
$\psi_{LK} > 1$		$\psi_{LK} = 1$	$\psi_{LK} < 1$		$\psi_{LK} > 1$		$\psi_{LK} = 1$	$\psi_{LK} < 1$
$\psi_{LK} > 1/s_K$	$1 < \psi_{LK} < 1/s_K$				$\psi_{LK} > 1/s_L$	$1 < \psi_{LK} < 1/s_L$		
$\hat{w}_L < 0, \hat{w}_K > 0$ *L-penalizing K-rewarding*	$0 < \hat{w}_L < \hat{w}_K$ *L- & K-rewarding*	$\hat{w}_L = \hat{w}_K > 0$ *L- & K-rewarding*	$\hat{w}_L > \hat{w}_K > 0$ *L- & K-rewarding*	$\hat{w}_L = \hat{w}_K = \mu > 0$ *L- & K-rewarding*	$\hat{w}_L > 0, \hat{w}_K < 0$ *L-rewarding K-penalizing*	$\hat{w}_L > \hat{w}_K > 0$ *L- & K-rewarding*	$\hat{w}_L = \hat{w}_K > 0$ *L- & K-rewarding*	$0 < \hat{w}_L < \hat{w}_K$ *L- & K-rewarding*
$\varepsilon_{LT} < 0, \varepsilon_{KT} > 0$ $\kappa_L < 0, \kappa_K > 0$ $\hat{s}_L < 0, \hat{s}_K > 0$ *ultra anti-labor, pro-capital biased*	$0 < \varepsilon_{LT} < \varepsilon_{KT}$ $\kappa_L < 0, \kappa_K > 0$ $\hat{s}_L < 0, \hat{s}_K > 0$ *anti-labor, pro-capital biased*	$\varepsilon_{LT} = \varepsilon_{KT} > 0$ $\kappa_L = \kappa_K = 0$ $\hat{s}_L = \hat{s}_K = 0$ *unbiased*	$\varepsilon_{LT} > \varepsilon_{KT} > 0$ $\kappa_L > 0, \kappa_K < 0$ $\hat{s}_L > 0, \hat{s}_K < 0$ *pro-labor, anti-capital biased*	$\varepsilon_{LT} = \varepsilon_{KT} = \mu > 0$ $\kappa_L = \kappa_K = 0$ $\hat{s}_L = \hat{s}_K = 0$ *unbiased*	$\varepsilon_{LT} > 0, \varepsilon_{KT} < 0$ $\kappa_L > 0, \kappa_K < 0$ $\hat{s}_L > 0, \hat{s}_K < 0$ *pro-labor, ultra anti-capital biased*	$\varepsilon_{LT} > \varepsilon_{KT} > 0$ $\kappa_L > 0, \kappa_K < 0$ $\hat{s}_L > 0, \hat{s}_K < 0$ *pro-labor, anti-capital biased*	$\varepsilon_{LT} = \varepsilon_{KT} > 0$ $\kappa_L = \kappa_K = 0$ $\hat{s}_L = \hat{s}_K = 0$ *unbiased*	$0 < \varepsilon_{LT} < \varepsilon_{KT}$ $\kappa_L < 0, \kappa_K > 0$ $\hat{s}_L < 0, \hat{s}_K > 0$ *anti-labor, pro-capital biased*

Table A2. Neutral, Disembodied, Factor-Augmenting Technological Change in the 2-Input Case: Cost-Function Setting

$$p_t = c(w_{L,t}e^{-\mu_L t}, w_{K,t}e^{-\mu_K t})$$

$\mu_L > 0, \mu_K = 0$ **Harrod-neutral** *(L-augmenting)*				$\mu_L = \mu_K (\equiv \mu) > 0$ **Hicks-neutral** *(L & K-augmenting)*	$\mu_L = 0, \mu_K > 0$ **Solow-neutral** *(K-augmenting)*			
$\hat{\tilde{v}}_L > 0, \hat{\tilde{v}}_K < 0$				$\hat{\tilde{v}}_L = \hat{\tilde{v}}_K = 0$	$\hat{\tilde{v}}_L < 0, \hat{\tilde{v}}_K > 0$			
$\sigma_{LK} > 1$		$\sigma_{LK} = 1$	$\sigma_{LK} < 1$		$\sigma_{LK} > 1$		$\sigma_{LK} = 1$	$\sigma_{LK} < 1$
$\sigma_{LK} > 1/s_K$	$1 < \sigma_{LK} < 1/s_K$				$\sigma_{LK} > 1/s_L$	$1 < \sigma_{LK} < 1/s_L$		
$\hat{v}_L > 0, \hat{v}_K < 0$ *L-using* *K-saving*	$0 > \hat{v}_L > \hat{v}_K$ *L- & K-* *saving*	$\hat{v}_L = \hat{v}_K < 0$ *L- & K-* *saving*	$\hat{v}_L < \hat{v}_K < 0$ *L- & K-* *saving*	$\hat{v}_L = \hat{v}_K = -\mu < 0$ *L- & K-* *saving*	$\hat{v}_L < 0, \hat{v}_K > 0$ *L-saving* *K-using*	$\hat{v}_L < \hat{v}_K < 0$ *L- & K-* *saving*	$\hat{v}_L = \hat{v}_K < 0$ *L- & K-* *saving*	$0 > \hat{v}_L > \hat{v}_K$ *L- & K-* *saving*
$\varepsilon_{LT} > 0, \varepsilon_{KT} < 0$ $\kappa_L > 0, \kappa_K < 0$ $\hat{s}_L > 0, \hat{s}_K < 0$ *ultra pro-labor, anti-capital biased*	$0 > \varepsilon_{LT} > \varepsilon_{KT}$ $\kappa_L > 0, \kappa_K < 0$ $\hat{s}_L > 0, \hat{s}_K < 0$ *pro-labor, anti-capital biased*	$\varepsilon_{LT} = \varepsilon_{KT} < 0$ $\kappa_L = \kappa_K = 0$ $\hat{s}_L = \hat{s}_K = 0$ *unbiased*	$\varepsilon_{LT} < \varepsilon_{KT} < 0$ $\kappa_L < 0, \kappa_K > 0$ $\hat{s}_L < 0, \hat{s}_K > 0$ *anti-labor, pro-capital biased*	$\varepsilon_{LT} = \varepsilon_{KT} < 0$ $\kappa_L = \kappa_K = 0$ $\hat{s}_L = \hat{s}_K = 0$ *unbiased*	$\varepsilon_{LT} < 0, \varepsilon_{KT} > 0$ $\kappa_L < 0, \kappa_K > 0$ $\hat{s}_L < 0, \hat{s}_K > 0$ *anti-labor, ultra pro-capital biased*	$\varepsilon_{LT} < \varepsilon_{KT} < 0$ $\kappa_L < 0, \kappa_K > 0$ $\hat{s}_L < 0, \hat{s}_K > 0$ *anti-labor, pro-capital biased*	$\varepsilon_{LT} = \varepsilon_{KT} < 0$ $\kappa_L = \kappa_K = 0$ $\hat{s}_L = \hat{s}_K = 0$ *unbiased*	$0 > \varepsilon_{LT} > \varepsilon_{KT}$ $\kappa_L > 0, \kappa_K < 0$ $\hat{s}_L > 0, \hat{s}_K < 0$ *pro-labor, anti-capital biased*

Chapter 7

MEASURING PRODUCTIVITY CHANGE WITHOUT NEOCLASSICAL ASSUMPTIONS: A CONCEPTUAL ANALYSIS

Bert M. Balk[1]

1. Introduction

The measurement of productivity change (or difference) is usually based on models that make use of strong assumptions such as competitive behaviour and constant returns to scale. This survey discusses the basics of productivity measurement and shows that one can dispense with most if not all the usual, neoclassical assumptions. By virtue of its structural features, the measurement model is applicable to individual establishments and aggregates such as industries, sectors, or economies.

The methodological backing of productivity measurement and growth accounting usually goes like this. The (aggregate) production unit considered has an input side and an output side, and there is a production function that links output quantities to input quantities. This production function includes a time variable, and the partial derivative of the production function with respect to the time variable is called technological change (or, in some traditions, multi- or total factor productivity change). Further, it is assumed that the production unit acts in a competitive environment; that is, input and output prices are assumed as given. Next, it is assumed that the production unit acts in a profit maximizing manner (or, it is said to be 'in equilibrium'), and that the production function exhibits constant returns to scale. Under these assumptions it then appears that output quantity growth (defined as the output-share-weighted mean of the individual output quantity growth rates) is equal to input quantity growth (defined as the input-share-weighted mean of the individual input quantity growth rates) plus the rate of technological change (or, multi- or total factor productivity growth).

For the empirical implementation one then turns to National Accounts, census and/or survey data, in the form of nominal values and deflators (price indices). Of course, one cannot avoid dirty hands by making various imputations where direct observations failed or were impossible (as in the case of labour input of self-employed workers). In the case of capital inputs the prices, necessary for the computation of input shares, cannot be observed, but must be computed as unit user costs. The single degree of freedom that is here available, namely the rate

---

[1] Rotterdam School of Management, Erasmus University, and Statistics Netherlands, The Hague. Email: bbalk@rsm.nl. The views expressed in this paper are those of the author and do not necessarily reflect any policy of Statistics Netherlands. The author thanks Dirk van den Bergen, Erwin Diewert and Marcel Timmer for helpful comments on an earlier version.

Citation: **Bert M. Balk (2011), "Measuring Productivity Change without Neoclassical Assumptions: A Conceptual Analysis," chapter 7, pp.133-184 in**
W.E. Diewert, B.M. Balk, D. Fixler, K.J. Fox and A.O. Nakamura,
***PRICE AND PRODUCTIVITY MEASUREMENT: Volume 6 -- Index Number Theory*. Trafford Press.**

© Alice Nakamura, 2011. Permission to link to, or copy or reprint, these materials is granted without restriction, including for use in commercial textbooks, with due credit to the authors and editors.

of return, is used to ensure that the restriction implied by the assumption of constant returns to scale, namely that profit equals zero, is satisfied. This procedure is usually rationalized by the assumption of perfect foresight, which in this case means that the ex post calculated capital input prices can be assumed as ex ante given to the production unit, so that they can be considered as exogenous data for the unit's profit maximization problem.

This account is, of course, somewhat stylized, since there occur many, smaller or larger, variations on this theme in the literature. Recurring, however, are a number of so-called neo-classical assumptions: 1) a technology that exhibits constant returns to scale, 2) competitive input and output markets, 3) optimizing behaviour, and 4) perfect foresight. A fine example from academia is provided by Jorgenson, Ho and Stiroh (2005, pp. 23, 37), while the Sources and Methods publication of Statistics New Zealand (2006) shows that the neo-classical model has also deeply invaded official statistical agencies.[2] An interesting position is taken by the EU KLEMS Growth and Productivity Accounts project. Though in their main text Timmer *et al.* (2007) adhere to the Jorgenson, Ho and Stiroh framework, there is a curious footnote saying:

> "Under strict neo-classical assumptions, MFP [multifactor productivity] growth measures disembodied technological change. *In practice* [my emphasis], MFP is derived as a residual and includes a host of effects such as improvements in allocative and technical efficiency, changes in returns to scale and mark-ups as well as technological change proper. All these effects can be broadly summarized as "improvements in efficiency", as they improve the productivity with which inputs are used in the production process. In addition, being a residual measure MFP growth also includes measurement errors and the effects from unmeasured output and inputs."

There are more examples of authors who exhibit similar concerns, without, however, feeling the need to adapt their conceptual framework.

I believe that for an official statistical agency, whose main task it is to provide statistics to many different users for many different purposes, it is discomforting to have such strong, and often empirically refuted, assumptions built into the methodological foundations of productivity and growth accounting statistics. This especially applies to the behavioral assumptions numbered 2, 3 and 4. There is ample evidence that, on average, markets are not precisely competitive; that producers' decisions frequently turn out to be less than optimal; and that managers almost invariably lack the magical feature of perfect foresight. Moreover, the environment in which production units operate is not so stable as the assumption of a fixed production function seems to claim.

But I also believe that it is possible, and even advisable, to avoid making such assumptions. In a sense I propose to start where the usual story ends, namely at the empirical side.[3] For any production unit, the total factor productivity index is then *defined* as an output

[2] The neo-classical model figured already prominently in the 1979 report of the U.S. National Research Council's Panel to Review Productivity Statistics (Rees 1979). An overview of national and international practice is provided by the regularly updated *OECD Compendium of Productivity Indicators*, available at www.oecd.org/statistics/productivity.

[3] There is another, minor, difference between my approach and the usual story. The usual story runs in the framework of continuous time in which periods are of infinitesimal short duration. When it then comes to implementation several approximations must be assumed. My approach does not need this kind of assumptions either, because this approach is entirely based on accounting periods of finite duration, such as years.

quantity index divided by an input quantity index. There are various options here, depending on what one sees as input and output, but the basic feature is that, given price and quantity (or value) data, this is simply a matter of index construction. There appear to be no behavioral assumptions involved, and this even applies -- as will be demonstrated -- to the construction of capital input prices. Surely, a number of imputations must be made (as in the case of the self-employed workers) and there is a fairly large number of more or less defendable assumptions involved (for instance on the depreciation rates of capital assets), but this belongs to the daily bread and butter of economic statisticians.

In my view, structural as well as behavioral assumptions enter the picture as soon as it comes to the *explanation* of productivity change. Then there are, depending on the initial level of aggregation, two main directions: 1) to explain productivity change at an aggregate level by productivity change and other factors operating at lower levels of aggregation; 2) to decompose productivity change into factors such as technological change, technical efficiency change, scale effects, input- and output-mix effects, and chance. In this case, to proceed with the analysis one cannot sidestep a technology model with certain specifications.

The contents of this paper unfold as follows. Section 2 outlines the architecture of the basic, KLEMS-Y, input-output model, with its total and partial measures of productivity change. This section also links productivity measurement and growth accounting. Section 3 proceeds with the KL-VA and K-CF models. Then it is time to discuss the measurement of capital input cost in sections 4 and 5. This gives rise to four additional input-output models, which are discussed in section 6. Section 7 is devoted to the rate of return: endogenous or exogenous, ex post or ex ante. Section 8 introduces the capital utilization rate. Section 9 considers a number of implementation issues, after which we take a look in section 10 at the Netherlands' system of productivity statistics. The conclusion can be brief.

2. The Basic Input-Output Model

Let us consider a single production unit. This could be an establishment or plant, a firm, an industry, a sector, or even an entire economy. I will simply speak of a 'unit'. For the purpose of productivity measurement, such a unit is considered as a (consolidated) input-output system. What does this mean?

For the output side as well as for the input side there is some list of commodities (according to some classification scheme). A commodity is thereby defined as a set of closely related items which, for the purpose of analysis, can be considered as "equivalent," either in the static sense of their quantities being additive or in the dynamic sense of displaying equal relative price or quantity changes. Ideally, then, for any accounting period considered (ex post), say a year, each commodity comes with a value (in monetary terms) and a price and/or a quantity. If value and price are available, then the quantity is obtained by dividing the value by the price. If value and quantity are available, then the price is obtained by dividing the value by the quantity. If both price and quantity are available, then value is defined as price times quantity. In any case, for every commodity it must be so that value equals price times quantity, the magnitudes of which of course must pertain to the same accounting period. Technically speaking, the price concept used here is the unit value. At the output side, the prices must be those received by the unit, whereas on the input side, the prices must be those paid. Consolidation (also referred to as taking a net-sector approach) means that the unit does not deliver to itself. Put otherwise, all the intra-unit deliveries are netted out.

The situation as pictured in the preceding paragraph is typical for a unit operating on the (output) market.[4] The question of how to deal with non-market units will be considered where appropriate.

The inputs are customarily classified according to the KLEMS format. The letter K denotes the class of owned, reproducible capital assets. The commodities here are the asset-types, sub-classified by age category. Cohorts of assets are assumed to be available at the beginning of the accounting period and, in deteriorated form (due to ageing, wear and tear), still available at the end of the period. Investment during the period adds entities to these cohorts, while disinvestment, breakdown, and retirement remove entities. Examples include buildings and other structures, machinery, transport and ICT equipment, and tools. As will be discussed later in detail, theory implies that the quantities sought are just the quantities of all these cohorts of assets (together representing the productive capital stock), whereas the relevant prices are their unit user costs (per type-age combination), constructed from imputed interest rates, depreciation profiles, (anticipated) revaluations, and tax rates. The sum of quantities times prices then provides the capital input cost of a production unit.[5]

The letter L denotes the class of labour inputs; that is, all the types of work that are important to distinguish, cross-classified for instance according to educational attainment, gender, and experience (which is usually proxied by age categories). Quantities are measured as hours worked (or paid), and prices are the corresponding wage rates per hour. Where applicable, imputations must be made for the work executed by self-employed persons. The sum of quantities times prices provides the labour input cost (or the labour bill, as it is sometimes called).[6]

The classes K and L concern so-called primary inputs. The letters E, M, and S denote three, disjunct classes of so-called intermediate inputs. First, E is the class of energy commodities consumed by a production unit: oil, gas, electricity, and water. Second, M is the class of all the (physical) materials consumed in the production process, which could be sub-classified into raw materials, semi-fabricates, and auxiliary products. Third, S is the class of all the business services which are consumed for maintaining the production process. Though it is not at all a trivial task to define precisely all the intermediate inputs and to classify them, it can safely be assumed that at the end of each accounting period there is a quantity and a price associated with each of those inputs.

Then, for each accounting period, production cost is defined as the sum of primary and intermediate input cost. Though this is usually not done, there are good reasons to exclude R&D

[4] Note that the role of inventories is disregarded.

[5] The productive capital stock may be underutilized, which implies that not all the capital costs are incurred in actual production. See Schreyer (2001, section 5.6) for a general discussion of this issue. For a treatment in the neo-classical framework the reader is referred to Berndt and Fuss (1986), Hulten (1986) and Morrison Paul (1999). We return to this issue later on.

[6] The utilization rate of the labour input factors is assumed to be 1. Over- or underutilization from the point of view of jobs or persons is reflected in the wage rates.

expenditure from production cost, the reason being that such expenditure is not related to the current but to future output. Put otherwise, by performing R&D, production units try to shift the technology frontier. When it then comes to explaining productivity change, the non-exclusion of R&D expenditure might easily lead to a sort of double-counting error.[7]

On the output side, the letter Y denotes the class of commodities, goods and/or services, which are produced by the unit. Though in some industries, such as services industries or industries producing mainly unique goods, definitional problems are formidable, it can safely be assumed that for each accounting period there are data on quantities produced. For units operating on the market there are also prices. The sum of quantities times prices then provides the production revenue, and, apart from taxes on production, revenue minus cost yields profit.

Profit is an important financial performance measure. A somewhat less obvious, but equally useful, measure is 'profitability,' defined as revenue *divided* by cost. Profitability gives, in monetary terms, the quantity of output per unit of input, and is thus a measure of return to aggregate input (called in some older literature 'return to the dollar').

Monitoring the unit's performance over time is here understood to mean monitoring the development of its profit or its profitability. Both measures are, by nature, dependent on price and quantity changes, at both sides of the unit. If there is (price) inflation and the unit's profit has increased then that mere fact does not necessarily mean that the unit has been performing better. Also, though general inflation does not influence the development of profitability, differential inflation does. If output prices have increased more than input prices then any increase of profitability does not necessarily imply that the unit has been performing better. Thus, for measuring the economic performance of the unit, one wants to get rid of the effect of price changes.

Profit and profitability are different, but equivalent, concepts. The first is a difference measure; the second is a ratio measure. Change of a variable through time, which will be our main focus, can also be measured by a difference or a ratio. Apart from technical details -- such as, that a ratio does not make sense if the variable in the denominator changes sign or becomes equal to zero -- these two ways of measuring change are equivalent. Thus there appear to be a number of ways of mapping the same reality in numbers, and differing numbers do not necessarily imply differing realities.

Profit change stripped of its price component will be called *real* profit change, and profitability change stripped of its price component will be called *real* profitability change.[8] Another name for real profit (-ability) change is (total factor) productivity change. Thus, productivity change can be measured as a ratio (namely as real profitability change) or as a difference (namely as real profit change). At the economy level, productivity change can be related to some measure of overall welfare change. A down-to-earth approach would use the National Accounts to establish a link between labour productivity change and real-income-per-capita change. A more sophisticated approach, using economic models and assumptions, was provided by Basu and Fernald (2002).

---

[7] See Diewert and Huang (2008) for more on this issue. A big problem seems to be the separation of the R&D part of labour input.

[8] Note that real change means nominal change deflated by some price index, not necessarily being a (headline) CPI.

For a non-market unit the story must be told somewhat differently. For such a unit, there are no output prices; hence, there is no revenue. Though there is cost, like for market units, there is no profit or profitability. National accountants usually resolve the problem here by *defining* the revenue of a non-market unit to be equal to its cost, thereby setting profit equal to 0 or profitability equal to 1.[9] But this leaves the problem that there is no natural way of splitting revenue change through time into real and monetary components. This can only be done satisfactorily when there is some output quantity index that is independent from the input quantity index.[10]

It is useful to remind the reader that the notions of profit and profitability, though conceptually rather clear, are difficult to operationalize. One of the reasons is that cost includes the cost of owned capital assets, the measurement of which exhibits a substantial number of degrees of freedom, as we will see in the remainder of this paper. Also, labour cost includes the cost of self-employed persons, for which wage rates and hours of work usually must be imputed. It will be clear that all these, and many other, uncertainties spill over to operational definitions of the profit and profitability concepts.

2.1 Notation

Let us now introduce some notation to define the various concepts we are going to use. As stated, on the output side we have M items, each with their price (received) p_m^t and quantity y_m^t, where $m = 1,\ldots,M$, and t denotes an accounting period (say, a year). Similarly, on the input side we have N items, each with their price (paid) w_n^t and quantity x_n^t, where $n = 1,\ldots,N$. To avoid notational clutter, simple vector notation will be used throughout. All the prices and quantities are assumed to be positive, unless stated otherwise. The ex post accounting point-of-view will be used; that is, quantities and monetary values of the so-called flow variables (output and labour, energy, materials, services inputs) are realized values, complete knowledge of which becomes available not before the accounting period has expired. Similarly, the cost of capital input is calculated ex post. This is consistent with statistical practice.

The unit's revenue, that is, the value of its (gross) output, during the accounting period t is defined as

$$(1) \qquad R^t \equiv p^t \cdot y^t \equiv \sum_{m=1}^{M} p_m^t y_m^t,$$

whereas its production cost is defined as

$$(2) \qquad C^t \equiv w^t \cdot x^t \equiv \sum_{n=1}^{N} w_n^t x_n^t.$$

The unit's *profit* (disregarding tax on production) is then given by its revenue minus its cost; that is,

[9] This approach goes back to Hicks (1940).

[10] See the insightful paper by Douglas (2006). Though written from a New Zealand perspective, its theme is generic.

(3) $\Pi^t \equiv R^t - C^t = p^t \cdot y^t - w^t \cdot x^t$.

The unit's profitability (also disregarding taxes on production) is defined as its revenue divided by its cost; that is,

(4) $R^t / C^t = p^t \cdot y^t / w^t \cdot x^t$.

Notice that profitability expressed as a percentage, $R^t / C^t - 1$, equals the ratio of profit to cost, Π^t / C^t. In some circles this is called the margin of the unit. Given positive prices and quantities, it will always be the case that $R^t > 0$ and $C^t > 0$. Thus, profitability R^t / C^t is always positive, but profit $\Pi^t = R^t - C^t$ can be positive, negative, or zero.

As stated, we are concerned with intertemporal comparisons. Moreover, in this paper, only bilateral comparisons will be considered, say comparing a certain period t to another, adjacent or non-adjacent period, t'. Without loss of generality it may be assumed that period t' precedes period t. To further simplify notation, the two periods will be labeled by $t = 1$ (which will be called the comparison period) and $t' = 0$ (which will be called the base period).

2.2 Productivity Index

The development over time of profitability is, rather naturally, measured by the ratio $(R^1 / C^1) / R^0 / C^0$. How to decompose this into a price and a quantity component? By noticing that

(5) $$\frac{R^1 / C^1}{R^0 / C^0} = \frac{R^1 / R^0}{C^1 / C^0},$$

we see that the question reduces to the question of how to decompose the revenue ratio (R^1 / R^0) and the cost ratio (C^1 / C^0) into two parts. The natural answer is to grab from the economic statistician's toolkit a pair of price and quantity indices that satisfy the Product Test:

(6) $$\frac{p^1 \cdot y^1}{p^0 \cdot y^0} = P(p^1, y^1, p^0, y^0) Q(p^1, y^1, p^0, y^0).$$

The Fisher price and quantity indices are a good choice, since these indices satisfy not only the basic axioms of price and quantity measurement (see appendix A), but also a number of other relatively important requirements (such as the Time Reversal Test). Thus we are using here the 'instrumental' or 'axiomatic' approach for selecting measures for aggregate price and quantity change, an approach that goes back to Fisher (1922); see Balk (1995) for a survey and Balk (2008) for an up-to-date treatment. When the time distance between the periods 1 and 0 is not too large, then any index that is a second-order differential approximation to the Fisher index may instead be used.[11]

Throughout this paper, when it comes to solving problems such as (6) we will assume that Fisher indices are used. Thus, in particular,

$$\frac{R^1}{R^0} = P^F(p^1, y^1, p^0, y^0)Q^F(p^1, y^1, p^0, y^0) \equiv P_R(1,0)Q_R(1,0), \tag{7}$$

where the second line serves to define our shorthand notation. In the same way, we decompose

$$\frac{C^1}{C^0} = P^F(w^1, x^1, w^0, x^0)Q^F(w^1, x^1, w^0, x^0) \equiv P_C(1,0)Q_C(1,0). \tag{8}$$

Of course, the dimensionality of the Fisher indices in expressions (7) and (8) is different.

The number of items distinguished on the output side (M) and the input side (N) of a production unit can be very high. To accommodate this, (detailed) classifications are used, by which all the items are allocated to hierarchically organized (sub-)aggregates. The calculation of output and input indices then proceeds in stages. Theoretically, it suffices to distinguish only two stages. At the first stage one calculates indices for the subaggregates at some level, and at the second stage these subaggregate indices are combined to aggregate indices.

Consequentially, in expressions (7) and (8), instead of one-stage, also two-stage Fisher indices may be used; that is, Fisher indices of Fisher indices for subaggregates (see appendix A for precise definitions). Since the Fisher index is not consistent-in-aggregation, a decomposition by two-stage Fisher indices will in general numerically differ from a decomposition by one-stage Fisher indices. Fortunately, one-stage and two-stage Fisher indices are second-order differential approximations of each other (as shown by Diewert, 1978).

Using the two relations (7) and (8), the profitability ratio can be decomposed as

$$\frac{R^1/C^1}{R^0/C^0} = \frac{R^1/R^0}{C^1/C^0} = \frac{P_R(1,0)}{P_C(1,0)}\frac{Q_R(1,0)}{Q_C(1,0)}. \tag{9}$$

The (total factor) productivity index (*IPROD*), for period 1 relative to 0, is now defined by

$$IPROD(1,0) \equiv \frac{Q_R(1,0)}{Q_C(1,0)}. \tag{10}$$

[11] Note, however, that this is not unproblematic. For instance, when the Törnqvist price index $P^T(.)$ is used, then the implicit quantity index $(p^1 \cdot y^1 / p^0 \cdot y^0)/P^T(.)$ does not necessarily satisfy the Identity Test $A3'$ (see appendix A).

Thus *IPROD*(1, 0) is the real or quantity component of the profitability ratio. Put otherwise, it is the ratio of an output quantity index to an input quantity index; *IPROD*(1, 0) is the factor with which the output quantities on average have changed relative to the factor with which the input quantities on average have changed. If the ratio of these factors is larger (smaller) than 1, there is said to be productivity increase (decrease).[12]

Notice that, using (7) and (8), there appear to be three other equivalent representations of the productivity index, namely

$$(11) \quad IPROD(1,0) = \frac{(R^1/R^0)/P_R(1,0)}{(C^1/C^0)/P_C(1,0)}$$

$$(12) \quad = \frac{(R^1/R^0)/P_R(1,0)}{Q_C(1,0)}$$

$$(13) \quad = \frac{Q_R(1,0)}{(C^1/C^0)/P_C(1,0)}.$$

Put in words, we are seeing here respectively a deflated revenue index divided by a deflated cost index, a deflated revenue index divided by an input quantity index, and an output quantity index divided by a deflated cost index.

Further, if the revenue change equals the cost change, $R^1/R^0 = C^1/C^0$ (for which zero profit in the two periods is a sufficient condition), then it follows from (9) that

$$(14) \quad IPROD(1,0) = \frac{P_C(1,0)}{P_R(1,0)};$$

that is, the productivity index is equal to an input price index divided by an output price index. In general, however, the dual productivity index $P_C(1,0)/P_R(1,0)$ will differ from the primal one, $Q_R(1,0)/Q_C(1,0)$.

2.3 Growth Accounting

The foregoing definitions are already sufficient to provide examples of simple but useful analysis. Consider relation (12), and rewrite this as

$$(15) \quad R^1/R^0 = IPROD(1,0) \times Q_C(1,0) \times P_R(1,0).$$

Recall that revenue change through time is only interesting in so far as it differs from general inflation. Hence, it makes sense to deflate the revenue index, R^1/R^0, by a general inflation measure such as the Consumer Price Index (CPI). Doing this, the last equation becomes

$$(16) \quad \frac{R^1/R^0}{CPI^1/CPI^0} = IPROD(1,0) \times Q_C(1,0) \times \frac{P_R(1,0)}{CPI^1/CPI^0}.$$

[12] This approach follows Diewert (1992), Diewert and Nakamura (2003), and Balk (2003).

Lawrence, Diewert and Fox (2006) basically use this relation to decompose 'real' revenue change into three factors: productivity change, input quantity change (which can be interpreted as measuring change of the unit's size), and 'real' output price change respectively.

Another example follows from rearranging expression (13) and taking logarithms. This delivers the following relation:

$$(17)\quad \ln\left(\frac{C^1/C^2}{Q_R(1,0)}\right) = \ln P_C(1,0) - \ln IPROD(1,0).$$

We see here that the growth rate of average cost can be decomposed into two factors, namely the growth rate of input prices and a residual which is the negative of productivity growth. Put otherwise, in the case of stable input prices the growth rate of average cost is equal to minus the productivity growth rate.

Both are examples of what is called *growth accounting*. The relationship between index number techniques and growth accounting can, more generally, be seen as follows. Recall the generic definition (10), and rewrite this expression as

$$(18)\quad Q_R(1,0) = IPROD(1,0) \times Q_C(1,0).$$

Using logarithms, this multiplicative expression can be rewritten as

$$(19)\quad \ln Q_R(1,0) = \ln IPROD(1,0) + \ln Q_C(1,0).$$

For index numbers in the neighborhood of 1, the logarithms thereof reduce to percentages, and the last expression can be interpreted as saying that the percentage change of output volume equals the percentage change of input volume plus the percentage change of productivity. Growth accounting economists like to work with equations expressing output volume growth in terms of input volume growth plus a residual that is interpreted as productivity growth, thereby suggesting that the last two factors cause the first. However, productivity change cannot be considered as an independent factor since it is *defined* as output quantity change minus input quantity change. A growth accounting table is just an alternative way of presenting productivity growth and its contributing factors. And decomposition does not imply anything about causality.[13]

2.4 Productivity Indicator

Let us now turn to profit and its development through time. This is naturally measured by the difference $\Pi^1 - \Pi^0$. Of course, such a difference only makes sense when the two money amounts involved, profit from period 0 and profit from period 1, are deflated by some general inflation measure (such as the headline CPI). In the remainder of this paper, when discussing difference measures, such a deflation is tacitly presupposed.

How to decompose the profit difference into a price and a quantity component? By noticing that

[13] Thus, saying that output growth outpaced input growth because TFP increased is "like saying that the sun rose because it was morning", to paraphrase Friedman (1988, p. 58).

$$(20) \quad \Pi^1 - \Pi^0 = (R^1 - R^0) - (C^1 - C^0),$$

we see that the question reduces to the question of how to decompose revenue change $(R^1 - R^0)$ and cost change $(C^1 - C^0)$ into two parts. We now grab from the economic statistician's toolkit a pair of price and quantity indicators that satisfy the Product Test:

$$(21) \quad p^1 \cdot y^1 - p^0 \cdot y^0 = \mathsf{P}(p^1, y^1, p^0, y^0) + \mathsf{Q}(p^1, y^1, p^0, y^0).$$

A good choice is the Bennet (1920) price and quantity indicator, since these indicators satisfy not only the basic axioms (see appendix A), but also a number of other relatively important requirements (such as the Time Reversal Test) (see Diewert 2005). But any indicator that is a second-order differential approximation to the Bennet indicator may instead be used. Thus,

$$(22) \quad \begin{aligned} R^1 - R^0 &= \mathsf{P}^B(p^1, y^1, p^0, y^0) + \mathsf{Q}^B(p^1, y^1, p^0, y^0) \\ &\equiv \mathsf{P}_R(1,0) + \mathsf{Q}_R(1,0), \end{aligned}$$

and similarly,

$$(23) \quad \begin{aligned} C^1 - C^0 &= \mathsf{P}^B(w^1, x^1, w^0, x^0) + \mathsf{Q}^B(w^1, x^1, w^0, x^0) \\ &\equiv \mathsf{P}_C(1,0) + \mathsf{Q}_C(1,0). \end{aligned}$$

Notice that the dimensionality of the Bennet indicators in these two decompositions is in general different.

The Bennet indicators are difference analogs to Fisher indices. Their aggregation properties, however, are much simpler. The Bennet price or quantity indicator for an aggregate is equal to the sum of the subaggregate indicators.

Using indicators, the profit difference can be written as

$$(24) \quad \begin{aligned} \Pi^1 - \Pi^0 &= \mathsf{P}_R(1,0) + \mathsf{Q}_R(1,0) - [\mathsf{P}_C(1,0) + \mathsf{Q}_C(1,0)] \\ &= \mathsf{P}_R(1,0) - \mathsf{P}_C(1,0) + \mathsf{Q}_R(1,0) - \mathsf{Q}_C(1,0). \end{aligned}$$

The first two terms at the right-hand side of the last equality sign provide the price component, whereas the last two terms provide the quantity component of the profit difference. Thus, based on this decomposition, the (total factor) productivity indicator (*DPROD*) is defined by

$$(25) \quad DPROD(1,0) \equiv \mathsf{Q}_R(1,0) - \mathsf{Q}_C(1,0);$$

that is, an output quantity indicator minus an input quantity indicator. Notice that productivity change is now measured as an amount of money. An amount larger (smaller) than 0 indicates productivity increase (decrease).[14]

The equivalent expressions for difference-type productivity change are

$$(26) \quad DPROD(1,0) = [R^1 - R^0 - \mathsf{P}_R(1,0)] - [C^1 - C^0 - \mathsf{P}_C(1,0)]$$

[14] This approach follows Balk (2003).

$$(27)\qquad = [R^1 - R^0 - \mathsf{P}_R(1{,}0)] - \mathsf{Q}_C(1{,}0)$$

$$(28)\qquad = \mathsf{Q}_R(1{,}0) - [C^1 - C^0 - \mathsf{P}_C(1{,}0)],$$

which can be of use in different situations. Notice further that, if $R^1 - R^0 = C^1 - C^0$, then

$$(29)\qquad DPROD(1{,}0) \equiv \mathsf{P}_C(1{,}0) - \mathsf{P}_R(1{,}0).$$

For a non-market production unit, a productivity indicator is difficult to define. Though one might be able to construe an output quantity indicator, it is hard to see how, in the absence of output prices, such an indicator could be given a money dimension.

2.5 Partial Productivity Measures

The productivity index $IPROD(1{,}0)$ and the indicator $DPROD(1{,}0)$ bear the adjective 'total factor' because all the inputs are taken into account. To define partial productivity measures, in ratio or difference form, additional notation is necessary.

All the items on the input side of our production unit are assumed to be allocatable to the five, mutually disjunct, categories mentioned earlier, namely capital (*K*), labour (*L*), energy (*E*), materials (*M*), and services (*S*). The entire input price and quantity vectors can then be partitioned as $w^t = (w_K^t, w_L^t, w_E^t, w_M^t, w_S^t)$ and $x^t = (x_K^t, x_L^t, x_E^t, x_M^t, x_S^t)$ respectively. Energy, materials and services together form the category of intermediate inputs, that is, inputs (denoted by EMS), which are acquired from other production units or imported. Capital and labour are called primary inputs. Consistent with this distinction the price and quantity vectors can also be partitioned as $w^t = (w_{KL}^t, w_{EMS}^t)$ and $x^t = (x_{KL}^t, x_{EMS}^t)$, or as $w^t = (w_K^t, w_L^t, w_{EMS}^t)$ and $x^t = (x_K^t, x_L^t, x_{EMS}^t)$. Since monetary values are additive, total production cost can be decomposed in a number of ways, such as

$$\begin{aligned} C^t &= \sum_{n\in K} w_n^t x_n^t + \sum_{n\in L} w_n^t x_n^t + \sum_{n\in E} w_n^t x_n^t + \sum_{n\in M} w_n^t x_n^t + \sum_{n\in S} w_n^t x_n^t \\ (30)\qquad &\equiv C_K^t + C_L^t + C_E^t + C_M^t + C_S^t \\ &\equiv C_K^t + C_L^t + C_{EMS}^t \\ &\equiv C_{KL}^t + C_{EMS}^t. \end{aligned}$$

Now, using as before Fisher indices, the labour cost ratio can be decomposed as

$$\begin{aligned} (31)\qquad \frac{C_L^1}{C_L^0} &= P^F(w_L^1, x_L^1, w_L^0, x_L^0) Q^F(w_L^1, x_L^1, w_L^0, x_L^0) \\ &\equiv P_L(1{,}0) Q_L(1{,}0). \end{aligned}$$

Then the labour productivity index (*ILPROD*) for period 1 relative to period 0 is defined by

(32) $$ILPROD(1,0) \equiv \frac{Q_R(1,0)}{Q_L(1,0)};$$

that is, the ratio of an output quantity index to a labour input quantity index. Notice that usually the labour productivity index is defined by specifying the labour input quantity index to be the Dutot or simple sum quantity index $Q^D(w_L^1, x_L^1, w_L^0, x_L^0) \equiv \sum_{n \in L} x_n^1 / \sum_{n \in L} x_n^0$. The ratio $Q^F(w_L^1, x_L^1, w_L^0, x_L^0) / Q^D(w_L^1, x_L^1, w_L^0, x_L^0)$ is then said to measure the shift in labour quality or composition.

In precisely the same way, one can define the capital productivity index

(33) $$IKPROD(1,0) \equiv \frac{Q_R(1,0)}{Q_K(1,0)},$$

and the other partial productivity indices $IkPROD$ for $k = E, M, S$. The ratio

(34) $$\frac{ILPROD(1,0)}{IKPROD(1,0)} = \frac{Q_K(1,0)}{Q_L(1,0)}$$

is called the index of 'capital deepening'. Loosely speaking, this index measures the change of the quantity of capital input per unit of labour input.

The relation between total factor and partial productivity indices is as follows. Let $Q_C(1,0)$ be a two-stage Fisher index; that is,

(35) $$Q_C(1,0) \equiv Q^F(Q_k(1,0), C_k^1, C_k^0; k = K, L, E, M, S),$$

where all the $Q_k(1,0)$ are Fisher indices. It is straightforward to check that then

(36)
$$\begin{aligned} IPROD(1,0) &= \frac{Q_R(1,0)}{Q_C(1,0)} \\ &= \frac{Q_R(1,0)}{(\sum_k Q_k(1,0) C_k^0 / C^0)^{1/2} (\sum_k Q_k(1,0)^{-1} C_k^1 / C^1)^{-1/2}} \\ &= \left(\sum_k \frac{Q_k(1,0)}{Q_R(1,0)} \frac{C_k^0}{C^0} \right)^{-1/2} \left(\sum_k \frac{Q_R(1,0)}{Q_k(1,0)} \frac{C_k^1}{C^1} \right)^{1/2} \\ &= \left(\frac{\sum_k C_k^0 (IkPROD(1,0))^{-1}}{C^0} \right)^{-1/2} \left(\frac{\sum_k C_k^1 IkPROD(1,0)}{C^1} \right)^{-1/2}, \end{aligned}$$

which is not a particularly simple relation. If instead as a second-stage quantity index the Cobb-Douglas functional form was chosen, that is,

(37) $$Q_C(1,0) \equiv \prod_k Q_k(1,0)^{\alpha_k} \quad \text{where} \sum_k \alpha_k = 1 \ (\alpha_k > 0),$$

then it appears that

$$\ln IPROD(1,0) = \sum_k \alpha_k \ln IkPROD(1,0). \quad (38)$$

This is a very simple relation between total factor productivity change and partial productivity change. Notice, however, that this simplicity comes at a cost. Definition (37) implies for the relation between aggregate and subaggregate input price indices that

$$P_C(1,0) = \prod_k P_k(1,0)^{\alpha_k} \frac{C^1/C^0}{\prod_k (C_k^1/C_k^0)^{\alpha_k}}. \quad (39)$$

Such an index does not necessarily satisfy the fundamental Identity Test A3; that is, if all prices are the same in period 1 as in period 0, then $P_C(1,0)$ does not necessarily deliver the outcome 1.

Let us now turn to partial productivity *indicators*. Using the Bennet indicators, the labour cost difference between periods 0 and 1 is decomposed as

$$\begin{aligned} C_L^1 - C_L^0 &= \mathsf{P}^B(w_L^1, x_L^1, w_L^0, x_L^0) + \mathsf{Q}^B(w_L^1, x_L^1, w_L^0, x_L^0) \\ &\equiv \mathsf{P}_L(1,0) + \mathsf{Q}_L(1,0). \end{aligned} \quad (40)$$

Similarly, one can decompose the capital, energy, materials, and services cost difference. However, costs are additive, the total factor productivity indicator can be written as

$$DPROD(1,0) = \mathsf{Q}_R(1,0) - \sum_{k=K,L,E,M,S} \mathsf{Q}_k(1,0). \quad (41)$$

By definition, the left-hand side is real profit change. The right-hand side gives the contributing factors. The contribution of category k to real profit change is simply measured by the amount $\mathsf{Q}_k(1,0)$. A positive amount, which means that the aggregate quantity of input category k has increased, means a negative contribution to real profit change.

3. Different Models, Similar Measures

The previous section laid out the basic features of what is known as the KLEMS model of production. This framework is currently used by the U.S. Bureau of Labor Statistics (BLS) and Statistics Canada for productivity measures at the industry level of aggregation (see Dean and Harper 2001, and Harchaoui *et al.* 2001 respectively). The KLEMS model, or, as I will denote it, the KLEMS-Y model delivers gross-output based total or partial productivity measures. However, there are more models in use, differing from the KLEMS-Y model by their input and output concepts. Since these models presuppose revenue as measured independently from cost, they are not applicable to non-market units.

3.1 The KL-VA model

The first of these models uses value added (VA) as its output concept. The production unit's value added (VA) is defined as its revenue minus the costs of energy, materials, and services; that is,

$$(42)\quad \begin{aligned} VA^t &\equiv R^t - C^t_{EMS} \\ &= p^t \cdot y^t - w^t_{EMS} \cdot x^t_{EMS}. \end{aligned}$$

The value-added concept subtracts the total cost of intermediate inputs from the revenue obtained, and in doing so essentially conceives the unit as producing value added (that is, money) from the two primary input categories capital and labour. It is assumed that $VA^t > 0$.

Although gross output, represented by y^t, is the natural output concept, the value-added concept is important when one wishes to aggregate single units to larger entities. Gross output consists of deliveries to final demand and intermediate destinations. The split between these two output categories depends very much on the level of aggregation. Value added is immune to this problem. It enables one to compare (units belonging to) different industries. From a welfare-theoretic point of view the value-added concept is important because value added can be conceived of as the income (from production) that flows into society.[15]

In this input-output model the counterpart to *profitability* is the ratio of value added to primary inputs cost, VA^t / C^t_{KL}, and the natural starting point for defining a productivity index is to consider the development of this ratio through time. Since $(VA^1 / C^1_{KL})/(VA^0 / C^0_{KL}) = (VA^1 / VA^0)/(C^1_{KL} / C^0_{KL})$, we need a decomposition of the value-added ratio and a decomposition of the primary inputs cost ratio.

The question of how to decompose a value-added ratio into price and quantity components cannot be answered unequivocally. There are several options here, the technical details of which are deferred to appendix B. Suppose, however, that a satisfactory decomposition is somehow available; that is,

$$(43)\quad \frac{VA^1}{VA^0} = P_{VA}(1,0)Q_{VA}(1,0).$$

Using one- or two-stage Fisher indices, the primary inputs cost ratio is decomposed as

$$(44)\quad \begin{aligned} \frac{C^1_{KL}}{C^0_{KL}} &= P^F(w^1_{KL}, x^1_{KL}, w^0_{KL}, x^0_{KL})Q^F(w^1_{KL}, x^1_{KL}, w^0_{KL}, x^0_{KL}) \\ &\equiv P_{KL}(1,0)Q_{KL}(1,0). \end{aligned}$$

The value-added based (total factor) productivity index for period 1 relative to period 0 is then defined as

$$(45)\quad IPROD_{VA}(1,0) \equiv \frac{Q_{VA}(1,0)}{Q_{KL}(1,0)}.$$

[15] In between the KLEMS-Y model and the KL-VA model there is the KLE"M"S-Margin model, applicable to distributive trade units. Here the set of material inputs M is split into two parts, M' denoting the goods for resale and M" the auxiliary materials. Likewise E, the set of energy inputs, is split into E' and E". The Margin is then defined as revenue minus the cost of the goods for resale and the cost of the first of the two energy components. See Inklaar and Timmer (2008).

This index measures the 'quantity' change of value added relative to the quantity change of primary input; or, can be seen as the index of real value added relative to the index of real primary input.

This is by far the most common model. It is used by the U. S. Bureau of Labor Statistics, Statistics Canada, the Australian Bureau of Statistics, Statistics New Zealand, and the Swiss Federal Statistical Office in their official productivity statistics.

In the KL-VA model the counterpart to *profit* is the difference of value added and primary inputs cost, $VA^t - C_{KL}^t$, and the natural starting point for defining a productivity indicator is to consider the development of this difference through time. However, since costs are additive, we see that, by using definition (42),

$$\begin{aligned} VA^t - C_{KL}^t &= R^t - C_{EMS}^t - C_{KL}^t \\ &= R^t - C^t . \end{aligned} \tag{46}$$

Thus, profit in the KL-VA model is the same as profit in the KLEMS-Y model, and the same applies to the price and quantity components of profit differences. Using Bennet indicators, one can easily check that

$$\begin{aligned} DPROD_{VA}(1,0) &\equiv \mathrm{Q}_{VA}(1,0) - \mathrm{Q}_{KL}(1,0) \\ &= \mathrm{Q}_R(1,0) - \mathrm{Q}_C(1,0) \\ &= DPROD(1,0); \end{aligned} \tag{47}$$

that is, the productivity indicators are the same in the two models. This, however, does not hold for the productivity indices. One usually finds that $IPROD_{VA}(1,0) \neq IPROD(1,0)$. Balk (2009) showed that if profit is zero in both periods, that is $R^t = C^t$ $(t = 0,1)$, then, for certain two-stage indices which are second-order differential approximations to Fisher indices,

$$\ln IPROD_{VA}(1,0) = D(1,0) \ln IPROD(1,0) , \tag{48}$$

where $D(1,0) \geq 1$ is the (mean) Domar-factor (= ratio of revenue over value added). Usually expression (48) is, in a continuous-time setting, derived under a set of strong neo-classical assumptions (see, for instance, Gollop (1979), Jorgenson *et al.* (2005, p. 298) or Schreyer (2001, p. 143)), so that it seems to be some deep economic-theoretical result. From the foregoing it may be concluded, however, that the inequality of the value-added based productivity index and the gross-output based productivity index is only due to the mathematics of ratios and differences. It does not point to any underlying economic phenomenon.

The value-added based labour productivity index for period 1 versus 0 is defined as

$$ILPROD_{VA}(1,0) \equiv \frac{Q_{VA}(1,0)}{Q_L(1,0)} , \tag{49}$$

where $Q_L(1,0)$ was defined by expression (31). The index defined by expression (49) measures the 'quantity' change of value added relative to the quantity change of labour input; or, can be seen as the index of real value added relative to the index of real labour input.

Recall that the labour quantity index $Q_L(1,0)$ is here defined as a Fisher index, acting on the prices and quantities of all the types of labour that are being distinguished. Suppose that the units of measurement of the various types are in some sense the same; that is, the quantities of all the types of labour are measured in hours, or in full-time equivalent jobs, or in some other common unit. Then one frequently considers, instead of the Fisher quantity index, the Dutot or simple sum quantity index,

$$(50) \quad Q_L^D(1,0) \equiv \sum_{n \in L} x_n^1 / \sum_{n \in L} x_n^0 .$$

The simple value-added based labour productivity index, defined as

$$(51) \quad ILPROD_{VA}^D(1,0) \equiv \frac{Q_{VA}(1,0)}{Q_L^D(1,0)},$$

has the alternative interpretation as an index of real value added per unit of labour. As such this measure frequently figures at the left-hand side (thus, as *explanandum*) in a growth accounting equation. However, for deriving such a relation nothing spectacular is needed, as will now be shown.

Consider the definition of the value-added based total factor productivity index, (45), and rewrite this as

$$(52) \quad Q_{VA}(1,0) = IPROD_{VA}(1,0) \times Q_{KL}(1,0).$$

Dividing both sides of this equation by the Dutot labour quantity index, and applying definition (51), one obtains[16]

$$(53) \quad ILPROD_{VA}^D(1,0) = ILPROD_{VA}(1,0) \times \frac{Q_{KL}(1,0)}{Q_L(1,0)} \times \frac{Q_L(1,0)}{Q_L^D(1,0)}.$$

Taking logarithms and, on the assumption that all the index numbers are in the neighborhood of 1, interpreting these as percentages, the last equation can be interpreted as: (simple) labour productivity growth equals total factor productivity growth plus ‘capital deepening’ plus ‘labour quality’ growth. Again, productivity change is measured as a residual and, thus, the three factors at the right-hand side of the last equation can in no way be regarded as causal factors.

If, continuing our previous example, the primary inputs quantity index was defined as a two-stage index of the form

$$(54) \quad Q_{KL}(1,0) \equiv Q_K(1,0)^{\alpha} Q_L(1,0)^{1-\alpha}, \qquad \text{for } 0 < \alpha < 1,$$

where the reader recognizes the simple Cobb-Douglas form, then the index of ‘capital deepening’ reduces to the particularly simple form

$$(55) \quad \frac{Q_{KL}(1,0)}{Q_L(1,0)} = \left[\frac{Q_K(1,0)}{Q_L(1,0)}\right]^{\alpha}.$$

---

16 This is a discrete time version of expression (23) of Baldwin, Gu and Yan (2007).

The 'labour quality' index, $Q_L(1,0)/Q_L^D(1,0)$, basically measures compositional shift or structural change among the labour types in the class *L*, because it is a ratio of two quantity indices.

3.2 The K-CF model

The next model uses cash flow (CF) as its output concept.[17] The unit's cash flow is defined as its revenue minus the costs of labour and intermediate inputs; that is

$$
\begin{aligned}
CF^t &\equiv R^t - C^t_{LEMS} \\
&= p^t \cdot y^t - w^t_{LEMS} \cdot x^t_{LEMS} \qquad (56)\\
&= VA^t - C^t_L.
\end{aligned}
$$

This input-output model basically sees cash flow as the return to capital input. It is assumed that $CF^t > 0$. Of course, if there is no owned capital (that is, all capital assets are leased), then $C^t_K = 0$, and this model does not make sense.

The counterpart to *profitability* is now the ratio of cash flow to capital input cost, CF^t / C^t_K, and the natural starting point for defining a productivity index is to consider the development of this ratio through time. Since $(CF^1/C^1_K)/(CF^0/C^0_K) = (CF^1/CF^0)/(C^1_K/C^0_K)$, we need a decomposition of the cash-flow ratio and a decomposition of the capital input cost ratio.

Decomposing a cash-flow ratio into price and quantity components is structurally similar to decomposing a value-added ratio (see appendix B). Thus, suppose that a satisfactory decomposition is somehow available; that is,

$$(57) \quad \frac{CF^1}{CF^0} = P_{CF}(1,0)Q_{CF}(1,0).$$

Using Fisher indices, the capital input cost ratio is decomposed as

$$
\begin{aligned}
(58) \quad \frac{C^1_K}{C^0_K} &= P^F(w^1_K, x^1_K, w^0_K, x^0_K)Q^F(w^1_K, x^1_K, w^0_K, x^0_K) \\
&\equiv P_K(1,0)Q_K(1,0).
\end{aligned}
$$

The cash-flow based (total factor) productivity index for period 1 versus 0 is then defined as

$$(59) \quad IPROD_{CF}(1,0) = \frac{Q_{CF}(1,0)}{Q_K(1,0)}.$$

[17] Cash flow is also called gross profit. The National Accounts term is 'gross operating surplus.'

This index measures the change of the quantity component of cash flow relative to the quantity change of capital input; or, it can be seen as the index of real cash flow relative to the index of real capital input.

In the K-CF model, the counterpart to *profit* is the difference of cash flow and capital input cost, $CF^t - C_K^t$, and the natural starting point for defining a productivity indicator is to consider the development of this difference through time. However, since costs are additive, we see that

$$\text{(60)} \quad \begin{aligned} CF^t - C_K^t &= R^t - C_{LEMS}^t - C_K^t \\ &= R^t - C^t. \end{aligned}$$

Thus, profit in the K-CF model is the same as profit in the KLEMS-Y model, and the same applies to the price and quantity components of profit differences. Using Bennet indicators, one easily checks that

$$\text{(61)} \quad \begin{aligned} DPROD_{CF}(1,0) &\equiv \mathrm{Q}_{CF}(1,0) - \mathrm{Q}_K(1,0) \\ &= \mathrm{Q}_R(1,0) - \mathrm{Q}_C(1,0) \\ &= DPROD(1,0); \end{aligned}$$

that is, the productivity indicators are the same in the two models. This, however, does not hold for the productivity indices. In general it will be the case that $DPROD_{CF}(1,0) \neq DPROD(1,0)$. Following the reasoning of Balk (2009), it is possible to show that, if profit is zero in both periods, that is, $R^t = C^t$ $(t = 0,1)$, then, for certain two-stage indices which are second-order differential approximations to Fisher indices,

$$\text{(62)} \quad \ln IPROD_{CF}(1,0) = E(1,0) \ln IPROD(1,0),$$

where $E(1,0) \geq 1$ is the ratio of mean revenue over mean cash flow. Since $CF^t \leq VA^t$, it follows that $E(1,0) \geq D(1,0)$.

4. Capital Input Cost

The K-CF model provides a good point of departure for a discussion of the measurement of capital input cost. Cash flow, as defined in the foregoing, is the (ex post measured) monetary balance of all the flow variables. Capital input cost is different, since capital is a stock variable. Basically, capital input cost is measured as the difference between the book values of the production unit's owned capital stock at beginning and end of the accounting period considered.

Our notation must therefore be extended. The beginning of period t is denoted by t^-, and its end by t^+. Thus a period is an interval of time $t = [t^-, t^+]$, where $t^- = (t-1)^+$ and $t^+ = (t+1)^-$. Occasionally, the variable *t* will also be used to denote the midpoint of the period.

All the assets are supposed to be economically born at midpoints of periods, whether this has occurred inside or outside the production unit under consideration. Thus the age of an asset of type i at (the midpoint of) period t is a non-negative integer number $j = 0,\ldots,J_i$. The age of this asset at the beginning of the period is $j-0.5$, and at the end is $j+0.5$. The economically maximal service life of asset type i is denoted by J_i.

The opening stock of capital assets is the inheritance of past investments and disinvestments; hence, this stock consists of cohorts of assets of various types, each cohort comprising a number of assets of the same age. By (Netherlands' National Accounts) convention, assets that are discarded (normally retired or prematurely scrapped) or sold during a certain period t are supposed to be discarded or sold at the end of that period; that is, at t^+. Second-hand assets that are acquired during period t from other production units are supposed to be acquired at the beginning of the next period, $(t+1)^-$. However, all other acquisitions of second-hand assets and those of new assets are supposed to happen at the midpoint of the period, and to be immediately operational.

Hence, all the assets that are part of the opening stock remain active through the entire period $[t^-,t^+]$. The period t investments are supposed to be active through the second half of period t, that is, $[t,t^+]$. Put otherwise, the stock of capital assets at t, the midpoint of the period, is the same as the stock at t^-, the beginning of the period, but 0.5 period older. At the midpoint of the period the investments, of various age, are added to the stock. Notice, however, that the closing stock at t^+, the end of the period, is not necessarily identical to the opening stock at $(t+1)^-$, because of the conventions regarding the sale, acquisition, and discard of assets.

Let K_{ij}^t denote the quantity (number) of asset type i ($i = 1,\ldots,I$) and age j ($j = 1,\cdots,J_i$) at the midpoint of period t. These quantities are nonnegative; some of them might be equal to 0. Further, let I_{ij}^t denote the (non-negative) quantity (number) of asset type i ($i = 1,\ldots,I$) and age j ($j = 0,\cdots,J_i$) that is added to the stock at the midpoint of period t. The following relations are useful to keep in mind:

(63) $$K_{i,j-0.5}^{t^-} = K_{ij}^t \quad \text{for } j = 1,\cdots,J_i,$$

(64) $$I_{i0}^t = K_{i,0.5}^{t^+},$$

(65) $$I_{ij}^t + K_{ij}^t = K_{i,j+0.5}^{t^+} \quad \text{for } j = 1,\cdots,J_i,$$

(66) $$K_{i,(j+1)-0.5}^{(t+1)^-} = K_{i,j+0.5}^{t^+} + B_{i,j+0.5}^{t^+} \quad \text{for } j = 1,\cdots,J_i - 1 \ ,$$

and

(67) $$K_{i,(J_i+1)-0.5}^{(t+1)^-} = 0,$$

where $B_{i,j+0.5}^{t^+}$ denotes the balance of sale, acquisition, and discard at t^+. We are now ready to define the concept of user cost for assets that are owned by the production unit.[18]

The first distinction that must be made is between assets that are part of the opening stock of a period, and investments that are made during this period. Consider an asset of type *i* that has age *j* at the midpoint of period *t*. Its price (or valuation) at the beginning of the period is denoted by $P_{i,j-0.5}^{t^-}$, and its price (or valuation) at the end of the period by $P_{i,j+0.5}^{t^+}$. For the time being, we consider such prices as being given, and postpone their precise definition to the next section. The prices are assumed to be non-negative; some might be equal to 0. In any case, $P_{i,J_i+0.5}^{t^+} = 0$; that is, an asset that has reached its economically maximal age in period *t* is valued with a zero price at the end of this period.

The (ex post) unit user cost over period *t* of an opening stock asset of type *i* that has age *j* at the midpoint of the period is then *defined* as

$$(68) \quad u_{ij}^t \equiv r^t P_{i,j-0.5}^{t^-} + (P_{i,j-0.5}^{t^-} - P_{i,j+0.5}^{t^+}) + \tau_{ij}^t, \qquad \text{for } j = 1, \cdots, J_i.$$

There are three components here. The first, $r^t P_{i,j-0.5}^{t^-}$, is the price (or valuation) of this asset at the beginning of the period, when its age is $j-0.5$, times an interest rate. This component reflects the premium that must be paid to the owner of the asset to prevent it from being sold, right at the beginning of the period, and the revenue used for immediate consumption; it is therefore also called the price of 'waiting.'[19] Another interpretation is to see this component as the actual or imputed interest cost to finance the monetary capital that is tied up in the asset; it is then called 'opportunity cost.' Anyway, it is a sort of remuneration which, since there might be a risk component involved, is specific for the production unit.[20]

The second part of expression (68), $P_{i,j-0.5}^{t^-} - P_{i,j+0.5}^{t^+}$, is the value change of the asset between the beginning and end of the accounting period. It is called (nominal) time-series depreciation, and combines the effect of the progress of time, from t^- to t^+, with the effect of ageing, from $j - 0.5$ to $j + 0.5$. In general, the difference between the two prices (valuations) comprises the effect of exhaustion, deterioration, and obsolescence.

The third component, τ_{ij}^t, denotes the specific tax(es) that is (are) levied on the use of an asset of type *i* and age *j* during period *t*.

[18] If there were no transactions in second-hand assets, then the number of assets K_{ij}^t would be equal to the number of new investments of *j* periods earlier, I_{i0}^{t-j}, adjusted for the probability of survival.

[19] According to Rymes (1983) this naming goes back to Pigou.

[20] The System of National Accounts 1993 prescribes that for non-market units belonging to the government sector the interest rate r^t must be set equal to 0.

Unit user cost as defined in expression (68) is also called 'rental price,' because it can be considered as the rental price that the owner of the asset would charge to the owner as user. Put otherwise, unit user cost is like a lease price.

Let us now turn to the unit user cost of an asset of type i and age j that is acquired at the midpoint of period t. To keep things simple, this user cost is, analogous to expression (68), defined as

$$(69) \quad v_{ij}^t \equiv (1/2)r^t P_{ij}^t + (P_{ij}^t - P_{i,j+0.5}^{t^+}) + (1/2)\tau_{ij}^t, \qquad \text{for } j = 0,\ldots,J_i.$$

The difference from the previous formula is that here the second half of the period instead of the entire period is taken into account.[21]

Total user cost over all asset types and ages, for period t, is then naturally defined by

$$(70) \quad C_K^t \equiv \sum_{i=1}^{I}\sum_{j=1}^{J_i} u_{ij}^t K_{ij}^t + \sum_{i=1}^{I}\sum_{j=0}^{J_i} v_{ij}^t I_{ij}^t.$$

The set of quantities $\{K_{ij}^t, I_{ij}^t; i = 1,\ldots,I; j = 0,\ldots,J_i\}$ represents the so-called productive capital stock of the production unit. This is an enumeration of the assets that make production possible. The total value of these assets at the midpoint of period t can be calculated as

$$(71) \quad \sum_{i=1}^{I}\sum_{j=1}^{J_i} P_{ij}^t K_{ij}^t + \sum_{i=1}^{I}\sum_{j=0}^{J_i} P_{ij}^t I_{ij}^t.$$

This value is called the net (or wealth) capital stock.[22]

We are now able to connect the variables in expression (70) with the notation introduced in the foregoing; see expression (30). We see that the set K consists of two subsets, corresponding respectively to the type-age classes of assets that are part of the opening stock and the type-age classes of assets that are acquired later. The dimension of the first set is $\sum_{i=1}^{I} J_i$, and the dimension of the second set is $\sum_{i=1}^{I}(1+J_i)$. The input prices w_n^t ($n \in K$) are given by expressions (68) and (69) respectively, while the quantities x_n^t ($n \in K$) are given by K_{ij}^t and I_{ij}^t respectively.

If all the variables occurring in expression (70) were observable, then our story would almost end here. However, this is not the case. Though the quantity variables are in principle observable, the price variables are not. To start with, the expressions (68) and (69) contain prices (valuations) for all asset types and ages, but, except for new assets and where markets for second-hand assets exist, these prices are not observable. Thus, we need models.

---

21 The factor $(1/2)r^t$ is meant as an approximation to $(1+r^t)^{1/2}-1$, and the factor $(1/2)\tau_{ij}^t$ as an approximation to $((1+\tau_{ij}^t / P_{i,j-0.5}^{t^-})^{1/2} - 1)P_{i,j}^t$.

22 Coremberg (2008) considers the difference between a quantity index based on expression (70) – capital services – and on expression (71) – capital stock.

5. The Relationship between Asset Price and Unit User Cost

Consider expression (68) and rewrite it in the form

$$(72)\quad u_{ij}^{t} - \tau_{ij}^{t} = (1 + r^{t})P_{i,j-0.5}^{t^-} - P_{i,j+0.5}^{t^+} \qquad \text{for } j = 1,\ldots,J_i.$$

For any asset that is not prematurely discarded it will be the case that its value at the end of period t is equal to its value at the beginning of period $t+1$; formally, $P_{i,j+0.5}^{t^+} = P_{i,(j+1)-0.5}^{(t+1)^-}$. Substituting this into expression (72), and rewriting again, one obtains

$$(73)\quad P_{i,j-0.5}^{t^-} = \frac{1}{1+r^{t}}(P_{i,(j+1)-0.5}^{(t+1)^-} + u_{i,j}^{t} - \tau_{i,j}^{t}) \qquad \text{for } j = 1,\ldots,J_i.$$

This expression links the price of an asset at the beginning of period t with its price at the beginning of period $t+1$, being then 1 period older. But a similar relation links its price at the beginning of period $t+1$ with its price at the beginning of period $t+2$, being then again 1 period older,

$$(74)\quad P_{i,(j+1)-0.5}^{(t+1)^-} = \frac{1}{1+r^{t+1}}(P_{i,(j+2)-0.5}^{(t+2)^-} + u_{i,j+1}^{t+1} - \tau_{i,j+1}^{t+1}) \qquad \text{for } j = 1,\ldots,J_i.$$

This can be continued until

$$(75)\quad P_{i,J_i-0.5}^{(t+J_i-j)^-} = \frac{1}{1+r^{t+J_i-j}}(P_{i,J_i+0.5}^{(t+J_i-j+1)^-} + u_{i,J_i}^{t+J_i-j} - \tau_{i,J_i}^{t+J_i-j}) \quad \text{for } j = 1,\ldots,J_i,$$

since we know that $P_{i,J_i+0.5}^{(t+J_i-j+1)^-} = P_{i,J_i+0.5}^{(t+J_i-j)^+} = 0$. Substituting expression (74) into (73), etcetera, one finally obtains

$$(76)\quad P_{i,j-0.5}^{t^-} = \frac{u_{i,j}^{t} - \tau_{i,j}^{t}}{1+r^{t}} + \frac{u_{i,j+1}^{t+1} - \tau_{i,j+1}^{t+1}}{(1+r^{t})(1+r^{t+1})} + \ldots + \frac{u_{i,J_i}^{t+J_i-j} - \tau_{i,J_i}^{t+J_i-j}}{(1+r^{t})\ldots(1+r^{t+J_i-j})}.$$

This is a materialization of the so-called fundamental asset price equilibrium equation. Notice, however, that there is no equilibrium assumed here -- whatever that may mean -- and there are no other economic behavioral assumptions involved; it is just a mathematical result. Expressions (72) and (76) are dual. The first derives the (ex tax) unit user cost from discounted asset prices, while the second derives the asset price as the sum of discounted future (ex tax) unit user costs; the discounting is executed by means of future interest rates.

A mathematical truth like expression (76), however, is not immediately helpful in the real world. At the beginning, or even at the end of period t, most if not all of the data that are needed for the computation of the asset prices $P_{i,j-0.5}^{t^-}$ and $P_{i,j+0.5}^{t^+}$ are *not* available. Thus, in practice, expression (76) must be filled in with expectations, and these depend on the point of time from which one looks at the future. A rather natural vantage point is the beginning of period t; thus, the operator E^{t^-} placed before a variable means that the expected value of the variable at t^- is taken. Modifying expression (76), the price at the beginning of period t of an asset of type i and age $j-0.5$ is given by

$$
\begin{aligned}
P^{t^-}_{i,j-0.5} &\equiv \frac{E^{t^-}(u^t_{i,j}-\tau^t_{i,j})}{1+E^{t^-}r^t} \\
&+ \frac{E^{t^-}(u^{t+1}_{i,j+1}-\tau^{t+1}_{i,j+1})}{(1+E^{t^-}r^t)(1+E^{t^-}r^{t+1})} + \ldots + \frac{E^{t^-}(u^{t+E^{t^-}J_i-j}_{i,E^{t^-}J_i}-\tau^{t+E^{t^-}J_i-j}_{i,E^{t^-}J_i})}{(1+E^{t^-}r^t)\ldots(1+E^{t^-}r^{t+E^{t^-}J_i-j})}.
\end{aligned} \tag{77}
$$

Notice in particular that in this expression the economically maximal age, as expected at the beginning of period t, $E^{t^-}J_i$, occurs. Put otherwise, at the beginning of period t the remaining economic lifetime of the asset is expected to be $E^{t^-}J_i-j-0.5$ periods.[23] For each of the coming periods, there is an expected (ex tax) rental, and the (with expected interest rates) discounted rentals are summed. This sum constitutes the price (value) of the asset.

Similarly, the price at the end of period t of an asset of type i and age $j+0.5$ is given by

$$
\begin{aligned}
P^{t^+}_{i,j+0.5} &= P^{(t+1)^-}_{i,(j+1)-0.5} \\
&\equiv \frac{E^{(t+1)^-}(u^{t+1}_{i,j+1}-\tau^{t+1}_{i,j+1})}{1+E^{(t+1)^-}r^{t+1}} + \frac{E^{(t+1)^-}(u^{t+2}_{i,j+2}-\tau^{t+2}_{i,j+2})}{(1+E^{(t+1)^-}r^{t+1})(1+E^{(t+1)^-}r^{t+2})} \\
&+ \ldots + \frac{E^{(t+1)^-}(u^{t+E^{(t+1)^-}J_i-j}_{i,E^{(t+1)^-}J_i}-\tau^{t+E^{(t+1)^-}J_i-j}_{i,E^{(t+1)^-}J_i})}{(1+E^{(t+1)^-}r^{t+1})\ldots(1+E^{(t+1)^-}r^{t+E^{(t+1)^-}J_i-j})}.
\end{aligned} \tag{78}
$$

Notice that this price depends on the economically maximal age, as expected at the beginning of period t+1 (which is the end of period t), $E^{(t+1)^-}J_i$, which may or may not differ from the economically maximal age, as expected one period earlier, $E^{t^-}J_i$. The last mentioned expected age plays a role in the price at the end of period t of an asset of type i and age $j+0.5$, as expected at the beginning of this period,

[23] See Erumban (2008a) on the estimation of expected lifetimes for three types of assets in a number of industries.

$$(79)\quad E^{t^-}P^{t^+}_{i,j+0.5} \equiv \frac{E^{t^-}(u^{t+1}_{i,j+1}-\tau^{t+1}_{i,j+1})}{1+E^{t^-}r^{t+1}} + \frac{E^{t^-}(u^{t+2}_{i,j+2}-\tau^{t+2}_{i,j+2})}{(1+E^{t^-}r^{t+1})(1+E^{t^-}r^{t+2})} + \ldots + \frac{E^{t^-}(u^{t+E^{t^-}J_i-j}_{i,E^{t^-}J_i} - \tau^{t+E^{t^-}J_i-j}_{i,E^{t^-}J_i})}{(1+E^{t^-}r^{t+1})\ldots(1+E^{t^-}r^{t+E^{t^-}J_i-j})}.$$

Expression (79) was obtained from expression (77) by deleting its first term as well as the first period discount factor $1+E^{t^-}r^t$. This reflects the fact that at the end of period t the asset's remaining lifetime has become shorter by one period. Generally one may expect that $E^{t^-}P^{t^+}_{i,j+0.5} \le P^{t^-}_{i,j-0.5}$.

Expression (78) differs from expression (79) in that expectations are at $(t+1)^-$ instead of t^-. Since one may expect that, due to technological progress, the remaining economic lifetime of any asset shortens, that is, $E^{(t+1)^-}J_i \le E^{t^-}J_i$, expression (78) contains fewer terms than expression (79). Generally one may expect that $P^{t^+}_{i,j+0.5} \le E^{t^-}P^{t^+}_{i,j+0.5}$; that is, the actual price of an asset at the end of a period is less than or equal to the price as expected at the beginning.

Armed with these insights we return to the unit user cost expressions (68) and (69). Natural decompositions of these two expressions are

$$(80)\quad u^t_{ij} = r^t P^{t^-}_{i,j-0.5} + (P^{t^-}_{i,j-0.5} - E^{t^-}P^{t^+}_{i,j+0.5}) + (E^{t^-}P^{t^+}_{i,j+0.5} - P^{t^+}_{i,j+0.5}) + \tau^t_{ij}, \quad \text{for } j=1,\ldots,J_i,$$

and

$$(81)\quad v^t_{ij} = (1/2)r^t P^t_{ij} + (P^t_{ij} - E^t P^{t^+}_{i,j+0.5}) + (E^t P^{t^+}_{i,j+0.5} - P^{t^+}_{i,j+0.5}) + (1/2)\tau^t_{ij}, \quad \text{for } j=0,\ldots,J_i.$$

As before, the first term at either right-hand side represents the price of waiting. The second term, between brackets, is called anticipated time-series depreciation, and could be decomposed into the anticipated effect of time (or, anticipated revaluation) and the anticipated effect of ageing (or, anticipated cross-section depreciation). The third term, also between brackets, is called unanticipated revaluation. We will come back to these terms later.

The underlying idea is that, at the beginning of each period or, in the case of investment, at the midpoint, economic decisions are based on anticipated rather than realized prices. The fourth term in the two decompositions is again the tax term. It is here assumed that with respect to waiting and tax, anticipated and realized prices coincide.

Substituting expressions (80) and (81) into expression (70), one obtains the following aggregate decomposition,

(82)
$$\begin{aligned}
C_K^t &= \sum_{i=1}^{I}\sum_{j=1}^{J_i} r^t P_{i,j-0.5}^{t^-} K_{ij}^t + \sum_{i=1}^{I}\sum_{j=0}^{J_i}(1/2) r^t P_{ij}^t I_{ij}^t \\
&+ \sum_{i=1}^{I}\sum_{j=1}^{J_i}(P_{i,j-0.5}^{t^-} - E^{t^-} P_{i,j+0.5}^{t^+}) K_{ij}^t + \sum_{i=1}^{I}\sum_{j=0}^{J_i}(P_{i,j}^t - E^t P_{i,j+0.5}^{t^+}) I_{ij}^t \\
&+ \sum_{i=1}^{I}\sum_{j=1}^{J_i}(E^{t^-} P_{i,j+0.5}^{t^+} - P_{i,j+0.5}^{t^+}) K_{ij}^t + \sum_{i=1}^{I}\sum_{j=0}^{J_i}(E^t P_{i,j+0.5}^{t^+} - P_{i,j+0.5}^{t^+}) I_{ij}^t \\
&+ \sum_{i=1}^{I}\sum_{j=1}^{J_i}\tau_{ij}^t K_{ij}^t + \sum_{i=1}^{I}\sum_{j=0}^{J_i}(1/2)\tau_{ij}^t I_{ij}^t .
\end{aligned}$$

On the first line after the equality sign we have the aggregate cost of waiting,

(83) $$C_{K,w}^t \equiv r^t \left(\sum_{i=1}^{I}\sum_{j=1}^{J_i} P_{i,j-0.5}^{t^-} K_{ij}^t + \sum_{i=1}^{I}\sum_{j=0}^{J_i}(1/2) P_{ij}^t I_{ij}^t \right).$$

Notice that the part between brackets differs slightly from expression (71). It can be interpreted as the production unit's productive capital stock *as used* during period t.

On the second line after the equality sign in expression (82) we have the aggregate cost of anticipated time-series depreciation,

(84) $$C_{K,e}^t = \sum_{i=1}^{I}\sum_{j=1}^{J_i}(P_{i,j-0.5}^{t^-} - E^{t^-} P_{i,j+0.5}^{t^+}) K_{ij}^t + \sum_{i=1}^{I}\sum_{j=0}^{J_i}(P_{i,j}^t - E^t P_{i,j+0.5}^{t^+}) I_{ij}^t .$$

On the third line we have the aggregate cost of unanticipated revaluation,

(85) $$C_{K,u}^t = \sum_{i=1}^{I}\sum_{j=1}^{J_i}(E^{t^-} P_{i,j+0.5}^{t^+} - P_{i,j+0.5}^{t^+}) K_{ij}^t + \sum_{i=1}^{I}\sum_{j=0}^{J_i}(E^t P_{i,j+0.5}^{t^+} - P_{i,j+0.5}^{t^+}) I_{ij}^t .$$

Finally, on the fourth line we have the aggregate cost of tax,

(86) $$C_{K,tax}^t = \sum_{i=1}^{I}\sum_{j=1}^{J_i}\tau_{ij}^t K_{ij}^t + \sum_{i=1}^{I}\sum_{j=0}^{J_i}(1/2)\tau_{ij}^t I_{ij}^t .$$

Using these definitions, expression (82) reduces to

(87) $$C_K^t = C_{K,w}^t + C_{K,e}^t + C_{K,u}^t + C_{K,tax}^t .$$

Thus, capital input cost can rather naturally be split into four meaningful components. As will be detailed in the next section, this leads to four additional input-output models.

6. More Models

6.1 The KL-NVA model

The first two models are variants of the KL-VA model. The idea is that the (ex post) cost of time-series depreciation plus tax should be treated like the cost of intermediate inputs, and subtracted from value added. Hence, the output concept is called net value added, and defined by

$$NVA^t \equiv VA^t - (C^t_{K,e} + C^t_{K,u} + C^t_{K,tax}). \tag{88}$$

The remaining input cost is the sum of labour cost, C^t_L, and waiting cost of capital, $C^t_{K,w}$. It is assumed that $NVA^t > 0$.

Some argue that this model is to be preferred from a welfare-theoretic point of view. If the objective is to hold owned capital (including investments during the accounting period) in terms of money intact, then depreciation -- whether expected or not -- and tax should be treated like intermediate inputs (see Spant 2003). This model was strongly defended by Rymes (1983). Apart from land, he considered labour and waiting as the only primary inputs, and connected this with a Harrodian model of technological change.

The counterpart to *profitability* in this model is

$$\frac{NVA^t}{C^t_{K,w} + C^t_L},$$

and the problem is to decompose the ratios NVA^1 / NVA^0 and $(C^1_{K,w} + C^1_L)/(C^0_{K,w} + C^0_L)$ into price and quantity components. The decomposition of the net-value-added ratio is structurally similar to the decomposition of the value-added ratio (see appendix B). Hence, let a solution be given by

$$\frac{NVA^1}{NVA^0} = P_{NVA}(1,0)Q_{NVA}(1,0). \tag{89}$$

Using one- or two-stage Fisher indices, the input cost ratio can be decomposed as

$$\frac{C^1_{K,w} + C^1_L}{C^0_{K,w} + C^0_L} = P_{KwL}(1,0)Q_{KwL}(1,0). \tag{90}$$

The net-value-added based (total factor) productivity index for period 1 relative to period 0 is then defined as

$$IPROD_{NVA}(1,0) \equiv \frac{Q_{NVA}(1,0)}{Q_{KwL}(1,0)}. \tag{91}$$

In general, $IPROD_{NVA}(1,0) \neq IPROD(1,0)$. Following the reasoning of Balk (2009) it is possible to show that, if profit is zero in both periods, that is, $R^t = C^t$ $(t = 0,1)$, then, for certain two-stage indices which are second-order differential approximations to Fisher indices,

(92) $\ln IPROD_{NVA}(1,0) = D'(1,0)\ln IPROD(1,0)$,

where $D'(1,0) \geq 1$ is the ratio of mean revenue over mean net value added. Since $NVA^t \leq VA^t$, it follows that $D'(1,0) \geq D(1,0)$.

The counterpart to *profit* in the KL-NVA model is $NVA^t - (C_{K,w}^t + C_L^t)$, but one easily checks that

(93) $NVA^t - (C_{K,w}^t + C_L^t) = R^t - C^t$.

Thus, profit in the KL-NVA model is the same as profit in the KLEMS-Y model, and the same applies to their price and quantity components. Hence, there is nothing really new here.

6.2 The KL-NNVA Model

Diewert, Mizobuchi and Nomura (2005), Diewert and Lawrence (2006) and Diewert and Wykoff (2011) suggested we should consider unanticipated revaluation, which is the unanticipated part of time-series depreciation, as a monetary component that must be added to profit. The result could be called "profit from normal operations of the production unit." Following this suggestion, the output concept becomes

(94) $NNVA^t \equiv VA^t - (C_{K,e}^t + C_{K,tax}^t)$,

which could be called normal net value added. The inputs considered are labour, C_L^t, and the waiting cost of capital, $C_{K,w}^t$. It is assumed that $NNVA^t > 0$.

The counterpart to *profitability* now is

$$\frac{NNVA^t}{C_{K,w}^t + C_L^t},$$

and the problem is to decompose the ratios $NNVA^1 / NNVA^0$ and $(C_{K,w}^1 + C_L^1)/(C_{K,w}^0 + C_L^0)$ into price and quantity components. The decomposition of the normal-net-value-added ratio is structurally similar to the decomposition of the value-added ratio (see appendix B). Hence, let a solution be given by

(95) $\frac{NNVA^1}{NNVA^0} = P_{NNVA}(1,0)Q_{NNVA}(1,0)$.

The decomposition of the input cost ratio was given by expression (90). The normal-net-value-added based (total factor) productivity index for period 1 relative to period 0 is then defined as

(96) $IPROD_{NNVA}(1,0) \equiv \frac{Q_{NNVA}(1,0)}{Q_{KwL}(1,0)}$.

In general it will be the case that $IPROD_{NNVA}(1,0) \neq IPROD_{NVA}(1,0)$.

The counterpart to *profit* in the KL-NNVA model is $NNVA^t - (C^t_{K,w} + C^t_L)$. However, one easily checks that

(97) $\quad NNVA^t - (C^t_{K,w} + C^t_L) = R^t - C^t + C^t_{K,u}$

Hence, the KL-NNVA model really differs from the KLEMS-Y model.

6.3 The K-NCF model

The last two models are variants of the K-CF model. Here also the idea is that the (ex post) cost of time-series depreciation plus tax should be treated like the cost of intermediate inputs, and subtracted from cash flow. The output concept is called net cash flow, and defined by

(98) $\quad NCF^t \equiv CF^t - (C^t_{K,e} + C^t_{K,u} + C^t_{K,tax})$.

The remaining input cost is the waiting cost of capital, $C^t_{K,w}$. It is assumed that $NCF^t > 0$.

The counterpart to profitability now is $NCF^t / C^t_{K,w}$ and the problem is to decompose the ratios NCF^1 / NCF^0 and $C^1_{K,w} / C^0_{K,w}$ into price and quantity components. The decomposition of the net-cash-flow ratio is structurally similar to the decomposition of the value-added ratio (see appendix B). Hence, let a solution be given by

(99) $$\frac{NCF^1}{NCF^0} = P_{NCF}(1,0)Q_{NCF}(1,0).$$

Using Fisher indices, the waiting cost of capital ratio can be decomposed as

(100) $$\frac{C^1_{K,w}}{C^0_{K,w}} = P_{Kw}(1,0)Q_{Kw}(1,0).$$

The net-cash-flow based (total factor) productivity index for period 1 relative to 0 is then defined as

(101) $$IPROD_{NCF}(1,0) \equiv \frac{Q_{NCF}(1,0)}{Q_{Kw}(1,0)}.$$

In general, it will be the case that $IPROD_{NCF}(1,0) \neq IPROD(1,0)$. Following the reasoning of Balk (2009), it is possible to show that, if profit is zero in both periods, that is, $R^t = C^t \ (t = 0,1)$, then, for certain two-stage indices which are second-order differential approximations to Fisher indices,

(102) $\quad \ln IPROD_{NCF}(1,0) = E'(1,0) \ln IPROD(1,0)$,

where $E'(1,0) \geq 1$ is the ratio of mean revenue over mean net cash flow. Since $NCF^t \leq CF^t$, it follows that $E'(1,0) \geq E(1,0)$.

The counterpart to *profit* in the K-NCF model is $NCF^t - C^t_{K,w}$, but one easily checks that

(103) $NCF^t - C^t_{K,w} = R^t - C^t$.

Thus, profit in the K-NCF model is the same as profit in the KLEMS-Y model, and the same applies to their price and quantity components. Hence, there is nothing really new here.

6.4 The K-NNCF Model

A variant of the K-NCF model is obtained by considering unanticipated revaluation, which is the unanticipated part of time-series depreciation, as a component that must be added to profit. Hence, the output concept becomes

(104) $NNCF^t \equiv CF^t - (C^t_{K,e} + C^t_{K,tax})$,

which could be called normal net cash flow. It is assumed that $NNCF^t > 0$. The only input category is the waiting cost of capital, $C^t_{K,w}$.[24]

The counterpart to profitability now is $NNCF^t / C^t_{K,w}$, and the problem is to decompose the ratios $NNCF^1 / NNCF^0$ and $C^1_{K,w} / C^0_{K,w}$ into price and quantity components. The decomposition of the normal-net-cash-flow ratio is structurally similar to the decomposition of the value-added ratio (see appendix B). Hence, let a solution be given by

(105) $$\frac{NNCF^1}{NNCF^0} = P_{NNCF}(1,0) Q_{NNCF}(1,0).$$

The decomposition of the input cost ratio was given by expression (100). The normal-net-value-added based (total factor) productivity index for period 1 relative to period 0 is then defined as

(106) $$IPROD_{NNCF}(1,0) \equiv \frac{Q_{NNCF}(1,0)}{Q_{Kw}(1,0)}.$$

In general it will be the case that $IPROD_{NNCF}(1,0) \neq IPROD_{NCF}(1,0)$.

The counterpart to *profit* in the K-NNCF model is $NNCF^t - C^t_{K,w}$. However, one easily checks that

(107) $NNCF^t - C^t_{K,w} = R^t - C^t + C^t_{K,u}$.

---

[24] In the model of Hulten and Schreyer (2006) total (= unanticipated plus anticipated) revaluation is added to profit. This is consistent with SNA93's prescription for non-market units.

Hence, the K-NNCF model really differs from the KLEMS-Y model. However, the K-NNCF model is the same as the KL-NNVA model, as can be concluded from a comparison of expressions (97) and (107).

7. The Rate of Return

It is useful to recall the various models in their order of appearance. We are using thereby the notation introduced gradually. Further, recall that $\Pi^t \equiv R^t - C^t$ denotes profit. The KLEMS-Y model is governed by the following accounting identity, where input categories are placed left and output categories are placed right of the equality sign:

$$(108) \quad C_{K,w}^t + C_{K,e}^t + C_{K,u}^t + C_{K,tax}^t + C_L^t + C_E^t + C_M^t + C_S^t + \Pi^t = R^t.$$

The $KL-VA$ model is then seen to be governed by

$$(109) \quad C_{K,w}^t + C_{K,e}^t + C_{K,u}^t + C_{K,tax}^t + C_L^t + \Pi^t = R^t - (C_E^t + C_M^t + C_S^t).$$

The $KL-NVA$ model is governed by

$$(110) \quad C_{K,w}^t + C_L^t + \Pi^t = R^t - (C_{K,e}^t + C_{K,u}^t + C_{K,tax}^t + C_E^t + C_M^t + C_S^t),$$

while the KL-NNVA model is governed by

$$(111) \quad C_{K,w}^t + C_L^t + \Pi^{*t} = R^t - (C_{K,e}^t + C_{K,tax}^t + C_E^t + C_M^t + C_S^t),$$

with $\Pi^{*t} \equiv \Pi^t + C_{K,u}^t$ being the profit from normal operations. In contrast, Π^t could be called the profit from all operations.

Similarly, departing from expression (108), the K-CF model is seen to be governed by

$$(112) \quad C_{K,w}^t + C_{K,e}^t + C_{K,u}^t + C_{K,tax}^t + \Pi^t = R^t - (C_L^t + C_E^t + C_M^t + C_S^t).$$

The K-NCF model is governed by

$$(113) \quad C_{K,w}^t + \Pi^t = R^t - (C_{K,e}^t + C_{K,u}^t + C_{K,tax}^t + C_L^t + C_E^t + C_M^t + C_S^t),$$

while the K-NNCF model is governed by

$$(114) \quad C_{K,w}^t + \Pi^{*t} = R^t - (C_{K,e}^t + C_{K,tax}^t + C_L^t + C_E^t + C_M^t + C_S^t).$$

The last two expressions provide an excellent point of departure for a discussion of the rate of return r^t, which determines the aggregate cost of waiting or opportunity cost $C_{K,w}^t$ according to expression (83). Using definition (98) and expression (83), the accounting identity of the K-NCF model can be rewritten as

$$(115)\quad r^t\left(\sum_{i=1}^{I}\sum_{j=1}^{J_i} P_{i,j-0.5}^{t^-}K_{ij}^t + \sum_{i=1}^{I}\sum_{j=0}^{J_i}(1/2)P_{i,j}^t I_{ij}^t\right) + \Pi^t = NCF^t.$$

Recall that the part between big brackets can be interpreted as the (value of the) production unit's capital stock as used during period t. Provided that $NCF^t \geq \Pi^t \geq 0$, the last equation then says that, apart from profit, net cash flow provides the return to the (owner of the) capital stock. This is the reason why r^t is also called the 'rate of return'.

In principle, the value of the capital stock as well as the net cash flow are empirically determined. That leaves an equation with two unknowns: the rate of return r^t and profit Π^t.

Setting $\Pi^t = 0$ and solving equation (115) for r^t delivers the so-called 'endogenous,' or 'internal' or 'balancing' rate of return. This solution is, of course, specific for the production unit. Net cash flow is calculated ex post, since it contains total time-series depreciation. Thus, the endogenous rate of return as calculated from expression (115) is also an ex post concept. The alternative is to specify some reasonable, *exogenous* value for the rate of return, say the annual percentage of headline CPI change plus something. Then, of course, profit follows from equation (115) and will in general be unequal to 0.

Thus, the endogenous rate of return is defined by the equation

$$(116)\quad r_{endo}^t\left(\sum_{i=1}^{I}\sum_{j=1}^{J_i} P_{i,j-0.5}^{t^-}K_{ij}^t + \sum_{i=1}^{I}\sum_{j=1}^{J_i}(1/2)P_{ij}^t I_{ij}^t\right) = NCF^t.$$

Combining this with expression (115) delivers the following relation between the endogenous and an exogenous rate of return:

$$(117)\quad r_{endo}^t = r^t + \Pi^t \Big/ \left(\sum_{i=1}^{I}\sum_{j=1}^{J_i} P_{i,j-0.5}^{t^-}K_{ij}^t + \sum_{i=1}^{I}\sum_{j=1}^{J_i}(1/2)P_{ij}^t I_{ij}^t\right).$$

Hence, profit Π^t is positive if and only if $r_{endo}^t > r^t$.

Alternatively, using definition (104), the accounting identity of the K-NNCF model can be rewritten as

$$(118)\quad r^t\left(\sum_{i=1}^{I}\sum_{j=1}^{J_i} P_{i,j-0.5}^{t^-}K_{ij}^t + \sum_{i=1}^{I}\sum_{j=0}^{J_i}(1/2)P_{i,j}^t I_{ij}^t\right) + \Pi^{*t} = NNCF^t.$$

Now, provided that $NNCF^t \geq \Pi^{*t} \geq 0$, normal net cash flow is seen as the return to the (owner of the) capital stock. Setting $\Pi^{*t} = 0$ and solving equation (118) for r^t delivers what can be called the 'normal endogenous' rate of return. In a sense, this rate absorbs not only profit but also the monetary value of all unanticipated asset revaluations. Alternatively, one can specify some reasonable, exogenous value for the rate of return. Then, of course, Π^{*t} follows from equation (118), and by subtracting the sum of all unanticipated asset revaluations, $C_{K,u}^t$, one obtains profit.

The two expressions (115) and (118) and their underlying models are polar cases. In the first, all unanticipated revaluations (that is, the whole of $C^t_{K,u}$) are considered as intermediate cost, whereas in the second they are considered as belonging to profit. Clearly, positions in between these two extremes are thinkable. For some asset types unanticipated revaluations might be considered as intermediate cost and for the remaining types these revaluations might be considered as belonging to profit.

This is a good moment to draw a number of conclusions. First, we have considered a number of input-output models: KLEMS-Y, KL-VA, KL-NVA, KL-NNVA, K-CF, K-NCF, and K-NNCF respectively. All these models lead to different (total factor) productivity *indices*. However, most of these differences are artifacts, caused by a different mixing of subtraction and division.[25] Thus, it depends on purpose and context of a study which particular model is chosen for the presentation of results. When productivity *indicators* are compared, the real difference turns up, namely between the KL-NNVA and K-NNCF models on the one hand and the rest on the other hand.

Second, there is no single concept of the endogenous rate of return. There is rather a continuum of possibilities, depending on the way one wants to deal with unanticipated revaluations.

Third, an endogenous rate of return, of whatever variety, can only be calculated ex post. Net cash flow as well as normal net cash flow require for their computation that the accounting period has expired.

Fourth, as the name suggests, a total factor productivity index or indicator suggests that all the inputs and outputs are correctly observed. Unobserved inputs and outputs and measurement errors lead to a distorted profit figure and have impacts on the interpretation of total factor productivity change. Since an endogenous rate of return can be said to absorb profit -- see expression (117) -- the extent of undercoverage has also implications for the interpretation of the rate of return (see also Schreyer 2011). Put otherwise, since an endogenous rate of return closes the gap between the input and the output side of the production unit, it is influenced by all sorts of measurement errors.

The question whether to use, for a certain production unit, an endogenous or an exogenous rate of return belongs, according to Diewert (2008), to the list of still unresolved issues. The practice of official statistical agencies is varied, as a brief survey reveals.

The U. S. Bureau of Labor Statistics uses endogenous rates (see Dean and Harper 2001),[26] as does Statistics Canada (see Harchaoui *et al*. 2001). The Australian Bureau of Statistics uses, per production unit considered, the maximum of the endogenous rate and a certain exogenous rate (set equal to the annual percentage change of the CPI plus 4 percent) (see Roberts 2006). Statistics New Zealand uses endogenous rates (according to their *Sources and Methods 2006* publication). The Swiss Federal Statistical office has the most intricate system: per production unit the simple mean of the endogenous rate and a certain exogenous rate is used

[25] Rymes (1983) would single out the KL-NVA model as the "best" one, but this is clearly not backed by the argument presented here.

[26] It seems to me that Jorgenson (2009) is also proposing endogenous rates of return for the four sectors considered.

as the final exogenous rate (see Rais and Sollberger 2008). Concerning the endogenous rates, however, these sources are not clear as to which concept is used precisely.

The fact that an endogenous rate of return can only be calculated ex post seems to imply that ex ante unit user costs can only be based on exogenous values for the rate of return. This, of course, implies some arbitrariness. However, since the anticipated unit user costs serve as data in economic decision processes, it is not unimportant to consider the question whether there is a sense in which such unit user costs can be based on an endogenous rate of return. This is a topic considered by Oulton (2007). The rather simple model he is using already makes clear that a fair amount of mental acrobatics is needed to combine the concept of endogeneity with that of anticipation. Let us consider the situation in our set-up.

The (at the beginning of period t) anticipated unit user cost for an asset of type i and age j over period t is, based on expression (77) and (79), given by

$$(119)\quad E^{t^-} u^t_{ij} = (E^{t^-} r^t) P^{t^-}_{i,j-0.5} + (P^{t^-}_{i,j-0.5} - E^{t^-} P^{t^+}_{i,j+0.5}) + E^{t^-} \tau^t_{ij} \qquad \text{for } j = 1,\ldots,J_i .$$

These unit user costs concern assets that are available at the beginning of period t. There are, however, also investments to be made. In our set-up these investments happen at the midpoint of each period. Then, compare expression (81), the (at the midpoint of period t) anticipated unit user cost for an asset of type i and age j over the second half of period t is given by

$$(120)\quad E^t v^t_{ij} = ((1/2)E^t r^t) P^t_{i,j} + (P^t_{i,j} - E^t P^{t^+}_{i,j+0.5}) + (1/2)E^t \tau^t_{ij} \qquad \text{for } j = 0,\ldots,J_i .$$

Anticipated total user cost over period t is now equal to

$$
\begin{aligned}
EC^t_K \equiv\ & (E^{t^-} r^t)\sum_{i=1}^{I}\sum_{j=1}^{J_i} P^{t^-}_{i,j-0.5} K^t_{ij} + (E^t r^t)\sum_{i=1}^{I}\sum_{j=0}^{J_i} (1/2) P^t_{ij} \hat{I}^t_{ij} \\
(121)\qquad & + \sum_{i=1}^{I}\sum_{j=1}^{J_i} (P^{t^-}_{i,j-0.5} - E^{t^-} P^{t^+}_{i,j+0.5}) K^t_{ij} + \sum_{i=1}^{I}\sum_{j=0}^{J_i} (P^t_{i,j} - E^t P^{t^+}_{i,j+0.5}) \hat{I}^t_{ij} \\
& + \sum_{i=1}^{I}\sum_{j=1}^{J_i} (E^{t^-} \tau^t_{ij}) K^t_{ij} + \sum_{i=1}^{I}\sum_{j=0}^{J_i} (1/2)(E^t \tau^t_{ij}) \hat{I}^t_{ij},
\end{aligned}
$$

where the quantities $\hat{I}^t_{ij}$ $(i = 1,\ldots,I;\ j = 0,\ldots,J_i)$ are as yet to be determined. Thus, given asset prices, expected asset prices, and expected amounts of tax-per-unit, expression (121) contains $\sum_{i=1}^{I}(1+J_i)$ unknown investment quantities, in addition to the two rate of return terms, $E^{t^-} r^t$ and $E^t r^t$. Now this expression corresponds to the left-hand side of the accounting identity of the K-CF model. For the right-hand side we need the anticipated value of period t's cash flow. Based on past experience, at the beginning of period t the production unit may have expectations about its output prices, and the prices of its labour, energy, materials, and services inputs. The corresponding quantities, however, are as yet to be determined. Taken together, we are having here a single equation with many unknowns and, except under heroic, simplifying assumptions, it seems difficult to get an indubitable solution for the required, endogenous rate of return.

Finally, the concept of an endogenous rate of return does not make sense for non-market units, since there is no accounting identity based on independent measures at the input and the output side.

8. Capital Utilization

Until now it was tacitly assumed that the productive capital stock was fully used in actual production. We want to make this assumption explicit. For introducing the capital utilization rate, let us return to the K-CF model, which is governed by the equation

$$(122)\quad C_K^t + \Pi^t = CF^t,$$

where C_K^t is given by expression (70). Cash flow, if positive, is seen as the return to the productive capital stock. But what if this stock is only partly used in productive operations?

Let $\{\theta_K^t K_{ij}^t, \theta_K^t I_{ij}^t; i = 1,\ldots, I; j = 0,\ldots, J_i\}$, where $0 < \theta_K^t < 1$, is the part of the productive capital stock that is actually used during period t. For ease of presentation the utilization rate θ_K^t is assumed to be the same for all asset types and ages. Then one easily checks that the foregoing equation, governing the K-CF model, can be written as

$$(123)\quad \theta_K^t C_K^t + (1-\theta_K^t)C_K^t + \Pi^t = CF^t$$

where $\theta_K^t C_K^t$ and $(1-\theta_K^t)C_K^t$ are the user costs of the used and unused parts of the capital stock, respectively.

Now, like unanticipated revaluation, one can argue that the cost of unused capital should be added to profit and that the measurement of productivity change should be based on the equation

$$(124)\quad \theta_K^t C_K^t + \Pi^{**t} = CF^t,$$

with $\Pi^{**t} \equiv (1-\theta_K^t)C_K^t + \Pi^t$ being the profit adjusted for underutilization of capital. Put otherwise, in this model the (total factor) productivity index for period 1 relative to period 0 is defined as

$$(125)\quad IPROD_{CFU}(1,0) \equiv \frac{Q_{CF}(1,0)}{(\theta_K^1/\theta_K^0)Q_K(1,0)}.$$

This is the index of real cash flow divided by the index of real capital input multiplied by the change of the capital utilization rate.

It is straightforward to check that the utilization rate can be introduced in any of the models discussed in this paper. This exercise is left to the reader.

9. Implementation Issues

There remain a number of implementation issues to discuss. For this, the reader is invited to return to expression (82). To ease the presentation, a period is now set equal to a year.

The quantities $\{K_{ij}^{t}; i=1,\ldots,I; j=1,\ldots,J_i\}$ and $\{I_{ij}^{t}; i=1,\ldots,I; j=0,\ldots,J_i\}$ are usually not available. Instead, as is the case in the Netherlands, the Perpetual Inventory Method generates estimates of the opening stock of assets at period $t-1$ prices $\{P_{i,j-0.5}^{t-1}K_{ij}^{t} = P_{i,j-0.5}^{t-1}K_{ij-0.5}^{t^-}; i=1,\ldots,I; j=1,\ldots,J_i\}$, and the Investment Survey generates estimates of mid-period values $\{P_{ij}^{t}I_{ij}^{t}; i=1,\ldots,I; j=0,\ldots,J_i\}$.

Models for time-series depreciation are briefly discussed in appendix C. The time-series depreciation for an asset of type i and age j that is available at the beginning of period t is in practice frequently modeled as

$$(126)\quad \frac{P_{i,j+0.5}^{t^+}}{P_{i,j-0.5}^{t^-}} = \frac{PPI_i^{t^+}}{PPI_i^{t^-}}(1-\delta_{ij}),$$

where PPI_i^{t} denotes the Producer Price Index (or a kindred price index) that is applicable to new assets of type i, and δ_{ij} is the annual cross-section depreciation rate that is applicable to an asset of type i and age j. This depreciation rate ideally comes from an empirically estimated age-price profile.

Thus, time-series depreciation is modeled as a simple, multiplicative function of two, independent factors. The first one, $PPI_i^{t^+} / PPI_i^{t^-}$, which is one plus the annual rate of price change of new assets of type i, concerns the effect of the progress of time on the value of an asset of type i and age j. The second one, $1-\delta_{ij} > 0$, concerns the effect of ageing by one year on the value of an asset of type i and age j. Ageing by one year causes the value to decline by $\delta_{ij} \times 100$ percent.

Similarly, anticipated time-series depreciation is modeled as

$$(127)\quad \frac{E^{t^-}P_{i,j+0.5}^{t^+}}{P_{i,j-0.5}^{t^-}} = E^{t^-}\left(\frac{PPI_i^{t^+}}{PPI_i^{t^-}}\right)(1-\delta_{ij}).$$

In this expression, instead of the annual rate of price change of new assets, as observed ex post , the annual rate as expected at the beginning of period t is taken.

But what to expect? There are, of course, several options here. The first that comes to mind is to use some past, observed rate of change of PPI_i or a more general PPI. Second, one could assume that expectedly the rate of price change of new assets is equal to the rate of change of the (headline) CPI, and use the 'realized expectation':

$$(128)\quad E^{t^-}\left(\frac{PPI_i^{t^+}}{PPI_i^{t^-}}\right)=\frac{CPI^{t^+}}{CPI^{t^-}}.$$

Under the last assumption, the anticipated time-series depreciation is measured as

$$(129)\quad \frac{E^{t^-}P_{i,j+0.5}^{t^+}}{P_{i,j-0.5}^{t^-}}=\frac{CPI^{t^+}}{CPI^{t^-}}(1-\delta_{ij}),$$

and, combining expressions (126) and (129), unanticipated revaluation is measured by

$$(130)\quad \frac{E^{t^-}P_{i,j+0.5}^{t^+}}{P_{i,j-0.5}^{t^-}}-\frac{P_{i,j+0.5}^{t^+}}{P_{i,j-0.5}^{t^-}}=\left(\frac{CPI^{t^+}}{CPI^{t^-}}-\frac{PPI_i^{t^+}}{PPI_i^{t^-}}\right)(1-\delta_{ij}).$$

Similar expressions hold for assets that are acquired at the midpoint of period t, except that we must make a distinction between new and used assets. The time-series depreciation for an asset of type i and age j is modeled as

$$\frac{P_{i,0.5}^{t^+}}{P_{i,0}^{t}}=\frac{PPI_i^{t^+}}{PPI_i^{t}}(1-\delta_{i0})$$

$$(131)\quad \frac{P_{i,j+0.5}^{t^+}}{P_{i,j}^{t}}=\frac{PPI_i^{t^+}}{PPI_i^{t}}(1-\delta_{ij}/2),\qquad \text{for } j=1,\dots,J_i.$$

The anticipated time-series depreciation is measured by

$$\frac{E^tP_{i,0.5}^{t^+}}{P_{i,0}^{t}}=\frac{CPI^{t^+}}{CPI^{t}}(1-\delta_{i0})$$

$$(132)\quad \frac{E^tP_{i,j+0.5}^{t^+}}{P_{i,j}^{t}}=\frac{CPI^{t^+}}{CPI^{t}}(1-\delta_{ij}/2),\qquad \text{for } j=1,\dots,J_i,$$

and unanticipated revaluation is measured by

$$(133)\quad \frac{E^t P^{t^+}_{i,0.5}}{P^t_{i,0}} - \frac{P^{t^+}_{i,0.5}}{P^t_{i,0}} = \left(\frac{CPI^{t^+}}{CPI^t} - \frac{PPI_i^{t^+}}{PPI_i^t} \right)(1-\delta_{i0})$$

$$\frac{E^t P^{t^+}_{i,j+0.5}}{P^t_{i,j}} - \frac{P^{t^+}_{i,j+0.5}}{P^t_{i,j}} = \left(\frac{CPI^{t^+}}{CPI^t} - \frac{PPI_i^{t^+}}{PPI_i^t} \right)(1-\delta_{ij}/2) \qquad \text{for } j = 1,\ldots,J_i.$$

An important question is in which circumstances the unit user costs u^t_{ij} and v^t_{ij} become non-positive? Consider, for instance, expression (80), and substitute expressions (129) and (130). This yields

$$(134)\quad \begin{aligned} \frac{u^t_{ij}}{P^{t^-}_{i,j-0.5}} &= r^t + 1 - \frac{CPI^{t^+}}{CPI^{t^-}}(1-\delta_{ij}) + \left(\frac{CPI^{t^+}}{CPI^{t^-}} - \frac{PPI_i^{t^+}}{PPI_i^{t^-}} \right)(1-\delta_{ij}) + \frac{\tau^t_{ij}}{P^{t^-}_{i,j-0.5}} \\ &= r^t + 1 - \frac{PPI_i^{t^+}}{PPI_i^{t^-}}(1-\delta_{ij}) + \frac{\tau^t_{ij}}{P^{t^-}_{i,j-0.5}}. \end{aligned}$$

Hence, $u^t_{ij} \le 0$ if and only if

$$(135)\quad \frac{PPI_i^{t^+}}{PPI_i^{t^-}} \ge \frac{1 + r^t + \tau^t_{ij} / P^{t^-}_{i,j-0.5}}{1-\delta_{ij}}.$$

In certain, extreme cases this can indeed happen. Consider assets with a very low cross-sectional depreciation rate (such as certain buildings or land) and a very high revaluation rate (or rate of price increase). A low interest plus tax rate can then lead to negative unit user costs. Put otherwise, when the ex post revaluation (as measured by a PPI) more than offsets interest plus tax plus depreciation then the unit user cost of such an asset becomes negative.

If the unanticipated revaluation is deleted from the user cost, that is, unit user cost is measured by

$$(136)\quad \frac{u^t_{ij}}{P^{t^-}_{i,j-0.5}} = r^t + 1 - \frac{CPI^{t^+}}{CPI^{t^-}}(1-\delta_{ij}) + \frac{\tau^t_{ij}}{P^{t^-}_{i,j-0.5}},$$

then $u^t_{ij} \le 0$ if and only if

$$(137)\quad \frac{CPI^{t^+}}{CPI^{t^-}} \geq \frac{1+r^t+\tau_{ij}^t / P_{i,j-0.5}^{t^-}}{1-\delta_{ij}}.$$

The likelihood that such a situation will occur is small. For this to happen, expected revaluation (as measured by a *CPI*) must more than offset interest plus tax plus depreciation.

10. The Netherlands' System in Perspective

Against the backdrop of the preceding analysis, I now briefly review the Netherlands' system of productivity statistics, as laid out in Van den Bergen *et al.* (2007). Basically the system is built on the KLEMS-Y and KL-VA models.

Revenue R (or the value of gross output), value added VA, and intermediate inputs cost C_{EMS} is obtained from National Accounts' supply and use tables at current and previous year prices. The level of detail is a cross classification of 120 industries and 275 commodity groups. When it comes to consolidation, imputations must be made for trade and transport margins. The reason is that inter-industry deliveries of these margins are not recorded, but must be estimated from column and row totals.

The quantity indices $Q_R(t,t-1)$, $Q_{VA}(t,t-1)$, and $Q_{EMS}(t,t-1)$ are, for the time being and to be consistent with National Accounts' practice, chosen as Laspeyres.

Labour cost, C_L, is based on a cross-classification of two types (employees and self-employed workers) and 49 industries. The unit of measurement is an hour worked. It is assumed that, with some exceptions, in each industry self-employed workers have the same annual income as employees. Again, the quantity index $Q_L(t,t-1)$ is Laspeyres.

The cost of capital input, C_K, is based on a cross-classification of 20 asset types by 60 industries by 18 institutional sectors. Beginning of year estimates of the available capital stock are generated by a version of the Perpetual Inventory Method, whereas the annual Investment Survey delivers the values of additions to and subtractions from the capital stock. User cost is calculated according to expression (70), with (68) and (69) substituted, except that at the level of asset type (and age) the tax (plus subsidies) components are not known. Thus, the tax (plus subsidies) components must be inserted at a higher level of aggregation. Wherever necessary, beginning and end of year price index numbers are approximated by geometric means of adjacent year (average) annual price index numbers. For instance, $PPI_i^{t^+}$ is approximated by $(PPI_i^t PPI_i^{t+1})^{1/2}$. The quantity index $Q_K(t,t-1)$ is Laspeyres. All the operational details are discussed by Balk and Van den Bergen (2006). The capital utilization rate is set equal to 1.

The interest rate r^t is set equal to the so-called Internal Reference Rate, which is the interest rate that banks charge to each other, plus 1.5 percent. For all the assets, unanticipated revaluation is retained as part of their unit user cost.[27]

Tying the various strands together, the gross output based total factor productivity index is computed as

$$(138)\quad IPROD(t,t-1) = \frac{Q_R(t,t-1)}{\left[\dfrac{C_K^{t-1}Q_K(t,t-1) + C_L^{t-1}Q_L(t,t-1) + C_{EMS}^{t-1}Q_{EMS}(t,t-1)}{C_K^{t-1} + C_L^{t-1} + C_{EMS}^{t-1}}\right]},$$

and the value-added based total factor productivity index as

$$(139)\quad IPROD_{VA}(t,t-1) = \frac{Q_{VA}(t,t-1)}{\left[\dfrac{C_K^{t-1}Q_K(t,t-1) + C_L^{t-1}Q_L(t,t-1)}{C_K^{t-1} + C_L^{t-1}}\right]}.$$

A number of sensitivity analyses were performed to gauge the influence of assumptions on outcomes. I review the main results:

1. Changing the index formula, from Laspeyres to Paasche and Fisher, did not lead to remarkable adjustments.
2. For all the assets, unanticipated revaluation was excluded from their unit user cost, which means that it was added to profit. This led to small, immaterial differences between the TFP index numbers.
3. Varying the exogenous interest rate, for instance by setting it equal to the annual rate of change of the headline CPI plus 4 percent, also caused relatively small changes.
4. Using endogenous interest rates, computed according to expression (115), had considerably more impact. The endogenous rates themselves showed a substantial variability, both cross-sectionally (over industries) and intertemporally. Moreover, there appeared to be a strong dependence on the imputation method used for the compensation of self-employed workers. The resulting TFP index numbers varied wildly, especially in agriculture and the mining industry.[28]

Interesting empirical results were obtained by Vancauteren *et al.* (2009). Over the years 1995 to 2007 these authors calculated total factor productivity changes according to the KLEMS-Y, KL-

[27] The only exception, by SNA93 conventions motivated, concerns the asset type "transfer of property rights."

[28] It is also interesting to look at the results of the sensitivity analyses carried out by Erumban (2008b), in particular those concerning the interest rate and the revaluation part of the user cost. MacGibbon (2008) compared results from endogenous and exogenous rates of return and from the in- and exclusion of revaluations. Also interesting are the numerical results obtained by Coremberg (2008). He compared results from using Laspeyres and Törnqvist indices, undifferentiated and differentiated labour input categories, and capital input quantity indices for stocks and services. The biggest effect came from the introduction of a capital utilization rate.

VA, KL-NVA, K-CF and K-NCF models, with exogenous and endogenous interest rates, for nine industrial sectors and their aggregate.

11. Conclusion

After measurement comes explanation. Depending on the initial level of aggregation, there appear to be two main directions. The first is disaggregation: the explanation of productivity change at an aggregate level (economy, sector, industry) by productivity change at a lower level (firm, plant) and other factors, collectively subsumed under the heading of re-allocation (expansion, contraction, entry, and exit of units). This topic was reviewed by Balk (2003, section 6). As the example of Balk and Hoogenboom-Spijker (2003) demonstrates, this type of research is of an economic-statistical nature, and there are no neoclassical assumptions involved.

The second direction is concerned with the decomposition of productivity change into factors such as technological change, technical efficiency change, scale effects, input- and output-mix effects, and chance. The basic idea can be explained as follows.

To start with, for each time period t the technology to which the production unit under consideration has access is defined as the set S^t of all the input-output quantity combinations which are feasible during t. Such a set is assumed to have nice properties like being closed, bounded, and convex. Of particular interest is the subset of S^t, called its frontier, consisting of all the efficient input-output combinations. An input-output quantity combination is called efficient when output cannot be increased without increasing some input and input cannot be decreased without decreasing some output.

From base period to comparison period our production unit moves from $(x^0, y^0) \in S^0$ to $(x^1, y^1) \in S^1$. Decomposition of productivity change means that between these two points some hypothetical path is constructed, the segments of which can be given a distinct interpretation.

In particular, we consider the projection of (x^0, y^0) on the frontier of S^0, and the projection of (x^1, y^1) on the frontier of S^1. Comparing the base period and comparison period distances between the original points and their projections provides a measure of efficiency change.

Two more points are given by projecting (x^0, y^0) also on the frontier of S^1, and (x^1, y^1) on the frontier of S^0. The distance between the two frontiers at the base and comparison period projection points provides a (local) measure of technological change. And, finally, moving over each frontier (which is a surface in $N+M$-dimensional space) from a base period to a comparison period projection point provides measures of the scale and input-output mix effects.

The construction of all those measures was discussed by Balk (2004). Since there is no unique path connecting the two observations, there is no unique decomposition either.

And here come the neoclassical assumptions, at the end of the day rather than at its beginning. Suppose that the production unit always stays on the frontier, that its input- and output-mix is optimal at the, supposedly given, input and output prices, and that the two technology sets exhibit constant returns to scale, then productivity change reduces to technological change (see Balk (1998, section 3.7) for a formal proof). The technology sets are thereby supposed to reflect the true state of nature, which rules out chance as a factor also contributing to productivity change.[29]

Appendix A. Indices and Indicators

The basic measurement tools used are price and quantity indices and indicators. The first are ratio-type measures, and the second are difference-type measures. What, precisely, are the requirements for good tools?

A1. Indices

A *price index* is a positive, continuously differentiable function $P(p^1,y^1,p^0,y^0):\Re^{4N}_{++}\rightarrow\Re_{++}$ that correctly indicates any increase or decrease of the elements of the price vectors p^1 or p^0, conditional on the quantity vectors y^1 and y^0. A *quantity index* is a positive, continuously differentiable function of the same variables $Q(p^1,y^1,p^0,y^0):\Re^{4N}_{++}\rightarrow\Re_{++}$ that correctly indicates any increase or decrease of the elements of the quantity vectors y^1 and y^0, conditional on the price vectors p^1 or p^0. The number N is called the dimension of the price or quantity index.

The basic requirements on price and quantity indices are:

A1. Monotonicity in prices. $P(p^1,y^1,p^0,y^0)$ is increasing in comparison period prices p^1_n and decreasing in base period prices p^0_n $(n=1,\ldots,N)$.

A1′. Monotonicity in quantities. $Q(p^1,y^1,p^0,y^0)$ is increasing in comparison period quantities y^1_n and decreasing in base period quantities y^0_n $(n=1,\ldots,N)$.

A2. Linear homogeneity in comparison period prices. Multiplication of all comparison period prices by a common factor leads to multiplication of the price index number by this factor; that is, $P(\lambda p^1,y^1,p^0,y^0)=\lambda P(p^1,y^1,p^0,y^0)$ $(\lambda>0)$.

A2′. Linear homogeneity in comparison period quantities. Multiplication of all comparison period quantities by a common factor leads to multiplication of the quantity index number by this factor; that is, $Q(p^1,\lambda y^1,p^0,y^0)=\lambda Q(p^1,y^1,p^0,y^0)$ $(\lambda>0)$.

[29] On stochastic productivity measurement see Chambers (2008).

A3. Identity test. If all the comparison period prices are equal to the corresponding base period prices, then the price index number must be equal to 1: $P(p^1, y^1, p^0, y^0) = 1$.

A3′. Identity test. If all the comparison period quantities are equal to the corresponding base period quantities, then the quantity index number must be equal to 1: $Q(p^0, y^0, p^0, y^0) = 1$.

A4. Homogeneity of degree 0 in prices. Multiplication of all comparison and base period prices by the same factor does not change the price index number; that is, $P(\lambda p^1, y^1, \lambda p^0, y^0) = P(p^1, y^1, p^0, y^0)$ $(\lambda > 0)$.

A4′. Homogeneity of degree 0 in quantities. Multiplication of all comparison period and base period quantities by the same factor does not change the quantity index number; that is, $Q(p^1, \lambda y^1, p^0, \lambda y^0) = Q(p^1, y^1, p^0, y^0)$ $(\lambda > 0)$.

A5. Dimensional invariance. The price index is invariant to changes in the units of measurement of the commodities: for any diagonal matrix Λ with elements of $\Re_{++}$ it is required that $P(p^1\Lambda, y^1\Lambda^{-1}, p^0\Lambda, y^0\Lambda^{-1}) = P(p^1, y^1, p^0, y^0)$.

A5′. Dimensional invariance. The quantity index is invariant to changes in the units of measurement of the commodities: for any diagonal matrix Λ with elements of $\Re_{++}$, it is required that $Q(p^1\Lambda, y^1\Lambda^{-1}, p^0\Lambda, y^0\Lambda^{-1}) = Q(p^1, y^1, p^0, y^0)$.

Product Test. $P(p^1, y^1, p^0, y^0)Q(p^1, y^1, p^0, y^0) = p^1 \cdot y^1 / p^0 \cdot y^0$.

Any function $P(p^1, y^1, p^0, y^0)$ that satisfies axiom A5 can be written as a function of only $3N$ variables, namely the price relatives p_n^1 / p_n^0, the comparison period values $v_n^1 \equiv p_n^1 y_n^1$, and the base period values $v_n^0 \equiv p_n^0 y_n^0$ $(n = 1, \ldots, N)$.

Similarly, any function $Q(p^1, y^1, p^0, y^0)$ that satisfies axiom A5′ can be written as a function of only $3N$ variables, namely the quantity relatives y_n^1 / y_n^0, the comparison period values $v_n^1 \equiv p_n^1 y_n^1$, and the base period values $v_n^0 \equiv p_n^0 y_n^0$ $(n = 1, \ldots, N)$.

Some simple examples might be useful to illustrate this. Consider the Laspeyres price index as a function of prices and quantities,

$$P^L(p^1, y^1, p^0, y^0) \equiv p^1 \cdot y^0 / p^0 \cdot y^0,$$

and notice that this index can be written as a function of price relatives and (base period) values,

$$P^L(p^1, y^1, p^0, y^0) = \sum_{n=1}^N (p_n^1 / p_n^0) v_n^0 / \sum_{n=1}^N v_n^0 .$$

Similarly, the Paasche price index

$$P^P(p^1, y^1, p^0, y^0) \equiv p^1 \cdot y^1 / p^0 \cdot y^1,$$

can be written as a function of price relatives and (comparison period) values,

$$P^P(p^1,y^1,p^0,y^0)=\left(\sum_{n=1}^{N}(p_n^0/p_n^1)v_n^1/\sum_{n=1}^{N}v_n^1\right)^{-1}.$$

Finally, the Fisher price index, defined as the geometric mean of the Laspeyres and Paasche indices, reads

$$P^F(p^1,y^1,p^0,y^0)\equiv\left[\frac{\sum_{n=1}^{N}(p_n^1/p_n^0)v_n^0/\sum_{n=1}^{N}v_n^0}{\sum_{n=1}^{N}(p_n^0/p_n^1)v_n^1/\sum_{n=1}^{N}v_n^1}\right]^{1/2}.$$

Such functional forms are useful for the definition of two-stage indices. Let the aggregate under consideration be denoted by A, and let A be partitioned arbitrarily into K subaggregates A_k,

$$A=\cup_{k=1}^{K}A_k,\quad A_k\cap A_{k'}=\phi,\qquad\text{for } k\neq k'.$$

Each subaggregate consists of a number of items. Let $N_k\geq 1$ denote the number of items contained in A_k ($k=1,\ldots,K$). Obviously $N=\sum_{k=1}^{K}N_k$. Let $(p_k^1,y_k^1,p_k^0,y_k^0)$ be the subvector of (p^1,y^1,p^0,y^0) corresponding to the subaggregate A_k. Recall that $v_n^t\equiv p_n^t y_n^t$ is the value of item n at period t. Then $V_k^t\equiv\sum_{n\in A_k}v_n^t$ ($k=1,\ldots,K$) is the value of the subaggregate A_k at period t, and $V^t\equiv\sum_{n\in A}v_n^t=\sum_{k=1}^{K}V_k^t$ is the value of aggregate A at period t.

Let $P(\cdot)$, $P^{(1)}(.)$, ..., $P^{(K)}(.)$ be price indices of dimension $K,N_1,\ldots,N_K$ respectively that satisfy A1,...,A5. Then the price index defined by

$$(140)\quad P^*(p^1,y^1,p^0,y^0)\equiv P(P^{(k)}(p_k^1,x_k^1,p_k^0,x_k^0),V_k^1,V_k^0;k=1,\ldots,K)$$

is of dimension N and also satisfies A1,...,A5. The index $P^*(\cdot)$ is called a two-stage index. The first stage refers to the indices $P^{(k)}(\cdot)$ for the subaggregates A_k ($k=1,\ldots,K$). The second stage refers to the index $P(.)$ that is applied to the subindices $P^{(k)}(\cdot)$ ($k=1,\ldots,K$). A two-stage index such as is defined by expression (140) closely corresponds to the calculation practice at statistical agencies. All the subindices are usually of the same functional form, for instance Laspeyres or Paasche indices. The aggregate, second stage index may or may not be of the same functional form. This could be, for instance, a Fisher index.

If the functional forms of the subindices $P^{(k)}(\cdot)$ ($k=1,\ldots,K$) and the aggregate index $P(\cdot)$ are the same, then $P^*(\cdot)$ is called a two-stage $P(\cdot)$ index. Continuing the example, the two-stage Laspeyres price index reads

$$P^{*L}(p^1,y^1,p^0,y^0)\equiv\sum_{k=1}^{K}P^L(p_k^1,y_k^1,p_k^0,y_k^0)V_k^0/\sum_{k=1}^{K}V_k^0,$$

and one simply checks that the two-stage and the single-stage Laspeyres price indices coincide. However, this is the exception rather than the rule. For most indices, two-stage and single-stage variants do not coincide.

Similarly, let $Q(\cdot)$, $Q^{(1)}(\cdot)$, ..., $Q^{(K)}(\cdot)$ be quantity indices of dimension $K, N_1, \ldots, N_K$ respectively that satisfy A1′,…, A5′.. Then the quantity index defined by

(141) $Q^*(p^1, y^1, p^0, y^0) \equiv Q(Q^{(k)}(p^1_k, y^1_k, p^0_k, y^0_k), V^1_k, V^0_k; k = 1,\ldots, K)$

is of dimension N and also satisfies A1′,…, A5′. The index $Q^*(\cdot)$ is called a two-stage index.

A2. Indicators

Provided that certain reasonable requirements are satisfied, the continuous functions $\mathsf{P}(p^1, y^1, p^0, y^0) : \Re^{4N}_{++} \to \Re$ and $\mathsf{Q}(p^1, y^1, p^0, y^0) : \Re^{4N}_{++} \to \Re$ will be called a price indicator and a quantity indicator respectively. Notice that these functions may take on negative or zero values. The basic requirements are:

AA1. Monotonicity in prices. $\mathsf{P}(p^1, y^1, p^0, y^0)$ is increasing in comparison period prices p^1_n and decreasing in base period prices p^0_n $(n = 1, \ldots, N)$.

AA1′. Monotonicity in quantities. $\mathsf{Q}(p^1, y^1, p^0, y^0)$ is increasing in comparison period quantities y^1_n and decreasing in base period quantities y^0_n $(n = 1, \ldots, N)$.

AA3. Identity test. If all the comparison period prices are equal to the corresponding base period prices, then the price indicator must deliver the outcome 0: $\mathsf{P}(p^0, y^1, p^0, y^0) = 0$.

AA3′. Identity test. If all the comparison period quantities are equal to the corresponding base period quantities, then the quantity indicator must deliver the outcome 0: $\mathsf{Q}(p^1, y^0, p^0, y^0) = 0$.

AA4. Homogeneity of degree 1 in prices. Multiplication of all comparison and base period prices by a common factor changes the price indicator outcome by this factor; that is, $\mathsf{P}(\lambda p^1, y^1, \lambda p^0, y^0) = \lambda \mathsf{P}(p^1, y^1, p^0, y^0)$ $(\lambda > 0)$.

AA4′. Homogeneity of degree 1 in quantities. Multiplication of all comparison period and base period quantities by a common factor changes the quantity indicator outcome by this factor; that is, $\mathsf{Q}(p^1, \lambda y^1, p^0, \lambda y^0) = \lambda \mathsf{Q}(p^1, y^1, p^0, y^0)$ $(\lambda > 0)$.

AA5. Dimensional invariance. The price indicator is invariant to changes in the units of measurement of the commodities: for any diagonal matrix Λ with elements of $\Re_{++}$, it is required that $\mathsf{P}(p^1\Lambda, y^1\Lambda^{-1}, p^0\Lambda, y^0\Lambda^{-1}) = \mathsf{P}(p^1, y^1, p^0, y^0)$.

AA5′. Dimensional invariance. The quantity indicator is invariant to changes in the units of measurement of the commodities: for any diagonal matrix Λ with elements of $\Re_{++}$, it is required that $\mathsf{Q}(p^1\Lambda, y^1\Lambda^{-1}, p^0\Lambda, y^0\Lambda^{-1}) = \mathsf{Q}(p^1, y^1, p^0, y^0)$.

Analogue of the Product Test. $\mathsf{P}(p^1, y^1, p^0, y^0) + \mathsf{Q}(p^1, y^1, p^0, y^0) = p^1 \cdot y^1 - p^0 \cdot y^0$.

Any function $\mathsf{P}(p^1, y^1, p^0, y^0)$ that satisfies axiom AA5 can be written as a function of only $3N$ variables, namely the price relatives p_n^1 / p_n^0, the comparison period values $v_n^1 \equiv p_n^1 y_n^1$, and the base period values $v_n^0 \equiv p_n^0 y_n^0$ $(n = 1,\ldots,N)$.

Similarly, any function $\mathsf{Q}(p^1, y^1, p^0, y^0)$ that satisfies axiom *AA5′* can be written as a function of only $3N$ variables, namely the quantity relatives y_n^1 / y_n^0, the comparison period values $v_n^1 \equiv p_n^1 y_n^1$, and the base period values $v_n^0 \equiv p_n^0 y_n^0$ $(n = 1,\ldots,N)$.

Also here some simple examples might be useful. Consider the Laspeyres price indicator as a function of prices and quantities,

$$\mathsf{P}^L(p^1, y^1, p^0, y^0) \equiv (p^1 - p^0) \cdot y^0,$$

and notice that this indicator can be written as a function of price relatives and (base period) values,

$$\mathsf{P}^L(p^1, y^1, p^0, y^0) \equiv \textstyle\sum_{n=1}^N (p_n^1 / p_n^0 - 1) v_n^0 .$$

Similarly, the Paasche price indicator,

$$\mathsf{P}^P(p^1, y^1, p^0, y^0) \equiv (p^1 - p^0) \cdot y^1,$$

can be written as a function of price relatives and (comparison period) values,

$$\mathsf{P}^P(p^1, y^1, p^0, y^0) \equiv \textstyle\sum_{n=1}^N (1 - p_n^0 / p_n^1) v_n^1 .$$

Finally, the Bennet indicator is usually defined as

$$\mathsf{P}^B(p^1, y^1, p^0, y^0) \equiv (1/2)(p^1 - p^0) \cdot (y^1 + y^0),$$

but can be written as

$$\mathsf{P}^B(p^1, y^1, p^0, y^0) = (1/2)\left[\sum_{n=1}^N (p_n^1 / p_n^0 - 1) v_n^0 + \sum_{n=1}^N (1 - p_n^0 / p_n^1) v_n^1\right].$$

The Bennet price indicator for an aggregate is a simple sum of Bennet price indicators for its subaggregates:

$$\mathsf{P}^B(p^1, y^1, p^0, y^0) = \textstyle\sum_{k=1}^K \mathsf{P}^B(p_k^1, y_k^1, p_k^0, y_k^0),$$

and a similar relation holds for quantity indicators.

Appendix B. Decompositions of the Value Added Ratio

Value added is defined as revenue minus the cost of intermediate inputs. For the logarithm of the value added ratio, we get by repeated application of the logarithmic mean[30] $L(a,b)$,

$$\ln\left(\frac{VA^1}{VA^0}\right) = \frac{VA^1 - VA^0}{L(VA^1,VA^0)}$$

$$(142) \quad = \frac{R^1 - R^0}{L(VA^1,VA^0)} - \frac{C^1_{EMS} - C^0_{EMS}}{L(VA^1,VA^0)}$$

$$= \frac{L(R^1,R^0)\ln(R^1/R^0)}{L(VA^1,VA^0)} - \frac{L(C^1_{EMS},C^0_{EMS})\ln(C^1_{EMS}/C^0_{EMS})}{L(VA^1,VA^0)}.$$

For R^1/R^0 recall expression (7) and decompose the ratio C^1_{EMS}/C^0_{EMS} by one- or two stage Fisher indices as

$$(143) \quad C^1_{EMS}/C^0_{EMS} = P^F(w^1_{EMS},x^1_{EMS},w^0_{EMS},x^0_{EMS})Q^F(w^1_{EMS},x^1_{EMS},w^0_{EMS},x^0_{EMS}) \equiv P_{EMS}(1,0)Q_{EMS}(1,0).$$

Then the logarithm of the value added ratio can be expressed as

$$(144) \quad \ln\left(\frac{VA^1}{VA^0}\right) = \frac{L(R^1,R^0)\ln(P_R(1,0)Q_R(1,0))}{L(VA^1,VA^0)} - \frac{L(C^1_{EMS},C^0_{EMS})\ln(P_{EMS}(1,0)Q_{EMS}(1,0))}{L(VA^1,VA^0)}.$$

This can be rearranged as

$$(145) \quad \frac{VA^1}{VA^0} = \frac{P_R(1,0)^{\phi}}{P_{EMS}(1,0)^{\psi}}\frac{Q_R(1,0)^{\phi}}{Q_{EMS}(1,0)^{\psi}},$$

where $\phi \equiv L(R^1,R^0)/L(VA^1,VA^0)$, that is, as mean revenue over mean value added, and $\psi \equiv L(C^1_{EMS},C^0_{EMS})/L(VA^1,VA^0)$, that is, as mean intermediate inputs cost over mean value added. Thus, value added price and quantity indices can rather naturally be defined by

$$(146) \quad P_{VA}(1,0) \equiv \frac{P_R(1,0)^{\phi}}{P_{EMS}(1,0)^{\psi}},$$

[30] For any two strictly positive real numbers a and b their logarithmic mean is defined by $L(a,b) = (a-b)/\ln(a/b)$ if $a \neq b$ and $L(a,a) = a$.

$$(147)\quad Q_{VA}(1,0) \equiv \frac{Q_R(1,0)^{\phi}}{Q_{EMS}(1,0)^{\psi}}.$$

These indices generalize the conventional Montgomery-Vartia indices (see Balk 2008, 87 for their definition). They are Consistent-in-Aggregation, but fail the Equality Test. The reason is that,

$$(148)\quad \phi - \psi = \frac{L(R^1,R^0) - L(C^1_{EMS},C^0_{EMS})}{L(VA^1,VA^0)} \leq 1,$$

because $L(a,1)$ is a concave function.

An alternative is to define $P_{VA}(1,0)$ as a Fisher-type index of the subindices $P_R(1,0)$ and $P_{EMS}(1,0)$; that is,

$$(149)\quad P_{VA}(1,0) \equiv \left[\frac{\frac{R^0}{VA^0} P_R(1,0) - \frac{C^0_{EMS}}{VA^0} P_{EMS}(1,0)}{\frac{R^1}{VA^1} (P_R(1,0))^{-1} - \frac{C^1_{EMS}}{VA^1} (P_{EMS}(1,0))^{-1}} \right]^{1/2}.$$

The numerator is a Laspeyres-type double deflator, and the denominator is the inverse of a Paasche-type double deflator. Similarly, $Q_{VA}(1,0)$ is defined as a Fisher-type index of the subindices $Q_R(1,0)$ and $Q_{EMS}(1,0)$. These indices satisfy the Equality Test, but fail the Consistency-in-Aggregation Test. Moreover, there are situations where Fisher-type indices are undefined.

Appendix C. Decompositions of Time Series Depreciation

Time-series depreciation of an asset of type i and age j over period t is, according to expression (68), defined by $P^{t^-}_{i,j-0.5} - P^{t^+}_{i,j+0.5}$, which is the (nominal) value change of the asset between the beginning and the end of the period. This value change combines the effect of the progress of time, from t^- to t^+, with the effect of ageing, from $j-0.5$ to $j+0.5$. Since value change is here measured as a difference, a natural decomposition of time-series depreciation according to these two effects is

$$(150)\quad \begin{aligned} P^{t^-}_{i,j-0.5} - P^{t^+}_{i,j+0.5} &= (1/2)[(P^{t^-}_{i,j-0.5} - P^{t^+}_{i,j-0.5}) + (P^{t^-}_{i,j+0.5} - P^{t^+}_{i,j+0.5})] \\ &+ (1/2)[(P^{t^-}_{i,j-0.5} - P^{t^-}_{i,j+0.5}) + (P^{t^+}_{i,j-0.5} - P^{t^+}_{i,j+0.5})]. \end{aligned}$$

This decomposition is symmetric. The first term on the right-hand side of the equality sign measures the effect of the progress of time on an asset of unchanged age; this is called revaluation. The revaluation, as measured here, is the arithmetic mean of the revaluation of a

$j-0.5$ periods old asset and a $j+0.5$ periods old asset, and may be said to hold for a j periods old asset.

The second term concerns the effect of ageing, which is measured by the price difference of two, otherwise identical, assets that differ precisely one period in age. This is called Hicksian or cross-section depreciation. The arithmetic mean is taken of cross-section depreciation at the beginning and end of the period, and, hence, may be said to hold at the midpoint of period t.

Since the Perpetual Inventory Method combines the beginning-of-period price with the corresponding cohort quantities, expression (150) is rewritten as

$$1-\frac{P_{i,j+0.5}^{t^+}}{P_{i,j-0.5}^{t^-}}=\frac{(1/2)[(P_{i,j-0.5}^{t^-}-P_{i,j-0.5}^{t^+})+(P_{i,j+0.5}^{t^-}-P_{i,j+0.5}^{t^+})]}{P_{i,j-0.5}^{t-}} \tag{151}$$
$$+\frac{(1/2)[(P_{i,j-0.5}^{t^-}-P_{i,j+0.5}^{t^-})+(P_{i,j-0.5}^{t^+}-P_{i,j+0.5}^{t^+})]}{P_{i,j-0.5}^{t^-}}.$$

At the left-hand side of this expression we have $(P_{i,j+0.5}^{t^+}/P_{i,j-0.5}^{t^-})$ as an inverse ratio-type measure of time-series depreciation. Considered as a decomposition, however, expression (151) is not symmetric. A symmetrical decomposition is given by

$$\frac{P_{i,j+0.5}^{t^+}}{P_{i,j-0.5}^{t^-}}=\left[\frac{P_{i,j-0.5}^{t^+}}{P_{i,j-0.5}^{t^-}}\frac{P_{i,j+0.5}^{t^+}}{P_{i,j+0.5}^{t^-}}\right]^{1/2}\left[\frac{P_{i,j+0.5}^{t^+}}{P_{i,j-0.5}^{t^+}}\frac{P_{i,j+0.5}^{t^-}}{P_{i,j-0.5}^{t^-}}\right]^{1/2}. \tag{152}$$

The first term on the right-hand side of the equality sign measures revaluation. The second term measures cross-section depreciation. As one can see, revaluation depends on age, and cross-section depreciation depends on time. In the usual model, these two dependencies are assumed away. Revaluation is approximated by $P_i^{t^+}/P_i^{t^-}$, the price change of a *new* asset of type i from beginning to end of period t. Cross-section depreciation is approximated by $1-\delta_{ij}$, where δ_{ij} is the percentage of annual depreciation that applies to an asset of type i and age j. The specific formulation highlights the fact that ageing usually diminishes the value of an asset.

Under these two assumptions, the basic time-series depreciation model for an asset of type i and age j, over period t, is given by

$$\frac{P_{i,j+0.5}^{t^+}}{P_{i,j-0.5}^{t^-}}=\frac{P_i^{t^+}}{P_i^{t^-}}(1-\delta_{ij}) \quad \text{for } j=1,\ldots,J_i. \tag{153}$$

For assets that are acquired at the midpoint of period t one must distinguish between new and used assets. Over the second half of period t, the model reads

$$(154)\quad \frac{P^{t^+}_{i,0.5}}{P^t_{i,0}} = \frac{P^{t^+}_i}{P^t_i}(1-\delta_{i0})$$

$$\frac{P^{t^+}_{i,j+0.5}}{P^t_{i,j}} = \frac{P^{t^+}_i}{P^t_i}(1-\delta_{ij}/2) \qquad \text{for } j=1,\ldots,J_i,$$

where $(1-\delta_{ij}/2)$ serves as an approximation to $(1-\delta_{ij})^{1/2}$. The percentage of annual depreciation, δ_{ij}, ideally comes from an empirically estimated age-price profile for asset-type *i*. Under a geometric profile one specifies $\delta_{i0} = \delta_i/2$ and $\delta_{ij} = \delta_i$ ($j=1,\ldots,J$).

References

Baldwin, J.R., W. Gu and B. Yan (2007), *Statistical Manual on the Annual Multifactor Productivity Program of Statistics Canada*, Micro Economic Analysis Division, Statistics Canada.

Balk, B.M. (1995), "Axiomatic Price Index Theory: A Survey," *International Statistical Review* 63, 69-93.

Balk, B.M. (1998), *Industrial Price, Quantity, and Productivity Indices: The Micro-Economic Theory and an Application*, Kluwer Academic Publishers.

Balk, B.M. (2003), "The Residual: On Monitoring and Benchmarking Firms, Industries, and Economies with Respect to Productivity," *Journal of Productivity Analysis* 20, 5-47.

Balk, B.M. (2004), "The Many Decompositions of Productivity Change," presented at the North American Productivity Workshop 2004, Toronto, and at the Asia-Pacific Productivity Conference 2004, Brisbane.

Balk, B. M. (2008), *Price and Quantity Index Numbers: Models for Measuring Aggregate Change and Difference*, Cambridge University Press.

Balk, B.M. (2009), "On the Relationship between Gross-Output and Value-Added Based Productivity Measures: The Importance of the Domar Factor," *Macroeconomic Dynamics* 13, S2, 241-267.

Balk, B.M. and D.A. van den Bergen (2006), The Cost of Capital Input: Calculation Methods, Revised version of a paper presented at the Capital Measurement Workshop, Ottawa, 22 May 2006.

Balk, B.M. and E. Hoogenboom-Spijker (2003), "The Measurement and Decomposition of Productivity Change: Exercises on the Netherlands Manufacturing Industry," Discussion paper 03001, Statistics Netherlands.

Basu, S. and J.G. Fernald (2002), "Aggregate Productivity and Aggregate Technology," *European Economic Review* 46, 963-991.

Bennet, T.L. (1920), "The Theory of Measurement of Changes in Cost of Living," *Journal of the Royal Statistical Society* 83, 455-462.

Bergen, D. van den, M. van Rooijen-Horsten, M. de Haan and B. M. Balk, 2007, Productivity Measurement at Statistics Netherlands. Report No. 2007-19-MNR (Statistics Netherlands, The Hague). Also in *Productivity Measurement and Analysis: Proceedings from OECD Workshops*, OECD/Swiss Federal Statistical Office, Paris/Neuchâtel, 2008.

Berndt, E.R. and M.A. Fuss, 1986, "Productivity Measurement with Adjustments for Variations in Capacity Utilization and Other Forms of Temporary Equilibrium," *Journal of Econometrics* 33, 7-29.

Chambers, R.G., 2008, "Stochastic Productivity Measurement," *Journal of Productivity Analysis* 30, 107-120.

Coremberg, A., 2008, "The Measurement of TFP in Argentina, 1990-2004: A Case of the Tyranny of Numbers, Economic Cycles and Methodology," *International Productivity Monitor* 17, 52-74.

Dean, E.R. and M.J. Harper (2001), "The BLS Productivity Measurement Program," in C. R. Hulten, E. R. Dean and M. J. Harper (eds.), *New Developments in Productivity Analysis*, Studies in Income and Wealth Volume 63, University of Chicago Press.

Diewert, W.E. (1978), "Superlative Index Numbers and Consistency in Aggregation," *Econometrica* 46, 883-900.

Diewert, W.E. (1992), "The Measurement of Productivity," *Bulletin of Economic Research* 44, 163-198.

Diewert, W.E. (2005), "Index Number Theory Using Differences Rather than Ratios," in R.W. Dimand and J. Geanakoplos (eds.), *Celebrating Irving Fisher: The Legacy of a Great Economist, American Journal of Economics and Sociology* 64 (2).

Diewert, W.E. (2008), "The Bern OECD Workshop on Productivity Analysis and Measurement: Conclusions and Future Directions", in *Productivity Measurement and Analysis: Proceedings from OECD Workshops*, OECD/Swiss Federal Statistical Office, Paris/Neuchâtel.

Diewert, W.E., and N. Huang (2008), Capitalizing R&D Expenditures, Paper presented at the EMG (Economic Measurement Group) Workshop 2007 held at the Crowne Plaza Hotel, Coogee Australia, December 12-14, 2007.

Diewert, W.E. and D. Lawrence (2006), "Measuring the Contributions of Productivity and Terms of Trade to Australia's Economic Welfare," Report by Meyrick and Associates to the Productivity Commission, Canberra.

Diewert, W. E., H. Mizobuchi and K. Nomura (2005), "On Measuring Japan's Productivity, 1955-2003," Discussion Paper No. 05-22, Department of Economics, University of British Columbia, Vancouver.

Diewert, W.E. and A.O. Nakamura (2003), "Index Number Concepts, Measures and Decompositions of Productivity Growth," *Journal of Productivity Analysis* 19, 127-159.

Diewert, W.E. and F.C. Wykoff (2011), "Depreciation, Deterioration and Obsolescence when there is Embodied or Disembodied Technical Change," forthcoming in W.E. Diewert, B.M. Balk, D. Fixler, K.J. Fox and A.O. Nakamura (eds.), *Price and Productivity Measurement, Volume 8: Capital and Income.*

Douglas, J. (2006), Measurement of Public Sector Output and Productivity. Policy Perspectives Paper 06/09, New Zealand Treasury.

Erumban, AA. (2008a), "Lifetimes of Machinery and Equipment: Evidence from Dutch Manufacturing", *Review of Income and Wealth* 54, 237-268.

Erumban, AA. (2008b), "Rental Prices, Rates of Return, Capital Aggregation and Productivity: Evidence from EU and US", *CESifo Economic Studies* 54, 499-533.

Fisher, I. (1922), *The Making of Index Numbers*, Houghton Mifflin.

Friedman, B.M. (1988) "Lessons on Monetary Policy from the 1980s", *Journal of Economic Perspectives* 2(3), 51-72.

Gollop, F.M. (1979), "Accounting for Intermediate Input: The Link between Sectoral and Aggregate Measures of Productivity Growth," in Rees (1979).

Harchaoui, T.M., M. Kaci and J.-P. Maynard (2001), *Productivity Growth in Canada*, "Statistics Canada Productivity Program: Concepts and Methods, Appendix 1," Catalogue no. 15-204, Statistics Canada.

Hicks, J. R. (1940), "The Valuation of Social Income," *Economica* 7, 105-124.

Hulten, C.R. (1986), "Productivity Change, Capacity Utilization, and the Sources of Efficiency Growth", *Journal of Econometrics* 33, 31-50.

Hulten, C.R. and P. Schreyer (2006), "Income, Depreciation and Capital Gains in an Intertemporal Economic Model," Fifth Ottawa Productivity Workshop, 23-24 May 2006.

Inklaar, R. and M.P. Timmer (2008), "Accounting for Growth in Retail Trade: An International Productivity Comparison", *Journal of Productivity Analysis* 29, 23-31.

Jorgenson, D. W. (2009), "A New Architecture for the U. S. National Accounts", *Review of Income and Wealth* 55, 1-42.

Jorgenson, D.W., M.S. Ho and K.J. Stiroh (2005), *Productivity Volume 3: Information Technology and the American Growth Resurgence*, MIT Press.

Lawrence, D., W. E. Diewert and K. J. Fox (2006), "The Contributions of Productivity, Price Changes and Firm Size to Profitability," *Journal of Productivity Analysis* 26, 1-13.

MacGibbon, N. (2008), "The User Cost of Capital in Statistics NZ's Multifactor Productivity Measures," Paper for Productivity Reference Group Feedback, Statistics New Zealand.

Morrison Paul, C.J., (1999), *Cost Structure and the Measurement of Economic Performance*, Kluwer Academic Publishers.

Oulton, N. (2007), "Ex Post versus Ex Ante Measures of the User Cost of Capital," *Review of Income and Wealth* 53, 295-317.

Rais, G. and P. Sollberger (2008), "Multi-Factor Productivity Measurement: From Data Pitfalls to Problem Solving — The Swiss Way", in *Productivity Measurement and Analysis: Proceedings from OECD Workshops*, OECD/Swiss Federal Statistical Office, Paris/Neuchâtel.

Rees, A. (chairman) (1979), *Measurement and Interpretation of Productivity,* Report of the Panel to Review Productivity Statistics, Committee on National Statistics, Assembly of Behavioral and Social Sciences, National Research Council, National Academy of Sciences, Washington DC.

Roberts, P. (2006), "Estimates of Industry Level Multifactor Productivity in Australia: Measurement Initiatives and Issues," in *Productivity Measurement and Analysis: Proceedings from OECD Workshops*, OECD/Swiss Federal Statistical Office, Paris/Neuchâtel.

Rymes, T.K. (1983), "More on the Measurement of Total Factor Productivity," *Review of Income and Wealth* 29, 297-316.

Schreyer, P. (2001), *Measuring Productivity: Measurement of Aggregate and Industry-Level Productivity Growth,* OECD Manual, OECD, Paris.

Schreyer, P. (2011), "Measuring Multi-Factor Productivity when Rates of Return are Exogenous," in W.E. Diewert, B.M. Balk, D. Fixler, K.J. Fox and A.O. Nakamura (eds.), *Price and Productivity Measurement, Volume 6: Index Number Theory*.

Spant, R. (2003), "Why Net Domestic Product Should Replace Gross Domestic Product as a Measure of Economic Growth," *International Productivity Monitor* 7 (Fall), 39-43.

Statistics New Zealand (2006), *Productivity Statistics: Sources and Methods*, www.stats.govt.nz.

Timmer, M.P., M. O'Mahoney and B. van Ark (2007), "EU KLEMS Growth and Productivity Accounts: An Overview," *International Productivity Monitor* 14 (Spring), 71-85.

Vancauteren, M., D. van den Bergen, E. Veldhuizen and B. M. Balk, 2009, Measures of Productivity Change: Which Outcome Do You Want?, Invited Paper for the 57th Session of the International Statistical Institute, 16-22 August 2009, Durban, South Africa.

PART II Index Number Formulas

Chapter 8
THE LOWE CONSUMER PRICE INDEX AND ITS SUBSTITUTION BIAS

Bert M. Balk and W. Erwin Diewert[1]

1. Introduction

Usually the substitution bias of an official CPI is assessed under the assumption that such an index is an estimator of a Laspeyres price index. The generic form of the Laspeyres price index is

$$(1) \qquad P_L(p^0, p^t, q^0) = \frac{\sum_{n=1}^{N} p_n^t q_n^0}{\sum_{n=1}^{N} p_n^0 q_n^0},$$

where $p^t(p^0)$ is the current (reference) period price vector and q^0 is the reference period quantity vector. The question then is how this index relates to its true cost of living counterpart.

Indeed, many statistical agencies are employing a Laspeyres price index as their conceptual target. For example, the Netherlands' CPI is modelled this way, where currently the reference period is the year 2006, and t is any month from January 2007 onwards. Nevertheless, the headline inflation figure is obtained as the percentage change between the current month and the corresponding month of the previous year. Put otherwise, the really interesting index number is the one given by

$$(2) \qquad \frac{P_L(p^0, p^t, q^0)}{P_L(p^0, p^{t-12}, q^0)} = \frac{\sum_{n=1}^{N} p_n^t q_n^0}{\sum_{n=1}^{N} p_n^{t-12} q_n^0},$$

which is a fixed basket price index, but definitely not a Laspeyres index. Actually, the right-hand side of this expression is an instance of the Lowe price index,[2] and will be denoted by $P_{Lo}(p^{t-12}, p^t, q^0)$. Thus it makes much more sense to inquire after the substitution bias of this index than the Laspeyres index.

---

[1] Bert Balk is with the Rotterdam School of Management, Erasmus University, and Statistics Netherlands, The Hague, and can be reached at email bbalk@rsm.nl.. Erwin Diewert is with the Department of Economics, University of British Columbia, Vancouver, B. C., Canada, email diewert@econ.ubc.ca.

[2] Named after Lowe (1823). See Diewert (1993a) or Balk (2008; Chapter 1) for Lowe's place in the history of index number theory.

Citation: **Bert M. Balk and W. Erwin Diewert (2011),**
"The Lowe Consumer Price Index and Its Substitution Bias,"
chapter 8, pp. 187-197 in
W.E. Diewert, B.M. Balk, D. Fixler, K.J. Fox and A.O. Nakamura,
PRICE AND PRODUCTIVITY MEASUREMENT: Volume 6 -- Index Number Theory. Trafford Press.

© Alice Nakamura, 2011. Permission to link to, or copy or reprint, these materials is granted without restriction, including for use in commercial textbooks, with due credit to the authors and editors.

There are also many statistical agencies which employ as conceptual target for their CPI a so-called modified Laspeyres index. This concept measures the price change between reference month 0 and current month t as a weighted average of price relatives

$$(3)\qquad \sum_{n=1}^{N} w_n(p_n^t / p_n^0) \text{ where } \sum_{n=1}^{N} w_n = 1.$$

The weights are then derived from consumer expenditures of some year b prior to month 0, which are price-updated to month 0. Formally written,

$$(4)\qquad w_n \equiv \frac{p_n^b q_n^b (p_n^0 / p_n^b)}{\sum_{n=1}^{N} p_n^b q_n^b (p_n^0 / p_n^b)},\ n = 1,\ldots,N.$$

But this means that

$$(5)\qquad \sum_{n=1}^{N} w_n(p_n^t / p_n^0) = \frac{\sum_{n=1}^{N} p_n^t q_n^b}{\sum_{n=1}^{N} p_n^0 q_n^b} = P_{Lo}(p^0, p^t, q^b);$$

that is, the target index is a Lowe index.

The foregoing is sufficient to motivate the question to be addressed in this paper: can the Lowe index $P_{Lo}(p^0, p^t, q^b)$, where typically $b \le 0 < t$, be related to one derived from the economic approach to index number theory? Note that when $b = 0$, the Lowe index reduces to the Laspeyres index. Thus our question is more general than the usual one. The lay-out of this paper is as follows. Section 2 considers in a very general way the Lowe index as an approximation to a cost of living index. Sections 3 and 4 respectively pursue first- and second-order approximations to its substitution bias. Section 5 concludes.

2. The Lowe Index as an Approximation to a Cost of Living Index

Assume that the consumer has preferences defined over consumption vectors $q \equiv (q_1,\ldots,q_N)$ that can be represented by the continuous increasing utility function $f(q)$. Thus if $f(q^1) > f(q^0)$, then the consumer prefers the consumption vector q^1 to q^0. Let q^b be the annual consumption vector for the consumer in the base year b. Define the base year utility level u^b as the utility level that corresponds to $f(q)$ evaluated at q^b:

$$(6)\qquad u^b \equiv f(q^b).$$

For any vector of positive commodity prices $p \equiv (p_1,\ldots,p_N)$ and for any feasible utility level u, the consumer's cost function, $C(u, p)$, can be defined in the usual way as the minimum expenditure required to achieve the utility level u when facing the prices p:

$$(7)\qquad C(u, p) \equiv \min_q \{\sum_{n=1}^{N} p_n q_n \,|\, f(q_1,\ldots,q_N) = u\}.$$

Let $p^b \equiv (p_1^b,\ldots,p_N^b)$ be the vector of annual prices that the consumer faced in the base year b. Assume that the observed base year consumption vector $q^b \equiv (q_1^b,\ldots,q_N^b)$ solves the following base year cost minimization problem:

$$C(u^b, p^b) = \sum_{n=1}^{N} p_n^b q_n^b . \tag{8}$$

The cost function will be used below in order to define the consumer's cost of living index.

Let p^0 and p^t be the monthly price vectors that the consumer faces in months 0 and t. Then the Konüs cost of living index, $P_K(p^0, p^t, q^b)$, between months 0 and t, using the base year utility level $u^b = f(q^b)$ as the reference standard of living, is defined as the following ratio of minimum monthly costs of achieving the utility level u^b:

$$P_K(p^0, p^t, q^b) \equiv \frac{C(f(q^b), p^t)}{C(f(q^b), p^0)} . \tag{9}$$

Using the definition of the monthly cost minimization problem that corresponds to the cost $C(f(q^b), p^t)$, it can be seen that the following inequality holds:

$$C(f(q^b), p^t) \le \sum_{n=1}^{N} p_n^t q_n^b \tag{10}$$

since the base year quantity vector q^b is feasible for the cost minimization problem. Similarly, using the definition of the monthly cost minimization problem that corresponds to the cost $C(f(q^b), p^0)$, it can be seen that the following inequality holds:

$$C(f(q^b), p^0) \le \sum_{n=1}^{N} p_n^0 q_n^b \tag{11}$$

since the base year quantity vector q^b is feasible for the cost minimization problem.

It will prove useful to rewrite the two inequalities (10) and (11) as equalities. This can be done if nonnegative substitution bias terms, e^t and e^0, are subtracted from the right-hand sides of these two inequalities. Thus (10) and (11) can be rewritten as follows:

$$C(f(q^b), p^t) = \sum_{n=1}^{N} p_n^t q_n^b - e^t \tag{12}$$

$$C(f(q^b), p^0) = \sum_{n=1}^{N} p_n^0 q_n^b - e^0 . \tag{13}$$

Using (12) and (13) and the definition of the Lowe index, the following approximate equality results:

$$(14)\quad P_{Lo}(p^0,p^t,q^b) \equiv \frac{\sum_{n=1}^N p_n^t q_n^b}{\sum_{n=1}^N p_n^0 q_n^b} = \frac{C(u^b,p^t)+e^t}{C(u^b,p^0)+e^0} \approx \frac{C(u^b,p^t)}{C(u^b,p^0)} = P_K(p^0,p^t,q^b).$$

Thus if the nonnegative substitution bias terms e^0 and e^t are small, then the Lowe index between months 0 and t, $P_{Lo}(p^0,p^t,q^b)$, will be an adequate approximation to the cost of living index between months 0 and t, $P_K(p^0,p^t,q^b)$.

A bit of algebraic manipulation shows that the Lowe index will be exactly equal to its cost of living counterpart if the substitution bias terms satisfy the following relationship:[3]

$$(15)\quad \frac{e^t}{e^0} = \frac{C(u^b,p^t)}{C(u^b,p^0)} = P_K(p^0,p^t,q^b).$$

Equations (14) and (15) can be interpreted as follows: if the rate of growth in the amount of substitution bias between months 0 and t is equal to the rate of growth in the minimum cost of achieving the base year utility level u^b between months 0 and t, then the observable Lowe index, $P_{Lo}(p^0,p^t,q^b)$, will be exactly equal to its cost of living index counterpart, $P_K(p^0,p^t,q^b)$.[4] It is difficult to know whether condition (15) will hold or whether the substitution bias terms e^0 and e^t will be small. Thus in the following two sections, first and second order Taylor series approximations to these substitution bias terms will be developed.

3. A First-Order Approximation to the Substitution Bias of the Lowe Index

The cost of living index between months 0 and t, using the base year utility level u^b as the reference utility level, is the ratio of two unobservable costs, $C(u^b,p^t)/C(u^b,p^0)$. However, both of these hypothetical costs can be approximated by first-order Taylor series approximations that can be evaluated using observable information on prices and base year quantities.

---

[3] This assumes that e^0 is greater than zero. If e^0 is equal to zero, then to have equality of P_K and P_{Lo}, it must also be the case that e^t is equal to zero.

[4] It can be seen that when month t is set equal to month 0, $e^t = e^0$ and $C(u^b,p^t) = C(u^b,p^0)$ and thus (15) is satisfied and $P_{Lo} = P_K$. This is not surprising since both indices are equal to unity when t = 0.

The first-order Taylor series approximation to $C(u^b, p^t)$ around the annual base year price vector p^b is given by the following approximate equation:[5]

$$
\begin{aligned}
C(u^b, p^t) &\approx C(u^b, p^b) + \sum_{n=1}^{N} \frac{\partial C(u^b, p^b)}{\partial p_n}(p_n^t - p_n^b) \\
(16)\qquad &= C(u^b, p^b) + \sum_{n=1}^{N} q_n^b (p_n^t - p_n^b) \\
&= \sum_{n=1}^{N} p_n^b q_n^b + \sum_{n=1}^{N} q_n^b (p_n^t - p_n^b) \\
&= \sum_{n=1}^{N} p_n^t q_n^b,
\end{aligned}
$$

where Shephard's Lemma and assumption (8) have been used. Similarly, the first-order Taylor series approximation to $C(u^b, p^0)$ around the annual base year price vector p^b is given by the following approximate equation:

$$
\begin{aligned}
C(u^b, p^0) &\approx C(u^b, p^b) + \sum_{n=1}^{N} \frac{\partial C(u^b, p^b)}{\partial p_n}(p_n^0 - p_n^b) \\
(17)\qquad &= C(u^b, p^b) + \sum_{n=1}^{N} q_n^b (p_n^0 - p_n^b) \\
&= \sum_{n=1}^{N} p_n^b q_n^b + \sum_{n=1}^{N} q_n^b (p_n^0 - p_n^b) \\
&= \sum_{n=1}^{N} p_n^0 q_n^b,
\end{aligned}
$$

Comparing (16) to (12), and (17) to (13), we see that to the accuracy of the first order the substitution bias terms e^t and e^0 will be zero. Using these results to reinterpret (14), it can be seen that if the month 0 and month t price vectors, p^0 and p^t, are not too different from the base year vector of prices p^b, then the Lowe index $P_{Lo}(p^0, p^t, q^b)$ will approximate the cost of living index $P_K(p^0, p^t, q^b)$ to the accuracy of the first order. This result is quite useful, since it indicates that if the monthly price vectors p^0 and p^t are just randomly fluctuating around the base year prices p^b (with modest variances), then the Lowe index will serve as an adequate approximation to a theoretical cost of living index. However, if there are systematic long term trends in prices and month t is fairly distant from month 0 (or the end of year b is quite distant from month 0), then the first-order approximations given by (16) and (17) may no longer be adequate and the Lowe index may have a considerable bias relative to its cost of living counterpart. The hypothesis of long run trends in prices will be explored in the following section.

[5] This type of Taylor series approximation was used in Schultze and Mackie (2002; 91) in the cost of living index context but it essentially dates back to Hicks (1941-42; 134) in the consumer surplus context. See also Diewert (1992; 568).

4. A Second-Order Approximation to the Substitution Bias of the Lowe Index

A second-order Taylor series approximation to $C(u^b, p^t)$ around the base year price vector p^b is given by the following approximate equation:

$$C(u^b, p^t) \approx C(u^b, p^b) + \sum_{n=1}^{N} \frac{\partial C(u^b, p^b)}{\partial p_n}(p_n^t - p_n^b)$$

$$(18) \qquad + (1/2)\sum_{n=1}^{N}\sum_{n'=1}^{N} \frac{\partial^2 C(u^b, p^b)}{\partial p_n \partial p_{n'}}(p_n^t - p_n^b)(p_{n'}^t - p_{n'}^b)$$

$$= \sum_{n=1}^{N} p_n^t q_n^b + (1/2)\sum_{n=1}^{N}\sum_{n'=1}^{N} \frac{\partial^2 C(u^b, p^b)}{\partial p_n \partial p_{n'}}(p_n^t - p_n^b)(p_{n'}^t - p_{n'}^b),$$

where the last equality follows using (16).[6] Similarly, a second-order Taylor series approximation to $C(u^b, p^0)$ around the base year price vector p^b is given by the following approximate equation:

$$C(u^b, p^0) \approx C(u^b, p^b) + \sum_{n=1}^{N} \frac{C(u^b, p^b)}{\partial p_n}(p_n^0 - p_n^b)$$

$$(19) \qquad + (1/2)\sum_{n=1}^{N}\sum_{n'=1}^{N} \frac{\partial^2 C(u^b, p^b)}{\partial p_n \partial p_{n'}}(p_n^0 - p_n^b)(p_{n'}^0 - p_{n'}^b)$$

$$= \sum_{n=1}^{N} p_n^0 q_n^b + (1/2)\sum_{n=1}^{N}\sum_{n'=1}^{N} \frac{\partial^2 C(u^b, p^b)}{\partial p_n \partial p_{n'}}(p_n^0 - p_n^b)(p_{n'}^0 - p_{n'}^b)$$

where the last equality follows using (17).

Comparing (18) to (12), and (19) to (13), it can be seen that to the accuracy of the second order, the month 0 and month t substitution bias terms, e^0 and e^t, will be equal to the following expressions involving the second-order partial derivatives of the consumer's cost function evaluated at the base year standard of living u^b and the base year prices p^b:

$$(20) \qquad e^0 \approx -(1/2)\sum_{n=1}^{N}\sum_{n'=1}^{N} \frac{\partial^2 C(u^b, p^b)}{\partial p_n \partial p_{n'}}(p_n^0 - p_n^b)(p_{n'}^0 - p_{n'}^b)$$

$$(21) \qquad e^t \approx -(1/2)\sum_{n=1}^{N}\sum_{n'=1}^{N} \frac{\partial^2 C(u^b, p^b)}{\partial p_n \partial p_{n'}}(p_n^t - p_n^b)(p_{n'}^t - p_{n'}^b).$$

Since the consumer's cost function $C(u, p)$ is a concave function in the components of the price vector p,[7] it is known[8] that the $N \times N$ (symmetric) matrix of second-order partial derivatives is

[6] This type of second-order approximation is due to Hicks (1941-42; 133-134) (1946; 331). See also Diewert (1992; 568) and Schultze and Mackie (2002; 91).

negative semidefinite.[9] Hence, for arbitrary price vectors p^b, p^0 and p^t, the right-hand sides of (20) and (21) will be nonnegative. Thus to the accuracy of the second order, the substitution bias terms e^0 and e^t will be nonnegative.

Now assume that there are systematic long run trends in prices. Assume that the last month of the base year for quantities occurs M months prior to month 0, the base month for prices, and assume that prices trend linearly with time, starting with the last month of the base year for quantities. Thus assume the existence of constants α_n ($n = 1,\ldots,N$) such that the price of commodity n in month t is given by:

$$(22) \qquad p_n^t = p_n^b + \alpha_n(M+t),\ n = 1,\ldots,N;\ t = 0,1,\ldots,T.$$

Substituting (22) into (20) and (21) leads to the following second-order approximations to the two substitution bias terms:

$$(23) \qquad e^0 \approx \gamma M^2$$

$$(24) \qquad e^t \approx \gamma(M+t)^2,$$

where γ is defined as

$$(25) \qquad \gamma \equiv -(1/2)\sum_{n=1}^{N}\sum_{n'=1}^{N}\frac{\partial^2 C(u^b, p^b)}{\partial p_n \partial p_{n'}}\alpha_n\alpha_{n'} \geq 0.$$

It should be noted that the parameter γ will be zero under two sets of conditions:[10]

- All of the second-order partial derivatives of the consumer's cost function equal zero.
- Each commodity price change parameter α_n is proportional to the corresponding commodity n base year price p_n^b.[11]

The first condition is empirically unlikely since it implies that the consumer will not substitute away from commodities whose relative price has increased. The second condition is

---

[7] See Diewert (1993b; 109-110).

[8] See Diewert (1993b; 149).

[9] A symmetric $N \times N$ matrix A with nn'-th element equal to $a_{nn'}$ is negative semidefinite if and only if for every vector $z \equiv (z_1,\ldots,z_N)$ it is the case that $\sum_{n=1}^{N}\sum_{n'=1}^{N} a_{nn'} z_n z_{n'} \leq 0$.

[10] A more general condition that ensures the positivity of γ is that the vector $(\alpha_1,\ldots,\alpha_N)$ is not an eigenvector of the matrix of second-order partial derivatives $\partial^2 C(u^b, p^b)/\partial p_n \partial p_{n'}$ that corresponds to a zero eigenvalue.

[11] It is known that $C(u,p)$ is linearly homogeneous in the components of the price vector p; see Diewert (1993b; 109) for example. Hence, using Euler's Theorem on homogeneous functions, it can be shown that p^b is an eigenvector of the matrix of second-order partial derivatives $\partial^2 C(u^b, p^b)/\partial p_n \partial p_{n'}$ that corresponds to a zero eigenvalue and thus $\sum_{n=1}^{N}\sum_{n'=1}^{N}[\partial^2 C(u^b, p^b)/\partial p_n \partial p_{n'}]p_n^b p_{n'}^b = 0$; see Diewert (1993b; 149) for a detailed proof.

also empirically unlikely, since it implies that the structure of relative prices remains unchanged over time. Thus in what follows, it will be assumed that γ is a positive number.

In order to simplify the notation in what follows, define the denominator and numerator of the month t Lowe index, $P_{Lo}(p^0,p^t,q^b)$, as a and b respectively; that is, define

$$a \equiv \sum_{n=1}^{N} p_n^0 q_n^b \tag{26}$$

$$b \equiv \sum_{n=1}^{N} p_n^t q_n^b \tag{27}$$

Using equations (22) leads to the following expressions for a and b:

$$a = \sum_{n=1}^{N} p_n^b q_n^b + \sum_{n=1}^{N} \alpha_n q_n^b M \tag{28}$$

$$b = \sum_{n=1}^{N} p_n^b q_n^b + \sum_{n=1}^{N} \alpha_n q_n^b (M+t) \tag{29}$$

It is assumed that

$$\sum_{n=1}^{N} \alpha_n q_n^b \geq 0, \tag{30}$$

which rules out a general decrease of prices. It is also assumed that $a-\gamma M^2$ is positive.

Define the bias in the month t Lowe index, B^t, as the difference between the cost of living index $P_K(p^0,p^t,q^b)$ defined by (9) and the corresponding Lowe index $P_{Lo}(p^0,p^t,q^b)$. Then,

$$\begin{aligned} B^t &\equiv P_K(p^0,p^t,q^b) - P_{Lo}(p^0,p^t,q^b) = \frac{C(u^b,p^t)}{C(u^b,p^0)} - \frac{b}{a} \\ &= \frac{b-e^t}{a-e^0} - \frac{b}{a} \approx \frac{b-\gamma(M+t)^2}{a-\gamma M^2} - \frac{b}{a} \\ &= \gamma\frac{(b-a)M^2 - 2aMt - at^2}{a(a-\gamma M^2)} \\ &= \gamma\frac{(\sum_{n=1}^{N}\alpha_n q_n^b)M^2 t - 2(\sum_{n=1}^{N} p_n^b q_n^b + \sum_{n=1}^{N}\alpha_n q_n^b M)Mt - at^2}{a(a-\gamma M^2)} \\ &= -\gamma\frac{(\sum_{n=1}^{N}\alpha_n q_n^b)M^2 t + 2(\sum_{n=1}^{N} p_n^b q_n^b)Mt + at^2}{a(a-\gamma M^2)} \\ &< 0, \end{aligned} \tag{31}$$

using respectively (26) and (27), (12) and (13), (23) and (24), (28) and (29), and (30).

Thus for $t \geq 1$, the Lowe index will have an upward bias (to the accuracy of a second order Taylor series) relative to the corresponding cost of living index, since the approximate bias defined by the last expression in (31) is the sum of one nonpositive and two negative terms. Moreover this approximate bias will grow quadratically in time t.[12]

In order to give the reader some idea of the magnitude of the approximate bias B^t defined by the last line of (31), a simple special case will be considered at this point. Suppose there are only 2 commodities and at the base year, all prices and quantities are equal to 1. Thus $p_n^b = q_n^b = 1$ for $n = 1,2$ and $\sum_{n=1}^{N} p_n^b q_n^b = 2$. Assume that M = 24 so that the base year data on quantities take 2 years to process before the Lowe index can be implemented. Assume that the monthly rate of growth in price for commodity 1 is $\alpha_1 = 0.002$ so that after 1 year, the price of commodity 1 rises 0.024 or 2.4%. Assume that commodity 2 falls in price each month with $\alpha_2 = -0.002$ so that the price of commodity 2 falls 2.4% in the first year after the base year for quantities. Thus the relative price of the two commodities is steadily diverging by about 5 percent per year. Finally, assume that $\partial^2 C(u^b, p^b) / \partial p_1 \partial p_1 = \partial^2 C(u^b, p^b) / \partial p_2 \partial p_2 = -1$ and $\partial^2 C(u^b, p^b) / \partial p_1 \partial p_2 = \partial^2 C(u^b, p^b) / \partial p_2 \partial p_1 = 1$. These assumptions imply that the own price elasticity of demand for each commodity is -1 at the base year consumer equilibrium. Making all of these assumptions means that:

$$(32) \qquad 2 = \sum_{n=1}^{N} p_n^b q_n^b = a = b\, ; \ \sum_{n=1}^{N} \alpha_n q_n^b = 0\, ; \ M = 24\, ; \ \gamma = 0.000008\, .$$

Thus the Lowe index keeps for all months t the value 1. Substituting the parameter values given in (32) into (31) leads to the following formula for the approximate amount that the Lowe index will exceed the corresponding true cost of living index at month t:

$$(33) \qquad -B^t = 0.000008 \frac{96t + 2t^2}{2(2 - 0.004608)}.$$

Evaluating (33) at t = 12, t = 24, t = 36, t = 48 and t = 60 leads to the following estimates for $-B^t$: 0.0029 (the approximate bias in the Lowe index at the end of the first year of operation); 0.0069 (the bias after 2 years); 0.0121 (3 years); 0.0185 (4 years); 0.0260 (5 years). Thus at the end of the first year of the operation of the Lowe index, it will only be above the corresponding cost of living index by approximately a third of a percentage point but by the end of the fifth year of operation, it will exceed the corresponding cost of living index by about 2.6 percentage points, which is no longer a negligible amount.[13]

The numerical results in the previous paragraph are only indicative of the approximate magnitude of the difference between a Lowe index and the corresponding cost of living index. The important point to note is that to the accuracy of the second order, the Lowe index will generally exceed its cost of living counterpart. However, the results also indicate that this difference can be reduced to a negligible amount if:

- the lag in obtaining the base year quantity weights is minimized, and

[12] If M is large relative to t, then it can be seen that the first two terms in the last equation of (31) can dominate the last term, which is the quadratic in t term.

[13] Note that the relatively large magnitude of M compared to t leads to a bias that grows approximately linearly with t rather than quadratically.

- the base year is changed as frequently as possible.[14]

It also should be noted that the numerical results depend on the assumption that long run trends in prices exist, which may not be true,[15] and on elasticity assumptions that may not be justified.[16] Thus statistical agencies should prepare their own carefully constructed estimates of the differences between a Lowe index and a cost of living index in the light of their own particular circumstances.

5. Conclusion

The conceptual target for measuring consumer price change appears to be a Lowe price index rather than a Laspeyres price index. In this paper we derived first- and second-order approximations to the substitution bias of the Lowe index. A simple, but not unreasonable, example was used to get some idea of the magnitude of this bias. The bias is seen to crucially depend on the time span between the year to which the quantities refer and the price reference month.

References

Balk, B. M. (2008), *Price and Quantity Index Numbers; Models for Measuring Aggregate Change and Difference*, New York: Cambridge University Press.

Diewert, W.E. (1992), "Exact and Superlative Welfare Change Indicators," *Economic Inquiry* 30, 565-582.

Diewert, W.E. (1993a), "The Early History of Price Index Research," in W.E. Diewert and A.O. Nakamura (eds.), *Essays in Index Number Theory, Volume 1*, Amsterdam: North-Holland.

Diewert, W.E. (1993b), "Duality Approaches to Microeconomic Theory", W.E. Diewert and A.O. Nakamura (eds.), *Essays in Index Number Theory, Volume 1*, Amsterdam: North-Holland.

Hicks, J.R. (1941-42), "Consumers' Surplus and Index Numbers," *Review of Economic Studies* 9, 126-137.

Hicks, J. R. (1946), *Value and Capital*, Second Edition, Oxford: Clarendon Press.

Lowe, J. (1823), *The Present State of England in Regard to Agriculture, Trade and Finance*, Second Edition, London: Longman, Hurst, Rees, Orme and Brown.

Schultze, C. L. and C. Mackie (eds.) (2002), *At What Price? Conceptualizing and Measuring Cost-of-Living and Price Indices*, Washington DC: National Academy Press.

[14] In our example, if M = 0, which means that the Lowe index reduces to the Laspeyres index, the approximate bias at $t = 12$ turns out to be 0.0006.

[15] For mathematical convenience, the trends in prices were assumed to be linear rather than the more natural assumption of geometric.

[16] Another key assumption that was used to derive the numerical results is the magnitude of the divergent trends in prices. If the price divergence vector is doubled to $\alpha_1 = 0.004$ and $\alpha_2 = -0.004$, then the parameter γ quadruples and the approximate bias will also quadruple.

Chapter 9
LOWE INDICES

Peter Hill[1]

1. Introduction

The Lowe price index is a type of index in which the quantities are fixed and predetermined. The Lowe quantity index is a type of index in which the prices are fixed and predetermined. Many of the indices produced by statistical agencies turn out to be Lowe indices. They range from Consumer Price Indices to the Geary-Khamis quantity indices used in the first three phases of the International Comparisons Project of the United Nations and the World Bank. Lowe indices have certain characteristic features that throw light on their underlying properties.

The name "Lowe Index" was introduced in the international *Consumer Price Index Manual: Theory and Practice* (2004) -- the 2004 CPI Manual hereafter -- and in a paper by Balk and Diewert (2003, 2011).[2] However, it is not a new index number formula. It makes its appearance in paragraph 1.17 of Chapter 1 of the 2004 CPI Manual where it is described as follows:

> "One very wide, and popular, class of price indices is obtained by defining the index as the percentage change, between the periods compared, in the total cost of purchasing a given set of quantities generally described as a 'basket'... This class of index is called a Lowe index after the index number pioneer who first proposed it in 1823" (see Chapter 15).

Such indices are often described loosely as Laspeyres indices or Laspeyres type indices. However, a true Laspeyres price index is one in which the quantities that make up the basket are the actual quantities of the price reference period. This is the earlier of the two periods compared, assuming that the price changes are being measured forwards in time. Consumer Price Indices, or CPIs, are not Laspeyres indices as just defined, even though they may officially be described as Laspeyres type indices. The expenditures and quantities used as weights for CPIs typically come from household budget surveys undertaken some years before the price reference period for the CPI. For practical reasons, the quantities always refer to a period which pre-dates the price reference period, possibly by a considerable length of time.

---

[1] The author would like to thank Bert Balk and Erwin Diewert for a number of helpful and constructive comments on an earlier draft of this paper.

[2] The 2004 international *CPI Manual* was produced under the auspices of a group of international agencies - the ILO, IMF, OECD, EU (Eurostat), UNECE, and World Bank - advised by an international group of experts that included Bert Balk, Erwin Diewert and the author. Erwin Diewert wrote the entire sequence of chapters on index number theory from Chapter 15 onwards.

Citation: **Peter Hill (2011), "Lowe Indices," chapter 9, pp. 197-216 in**
W.E. Diewert, B.M. Balk, D. Fixler, K.J. Fox and A.O. Nakamura,
***PRICE AND PRODUCTIVITY MEASUREMENT: Volume 6 -- Index Number Theory*. Trafford Press.**

© Alice Nakamura, 2011. Permission to link to, or copy or reprint, these materials is granted without restriction, including for use in commercial textbooks, with due credit to the authors and editors.

In the interest of greater accuracy and precision, and to avoid confusion about the actual status of CPIs, it was decided to introduce the concept of a 'Lowe index' in the 2004 CPI Manual. The term 'Lowe index' will not be found in the index number literature before 2003. In a Lowe price index the quantities are not restricted to those in one or another of the periods compared. Any set of quantities may be used. They could even be hypothetical quantities that do not refer to any actual period of time.

This paper is not just concerned with CPIs. Lowe indices are used extensively throughout the entire field of economic statistics. This paper introduces the concept of the Lowe quantity index which is defined as the ratio of total costs, or values, of two different baskets of goods and services valued at the same set of prices. Any set of prices may be used and they do not have to be those observed in either of the two periods compared. Lowe quantity indices are used extensively by statistical agencies. They are commonly used in national accounts.

Moreover, Lowe indices are not confined to inter-temporal comparisons. As they are transitive, Lowe indices have been widely used in multilateral comparisons of real product between countries. For example, the Geary-Khamis method used in the first three phases of the International Comparisons Project of the United Nations and World Bank uses a Lowe quantity index in which the prices are the average prices for the group of countries as a whole[3]. Other types of Lowe indices have also been used for international comparisons.

The first section of the paper focuses on the use of Lowe price indices as CPIs drawing upon material contained in the 2004 CPI Manual. Later sections focus mainly on Lowe quantity indices, particularly as used in international comparisons.

2. CPIs as Lowe Price Indices

An inter-temporal Lowe price index compares the total value of a given set, or basket, of quantities in two different time periods. The quantities that make up the basket are described as the reference quantities and are denoted by q_i^r $(i = 1,2,\ldots,n)$. The period with which prices in other periods are compared is described as the price reference period. The Lowe index for period t with period 0 as the price reference period, $P_{LO}^{0,t}$, is defined as follows:

$$(1) \qquad P_{LO}^{0,t} \equiv \frac{\sum_{i=1}^{n} p_i^t q_i^r}{\sum_{i=1}^{n} p_i^0 q_i^r}$$

In a Lowe index, any set of quantities could serve as the reference quantities. They do not have to be the quantities purchased in one or other of the two periods compared, or indeed in any other period of time. They could, for example, be arithmetic or geometric averages of the quantities in the two periods compared or purely hypothetical quantities.

[3] See Kravis, Heston and Summers (1982, pp. 89-94) and Hill (1997, pp. 57, 58).

In CPIs, the quantities selected to serve as the reference quantities are generally those actually purchased by households over the course of a year or possibly over a longer period. The data source is typically a survey of household consumption expenditures conducted well in advance of the period which is to serve as the price reference period. For example, if Jan. 2000 is chosen as the price reference period for a monthly CPI, the quantities may be derived from an annual expenditure survey carried out in 1997 or 1998, or perhaps spanning both years. As it takes a long time to collect and process expenditure data, there is usually a considerable time lag before such data can be introduced into the calculation of CPIs. The basket may also refer to a year, whereas the periodicity of the index may be a month or quarter.

When the reference quantities in a CPI belong to an actual time period it is described as the quantity reference period. It will be denoted as period b. As just noted, the quantity reference period b is likely to precede price reference period 0 and it will be assumed throughout this section that the order of the three time periods is $b < 0 < t$. The Lowe index for period t with period b as the quantity reference period and period 0 as the price reference period is written as follows:

$$(2) \qquad P_{LO}^{0,t} = \frac{\sum_{i=1}^{n} p_i^t q_i^b}{\sum_{i=1}^{n} p_i^0 q_i^b} = \sum_{i=1}^{n} \left(\frac{p_i^t}{p_i^0} \right) s_i^{0b} \quad \text{where} \quad s_i^{0b} = \frac{p_i^0 q_i^b}{\sum_{i=1}^{n} p_i^0 q_i^b}.$$

The index can be written, and calculated, in two ways: either as the ratio of two value aggregates, or as an arithmetic weighted average of the price ratios, or price relatives, p_i^t / p_i^0, for the individual products using the hybrid expenditures shares s_i^{0b} as weights. They are described as hybrid because the prices and quantities belong to two different time periods, 0 and b respectively. The hybrid weights may be obtained by updating the actual expenditure shares in period b, namely $p_i^b q_i^b / \sum p_i^b q_i^b$, for the price changes occurring between periods b and 0 by multiplying them by the price relatives p_i^0 / p_i^b and then normalising them to sum to unity.

3. Laspeyres and Paasche Indices

Laspeyres and Paasche indices are special cases of the Lowe index. The Laspeyres price index is the Lowe index in which the reference quantities are those of the price reference period 0 -- that is, period b coincides with period 0 in equation (2).[4] The Paasche price index is the Lowe index in which the reference quantities are those of period t -- that is, period b coincides

[4] When the quantity reference period is not the same as the price reference period, the term 'base period' can be ambiguous as it could mean either period. The term 'base period' is therefore avoided here where possible. In a Laspeyres index the price and quantity reference periods are the same so that it can unambiguously be described as the base period.

with t. Assuming that $0 < t$, the Laspeyres index uses the basket of the earlier of the two periods while the Paasche uses that of the later period.

The properties of Laspeyres and Paasche indices are well known and discussed extensively in the index number literature. When the price and quantity relatives for period t based on period 0 are negatively correlated, which happens when consumers substitute goods that are becoming relatively cheaper for goods that are becoming relatively dearer, the Laspeyres index exceeds the Paasche.[5] This almost invariably happens in practice, at least with CPIs. For a more detailed and rigorous discussion of the inter-relationships between Laspeyres and Paasche indicies, see paragraphs 15.11 to 15.17 and Appendix 15.1 by Erwin Diewert in the 2004 CPI Manual. In the present context, it is necessary to consider the relationships beween Lowe, Laspeyres and Paasche indices.

A Lowe price index can be expressed as the ratio of two Laspeyres prices indices based on the quantity reference period b. For example, the Lowe index for period t with price reference period 0 is equal to the Laspeyres index for period t based on period b divided by the Laspeyres index for period 0 also based on period b. Thus,

$$(3) \quad P_{LO}^{0,t} = \frac{\sum_{i=1}^{n} p_i^t q_i^b}{\sum_{i=1}^{n} p_i^0 q_i^b} = \left[\frac{\sum_{i=1}^{n} p_i^t q_i^b}{\sum_{i=1}^{n} p_i^b q_i^b} \Bigg/ \frac{\sum_{i=1}^{n} p_i^0 q_i^b}{\sum_{i=1}^{n} p_i^b q_i^b} \right] = \frac{P_{LA}^{b,t}}{P_{LA}^{b,0}},$$

where the subscript $_{LA}$ denotes Laspeyres.

Equation (3) also implies that the Laspeyres index for period t based on period b can be factored into the product of two Lowe indices, namely for period 0 on period b multiplied by that for period t on period 0. Re-arranging (3) we have

$$(4) \quad P_{LA}^{b,t} = P_{LA}^{b,0} \cdot P_{LO}^{0,t} = P_{LO}^{b,0} \cdot P_{LO}^{0,t} = P_{LO}^{b,t},$$

since $P_{LO}^{b,0}$ is identical to $P_{LA}^{b,0}$ and $P_{LO}^{b,t}$ is identical to $P_{LA}^{b,t}$. Equation (4) illustrates an important property of Lowe price indices, namely that they are transitive. The Lowe (=Laspeyres) index for period t based on the quantity reference period b can be viewed as a chain Lowe index in which periods b and t are linked through the intermediate period 0.

It is more interesting and important to consider the case where the link is through a period that does not lie between the two periods compared. The Lowe index for period for period t on period 0 can be factored as follows by rearranging (3):

[5] This result was first derived by von Bortkiewicz (1923). The proof is given in Appendix 15.9 by Erwin Diewert in the 2004 CPI Manual. See also Hill (2006), pp. 315- 323.

$$(5)\qquad P_{LO}^{0,t} \equiv \frac{\sum_{i=1}^{n} p_i^t q_i^b}{\sum_{i=1}^{n} p_i^0 q_i^b} = \frac{\sum_{i=1}^{n} p_i^b q_i^b}{\sum_{i=1}^{n} p_i^0 q_i^b} \cdot \frac{\sum_{i=1}^{n} p_i^t q_i^b}{\sum_{i=1}^{n} p_i^b q_i^b} = P_{LO}^{0,b} \cdot P_{LO}^{b,t} = P_{PA}^{0,b} \cdot P_{LA}^{b,t}.$$

This shows that the direct Lowe index for t on 0 is identical to the chain Lowe index that links t with 0 via period b. This reflects the fact that Lowe indices are transitive. However, as just noted, $P_{LO}^{b,0}$ is identical to $P_{LA}^{b,0}$ and $P_{LO}^{b,t}$ is identical to $P_{LA}^{b,t}$. Thus, the direct Lowe index is also identical to the Paasche index for b based on 0 multiplied by the Laspeyres index for t based on b. Given that the order of the three periods is $b < 0 < t$, the Paasche index for b with period 0 as the price reference period measures the price change *backwards* from 0 to b. Thus, (5) can be interpreted as showing that the Lowe index for t on 0 is a chain index in which the first link is the backwards Paasche[6] from 0 to b while the second link is the forwards Laspeyres from b to t.

This roundabout way of measuring the change between 0 and t via period b becomes increasingly arbitrary and unsatisfactory the further back in time the quantity reference period b is from the price reference period 0.

4. Short Term Price Movements

Most users of CPIs are more interested in short term price movements in the recent past than in the total price change between the possibly remote price reference period 0 and period t. Consider the index for period $t+1$ on period t with price reference period 0 and quantity reference period b. The order of the periods remains $b < 0 < t < t+1$. The change between t and t+1 is obtained indirectly by dividing the index of t+1 by the index for t, as follows:

$$(6)\qquad P_{LO}^{t,t+1} = \left[\frac{\sum_{i=1}^{n} p_i^{t+1} q_i^b}{\sum_{i=1}^{n} p_i^0 q_i^b} \Bigg/ \frac{\sum_{i=1}^{n} p_i^t q_i^b}{\sum_{i=1}^{n} p_i^0 q_i^b} \right] = \frac{\sum_{i=1}^{n} p_i^{t+1} q_i^b}{\sum_{i=1}^{n} p_i^t q_i^b}.$$

In general, the ratio of two Lowe indices is also a Lowe index. Here, the index for t+1 on t is a Lowe index with period b as the quantity reference period. It does not depend on the quantities in the original price reference period 0.

As just shown above, this index can also be viewed as a chain index in which the first link is $P_{PA}^{t,b}$, the *backwards* Paasche index that measures the price change from period t back to period b, while the second link is $P_{PA}^{t,b+1}$, the *forwards* Laspeyres from b to t+1. Linking two

[6] The backwards Paasche index is equal to $1/P_{LA}^{0,b}$. It is the reciprocal of the Laspeyres index for period 0 that uses period b as the price (and quantity) reference period.

consecutive time periods in this roundabout way through some third period in the past is inherently arbitrary and unreasonable. There can be no economic rationale for such a procedure. With the passage of time, the relative quantities in periods t and t+1 are likely to diverge increasingly from the relative quantities in period b. In this case, the quantities of period b become increasingly irrelevant to a price comparison between t and t+1 the longer the lapse of time between period b and period t.[7]

In order to have short term Lowe indices whose reference quantities are of some relevance to the two periods compared, the gap between the quantity reference period b and period t should be kept to a minimum. This implies that the quantity reference period itself should be updated as frequently as possible. The Lowe indices themselves need to be chained.

5. Lowe, Laspeyres and Cost of Living Indices

A cost of living index, or COLI, may be defined as the ratio of minimum expenditures needed to attain the same level of utility in two time periods. Assuming that the actual expenditures in the first period are minimal, the COLI measures the minimum amount by which expenditures need to change in order to maintain the level of utility in the first period.

COLIs cannot be calculated exactly because the second set of expenditures cannot be observed. However, a COLI may be approximated by means of a superlative index. The concept of a superlative index was introduced by Erwin Diewert (1976). Superlative indices treat both periods symmetrically, the two most widely used examples of superlative indices being the Fisher index and the Törnqvist index. These indices and their properties are explained in some detail in Chapters 1, 15, 16 and 17 of the 2004 CPI Manual.

A well known result in index number theory is that the Laspeyres price index places an upper bound on the COLI based on the first period, while the Paasche index places a lower bound on the COLI based on the second period.[8] It useful therefore to establish how a Lowe index that uses as reference quantities the quantities of period b may be expected to relate to the Laspeyres based on period 0 where, as usual, b is earlier than 0.

This relationship is examined in paragraphs 15.44 to 15.48 and Appendix 15.2 of the 2004 CPI Manual. As it depends on the behaviour of prices and quantities over time, no unconditional generalizations can be made. However, it is possible to make generalizations that are conditional on particular types of behaviour, just as it can predicted that a Laspeyres index will exceed the corresponding Paasche index if there is a negative correlation between the price and quantity relatives. The conclusion reached in paragraph 15.45 of the 2004 CPI Manual is that "under the assumptions that there are long-term trends in prices and normal consumer substitution responses, the Lowe index will normally be greater than the corresponding Laspeyres index."

---

[7] In a paper on the relative merits of direct and chained indices included in the present volume, Balk (2011) also concludes that when measuring the change between consecutive time periods "it is not at all clear why period *0* price and/or quantity data should play a role in the comparison of periods τ and $\tau-1$ ($\tau = 2,\ldots,t$)."

[8] The proof is given in paragraphs 17.9 to 17.17 of the 2004 CPI Manual. The proof is attributable to Konüs (1924).

It is reasonable to conclude that, in most cases, the Lowe index will exceed the corresponding Laspeyres index, and that the gap between them is likely to increase the further back in time period b for the Lowe reference quantities is compared with period 0, the base period for the Laspeyres index.

Given that period b precedes period 0, the ranking of the indices for period t on period 0 under the assumed conditions will be:

Lowe ≥ Laspeyres ≥ Fisher ≥ Paasche.

As the Fisher is a superlative index it may be expected to approximate a COLI.

Statistical offices need to take these relationships into consideration. There may be practical advantages and financial savings from continuing to make repeated use over many years of the same fixed set of quantities to calculate a CPI. However, the amount by which such a CPI exceeds some conceptually preferred target index, such as a COLI, is likely to get steadily larger the longer the same set of reference quantities is used. Many users are likely to interpret the difference as upward bias, which may eventually undermine the credibility and acceptability of the index.

Assuming long term trends in prices and normal consumer substitution, Balk and Diewert (2003) conclude that, the difference between a Lowe index and a COLI may be "reduced to a negligible amount if:

- the lag in obtaining the base year quantity weights is minimized, and

- the base year is changed as frequently as possible."

Essentially the same recommendation was made at the end of the previous section but on slightly different grounds.

6. Lowe Price Indices as Deflators and Their Associated Implicit Quantity Indices

Lowe price indices may be used to deflate time series of consumption expenditures at current prices in order to obtain the implicit quantity indices. The two implicit quantity indices of main interest are the index for period t on period 0 and for period t+1 on period t. Deflating the change in current expenditures between period 0 and period t by the Lowe index for period t, we have:

$$(7)\quad \left[\frac{\sum_{i=1}^{n} p_i^t q_i^t}{\sum_{i=1}^{n} p_i^0 q_i^0} \Bigg/ \frac{\sum_{i=1}^{n} p_i^t q_i^b}{\sum_{i=1}^{n} p_i^0 q_i^b}\right] = \left[\frac{\sum_{i=1}^{n} p_i^t q_i^t}{\sum_{i=1}^{n} p_i^t q_i^b} \Bigg/ \frac{\sum_{i=1}^{n} p_i^0 q_i^0}{\sum_{i=1}^{n} p_i^0 q_i^b}\right] = \frac{Q_{PA}^{b,t}}{Q_{PA}^{b,0}}$$

where Q_{PA} denotes a Paasche quantity index. The implicit quantity index is therefore equal to the ratio of the Paasche quantity index for t on b divided by that for 0 on b.

In the likely case in which the Lowe price index for t on 0 exceeds the Laspeyres index for t on 0, then the implicit quantity index for t on 0 will be less than the Paasche index for t on 0.

The implicit quantity index between period t and period t+1 is as follows.

$$(8)\quad \left[\frac{\sum_{i=1}^{n} p_i^{t+1} q_i^{t+1}}{\sum_{i=1}^{n} p_i^{t} q_i^{t}} \bigg/ \frac{\sum_{i=1}^{n} p_i^{t+1} q_i^{b}}{\sum_{i=1}^{n} p_i^{t} q_i^{b}}\right] = \left[\frac{\sum_{i=1}^{n} p_i^{t+1} q_i^{t+1}}{\sum_{i=1}^{n} p_i^{t+1} q_i^{b}} \bigg/ \frac{\sum_{i=1}^{n} p_i^{t} q_i^{t}}{\sum_{i=1}^{n} p_i^{t} q_i^{b}}\right] = \frac{Q_{PA}^{b,t+1}}{Q_{PA}^{b,t}}$$

Thus, it equals the ratio of the Paasche quantity index for t+1 on b to the Paasche index of t on b. It does not depend on the prices or quantities in the price reference period 0.

The ratio of two Paasche quantity indices is a conceptually complex measure whose meaning is not intuitively obvious. Such indices are not common and Lowe price indices do not seem to be widely used as deflators.[9]

6. Inter-temporal Lowe Quantity Indices

Consider a set of n products with quantities q_i $(i = 1,2,\ldots,n)$. A Lowe quantity index is defined as the ratio of the total values of the quantities in two different time periods valued at the same set of reference prices. Any set of prices may be chosen as the reference prices. They do not have to be those observed in some actual period.

The inter-temporal Lowe quantity index, $Q_{LO}^{0,t}$, for period t with period 0 as the quantity reference period is defined as follows:

$$(9)\quad Q_{LO}^{0,t} = \frac{\sum_{i=1}^{n} p_i^{r} q_i^{t}}{\sum_{i=1}^{n} p_i^{r} q_i^{0}}$$

where the p_i^r denote the reference prices. When the reference prices are those observed in some actual time period b it will be described as the price reference period.

The Lowe quantity index for period t with period 0 as the quantity reference period and period b as the price reference period is defined as follows:

[9] Although aggregate Lowe price indices, such as the overall CPI, may not be widely used to deflate expenditure aggregates, the detailed disaggregated price indices of which they are composed are commonly used to deflate individual components of final expenditures or output in national accounts. The disaggregated component indices may be reweighted as required or appropriate.

$$(10) \qquad Q_{LO}^{0,t} = \frac{\sum_{i=1}^{n} p_i^b q_i^t}{\sum_{i=1}^{n} p_i^b q_i^0} = \sum_{i=1}^{n} \left(\frac{q_i^t}{q_i^0} \right) s_i^{b0}, \qquad \text{where} \quad s_i^{b0} = \frac{p_i^b q_i^0}{\sum_{i=1}^{n} p_i^b q_i^0}.$$

Like the Lowe price index, the Lowe quantity index can be written, and calculated, in two ways: either as the ratio of two value aggregates, or as an arithmetic weighted average of the quantity relatives, q_i^t / q_i^0, using the hybrid expenditures shares s_i^{0b} as weights. The hybrid weights may be obtained by updating the actual expenditure shares in period b, namely $p_i^b q_i^b / \sum p_i^b q_i^b$, by multiplying them by the quantity relatives q_i^0 / q_i^b and then normalising them to sum to unity.

7. Lowe, Laspeyres and Paasche Quantity Indices

The properties and behaviour of Lowe quantity indices match those of the corresponding price indices and will therefore only be summarized here.

First, the Laspeyres and Paasche quantity indices are special cases of the Lowe quantity index. Second, any Lowe quantity index can be expressed as the ratio of two Laspeyres quantity indices based on the price reference period b.

Third, the Lowe quantity index is transitive. Consider a pair of Lowe quantity indices using the same set of reference prices such as those of period b. The Lowe quantity index for period k with period j as the quantity reference period multiplied by the index for period l with period k as the quantity reference period is identical with the Lowe quantity index for period l with period j as the quantity reference period:

$$(10) \qquad \frac{\sum_{i=1}^{n} p_i^b q_i^k}{\sum_{i=1}^{n} p_i^b q_i^j} \frac{\sum_{i=1}^{n} p_i^b q_i^l}{\sum_{i=1}^{n} p_i^b q_i^k} \equiv \frac{\sum_{i=1}^{n} p_i^b q_i^l}{\sum_{i=1}^{n} p_i^b q_i^j}, \qquad \text{or} \qquad Q_{LO}^{j,k} \cdot Q_{LO}^{k,l} \equiv Q_{LO}^{j,l}.$$

8. Time series at Constant Prices

It is common in national accounts to publish time series for an aggregate such as Household Consumption Expenditures at constant prices. A convenient year such as 2,000 is chosen as the base year and the values of the aggregate in subsequent years are given by revaluing the quantities at the reference prices of year 2,000. The constant price series is usually obtained by deflating the values of the aggregate at current prices by Paasche price indices based on 2,000. The movements in the resulting constant prices series are, of course, identical with those of a Laspeyres quantity index based on 2,000. The base year 2,000 will be denoted here simply as year 0.

The proportionate change in the constant price series between any pair of consecutive years, such as t and t+1, that do not include the base year is a Lowe quantity index: namely,

$$(11) \qquad Q_{LO}^{t,t+1} = \frac{\sum_{i=1}^{n} p_i^0 q_i^{t+1}}{\sum_{i=1}^{n} p_i^0 q_i^t}$$

where p_i^0 is the price of product i in 2,000. It equals the Laspeyres quantity index for year t+1 divided by that for year t. In practice, the change between t and t+1 may be of greater interest to users and of more relevance for policy purposes than the total change between the price reference year 2,000 and year t+1.

As in the corresponding case of a Lowe price index, this Lowe quantity index can be viewed as a chain index that links t and t+1 via the base year 0:

$$(12) \qquad Q_{LO}^{t,t+1} = \frac{\sum_{i=1}^{n} p_i^0 q_i^0}{\sum_{i=1}^{n} p_i^0 q_i^t} \cdot \frac{\sum_{i=1}^{n} p_i^0 q_i^{t+1}}{\sum_{i=1}^{n} p_i^0 q_i^0} = \frac{Q_{LA}^{0,t+1}}{Q_{LA}^{0,t}}$$

The first term on the right of (12) is the (backwards) Paasche quantity index for year 0 with year t as the quantity reference period. It measures the quantity change from t back to 0. The second term in (12), the Laspeyres for t+1 based on 0, then measures the forward change from 0 up to t+1. As in the case of the corresponding Lowe price index, this roundabout way of measuring the change between t and t+1 is inherently arbitrary and unsatisfactory. The reference prices for year 0 are likely to become increasingly inappropriate for a comparison between t and t+1 with the passage of time.

For this reason, it is generally accepted that, despite the convenience of constant price series for many uses, it not desirable to permit the series to continue for more than a few years before moving the price reference year forwards. Each new price reference year then acts as the link between the previous series and the new series[10].

9. Lowe Indices in International Comparisons

As Lowe indices are transitive, they are widely used for purposes of multilateral comparisons within groups of countries. There are many ways in which the reference quantities

[10] The *1993 SNA Manual* remarks in paragraph 16.77 that "… the underlying issue is not whether to chain or not but how often to rebase. Sooner or later the base year for fixed weight Laspeyres volume indices and their associated constant price series has to be updated because the prices in the base year become increasingly irrelevant."

or prices might be specified. Two important classes of multilateral price and quantity indices actually used in international comparisons are the average quantity methods and the average price methods[11].

The average quantity methods use as reference quantities a basket whose quantities consist of some kind of average of the quantities in all the countries in the group. The purchasing power parity, or PPP, for a pair of countries is then defined as the ratio of the values of the reference basket in the two countries valued at their own prices in their own national currencies. Either country may serve as the reference country. The average price methods use a set of average prices for the group as a whole as the reference prices to construct international quantity indices.

The average quantity methods generate Lowe PPPs while the average price methods generate international Lowe quantity indices. However, they are not described as 'Lowe' PPPs or indices in the existing literature on PPPs and International Comparisons as the term 'Lowe' index was only introduced in 2003, as already mentioned.

10. Lowe PPPs

Consider first the PPP between a single pair of countries, j and k. A basket of n reference quantities is specified, the quantities being denoted by q_i^r. The prices in each country denoted by p_i^j, are denominated in the national currency of the country. The Lowe PPP, or PPP_{LO}, for country k with country j as the reference country is defined as follows:

$$(13) \qquad PPP_{LO}^{j,k} = \frac{\sum_{i=1}^{n} p_i^k q_i^r}{\sum_{i=1}^{n} p_i^j q_i^r}$$

Any set of quantities could serve as the reference quantities. They do not have to be the quantities purchased in one or other of the two countries compared, or indeed in any actual country. They could be arithmetic or geometric averages of the quantities in the two countries compared or averages over a larger group of countries for which multilateral PPPs are required.

If the reference quantities are specified to be those of the reference country j the PPP becomes a Laspeyres PPP. If the reference quantities are those of country k, it becomes a Paasche PPP.[12] As in inter-temporal indices, Laspeyres and Paasche indices are special cases of Lowe indices.

[11] See Kravis, Heston and Summers (1982) pp. 77-79 and Hill (1997, pp. 54-62).

[12] See, for example, Table 7.2 of Kravis, Heston and Summers (1982) which lists all the Laspeyres and Paasche indices between 34 countries.

11. Multilateral PPPs Using the Star method

The attraction of a Lowe PPP in the context of a set of multilateral comparisons for a group of countries is that the Lowe index is transitive. There are many possible sets of reference quantities to choose from. One possibility to select the quantities in one of the countries in the group, say country b, and to use them as the reference quantities for the PPPs between every pair of countries in the group. In this case, country b acts as the base country for the multilateral comparisons. The reference quantities q_i^r become the actual quantities in country b or q_i^b. The Lowe PPP between country k and country j is then equal to the ratio of their Laspeyres PPPs based on country b:

$$(14) \qquad PPP_{LO}^{j,k} = \frac{\sum_{i=1}^{n} p_i^k q_i^b}{\sum_{i=1}^{n} p_i^j q_i^b} = \left[\frac{\sum_{i=1}^{n} p_i^k q_i^b}{\sum_{i=1}^{n} p_i^b q_i^b} \Big/ \frac{\sum_{i=1}^{n} p_i^j q_i^b}{\sum_{i=1}^{n} p_i^b q_i^b} \right] = \frac{PPP_{LA}^{r,k}}{PPP_{LA}^{r,j}}.$$

In practice, Laspeyres PPPs are calculated between every country and the base country b. The various Lowe PPPs between pairs of countries that do not include the base country are all derived indirectly by dividing one Laspeyres by another.

This arrangement can be portrayed graphically by a star in which the base country is placed at the centre and every other country is placed in a ring around the centre. This kind of method is therefore described as a star method.

Star methods in which an individual country is chosen to be at the centre of the star have been used in the past.[13] However, the results obtained obviously vary according to the subjective choice of country to act as the base country. For this reason, star methods that place an actual country at the centre of the star are generally considered to be unacceptable. A less arbitrary method is needed.

As quantities of the same product can be summed across countries, another obvious possibility is to choose the total quantities of each product over the group of countries concerned as the reference quantities. This makes the reference quantities characteristic of the group of countries as a whole, which may be considered a desirable property for a set of multilateral comparisons. Alternatively, the total quantities may be replaced by the average quantities obtained by dividing the total quantities by the number of countries. Dividing by a constant does not change the relative quantities of different kinds of product and it is immaterial whether the average or the total quantities are used in Lowe PPPs.

The use of such average or total quantities as reference quantities for international Lowe PPPs was first proposed by Walsh (1901) and also considered as a possibility by Van Ijzeren (1956)[14]. Both Walsh and Van Ijzeren also examined the possibility of using other kinds of

[13] For example, a type of star method was used to calculate PPPs among the so-called Group II countries of Eastern Europe in the 1980's with Austria at the centre of the star.

[14] See Diewert (1993) and Hill (1997, p. 55).

averages such as geometric averages. Lowe PPPs that use arithmetic average quantities as reference quantities have been calculated by the United Nations Economic Commission for Latin America and the Caribbean.

When average quantities are used as the reference quantities, the method still remains a star method, but one in which an 'average country' is placed at the centre of the star instead of an actual country.[15] This is explained more fully below.

12. Lowe PPPs as deflators

Using Lowe PPPs as deflators produces derived or implicit measures of relative real expenditures that are conceptually complex. As illustrated in equation (15), if the ratio of the expenditures in national currencies for countries k and j is divided by a Lowe PPP with reference quantities q^b, the result is the ratio of two Paasche quantity indices based on country b. Country b may be an average country or an actual country:

$$(15)\qquad \left[\frac{\sum_{i=1}^{n} p_i^k q_i^k}{\sum_{i=1}^{n} p_i^j q_i^j} \Bigg/ \frac{\sum_{i=1}^{n} p_i^k q_i^b}{\sum_{i=1}^{n} p_i^j q_i^b}\right] = \left[\frac{\sum_{i=1}^{n} p_i^k q_i^k}{\sum_{i=1}^{n} p_i^k q_i^b} \Bigg/ \frac{\sum_{i=1}^{n} p_i^j q_i^j}{\sum_{i=1}^{n} p_i^j q_i^b}\right] = \frac{Q_{PA}^{b,k}}{Q_{PA}^{b,j}}.$$

In international comparisons, there is typically more interest in the quantity comparisons than in the PPPs and the international agencies tend to give quantity comparisons priority over PPPs. Lowe quantity indices which provide conceptually simple and meaningful comparisons of real expenditures have therefore been preferred to the kinds of complex implicit quantity measures given in (14).

13. International Lowe Quantity Indices

Let the two countries compared be j and k and let the selected reference prices be denoted by p_i^r. The Lowe quantity index for country k based on country j, or $Q_{LO}^{j,k}$, is defined as follows:

$$(16)\qquad Q_{LO}^{j,k} = \frac{\sum_{i=1}^{n} p_i^r q_i^k}{\sum_{i=1}^{n} p_i^r q_i^j}.$$

[15] The fact that all average quantity and average price methods are examples of the star method was pointed out by Hill (1997, pp. 54-60).

Any set of prices could be selected as the reference prices, p_i^r.

In a set of multilateral comparisons, if the prices of one of the countries, say country b, are selected as the reference quantities, the method becomes a star method in which that country is placed at the centre of the star. As shown above in the corresponding case of Lowe PPPs, the Lowe quantity index between countries j and k can then be obtained as the ratio of the Laspeyres quantity indices for countries k and j based on b.

Each Lowe quantity index can also be interpreted as a chain index in which country j is compared indirectly with country k via country b at the centre of the star:

$$(17) \qquad Q_{LO}^{j,k} \equiv \frac{\sum_{i=1}^{n} p_i^b q_i^k}{\sum_{i=1}^{n} p_i^b q_i^j} = \frac{\sum_{i=1}^{n} p_i^b q_i^b}{\sum_{i=1}^{n} p_i^b q_i^j} \cdot \frac{\sum_{i=1}^{n} p_i^b q_i^k}{\sum_{i=1}^{n} p_i^b q_i^b} = Q_{PA}^{j,b} \cdot Q_{LA}^{b,k}.$$

The Lowe index in (17) is the product of the Paasche quantity index for country b based on country j multiplied by the Laspeyres index for country k based on country b. If countries j and k are very different from each other while country b is intermediate between them, the chain index may provide a satisfactory quantity measure. However, if countries j and k are very similar to each other while country b is very different from both of them, the chain index is not likely to provide a satisfactory quantity measure. In any case, the arbitrary selection of the prices of one country to act as the reference prices is not generally consider to be an acceptable method. In practice, some kind of average prices for the group are preferred.

14. The Geary Khamis quantity index

The Geary Khamis, or GK, quantity index is a Lowe index that uses average international prices as the reference prices. The GK index has been widely used. It was used in the first three phases of the International Comparisons Project, or ICP, of the United Nations and World Bank that started in 1970. It has also been used by the OECD as one of the methods for making comparisons among OECD countries. The GK method may be described as follows.

Assume there are C countries in the group. The GK quantity index for country k on country j, Q_{GK}^{jk}, is defined as follows.

$$(18) \qquad Q_{GK}^{j,k} = \frac{\sum_{i=1}^{n} \bar{p}_i^G q_i^k}{\sum_{i=1}^{n} \bar{p}_i^G q_i^j} \quad \text{where} \quad \bar{p}_i^G = \sum_{c=1}^{C} \frac{p_i^c}{PPP^c} \frac{q_i^c}{Q_i^G} \quad \text{and} \quad Q_i^G = \sum_{c=1}^{C} q_i^c .$$

The aggregate purchasing power parity for country c, PPP^c, is defined as follows:

$$(19) \qquad PPP^c = \frac{\sum_{i=1}^{n} p_i^c q_i^c}{\sum_{i=1}^{n} \bar{p}_i^G q_i^c}$$

The average prices and the PPPs are determined simultaneously in the GK method[16]. The average prices are denominated in the numeraire currency for the group. The method is invariant to the choice of numeraire currency,

The GK average international price has a simple interpretation because it is defined in the same way as the national average price for a single country. A national average price is defined as the total value of the transactions in the product divided by the total quantity of the product. It is a quantity weighted arithmetic average of the prices at which the product is sold within the country. Similarly, a GK average international price as defined in (18) is a quantity weighted average of the prices at which the product is sold across the entire group of countries after the prices have all been converted into the designated numeraire currency. The group can therefore be regarded as if it were a super country with average prices p_i^G and total quantities Q_i^G, the p_i^G s serving as the reference prices for the Lowe quantity index.

The PPP for country c in (19) is a Paasche price index for country c based on the group G. This means that the PPP between any two countries, such as countries j and k, is the ratio of the two Paasche indices based on the group G:

$$(20) \qquad PPP_{GK}^{j,k} = \frac{\sum_{i=1}^{n} p_i^k q_i^k}{\sum_{i=1}^{n} \bar{p}_i^G q_i^k} \Bigg/ \frac{\sum_{i=1}^{n} p_i^j q_i^j}{\sum_{i=1}^{n} \bar{p}_i^G q_i^j}$$

This expression does not simplify. The properties of GK PPPs are not so simple and transparent as those of GK quantity indices.

As it is a Lowe index, the GK quantity index can be expressed as the ratio of two Laspeyres quantity indices based on the group G:

$$(21) \qquad Q_{GK}^{j,k} \equiv \frac{\sum_{i=1}^{n} \bar{p}_i^G q_i^k}{\sum_{i=1}^{n} \bar{p}_i^G q_i^j} = \left[\frac{\sum_{i=1}^{n} \bar{p}_i^G q_i^k}{\sum_{i=1}^{n} \bar{p}_i^G Q_i^G} \Bigg/ \frac{\sum_{i=1}^{n} \bar{p}_i^G q_i^j}{\sum_{i=1}^{n} \bar{p}_i^G Q_i^G} \right] = \frac{Q_{LA}^{G,k}}{Q_{LA}^{G,j}}.$$

The GK method can be viewed as a star method which places the group itself at the centre of the star.[17] The denominator in each of the two Laspeyres indices in (21) is the total value of all

[16] See Kravis, Heston and Summers (1982), pp. 89-94 for a full explanation of the GK method and its properties.

[17] See Hill (1997) pp. 54-60.

transactions in all products in all countries of the group valued at the average prices for the group expressed in the numeraire currency. The resulting GK indices do not actually depend on the total quantities Q_i^G, however, as the two denominators in (21) cancel each other out.[18]

Alternatively, the GK quantity index can be viewed as chain index as follows.

$$(22) \qquad Q_{GK}^{j,k} = \frac{\sum_{i=1}^{n} \bar{p}_i^G Q_i^G}{\sum_{i=1}^{n} \bar{p}_i^G q_i^j} \cdot \frac{\sum_{i=1}^{n} \bar{p}_i^G q_i^k}{\sum_{i=1}^{n} \bar{p}_i^G Q_i^G} = Q_{PA}^{j,G} \cdot Q_{LA}^{G,k} \,.$$

Q_{GK}^{jk} is a chain index in which k is linked to j via the group G. It equals the Paasche quantity index for G on j multiplied by the Laspeyres quantity index for k on G.

15. Missing Products

Linking countries through the group G can have advantages over direct comparisons between the countries concerned. One of the main problems encountered in constructing international price and quantity indices is the fact that not all the products that can be found in the group as a whole are to be found in every country. On the contrary, in any one country, many products are likely to be missing, especially if the group of countries is large and economically diverse and patterns of consumption vary considerably among the countries.

There are obviously no prices to be observed for products whose quantities are zero. As the number products available varies from country to country, the sets of country prices that might potentially be used as reference prices for Lowe quantity indices also vary in size from country to country. The largest and most comprehensive set of prices consists of the average prices for the group as a whole. This set must include every product in every country.

A direct binary comparison between two countries carried out independently of other countries uses only the prices and quantities of those two countries. However, it may not be possible to use all the quantity information if there are some products that are found in only one of the two countries. For example, it is not possible to include products that are found in country k but not in country j in the direct Laspeyres quantity index for k based on j because there are no prices for them in j. Similarly, it is not possible to include products found in j but not in k in the Paasche quantity index for k on j as there are no prices for them in k. In these circumstances, the Laspeyres and Paasche quantity indices may be regarded as being subject to bias.

---

[18] In the UN / World Bank *International Comparisons Project*, the denominator in each of the two Laspeyres indices in (21) could be interpreted as the total GDP of the group of countries as a whole expressed in the numeraire currency. If the group included all countries in the world, the denominator would be World GDP. Implicitly, in the GK method the Laspeyres index for the GDP of each individual country is calculated based on the total GDP for the group. The GDP quantity indices for pairs of countries are then obtained indirectly as the ratios of the corresponding Laspeyres indices based on the group as a whole.

However, all the products in both countries can be included in the Lowe quantity index between them that uses the average international prices for the group of countries to which they belong as the reference prices. As already noted, there must be an average international price for every product that is found in any country in the group. Thus, a Lowe quantity index that uses international prices is able to utilize all the quantities in both countries. For this reason it might provide a better measure of the relative quantities in the two countries than a direct binary index that has to ignore certain quantities. .

Much depends on how appropriate or relevant the average international prices are considered to be for a comparison between two countries. The GK average international prices have a clear economic interpretation and must be relevant for comparisons between countries within the group. As already explained, the GK index can be viewed as the ratio of the two Laspeyres quantity indices based on the group as a whole. Each index is able to include all the quantities in that country irrespectively of whether they are found in the other country. As shown in (22), the GK quantity index can also be viewed as a chain index that links the two countries though the group. Each link covers all the products in the country in question even though the coverage is not the same in the two links. However, this is an advantage. The main reason for chaining is that this approach is able to deal with situations, whether over time periods or countries, in which the set of products covered is variable.

If the two countries are very different with a relatively small overlap of products between them, chaining through the group as a whole is likely to produce a better quantity index than a direct comparison between them that is restricted to using only the price and quantities in the two countries concerned. On the other hand, if the sets of products available in the two countries largely coincide, the direct quantity index between them may be preferable to a chain index through the group. The argument is similar to that used earlier to argue that consecutive time periods for the same country, which are likely to have almost identical sets of products, should not be linked through some earlier time period, and especially not through some period in the remote past. In some circumstances chain indices are superior to direct indices while in other circumstances, direct indices are superior. The choice of preferred index depends on the circumstances.

16. Other Average Price Methods

Any set of prices can serve as the reference prices in a Lowe quantity index. Although a GK average price, being the international equivalent of a national average price, has a meaningful economic interpretation, there are other ways in which an average international price might be defined. Different types of averages might be used instead of an arithmetic average, and different kinds of weighting may be used.

For example, one possibility would be to use unweighted geometric means of the national average prices as the reference prices in an international Lowe quantity index. This method was advocated by Gerardi (1982), but it was first proposed by Walsh (1901).[19] An intriguing feature

[19] See Diewert (1993).

of this method is that it makes no difference to the quantity indices whether the national average prices are converted into a common numeraire currency or not.

When considering the relative merits of the different methods, the key issue is what effect the different kinds of average prices may be expected to have on the international quantity indices. This depends on how closely the various sets of national prices are correlated with the average international prices. Whatever international prices are used, they must be closer to some sets of national prices than others. Because of ordinary substitution effects, for a given set of quantities, the Lowe quantity index for a country may be expected to be lower the more closely the pattern of the reference prices resembles the pattern for the prices of that country.[20]

Consider the example of two countries. Suppose the initial vector of average international prices used as the reference prices for the Lowe quantity index is roughly equidistant from the price vectors for countries k and j. Next, suppose the vector of reference prices is changed to bring it closer to country k's vector and further away from j's vector, the quantities in both countries remaining unchanged. As the vector of reference prices approaches the actual pattern of relative prices in k that was responsible for generating the actual quantities in k, the Laspeyres quantity index for k based on the group G will tend to fall. Conversely, as the vector of reference prices moves away from the actual prices in j, the Laspeyres index for j will tend to rise. Thus, the Lowe quantity index for k on j will tend to fall.

The effects on the Lowe quantity indices of defining the average international prices in different ways are sometimes predictable for reasons just given. Suppose the average prices are weighted according to the economic size of the country as in the GK method. The vector of average international prices will tend to be closer to the vectors of actual prices for the richest countries than if the average prices are unweighted, as in the Gerardi method. Thus, the GK quantity indices for the richest countries will tend to be lower than if unweighted Gerardi prices are used.

This is an illustration of the Gerschenkron effect. It does not demonstrate which of the two types of index is biased. If unweighted average prices are preferred on the grounds that each country should be given equal weight as a matter of principle, then the Lowe quantity indices for the richest countries using GK prices as reference prices may be regarded as having a downward bias, thereby understating the gap between rich and poor countries. On the other hand, in reality countries are not all the same size and some countries account for much larger shares of total world income and output than others. From this perspective, Lowe quantity indices that use unweighted average international prices may be regarded as having an upward bias for the largest and richest countries. These are issues that cannot be decided on technical grounds alone. Value judgments are inevitably involved.

[20] This phenomenon is described in the literature as the 'Gerschenkron effect.' It occurs with all multilateral indices that use some kind of average group prices as the reference prices.

17. Conclusions

Lowe indices are popular for several reasons. They are conceptually simple and meaningful. They enable statistical agencies to economize by continuing to make use of the same set of reference prices of quantities over many years. They are transitive and additive. These two properties are particularly attractive to users of both inter-temporal and international Lowe quantity indices.

Very many of the price and quantity indices produced by statistical agencies turn out to be Lowe indices although their generic similarity has not been so obvious until recently because of the lack of a common name.

Lowe indices have two closely interrelated characteristics. They can be expressed as ratios of Laspeyres indices and they can be viewed as chain indices that link through some other period, country or group of countries. The quality of a Lowe index depends on the relevance or suitability of the link. In the case of temporal price or quantity indices where the link is some past period, its relevance must diminish as it recedes into the past. In these circumstances, a Lowe price index is also likely to be subject to increasing upward bias as compared with a cost of living index. In the case of international Lowe quantity indices, the situation is complicated. Linking a pair of countries through the group of countries to which they belong may be regarded as strengthening or weakening the comparison between them depending on circumstances.

References

Balk, B.M. (2011), “Direct and Chained Indices: A Review of Two Paradigms”, chapter 10 in W.E. Diewert, B.M. Balk, D. Fixler, K.J. Fox, and A.O. Nakamura (eds.), *Price and Productivity Measurement: Volume 6 -- Index Number Theory*, Trafford Press.

Balk, B.M. and W.E. Diewert (2011), “The Lowe Consumer Price Index and its Substitution Bias,” chapter 7 in W.E. Diewert, B.M. Balk, D. Fixler, K.J. Fox, and A.O. Nakamura (eds.), *Price and Productivity Measurement: Volume 6 -- Index Number Theory*, Trafford Press.

Bortkiewicz, L. von (1923), “Zweck und Struktur einer Preisindexzahl”, *Nordic Statistical Journal*, 2.

Diewert, W.E. (1976), “Exact and Superlative Index Numbers”, *Journal of Econometrics*, Vol. 4, pp. 224-245.

Diewert, W.E. (1993), “The Early History of Price Index Research”, in *Essays in Index Number Theory, Volume 1*, edited by W.E. Diewert and A.O. Nakamura, North Holland.

EU, IMF, OECD, UN, World Bank, 1993, *System of National Accounts, 1993*, Brussels/Luxembourg, New York, Paris, Washington D.C., 1993 chapters can be downloaded for free at http://unstats.un.org/unsd/sna1993/toctop.asp?L1=1

Gerardi, D. (1982), “Selected Problems of Inter-County Comparisons on the Basis of the Experience of the EEC”, *Review of Income and Wealth*, Series 28, December 1092, pp. 381-405.

Hill, R.J. (1997), “A Taxonomy of Multilateral Methods for Making International Comparisons of Prices and Quantities”, *Review of Income and Wealth*, Series 43 (1) March, 49-69.

Hill, R.J. (2006), “When Does Chaining Reduce the Paasche-Laspeyres Spread? An Application to Scanner Data”, *Review of Income and Wealth*, Series 52, No 2, June, 309-325.

ILO, IMF, OECD, Eurostat, UNECE, and the World Bank (2004), *Consumer Price Index Manual: Theory and Practice*, International Labour Office.

Konüs, A.A. (1924), “The Problem of the True Index of the Cost of Living”, *The Economic Bulletin of the Institute of Economic Conjuncture*, No. 9-10 reprinted in English in *Econometrica*, volume 7, 1939.

Kravis, I.B, A.W. Heston and R. Summers (1982), *World Product and Income: International Comparisons of Real Gross Product*, Johns Hopkins University Press.

Van Ijzeren, J. (1956), "Three Methods of Comparing the Purchasing Power of Currencies," *Statistical Studies* No.7, The Netherlands Central Bureau of Statistics.

Walsh, C.M. (1901), *The Measurement of the General Exchange Value*, Macmillan and Co.

Chapter 10
DIRECT AND CHAINED INDICES: A REVIEW OF TWO PARADIGMS

Bert M. Balk[1]

1. Introduction

A recurrent theme when measuring aggregate price and quantity change between more than two periods is the choice between the computation of direct or chained index numbers. Suppose we consider periods 0, 1, 2, …,T and want to measure change relative to the base period *0*. A direct index number comparing period t $(t = 1,...,T)$ to period *0* results from inserting period t and period 0 data into a bilateral index formula. A chained index number comparing period t to period 0 results from successively inserting period 1 and period 0 data, period 2 and period 1 data, …., and period t and period t-1 data into a bilateral index formula and multiplying the outcomes with each other.

A commonly claimed advantage of the method of chaining is the reduction of so-called index number spread. As the *CPI Manual* (2004) states:

> "The main advantage of the chain system is that under normal conditions, chaining will reduce the spread between the Paasche and Laspeyres indices." (par. 15.83)
>
> "Basically, chaining is advisable if the prices and quantities pertaining to adjacent periods are *more similar* than the prices and quantities of more distant periods, since this strategy will lead to a narrowing of the spread between the Paasche and Laspeyres indices at each link." (par. 15.85)

The detailed numerical example discussed in chapter 19 of the *CPI Manual* also reflects this viewpoint, as the following quotations make clear:

> "… if the underlying price and quantity data are subject to reasonably smooth trends over time, then the use of chain indices will narrow considerably the dispersion in the asymmetrically weighted indices." (par. 19.16)

---

[1] Rotterdam School of Management, Erasmus University, and Statistics Netherlands, The Hague. Email: bbalk@rsm.nl. The views expressed in this paper are those of the author and do not necessarily reflect those of Statistics Netherlands. The author thanks Erwin Diewert for comments on a previous version.

Citation: **Bert M. Balk (2011),**
"Direct and Chained Indices: A Review of Two Paradigms,"
chapter 10, pp. 217-234 in
W.E. Diewert, B.M. Balk, D. Fixler, K.J. Fox and A.O. Nakamura,
PRICE AND PRODUCTIVITY MEASUREMENT: Volume 6 -- Index Number Theory. Trafford Press.

© Alice Nakamura, 2011. Permission to link to, or copy or reprint, these materials is granted without restriction, including for use in commercial textbooks, with due credit to the authors and editors.

"... the combined effect of using both the chain principle as well as symmetrically weighted indices is to dramatically reduce the spread between all indices constructed using these two principles." (par. 19.21)

The overall impression one gets is that chained index numbers are somehow closer to the truth than direct index numbers. But is this impression warranted?

The technique of chaining index numbers was introduced by Lehr (1885) and Marshall (1887) primarily as a means to overcome the problems of making comparisons for distant periods when there are many disappearing and newly appearing commodities through time. Statistical agencies were reluctant to officially use chained index numbers. However, during the last two decades this situation has started to change.

The growing acceptance of chained index numbers was not brought about by some convincing theoretic demonstration of the 'verisimilitudiness' of the method of chaining. Instead, under the influence of a small number of researchers, some important agencies in the field of economic measurement changed their ways.

Both the use of chaining and the replacement of the Laspeyres and Paasche indices (which are asymmetrically weighted) by Fisher indices (which are symmetrically weighted) are practices that have met with criticism from some, notably Peter von der Lippe[2]. Certainly it would be helpful to know more about how the approaches compare.

The plan of this paper is as follows. Section 2 summarizes the traditional point of view that is based on the use of direct Laspeyres and Paasche indices. Section 3 summarizes the modern point of view based on the use of chained Fisher indices. In section 4, the two views are compared. The conclusion that emerges is that, mathematically at least, a unification of the two approaches is impossible. A related question that remains to be answered is: What precisely does a chained price or quantity index measure? I search for an answer in section 5 using micro-economic theory, and in section 6 using Divisia index theory. Section 7 concludes.

2. The Traditional Point of View

I consider an economic aggregate consisting of a number of transaction categories that I will call 'commodities'. For the time being, I will assume that these commodities do not change through time. Each commodity ($n = 1,\ldots,N$) has an (average) price p_n^t per unit in each period t and a corresponding quantity q_n^t measured using the same units. The superscript t denotes the time period (thought of here as being a year). The (transaction) value of commodity n in period t is then $v_n^t \equiv p_n^t q_n^t$, and the value of the entire aggregate is $V^t \equiv \sum_{n=1}^{N} p_n^t q_n^t$. It is efficient to use from hereon simple vector notation. Hence, $p^t \cdot q^{t'} \equiv \sum_{n=1}^{N} p_n^t q_n^{t'}$, where t and t' denote two, not necessarily different, time periods.

[2] See Von der Lippe (2000), (2001a), (2001b), Reich (2000), and Rainer (2002). The discussion appears to be by and large limited to the readership of the *Allgemeines Statistisches Archiv*. A recent summary of Von der Lippe's position is provided by Von der Lippe (2007, Chapter 7).

Consider now the development of this aggregate through a number of consecutive periods, say $t = 0, 1, 2, \ldots, T$. The associated sequence of nominal values is given by

(1) $$p^0 \cdot q^0,\ p^1 \cdot q^1,\ p^2 \cdot q^2, \ldots,\ p^T \cdot q^T.$$

It is clear that the nominal value development is caused by both price and quantity changes. The problem is to disentangle the two components in order to get a picture of the 'real', quantity part of the development.

The traditional solution[3] involves transforming the sequence of nominal values into a sequence of values-at-constant-prices. If one employs the period 0 prices as constant prices, the solution becomes that of computation of the sequence

(2) $$p^0 \cdot q^0,\ p^0 \cdot q^1,\ p^0 \cdot q^2, \ldots,\ p^0 \cdot q^T.$$

In practice, the computation is carried out elementwise in two ways. One way is to multiply (inflate) each commodity's nominal period 0 value by its quantity change,

(3) $$p_n^0 q_n^0 (q_n^t / q_n^0) = p_n^0 q_n^t \quad (t = 1,\ldots,T).$$

The other way is to divide (deflate) each commodity's period t value by its price change,

(4) $$p_n^t q_n^t / (p_n^t / p_n^0) = p_n^0 q_n^t \quad (t = 1,\ldots,T).$$

The adding-up of $p_n^0 q_n^t$ for $n = 1,\ldots,N$ delivers $p^0 \cdot q^t$ for each period t. Recall that the Laspeyres price index is defined by $P_L(t,t') \equiv p^t \cdot q^{t'} / p^{t'} \cdot q^{t'}$, the Paasche price index is defined by $P_P(t,t') \equiv p^t \cdot q^t / p^{t'} \cdot q^t$, the Laspeyres quantity index is defined by $Q_L(t,t') \equiv p^{t'} \cdot q^t / p^{t'} \cdot q^{t'}$, and the Paasche quantity index is defined by $Q_P(t,t') \equiv p^t \cdot q^t / p^t \cdot q^{t'}$. With hindsight, the sequence (2) can be considered as having been obtained by taking the sequence of nominal values given in (1) and deflating these using the Paasche price index numbers, or by inflating these using the Laspeyres quantity index numbers, since

(5) $$p^0 \cdot q^t = p^t \cdot q^t / P_P(t,0) = p^0 \cdot q^0 Q_L(t,0) \quad (t = 1,\ldots,T).$$

The aggregate quantity change between any two periods can now be computed simply by taking the ratio of the corresponding two values from the sequence (2). For instance, if one is interested in the change between two adjacent periods t-1 and t, this is given by

(6) $$p^0 \cdot q^t / p^0 \cdot q^{t-1} = Q_{Lo}(t,t-1;0) \quad (t = 1,\ldots,T).$$

This formula is an instance of what in the literature is known as a Lowe quantity index[4]. Its interpretation is straightforward: the numerator contains the period t quantities evaluated at their base period prices, and the denominator contains the period t-1 quantities evaluated at the same prices.

[3] I associate this view with the *SNA* 1968, the relevant paragraph being 4.46.

[4] Some are accustomed to calling this a 'modified Laspeyres quantity index'.

The framework provided by (1), (2) and (6) has the virtue of simplicity. This simplicity does not carry through, however, to the price index counterpart to the Lowe quantity index given in (6). This price index, which can be obtained by dividing the value change by the quantity change, is given by:

$$(7)\qquad \frac{p^t \cdot q^t / p^{t-1} \cdot q^{t-1}}{p^0 \cdot q^t / p^0 \cdot q^{t-1}} \quad (t = 1,\ldots,T).$$

This formula not only is less simple than (6), but also has an important disadvantage. Suppose that between periods t-1 and t all the prices change by the same factor, that is, $p_n^t = \lambda p_n^{t-1}$ (n = 1,…,N) for a certain $\lambda > 0$. In this situation, formula (7) in general will exhibit an outcome different from λ.

In practice one also has to face all the difficulties connected with the fact that our assumption of (an) unchanging (set of) commodities is not valid. First, in the course of time, new commodities enter the aggregate. The problem becomes clear by looking at formulas (3) and (4). For any new commodity, its base period value as well as quantity equal zero; hence, formula (3) cannot be used. Although the period t value and price are known, the base period price does not exist; hence, formula (4) cannot be used either. Of course, for commodities that in the course of time have disappeared from the aggregate an analogous problem.

Second, even when there are no (dis-) appearing commodities, usually it is still necessary to deal with quality change. Quality change of commodity n occurs when its period t price cannot be compared to its base period price without allowing for changes in the nature of the commodity; or, equivalently, when its period t quantity cannot immediately be compared to its base period quantity. Dependent on the calculation method chosen – according to formula (3) or (4) – the quantity or price change must somehow be adjusted for the quality change that has occurred.

The important point is that in all these cases, imputations or estimates must be made, and this becomes more difficult and more dubious the longer the time span becomes between the base period and period t. In addition, with the lapse of time it becomes less and less meaningful to aggregate recent quantities with prices from a past period, as in expression (6). Therefore, every five or ten years, a new set of constant prices must be taken to act as base prices, which causes structural breaks in the time series of values-at-constant-prices.

3. The Modern Point of View

The modern view is rooted in the perspective that primary interest lies in measuring the real change between two adjacent periods. Stated more formally, according to the modern view, the primary problem is to decompose the value change,

$$(8)\qquad p^t \cdot q^t / p^{t-1} \cdot q^{t-1} \quad (t = 1,\ldots,T),$$

into price and quantity change components. There are various ways to do this. One frequently used approach decomposes the value change into a Paasche price index and a Laspeyres quantity index; that is, the value change is decomposed as:

$$\frac{p^t \cdot q^t}{p^{t-1} \cdot q^{t-1}} = P_P(t,t-1)Q_L(t,t-1) \quad (t = 1,\ldots,T). \tag{9}$$

Alternatively, the axiomatic approach leads to the recommendation[5] to use Fisher price and quantity indices for this decomposition. Using Fisher indices, the value change can be decomposed as follows:

$$\frac{p^t \cdot q^t}{p^{t-1} \cdot q^{t-1}} = \left[\frac{p^t \cdot q^{t-1}}{p^{t-1} \cdot q^{t-1}} \frac{p^t \cdot q^t}{p^{t-1} \cdot q^t}\right]^{1/2} \left[\frac{p^{t-1} \cdot q^t}{p^{t-1} \cdot q^{t-1}} \frac{p^t \cdot q^t}{p^t \cdot q^{t-1}}\right]^{1/2}$$

$$\equiv P_F(t,t-1)Q_F(t,t-1) \quad (t = 1,\ldots,T). \tag{10}$$

The first term in square brackets on the right-hand side of the first equality sign in (10) is the price index and the second one is the quantity index.[6]

New commodities, disappearing commodities, and quality change also cause problems in the computation of the components of (10). However, since the time span between periods t-1 and t is quite small – usually a year – the extent of the problems that must be solved is smaller than in the case discussed in the previous section: there are fewer new and disappearing commodities, and fewer (and probably smaller) quality changes to account for when comparing two adjacent periods than two periods far apart.

Not so well known, but extremely useful, is the fact that the Fisher quantity index can be written in a form comparable to formula (6). This result, for the first time discovered by Jan van IJzeren (1952), reads

$$Q_F(t,t-1) = \frac{\frac{1}{2}(p^{t-1} + p^t / P_F(t,t-1)) \cdot q^t}{\frac{1}{2}(p^{t-1} + p^t / P_F(t,t-1)) \cdot q^{t-1}} \quad (t = 1,\ldots,T). \tag{11}$$

The numerator contains the period t quantities valued at the average, deflated prices for periods t-1 and t, whereas the denominator contains the period t-1 quantities valued at the same deflated prices as appear in the numerator. Notice that each individual component of the price vector $p^{t-1} + p^t / P_F(t,t-1)$ depends on all the prices and all the quantities. This formula enables one to view the measure for the aggregate quantity change, $Q_F(t,t-1)$, as a weighted arithmetic average of individual quantity changes, q_n^t / q_n^{t-1} $(n = 1,\ldots,N)$.[7] This makes clear to what extent the various commodities contribute to the aggregate quantity change.

Does there exist in this approach a more general analogue to the sequence of values-at-constant-prices (2)? The answer appears to be: yes. Based on expression (5), the analogue to (2) is given by the sequence of real values

---

[5] A summary of the underlying literature can be found in Diewert (1996).

[6] Because these are Fisher indices, the price and quantity indices have the same functional form; that is, by interchanging prices and quantities the indices transform into each other.

[7] See Balk (2004) for alternatives. Formula (11) has been in use since 1999 by the U.S. Bureau of Economic Analysis; see Ehemann *et al.* (2002). Of course, a similar formula holds for the Fisher price index.

(12) $$p^t \cdot q^t / P(t,0) = p^0 \cdot q^0 Q(t,0) \quad (t = 1,\ldots,T),$$

where $P(t,t')$ is some price index and $Q(t,t')$ is some quantity index. Notice that (12) expresses in a slightly different form what in the axiomatic approach is called the Product Test.

The *SNA* 1993 recommends either of two methods. One is to start at the left-hand side of (12) and to deflate nominal values by chained Fisher price index numbers; that is, to replace $P(t,0)$ by

(13) $$P_F^c(t,0) \equiv \prod_{\tau=1}^{t} P_F(\tau,\tau-1) \quad (t = 1,\ldots,T).$$

The other is to start at the right-hand side of (12) and to inflate the nominal base period value by chained Fisher quantity index numbers; that is, to replace $Q(t,0)$ by

(14) $$Q_F^c(t,0) \equiv \prod_{\tau=1}^{t} Q_F(\tau,\tau-1) \quad (t = 1,\ldots,T).$$

The real values obtained in this manner correspond to what in the United States have come to be called 'chained dollars'[8]. The use of chained Fisher price index numbers in (13) is consistent with (10). This follows because, dividing the real values of two adjacent periods into each other yields

(15) $$\frac{p^t \cdot q^t / P_F^c(t,0)}{p^{t-1} \cdot q^{t-1} / P_F^c(t-1,0)} = \frac{p^t \cdot q^t / p^{t-1} \cdot q^{t-1}}{P_F(t,t-1)} = Q_F(t,t-1) \quad (t = 1,\ldots,T),$$

which is an expression for the quantity change that has occurred between the two periods. The same holds for the use of chained Fisher quantity index numbers as in (14).

An unsatisfactory alternative was proposed by Hillinger (2002); see the Appendix for details.

4. Comparison

The traditional approach gives priority to the construction of sequences of values-at-constant-prices according to expression (5). Quantity changes between adjacent periods are then evaluated using expression (6). The modern approach gives priority to the computation of quantity index numbers for adjacent periods according to expression (10). Real values can then be computed using expression (12) and chained index numbers. These are two distinct paradigms.

The core of Von der Lippe's critique (mentioned in the text and footnote 2 in section 1 above) is that the properties of the sequence of real values given in (5) differ from those of (12), and that the properties of the Lowe quantity index given in (6) differ from those of the Fisher

[8] The practice in other countries is to use chained Paasche price index numbers and Laspeyres quantity index numbers respectively, as was recommended by Al *et al.* (1986); see also De Boer *et al.* (1997). The *ESA* 1995 considers this practice to be acceptable. The use of chained Fisher index numbers was already mentioned in the *SNA* 1968, par. 4.47.

quantity index in (10). One important difference is that the real values computed according to (12) by chained index numbers are not additive, whereas the real values in (5) do exhibit additivity. Thus, the chained index numbers (can) exhibit behavior that is different from the direct index numbers.

It is relatively simple to show that the two approaches cannot be unified; that is done in this section.

The first key question is whether there exists a quantity index $Q(t,t')$ such that

(16) $$Q(t,t') = Q(t,0)/Q(t',0).$$

A quantity index that satisfies this condition exhibits the property of circularity and can be written as

(17) $$Q(t,t') = f(t)/f(t').$$

The fundamental requirement that $Q(t,t') = 1$ if the quantity vectors of the two periods are equal leads to the conclusion that $f(t)$ in (17) must be a function of the quantities only. Hence, prices cannot play any role in $Q(t,t')$.[9] This implies that the price index corresponding to $Q(t,t')$, $(p^t \cdot q^t / p^{t'} \cdot q^{t'})/Q(t,t')$, does *not* pass the fundamental Identity Test; that is, if the price vectors of the two periods are equal, then this last expression will not necessarily equal 1.

The second key question concerns the additivity, or, more generally, the consistency-in-aggregation, of price and quantity indices. Suppose that our aggregate can be partitioned into K subaggregates and let (after permutation of commodities) the price and quantity vectors be partitioned as $p^t = (p_1^t,...,p_K^t)$ and $q^t = (q_1^t,...,q_K^t)$ respectively, where (p_k^t, q_k^t) is the subvector corresponding to the subaggregate $k = 1,...,K$. Let $P_k(t,t')$ be a price index with the same functional form as $P(t,t')$, but with its number of variables reduced to the number of commodities of subaggregate k. Similarly, let $Q_k(t,t')$ be a quantity index with the same functional form as $Q(t,t')$, but with its number of variables reduced to the number of commodities of subaggregate k. Now the real values computed according to (12) are called *additive* if

(18a) $$\sum_{k=1}^{K} \frac{p_k^t \cdot q_k^t}{P_k(t,0)} = \frac{p^t \cdot q^t}{P(t,0)};$$

or, in other words, if the real subaggregate values add up to the real aggregate value. In terms of quantity indices, additivity means that

(18b) $$\sum_{k=1}^{K} p_k^0 \cdot q_k^0 Q_k(t,0) = p^0 \cdot q^0 Q(t,0).$$

[9] A more formal proof is given by Balk (1995); see also Balk (2008).

The more general concept of consistency-in-aggregation for price and quantity indexes was defined by Balk (1995), (1996), (2008)[10]. A price index $P(t,t')$ is called consistent-in-aggregation if

$$\text{(19a)} \qquad \sum_{k=1}^{K} \psi(P_k(t,t'), p_k^t \cdot q_k^t, p_k^{t'} \cdot q_k^{t'}) = \psi(P(t,t'), p^t \cdot q^t, p^{t'} \cdot q^{t'}),$$

where $\psi(.)$ is a function that is continuous and strictly monotonic in its first variable. Likewise, a quantity index $Q(t,t')$ is called consistent-in-aggregation if

$$\text{(19b)} \qquad \sum_{k=1}^{K} \zeta(Q_k(t,t'), p_k^t \cdot q_k^t, p_k^{t'} \cdot q_k^{t'}) = \zeta(Q(t,t'), p^t \cdot q^t, p^{t'} \cdot q^{t'}),$$

where $\zeta(.)$ is a function that is continuous and strictly monotonic in its first variable.

There are many, in fact infinitely many, functional forms for price and quantity indices that satisfy (19a) or (19b). As an example, the reader is invited to consider the generalized mean price index $P(t,t') = [\sum_{n=1}^{N} (v_n^{t'} / V^{t'})(p_n^t / p_n^{t'})^{\rho}]^{1/\rho}$ where $\rho \neq 0$. However, problems arise as soon as a number of very basic requirements are imposed on the price and quantity indices.

Suppose it is assumed that

- the price and quantity indices satisfy the Product Test (12);
- the price index satisfies the Equality Test; that is, if all the subaggregate price index numbers are equal – that is, if $P_k(t,t') = \lambda$ for all $k = 1,\ldots,K$ – then the aggregate price index number takes on the same magnitude, $P(t,t') = \lambda$;
- the quantity index satisfies the Equality Test; that is, if $Q_k(t,t') = \lambda$ for all $k = 1,\ldots,K$, then $Q(t,t') = \lambda$;
- the price index $P(t,t')$ is linearly homogeneous in current period prices p^t;
- when the number of commodities in an aggregate reduces to 1, then the price index reduces to a price relative; that is, $P(t,t') = p^t / p^{t'}$ whenever $N = 1$.

Under these assumptions it can be shown that the only price indices satisfying the consistency-in-aggregation requirement (19a) are the Laspeyres and Paasche.[11] Moreover, it is straightforward to show that any chained price index deviates from these two functional forms. For instance, for the chained Laspeyres price index it can be shown that

$$\text{(20)} \qquad P_L^c(t,0) = \prod_{\tau=1}^{t} \frac{p^{\tau} \cdot q^{\tau-1}}{p^{\tau-1} \cdot q^{\tau-1}} = \frac{p^* \cdot q^0}{p^0 \cdot q^0} \neq \frac{p^t \cdot q^0}{p^0 \cdot q^0},$$

since

[10] Pursiainen (2005) proposed a more general definition of consistency-in-aggregation, which appears to reduce to the one presented here for the situations considered here.

[11] See Balk (1995), (2008).

(21) $$p^* = p^1\prod_{\tau=2}^{t}\frac{p^\tau \cdot q^{\tau-1}}{p^{\tau-1}\cdot q^{\tau-1}} \neq p^t.$$

Given this mathematical, state-of-affairs, it seems justified that priority is given to decomposing the value change between adjacent periods into price and quantity index components. If one is to construct real values for a sequence of periods, then chained index numbers must be used for deflating or inflating.[12] With the present day computation facilities and the basic data, however, it should be relatively simple, for analytical purposes, to compute alternative price and quantity index numbers, as well as alternative sequences of real values, among which are included values-at-constant-prices.

5. On the Economic Theoretic Interpretation of Chained Index Numbers

The strategy of chaining has primarily been motivated by practical considerations. The question considered in this, and the next, section is: what precisely does a chained index measure? This section approaches the question from the economic-theoretic point of view. For direct (bilateral) price and quantity indexes there is a well-established body of theory. Can this theory be used to provide an answer to our question? That question is addressed here.

5.1 Constant homothetic preference ordering

Suppose our price and quantity data (p^t, q^t) for $t = 0,1,\ldots,T$ can be rationalized by a utility function. That is, suppose there exists a continuous function $U(q)$ representing a preference ordering that satisfies mild regularity conditions. More specifically, suppose that

(22) $$p^t \cdot q^t = C(p^t, U(q^t)),$$

where $C(p,u) \equiv \min_q\{p \cdot q \mid U(q) \geq u\}$ is the cost function that is dual to $U(q)$. Duality theory tells us that U(q) is homothetic if and only if the cost function can be decomposed as

(23) $$C(p,u) = F(u)C(p,1) \equiv F(u)c(p),$$

where *F(u)* is a function that is monotonicly increasing in *u*, and $c(p)$ is called the unit cost function. Varian (1983), based on earlier work by Diewert (1973), showed that there exists a data rationalizing utility function, which is homothetic if and only if a condition called the Homothetic Axiom of Revealed Preference (HARP) is satisfied. The specific form of this function is of no concern here.

As is well known, the Konüs cost of living index for period *t* relative to period *t'*, conditional on the utility level *u*, is defined by

(24) $$P_K(t,t';u) \equiv \frac{C(p^t,u)}{C(p^{t'},u)} \qquad u \in \text{Range}(U).$$

[12] A practical way of dealing with the additivity problem was developed by Balk and Reich (2008).

If the utility function is homothetic, then the Konüs cost of living index can be expressed as the ratio of values of the unit cost function; that is, the Konüs cost of living index can be expressed as

$$(25) \qquad P_K(t,t';u) = c(p^t)/c(p^{t'}) \equiv P_K(t,t')$$

for any two periods t, t'. Using relations (25), (22), and the definition of the cost function, it is straightforward to derive the well-known Laspeyres and Paasche bounds:

$$(26) \qquad P_K(t,t') = \frac{C(p^t, U(q^{t'}))}{C(p^{t'}, U(q^{t'}))} \leq \frac{p^t \cdot q^{t'}}{p^{t'} \cdot q^{t'}} = P_L(t,t')$$

$$(27) \qquad P_K(t,t') = \frac{C(p^t, U(q^t))}{C(p^{t'}, U(q^t))} \geq \frac{p^t \cdot q^t}{p^{t'} \cdot q^t} = P_P(t,t').$$

Based on this double inequality, it is reasonable to view the Fisher price index, $P_F(t,t') = [P_L(t,t')P_P(t,t')]^{1/2}$, as an approximation to the Konüs index $P_K(t,t')$. In fact, $P_F(t,t') = P_K(t,t')$ if and only if the unit cost function $c(p)$ is quadratic.[13]

However, many other sets of bounds can also be derived. Consider for instance an arbitrary third period $0 \leq s \leq T$. Then, by the same method, we find that also

$$(28) \qquad P_K(t,t') = \frac{c(p^t)}{c(p^s)} \frac{c(p^s)}{c(p^{t'})} \leq \frac{p^t \cdot q^s}{p^s \cdot q^s} \frac{p^s \cdot q^{t'}}{p^{t'} \cdot q^{t'}} = P_L(t,s)P_L(s,t'),$$

and

$$(29) \qquad P_K(t,t') = \frac{c(p^t)}{c(p^s)} \frac{c(p^s)}{c(p^{t'})} \geq \frac{p^t \cdot q^t}{p^s \cdot q^t} \frac{p^s \cdot q^s}{p^{t'} \cdot q^s} = P_P(t,s)P_P(s,t').$$

The obvious generalization of the above procedure is to consider all spanning trees connecting the periods 0,1,…,*T*. A spanning tree is a connected graph without cycles. Suppose that on such a tree the periods t' and t are connected via the periods $s(2),\ldots,s(L-1)$, where $L \geq 3$, and call $t' = s(1)$ and $t = s(L)$. Let $L=2$ represent the case where t' and t are adjacent (hence the number of intermediate periods equals zero). Then

$$(30) \qquad P_K(t,t') = \prod_{\ell=2}^{L} \frac{c(p^{s(\ell)})}{c(p^{s(\ell-1)})} \leq \prod_{\ell=2}^{L} P_L(s(\ell), s(\ell-1)).$$

Taking the minimum of the right-hand side of this expression over all spanning trees delivers the tightest upper bound for $P_K(t,t')$. Similarly, one obtains that

$$(31) \qquad P_K(t,t') = \prod_{\ell=2}^{L} \frac{c(p^{s(\ell)})}{c(p^{s(\ell-1)})} \geq \prod_{\ell=2}^{L} P_P(s(\ell), s(\ell-1)),$$

[13] See Konüs and Byushgens (1926), Diewert (1976), and Lau (1979).

and taking the maximum of the right-hand side of this expression over all spanning trees delivers the tightest lower bound for $P_K(t,t')$. Both of these tightest bounds can be computed by employing Warshall's algorithm. This algorithm also checks whether HARP is satisfied and, if so, computes the tightest upper and lower bounds.

It is clear that, given that HARP is satisfied, the (direct) Laspeyres price index $P_L(t,t')$ as well as the chained Laspeyres price index $P_L^c(t,t')$ are elements of the set of upper bounds for the Konüs cost of living index $P_K(t,t')$. Similarly, the (direct) Paasche price index $P_P(t,t')$ as well as the chained Paasche price index $P_P^c(t,t')$ are elements of the set of lower bounds. If $P_L^c(t,t') < P_L(t,t')$ then the chained Laspeyres price index is a tighter upper bound for the Konüs index than the (direct) Laspeyres price index. Similarly, if $P_P^c(t,t') > P_P(t,t')$ then the chained Paasche price index is a tighter lower bound for the Konüs index than the (direct) Paasche price index.

We may conclude that, if both conditions are satisfied, then the chained Fisher price index $P_F^c(t,t') = [P_L^c(t,t')P_P^c(t,t')]^{1/2}$ is a better approximation to $P_K(t,t')$ than the (direct) Fisher price index.

5.2 Constant preference ordering

However, the nice result just derived only holds when HARP is satisfied. When HARP is not satisfied, it is still possible that there exists a data rationalizing utility function such that (22) holds; however, this function is not necessarily homothetic. Varian (1982), based on earlier work by Afriat and Diewert (1973), showed this to be the case if and only if a condition called the Generalized Axiom of Revealed Preference (GARP) is satisfied. Under this weaker assumption, the standard bounding result reads:

(32) $$P_K(t,t';U(q^{t'})) \leq P_L(t,t')$$

(33) $$P_K(t,t';U(q^t)) \geq P_P(t,t').$$

It can then be shown[14] that there exists a utility level u^* between $U(q^{t'})$ and $U(q^t)$ such that $P_K(t,t';u^*)$ lies between $P_L(t,t')$ and $P_P(t,t')$. $P_F(t,t')$ is a symmetric average of $P_L(t,t')$ and $P_P(t,t')$. Hence, if the interval between $P_L(t,t')$ and $P_P(t,t')$ is small, it would be expected that

(34) $$P_F(t,t') \approx P_K(t,t';u^*) \text{ for some } u^* \text{ between } U(q^{t'}) \text{ and } U(q^t).$$

The result given above is interesting, but not very useful if the periods t and t' are far apart and the difference between the Laspeyres and Paasche price index numbers is large. If this is the case, it may be better to consider the chained Fisher price index, which is built up from

[14] The proof by Diewert (1981) goes back to Konüs.

comparisons of adjacent periods. For these comparisons, the Laspeyres-Paasche spread may be more likely to be small enough to justify the use of (34). Hence,

(35) $$P_F^c(t,t') = \prod_{\tau=t'+1}^{t} P_F(\tau,\tau-1) \approx \prod_{\tau=t'+1}^{t} P_K(\tau,\tau-1;u^{\tau*})$$

for some $u^{\tau*}$ between $U(q^{\tau-1})$ and $U(q^{\tau})$.

This result is still not very insightful. Equation (35) means that the chained Fisher price index approximates a chained Konüs index where the levels of utility vary over time. Getting rid of the variation in levels of utility would be helpful. This can be accomplished by noticing that the Konüs index defined in (24) is continuous in the utility level u. Choose $s=(t+t'+1)/2$ and assume that

(36) $$P_K(\tau,\tau-1;u^{\tau*}) = P_K(\tau,\tau-1;U(q^s))\exp\{a(\tau-s)\} \text{ for some } a \neq 0,$$

which means that, conditional on prices p^{τ} and $p^{\tau-1}$, $P_K(\tau,\tau-1;u^{\tau*})$ is a loglinear function of the time variable associated with the reference utility level. By elementary analytical methods, one can then show that

(37) $$\prod_{\tau=t'+1}^{t} P_K(\tau,\tau-1;u^{\tau*}) = \prod_{\tau=t'+1}^{t} P_K(\tau,\tau-1;U(q^s)) = P_K(t,t';U(q^s)),$$

where the last equality follows from the transitivity of the Konüs index for some fixed u. Thus, if (36) holds, then the chained Fisher price index $P_F^c(t,t')$ can be viewed as approximating the Konüs cost of living index $P_K(t,t';U(q^s))$, where s is an intermediate time period. Notice that assumption (36) rules out any cycles.

5.3 Variable preference ordering

A still weaker, but not testable, assumption is that the preference ordering is changing over time, so that (22) must be replaced by

(38) $$p^t \cdot q^t = C^t(p^t, U^t(q^t))$$

where $U^t(q)$ represents the period t preference ordering and $C^t(p,u)$ represents the period t dual cost function. The Laspeyres and Paasche bounds still apply, but must be reformulated as

(39) $$P_K^{t'}(t,t';U^{t'}(q^{t'})) \leq P_L(t,t')$$

(40) $$P_K^{t}(t,t';U^{t}(q^{t})) \geq P_P(t,t').$$

A result such as (34), however, is now impossible because the utility functions $U^{t'}(q)$ and $U^t(q)$ represent different preference orderings. It is meaningless to compare their numerical values across periods. There is a way out, however. A cost of living index including the preference change effect was defined by Balk (1989) as

(41) $$P^{t,t'}(t,t';q) \equiv \frac{C^t(p^t,U^t(q))}{C^{t'}(p^{t'},U^{t'}(q))}.$$

This index conditions on the quantity vector q and compares the period t cost of the period t indifference class of q to the period t' cost of the period t' indifference class of q. It is a natural extension of the Konüs cost of living index: if the period t and t' preference orderings are identical, then $P^{t,t'}(t,t';q) = P_K(t,t';U(q))$. The index (41) can be decomposed into two parts relating, respectively, to the effects of price change and preference change. The effect of preference change is measured by $P^{t,t'}(t,t';q)$ by setting $p^t = p^{t'}$. This effect is not necessarily equal to 1, but, as argued by Balk (1989), has the right sign.

Balk (1989) also showed that the Laspeyres and Paasche bounds still apply, so that:

(42) $P^{t,t'}(t,t';q^{t'}) \leq P_L(t,t')$

(43) $P^{t,t'}(t,t';q^{t}) \geq P_P(t,t')$.

In this case, Diewert's (1981) proof can be used to show that there exists a quantity vector q^* between $q^{t'}$ and q^t such that $P^{t,t'}(t,t';q^*)$ lies between $P_L(t,t')$ and $P_P(t,t')$. If the interval between $P_L(t,t')$ and $P_P(t,t')$ is small, then one may expect the following result to hold for the Fisher price index:

(44) $P_F(t,t') \approx P^{t,t'}(t,t';q^*)$ for some q^* between $q^{t'}$ and q^t.

Assuming now that for adjacent periods the Laspeyres-Paasche spread is indeed small, the following approximation using the chained Fisher price index may be close enough to be useful:

(45) $$P_F^C(t,t') = \prod_{\tau=t'+1}^{t} P_F(\tau,\tau-1) \approx \prod_{\tau=t'+1}^{t} P^{\tau,\tau-1}(\tau,\tau-1;q^{\tau*})$$

for some $q^{\tau*}$ between $q^{\tau-1}$ and q^τ.

The right-hand side of expression (45) contains indices that are conditional on quantity vectors that vary through time. Using the continuity of $P^{\tau,\tau-1}(\tau,\tau-1;q)$ in q, we assume that

(46) $$P^{\tau,\tau-1}(\tau,\tau-1;q^{\tau*}) = P^{\tau,\tau-1}(\tau,\tau-1;q^{s})\exp\{b(\tau-s)\} \text{ for some } b \neq 0;$$

that is, conditional on prices p^τ and $p^{\tau-1}$, $P^{\tau,\tau-1}(\tau,\tau-1;q^{\tau*})$ is a loglinear function of the time variable associated with the reference quantity vector. Then, as in the previous subsection, it can be shown that

(47) $$\prod_{\tau=t'+1}^{t} P^{\tau,\tau-1}(\tau,\tau-1;q^{\tau*}) = \prod_{\tau=t'+1}^{t} P^{\tau,\tau-1}(\tau,\tau-1;q^{s}) = P^{t,t'}(t,t';q^{s}),$$

where the last equality follows from the transitivity of (41) for fixed q. Thus, if (46) holds, the chained Fisher price index $P_F^c(t,t')$ may be considered to provide an approximation to the cost of living index including the preference change effect $P^{t,t'}(t,t';q^s)$, where s is an intermediate time period. Notice that assumption (46) also rules out any cycles.

Recall that $P^{t,t'}(t,t';q^s)$ is not necessarily equal to 1 when $p^t = p^{t'}$. This feature is shared by a chained index such as $P_F^c(t,t')$. Put otherwise, the fact that a chained index violates the (bilateral) Identity Test reflects the fact that such an index encompasses the effect of preference change.

6. A Divisia Index Theory Perspective

For those who do not believe in well-behaved preference orderings and optimization, Divisia index theory might be used to shed light on the relation between direct and chained indices. This theory, however, requires a mental leap: time periods must be considered as being of infinitesimal length and time itself as a continuous variable. Prices and quantities are supposed to be strictly positive, continuous and piecewise differentiable functions of time. Thus, when time τ moves from period 0 to period T, prices and quantities $\langle p(\tau),q(\tau)\rangle$ map out a path through the 2N-dimensional, strictly positive, Euclidean orthant. It is also assumed that observations are available at periods 0, 1, 2, …, T; that is, it is assumed that we observe

(48) $$p(\tau)=p^\tau \text{ and } q(\tau)=q^\tau \text{ for } \tau=0,1,...,T.$$

The starting point for Divisia index theory is the Product Test equation (12). It is straightforward to show, using elementary integral calculus, that this equation can be written as

(49) $$p^t\cdot q^t/p^0\cdot q^0 = p(t)\cdot q(t)/p(0)\cdot q(0) = P^{Div}(t,0)Q^{Div}(t,0) \quad (t=1,\ldots,T)$$

where

(50) $$\ln P^{Div}(t,0) \equiv \int_{\tau=0}^{t} \sum_{n=1}^{N} s_n(\tau)\frac{d\ln p_n(\tau)}{d\tau}d\tau,$$

(51) $$\ln Q^{Div}(t,0) \equiv \int_{\tau=0}^{t} \sum_{n=1}^{N} s_n(\tau)\frac{d\ln q_n(\tau)}{d\tau}d\tau,$$

and

(52) $$s_n(\tau) \equiv p_n(\tau)q_n(\tau)/p(\tau)\cdot q(\tau) \quad (n=1,\ldots,N).$$

The problem is how to estimate these index numbers, given that one only has observations on prices and quantities for a finite number of periods. Integral calculus provides us with the following two useful decompositions:

(53) $$P^{Div}(t,0) \equiv \prod_{\tau=1}^{t} P^{Div}(\tau,\tau-1) \quad (t=1,\ldots,T)$$

and

(54) $$Q^{Div}(t,0) \equiv \prod_{\tau=1}^{t} Q^{Div}(\tau,\tau-1) \quad (t=1,\ldots,T).$$

Now, as demonstrated by Balk (2005), (2008, Chapter 6), for any pair of bilateral price and quantity indices $\langle P(t,t'),Q(t,t')\rangle$ there exists a (hypothetical) vector of functions $C \equiv \langle \hat{p}(\tau),\hat{q}(\tau)\rangle$, defined over the interval [t',t] such that $\hat{p}(t')=p(t')$, $\hat{q}(t')=q(t')$, $\hat{p}(t)=p(t)$, and $\hat{q}(t)=q(t)$, and such that

(55) $$P(t,t') = P_C^{Div}(t,t')$$

(56) $$Q(t,t') = Q_C^{Div}(t,t'),$$

where the subscript C indicates that the integrals are computed using the functions defined by C rather than the true, but unknown, functions occurring in (50) and (51). The closer one believes that C approximates these unknown functions, the better $\langle P(t,t'),Q(t,t')\rangle$ will approximate $\langle P^{Div}(t,t'),Q^{Div}(t,t')\rangle$. The survey quoted makes clear as well that $\langle P_F(t,t'),Q_F(t,t')\rangle$ corresponds to a more reasonable price-quantity path than, say, $\langle P_P(t,t'),Q_L(t,t')\rangle$.

Given this theoretical knowledge, there are two distinct ways of approximating $\langle P^{Div}(t,0),Q^{Div}(t,0)\rangle$. The first is by calculating direct index numbers $\langle P_F(t,0),Q_F(t,0)\rangle$, which use only the period 0 and t data and map out a path over the whole time interval. The second is, according to expressions (53) and (54), by calculating chained index numbers $\langle P_F^c(t,0),Q_F^c(t,0)\rangle$. These chained index numbers also use the available data for the intermediate periods and map out a segmented path that coincides with the true one at the observation points. It seems clear that this second option should be preferred, since all available observations are used this way and the hypothesized path will stay closer to the true one.

7. Conclusion

By way of conclusion I return to the main problem: that of decomposing a value ratio into price and quantity components. Let $\langle P(t,t'),Q(t,t')\rangle$ be a pair of bilateral price and quantity indices that satisfy the Product Test. Then we have for any period t = 2, …, T the choice between the decompositions

(57) $$V^t/V^0 = P(t,0)Q(t,0)$$

and

$$V^t/V^0 = \prod_{\tau=1}^{t} V^\tau/V^{\tau-1} = \prod_{\tau=1}^{t} P(\tau,\tau-1)Q(\tau,\tau-1)$$

$$(58) \qquad = \prod_{\tau=1}^{t} P(\tau,\tau-1) \prod_{\tau=1}^{t} Q(\tau,\tau-1);$$

that is, we have the choice between using direct indices or chained indices. Notice, however, that expression (57) can easily be rewritten as

$$(59) \qquad V^t / V^0 = \left[\prod_{\tau=1}^{t} \frac{P(\tau,0)}{P(\tau-1,0)} \right] \left[\prod_{\tau=1}^{t} \frac{Q(\tau,0)}{Q(\tau-1,0)} \right],$$

the form of which is comparable to that of expression (58). From this point of view, the question is not so much whether to decompose the value ratio between periods t and 0 by direct or chained indices, but whether adjacent periods should be compared by indices of the form $\langle P(\tau,0)/P(\tau-1,0), Q(\tau,0)/Q(\tau-1,0) \rangle$ or $\langle P(\tau,\tau-1), Q(\tau,\tau-1) \rangle$. Posed in this way, the answer seems obvious, because it is not at all clear why period 0 price and/or quantity data should play a role in the comparison of periods τ and $\tau-1$ ($\tau = 2, \ldots, t$).

As advanced in section 5.3, micro-economic theory suggests the use of Fisher indices for the comparison of adjacent periods, since in that case the chained price and quantity indices admit the respective interpretation of being approximations to cost of living and standard of living indices under changing preferences. The main condition on which this result is predicated is that the observed quantities do not exhibit cyclical behavior.

Appendix: A Note on Hillinger's (2002) Proposal

Hillinger (2002) proposed to replace chained Fisher price index numbers by chained Marshall-Edgeworth price index numbers; that is, he proposed to replace formula (13) by

$$(A.1) \qquad P_{ME}^{c}(t,0) \equiv \prod_{\tau=1}^{t} P_{ME}(\tau,\tau-1) \quad (t = 1,\ldots,T),$$

where the Marshall-Edgeworth price index is defined as

$$(A.2) \qquad P_{ME}(t,t') = \frac{\frac{1}{2}(q^{t'} + q^t) \cdot p^t}{\frac{1}{2}(q^{t'} + q^t) \cdot p^{t'}} \quad (t = 1,\ldots,T).$$

This proposal has the disadvantage that the equality of deflation and inflation – see expression (12) – gets lost, since

$$(A.3) \qquad \frac{p^t \cdot q^t / p^0 \cdot q^0}{P_{ME}^{c}(t,0)} \neq Q_{ME}^{c}(t,0)$$

where $Q_{ME}^{c}(t,0)$ is a chained Marshall-Edgeworth quantity index defined by (A.1) and (A.2) after interchanging prices and quantities.

It appears that for two adjacent periods the quantity component,

$$(A.4) \qquad \frac{p^t \cdot q^t / p^{t-1} \cdot q^{t-1}}{P_{ME}(t,t-1)} = \frac{1+Q_L(t,t-1)}{1+1/Q_P(t,t-1)},$$

is dual to the "true factorial price index" and has the disadvantage of being not linearly homogeneous in q^t. By mimicking the proof of Balk (1983), it is straightforward to show that the quantity index (A.4) is exact for a linear utility function.

Interestingly, the difference of two real values can be rewritten as

$$(A.5) \qquad \frac{p^t \cdot q^t}{P^c_{ME}(t,0)} - \frac{p^{t-1} \cdot q^{t-1}}{P^c_{ME}(t-1,0)}$$

$$= \frac{1}{P^c_{ME}(t-1,0)}\left[\frac{1}{2}\left(\frac{p^t}{P_{ME}(t,t-1)} + p^{t-1}\right) \cdot \left(q^t - q^{t-1}\right) + \frac{1}{2}\left(q^t + q^{t-1}\right) \cdot \left(\frac{p^t}{P_{ME}(t,t-1)} - p^{t-1}\right)\right]$$

$$= \frac{1}{P^c_{ME}(t-1,0)}\left[\frac{1}{2}\left(\frac{p^t}{P_{ME}(t,t-1)} + p^{t-1}\right) \cdot \left(q^t - q^{t-1}\right)\right]$$

$$= \frac{1}{2}\left(\frac{p^t}{P^c_{ME}(t,0)} + \frac{p^{t-1}}{P^c_{ME}(t-1,0)}\right) \cdot \left(q^t - q^{t-1}\right),$$

where the next to last equality is based on definition (A.2). The difference of two real values can thus be written as a weighted average of individual quantity differences, $q_n^t - q_n^{t-1}$, which provides a nice interpretation.

The second component of Hillinger's (2002) proposal is to also use the deflator (A.1) for the computation of real values of subaggregates. The additivity problem is thereby not solved, but circumvented. Hillinger's argument is, however, not convincing. As Ehemann *et al.* (2002) see it, Hillinger's proposal "appears to provide data users with very little information beyond what is already provided in the aggregates valued at current prices.". These authors also show that the Hillinger proposal can lead to perverse outcomes.

References

Al, P.G., B.M. Balk, S. de Boer and G.P. den Bakker (1986), "The Use of Chain Indices for Deflating the National Accounts", *Statistical Journal of the United Nations ECE* 4, 347-368.

Balk, B.M. (1983), "A Note on the True Factorial Price Index", *Statistische Hefte / Statistical Papers* 24, 69-72.

Balk, B.M. (1989), "Changing Consumer Preferences and the Cost-of-Living Index: Theory and Nonparametric Expressions", *Journal of Economics* 50, 157-169.

Balk, B.M. (1995), "Axiomatic Price Index Theory: A Survey", *International Statistical Review* 63, 69-93.

Balk, B.M. (1996), "Consistency-in-Aggregation and Stuvel Indices", *Review of Income and Wealth* 42, 353-363.

Balk, B.M. (2004), "Decompositions of Fisher Indexes", *Economics Letters* 82, 107-113.

Balk, B.M. (2005), "Divisia Price and Quantity Indices: 80 Years After", *Statistica Neerlandica* 59, 119-158.

Balk, B.M. (2008), *Price and Quantity Index Numbers: Models for Measuring Aggregate Change and Difference*, Cambridge University Press.

Balk, B.M. and U.P. Reich (2008), "Additivity of National Accounts reconsidered," *Journal of Economic and Social Measurement* 33, 165-178.

Boer, S. de, J. van Dalen and P. Verbiest (1997), Chain Indices in the National Accounts: The Dutch Experience, National Accounts Occasional Paper Nr. NA-087, Statistics Netherlands.

CPI Manual (2004), *Consumer Price Index Manual: Theory and Practice*, International Labour Office, International Monetary Fund, Organisation for Economic Co-operation and Development, Eurostat, United Nations, The World Bank.

Diewert, W.E. (1973), "Afriat and Revealed Preference Theory," *Review of Economic Studies* 40, 419-425.

Diewert, W.E. (1976), "Exact and Superlative Index Numbers", "Exact and Superlative Index Numbers," *Journal of Econometrics* 4, 115-145; reprinted as chapter 8 in W.E. Diewert and A.O. Nakamura (eds.) (1993, pp. 223-252), North-Holland.

Diewert, W.E. (1981), "The Economic Theory of Index Numbers: A Survey", in A. Deaton (ed.), *Essays in the Theory and Measurement of Consumer Behaviour in Honour of Sir Richard Stone*, Cambridge University Press, pp. 163-208; reprinted as chapter 7 in Diewert and Nakamura (1993, pp. 177-221).

Diewert, W.E. (1996), "Price and Volume Measures in the System of National Accounts", in *The New System of National Accounts*, edited by J. Kendrick, Kluwer Academic Publishers.

Diewert, W. E. and A. O. Nakamura (1993), Essays in Index Number Theory, Vol. I, North-Holland.

Ehemann, C., A.J. Katz and B.R. Moulton (2002), "The Chain-Additivity Issue and the US National Economic Accounts", *Journal of Economic and Social Measurement* 28, 37-49.

ESA (1995), *European System of Accounts* (Eurostat, 1996).

Hillinger, C. (2002), "Consistent Aggregation and Chaining of Price and Quantity Measures", *Journal of Economic and Social Measurement* 28, 1-20.

Konüs, A.A. and S.S. Byushgens (1926), "On the Problem of the Purchasing Power of Money" (in Russian), *Voprosi Konyunkturi* II(1), 151-172.

Lau, L.J. (1979), "On Exact Index Numbers", *The Review of Economics and Statistics* 61, 73-82.

Lehr, J. (1885), *Beiträge zur Statistik der Preise* (J. D. Sauerlander, Frankfurt).

Lippe, P. von der (2000), "Der Unsinn von Kettenindizes", *Allgemeines Statistisches Archiv* 84, 67-82.

Lippe, P. von der (2001a), *Chain Indices: A Study in Price Index Theory.* Spectrum of Federal Statistics, Volume 16 (Metzler-Poeschel, Stuttgart).

Lippe, P. von der (2001b), "Zur Interpretation von Kettenindizes: Wie U. P. Reich Widersinn bei Kettenindizes zum Verschwinden bringt", *Allgemeines Statistisches Archiv* 85, 343-347.

Lippe, P. von der (2007), *Index Theory and Price Statistics*, Peter Lang, Frankfurt am Main.

Marshall, A. (1887), "Remedies for Fluctuations of General Prices", *Contemporary Review* 51, 355-375.

Pursiainen, H. (2005), Consistent Aggregation Methods and Index Number Theory, Research Report No. 106, Department of Economics, University of Helsinki.

Rainer, A. (2002), "Verkettung gegensätzlicher Positionen zu Indexfragen", *Allgemeines Statistisches Archiv* 86, 385-389.

Reich, U.P. (2000), "Messung des Geldwertes: Zur Statistik und Theorie der reinen Preisbewegung," *Allgemeines Statistisches Archiv* 84, 461-478.

SNA (1968), *A System of National Accounts*, Studies in Methods, Series F, No. 2, Rev. 3, Department of Economic and Social Affairs, Statistical Office of the United Nations, New York.

SNA (1993), *System of National Accounts 1993,* Prepared under the auspices of the Inter-Secretariat Working Group on National Accounts (Commission of the European Communities, International Monetary Fund, Organisation for Economic Co-operation and Development, United Nations, Worldbank).

Varian, H.R. (1982), "The Nonparametric Approach to Demand Analysis", *Econometrica* 50, 945-973.

Varian, H.R. (1983), "Nonparametric Tests of Consumer Behaviour", *Review of Economic Studies* 50, 99-110.

IJzeren, J. van (1952), "On the Plausibility of Fisher's Ideal Indices" (in Dutch), *Statistische en Econometrische Onderzoekingen (CBS)*, Nieuwe Reeks, 7, 104-115.

Chapter 11

ON THE STOCHASTIC APPROACH TO INDEX NUMBERS

W. Erwin Diewert[1]

> "In mathematics disputes must soon come to an end, when the one side is proved and the other disproved. And where mathematics enters into economics, it would seem that little room could be left for long-continued disputation. It is therefore somewhat surprising that one economist after another takes up the subject of index-numbers, potters over it for a while, differs from the rest if he can, and then drops it. And so nearly sixty years have gone by since Jevons first brought mathematics to bear upon this question, and still economists are at loggerheads over it. Yet index-numbers involve the use of means and averages, and these being a purely mathematical element, demonstration ought soon to be reached, and then agreement should speedily follow."
>
> Walsh [1921; preface].

1. Introduction

The recent appearance of a book on the stochastic approach to index number theory by Selvanathan and Prasada Rao [1994] marks an appropriate occasion to provide a critical review of this approach. This is the primary purpose of the present paper.

The stochastic approach[2] to index number theory originated with Jevons [1863; 23-26] [1865; 121-122] [1869; 156-157], Edgeworth [1887; 245] [1888a] [1888b] [1889; 286-292] and Bowley [1901; 219] [1911] [1919; 346] [1926] [1928; 217]. Basically, this approach was driven by the quantity theory of money: as the quantity of gold or money is increased, all prices should increase approximately proportionally. Thus a measure of the general increase in prices going from period 0 to period t could be obtained by taking an appropriate average of price relatives, p_{it}/p_{i0}, where p_{it} denotes the price of commodity i in period t. This average of the price relatives can be regarded as an index number of price change going from period 0 to t. Selvanathan and Prasada Rao [1994; 5-6] express this ancient theory in more modern language as follows:

---

[1] W. Erwin Diewert is with the Department of Economics at the University of British Columbia and can be reached at diewert@econ.ubc.ca. This research was supported by a Strategic Grant from the Social Sciences and Humanities Research Council of Canada. Thanks are due to Louise Hebert and Keltie Stearman for typing a difficult manuscript.

[2] This term is due to Frisch [1936; 3-4].

Citation: **W. Erwin Diewert (2011), "On the Stochastic Approach to Index Numbers," chapter 11, pp. 235-262 in**
W.E. Diewert, B.M. Balk, D. Fixler, K.J. Fox and A.O. Nakamura,
***PRICE AND PRODUCTIVITY MEASUREMENT: Volume 6 -- Index Number Theory*. Trafford Press.**

© Alice Nakamura, 2011. Permission to link to, or copy or reprint, these materials is granted without restriction, including for use in commercial textbooks, with due credit to the authors and editors.

> "The stochastic approach considers the index number problem as a signal extraction problem from the messages concerning price changes for different commodities. Obviously the strength of the signal extracted depends upon the messages received and the information context of the messages."

The recent resurrection of the stochastic approach to index number theory is due to Balk [1980], Clements and Izan [1981] [1987], Bryan and Cecchetti [1993] and Selvanathan and Prasada Rao [1994][3]. The main attraction of the approach over competing approaches to index number theory is its ability to provide confidence intervals for the estimated inflation rates:

> "Accordingly, we obtain a point estimate of not only the rate of inflation, but also its sampling variance. The source of the sampling error is the dispersion of relative prices from their trend rates of change -- the sampling variance will be larger when the deviations of the relative prices from their trend rates of change are larger. This attractive result provides a formal link between the measurement of inflation and changes in relative prices."
>
> Clements and Izan [1987; 339].

Selvanathan and Prasada Rao note the above advantage but go further and claim that the stochastic approach can be utilized to derive standard errors for many well known index number formulae:

> "The attraction of this approach is that is provides an alternative interpretation to some of the well known index numbers as the estimators of parameters of specific regression models. For example, the Laspeyres, Paasche, Theil-Törnqvist and other index numbers can be derived from various regression models. Further this approach provides standard errors for these index numbers."
>
> Selvanathan and Prasada Rao [1994; 6].

At this point, it should be mentioned that the two main competing approaches to index number theory are the test approach and the economic approach.

The test approach can apply to two periods (the bilateral case) or to many periods (the multilateral case). The bilateral test approach assumes that complete price and quantity information on the relevant set of commodities is available for the two periods under consideration, say periods s and t. Denote the price and quantity vectors for these two periods by p^s, p^t and q^s, q^t, where $p^s = [p_{1s}, \ldots, p_{Ns}]$, etc. A bilateral price index is defined as a function P of the four sets of variables, $P(p^s, p^t, q^s, q^t)$. The bilateral test approach attempts to determine the functional form for P by assuming that P satisfies certain plausible tests, axioms or mathematical properties. In the case of only one commodity in the set of commodities to be aggregated, the imposed tests generally cause the price index $P(p_{1s}, p_{1t}, q_{1s}, q_{1t})$ to collapse down to the single price ratio, p_{1t}/p_{1s}. There is an analogous bilateral test approach for the quantity index $Q(p^s, p^t, q^s, q^t)$. Fisher [1911; 403] observed that in the present context of complete information on prices and quantities, the price and quantity indexes, P and Q, should satisfy the following conservation of value equation:

---

[3] See Selvanathan and Prasada Rao [1994; 6] for an extensive list of their recent contributions.

(1) $P(p^s,p^t,q^s,q^t)Q(p^s,p^t,q^s,q^t) = p^t \cdot q^t / p^s \cdot q^s$

where $p^t \cdot q^t = \Sigma_{n=1}^{N} p_{nt} q_{nt}$. The importance of (1) is that once the functional form for P has been determined, then (1) automatically determines the functional form for Q. Moreover, tests for the quantity index Q can be translated into tests for the corresponding price index P defined via (1). Useful references for the test approach are Walsh [1901] [1921] [1924], Fisher [1911] [1921] [1922], and Diewert [1992a] [1993a; 6-10]. The early history of the test approach is reviewed by Frisch [1936; 5-7] and Diewert [1993b; 38-41].

In the test approach, the vectors of prices and quantities for the two periods are regarded as independent variables. In the economic approach, the two price vectors are regarded as independent variables but the quantity vectors are regarded as solutions to various economic maximization or minimization problems. In the consumer price context, it is assumed that the consumer has preferences over N commodities and these preferences can be represented by an aggregator or utility function $f(q_1,...,q_N) \equiv f(q)$. It is also assumed that in each period t, the consumer minimizes the cost $C[f(q^t),p^t]$ of achieving the utility level $f(q^t)$ when facing the period t vector of prices $p^t[p_{1t},p_{2t},...,p_{Nt}]$. The Konüs [1924] true cost of living index between periods s and t, using the reference utility level $f(q)$, is defined as the ratio of costs of achieving the reference utility level when facing the period s and t prices, $C[f(q),p^t]/C[f(q),p^s]$. If the consumer's utility function is linearly homogeneous, then the cost function $C[f(q),p]$ factors into two components, $f(q)c(p)$, where $c(p)$ is defined as the unit (utility level) cost function, $C[1,p]$. In this homogeneous case, the Konüs true cost of living index reduces to the unit cost ratio, $c(p^t)/c(p^s)$ and the corresponding quantity index is the utility ratio, $f(q^t)/f(q^s)$.

Finally, consider a given formula for the price index, say $P(p^s,p^t,q^s,q^t)$. We say that P is *exact* for the consumer preferences dual to the unit cost function c if under the assumption of cost minimizing behavior on the part of the consumer for periods s and t, we have

(2) $P(p^s,p^t,q^s,q^t) = c(p^t)/(c(p^t)$.

Similarly, a given functional form for the quantity index, $Q(p^s,p^t,q^s,q^t)$, is exact for the linearly homogeneous utility function f if, under the assumption of cost minimizing behavior for periods s and t, we have

(3) $Q(p^s,p^t,q^s,q^t) = f(q^t)/f(q^s)$.

The economic approach to index number theory concentrates on finding functional forms for price indexes P that are exact for flexible[4] unit cost functions c and on finding functional forms for quantity indexes Q that are exact for flexible linearly homogeneous utility functions f. Index number formulae that are exact for flexible functional forms are called superlative.[5] The theory

[4] A flexible functional form is one that has a second order approximation property; see Diewert [1974; 115].

[5] See Diewert [1976; 117].

of exact index numbers was developed by Konüs and Byushgens [1926], Afriat [1972; 44-47], Samuelson and Swamy [1974] and Pollak [1989; 15-32]. The early history of exact index numbers is reviewed in Diewert [1993b; 45-50]. For examples of superlative indexes, see Diewert [1976] [1978] [1992b; 576].

As can be seen from the above brief reviews of the test and economic approaches to index number theory,[6] these approaches are silent on the problem of providing an estimate of the reliability of the suggested bilateral index number formulae. Thus the new champions of the stochastic approach appear to have a strong a priori argument in favor of their approach.

In section 2 below, we review the original approaches of Jevons, Edgeworth and Bowley. In section 3, we review the initial new stochastic approaches of Clements and Izan [1981] and Selvanathan and Prasada Rao [1994; 51-61]. In section 4, we review the more sophisticated stochastic approaches of Balk [1980], Clements and Izan [1987] and Selvanathan and Prasada Rao [1994; 61-110]. The stochastic specifications that are utilized in the models presented in sections 3 and 4 are easily rejected from an empirical point of view. Thus in section 5, we present a new stochastic model that seems to be in the spirit of the type of model that Edgeworth had in mind but was never able to implement. In section 6, we present some practical criticisms of the new stochastic approaches to index number theory that will make it difficult for Statistical Agencies to embrace these approaches. Section 7 concludes by reconsidering the problems involved in providing measures of reliability for based on the test or economic approaches.

2. The Early Statistical Approaches to Index Number Theory

We assume that we are given price and quantity data, p_{it} and q_{it}, for periods t=0,1,...,T and for commodities i=1,2,...,N. The first stochastic index number model that Selvanathan and Prasada Rao [1994; 49-51] consider is given by the following equations for t=1,2,...T:

$$(4) \quad p_{it}/p_{i0} = \alpha_t + \varepsilon_{it};\ i=1,2,...,N;$$

where α_t represents the systematic part of the price change going from period 0 to t and the independently distributed random variables ε_{it} satisfy the following assumptions:

$$(5) \quad E\varepsilon_{it} = 0;\ \mathrm{Var}\,\varepsilon_{it} = \sigma_t^2;\ i=1,2,...,N;$$

i.e., ε_{it} has mean 0 and variance $\sigma_t^2 > 0$. The least squares and maximum likelihood estimator for α_t in Model 1 defined by (4) and (5) is the Carli [1764] price index:

$$(6) \quad \hat{\alpha}_t = \sum_{i=1}^{N} (1/N) p_{it}/p_{i0},$$

[6] Selvanathan and Prasada Rao [1994; 15-44] provide a rather inadequate review of the test and economic approaches. For example on page 17, they attribute Walsh's [1901] [1921; 97] price index to Drobisch, they misspell Marshall and they cite an incorrect reference to Marshall [1887], the cofounder of the Edgeworth-Marshall index.

which is the unweighted arithmetic mean of the period 0 to t price relatives, p_{it}/p_{i0}. The variance of $\hat{\alpha}_t$ is

(7) $\quad \text{Var}\, \hat{\alpha}_t = (1/N)\sigma_t^2$

and Selvanathan and Prasada Rao [1994; 51] note that an unbiased estimator for the variance is

(8) $\quad \sigma_t^2 = [1/(N-1)]\Sigma_{i=1}^N [(p_{it}/p_{i0}) - \hat{\alpha}_t]^2 .$

Using (7) and (8), a confidence interval for the Carli price index $\hat{\alpha}_t$ can be calculated under the assumption of normally distributed errors. As Selvanathan and Prasada Rao [1994; 51] note, if the dispersion of the price relatives p_{it}/p_{i0} increases, then the precision of our period t fixed base price index $\hat{\alpha}_t$ will decline.

Instead of assuming that the independent errors ε_{it} are additive, we could more plausibly assume that the errors are multiplicative.[7] This leads to Model 2, which is defined by the following equations for t=1,...,T:

(9) $\quad \ell n[p_{it}/p_{i0}] = \pi_t + \varepsilon_{it}$; i=1,...,N;

(10) $\quad E\varepsilon_{it} = 0; \quad \text{Var}\, \varepsilon_{it} = \sigma_t^2$; i=1,...,N.

The least squares and maximum likelihood estimator for π_t in Model 2 is

(11) $\quad \hat{\pi}_t = [1/N]\Sigma_{i=1}^N \ell n[p_{it}/p_{i0}].$

A variance estimator for $\hat{\pi}_t$ can be constructed in a manner analogous to the use of (7) and (8) in Model 1. If we define α_t to be the exponential of π_t, we can exponentiate $\hat{\pi}_t$ to obtain the following estimator for α_t:

(12) $\quad \exp[\hat{\pi}_t] = \Pi_{i=1}^N [p_{it}/p_{i0}]^{1/N}.$

The right hand side of (12) is the Jevons [1863; 53] geometric mean price index. Jevons [1869; 157] later applied least squares theory to equation (9) and calculated a "probable error" (or confidence interval in modern terminology) for his estimator $\hat{\pi}_t$ defined by (11). This appears to be the first relatively complete exposition of the stochastic approach to index number theory.

Jevons [1865; 120-122] also used the arithmetic mean index number (6) in his empirical work but he did not report any confidence intervals for his Carli indexes. Edgeworth [1887; 226-246] considered both arithmetic and geometric mean (unweighted) index numbers and Edgeworth [1888a] was entirely devoted to the problems involved in constructing confidence intervals for these indexes. Bowley [1901; 203-229] [1919; 345-346] [1928; 216-222] was very

[7] Edgeworth [1887; 237-243] argued on empirical and logical grounds that Model 2 was more plausible than Model 1, assuming normally distributed errors. His logical argument was based on the positivity of prices; hence a price relative could have any upper bound but had a definite lower bound of zero, leading to an asymmetric distribution of price relatives. However, the logarithm of a price relative could be symmetrically distributed.

much concerned with the problems involved in determining the precision of index numbers.[8] Bowley [1911] was concerned with the precision of weighted index numbers while Bowley [1926] extended his earlier work to cover the case of correlated price relatives. Finally, Bowley was aware that precision in official indexes was rather important, since so many government expenditures were indexed to official price indexes. The following quotation refers to a potential upward bias of 18 percentage points in the Ministry of Labour index numbers for the UK over the years 1914-1918:

> "Every 4 points cost over a million pounds in the annual railway wage bill."
>
> Bowley [1919; 348]

We turn now to an exposition of the new stochastic models.

3. The New Stochastic Approach to Index Numbers

Model 3 consists of equations (4) again but our old assumptions (5) on the independently distributed errors ε_{it} are now replaced by the following assumptions:

$$(13) \quad E\varepsilon_{it} = 0; \quad \mathrm{Var}\,\varepsilon_{it} = \sigma_t^2 / w_i; \qquad i=1,\ldots,N$$

where the w_i are nonrandom fixed shares to be determined later; i.e. the w_i satisfy

$$(14) \quad w_i > 0 \text{ for } i=1,2,\ldots,N \text{ and } \Sigma_{i=1}^N w_i = 1.$$

Since the w_i are positive, we can multiply both sides of equation i in (4) by the square root of w_i, $w_i^{1/2}$, in order to obtain homoscedastic errors. The resulting least squares and maximum likelihood estimator for the period 0 to t inflation rate α_t is

$$(15) \quad \hat{\alpha}_1 = \Sigma_{i=1}^N w_i[p_{it}/p_{i0}] \big/ \Sigma_{n=1}^N w_n = \Sigma_{i=1}^N w_i[p_{it}/p_{i0}]$$

where the second equality follows using (14). Using (13), it can be seen that $\hat{\alpha}_t$ is an unbiased estimator for α_t and its variance is

$$(16) \quad \mathrm{Var} \quad \hat{\alpha}_t = \Sigma_{i=1}^N w_i^2[\sigma_i^2 / w_i] = \sigma_i^2$$

where the second equality follows using (14). An unbiased estimator for σ_t^2 is

$$(17) \quad \hat{\sigma}_t^2 \equiv [1/(N-1)]\Sigma_{i=1}^N w_i[(p_{it}/p_{i0}) - \hat{\alpha}]^2.$$

[8] Mills [1927; 240-247] succinctly reviewed the above literature and also computed standard errors for various index number formulae using BLS data on US wholesale prices.

Under the added assumption that the residuals ε_{it} are normally distributed, (16) and (17) may be used to obtain confidence intervals for the share weighted index numbers $\hat{\alpha}_t$ given by (15).

Selvanathan and Prasada Rao [1994; 51-55] consider the following special cases:

(18) $w_i \equiv p_{i0}q_{i0} \big/ \sum_{n=1}^{N} p_{n0}q_{n0}$; i=1,...,N;

(19) $w_i \equiv p_{i0}q_{it} \big/ \sum_{n=1}^{N} p_{n0}q_{nt}$; i=1,...,N.

In order to make the w_i fixed variables, we need to assume that base period prices and quantities, p_{i0} and q_{i0}, and current period quantities, q_{it}, are fixed. Thus in equations (4), the only random variables are the current period prices p_{it}.

Substituting (18) into (15) causes $\hat{\alpha}_t$ to become the fixed base Laspeyres price index, $p^t \cdot q^0 / p^0 \cdot q^0$, and substituting (19) into (15) leads to the Paasche price index, $p^t \cdot q^t / p^0 \cdot q^t$. Furthermore, substitution of (18) and (19) into (15)-(17) yields estimators for the variances of the fixed base Laspeyres and Paasche price indexes. Thus the new stochastic approach of Selvanathan and Prasada Rao does lead to estimates of the precision of these well known indexes (provided that their stochastic assumptions (13) are correct).

We turn now to the new stochastic approach of Clements and Izan [1981]. Consider two distinct periods s and t where $0 \le s < t \le T$. Let π_{st} be the logarithm of the price change going from period s to t. The equations that define Model 4 are:

(20) $\ell n[p_{it}/p_{is}] = \pi_{st} + \varepsilon_{ist}$; i=1,...,N;

(21) $E\varepsilon_{ist} = 0$; Var $\varepsilon_{ist} = \sigma_{st}^2 / w_i$; i=1,...,N

where the weights w_i again satisfy (14). Multiplying both sides of (20) through by $(w_i)^{1/2}$ leads to homoscedastic variances. The least squares and maximum likelihood estimator for π_{st} in this transformed model is

(22) $\hat{\pi}_{st} = \sum_{i=1}^{N} w_i \ell n[p_{it}/p_{is}]$.

Using (21), the variance of $\hat{\pi}_{st}$ is σ_{st}^2. An unbiased estimator for σ_{st}^2 is

(23) $\hat{\sigma}_{st}^2 \equiv [1/(N-1)] \sum_{i=1}^{N} w_i [\ell n(p_{it}/p_{is}) - \hat{\pi}_{st}]^2$.

Let $w_{it} \equiv p_{it}q_{it} / \sum_{n=1}^{N} p_{nt}q_{nt}$ be the expenditure share of commodity i in period t. Clements and Izan [1981; 745-746] and Selvanathan and Prasada Rao [1994; 76-77] choose the weights w_i that appear in (21) as follows:[9]

(24) $w_i \equiv (1/2)w_{is} + (1/2)w_{it}$; i=1,...,N;

[9] These authors choose period s to be period t-1 but this choice is not essential to their argument.

i.e., w_i is chosen to be the average expenditure share on commodity i over periods s and t. Substituting (24) into (22) yields

$$(25)\quad \exp[\hat{\pi}_{st}] = \prod_{i=1}^{N}[p_{it}/p_{is}]^{(1/2)w_{is}+(1/2)w_{it}} .$$

The right hand side of (25) is known as the Törnqvist [1936] price index.[10]

Under the assumption of normally distributed errors, (23) can be used to form confidence intervals for $\hat{\pi}_{st}$, the logarithm of the Persons-Törnqvist price index. However, since the weights w_i defined by (24) depend on p_{is} and p_{it}, it will be necessary to assume that the conditional (on w_i) distribution of $\ell n(p_{it}/p_{is})$ is normal and satisfies assumptions (21). Thus the stochastic assumptions justifying Model 4 are more tenuous than those for Model 3 above.

The variance assumptions (13) and (21), $\operatorname{Var} \varepsilon_{it} = \sigma_t^2 / w_i$ and $\operatorname{Var} \varepsilon_{ist} = \sigma_{st}^2 / w_i$, require some justification.[11] The following quotation indicates how Clements and Izan justify their assumptions on the variances of the log price relatives:

> "If all goods were equally important, the assumption that var ε_i is the same for all i would be acceptable. However, this is not so, since the budget share $\overline{w}_i$ varies with i. If we think in terms of sampling the individual prices to form Dp_i for each commodity group, then it seems reasonable to postulate that the collection agency invests more resources in sampling the prices of those goods more important in the budget. This implies that var ε_i is inversely proportional to $\overline{w}_i$."
>
> Clements and Izan [1981; 745]

In contrast to the explicit sampling approach of Clements and Izan [1981], Selvanathan and Prasada Rao [1994] (with the exception of their section 7.4) regarded their prices as being accurately known, or in any case, they wanted their analysis to apply to this case.[12] They justify their variance assumptions in (13) and (18) as follows:[13]

---

[10] This index first appeared as formula 123 in Fisher [1922; 473]. Fisher [1922; 265] listed it as number 15 in his list of the 29 best formulae, but he did not otherwise distinguish it. Walsh [1921; 97] almost recommended (25), but he used the geometric average of the weight, $(w_{is}w_{it})^{1/2}$, in place of the arithmetic average. Finally, Persons [1928; 21-22] recommended (25), the Fisher ideal index, $(p^t \cdot q^t p^t \cdot q^s / p^s \cdot q^t p^s \cdot q^s)^{1/2}$ and seven other indexes as being the best from the viewpoint of his test approach. Thus (25) should perhaps be known as the Persons-Törnqvist formula.

[11] The first person to make a variance specification of this form appears to have been Edgeworth [1887; 247] as the following quotation indicates: "Each price which enters into our formula is to be regarded as the mean of several prices, which vary with the differences of time, of place, and of quality; by the mere friction of the market, and, in the case of 'declared values', through errors of estimation, it is reasonable to support that this heterogeneity is greater the larger the volume of transactions." Edgeworth did not make any formal use of these observations.

[12] "Even in the case where prices of all the commodities of relevance are measured, and measured without any errors, the question of reliability of a given index arises." (Selvanathan and Prasada Rao [1994; 4]).

[13] The reader will deduce that, in the interests of a homogeneous presentation, I have modified the original notation of Clements and Izan and Selvanathan and Prasada Rao.

"Under this assumption we have that the variance of the price relative of i is λ_t^2 / w_{i0} and is inversely proportional to w_{i0}. This means that the variability of a price relative falls as the commodity becomes more important in the consumer's budget."

Selvanathan and Prasada Rao [1994; 52]

In their more sophisticated stochastic model to be discussed in the next section, Clements and Izan [1987] no longer relied on their earlier sampling theory justification for their variance assumptions of the form (21). Instead, they provided the following justification:

"As e_{it} is the change in the ith relative price, specification (7) implies that the variability of a relative price falls as the commodity becomes more important in the consumer's budget. Thus the variability of a relative price of a good having a large budget share, such as food, will be lower than that of a commodity with a smaller share, such as cigarettes. This is a plausible specification, since there is less scope for a relative price to change as the commodity in question grows in importance in the budget."

Clements and Izan [1987; 341]

As can be seen from the above quotations, the justifications presented for the variance assumptions in the new stochastic approaches are rather weak.[14] We will return to this point in section 5 below.

Clements and Izan [1981; 747] and Selvanathan and Prasada Rao [1994; 89] point out a positive feature of the new stochastic models such as Model 3 or 4: the resulting index numbers such as (15) or (22) are invariant to the level of commodity aggregation, provided that the same shares w_i that appear in the variance specifications (13) or (21) are used to do the aggregation. To see this, consider Model 3 represented by (4) and (13) and suppose that commodities 1 and 2 are aggregated together. Let p_{At} be the price of the aggregate commodity in period t. The weights w_1 and w_2 are used to define the following aggregate period 0 to t price relative:

(26) $$p_{At}/p_{A0} \equiv [w_1/(w_1+w_2)][p_{it}/p_{i0}]+[w_2/(w_1+w_2)][p_{2t}/p_{20}].$$

Replace the first two equations in (4) by the new aggregated equation $p_{At}/p_{A0} = \alpha_t + \varepsilon_{At}$. Using the first two equations in (4) as well as (26), it can be seen that the new aggregate error is equal to

(27) $$\varepsilon_{At} = [w_1/(w_1+w_2)]\varepsilon_{it} + [w_2/(w_1+w_2)]\varepsilon_{2t}.$$

Using (13) and (27), the expectation of p_{At}/p_{A0} is equal to α_t, the expectation of ε_{At} is 0 and the variance of ε_{At} is

(28) $$\text{Var}\,\varepsilon_{At} = [w_1/(w_1+w_2)]^2[\sigma_t^2/w_1]+[w_2/(w_1+w_2)]^2[\sigma_t^2/w_2] = [\sigma_t^2/(w_1+w_2)].$$

[14] In his new stochastic model, Balk [1980; 72] simply assumed a variance specification analogous to (13) or (21) without any justification other than mathematical convenience.

Thus the mean and variance of the aggregated error are of the same form as the means and variances of the original errors, ε_{it} and ε_{2t}, see (13). It is straightforward to show that the maximum likelihood estimator $\hat{\alpha}_1^*$ for α_t in the aggregated model is equal to the disaggregated estimator $\hat{\alpha}_t$ defined by (15).

We turn now to more sophisticated new stochastic approaches to price indexes.

4. A Specific Price Trends Stochastic Approach

The models presented in the previous section are similar to the classical stochastic models presented in section 2, except that the variance assumptions were different. These simple signal extraction models were effectively criticized by Keynes [1930; 58-84]. Clements and Izan summarize this Keynsian criticism as follows:

> "Thus the rate of inflation can be estimated by averaging over these n observations. This approach was correctly criticized by Keynes (1930, pp. 85-88) on the basis that it requires the systematic component of each price change to be identical. In other words, all prices must change equiproportionally so that there can be no changes in relative prices. The objective of this article is to rehabilitate the stochastic approach by answering Keynes's criticism by allowing for systematic changes in relative prices."
>
> Clements and Izan [1987; 339]

Selvanathan and Prasada Rao [1994; 61] also acknowledge that the Keynesian criticism applies to their Laspeyres and Paasche models (Model 3 with the w_i defined by (18) and (19) respectively). In order to rectify this deficiency in their Laspeyres model, Selvanathan and Prasada Rao [1994; 61-73] generalize their model as follows: assume that the period t over period 0 price ratios satisfy

$$p_{it}/p_{i0} = \alpha_t + \beta_i + \varepsilon_{it} \quad i=1,...,N; t=1,...,T \tag{29}$$

where the independently distributed residuals ε_{it} satisfy the following assumptions:

$$E\,\varepsilon_{it} = 0; \quad \text{Var}\,\varepsilon_{it} = \sigma_t^2/w_i; \; i=1,...,N; t=1,...,T. \tag{30}$$

As usual, the positive variance weights w_i are assumed to be shares; i.e., the w_i satisfy (14). Selvanathan and Prasada Rao [1994; 62] interpret β_i as the expectation of the change in the ith relative price in addition to general inflation; i.e., it is the systematic part of commodity i price change in addition to the overall period 0 to t price change α_t [15] Selvanathan and Prasada Rao

---

[15] It is immediately evident that the specification (29) is not very satisfactory. As we go from period 0 to 1, it is reasonable to postulate that β_1 is the systematic part of the commodity 1 price change p_{11}/p_{10} in addition to the general period 0 to 1 price change α_1 but it is <u>not</u> reasonable to assume that this same β_1 will characterize the systematic part of the commodity 1 relative price changes p_{11}/p_{10} for later periods, t=2,3,...,T, since as t increases, these fixed base systematic trends will tend to increase in magnitude.

[1994; 62] note that the parameters α_t and β_i are not identified. Thus they add an identifying restriction of the following form:

(31) $\sum_{i=1}^{N} w_i\beta_i = 0.$

The restriction (31) says that a share weighted average of the specific commodity price trends β_i sums to zero, a very reasonable assumption since the parameter α_t contains the general period t trend. What is not so reasonable, however, is the assumption that the w_i which appears in (31) is the <u>same</u> as the w_i which appear in (30).

Let us call the model that consists of (14) and (29)-(31) Model 5. Maximum likelihood estimators, $\hat{\alpha}_t$, $\hat{\beta}_i$, and $\hat{\sigma}_t^2$, for the parameters which appears in this model can be obtained in a manner analogous to the way Selvanathan and Prasada Rao [1994; 63-66] derived estimators for their specific version of this model. Define the maximum likelihood residuals $\hat{e}_{it}$ by:

(32) $\hat{e}_{it} \equiv (p_{it}/p_{i0}) - \hat{\alpha}_t - \hat{\beta}_i$; i-1,...,N; t=1,...,T.

The maximum likelihood estimators for the parameters of Model 5 can be obtained by solving the following system of equations, along with equations (32):

(33) $\hat{\alpha}_t \equiv \sum_{i=1}^{N} w_i\, p_{it}/p_{i0}$; t=1,...,T;

(34) $\sigma_t^2 = (1/N)\sum_{i=1}^{N} w_i\hat{e}_{it}^2$; t=1,...,T;

(35) $\hat{\beta}_i = \sum_{i=1}^{T}[1/\hat{\sigma}_t^2][(p_{it}/p_{i0}) - \hat{\alpha}_t]/\sum_{i=1}^{T}[1/\hat{\sigma}_t^2]$ i=1,...,N.

Substitution of equations (33) into (35) shows that the $\hat{\beta}_i$ satisfy the restriction (31). Equations (34) show that the period t variance estimator $\hat{\sigma}_t^2$ is a weighted sum of the squares of the period t maximum likelihood residuals, $\hat{e}_{it}^2$. Equations (35) show that the ith commodity effect $\hat{\beta}_i$ is a weighted average over T periods of the deviations of the period 0 to t price relatives p_{11}/p_{10} from the period t general inflation rates α_t, where the weights are inversely proportional to the period t variance estimates, $\hat{\alpha}_t^2$. Equations (33) show that the estimator for the period 0 to t general inflation rate $\hat{\alpha}_t$ is a simple weighted average of the period 0 to t price relatives, p_{it}/p_{i0} -- an amazingly simple result!

If we let the weights w_i equal the base period expenditure shares w_{i0}, we obtain the specific price trends stochastic model of Selvanathan and Prasada Rao [1994; 61-67] and the period 0 to t inflation estimate $\hat{\alpha}_t$ defined by (33) collapses down to the fixed base Laspeyres price index, $p^t \cdot q^0/p^0 \cdot q^0$. It is easy to show that $\hat{\alpha}_t$ is an unbiased estimator for α_t with the variance σ_t^2. Thus Selvanathan and Prasada Rao feel that they have justified the use of the fixed base Laspeyres price index (and provided measures of its variability) from the viewpoint of a sophisticated stochastic approach that blunts the force of the Keynesian objection to stochastic index number models.

However, a problem with Model 5 is that its specification for the specific commodity effects β_i in equations (29) is not very compelling. A more credible specific price trends stochastic model was developed by Clements and Izan [1987; 341-345] and repeated by Selvanathan and Prasada Rao [1994; 78-87]. The equations that characterize the model of these authors are:

$$(36) \quad \ell n[p_{it}/p_{it-1}] = \pi_t + \beta_i + \varepsilon_{it} \qquad i=1,...,N; t=1,...,T;$$

$$(37) \quad E\,\varepsilon_{it} = 0;\ \mathrm{Var}\,\varepsilon_{it} = \sigma_i^2/w_i; \qquad i=1,...,N; t=1,...,T;$$

As usual, the variance weights w_i that appear in (37) are assumed known and assumed to satisfy (14). As in the previous model, the π_t and β_i are not identified. Hence Clements and Izan [1987; 342] assume that the β_i satisfy the following restriction:

$$(38) \quad \Sigma_{i=1}^N w_i\beta_i = 0$$

where the w_i weights that appear in (38) are the same as those appearing in (37). It is this coincidence that leads to the following elegant formulae for the maximum likelihood estimators for the parameters of Model 6, consisting of (14) and (36)-(38):

$$(39) \quad \hat{e}_{it} \equiv \ell n[p_{it}/p_{it-1}] - \hat{\pi}_t - \hat{\beta}_i; \qquad i=1,...N; t=1,...,T;$$

$$(40) \quad \hat{\pi}_t = \Sigma_{i=1}^N w_i \ell n[p_{it}/p_{it-1}]; \qquad t=1,...,T;$$

$$(41) \quad \hat{\sigma}_t^2 = (1/N)\Sigma_{i=1}^N w_i\hat{e}_{it}^2; \qquad t=1,...,T;$$

$$(42) \quad \hat{\beta}_i = \Sigma_{i=1}^T[1/\sigma_s^2][\ell n(p_{it}/p_{it-1}) - \pi_t]/\sum_{i=1}^T[1/\sigma_s^2]; \qquad i=1,...,N.$$

The interpretation of (40) to (42) is analogous to the earlier interpretation of (33)-(35). However, the interpretation of the specific commodity price trend parameters β_i is much more reasonable for Model 6 than for Model 5: the β_i in the ith equation of (36) can be thought of as an average (multiplicative) price trend in the commodity i chain price relatives p_{it}/p_{it-1} around the general period t-1 to t inflation rates, $\exp[\pi_t]$, over all T periods in the sample; i.e., exponentiating both sides on the equation in (36) that corresponds to commodity i and period t and dropping the error term yields p_{it}/p_{it-1} approximately equal to $\exp[\pi_t]$ times $\exp[\beta_i]$. Thus the specification (36) will capture constant commodity specific growth rates over the sample period in prices (in addition to the general growth in prices).

Note that the logarithm of the period t-1 to t inflation rate, π_t, is estimated by the right hand side of (40), which is identical to the right hand side of (22) if we set s=t-1 and use the same weights w_i in each formula.

Recall that $w_{it} \equiv p_{it}q_{it} / \sum_{n=1}^{N} p_{nt}q_{nt}$ is the ith expenditure share in period t. Clements and Izan [1987; 342] make the following specification for the w_i which appear in (37) and (38):

$$(43) \quad w_i \equiv \Sigma_{i=0}^{T} w_{it} \big/ (T+1); \; i=1,\ldots,N;$$

i.e., the w_i are the mean expenditure shares over the entire sample period.

Of course, since the w_i defined by (43)[16] are not generally equal to the w_i defined by (24) when s=t-1, the Model 6 period t-1 to t inflation estimates $\hat{\pi}_t$ defined by (40) will not coincide precisely with the Model 4 estimates $\hat{\pi}_{t-1,t}$ defined by (22) when s=t-1. Thus Model 6 does not lead to a precise justification for the Törnqvist price index of Model 4, but Clements and Izan [1987; 343] argue that since the shares defined by (43) will not differ much from the shares defined by (24) when s=t-1, their specific price trends model provides an approximate justification for the use of the Persons-Törnqvist price index.

Clements and Izan [1987; 344-350] go on to show how variance estimates for the price indexes $\hat{\pi}_t$ defined by (40) can be derived. However, as in Model 4, the w_i defined by (43) depend on the prices p_{it} and hence the "fixed" weights w_i which appear in (37) and (38) are not really independent of the price relatives p_{it}/p_{it-1}. Hence the applicability of Model 6 when the w_i are defined by (43) is in doubt.[17]

This completes our review of the new stochastic approaches to index number theory. In the following two sections, we subject these approaches to a critical appraisal.

5. A Formulation of Edgeworth's Stochastic Approach to Index Numbers

The new stochastic models presented in the previous two sections suffer from a rather major defect: the variance assumptions of the type $\text{Var}\,\varepsilon_{it} = \sigma_t^2 / w_i$ where w_i is an observed expenditure share of some sort are simply not supported empirically. Clements and Izan [1987; 345] note explicitly that their variance assumptions (37) and (43) are not supported by their empirical example.[18] However, formal statistical tests are not required to support the common observation that the food and energy components of the consumer price index are more volatile

---

[16] It is interesting to note that Walsh [1901; 398] almost derived the transitive multilateral system of index numbers defined by (40) and (43): in place of the arithmetic means of the sample expenditure shares defined by (43), Walsh recommended the use of the corresponding geometric means. It should also be noted that Balk's [1980; 71] specialization of his seasonal model is a special case of Model 6 with w_i defined as $\Sigma_{t=0}^{T} p_{it}q_{it} \big/ \Sigma_{s=0}^{T} p_{js}q_{js}$.

[17] Note that Model 5 when $w_i \equiv w_{i0}$ does not suffer from this difficulty. However, the interpretation of the β_i in Model 5 is more problematic.

[18] "As can be seen, the variances are not inversely proportional to the budget shares as required by (16")." (Clements and Izan [1987; 345]).

than many of the remaining components. Food has a big share while energy has a small share -- volatility of price components is not highly correlated with the corresponding expenditure shares.

The observation that different price components have widely differing volatility dates back to the origins of index number theory. For example, Edgeworth [1887; 244] observed:

> "Cotton and Iron, for example, fluctuate in this sense much more than Pepper and Cloves."

Later, Edgeworth [1918; 186] commenting on Mitchell's work observed:

> "...that the fluctuation in price from year to year is much greater for some kinds of commodities than for others... Thus manufactured goods are steadier than raw materials. There are characteristic differences among the price fluctuations of the groups consisting of mineral products, forest products, animal products, and farm crops. Again, consumers' goods are steadier in price than producers' goods, the demand for the farmer being less influenced by vicissitudes in business conditions."

For a summary of Mitchell's evidence on the variability of different components of US wholesale prices over the years 1890-1913, see Mitchell [1921; 40-43]. Finally, Mills [1927; 46] summarizes his evidence on the monthly variability of commodity prices as follows:

> "It is clear from Table 4 that individual commodities differ materially in the matter of price variability and, also, that the variability of specific commodities has changed from period to period."

In the light of the above criticism of Models 3 through 6, let us reconsider the classical stochastic models presented in section 2. However, instead of assuming that the period 5 residuals have a common variance, we now assume that the log of each chain commodity price relative, $\ell n[p_{it}/p_{it-1}]$, after adjusting for a common period t inflation factor π_t has its own commodity specific variance σ_i^2. Thus Model 7 is defined by the following equations:

$$(44) \quad \ell n[p_{it}/p_{it-1}] = \pi_i + \varepsilon_{it}; \qquad i=1,...,N;\ t=1,...,T;$$

$$(45) \quad E\,\varepsilon_{it} = 0;\ \mathrm{Var}\,\varepsilon_{it} = \sigma_i^2; \qquad i=1,...,N;\ t=1,...,T.$$

The parameter π_t is the logarithm of the period t-1 to t price index for t=1,...,T and for i=1,...,N. The parameter σ_i^2 is the variance of the inflation adjusted logarithmic price ratios $\ell n[p_{it}/p_{it-1}] - \pi_t$ for t=1,...,T.

It is interesting to note that a model similar to that defined by (44) and (45) was first vaguely suggested by Edgeworth as the following quotations indicate:

> "A third principle is that less weight should be attached to observations belonging to a class which are subject to a wider deviation from the mean."
>
> Edgeworth [1887; 224].

> "Or, if more weight attaches to a change of price in one article rather than another, it is not on account of the importance of that article to the consumer or to the

shopkeeper, but on account of its importance to the calculator of probabilities, as affording an observation which is peculiarly likely to be correct..."

Edgeworth [1889; 287].

"In combination of these values derived from observation, less weight should be attached to one belonging to a class which is subject to a wider deviation from the mean, for which the mean square of deviation is greater."

Edgeworth [1923; 574].

"The term may include weighting according to 'precision' in the sense in which that term is attributed to errors of observation; a sense in which the price of pepper might deserve more weight than that of cotton, as M. Lucien March has the courage to maintain."

Edgeworth [1925; 383].

In the last quotation, Edgeworth is referring to March [1921; 81] who endorsed Edgeworth.[19] Irving Fisher summarized Edgeworth's vague suggestions efficiently as follows:

"Professor Edgeworth has made somewhat analogous, though less definite, proposals. He suggests that any commodity belonging to a class that is subject to wide scattering is a less reliable indicator than one belonging to a class not so subject. To take account of such differences in reliability he suggests that weights be assigned to each commodity in inverse proportion to the square of some variability-measure of the class to which it belongs.

This idea is scarcely capable of specific application, partly because the classification of commodities is so arbitrary and multiform, partly because of the difficulty of calculating any useful variability-measure for each class when determined. I wish Professor Edgeworth would take my 36 commodities, assign each to what he believes is its proper class, estimate each class-variability-measure, and calculate an index number accordingly."

Fisher [1922; 380]

We now show how estimators for our neo-Edgeworthian model defined by (44) and (45) can be obtained. The log of the likelihood function corresponding to Model 7 is, apart from inessential constants,

$$(46)\quad L(\pi_1,\ldots,\pi_T;\sigma_i^2,\ldots,\sigma_N^2) \equiv -\sum_{i=1}^{N} T\ell n\sigma_i^2 - \sum_{i=1}^{N}\sum_{i=1}^{T} \sigma_i^2[\ell n(p_{it}/p_{it-1})-\pi_t]^2 .$$

Differentiating (46) with respect to the parameters and setting the resulting partial derivatives equal to 0 leads to the following system of T+N simultaneous non linear equations to determine the maximum likelihood estimators for Model 7 (assuming that the $\hat{\sigma}_i^2$ are all strictly positive):

$$(47)\quad \hat{\pi}_t = \sum_{n=1}^{N}[1/\hat{\sigma}_n^2]\ell n(p_{it}/p_{it-1})/\sum_{i=1}^{N}[1/\hat{\sigma}_i^2]; \qquad t=1,\ldots,T;$$

[19] March [1921; 81] observed that if the price of paper varied less than the price of wheat, then the former price should be given more weight in the index number formula.

$$(48)\quad \hat{\sigma}_i^2 = [1/T]\Sigma_{i=1}^{T}[\ell n(p_{it}/p_{it-1}) - \hat{\pi}_t]^2 \qquad i=1,...,N.$$

The interpretation of the specific commodity price variance estimators $\hat{\sigma}_i^2$ defined by (48) is straightforward. Equation t in (47) says that the estimator for the logarithm of the period t-1 to t inflation rate, π_t, is a weighted average of the individual period t-1 to t log price changes, $\ell n[p_{it}/p_{it-1}]$, with the weight for the ith log price change being inversely proportional to its estimated variance, $\hat{\sigma}_i^2$. Thus Model 7 seems to capture the essence of Edgeworth's suggested stochastic approach to index number theory.

There can be at most one finite solution to equations (47) and (48) that has all $\hat{\sigma}_i^2$ strictly positive. A suggested algorithm for finding this solution if it exists is the following one. Begin iteration 1 by estimating $\hat{\pi}_t$ as the mean of the unweighted log price changes:

$$(49)\quad \hat{\pi}_t^{(1)} \equiv \Sigma_{i=1}^{N}(1/N)\ell n(p_{it}/p_{it-1});\ t=1,...,T.$$

Thus $\exp[\hat{\pi}^{(1)}]$ is the Jevons geometric mean price index for the t-1 to t price change. Once the $\hat{\pi}_t^{(1)}$ have been defined, define the iteration 1 variances $[\hat{\sigma}_i^{(1)}]^2$ by (48) replacing $\hat{\pi}_t$ by $\hat{\pi}_t^{(1)}$. At the first stage of iteration 2, define the $\hat{\pi}_t^{(2)}$ by (47) using the iteration 1 $[\hat{\sigma}_i^{(1)}]^2$ in the right hand sides of (47). At the second stage of iteration 2, define the $[\hat{\sigma}_i^{(2)}]^2$ by (48) using the $\hat{\pi}_t^{(1)}$ in the right hand sides of (48). Now carry on repeating these first and second stage iterations until the estimates converge. It can be shown that if the $\hat{\sigma}_i^{(k)}$ remain positive, then each stage of each iteration will lead to a strict increase in the log likelihood function (46) until convergence has been achieved.

Unfortunately, the above algorithm may not always work in degenerate cases. For example, consider the case where the period t prices are proportional to the base period prices for all t. In this case, the $\hat{\pi}_t$ are explicit functions of the proportionality factors and all of the commodity variances defined by (48) will be 0. There are other problems as well: if we pick any i and define $\hat{\pi}_t = \ell n[p_{it}/p_{it-1}]$ for t=1,...,T and let σ_i^2 tend to 0 (with the other σ_j^2 positive and finite), we find that the log likelihood function approaches plus infinity. To rule out degenerate solutions of this type, it may be necessary to add a positive lower bound to the admissible variances in our model; i.e., we may need to add to (44) and (45) the following restrictions:

$$(50)\quad \sigma_i^2 \geq \sigma^2 > 0;\ i=1,...,N$$

for some σ^2 chosen a priori.

We now turn to a critical evaluation of these new stochastic models for price indexes.

6. A Critical Evaluation of the New Stochastic Approaches

Our first criticism of the new stochastic models presented in sections 3 and 4 has already been made: the variance assumptions made in these models are not consistent with the observed behavior of prices. This is a very fundamental criticism that has not been addressed by the proponents of these new models. The assertion of Selvanathan and Prasada Rao [1994; 6] that their stochastic approach has provided standard errors for several well known index number formulae is correct only if their stochastic assumptions are correct, which seems very unlikely!

Our second criticism is directed towards the specific price trend models of Balk [1980], Clements and Izan [1987] and Selvanathan and Prasada Rao [1994; 63-66]: these models force the same weights w_i to serve two distinct purposes and it is unlikely that their choice of weights could be correct for both purposes. In particular, their expenditure based weights are unlikely to be correct for the first purpose (which is criticism 1 again).

Our third criticism of the new stochastic approaches presented in sections 4 and 5 is that the resulting price indexes are not invariant to the number of periods T in the sample. Balk [1980; 72-73] was very concerned with this problem (since he works in a Statistical Agency and hence must suggest "practical" solutions to problems) and he presented some evidence on the stability of his estimated index numbers as T was increased. His evidence indicates that our third criticism is empirically important. Due to the fact that variances of price relatives can change considerably over time (recall Mills [1927; 46]), our neo-Edgeworthian Model 7 presented in the previous section will be particularly subject to this instability criticism.

The above invariance problem also occurs in the multilateral context and in the multiperiod time series context when we want our estimated index numbers to satisfy the circularity test; i.e., to be transitive. Walsh, after noting how multilateral transitivity can be achieved by using weights that pertain to all of the periods in the sample (e.g., recall equations (43) in Model 6), draws attention to the above invariance problem and also notes why the multilateral case is more difficult than the bilateral case:

> "In no case is this remedy satisfactory, for two principle reasons: (1) Because the present epoch is extending every year, requiring recalculations; and it does not appear that a later recalculation will be more correct than an earlier. Besides, how is a past variation between two years several years ago to be affected by present variations? (2) Because we really do not know how to calculate weights, or to determine equivalence of mass-units, or to average mass-quantities, over more than two periods, since the geometric average loses its virtue when applied to more than two figures."
>
> Walsh [1901; 399]

Our fourth criticism of the new stochastic approaches is simply a restatement of the fundamental objection of Keynes:

> "The hypothetical change in the price level, which would have occurred if there had been no changes in relative prices, is no longer relevant if relative prices have in fact changed -- for the change in relative prices has in itself affected the price level.

> I conclude, therefore, that the unweighted (or rather the randomly weighted) index number of prices -- Edgeworth's 'indefinite' index number -- ...has no place whatever in a rightly conceived discussion of the problems of price levels."
>
> Keynes [1930; 78]

Thus if price relatives are different, then an appropriate definition of average price change cannot be determined independently of the economic importance of the corresponding goods. What is an appropriate definition of aggregate price change? Earlier in his book, Keynes [1930; 59-61] indicated that the price relatives in a producer or consumer price index should be weighted according to their relative importance as indicated by a census of production or by a consumer budget study. Thus the best index number formula according to Keynes is an expenditure weighted sum of relative prices; i.e., the price relatives must be weighted according to their economic importance, not according to their statistical importance, a la Edgeworth.[20] Of course, in the approach advocated by Keynes, there is still the problem of choosing the "best" economic weights (base or current period expenditure shares or a mixture of them), but precise answers to this question simply lead back to the test or economic approaches to index number theory.

Criticism four can be restated as follows. The early statistical approaches of Jevons and Edgeworth (see section 2) treated each price relative as an equally valid signal of the general inflation rate: the price relative for pepper is given the same weight as the price relative for bread. This does not seem reasonable to "Keynesians" if the quantity of pepper consumed is negligible.

Another more technical way of restating the Keynesian objection to stochastic approaches can be accomplished by drawing on the models presented in section 5: if we make more reasonable variance assumptions, models of the form (36)-(38) are reasonable, except that the constant β_i's should be replaced by sets of period specific β_{it}'s. But then the resulting model has too many parameters to be identified.

Our conclusion at this stage is: in the present context where all prices and quantities are known without sampling error, signal extraction approaches to index number theory should be approached with some degree of caution.[21]

Of course, there is a huge role for statistical approaches when we change our terms of reference and assume that the given price and quantity data are samples. The founders of the test approach, Walsh [1924; 516-517] and Fisher [1922; 336-340], did not deny a strong role for statistical techniques in the sampling context. In addition to the work of Bowley [1901] [1911] [1919] [1926] [1928], more recent references on the sampling aspects of price indexes include Mudgett [1951; 51-54], Adelman [1958], McCarthy [1961], Kott [1984] and the BLS [1988].

---

[20] Keynes' belief in the importance of economic weighting (as opposed to Edgeworth [1901; 410] and Bowley [1901; 219] who at times believed that weighting was unimportant) dates back at least to Keynes [1911; 46].

[21] The dynamic factor index approach of Bryan and Cecchetti [1993; 19] is an example of a signal extraction approach to index numbers that we did not cover due to its complexity. Their approach is only subject to our criticisms 3 and 4. Their approach is also subject to a criticism that can be leveled against the specific price trend models of section 4: the nonstationary components of their specific price trends (their counterparts to the β_1 which appear in Models 5 and 6 above) are assumed to be constant over the sample period.

7. Other Approaches to the Determination of the Precision of an Index

Having rejected the new stochastic approaches to index number theory (when all prices and quantities are known with certainty over the sample period), we have to admit that the proponents of these new approaches have a point: if all of the price relatives pertaining to two periods are identical, it must be the case that the "precision" of the index number computation for those two periods is greater than when the price relatives are widely dispersed. On the other hand, the proponents of the test and economic approaches to index number theory use their favorite index number formula and thus provide a precise answer whether the price relatives are widely dispersed or not. Thus the test and economic approaches give a false sense of precision.

The early pioneers of the test approach addressed the above criticism. Their method works as follows: (i) decide on a list of desirable tests that an index number formula should satisfy; (ii) find some specific formulae that satisfy these tests (if possible); (iii) evaluate the chosen formulae with the data on hand and (iv) table some measure of the dispersion of the resulting index number computations (usually the range or standard deviation was chosen). The resulting measure of dispersion can be regarded as a measure of functional form error.

Fisher [1922; 226-229] applied the above method to address the charge that the test approach gave a false precision to index numbers. He found 13 index number formulae (including the ideal) that satisfied the commodity, time and factor reversal tests and were not "freakish"; i.e., descended from modes or medians (and hence discontinuous). Fisher [1922; 227] found that the standard deviations between his 13 best fixed base indexes increased as the two periods being compared grew further apart; his "probable error" reached a maximum of about .1% when his 13 indexes were compared between 1913 and 1918. Fisher called this functional form error, instrumental error. In response to outraged criticisms from Bowley, Fisher later summarized his results as follows:

> "What I do claim to have demonstrated is something quite different, namely, that the 'instrumental' error, i.e., that part of the total error which may be ascribed to any inaccuracy in the mathematical formula used, is, in the case of the ideal formula (and, in fact, in the case of a score of other formulae as well), usually less than one part in 1000."
>
> Fisher [1923; 248]

Warren Persons [1928; 19-23] also implemented the above test approach to the determination of functional form error. Persons looked for index number formulae that satisfied the time reversal test and his new test, the absence of weight correlation bias test. He found nine admissible index number formulae (including the Persons-Törnqvist and the Fisher ideal) and used Fisher's [1922] data to numerically evaluate these nine. Finally, Persons [1928; 23] tabled the range of the resulting indexes over the sample period; he found the range was a maximum in 1917 when it slightly exceeded 1%. It turned out that indexes satisfying Fisher's tests had a narrower range of dispersion than the indexes satisfying Persons' tests for the same data set.

Walsh [1921; 97-107] almost recommended the above approach to functional form error. He chose six index number formulae on the basis of how close they came empirically to satisfying his multiperiod identity test.[22] Walsh [1921; 106] used a small but somewhat extreme data set from Bowley [1901; 226] to evaluate his six index number formulae; he found that their range was about 2%. However, Walsh did not stop at this point; he went on to choose a single best index number formula:

> "To return to theory: would anything be gained by drawing an average of the results yielded by several methods? Hardly, as they have different merits. All that we can do is choose the best, after testing all the candidates; for to average the others with the best, would only vitiate the result."
>
> Walsh [1921; 106-107]

What was Walsh's [1921; 102] theoretically best index number formula? None other than Irving Fisher's [1922] ideal index![23]

It is clear that there are some problems in implementing the above test approach to the determination of functional form error; i.e., what tests should we use and how many index number formulae should be evaluated in order to calculate the measure of dispersion? However, it is interesting to note that virtually all of the above index number formulae suggested by Fisher, Persons and Walsh approximate each other to the second order around an equal price and quantity point.[24]

The above approach may be used to estimate the functional form error that arises from choosing an index number formula that is based on the economic approach. The economic approach recommends the use of a superlative index number formula, such as the Fisher-Walsh ideal formula[25] or the Persons-Törnqvist formula[26] or the direct and implicit quadratic mean of order r families of price indexes that include two indexes recommended by Walsh [1901; 105].[27] Many of these superlative indexes appear in the list of best test approach index number formulae recommended by Fisher, Persons and Walsh.[28] As was done for the test approach, the functional form error involved in using any specific superlative index could be approximated by evaluating a number of superlative indexes and then tabling a measure of their dispersion.

---

[22] Walsh [1921; 104] called his test the circular test but it is slightly different from the Westergaard-Fisher [1922; 413] circular test; see Diewert [1993b; 39]

[23] Walsh [1901] [1921] was an originator of the test approach to index number theory and he also proposed the use of the ideal index either before Fisher [1921] or coincidentally. Perhaps the reason why Walsh has been forgotten but Fisher lives on is due to the rather opaque writing style of Walsh whereas Fisher wrote in a very clear style.

[24] Thus these indexes are either superlative or pseudo-superlative; i.e., they approximate superlative indexes to the second order around an equal price and quantity point; see Diewert [1978; 896-898].

[25] See Diewert [1976; 134].

[26] See Diewert [1976; 121].

[27] See Diewert [1976; 134-135]. The two Walsh indexes are obtained when we set r=1. Walsh [1921; 97] listed his two recommended indexes as formulae (5) and (6). The right hand side of (5) needs to be multiplied by the expenditure ratio for the two periods under consideration, since on the previous page, Walsh [1921; 96] assumed that these expenditures were equal.

[28] On the basis of its consistency with revealed preference theory and its consistency with linear and Leontief aggregator functions, Diewert [1976; 137-138] recommended the Fisher-Walsh ideal index as the best superlative index number formula. Allen and Diewert [1981; 435] also endorse this index number formula as being the best superlative one since it is consistent with both Hicks' [1946; 312-313] Composite Commodity Theorem and Leontief's [1936; 54-57] Aggregation Theorem.

A specific proposal to measure the dispersion of superlative indexes is the following one. Choose the following members of Diewert's [1976; 131] quadratic mean of order r price indexes $P_r : P_2$ (the Fisher-Walsh ideal price index), P_1 (Walsh), P_0 (Persons-Törnqvist), and P_{-2}. Choose the following members from Diewert's [1976; 132] implicit quadratic mean of order r prices indexes $\widetilde{P}_r : \widetilde{P}_2$ (implicit Walsh), $\widetilde{P}_0$ (implicit Törnqvist) and $\widetilde{P}_{-2}$.[29] These formulae include the most frequently used superlative indexes. To measure the dispersion of these indexes, consider the following dispersion measure D, which is the range of the seven indexes divided by the minimum index:

$$(51)\quad D(p^s,p^t,q^s,q^t) \equiv [\max\{P_2,P_1,P_0,P_{-2},\widetilde{P}_1,\widetilde{P}_0,\widetilde{P}_{-2}\}/\min\{P_2,P_1,P_0,P_{-2},\widetilde{P}_1,\widetilde{P}_0,\widetilde{P}_{-2}\}]^{-1}$$

where $P_i \equiv P_i(p^s,p^t,q^s,q^t)$ and $\widetilde{P}_j \equiv \widetilde{P}_j(p^s,p^t,q^s,q^t)$ D can be interpreted as the percentage difference between the highest and lowest price indexes in the set of admissible indexes.

Note that $D(p^s,p^t,q^s,q^t) \geq 0$. Moreover, since each of the seven indexes that appear on the right hand side of (1) satisfy the Fisher [1911; 534] [1922; 64]-Walsh [1901; 368] <u>time reversal test</u>:

$$(52)\quad P(p^s,p^t,q^s,q^t) = 1/(p^s,p^t,q^s,q^t),$$

it can be verified that the dispersion measures defined by (51) will satisfy the following <u>base period invariance property</u>:

$$(53)\quad D(p^s,p^t,q^s,q^t) = D(p^t,p^s,q^t,q^s);$$

i.e., if we interchange periods, the dispersion remains unchanged.

The dispersion measure defined by (51) can be adapted to the test approach: the set of index number formulae that would appear in (51) would be restricted to formulae that satisfied the appropriate set of tests. In particular, assume that the admissible P satisfy the time reversal test (52) and Walsh's [1901; 385] <u>strong proportionality test</u>:

$$(54)\quad P(p^s,\lambda p^s,q^s,q^t) = \lambda \text{ for } \lambda > 0;$$

i.e., if the period t price vector p^t is proportional to the period s price vector p^s, then the index equals the common proportional factor. Under these hypotheses on the class of admissible price indexes in (51), the dispersion measure defined by the appropriate version of (51) would satisfy the base period invariance test (53) and would equal 0 if all the price relatives were identical.

Returning to the economic approach to index numbers and the specific measure of formula error defined by (51), it can be verified that if both prices and quantities are proportional during the two periods under consideration, so that $p^t = \alpha p^s$ and $q^t = \beta q^s$ for some $\alpha > 0, \beta > 0$, then each of the seven indexes which appears in the right hand side of (51) is equal

[29] Fisher's [1922; 461-487] identification numbers for these formulae are: 353, 1153, 123, the geometric mean of 13 and 19, 1154, 124, and the geometric mean of 14 and 20.

to α and hence the dispersion measure $D(p^s,\alpha p^s,q^s,\beta q^s)$ will attain its lower bound of 0. However, if only prices are proportional, then $D(p^s,\alpha p^s,q^s,q^t)$ will not necessarily equal 0. If we want a measure of dispersion that will equal zero when only prices are proportional, a different approach is required, which we now turn to.

A more direct approach to the reliability of a price index, $P(p^s,p^t,q^s,q^t)$, is to simply look at the variability of the individual price relatives, p_{it}/p_{is}, around the index number "average" value, $P(p^s,p^t,q^s,q^t)$. In order to implement this approach, define the ith absolute deviation by

$$(55)\quad d_i(p^s,p^t,q^s,q^t) \equiv \left|(p_{it}/p_{is}) - P(p^s,p^t,q^s,q^t)\right| \quad i=1,\ldots,N.$$

A <u>measure of relative price variability</u>, V, could be defined as an appropriate function of the deviations d_i defined by (55), say:

$$(56)\quad V(p^s,p^t,q^s,q^t) \equiv M[d_1(p^s,p^t,q^s,q^t),\ldots,d_N(p^s,p^t,q^s,q^t)]$$

where M is a linearly homogeneous symmetric mean.[30]

A desirable property for a price variability measure V is that it satisfy the base period invariance property (53) (where we replace D by V). Unfortunately, the V defined by (56) and (55) will not generally have this property.

In order to obtain a base period invariant measure of price variability between two periods, define the ith absolute logarithmic deviation e_i by

$$(57)\quad e_i(p^s,p^t,q^s,q^t) \equiv \left|\ell n(p_{it}/p_{is}) - \ell nP(p^s,p^t,q^s,q^t)\right|, \quad i=1,\ldots,N.$$

Define a <u>logarithmic price variability measure</u> V by

$$(58)\quad V(p^s,p^t,q^s,q^t) \equiv M[e_1(p^s,p^t,q^s,q^t),\ldots,e_N(p^s,p^t,q^s,q^t)]$$

where again M is a homogeneous symmetric mean. If the index number formula P satisfies the time reversal test (52), then it can be verified that $e_i(p^s,p^t,q^s,q^t) = e_i(p^t,p^s,q^t,q^s)$ and hence the V defined by (58) satisfies the base period invariance property (53) (with V replacing D).

Define the mean of order r of N positive numbers $x_1,\ldots,x_N$ for $r \neq 0$ by[31]

$$(59)\quad M_r(x_1,\ldots,x_N) \equiv [\Sigma_{i=1}^N (1/N)x_i^r]^{1/r}.$$

[30] A symmetric mean $M(x_1,\ldots,x_N)$ is defined to be a continuous, symmetric increasing function of N real variables that has the mean value property, $M(\lambda_1,\ldots,\lambda_N) = \lambda$. $M(x_1,\ldots,x_N)$ will also satisfy the following min-max property: $\min_i\{x_i\} \le M(x_1,\ldots,x_N) \le \max_i\{x_i\}$ This last property and (55) imply that V will be nonnegative.

[31] See Hardy, Littlewood and Polya [1934; 12].

The means of order r, M_r, are homogeneous symmetric means and hence can be used as M's in (58). For example, if we choose r=2 and substitute M_2 into (58), we obtain the following logarithmic price variability measure:

$$(60)\quad V_2(p^s,p^t,q^s,q^t) \equiv [(1/N)\sum_{i=1}^{N}\{\ell n(p_{it}/p_{is}) - \ell nP(p^s,p^t,q^s,q^t)\}^2]^{1/2}.$$

Note that (60) bears some resemblance to the earlier stochastic measure of reliability, $\hat{\sigma}_{st}$ defined by the square root of (23). It should also be noted that a monotonic transformation of the measure of relative price variability defined by (60), $N[V_2(p^s,p^t,q^s,q^t)]^2$, was suggested as a measure of the nonproportionality of prices by Allen and Diewert [1981; 433]: the price index P that they used in (60) was the Jevons equally weighted geometric mean defined by the right hand side of (12) (with p^s replacing p^0).

Unfortunately, the measures of price variability defined by (58) or (60) are still not satisfactory in the present context. The problem is that some price relatives are completely unimportant and hence should not be given the same weight as items that are important in the budgets of the consumer or producer for the two periods under consideration: recall Edgeworth and March's discussion about the relative importance of pepper versus wheat or cotton. We could use the budget shares of period s, w_{is}, or the budget shares of period t, w_{it}, as weights, but it seems less arbitrary to use an even handed average of these two sets of weights.[32] Thus we will weight the ith absolute logarithmic price deviation e_i defined by (57) by $m(w_{is}, w_{it})$, where m is a linearly homogeneous symmetric mean of two variables. Note that the symmetry property of m implies that

$$(61)\quad m(w_{is}, w_{it}) = m(w_{it}, w_{is}),\ i=1,...,N.$$

Thus our final class of price variability measures is defined as follows:

$$(62)\quad V(p^s,p^t,q^s,q^t) \equiv M[m(w_{1s},w_{1t})e_1(p^s,p^t,q^s,q^t),\ldots,m(w_{Ns},w_{Nt})e_N(p^s,p^t,q^s,q^t)]$$

where the e_i are defined by (57) and M is again a homogeneous symmetric mean. If the price index P satisfies the time reversal test (52) and the share aggregator function m satisfies (61), then it can be verified that the V defined by (62) satisfies the base period invariance test (53).

[32] Our reasoning is similar to that of Walsh [1921; 90], who made the case for the use of average weights in a price index as follows: "Commodities are to be weighted according to their importance, or their full values. But the problem of axiometry always involves at least two periods. There is a first period, and there is a second period that is compared with it. Price-variations have taken place between the two, and these are to be averaged to get the amount of their variation as a whole. But the weights of the commodities at the second period are apt to be different from their weights at the first period. Which weights, then, are the right ones -- those of the first period? or those of the second? or should there be a combination of the two sets? There is no reason for preferring either the first or the second. Then the combination of both would seem to be the proper answer. And this combination itself involves an averaging of the weights of the two periods."

This V will also be nonnegative.[33] Moreover, if the price index P satisfies the strong proportionality test (54), then V will equal 0 if prices are proportional so $V(p^s,\lambda p^t,q^s,q^t)=0$.

The most straightforward special case of (62) is obtained if we let M and m be means of order 1; i.e., arithmetic means. In this case, V becomes

$$(63) \quad V_1(p^s,p^t,q^s,q^t) \equiv \Sigma_{i=1}^N (1/N)\overline{w}_{ist}\left|\ell n(p_{it}/p_{is}) - \ell nP(p^s,p^t,q^s,q^t)\right|$$

where $\overline{w}_{ist} \equiv (1/2)(w_{is}+w_{it})$ is the average expenditure share on commodity i during periods s and t. The measure (63) is simply the arithmetic average of the weighted absolute logarithmic deviations, $\overline{w}_{ist}e_i(p^s,\lambda p^t,q^s,q^t)$. The only disadvantage of this measure is that it is not differentiable. A differentiable special case of (62) is obtained if we set $M = M_2$ and still let m be the arithmetic mean:

$$(64) \quad V_2(p^s,p^t,q^s,q^t) \equiv \{\sum_{i=1}^N (1/N)\Sigma_{i=1}^N (1/N)w_{ist}[\ell n(p_{it}/p_{is}) - \ell nP(p^s,p^t,q^s,q^t)]^2\}^{1/2}.$$

Note the resemblance of (64) to the square root of (23). Comparing (64) to (63), V_2 gives larger weight to the larger weighted absolute logarithmic deviations, $\overline{w}_{ist}e_i(p^s,\lambda p^t,q^s,q^t)$. Both of the measures V_1 and V_2 will serve as satisfactory measures of variability or degree of nonproportionality of relative prices relative to the index number formula $P(p^s,p^t,q^s,q^t)$.

There is another approach to the measurement of relative price variability that has the advantage that it is simultaneously a measure of relative quantity variability. Consider the following variability measure due to Robert Hill [1995; 81][34]:

$$(65) \quad V_H(p^s,p^t,q^s,q^t) = \ell n(p^s \cdot q^t\; p^t \cdot q^s / p^t \cdot q^t\; p^s \cdot q^s)] \geq 0$$

$$(66) \quad \equiv [\ell n(P_L/P_P)]$$

$$(67) \quad \equiv [\ell n(Q_L/Q_P)]$$

where $P_L \equiv p^t \cdot q^s / p^s \cdot q^s$ and $P_P \equiv p^t \cdot q^t / p^s \cdot q^t$ are the Laspeyres and Paasche price indexes and $Q_L \equiv p^s \cdot q^t / p^s \cdot q^s$ and $Q_P \equiv p^t \cdot q^t / p^t \cdot q^s$ are the Laspeyres and Paasche quantity indexes. Equation (66) shows that the variability measure defined by (65) can be written as the absolute value of the log of the ratio of the Laspeyres and Paasche price indexes while (67) shows a similar equality involving the ratio of the Laspeyres and Paasche quantity indexes. Thus if prices in the two periods are proportional (so that $p^t = \alpha p^s$), then $P_L = P_P = \alpha$ and using (66), $V_H = 0$. Similarly, if quantities in the two periods are proportional (so that $q^t = \beta q^s$), then

[33] If P satisfies the usual homogeneity properties with respect to prices and quantities (e.g., see tests PT5-PT8 in Diewert [1992a; 215-216]), then it can be shown that $V(p^s,p^t,q^s,q^t)$ will be homogeneous of degree zero in each of its four sets of variables.

[34] Hill defined $V_H \equiv \ell n[\max\{Q_L,Q_P\}]/\min\{Q_L,Q_P\}$. It can be shown that this definition is equivalent to (67).

$Q_L = Q_P = \beta$ and using (67), $V_H = 0$. Hence as Hill [1995; 81] observed, if either prices are proportional (recall Hicks' [1946; 312-313] Aggregation Theorem) or quantities are proportional (recall Leontief's [1936; 54-57] Aggregation Theorem), then the variability measure V_H defined by (65) attains its lower bound of 0. Note also that if we interchange periods, V_H remains unchanged; i.e., it satisfies the base period invariance property (53).

If x is close to 1, then $\ln x$ can be closely approximated by the first order approximation, $x-1$. Hence the Hill variability measure V_H can be approximated by the following measure:

$$(68) \quad \overline{V}(p^s,p^t,q^s,q^t) \equiv [(P_L/P_P)-1] = [(Q_L/Q_P)-1].$$

This variability measure has the same mathematical properties that were noted for V_H. Both measures are base period invariant measures of the spread between the Paasche and Laspeyres price (or quantity) indexes; both measures are approximately equal to the absolute value of the percentage difference between the Paasche and Laspeyres indexes. From the viewpoint of the test approach to index numbers, Bowley [1901; 227], Fisher [1922; 403] and Diewert [1992a; 219-220] proposed that the price index P should be between the Paasche and Laspeyres price indexes. These bounds are also valid from the economic point of view if we have a homothetic or linearly homogeneous aggregator function. Thus the variability measures defined by (65) and (68) provide convenient methods of describing the width of these index number bounds.

Note that the variability or nonproportionality measures V_H and V do not depend on a particular index number formula P. However, if the index number formula P is a symmetric mean of the Paasche and Laspeyres indexes (e.g., $P=(P_L P_P)^{1/2}$, the Fisher Walsh ideal index), then P will lie between P_L and P_P and V_H or $\overline{V}$ may be used as reliability measures for P.

We have presented three classes of dispersion measures (see (51), (62) and (65) or (68) above) that could be used to measure the reliability of an index number formula. The use of (62), (65) or (68) as measures of dispersion would meet some of the criticisms of the test and economic approaches that have been made by the proponents of the stochastic approach. If all of the relative prices were identical, the above dispersion measures would attain their lower bounds of zero, but if the price relatives were dispersed, nonzero measures of dispersion or variability would be obtained if (51) or (62) were used.

It is now almost 75 years after Walsh [1921] made his comments on the diversity of approaches to index number theory and economists are still "at loggerheads." However, perhaps this diversity is a good thing. The new stochastic approach to index numbers has at least caused this proponent of the test and economic approaches to think more deeply about the foundations of the subject.

References

Adelman, I. [1958], "A New Approach to the Construction of Index Numbers," *Review of Economics and Statistics* 40, 240-249.

Afriat, S.N. [1972], "The Theory of International Comparisons of Real Income and Prices," pp. 13-69 in D.J. Daly (ed.), *International Comparisons of Prices and Outputs*, New York: Columbia University Press.

Allen, R.C. and W.E. Diewert [1981], "Direct versus Implicit Superlative Index Number Formulae," *The Review of Economics and Statistics* 63, 430-435.

Balk, B.M. [1980], "A Method for Constructing Price Indices for Seasonal Commodities," *Journal of the Royal Statistical Society* A, 143, 68-75.

Bowley, A.L. [1901], *Elements of Statistics*, Westminster England: P.S. King and Son.

Bowley, A.L. [1911], "The Measurement of the Accuracy of an Average," *Journal of the Royal Statistical Society* 75, 77-88.

Bowley, A.L. [1919], "The Measurement of Changes in the Cost of Living," *Journal of the Royal Statistical Society* 82, 343-372.

Bowley, A.L. [1926], "The Influence on the Precision of Index-Numbers of Correlation between the Prices of Commodities," *Journal of the Royal Statistical Society* 89, 300-319.

Bowley, A.L. [1928], "Notes on Index Numbers," *The Economic Journal* 38, 216-237.

Bryan, M.F. and S.G. Cecchetti [1993], "The Consumer Price Index as a Measure of Inflation," *Economic Review, Federal Reserve Bank of Cleveland* 29, 15-24.

Bureau of Labor Statistics [1988], *BLS Handbook of Methods*, Bulletin 2285, Washington: U.S. Government Printing Office.

Carli, Gian-Rinaldo [1764], "Del valore e della proporzione de'metalli monetati," reprinted in pp. 297-336 in *Scrittori classici italiani di economia politica*, Volume 13, Milano: G.G. Destefanis, 1804.

Clements, K.W. and H.Y. Izan [1981], "A Note on Estimating Divisia Index Numbers," *International Economics Review* 22, 745-747.

Clements, K.W. and H.Y. Izan [1987], "The Measurement of Inflation: A Stochastic Approach," *Journal of Business and Economic Statistics* 5, 339-350.

Diewert, W.E. [1974], "Applications of Duality Theory," pp. 106-171 in M.D. Intriligator and D.A. Kendrick (eds.), *Frontiers of Quantitative Economics*, Vol. II, Amsterdam: North-Holland.

Diewert, W.E. [1976], "Exact and Superlative Index Numbers," *Journal of Econometrics* 4, 115-145.

Diewert, W.E. [1978], "Superlative Index Numbers and Consistency in Aggregation," *Econometrica* 46, 883-900.

Diewert, W.E. [1992a], "Fisher Ideal Output, Input and Productivity Indexes Revisited," *The Journal of Productivity Analysis* 3, 211-248.

Diewert, W.E. [1992b], "Exact and Superlative Welfare Change Indicators," *Economic Inquiry* 30, 565-582.

Diewert, W.E. [1993a], "Overview of Volume 1," pp. 1-31 in *Essays in Index Number Theory*, Vol. 1, W.E. Diewert and A.O. Nakamura (eds.). Amsterdam: North-Holland.

Diewert, W.E. [1993b], "The Early History of Price Index Research," pp. 33-65 in *Essays in Index Number Theory*, Vol. 1, W.E. Diewert and A.O. Nakamura (eds.), Amsterdam: North-Holland.

Diewert, W.E. [1993c], "Symmetric Means and Choice Under Uncertainty," pp. 355-433 in *Essays in Index Number Theory*, Vol. 1, W.E. Diewert and A.O. Nakamura (eds.), Amsterdam: North-Holland.

Edgeworth, F.Y. [1887], *Measurement of Change in Value of Money I*, the first Memorandum presented to the British Association for the Advancement of Science; reprinted as pp. 198-259 in *Papers Relating to Political Economy*, Vol. 1, New York: Burt Franklin, 1925.

Edgeworth, F.Y. [1888a], *Tests of Accurate Measurement*, the second Memorandum presented to the British Association for the Advancement of Science; reprinted as pp. 304-343 in *Papers Relating to Political Economy*, Vol. 1, New York: Burt Franklin, 1925.

Edgeworth, F.Y. [1888b], "Some New Methods of Measuring Variation in General Prices," *Journal of the Royal Statistical Society* 51, 346-368.

Edgeworth, F.Y. [1889], *Measurement of Change in Value of Money*, the third Memorandum presented to the British Association for the Advancement of Science; reprinted as pp. 259-297 in *Papers Relating to Political Economy*, Vol. 1, New York: Burt Franklin, 1925.

Edgeworth, F.Y. [1901], "Mr. Walsh on the Measurement of General Exchange Value," *The Economic Journal* 11, 404-416.

Edgeworth, F.Y. [1918], "The Doctrine of Index-Numbers according to Professor Wesley Mitchell," *The Economic Journal* 28, 176-197.

Edgeworth, F.Y. [1923], "Mr. Correa Walsh on the Calculation of Index-Numbers," *Journal of the Royal Statistical Society* 86, 570-590.

Edgeworth, F.Y. [1925], "The Plurality of Index-Numbers," *The Economic Journal* 35, 379-388.

Eichhorn, W. [1978], *Functional Equations in Economics*, Reading, Massachusetts: Addison-Wesley.

Eichhorn, W. and J. Voeller [1976], *Theory of the Price Index*, Berlin: Springer-Verlag.

Fisher, I. [1911], *The Purchasing Power of Money*, London: Macmillan.

Fisher, I. [1921], "The Best Form of Index Number," *Journal of the American Statistical Association* 17, 533-537.

Fisher, I. [1922], *The Making of Index Numbers*, Boston: Houghton Mifflen.

Fisher, I. [1923], "Professor Bowley on Index-Numbers" (with a comment by Bowley), *The Economic Journal* 33, 246-252.

Frisch, R. [1936], "Annual Survey of General Economic Theory: The Problem of Index Numbers," *Econometrica* 4, 1-39.

Hardy, G.H., J.E. Littlewood and E. Polya [1934], *Inequalities*, London: Cambridge University Press.

Hicks, J.R. [1946], *Value and Capital*, Second Edition, Oxford: Clarendon Press.

Hill, R.J. [1995], "Purchasing Power Parity Methods of Making International Comparisons," Ph.D. Thesis, Economics Department, University of British Columbia, Vancouver, Canada.

Jevons, W.S. [1863], "A Serious Fall in the Value of Gold Ascertained and its Social Effects Set Forth," reprinted as pp. 13-118 in *Investigations in Currency and Finance*, London: Macmillan and Co., 1884.

Jevons, W.S. [1865], "The Variation of Prices and the Value of the Currency since 1782," *Journal of the Statistical Society of London* 28, 294-320; reprinted as pp. 119-150, *Investigations in Currency and Finance*, Macmillan and Co., 1884.

Jevons, W.S. [1869], "The Depreciation of Gold," *Journal of the Statistical Society of London* 32, 445-449; reprinted as pp. 151-159 in *Investigations in Currency and Finance*, London: Macmillan and Co., 1884.

Konüs, A.A. [1924], "The Problem of the True Index of the Cost of Living," translated in *Econometrica* 7, (1939), 10-29.

Konüs, A.A. and S.S. Byushgens [1926], "K. Probleme Pokupatelnoi Cili Deneg," *Voprosi Konyunkturi* II:1, 151-172.

Keynes, J.M. [1911], "Comment on the Course of Prices at Home and Abroad, 1890-1910," *Journal of the Royal Statistical Society* 75, 45-47.

Keynes, J.M. [1930], *A Treatise on Money* Vol. 1, New York: Harcourt, Brace and Company.

Kott, P.S. [1984], "A Superpopulation Theory Approach to the Design of Price Index Estimators with Small Sampling Biases," *Journal of Business and Economic Statistics* 2, 83-90.

Leontief, W. [1936], "Composite Commodities and the Problem of Index Numbers," *Econometrica* 4, 39-59.

March, L. [1921], "Les modes de mesure du mouvement général des prix," Metron 1, 57-91.

Marshall, A. [1887], "Remedies for Fluctuations of General Prices," *Contemporary Review* 51, 355-375.

McCarthy, P.J. [1961], "Sampling Considerations in the Construction of Price Indexes with particular Reference to the United States Consumer Price Index," pp. 197-232 in *The Price Statistics of the Federal Government*, George J. Stigler, chairman of commission and editor, New York: National Bureau of Economic Research.

Mills, F.C. [1927], *The Behavior of Prices*, New York: The National Bureau of Economic Research.

Mitchell, W.C. [1921], "The Making and Using of Index Numbers," pp. 7-114 in *Index Numbers of Wholesale Prices in the United States and Foreign Countries*, Revision of Bulletin 173, Bureau of Labor Statistics, Washington D.C.: Government Printing Office.

Mudgett, B.D. [1951], *Index Numbers*, New York: John Wiley and Sons.

Persons, W.M. [1928], *The Construction of Index Numbers*, Cambridge, Massachusetts: The Riverside Press.

Pollak, R.A. [1989], *The Theory of the Cost-of-Living Index*, Oxford: Oxford University Press.

Samuelson, P.A. and S. Swamy [1974], "Invariant Economic Index Numbers and Canonical Duality: Survey and Synthesis," *American Economic Review*, 24, 566-597.

Selvanathan, E.A. and D.S. Prasada Rao [1994], *Index Numbers: A Stochastic Approach*, University of Michigan Press.

Törnqvist, L. [1936], "The Bank of Finland's Consumption Price Index," *Bank of Finland Monthly Bulletin* 10, 1-8.

Walsh, C.M. [1901], *The Measurement of General Exchange Value*, New York: Macmillan and Co.

Walsh, C.M. [1921], *The Problem of Estimation*, London: P.S. King and Son.

Walsh, C.M. [1924], "Professor Edgeworth's Views on Index-Numbers," *Quarterly Journal of Economics* 38, 500-519.

Westergaard, H. [1890], *Die Grundzüge der Theorie der Statistik*, Jena: Gustav Fischer.

Chapter 12

ALTERNATIVE APPROACHES TO INDEX NUMBER THEORY

W. Erwin Diewert and Robert J. Hill[1]

1. Introduction

The present paper reconsiders the fundamental concepts of true and exact indexes, as these concepts are defined in the index number literature. These concepts form the bedrock of the economic approach to index number theory. A true index is the underlying target – the thing we are trying to measure. An empirically calculable index is exact when, under certain conditions, it exactly equals the true index. Also discussed briefly is the fundamental distinction between the axiomatic and economic approaches.

This paper was inspired by the 2008 *American Economic Review* paper of Van Veelen and van der Weide, henceforth VW. VW provide some interesting new perspectives on these issues.

VW have two main objectives. First, they attempt to give precise meanings to the concepts of exact and true indexes. A few definitions of a true index have been provided in the literature. VW propose some new and broader definitions that aim to include all of these as special cases. Some of the existing definitions, however, are more established than others. In particular, a broad consensus is already established in favor of the Konüs (1924) and Allen (1949) index definitions (which are closely related). One problem with VW's new definitions are that by seeking to embrace also the less established definition associated with Afriat (1981), they end up with outcomes that are quite abstract and differ considerably from the consensus position. Hence it might have been better if VW had introduced a new terminology rather than adding to the existing definitions of true indexes. VW also identify some problems with the standard definition of exactness, most notably that for some well known index number formulae the exactness property does not always hold for all strictly positive prices. This is an important finding. However, rather than changing the definition of exactness, we argue that what is required is a more careful analysis of the regularity region of exact indexes.

Second, VW reinterpret the distinction between the axiomatic and economic approaches. Their findings rely on the perceived limitations of the economic approach. In our opinion their reinterpretation is problematic. In our view, the economic approach is more flexible than the

[1] W. Erwin is with the Department of Economics at the University of British Columbia, Vancouver B.C., Canada, V6T 1Z1 and can be reached at diewert@econ.ubc.ca). Robert J. Hill is with the Department of Economics at the University of Graz, Universitaetsstrasse 15/F4, 8010 Graz, Austria and also with the School of Economics, University of New South Wales, Sydney 2052, Australia. He can be reached at robert.hill@uni-graz.at.

Citation: **W. Erwin Diewert and Robert J. Hill (2011), "Alternative Approaches to Index Number Theory," chapter 12, pp. 263-278 in W.E. Diewert, B.M. Balk, D. Fixler, K.J. Fox and A.O. Nakamura, *PRICE AND PRODUCTIVITY MEASUREMENT: Volume 6 -- Index Number Theory*. Trafford Press.**

© Alice Nakamura, 2011. Permission to link to, or copy or reprint, these materials is granted without restriction, including for use in commercial textbooks, with due credit to the authors and editors.

analysis of VW suggests, thus potentially invalidating their demarcations between the two approaches.

Nevertheless, even though we disagree with some of their conclusions, VW's method is novel and raises a number of issues relating to fundamental concepts of index number theory that deserve closer scrutiny. The differences distinguishing the various approaches are explained in the present paper in the context of earlier work of others.

2. Existing Definitions of True Indexes

The first concept of a true index was introduced into the literature in the price index context by Konüs (1924). The theory assumes that a consumer has well defined *preferences* over different combinations of N consumer commodities or items. The consumer's preferences over alternative possible nonnegative consumption vectors **q** are assumed to be representable by a nonnegative, continuous, increasing and concave utility function $U(\mathbf{q})$. It is further assumed that the consumer minimizes the cost of achieving the period t utility level $u^i \equiv U(\mathbf{q}^i)$ for periods (or situations) $i = 1,2$. Thus it is assumed that the observed (nonzero) period i consumption vector $\mathbf{q}^i$ solves the following *period i cost minimization problem*:

$$(1) \quad C(u^i,p^i) \equiv \min_q\{\mathbf{p}^i\mathbf{q} : U(\mathbf{q}) = u^i \equiv U(\mathbf{q}^i)\} = \mathbf{p}^i\mathbf{q}^i;\ i = 1,2$$

where the period t price vector $\mathbf{p}^i$ is strictly positive for $i = 1,2$ and $p^iq^i \equiv \sum_{n=1}^{N} p_n^i q_n^i$.

The Konüs (1924) family of *true cost of living indexes*, pertaining to two periods where the consumer faces the strictly positive price vectors $\mathbf{p}^0$ and $\mathbf{p}^1$ in periods 0 and 1 respectively, is defined as the ratio of the minimum costs of achieving the same utility level $u \equiv U(\mathbf{q})$ where **q** is a positive reference quantity vector. Thus, the Konüs true cost of living index with reference quantity vector **q** is defined as follows:

$$(2) \quad P_K(\mathbf{p}^1,\mathbf{p}^2,\mathbf{q}) \equiv C[U(\mathbf{q}),\mathbf{p}^2]/C[U(\mathbf{q}),\mathbf{p}^1].$$

We say that definition (2) defines a *family* of true price indexes because there is one such index for each reference quantity vector **q** chosen.

If the utility function U happens to be linearly homogeneous (or can be monotonically transformed into a linearly homogeneous function[2]), then definition (2) simplifies to[3]

$$(3) \quad P_K(\mathbf{p}^1,\mathbf{p}^2,\mathbf{q}) = \{U(\mathbf{q})C[1,\mathbf{p}^2]\}/\{U(\mathbf{q})C[1,\mathbf{p}^1]\} = c(\mathbf{p}^2)/c(\mathbf{p}^1),$$

[2] Shephard (1953) defined a *homothetic* function to be a monotonic transformation of a linearly homogeneous function. However, if a consumer's utility function is homothetic, we can always rescale it to be linearly homogeneous without changing consumer behavior. Hence in what follows, we will simply identify the homothetic preferences assumption with the linear homogeneity assumption.

[3] See Afriat (1972) or Pollak (1983).

where $c(\mathbf{p}^i)$ is the unit cost function $C(1,\mathbf{p}^i)$. Thus in the case of homothetic preferences, the family of true cost of living indexes collapses to a unit cost or expenditure ratio.

The second concept of a true index is the *Allen* (1949) *family of true quantity indexes*, which also uses the consumer's cost or expenditure function in order to define these true indexes. Again, it is assumed that the consumer engages in cost minimizing behavior in each period so that assumptions (1) hold. For each choice of a strictly positive reference price vector **p**, the Allen true quantity index, $Q_A(\mathbf{q}^1,\mathbf{q}^2,\mathbf{p})$ is defined as

$$(4) \qquad Q_A(\mathbf{q}^1,\mathbf{q}^2,\mathbf{p}) \equiv C[U(\mathbf{q}^2),\mathbf{p}]/C[U(\mathbf{q}^1),\mathbf{p}].$$

The basic idea of the Allen quantity index dates back to Hicks (1942) who observed that if the price vector **p** were held fixed and the quantity vector **q** is free to vary, then $C[U(\mathbf{q}),\mathbf{p}]$ is a perfectly valid cardinal measure of utility.[4]

As with the true Konüs cost of living, the Allen definition simplifies considerably if the utility function happens to be linearly homogeneous. In this case, (4) simplifies to:[5]

$$(5) \quad Q_A(\mathbf{q}^1,\mathbf{q}^2,\mathbf{p}) = \{U(\mathbf{q}^2)C[1,\mathbf{p}]\}/\{U(\mathbf{q}^1)C[1,\mathbf{p}]\} = U(\mathbf{q}^2)/U(\mathbf{q}^1).$$

Thus in the case of homothetic preferences (where preferences can be represented by a linearly homogeneous utility function), the family of Allen quantity indexes collapses to the utility ratio between the two situations.

Note that in the homothetic preferences case, the Allen quantity aggregate for the vector **q** is simply the utility level $U(\mathbf{q})$ and the Konüs price aggregate for the price vector **p** is the unit cost or expenditure $c(\mathbf{p})$.[6]

A third concept for a true index that appears frequently in the literature is the *Malmquist* (1953) *quantity index*. This index can be defined using only the consumer's utility function $U(\mathbf{q})$ but we will not study this index in any detail[7] since we will use the Allen quantity index concept to distinguish VW's concept of a true quantity index from true quantity indexes that have been defined in the literature.

A fourth and somewhat different concept for a true index is associated with Afriat (1981) and Dowrick and Quiggin (1997). If for each bilateral comparison subsumed within a broader multilateral comparison, the maximum of all the chained Paasche paths between the two periods or regions is less than the minimum of all the chained Laspeyres paths, then any index that for all pairs of bilateral comparisons lies between these so-called Afriat bounds is defined as true. The resulting index is true in the sense that there exists a nonparametric utility function that rationalizes the data and generates Konüs indexes that are identically equal to it. In our opinion, however, this alternative usage of the word "true" is misleading because it is at odds with a large literature that uses this term differently. VW seem to have been influenced by this fourth concept.

---

[4] Samuelson (1974) called this a money metric measure of utility.

[5] See Diewert (1981) for references to the literature.

[6] Shephard (1953) was an early pioneer in developing this theory of aggregation.

[7] See Diewert (1981) and Caves, Christensen and Diewert (1982) for additional material on this index concept.

Note that the concepts of a Konüs true price index and an Allen true quantity index are not immediately "practical" concepts since they assume that the functional form for the consumer's utility function (or its dual cost function) is known.[8] Note also that definition (2) for a true Konüs price index is defined for any given utility function U satisfying the regularity conditions listed above (with dual cost function C) for all strictly positive price vectors $\mathbf{p}^1$ and $\mathbf{p}^2$ and for all strictly positive reference quantity vectors $\mathbf{q}$. Similarly, definition (4) for a true Allen quantity index is defined for any given utility function U satisfying the regularity conditions listed above (again with dual cost function C), for all strictly positive quantity vectors $\mathbf{q}^1$ and $\mathbf{q}^2$ and for all strictly positive reference price vectors $\mathbf{p}$.

3. The VW System of True Quantity Indexes

Having reviewed the literature on bilateral true indexes, we are now ready to consider van Veelen and van der Weide's (VW's) (2008) multilateral concepts for a system of true quantity indexes. They assume that price and quantity data, $\mathbf{p}^m$ and $\mathbf{q}^m$ for $m = 1,\ldots,M$ are available for say M countries. Denote the N by M matrix of country price data by $\mathbf{P} \equiv [\mathbf{p}^1,\mathbf{p}^2,\ldots,\mathbf{p}^M]$ and the N by M matrix of country quantity data by $\mathbf{Q} \equiv [\mathbf{q}^1,\mathbf{q}^2,\ldots,\mathbf{q}^M]$. A *system of VW multilateral quantity indexes* is a set of M functions, $[F_1(\mathbf{P},\mathbf{Q}),F_2(\mathbf{P},\mathbf{Q}),\ldots,F_M(\mathbf{P},\mathbf{Q})] \equiv F(\mathbf{P},\mathbf{Q})$ where F is a vector valued function whose components are the country relative quantity aggregates, the $F_m(\mathbf{P},\mathbf{Q})$.

VW (2008; 1724-1725) provide three alternative definitions for the concept of a true quantity index in the multilateral context. These definitions are of interest, but none of their definitions coincide with the definitions for a true index that already exist in the literature. Their third definition of a true multilateral system is closest to what we think is the definition in the literature on true indexes and so we will repeat it here:

VW's Third Definition: The vector valued function $F(\mathbf{P},\mathbf{Q})$ is a *true system of multilateral quantity indexes* for the utility function U if for all data sets $(\mathbf{P},\mathbf{Q})$ that U rationalizes, the following inequalities hold:

(6) $$F_j(\mathbf{P},\mathbf{Q}) > F_k(\mathbf{P},\mathbf{Q}) \leftrightarrow U(\mathbf{q}^j) > U(\mathbf{q}^k) \quad \text{for all } 1 \le j,k \le M.$$

[8] However, if preferences have been estimated econometrically, then these true index number concepts do become "practical". Moreover, one can construct observable nonparametric bounds to these indexes and under certain conditions, these bounds again become practical; see Pollak (1983) and Diewert (1981) for expositions of this bounds approach to true indexes. The working paper version of Pollak (1983) was issued in (1971).

4. An Allen True Multilateral System of Quantity Indexes

Now we consider alternative definitions for a true multilateral system of quantity indexes based on the existing literature on true indexes. In the case where preferences are nonhomothetic, the *system of true Allen multilateral quantity indexes* consists of the following M functions where the positive price vector $\mathbf{p}$ is an arbitrarily chosen reference price vector:

$$(7)\qquad C(U(\mathbf{q}^1),\mathbf{p}),C(U(\mathbf{q}^2),\mathbf{p}),\ldots,C(U(\mathbf{q}^M),\mathbf{p})$$

where as usual, C is the cost or expenditure function that is dual to the utility function U. In the case where preferences are linearly homogeneous, then it is not necessary to specify a reference price vector and the *system of true multilateral quantity indexes* in this case becomes just the vector of country utilities:

$$(8)\qquad U(\mathbf{q}^1),U(\mathbf{q}^2),\ldots,U(\mathbf{q}^M).$$

Comparing (6), (7) and (8), it can be seen that (8) could be regarded as a special case of the VW definition; i.e., if we set $F_j(\mathbf{P},\mathbf{Q})$ equal to $U(\mathbf{q}^j)$, then it can be seen that the VW definition of a true multilateral index is equivalent to the definition of a true index that is in the traditional literature but of course, we need the homothetic preferences assumption in order to get this equivalence. In the general case where preferences are not homothetic, then it can be seen that the "traditional" definition of a true set of multilateral indexes (7) cannot be put into the VW form (6). Using the VW definition of a true system, their functions F_j depend on two matrices of observed price and quantity data, $\mathbf{P}$ and $\mathbf{Q}$. In contrast, using the Allen definition of a true system, the counterpart functions to the F_j depend only on the observed country j quantity vector $\mathbf{q}^j$ and the reference price vector $\mathbf{p}$. Thus, the definition that VW suggest differs from the literature's existing definition of a true index.[9]

5. Traditional Definitions for Exact Indexes

We now turn our attention to the concept of an exact index as it exists in the index number literature. We will first look at the concept of an exact index in the bilateral context; i.e., where we are comparing only two price quantity situations.

The concept of an exact index number formula dates back to the pioneering contributions of Konüs and Byushgens (1926) in the context of bilateral index number theory.[10] In the price index context, the theory starts with a given bilateral index number formula for an axiomatic price index P which is a function of the price and quantity vectors pertaining to two situations

[9] Of course, VW are entitled to make whatever definitions they find convenient. Our point is that they should carefully note that they are changing a well established definition of a true index.

[10] For additional material on the contributions of Konüs and Byushgens, see Afriat (1972) and Diewert (1976).

(time periods or countries) where the prices are positive, say $P(\mathbf{p}^1,\mathbf{p}^2,\mathbf{q}^1,\mathbf{q}^2)$. The function P is supposed to reflect the price level in, say, country 2 relative to the price level in country 1.

Now assume that the data $\mathbf{p}^1,\mathbf{p}^2,\mathbf{q}^1,\mathbf{q}^2$ pertaining to the two countries is generated by utility maximizing behavior on the part of an economic agent, where the utility function $U(\mathbf{q})$ is defined over the nonnegative orthant, and is nonnegative, linearly homogeneous, increasing (if all components of $\mathbf{q}$ increase) and concave. The unit cost function that is dual to $U(\mathbf{q})$ is $c(\mathbf{q})$.

The existing literature defines $P(\mathbf{p}^1,\mathbf{p}^2,\mathbf{q}^1,\mathbf{q}^2)$ to be an *exact price index* for $U(\mathbf{q})$ and its dual unit cost function $c(\mathbf{p})$ if

$$(9) \quad P(\mathbf{p}^1,\mathbf{p}^2,\mathbf{q}^1,\mathbf{q}^2) = c(\mathbf{p}^2)/c(\mathbf{p}^1).$$

The equality (9) is supposed to hold for all strictly positive price vectors $\mathbf{p}^1$ and $\mathbf{p}^2$ (and, of course, the corresponding $\mathbf{q}^1$ and $\mathbf{q}^2$ are assumed to be solutions to the cost minimization problems defined by (1).

There is an analogous theory for exact quantity indexes, $Q(\mathbf{p}^1,\mathbf{p}^2,\mathbf{q}^1,\mathbf{q}^2)$. Under the homothetic (actually linearly homogeneous) preference assumptions made in the previous paragraph and under the assumption that the data are consistent with cost minimizing behavior (1), the existing literature says that $Q(\mathbf{p}^1,\mathbf{p}^2,\mathbf{q}^1,\mathbf{q}^2)$ is an *exact quantity index* for $U(\mathbf{q})$ if

$$(10) \quad Q(\mathbf{p}^1,\mathbf{p}^2,\mathbf{q}^1,\mathbf{q}^2) = U(\mathbf{q}^2)/U(\mathbf{q}^1).$$

Many examples of exact bilateral price and quantity indexes are presented in Konüs and Byushgens (1926), Afriat (1972), Pollak (1983) and Diewert (1976).

Note that the above theory of exact quantity indexes does not guarantee that a given set of bilateral price and quantity vectors, $\mathbf{p}^1,\mathbf{p}^2,\mathbf{q}^1,\mathbf{q}^2$, are actually consistent with utility maximizing (or cost minimizing) behavior. The theory only says that given a particular functional form for U, given arbitrary strictly positive price vectors $\mathbf{p}^1$ and $\mathbf{p}^2$, and given that $\mathbf{q}^i$ solves the cost minimization problem (1) for $i = 1,2$, then a given function of 4N variables $Q(\mathbf{p}^1,\mathbf{p}^2,\mathbf{q}^1,\mathbf{q}^2)$ is an exact quantity index for the preferences defined by U if (10) holds. The problem that VW have uncovered with this definition has to do with the assumption that (10) holds for *all* strictly positive price vectors $\mathbf{p}^1$ and $\mathbf{p}^2$: this is not always the case for many of the commonly used exact index number formulae. We will return to this important point later.

The theory of exact quantity indexes in the multilateral situation is not as well developed as in the bilateral context. Note that in the bilateral context, an exact index number formula is exact for a utility ratio; i.e., the exact index number literature does not attempt to determine utility up to a cardinal scale but rather it only attempts to determine the utility ratio between the two situations. In the multilateral context, we could attempt to determine utility ratios relative to a numeraire country but then one country would be asymmetrically singled out to play the role of the numeraire country. Thus Diewert (1988) developed an axiomatic approach to multilateral quantity indexes that is based on a system of *country share functions*,

$[S_1(\mathbf{P},\mathbf{Q}),S_2(\mathbf{P},\mathbf{Q}),\ldots,S_M(\mathbf{P},\mathbf{Q})] \equiv S(\mathbf{P},\mathbf{Q})$ where S is a vector valued function whose components are the country relative quantity aggregates, the $S_m(\mathbf{P},\mathbf{Q})$, where each S_m represents the share of country m in world output (or consumption).[11] For all practical purposes, Diewert's system of share functions, $S(\mathbf{P},\mathbf{Q})$, is equivalent to VW's system of multilateral indexes, $F(\mathbf{P},\mathbf{Q})$.

Diewert (1999; 20-23) developed a theory of exact indexes in the multilateral context and we will explain his theory below.[12]

The basic assumption in Diewert's economic approach to multilateral indexes is that the country m quantity vector $\mathbf{q}^m$ is a solution to the following country m utility maximization problem:

$$(11) \quad \max_{\mathbf{q}}\{U(\mathbf{q}) : \mathbf{p}^m\mathbf{q} = \mathbf{p}^m\mathbf{q}^m\} = u^m,$$

for $m = 1,\ldots,M$ where $u^m \equiv U(\mathbf{q}^m)$ is the utility level for country m, $\mathbf{p}^m$ is the vector of strictly positive prices for outputs that prevail in country m for $m = 1,\ldots,M$, and U is a linearly homogeneous, increasing and concave utility function that is assumed to be the same across countries.[13] As usual, the utility function has a *dual unit cost or expenditure function* $c(\mathbf{p})$ which is defined as the minimum cost or expenditure required to achieve a unit utility level if the consumer faces the positive commodity price vector **p**.[14] Since consumers in country m are assumed to face the positive prices $\mathbf{p}^m$, we have the following equalities:

$$(12) \quad c(\mathbf{p}^m) \equiv \min_{\mathbf{q}}\{\mathbf{p}^m\mathbf{q} : U(\mathbf{q}) \geq 1\} \equiv P^m; \qquad m = 1,\ldots,M,$$

where P^m is the (unobserved) minimum expenditure that is required for country m to achieve a unit utility level when it faces its prices $\mathbf{p}^m$, which can also be interpreted as country m's PPP, or Purchasing Power Parity. Under the above assumptions, it can be shown that the country data satisfy the following equations:

$$(13) \quad \mathbf{p}^m\mathbf{q}^m = c(\mathbf{p}^m)U(\mathbf{q}^m) = P^m u^m; \qquad m = 1,\ldots,M.$$

In order to make further progress, we assume that the unit cost function $c(\mathbf{p})$ is once continuously differentiable with respect to the components of $\mathbf{p}$. Then Shephard's Lemma implies the following equations which relate the country m quantity vectors $\mathbf{q}^m$ to the country m price vectors $\mathbf{p}^m$ and utility levels u^m:

$$(14) \quad \mathbf{q}^m = \nabla c(\mathbf{p}^m)u^m; \qquad m = 1,\ldots,M.$$

---

[11] This multilateral axiomatic approach was further refined by Balk (1996) and Diewert (1999).

[12] See also Diewert (2008).

[13] Note that in Diewert's multilateral approach to exact indexes (1999) (2008), he did not consider the case of nonhomothetic preferences whereas in the bilateral case, Diewert (1976) did consider the nonhomothetic case.

[14] The unit cost function $c(\mathbf{p})$ is an increasing, linearly homogeneous and concave function in p for $p >> 0_N$.

Now we are ready to define the concept of exactness for a multilateral share system. We say that *the multilateral system of share functions*, $S(\mathbf{P},\mathbf{Q})$, *is exact* for the linearly homogeneous utility function U and its differentiable dual unit cost function c if the following system of equations is satisfied for all strictly positive country price vectors $\mathbf{P} \equiv [\mathbf{p}^1,\ldots,\mathbf{p}^M]$ and all positive utility levels $u^1,\ldots,u^M$:

$$(15)\qquad \frac{S_i(P,\nabla c(\mathbf{p}^1)u^1,\nabla c(\mathbf{p}^2)u^2,\ldots,\nabla c(\mathbf{p}^M)u^M}{S_j(P,\nabla c(\mathbf{p}^1)u^1,\nabla c(\mathbf{p}^2)u^2,\ldots,\nabla c(\mathbf{p}^M)u^M} = \frac{u^i}{u^j}; \qquad i,j=1,\ldots,M.$$

Thus an exact multilateral share system gives us exactly the underlying utilities up to an arbitrary positive scaling factor. Diewert (1999, 2008) gives many examples of exact multilateral systems. Diewert also goes on to define a *superlative multilateral system* to be an exact system where the underlying utility function U or dual unit cost function can approximate an arbitrary linearly homogeneous function to the second order around any given data point.

As in the bilateral case, VW have uncovered a problem with our definition (15) above for an exact multilateral system. The problem is that it is assumed that (15) holds for *all* strictly positive price vector matrices $\mathbf{P}$: this is not always the case for many of the commonly used exact index number formulae. We will return to this important point in the following section.

Van Veelen and van der Weide (2008; 1723) also give their definition of an exact multilateral system (which we will not reproduce here due to its complexity). However, their definition is rather far from the above definition of multilateral exactness that is out there in the literature.[15]

In our view, the "problem" with the VW definitions of true and exact indexes is that they are mixing up these theoretical concepts (as they exist in the index number literature) with a related but different question: namely, is a given set of, say, M price and quantity vectors consistent with utility maximizing behavior under various assumptions? This latter question is an interesting one and there is certainly room for more research in this area. However, some care should be taken to not redefine well established concepts as this research takes place.

6. The Problems Associated with Finding the Regularity Region for Exact Indexes

In the previous section, we noted that there can be a problem with some well known exact index number formulae in that the exactness property does not always hold for *all* strictly positive prices. We will explain the problem by giving two examples of exact index number formulae: one where there is no problem, and a second where there could be a problem.

[15] A major problem with their definition is this: the VW definition is conditional on a set of admissible price and quantity vectors D but this admissible set is not well specified. If we take the set D to be a single price quantity point for each country where the country price vectors are all equal to the same **p** and the country quantity vectors are all equal to the same **q**, and the function F treated countries in a symmetric manner, then F would be exact for any utility function.

Example 1: The Jevons Price Index

Suppose each consumer's unit cost function c has the following Cobb-Douglas functional form:[16]

$$(16) \quad c(\mathbf{p}) \equiv \beta \prod_{n=1}^{N} p_n^{\alpha_n} \,,$$

where the α_n are positive constants which sum to one and β is a positive constant. If we are comparing the level of prices in country 2 relative to country 1, then the Jevons (1865) price index, P_J is defined as the first line in (17):

$$(17) \quad \begin{aligned} P_J(\mathbf{p}^1,\mathbf{p}^2,\mathbf{q}^1,\mathbf{q}^2) &\equiv \prod_{n=1}^{N} (p_n^2/p_n^1)^{s_n^1} \\ &= c(\mathbf{p}^2)/c(\mathbf{p}^1), \end{aligned}$$

where the unit cost function c is defined by (16) and the nth expenditure share for country 1, s_n^1, is defined as $p_n^1 q_n^1/\mathbf{p}^1 \mathbf{q}^1$ for $n = 1,\ldots,N$. Thus under the assumption that consumers in the two countries have identical Cobb Douglas preferences $U(\mathbf{q})$ that are dual to the unit cost function c defined by (16) and assuming cost minimizing behavior on the part of consumers in both countries, then (17) tells us that the true Konüs price index between the two countries is *exactly* equal to the observable Jevons price index $P_J(\mathbf{p}^1,\mathbf{p}^2,\mathbf{q}^1,\mathbf{q}^2)$ and that *this equality will hold for all strictly positive price vectors* $\mathbf{p}^1$ and $\mathbf{p}^2$ for the two countries. The corresponding Jevons quantity index $Q_J(\mathbf{p}^1,\mathbf{p}^2,\mathbf{q}^1,\mathbf{q}^2)$ is defined as the expenditure ratio divided by the Jevons price index and we have the following equalities:

$$(18) \quad \begin{aligned} Q_J(p^1,p^2,q^1,q^2) &\equiv p^2q^2/p^1q^1 P_J(p^1,p^2,q^1,q^2) \\ &= U(q^2)/U(q^1). \end{aligned}$$

Thus under our assumptions on consumer behavior, (18) tells us that the true Allen quantity index between the two countries is *exactly* equal to the observable Jevons quantity index $Q_J(\mathbf{p}^1,\mathbf{p}^2,\mathbf{q}^1,\mathbf{q}^2)$ and again, this equality will hold for all strictly positive price vectors $\mathbf{p}^1$ and $\mathbf{p}^2$ for the two countries (with the corresponding quantity vectors $\mathbf{q}^1$ and $\mathbf{q}^2$ being endogenously determined). If we want to put the above results into the format that VW use, then the VW system of country quantity indexes could be defined as follows:

$$(19) \quad F_1(\mathbf{p}^1,\mathbf{p}^2,\mathbf{q}^1,\mathbf{q}^2) \equiv 1; \; F_2(\mathbf{p}^1,\mathbf{p}^2,\mathbf{q}^1,\mathbf{q}^2) \equiv Q_J(\mathbf{p}^1,\mathbf{p}^2,\mathbf{q}^1,\mathbf{q}^2).$$

Thus the theory of exact indexes works well under the assumption of Cobb Douglas preferences. However, note that the theory does not investigate whether consumers in the two countries actually minimize their costs of achieving their utility targets and whether they actually

[16] The Cobb Douglas case is treated in some detail by Afriat (1972) and Pollak (1983).

have Cobb Douglas preferences.[17] The theory is a conditional one: if consumers have certain preferences and if they engage in cost minimizing behavior, then their true price (or quantity) index will be exactly equal to a certain index number formula which in turn is a function of the observable price and quantity data pertaining to the two countries.

We turn to our second example of an exact index.

Example 2: The Fisher Price Index

Suppose each consumer has preferences that are dual to the following unit cost function:[18]

$$(20) \quad c(\mathbf{p}) \equiv (\mathbf{p}^T\mathbf{B}\mathbf{p})^{1/2}; \ \mathbf{B} = \mathbf{B}^T,$$

where **B** is an N by N symmetric matrix which has one positive eigenvalue (with a strictly positive eigenvector) and the remaining N−1 eigenvalues are negative or zero. The vector of first order partial derivatives of this unit cost function, $\nabla c(\mathbf{p})$, and the matrix of second order partials, $\nabla^2 c(\mathbf{p})$, are equal to the following expressions:

$$(21) \quad \nabla c(\mathbf{p}) = \mathbf{B}\mathbf{p}/(\mathbf{p}^T\mathbf{B}\mathbf{p})^{1/2};$$

$$(22) \quad \nabla^2 c(\mathbf{p}) = (\mathbf{p}^T\mathbf{B}\mathbf{p})^{-1/2}\{\mathbf{B} - \mathbf{B}\mathbf{p}(\mathbf{p}^T\mathbf{B}\mathbf{p})^{-1}\mathbf{p}^T\mathbf{B}\}.$$

At this point, we encounter the problem which we believe bothered VW; namely, that the unit cost function defined by (20) will generally not provide a representation of well behaved consumer preferences for all strictly positive price vectors **p**. In order for a unit cost function to provide a valid global representation of homothetic preferences, it must be a nondecreasing, linearly homogeneous and concave function over the positive orthant. However, in order for c to provide a valid local representation of preferences, we need only require that $c(\mathbf{p})$ be positive, nondecreasing, linearly homogeneous and concave over a convex subset of prices, say S, where S has a nonempty interior.[19] It is obvious that $c(\mathbf{p})$ defined by (20) is linearly homogeneous. The nondecreasing property will hold over S if the gradient vector $\nabla c(\mathbf{p})$ defined by (21) is strictly positive for $p \in S$ and the concavity property will hold if $\nabla^2 c(\mathbf{p})$ defined by (22) is a negative semidefinite matrix for $p \in S$. We will show how the regularity region S can be determined shortly but first, we will indicate why the $c(\mathbf{p})$ defined by (20) is a flexible functional form[20] since this explanation will help us to define an appropriate region of regularity.

---

[17] An implication of the Cobb Douglas preferences model is that the expenditure shares in the two countries should be equal; i.e., we should have $s_n^1 = s_n^2$ for $n=1,\cdots,N$. Of course, in the real world, these restrictions are unlikely to be satisfied.

[18] This is a special case of a functional form due to Denny (1974), which Diewert (1976; 131) called the quadratic mean of order r unit cost function, with r=2.

[19] See Blackorby and Diewert (1979) for more details on local representations of preferences using duality theory.

[20] A flexible functional form is one that is capable of providing a second order approximation to an arbitrary function in the class of functions under consideration; see Diewert (1976; 115) who introduced the term into the economics literature.

Let $\mathbf{p}^* >> 0_N$ be a strictly positive reference price vector and suppose that we are given an arbitrary unit cost function $c^*(\mathbf{p})$ that is twice continuously differentiable in a neighborhood around $\mathbf{p}^*$.[21] Let $\mathbf{q}^* \equiv \nabla c^*(\mathbf{p}) >> \mathbf{0}_N$ be the strictly positive vector of first order partial derivatives of $c^*(\mathbf{p}^*)$ and let $\boldsymbol{\Sigma} \equiv \nabla^2 c^*(\mathbf{p}^*)$ be the negative semidefinite symmetric matrix of second order partial derivatives of c^* evaluated at $\mathbf{p}^*$. Euler's Theorem on homogeneous functions implies that Σ satisfies the following matrix equation:

$$\boldsymbol{\Sigma}\mathbf{p}^* = \mathbf{0}_N. \tag{23}$$

In order to establish the flexibility of the c defined by (20), we need only show that there are enough free parameters in the **B** matrix so that the following equations are satisfied:

$$\nabla c(\mathbf{p}^*) = \mathbf{q}^*; \tag{24}$$

$$\nabla^2 c(\mathbf{p}^*) = \boldsymbol{\Sigma} \tag{25}$$

In order to prove the flexibility of c defined by (20), it is convenient to reparameterize the **B** matrix. Thus we now set **B** equal to:

$$\mathbf{B} = \mathbf{b}\mathbf{b}^T + \mathbf{A}, \tag{26}$$

where $\mathbf{b} >> \mathbf{0}_N$ is a positive vector and **A** is a negative semidefinite matrix which has rank equal to at most $N-1$ and it satisfies the following restrictions:

$$\mathbf{A}\mathbf{p}^* = \mathbf{0}_N. \tag{27}$$

Note that $\mathbf{b}\mathbf{b}^T$ in (26) is a rank one positive semidefinite matrix with $\mathbf{p}^{*T}\mathbf{b}\mathbf{b}^T\mathbf{p}^* = (\mathbf{b}^T\mathbf{p}^*)^2 > 0$ and **A** is a negative semidefinite matrix and satisfies $\mathbf{p}^{*T}\mathbf{A}\mathbf{p}^* = \mathbf{0}$. Thus it can be seen that **B** is a matrix with one positive eigenvalue and the other eigenvalues are negative or zero.

Substitute (21) into (24) in order to obtain the following equation:

$$\mathbf{q}^* = \mathbf{B}\mathbf{p}^*/(\mathbf{p}^{*T}\mathbf{B}\mathbf{p}^*)^{-1/2} \tag{28}$$

$$= [\mathbf{b}\mathbf{b}^T + \mathbf{A}]\mathbf{p}^*/(\mathbf{p}^{*T}[\mathbf{b}\mathbf{b}^T + \mathbf{A}]\mathbf{p}^*)^{-1/2} \quad \text{using (26)}$$

[21] Of course, in addition, we assume that c^* satisfies the appropriate regularity conditions for a unit cost function. Using Euler's Theorem on homogeneous functions, the fact that c^* is linearly homogeneous and differentiable at $\mathbf{p}^*$ means that the derivatives of c^* satisfy the following restrictions: $c^*(\mathbf{p}^*) = \mathrm{p}^{*T}\nabla c^*(\mathbf{p}^*)$ and $\nabla^2 c^*(\mathbf{p}^*)\mathbf{p}^* = \mathbf{0}_N$. The unit cost function c defined by (20) satisfies analogous restrictions at $\mathbf{p} = \mathbf{p}^*$. These restrictions simplify the proof of the flexibility of c at the point $\mathbf{p}^*$.

$$= \mathbf{b}\mathbf{b}^T\mathbf{p}^*/(\mathbf{p}^{*T}\mathbf{b}\mathbf{b}^T\mathbf{p}^*)^{1/2} \qquad \text{using (27)}$$

$$= \mathbf{b}\,.$$

Thus if we choose $\mathbf{b}$ equal to $\mathbf{q}^*$, equation (24) will be satisfied. Now substitute (22) into (23) and obtain the following equation:

$$(29)\quad \mathbf{\Sigma} = (\mathbf{p}^{*T}\mathbf{B}\mathbf{p}^*)^{-1/2}\{\mathbf{B} - \mathbf{B}\mathbf{p}^*(\mathbf{p}^{*T}\mathbf{B}\mathbf{p}^*)^{-1}\mathbf{p}^{*T}\mathbf{B}\}$$

$$= (\mathbf{p}^{*T}\mathbf{b}\mathbf{b}^T\mathbf{p}^*)^{-1/2}\{\mathbf{b}\mathbf{b}^T + \mathbf{A} - \mathbf{b}\mathbf{b}^T\mathbf{p}^*(\mathbf{p}^{*T}\mathbf{b}\mathbf{b}^T\mathbf{p}^*)^{-1}\mathbf{p}^{*T}\mathbf{b}\mathbf{b}^T \qquad \text{using (26) and (27)}$$

$$= (\mathbf{b}^T\mathbf{p}^*)^{-1}\mathbf{A} \qquad \text{using } \mathrm{b}^T\mathrm{p}^* > 0\,.$$

Thus if we choose $\mathbf{A}$ equal to $(\mathbf{b}^T\mathbf{p}^*)\mathbf{\Sigma}$, equation (25) will be satisfied and the flexibility of c defined by (20) is established.[22]

Now we can define the region of regularity for c defined by (20).[23] Consider the following set of prices:

$$(30)\quad \mathrm{S} \equiv \{\mathbf{p} : \mathbf{p} >> \mathbf{0}_N ; \mathbf{B}\mathbf{p} >> 0_N\}\,.$$

If $\mathbf{p} \in \mathrm{S}$, then it can be seen that $c(\mathbf{p}) = (\mathbf{p}^T\mathbf{B}\mathbf{p})^{1/2} > 0$ and using (21), $\nabla c(\mathbf{p}) >> \mathbf{0}_N$. However, it is much more difficult to establish the concavity of $c(\mathbf{p})$ over the set S. We first consider the case where the matrix $\mathbf{B}$ has full rank so that it has one positive eigenvalue and $N-1$ negative eigenvalues. Let $\mathbf{p} \in \mathrm{S}$ and using equation (22), we see that $\nabla^2 c(\mathbf{p})$ will be negative semidefinite if and only if the matrix $\mathbf{M}$ defined as:

$$(31)\quad \mathbf{M} \equiv \mathbf{B} - \mathbf{B}\mathbf{p}(\mathbf{p}^T\mathbf{B}\mathbf{p})^{-1}\mathbf{p}^T\mathbf{B}$$

is negative semidefinite. Note that $\mathbf{M}$ is equal to the matrix $\mathbf{B}$ plus the rank 1 negative semidefinite matrix $-\,\mathbf{B}\mathbf{p}(\mathbf{p}^T\mathbf{B}\mathbf{p})^{-1}\mathbf{p}^T\mathbf{B}$. $\mathbf{B}$ has one positive eigenvalue and the remaining eigenvalues are 0 or negative. Since $\mathbf{M}$ is $\mathbf{B}$ plus a negative semidefinite matrix, the eigenvalues of $\mathbf{M}$ cannot be greater than the eigenvalues of $\mathbf{B}$. Now consider two cases; the first case where $\mathbf{B}$ has one positive and $N-1$ negative eigenvalues and the second case where $\mathbf{B}$ has $N-1$ negative or zero eigenvalues in addition to its positive eigenvalue. Consider case 1, let $\mathbf{p} \in \mathrm{S}$ and calculate $\mathbf{M}\mathbf{p}$:

$$(32)\quad \mathbf{M}\mathbf{p} = [\mathbf{B} - \mathbf{B}\mathbf{p}(\mathbf{p}^T\mathbf{B}\mathbf{p})^{-1}\mathbf{p}^T\mathbf{B}]\mathbf{p} = \mathbf{0}_N\,.$$

The above equation shows that $\mathbf{p} \neq \mathbf{0}_N$ is an eigenvector of $\mathbf{M}$ that corresponds to a 0 eigenvalue. Now the addition of a negative semidefinite matrix to $\mathbf{B}$ can only make the $N-1$ negative eigenvalues of $\mathbf{B}$ more negative (or leave them unchanged) so we conclude that the

---

[22] We need to check that $\mathbf{A}$ is negative semidefinite (which it is since it is a positive multiple of the negative semidefinite substitution matrix $\mathbf{\Sigma}$) and that $\mathbf{A}$ satisfies the restrictions in (27), since we used these restrictions to derive (28) and the second line in (29). But $\mathbf{A}$ does satisfy (27) since $\mathbf{\Sigma}$ satisfies (23).

[23] The region of regularity can sometimes be extended to the closure of the set S.

addition of the negative semidefinite matrix $-\mathbf{Bp}(\mathbf{p}^T\mathbf{Bp})^{-1}\mathbf{p}^T\mathbf{B}$ to $\mathbf{B}$ has converted the positive eigenvalue of $\mathbf{B}$ into a zero eigenvalue and hence $\mathbf{M}$ is negative semidefinite. Case 2 follows using a perturbation argument.

We are now in a position to exhibit an index number formula that is consistent with the preferences that are dual to c defined by (20). Thus we again consider the two country case and define the Fisher (1922) ideal price index P_F as follows:

$$(33)\quad F_F(\mathbf{p}^1,\mathbf{p}^2,\mathbf{q}^1,\mathbf{q}^2) \equiv [\mathbf{p}^2\mathbf{q}^1\mathbf{p}^2\mathbf{q}^2/\mathbf{p}^1\mathbf{q}^1\mathbf{p}^1\mathbf{q}^2]^{1/2}.$$

Assume that c(**p**) is defined by (20) and S defined by (30) is nonempty. Suppose that consumers in the two countries have preferences U(**q**) that are locally dual to c(**p**) and that the country price vectors, $\mathbf{p}^1$ and $\mathbf{p}^2$, both belong to S. Finally, assume that consumers in both countries engage in cost minimizing behavior. Then, under all these hypotheses, we have the following equality:[24]

$$(34)\quad F_F(\mathbf{p}^1,\mathbf{p}^2,\mathbf{q}^1,\mathbf{q}^2) = c(\mathbf{p}^2)/c(\mathbf{p}^1).$$

Thus under our hypotheses, (34) tells us that the true Konüs price index between the two countries is *exactly* equal to the observable Fisher price index $P_F(\mathbf{p}^1,\mathbf{p}^2,\mathbf{q}^1,\mathbf{q}^2)$ and that *this equality will hold for all strictly positive price vectors* $\mathbf{p}^1$ and $\mathbf{p}^2$ for the two countries that belong to the set S. As was the case for the Jevons index, the corresponding Fisher quantity index $Q_F(\mathbf{p}^1,\mathbf{p}^2,\mathbf{q}^1,\mathbf{q}^2)$ can be defined as the expenditure ratio divided by the Fisher price index and we have the following equalities:

$$(35)\quad \begin{aligned} Q_F(\mathbf{p}^1,\mathbf{p}^2,\mathbf{q}^1,\mathbf{q}^2) &\equiv \mathbf{p}^2\mathbf{q}^2/\mathbf{p}^1\mathbf{q}^1 P_F(\mathbf{p}^1,\mathbf{p}^2,\mathbf{q}^1,\mathbf{q}^2) \\ &= U(\mathbf{q}^2)/U(\mathbf{q}^1), \end{aligned}$$

where U is the utility function that is locally dual to c.

What are we to make of the above results in the light of the criticisms of VW? We think that VW are justified in noting the limitations of the above theory of exact index numbers. Some of these limitations are:

- All consumers in all countries in the comparison are generally assumed to have the same homothetic preferences;
- There are no checks done on the data to see if consumers really are maximizing a common linearly homogeneous utility function and finally,
- The exact result (for example (34)) may not hold for all positive price vectors pertaining to the countries in the comparison but may only hold for a subset **S** of prices and it will usually be difficult to figure out exactly what this set is.

[24] See Diewert (1976; 134) and specialize his result to the case where r=2 .

Our response to these valid criticisms is the following one. We regard exact superlative indexes (indexes which are exact for flexible functional forms) as a useful screening device. There are an infinite number of index number formulae out there and it is useful to distinguish formulae that have "good" economic properties under at least some conditions.[25] However, it is always useful to consider other noneconomic approaches to index number theory and it is perhaps "ideal" if the different approaches lead to the same index number formulae. Thus North American price statisticians tend to favor the use of the Fisher or Törnqvist Theil (1967) bilateral formula because of the connection of these indexes with the economic approach to index number theory whereas European statisticians tend to favor the axiomatic approach or the stochastic approach[26] to index number theory. However, strong axiomatic justifications for the use of the Fisher index can be given[27] and a strong axiomatic for the Törnqvist Theil formula can also be given.[28] Furthermore, the Törnqvist Theil formula also does well from the viewpoint of the stochastic approach. Thus at the current state of index number theory, it appears that the Fisher and the Törnqvist Theil indexes are pretty good choices from multiple points of view.[29]

7. The Distinction Between the Axiomatic and Economic Approaches

Although VW make many good points in their note, they make some points which we find are problematical. Consider the following quotation:

> "In the literature, two approaches to index numbers are distinguished: the axiomatic approach and the economic approach. ... In Neary's paper the difference is described as one between an approach that does and an approach that does not assume that quantities arise from optimizing behavior. ... We will argue that a more accurate description is that the difference lies in whether or not optimizing agents, or representative consumers, are assumed to optimize the *same* utility function." Matthijs van Veelen and Roy van der Weide (2008; 1722).

We do not agree with the above assertions: it seems to us that the economic approach definitely takes prices as exogenous variables and treats quantities as being endogenous, whereas the axiomatic approach treats both prices and quantities as being exogenous. That is, we agree with the consensus view, as stated in Neary (2004) and Balk (2008), which can be traced back at least to Frisch (1936). We do not think it is particularly helpful to try and blend the two approaches (although in the end, they may lead to the same index number formulae).

VW argue that an advantage of the axiomatic approach is that it allows for heterogeneity in preferences. We take issue with this claim. The economic approach allows for heterogeneity

---

[25] There are even an infinite number of superlative formulae as indicated by Diewert (1976) but Hill (2006) noted that not all of these formulae are really that super.

[26] See Theil (1967), Selvanathan and Rao (1994) and Clements, Izan and Selvanathan (2006) on the stochastic approach to index numbers.

[27] See Diewert (1992) and Balk (1995).

[28] See Diewert (2004).

[29] This argument follows along similar arguments made by Diewert (1997). Also Diewert (1978) showed that the Fisher and Törnqvist Theil indexes will numerically approximate each other to the second order around an equal price and quantity point. Thus, in the time series context, it will often not matter which of these indexes is used.

too, across households in each period and in tastes across periods. Pollak (1980, 1981, 1983) and Diewert (1984, 2001) extend the Konüs true index to the case of heterogeneous agents. For example, a plutocratic Konüs true index is defined as follows:

$$(36) \quad P_K(\mathbf{p}^1, \mathbf{p}^2, \mathbf{q}_1, \ldots, \mathbf{q}_H) \equiv \sum_{h=1}^{H} C_h[U_h(\mathbf{q}_h), \mathbf{p}^2] / \sum_{h=1}^{H} C_h[U_h(\mathbf{q}_h), \mathbf{p}^1],$$

where h indexes the households.[30] A plutocratic Konüs true index measures the change in the minimum cost of each household h achieving its reference utility level $U_h(\mathbf{q}_h)$ from period 1 to period 2. The plutocratic Konüs true index as formulated in (36) therefore explicitly allows preferences to differ across households. Similarly, true indexes that allow preferences to change over time are derived by Caves, Christensen and Diewert (1982) and Balk (1989). In short, the economic approach is more flexible than VW's analysis suggests.

8. Conclusion

Van Veelen and van der Weide (2008) have raised a number of contentious issues that deserve closer scrutiny. While we take issue with some of their findings, we commend them for providing a fresh perspective on an old topic.

References

Afriat, S.N. (1972), "The Theory of International Comparisons of Real Income and Prices", pp. 13-69 in *International Comparisons of Prices and Outputs*, D.J. Daly (ed.), Chicago: University of Chicago Press.

Afriat, S.N. (1981), "On the Constructability of Consistent Price Indices between Periods Simultaneously," in *Essays in the Theory and Measurement of Consumer Behaviour in Honour of Sir Richard Stone*, ed. Angus S. Deaton, 133-161, Cambridge University Press.

Allen, R.G.D. (1949), "The Economic Theory of Index Numbers", *Economica* 16, 197-203.

Balk, B.M (1989), "Changing Consumer Preferences and the Cost of Living Index: Theory and Nonparametric Expressions", *Journal of Economics* 50:2, 157-169.

Balk, B.M. (1995), "Axiomatic Price Index Theory: A Survey", *International Statistical Review* 63, 69-93.

Balk, B.M. (1996), "A Comparison of Ten Methods for Multilateral International Price and Volume Comparisons", *Journal of Official Statistics* 12, 199-222.

Balk, B.M. (2008), Price and Quantity Index Numbers: Models for Measuring Aggregate Change and Difference, Cambridge University Press.

Blackorby, C. and W.E. Diewert (1979), "Expenditure Functions, Local Duality and Second Order Approximations", *Econometrica* 47, 579-601.

Caves, D., L.R. Christensen and W.E. Diewert (1982), "The Economic Theory of Index Numbers and the Measurement of Input, Output, and Productivity', *Econometrica* 50, 1392-1414.

Clements, K.W., H.Y. Izan and E.A. Selvanathan (2006), "Stochastic Index Numbers: A Review," *International Statistical Review* 74, 235-270.

Denny, M. (1974), "The Relationship between Functional Forms for the Production System", *Canadian Journal of Economics* 7, 21-31.

Diewert, W.E. (1976), "Exact and Superlative Index Numbers", *Journal of Econometrics* 4, 114-145.

[30]Pollak (1989) and Diewert (2001) also consider generalizations that allow for environmental variables. An index that allows for changes in environmental variables is sometimes referred to as unconditional, while one that does not is referred to as conditional.

Diewert, W.E. (1978), "Superlative Index Numbers and Consistency in Aggregation", *Econometrica* 46, 883-900.

Diewert, W.E. (1981), "The Economic Theory of Index Numbers: A Survey", pp. 163-208 in *Essays in the Theory and Measurement of Consumer Behaviour in Honour of Sir Richard Stone*, edited by A. Deaton, Cambridge University Press.

Diewert, W.E. (1984), "Group Cost of Living Indexes: Approximations and Axiomatics," *Methods of Operations Research* 48, 23-45.

Diewert, W.E. (1988), "Test Approaches to International Comparisons", pp. 67-86 in *Measurement in Economics: Theory and Applications of Economic Indices*, W. Eichhorn (ed.), Heidelberg: Physica-Verlag.

Diewert, W.E. (1992), "Fisher Ideal Output, Input and Productivity Indexes Revisited", *Journal of Productivity Analysis* 3, 211-248.

Diewert, W.E. (1997), "Commentary on Mathew D. Shapiro and David W. Wilcox: Alternative Strategies for Aggregating Prices in the CPI", *The Federal Reserve Bank of St. Louis Review,* Vol. 79:3, 127-137.

Diewert, W.E. (1999), "Axiomatic and Economic Approaches to International Comparisons", pp. 13-87 in *International and Interarea Comparisons of Income, Output and Prices*, A. Heston and R.E. Lipsey (eds.), Studies in Income and Wealth, Volume 61, University of Chicago Press.

Diewert, W.E. (2001), "The Consumer Price Index and Index Number Purpose," *Journal of Economic and Social Measurement* 27, 167-248.

Diewert, W.E. (2004), "A New Axiomatic Approach to Index Number Theory", Discussion Paper 04-05, Department of Economics, University of British Columbia, Vancouver, Canada, V6T 1Z1.

Diewert, W.E. (2008), "New Methodological Developments for the International Comparison Program," Discussion Paper 08-08, Department of Economics, University of British Columbia, Vancouver Canada, V6T 1Z1, September.

Dowrick, S. and J. Quiggin (1997), "True Measures of GDP and Convergence," *American Economic Review* 87, 41-64.

Fisher, I. (1922), *The Making of Index Numbers*, Boston: Houghton-Mifflin.

Frisch, R. (1936), "Annual Survey of General Economic Theory: The Problem of Index Numbers," *Econometrica* 4, 1-39.

Hicks, J.R. (1942), "Consumers' Surplus and Index Numbers", *The Review of Economic Studies* 9, 126-137.

Hill, R.J. (2006), "Superlative Indexes: Not All of Them are Super", *Journal of Econometrics* 130, 25-43.

Jevons, W.S. (1865), "Variations of Prices and the Value of Currency since 1762", *Journal of the Royal Statistical Society* 28, 294-325.

Konüs, A.A. (1924), "The Problem of the True Index of the Cost of Living", translated in *Econometrica* 7, (1939), 10-29.

Konüs, A.A. and S.S. Byushgens (1926), "K probleme pokupatelnoi cili deneg", *Voprosi Konyunkturi* 2, 151-172.

Malmquist, S. (1953), "Index Numbers and Indifference Surfaces", *Trabajos de Estatistica* 4, 209-242.

Neary, J. P. (2004), "Rationalizing the Penn World Table: True Multilateral Indices for International Comparison of Real Income," *American Economic Review* 94(5), 1411-1428.

Pollak, R.A. (1980), "Group Cost-of-Living Indexes", *American Economic Review*70, 273-278.

Pollak, R.A. (1981), "The Social Cost-of-Living Index", *Journal of Public Economics* 15, 311-336.

Pollak, R.A. (1983), "The Theory of the Cost-of-Living Index", pp. 87-161 in *Price Level Measurement*, W.E. Diewert and C. Montmarquette (eds.), Ottawa: Statistics Canada; reprinted as pp. 3-52 in R.A. Pollak, *The Theory of the Cost-of-Living Index*, Oxford: Oxford University Press, 1989.

Pollak, R.A. (1989), "The Treatment of the Environment in the Cost–of–Living Index", pp. 181-185 in R.A. Pollak, *The Theory of the Cost-of-Living Index*, Oxford: Oxford University Press.

Samuelson, P.A. (1974), "Complementarity—An Essay on the 40th Anniversary of the Hicks-Allen Revolution in Demand Theory", *Journal of Economic Literature* 12, 1255-1289.

Selvanathan, E.A. and D.S. Prasada Rao (1994), *Index Numbers: A Stochastic Approach*, Ann Arbor: The University of Michigan Press.

Shephard, R.W. (1953), *Cost and Production Functions*, Princeton University Press.

Theil, H. (1967), *Economics and Information Theory*, North-Holland.

Van Veelen, M. and R. van der Weide (2008), "A Note on Different Approaches to Index Number Theory", *American Economic Review* 98 (4), 1722-1730.

Chapter 13
CHAIN PRICE AND VOLUME AGGREGATES FOR THE SYSTEM OF NATIONAL ACCOUNTS

Andrew Baldwin[1]

1. Summary and Introduction

This paper constitutes a critique of the recommendations for changing the System of National Accounts 1968 (SNA68) contained in the Systems of National Accounts 1993 (SNA93) on volume measures of gross domestic product (GDP). These recommendations are contained in Chapter XVI of the SNA93, authored by the distinguished English economist Peter Hill. Basically, this paper endorses the SNA93 recommendation for annual chain linking, but not its support for chain Fisher aggregates, nor, as a second-best solution, chain Laspeyres aggregates. I argue it is both feasible and desirable to calculate chain fixed-price aggregates that do not have the dangerous propensity to chain drift exhibited by chain Laspeyres aggregates. And these fixed-price aggregates can be calculated as direct series for the most recent period and so be additive over commodities, industries or regions, unlike their chain Fisher counterparts.

Perhaps the best way to summarize the present paper is to list Hill's five recommendations (H1-H5), followed, one by one, by my proposed amendments (B1-B5):

(H1) Original: *The preferred measure of year-to-year movements of GDP volume is a Fisher volume index; changes over longer periods being obtained by chaining; i.e., by cumulating the year-to-year movements.*

(B1) Amended: The preferred measure of year-to-year movements of GDP volume is an Edgeworth-Marshall[2] volume aggregate (see formula (4-1) below) changes over longer periods being obtained by chaining; i.e., by cumulating the year-to-year movements.

---

[1] The author is with Statistics Canada and can be reached at Andy.Baldwin@statcan.ca. The author acknowledges and thanks Ludwig von Auer of the University of Magdeburg, Bert Balk of Statistics Netherlands, Michel Chevalier of Statistics Canada, Christopher Ehemann and Marshall Reinsdorf of the U.S. BEA, and Amanda Tuke of the U.K.'s Office of National Statistics for helpful information and other input. Special thanks go to Jörgen Dalén, formerly with Statistics Sweden and Manfred Krtscha of the University of Karlsruhe for their papers, which have had such an influence on this one.

[2] I have referred to index formulae by their inventors. For formulae with multiple inventors, they are listed in alphabetical order without any attempt to assign a primacy among them. Thus, Edgeworth-Marshall instead of Edgeworth or Marshall-Edgeworth, Montgomery-Vartia instead of VartiaI, Sato-Vartia instead of VartiaII, and Bowley-Sidgwick instead of Sidgwick. Bowley was actually a propogandist rather than a discoverer of the Bowley-Sidgwick formula, but he should share the credit since Sidgwick did little more than note the possibility of an

Citation: **Andrew Baldwin (2011), "Chain Price and Volume Aggregates for the System of National Accounts," chapter 13, pp. 279-316 in**
W.E. Diewert, B.M. Balk, D. Fixler, K.J. Fox and A.O. Nakamura,
PRICE AND PRODUCTIVITY MEASUREMENT: Volume 6 -- Index Number Theory. Trafford Press.

© Alice Nakamura, 2011. Permission to link to, or copy or reprint, these materials is granted without restriction, including for use in commercial textbooks, with due credit to the authors and editors.

(H2) Original: *The preferred measure of year-to-year inflation for GDP is, therefore, a Fisher price index; price changes over longer periods being obtained by chaining the year-to-year price movements: the measurement of inflation is accorded equal priority with the volume movements.*

(B2) Amended: The preferred measure of year-to-year inflation for GDP is an Edgeworth-Marshall price index (see formula (7-1) below).

However, as the Edgeworth-Marshall formula does not satisfy the strong factor reversal test, direct and chain implicit price indexes should also be calculated and published. The direct implicit price index should be based on the ratio of the expenditure series at current prices to the expenditure series at constant prices (i.e., the weighted average of prices over two years).

For highly cyclical commodities, a modification of the Edgeworth-Marshall formula will be required for the inflation indicator, and the basket reference period can span three to five years as required. (This may also be necessary for the cyclical components of the GDP volume measure.) To accommodate seasonal commodities, the price index could incorporate a seasonal weighting pattern, preferably using the Rothwell or Balk formula.

(H3) Original: *Chain indexes that use Laspeyres volume indices to measure year-to-year movements in the volume of GDP and Paasche price indices to measure year-to-year inflation provide acceptable alternatives to Fisher indices.*

(B3) Amended: Countries too small or too poor to implement annual-link chain measures should calculate chain Laspeyres volume aggregates, with rebasing of these every five years, the base year of each five-year span being its central year. In addition to the chain Paasche price indexes that would be the counterpart of these chain volume aggregates, they should also calculate chain Laspeyres price indexes which would also be rebased every five years, with the central year of the five-year span serving as the basket reference year.

(H4) Original: *The chain indices for total final expenditures, imports and GDP cannot be additively consistent whichever formula is used, but this need not prevent time series of values being compiled by extrapolating base year values by the appropriate chain indices.*

(B4) Amended: The chain volume aggregates for total final expenditures, imports and GDP will continue to be additive because they will be linked backward and not forward.

(H5) *Original: Chain indices should only be used to measure year-to-year movements and not quarter to quarter movements.*

(B5) Amended: Chain volume aggregates should be calculated both annually and quarterly (or monthly). The fixed-price structure of the volume aggregates (i.e., using average prices over two years) will apply to both annual and quarterly (or monthly) series, ensuring that meaningful measures of quarterly (or monthly) volume change can be derived for all consecutive quarters (or months) for the direct series, and for all but the Q4-to-Q1 movements (December-to-January movements) of the chain series. Similarly, chain volume price indexes should be calculated both annually and quarterly (or monthly). The fixed-basket structure of the price indexes (i.e. using a two-year basket) will apply to both annual and quarterly (or monthly) series, ensuring that

---

arithmetic cross between the Laspeyres and Paasche formulae, whereas Bowley somewhat advocated it. Auer (2004) and others refer to the Bowley-Sidgwick formula as the Drobisch formula, but I follow Diewert (1993) in attributing it to these two English-speaking economists. However, the Fisher formula remains the Fisher formula out of deference to established custom, even though others, including Bowley, wrote about it before he did.

meaningful measures of quarterly (or monthly) price change can be derived for all consecutive quarters (or months) for the direct series, and for all but the Q4-to-Q1 movements (December-to-January movements) of the chain series.

However direct volume aggregates (fixed-basket price indexes) would also be calculated over longer periods of up to 10-11 years, and linked backward to form chain series whose base prices (basket) would change every five years, with the base period (basket) always representing the central years of the five-year span. These series would provide meaningful measures of quarterly or month change when the chain measures failed to do so.

The most controversial of the proposed amendments may well be (A1) and (A2). Some economists would reject the Edgeworth-Marshall formula because it is not exact for any aggregator function, i.e. it is not a "superlative" formula, like the Fisher formula. If the choice of a formula must be limited to those defined as "superlative", then (A1) and (A2) should be rewritten to replace the Edgeworth-Marshall formula with the linear Walsh formula[3]. The Walsh formula is exact for the Generalized Linear aggregator function. Because of its matrix consistency properties, it would still be a better choice than the Fisher formula. This has been suggested by Diewert (1996) in his critique of Hill's paper.

However, the Edgeworth-Marshall formula would seem to be the better choice as, unlike the Walsh formula (or the Fisher formula), it respects the property of transactions equality (i.e., the importance of a transaction in the formula does not depend on the period in which it occurs.) Also, unlike the Walsh formula, it does not discard commodities from a volume aggregate if the price goes to zero from a positive price or vice-versa, nor does it discard commodities from a price index if the quantity goes to zero from a positive quantity or vice-versa.

2. The SNA68 Volume Measures

In the 1968 System of National Accounts (SNA68) the prescribed volume measures are Laspeyres volume aggregates. These are direct measures over the recent period, but linked backward prior to the base year. Thus additive consistency is preserved for the most recent history of the series, but not prior to the base year.

Eight features of the direct Laspeyres volume aggregates are worthy of note.

First, they are expenditure totals and not index numbers, with the formula:

$$\sum p_0 q_t .$$

Thus, they are Laspeyres volume aggregates, rather than Laspeyres volume indexes. (Here and elsewhere, summation is assumed to be over commodities unless otherwise indicated.)

The Laspeyres volume aggregates can be defined as measuring period t expenditures at base year 0 prices. When these aggregates are indexed to base year expenditures, the result is a Laspeyres volume index given by

[3] Hereafter this is referred to simply as the Walsh formula; there is also a logarithmic Walsh formula, but it is not discussed in this paper.

$$Q^L_{t/0} = \sum p_0 q_t / \sum p_0 q_0 .$$

In actual statistical practice, it is more common to publish expenditure series at constant prices than Laspeyres volume index values.[4]

Second, for each commodity, the base year price is defined as a unit value ($\bar{p}_0$) so that when multiplied by the corresponding quarterly quantities for the base year and aggregated over quarters ($q = 1,\ldots,4$), the total will equal base year expenditure; i.e.,

$\sum_q p_{0q} q_{0q} = \sum_q \bar{p}_0 q_{0q}$, which requires that

$$(2\text{-}0) \quad \bar{p}_0 = \sum_q p_{0q} q_{0q} / \sum_q q_{0q} = \sum_q p_{0q} \left(q_{0q} / \sum_q q_{0q} \right).$$

Thus, the base price is calculated as the unit value of all base year transactions, which is a weighted arithmetic mean of quarterly prices with quarterly quantities used as the weights. This is the uniquely optimal estimate of the average price for any homogeneous commodity, a point that should be underlined.[5]

It can be seen that if the production of a commodity were completely inelastic with respect to price, all of the quantities in (2.0) would be equal and the unit value would reduce to an arithmetic mean of prices, which always exceeds the geometric mean of prices.

As a mean of quarterly base prices weighted by quantities, the base year unit value can also be interpreted as a harmonic mean of prices weighted by expenditures; that is:

$$(2.1) \quad \bar{p}_0 = 1 / \sum_q w_{0q} (1/p_{0q}), \text{ where } w_{0j} = p_{0q} q_{0q} / \sum_q p_{0q} q_{0q} = v_{0q} / \sum_q v_{0q} .$$

In (2.1), $v_{0q} = p_{0q} q_{0q}$ denotes the transactions value. It can be seen that if production of the commodity were unit-elastic with respect to price, so that whatever the change in price, the same revenues were generated, the base year unit value would reduce to a simple harmonic mean of quarterly base prices, which is always less than the geometric mean of base prices. Note, in particular, that the unit value is not consistently higher or lower than the geometric mean; it is higher for commodities with higher price elasticities and lower for commodities with lower price elasticities.

---

[4] Until recently, the only important volume index that used to be published by the Canadian System of National Accounts (CSNA) was the index of industrial production. Even for this series, a chain volume aggregate, rather than a volume index, is now published instead.

[5] Suppose that exactly the same transactions occurred two years in a row at the same set of prices. The same amount of money would be required for these expenditures in both years. Suppose further that the budget for year 1 is established as the number of units purchased multiplied by the average price in year 0. If one chose an average price less than the unit value, the budget would be inadequate to make all the transactions required. If one chose a price greater than the unit value, then the budgeted funds would be more than needed. The resulting surplus would be greater the larger the discrepancy between the unit value and the overestimated annual price. The same would be true if there were an increase in the volume of transactions but the seasonal profile of volumes and prices remained constant.

In actual national accounting practice, one would rarely have actual price and quantity data to work with. Usually one would be dealing with value series and independently derived price indexes that serve as deflators. In this case, what would replace (2.1) is:

$$(2.2) \quad \sum_q v_{0q} = \sum_q v_{0q} / P_{0q/0},$$

where $P_{0q/0}$ is the price index for a given quarter of year 0 with base year 0. Generally, the identity in (2.2) does not hold and it must be forced; i.e., the quarterly values for the base year must be prorated so that the value for quarter q is given by

$$(2.3) \quad f \times v_{0q} / P_{0q/0}$$

where $f = \sum_q v_{0q} / (\sum_q v_{0q} / P_{0q/0})$.

(Strictly speaking, the adjustment factor f should be applied to all quarterly values, but in practice it is usually applied only to the base year quarterly values, creating a discontinuity between the base year estimates and the estimates to follow that is presumed to be slight.)

<u>Third</u>, the ratio of the expenditures at current prices to the expenditures at constant prices provides an implicit price index that has the Paasche formula:

$$P^P_{t/0} = \sum p_t q_t / \sum p_0 q_t.$$

This can serve as a price indicator for GDP. In production, Paasche price indexes offer official statisticians the choice of calculating volume aggregates directly or by deflating using the Paasche deflator. More specifically, volume aggregates have usually been calculated indirectly as seasonally adjusted series at current prices deflated by raw or seasonally adjusted Paasche price indexes.

However, the importance of this association of Laspeyres volume aggregates with Paasche price indexes should not be exaggerated. A Paasche price index is a poor indicator of price change except for binary or two-period comparisons since quarterly price changes are always distorted by changes from one basket to another. In Canada, dissatisfaction with the Paasche deflators led to the development of Laspeyres price measures, and then to the use of chain Laspeyres series, years before the current chain volume measures were introduced.

<u>Fourth</u>, there is additivity of the components of GDP in the volume aggregates, as one would expect, since they are simply the expenditures of each quarter at a common set of prices. That is, expenditures on consumer goods and services sum to total consumer expenditure, construction expenditures and investment in machinery and equipment sum to gross fixed capital formation, and so forth.

There is also additivity of the monthly or quarterly GDP estimates, which sum to equal the annual estimates, and the same applies for all major components of GDP.

Finally, there is at least the possibility with this kind of structure of having additivity of provincial or regional GDP estimates to the national total. In Canada, this was imposed. Hence, the provincial GDP estimates by industry at 1997 prices sum to the all-Canada totals. This multi-dimensional additivity over commodities, industries, months or quarters, and regions can be characterized as *matrix consistency*. Thus, a desirable feature of GDP volume aggregates is additivity along any dimension of a matrix of values at constant prices.

Fifth, the change between any two quarters or any two years of the volume aggregates satisfies the *proportionality test*: i.e., if all of the quantities in a given period are k times the corresponding quantities in the comparison period, then the volume aggregate shows a k-fold increase between the two periods. As a special case of this, the volume aggregates satisfy the identity test. Hence, if all the quantities in a given period are identical with the corresponding quantities in the comparison period, then the level of the volume aggregate will be the same in the given period as in the comparison period. (The identity test is just the proportionality test for k=1.) This is a consequence of all expenditures for all periods being converted to the same set of fixed prices.

Sixth, the Laspeyres volume aggregates are strictly or strongly consistent in aggregation; that is, they can be equally well calculated in a single stage from basic components, or in two stages by first using the basic components and then using higher level subaggregates, with the same formula applied at both stages (see also the appendix).

Seventh, the Laspeyres volume aggregates have the new commodity property alluded to by Irving Fisher in *The Making of Index Numbers*:

> "The introduction of a new commodity ought, evidently, to change, in some degree, any price index which pretends to be a sensitive expression of the data from which it is computed (*unless,* of course, *the new commodity happens to have a price relative exactly equal to the index number*)" [emphasis added].[6]

If a new commodity is added to the volume aggregate with the identical volume movements as the aggregate, the movement of the aggregate will not change. Although this seems like a banal property, it is quite useful in actual statistical work since frequently one may have weighting information of some kind for a new commodity for a reference year, but lack detailed price or quantity data. It is possible to create a volume series for a new commodity, explicitly or implicitly by imputing the group movement in a straightforward way. Of course, given detailed data for a new commodity, one would immediately know if it would push the aggregate series up or drag it down. This is quite important for agencies concerned with making their GDP by industry and GDP by expenditure estimates mesh, where the implementation of a methodology change in a given revision cycle could depend on whether it tended to increase or decrease an aggregate growth rate, and decisions are often made under severe time pressure.

Eighth, SNA68 recommended rebasing of the volume aggregates every five or ten years. Although the manual is vague about the mechanics involved, it clearly favoured retaining the same movements of historical series when the relative price structure was updated. It also favoured, if not quite so clearly, calculating volume aggregates at new base year prices starting from the base year itself, which became the Canadian practice for all rebasings that followed the publication of the SNA68 manual until the CSNA moved to chain Fisher estimates in 2001. For example, the 1961 base year was introduced for the period 1961 and after in the second quarter of 1969. Note that although quarterly estimates for the base year would be at base year prices, the annual benchmark estimates would reflect the previous base year. In terms of the previous

[6] Quoted by Krtscha (1984, p.136).

example, while CSNA calculated a quarterly series at 1961 prices from 1961 forward, the movement of the annual volume series for 1961 was based on 1957 prices. It should be noted that until the publication of the SNA68 manual, the CSNA had always applied the new base earlier than the base year itself, the 1949 base being applied starting in 1947 and the 1957 base starting in 1956.

Introducing a new base year only in the following year, in terms of the annual movement, certainly reduces the magnitude of the revisions of the volume aggregate series, but generally at a heavy price in terms of representativeness. Even with updatings of the base year every five years, the finalized estimates for the last year of a span will be five years removed from their reference year,.

The historical volume aggregates would be linked to the new volume aggregates using a rebasing factor for each series as follows:

$$(\sum p_5q_5/\sum p_0q_5)\times\sum p_0q_t; \quad t=0,1,\ldots,4.$$

Hence expenditures at year 0 prices are linked to the new series at year 5 prices. Typically, there would be a loss of additivity when this rebasing was carried out for the historical period (e.g., the sum of expenditures on consumer services and consumer goods would no longer equal total consumer expenditure). In Canada, this was handled with an elaborate set of adjusting entries that re-establish additivity between the sum of components and their aggregate, although it would probably have been simpler just to publish a note of warning that due to chain linking, additivity did not hold.[7]

3. Major Weaknesses of the SNA68 Measures

The principal weakness of the SNA68 methodology was obvious to its framers even at the time it was promulgated. In a rapidly changing world, a set of constant prices can get out of date even after a five-year interval, and will be unrepresentative of the economy whose output it is supposed to measure. Thus, SNA68-type estimates frequently lack the quality of representativeness. Also, given a negative correlation between prices and quantities, there will tend to be a positive bias in direct Laspeyres volume measures, and this bias will be more serious the longer a single set of constant prices is retained. For this reason, those who decided on the procedures for the SNA68 considered the possibility of chaining volume series every year instead of every five or ten years, but finally rejected the idea for general application because of its onerous data requirements.

The SNA68 manual did give lukewarm support to the idea of calculating Fisher index numbers for the years between the new base year and the old base year, but this was probably never done in any country and certainly not in Canada. The problem was that, for example, between 1961 and 1971, two successive base years of the CSNA, one could only calculate one true Fisher volume index number, for 1971 as compared to 1961. One could of course, calculate index numbers for the intervening years from 1962 to 1970, that would also reflect a geometric

[7] This was the practice for the quarterly estimates of GDP by expenditure category. There were never any adjusting entries published for the monthly estimates of GDP by industry.

mean of indexes at 1961 prices and indexes at 1971 prices, but it didn't make any sense to give 1961 prices and 1971 prices the same influence on volume movements in 1962 as compared to 1961, when the price structure in 1962 was so much more like that of 1961.

A second major weakness of SNA68 is that the Laspeyres formula does not pass the time reversal test; i.e., the Laspeyres quantity index for year t with base year 0 is not equal to the reciprocal of the Laspeyres quantity index for year t with base year t as required by the time reversal test; i.e.,

$$Q^L_{t/0} = \frac{\sum p_0 q_t}{\sum p_0 q_0} \neq 1/Q^L_{0/t} = 1/\frac{\sum p_t q_0}{\sum p_t q_t} = \frac{\sum p_t q_t}{\sum p_t q_0} = Q^P_{t/0}$$

In fact, the reciprocal of the Laspeyres quantity index is the Paasche volume index, which shows the dual nature of the two formulae, one being the complement of the other. Suppose that prices and quantities, after changing in year 1, revert to their previous year 0 values in year 2. A chain Laspeyres volume index with a link at year 1 would show:

$$\frac{\sum p_0 q_1}{\sum p_0 q_0} \times \frac{\sum p_1 q_2}{\sum p_1 q_1} = \frac{\sum p_0 q_1}{\sum p_0 q_0} \times \frac{\sum p_1 q_0}{\sum p_1 q_1} \neq 1$$

Generally one would expect prices and quantities to be negatively correlated. The import of this is that a chain Laspeyres volume index may be subject to *chain index drift*, tending to drift upward due to a negative correlation between prices and quantities even if the overall level of output between two years at the same point in the business cycle is identical. More frequent chaining will not help this situation, but only worsen it, by strengthening the negative correlation between the index weights and quantity relatives.

The time reversal test has been dismissed as a useful criterion for index number formulae because in our world time never does run in reverse, but for statisticians who are more interested in producing reliable indexes than in clever word play, the failure of the Laspeyres formula to pass the time reversal test constitutes a serious problem.

A third weakness of the SNA68 is that the recommended volume estimates would not pass the *transactions equality test*, which states that, "the relative importance of each transaction is dependent only on its magnitude."[8] This is quite obvious, since the relative importance of all commodities in the Laspeyres volume estimates would be based only on the expenditures of base year 0. Base year transactions would consequently have a considerably greater influence on the estimates than those of other years.

This is similar to the property of representativeness already discussed but is not identical with it. For example, if one calculated a 20-year output series with base prices equal to the average annual prices over the entire 20-year period, such estimates would pass the transactions equality test (with transactions from every month of every year determining the base prices). However, by taking them from all years, the base prices would be poorly representative of any particular year, especially (if relative prices were strongly trending) the initial and final years.

[8] See Dikhanov (1994, p.3).

This particular weakness has not bothered most national accountants. The emphasis has been on finding a base year that was a normal year with a representative price structure. For example, in a comparison between output levels in 1913 and 1918, 1913 constant prices would be preferred over 1918 constant prices, since 1913 was a normal peacetime year and 1918 was a war year.[9] However, experience has shown that it is not that easy to find a "normal" year to serve as base. In the Canadian System of National Accounts (CSNA), some of the recent base years have proven less than optimal, including 1981 and 1992 which were both recession years. The year 1981 was especially poor as it was also a year when relative prices of important commodities were much higher than usual, as were nominal interest rates..

The use of a single year's base prices is especially problematical for industries such as agriculture where relative prices are persistently volatile. (It was to avoid the difficulty in finding a single representative base year that 1935-1939 base prices were adopted by the CSNA for its initial set of output estimates at constant prices, but subsequently base prices were always taken from a single year.)

4. The Natural Remedies for These Weaknesses

In summary, the SNA68 measures had three major weaknesses: lack of representativeness, an upward bias due to the use of the Laspeyres formula, and failure to pass the transactions equality test. All of these weaknesses can be corrected by calculating annually-linked volume series, where each year's expenditures are evaluated at the average of a given and the previous year's prices. Technically speaking, this would involve calculating a chain Edgeworth-Marshall volume series rather than a direct Laspeyres volume series. To make it clear how the proposed measures would differ from the SNA68 measures as well as the Hill SNA93 proposals, Hill's eight points will be rewritten in detail to reflect my proposals.

First, the Laspeyres volume aggregates would be replaced with expenditures at constant prices for years 0 and 1 combined, denoted hereafter by

$$\sum \bar{p}_{01} q_t$$

The annual index for year 1 for the above series is an Edgeworth-Marshall volume index, given as:

$$\text{(4-1)} \quad Q^{EM}_{1/0} = \sum \bar{p}_{01} q_1 / \sum \bar{p}_{01} q_0 \, .$$

It can be readily seen that such an index, in contrast with the Laspeyres volume index, passes the time reversal test; i.e.,

$$Q^{EM}_{1/0} = \frac{\sum \bar{p}_{01} q_1}{\sum \bar{p}_{01} q_0} = 1/Q^{EM}_{0/1} = 1/\frac{\sum \bar{p}_{01} q_0}{\sum \bar{p}_{01} q_1} \, .$$

[9] See Bowley (1924, p.92) where this argument is made in the context of a price index, with the Laspeyres formula favoured over the Fisher.

Therefore, chain Edgeworth-Marshall indexes will be less subject to chain drift than chain Laspeyres indexes.

Second, the use of base period prices defined over two years rather than one provides a more stable reference than a single year's prices would. Commodity by commodity, the base period price is defined so that the following equality holds:

$$\sum_q p_{0q} q_{0q} + \sum_q p_{1q} q_{1q} = \sum_{y=0}^{1} \sum_q \bar{p}_{01} q_{yq}.$$

For this to be true, it must also be so that:

$$\text{(4-2)} \quad \bar{p}_{01} = \left(\sum_{y=0}^{1} \sum_q p_{yq} q_{yq}\right) / \left(\sum_{y=0}^{1} \sum_q q_{yq}\right) = \sum_{y=0}^{1} \sum_q p_{yq} \left(q_{yq} / \left(\sum_{y=0}^{1} \sum_q q_{yq}\right)\right);$$

that is, the base price must be calculated as the unit value for the two years 0 and 1, which is the mean of the quarterly prices using quantities as weights. As discussed in section 2, this is the only appropriate way to calculate the average price for a homogeneous product. This base price can also be interpreted as a harmonic mean of the quarterly prices, with the weighting based on expenditures; i.e.,

$$\bar{p}_{01} = 1 / \sum_{y=0}^{1} \sum_q w_{yq} (1/p_{yq}) \text{ where } w_{yj} = p_{yq} q_{yj} / \sum_{y=0}^{1} \sum_q p_{yq} q_{yq}$$

As in the SNA68 case, if one were working with value series and independently derived price indexes rather than prices and quantities, the requirement would be somewhat different. For base prices defined over years 0 and 1, one would require that:

$$\text{(4-3)} \quad \sum_{y=0}^{1} \sum_q v_{yq} = \sum_{y=0}^{1} \sum_q v_{yq} / P_{yq/01},$$

where $P_{yq/01}$ is the price index for a given quarter with a two-year base period covering years 0 and 1. Generally, the identity in (4-3) does not hold. Instead, the quarterly values for the base period must be prorated so that the value for quarter q of year y at constant prices for years 0 and 1 will be equal to the following:

$$\text{(4-4)} \quad f \times v_{yq} / P_{0q/0},$$

$$\text{where } f = \left(\sum_{y=0}^{1} \sum_q v_{yq}\right) / \left(\sum_{y=0}^{1} \sum_q v_{yq} / P_{yq/01}\right).$$

As will be seen in the seventh point, the official chain volume estimates are to be based on annual links, so for the finalized estimates there is no issue of whether the adjustment factor should be applied to years 0 and following, or only to years 0 and 1.

Close inspection will show that this calculation of base prices for a two-year base period is completely analogous with the calculation of base prices for a one-year base period in the SNA68. Thus, it is somewhat surprising that this option seems to have been ignored in the literature on chain volume measures. The principle of Ockham's razor would suggest that the problems that plagued the SNA68 world should be solved with the least possible deviation from it. Instead the proposed solutions have usually related to different formulae than the fixed-price volume formula, notably the SNA93 recommendation in favour of the Fisher formula. When interest has been expressed in a fixed price formula, it usually relates to base prices defined as another average of the prices of years 0 and 1. In particular, the Walsh volume index, defined as:

$$(4\text{-}5)\quad Q_{01}^{W} = \frac{\sum \bar{p}_{01}^{W} q_1}{\sum \bar{p}_{01}^{W} q_0}$$

$$\text{where } \bar{p}_{01}^{W} = \sqrt{\bar{p}_0 \times \bar{p}_1} = \sqrt{1 \Big/ \left(\sum_q w_{0q}(1/p_{0q})\right) \times \left(\sum_q w_{1q}(1/p_{1q})\right)}$$

has received favourable attention, notably from Erwin Diewert (1996). Note that in the Walsh volume index, the base prices represent geometric means of the average annual prices for years 0 and 1, but since these are calculated as in the SNA68 system, the Walsh base prices represent an odd hybrid: the unweighted geometric means of weighted harmonic means.

Formula (4-5) does not satisfy the property of transactions equality between the two years 0 and1 because both years have about the same impact on the calculation of the average base prices even if the volume of transactions was much greater in one year than the other. (This is a real possibility for new commodities, outmoded commodities or highly cyclical ones, as discussed in section 8.)

If the price of a commodity were zero in either year using (4-5), the Walsh base price would be zero, and the commodity would have no influence on the estimate of volume change for the year. If there are no sales of the commodity in a given year one must impute a price for it anyway; it does not simply disappear from the calculation. The Edgeworth-Marshall base prices are much better behaved in this respect. At the limit, if all transactions were in year 0 and none in year 1, the unit value for years 0 and 1 would reduce to the unit value for year 0 only.

Third, the ratio of the expenditures at current prices to the expenditures at constant prices provides an implicit price index:

$$(4\text{-}6)\quad P_{1/01}^{EMIPI} = \frac{\sum p_1 q_1}{\sum \bar{p}_{01} q_0} \div \frac{\sum \bar{p}_{01} q_1}{\sum \bar{p}_{01} q_0} = \frac{\sum p_1 q_1}{\sum \bar{p}_{01} q_1}.$$

This is the Edgeworth-Marshall counterpart to the Paasche price index and would serve much the same purpose. Operationally, one can choose between calculating volume aggregates directly or by deflating value observations using implicit price indexes. However, like the Paasche price indexes, these Edgeworth-Marshall implicit price indexes would be poor indicators of price change in and of themselves, since all quarterly changes would be distorted by changes in the index basket from one quarter to the next.

Note that the first term after the first equal sign in (4-6) represents, not an index of values at current prices, as in a formula for a Paasche price index, but rather the index of values for the current year t to the base year values re-expressed in terms of average prices for years 0 and 1. Although this may look a little strange to someone used to the standard formulas, it is quite logical. If one rejects a single year's prices for making volume comparisons why would one wish to index current expenditures to base year expenditures at their own prices, rather than at a more normal set of prices?

Note also that while the counterpart of a Laspeyres volume index number with base year 0 is a Paasche price index number with the same base, the counterpart of an Edgeworth-Marshall volume index number with base year 0 is an implicit price index with a multi-year base covering years 0 and 1.

Fourth, as with the Laspeyres volume aggregates, these volume series would be additive across all important dimensions, and so would satisfy the property of matrix consistency. This point cannot be stressed enough, since the biggest drawback of SNA93's proposed Fisher aggregates is that they are not additive or matrix consistent.

Fifth, the change between any two quarters, or between the base year and the following year, of the Edgeworth-Marshall volume aggregates satisfies the *proportionality test*. This is because, like the Laspeyres aggregates, all expenditures for all periods are converted to the same set of fixed prices.

Sixth, the Edgeworth-Marshall volume aggregates are weakly consistent in aggregation; i.e., they can be equally well calculated in a single stage from basic components or in two stages, by first calculating subaggregates from basic components using the Edgeworth-Marshall formula, and then adding up the volume subaggregates to get the aggregate series. The Edgeworth-Marshall formula is weakly consistent in aggregation. At the second stage of aggregation the Edgeworth-Marshall formula would not be used to calculate the aggregate from the subaggregates; that would yield an incorrect result. In this respect, Edgeworth-Marshall aggregates differ from SNA68's Laspeyres volume measures, which were strongly consistent in aggregation. However, the Edgeworth-Marshall aggregates are superior to their Fisher aggregates which are not even weakly consistent in aggregation.[10]

Seventh, the Edgeworth-Marshall formula also has the new good property possessed by the Laspeyres formula. This is logical, since any formula that can be expressed as a weighted average of its component indexes will satisfy the new good property. It is one of the weaknesses of the Fisher formula that, being a geometric mean of the Laspeyres and Paasche indexes, it does not satisfy the new good property. This is obvious if one thinks of a new good being added for year 2004, with an imputed growth ratio equal to the Fisher volume index number for 2004 that was calculated without it. Since this Fisher index number will differ from its Laspeyres or Paasche components, both of these components will change when the new good is included, and so will the Fisher aggregate. To include the new good without it making a difference to the overall index, it would be necessary to treat the same new good as having two distinct movements: a movement equal to that of the Laspeyres measure for the Laspeyres calculation, and a movement equal to that of the Paasche measure for the Paasche calculation, so that, overall, the Fisher measure would remain unchanged. This would be possible, but would also be messy and error-prone.

[10] The failure of the Fisher formula to be even weakly consistent in aggregation, is not, as is sometimes alleged, empirically insignificant; the erroneous calculation of a Fisher aggregate in two or more stages instead of in a single stage can even reverse the direction of measured growth of an aggregate.

Eighth, Edgeworth-Marshall volume aggregates would be calculated as a chain volume series whose base would change every year. This would also be true of the Edgeworth-Marshall price aggregate. For the current year the estimate would be given by:

$$(4\text{-}7)\quad \sum \bar{p}_{t-1t} q_t .$$

Earlier years would follow the recursion:

$$(4\text{-}8)\quad \frac{\sum \bar{p}_{t-1t} q_t}{\sum \bar{p}_{t-2t-1} q_t} \times \sum \bar{p}_{t-2t-1} q_{t-1} .$$

That is, the volume aggregate would always be linked backwards, so that the additivity of the most recent periods would be preserved. This is different from what is recommended in the SNA93 where chaining is forward and additivity is not preserved for the most recent volume estimates even if a Laspeyres formula rather than a Fisher formula is used to calculate them.

In an era of electronic publications, there is no great difficulty in changing the base of volume estimates every year as this proposal would require. This has been proven by the Australian and British National Accounts programs that have adopted backward linking for their annually-linked chain volume measures based on the Laspeyres formula. For the Statistics Canada monthly GDP by industry estimates on which the present author worked, this proposal would entail the publication of from 43 to 54 months of data that were additive over an annual production cycle with backward linking in place. The time span is so long due to delays in the updating of annual benchmark price and volume estimates.

These estimates would be representative in a way that the old volume estimates were not, since the base prices would be updated every year. They would also satisfy the requirement of transactions equality, since every year y would be used to calculate the base prices for two annual comparisons: y-1 to y and y to y+1, and the importance of year y in the pooled set of base prices would depend on the volume of transactions associated with year y.

This is in contrast with the Fisher case recommended by SNA93 where the principle of transactions equality is violated. Instead, each year's transactions have about the same influence on the measure of base prices regardless of their volume. As can be seen from (4-1), if the volume of transactions in year 0 is very small compared to year 1, the base prices for years 0-1 will essentially be year 1 base prices. In the Fisher case, by contrast, one would have:

$$(4\text{-}9)\quad Q^F_{1/0} = \left[\frac{\sum p_0 q_1}{\sum p_0 q_0} \frac{\sum p_1 q_1}{\sum p_1 q_0} \right]^{1/2}$$

and prices for both years would have essentially the same influence on the measured volume movement even though the volume of transactions in year 0 is far less than what it is in year 1. Given a negative correlation between prices and quantities, this would imply much higher measured rates of growth using the Fisher measure than using the Edgeworth-Marshall measure. This is illustrated with an example in section 8.

Note also that another index number formula often associated with the Edgeworth-Marshall formula, the Bowley-Sidgwick formula, does not satisfy the transactions equality principle either. It is the arithmetic equivalent of the Fisher formula, defined as the arithmetic mean of the Laspeyres and Paasche indexes:

$$Q^{BS}_{1/0} = \left[\frac{\sum p_0 q_1}{\sum p_0 q_0} + \frac{\sum p_1 q_1}{\sum p_1 q_0}\right] / 2$$

Again, it can be seen that even if the volume of transactions is much larger in period 1 than in period 0, with this kind of a case, prices of period 0 and period 1 have about the same impact on the index. (In fact, the Bowley-Sidgwick formula would give an even worse result in this respect than the Fisher formula. Since the geometric mean is always less than the arithmetic mean of two estimates, the higher estimate based on the period 0 prices would have a greater influence on the Bowley-Sidgwick estimate than on the Fisher one.)

Moreover, like the Laspeyres formula, the Bowley-Sidgwick formula is also biased. It does not pass the time reversal test, so that we have:

$$Q^{BS}_{0/1} = \left[\frac{\sum p_1 q_0}{\sum p_1 q_1} + \frac{\sum p_0 q_0}{\sum p_0 q_1}\right] / 2 \neq 1/Q^{BS}_{1/0} = 2 / \left[\frac{\sum p_0 q_1}{\sum p_0 q_0} + \frac{\sum p_1 q_1}{\sum p_1 q_0}\right]$$

and so, like the Laspeyres formula, although much less so, it is subject to chain index drift.

The SNA93 manual recommends (see 16.76) that a set of fixed-price estimates be calculated in addition to the chain Fisher estimates, which would be rebased and (backward) linked about every five years. This is an excellent recommendation, which recognizes the limitations of annual-linked chain measures for certain kinds of analysis.

The SNA93 manual says nothing on where the base year should be in the finalized estimates for a five-year span in such a chain volume measure, although a seminal study by Szulc (1998) indicated that this is a matter of considerable importance. Comparisons using Canadian data on gross domestic expenditures showed that price indexes calculated according to an annual-link chain Fisher formula were poorly approximated by chain Laspeyres indexes with five-year or ten-year links, but were quite well approximated by chain fixed-basket indexes with the same linking frequency if these employed a mid-year basket. It is reasonable to assume that a similar relationship would hold for volume comparisons, favouring the choice of mid-period base prices for constant-price volume aggregates.

In fact, such was the practice of the Office of National Statistics in the United Kingdom in compiling their volume estimates until they moved to an annual-link chain Laspeyres format.[11] Expenditures for 1983 to 1987 were at 1985 prices, expenditures for 1988 to 1992 at 1990 prices and so on. Because a given year was never more than two years removed from the base year, the base year prices were more likely to be representative of that year, than they would have been if the base year were the initial year of a five-year span, and the given year were the final year or penultimate year of the span.

In their analysis of the differences between annual-linked and published estimates for both expenditure categories and industry estimates Tuke and Brown (2003) note that from 1995 to 2001 these are never larger than 0.2% in absolute terms. These remarkably small differences provide a good indication of the extent to which the choice of a central base year secures a lot of the benefits that can be derived from annual linking. It is likely that the differences would have

[11] See Lynch (2003).

been considerably greater had the Office of National Statistics followed SNA68 conventions and made the base year of their volume estimates the initial year of each span.

Given that the official chain measures should be Edgeworth-Marshall measures, the fixed-price volume measures should not be Laspeyres aggregates, but should be extensions of the series used to calculate the Edgeworth-Marshall links, i.e. for the most recent period they would have the formula:

(4-10) $\sum p_{01}q_y; y = -2,-1,2,0,1,2...$

These estimates would have to be calculated up to year 6, and possibly to year 10, before they were replaced by new volume series with base prices of years 5 and 6. For the five preceding years, the chained volume estimates would have the formula:

(4-11) $f \times \sum p_{-5-4}q_y = (\sum p_{01}q_{-2} / \sum p_{-5=4}q_{-2}) \times \sum p_{-5-4}q_y; y = -7,-6,-5,-4,-3$

where the series are at constant prices of the years -5 and -4. Extension to earlier five year spans is obvious. Note that with these links the annual movement for the year -2 is based on base prices for the years -5 and -4, and not those of years 0 and 1.

Generally speaking, calculating fixed-price volume aggregates using base prices over two years rather than a single year would tend to create smoother volume estimates with reduced amplitude, any anomalies in a single year base being smoothed out in a two-year base period. So in two respects, the centrality of the base period, and the fact that a double year base is used, these fixed-price aggregates would be superior to the old SNA68 Laspeyres volume aggregates.

Although the ultimate length of any fixed-price span would only be five years, due to the inevitable lags in rebasing the length of the current span would be much longer. For example, in Canada the monthly GDP estimates could probably only have been switched to 1997-8 prices with the July 2001 update, replacing 1992-93 prices that would have been taken back to January 1992. So the series at 1992-93 prices would have been calculated for January 1990 to June 2001, a period of 11 years and six months. (If the fixed-price series were a Laspeyres series with a 1992 base, it would be a year shorter, ending in June 2000.)

5. Subannual Values of Annually Linked Chain Aggregates

Most countries publish GDP estimates at constant prices both quarterly or monthly, and these subannual estimates are of at least as great interest to users as the annual estimates. Unfortunately, papers on chain volume aggregates written by interested economists or even by official statisticians have tended to ignore the difficulties in creating quarterly series with annual links. Most papers on the subject deal with the characteristics of different formulae -- Fisher, Montgomery-Vartia and so forth -- for individual (read annual) links and one is left with the impression that these same properties of the annual links also exist for the quarterly growth ratios. As a general rule, this is not so, and some formulae which look good in terms of annual links nevertheless look much worse if one considers what kind of quarterly estimates they will generate.

One of the few works that does recognize this problem is chapter XVI of SNA93. Unfortunately, its conclusion, that "chain indices should only be used to measure year-to-year movements and not quarter to quarter movements" is unduly defeatist. This conclusion seems to be based on its observation "that if it is desired to measure the change in prices or volumes between a given month, or quarter, and the same month, or quarter, in the following year, the change should be measured directly and not through a chain index linking the data over all the intervening months, or quarters" (SNA93, section 16.49).

However, annually linked volume aggregates whose constant price structure changes every year are not much different from the old SNA68 volume measures. The growth rates measured between consecutive quarters would all be comparable (i.e., they would satisfy the proportionality test) except for the first quarter. Over a 15-year span covering 59 quarterly changes, the SNA68 aggregates would provide 57 comparable quarterly changes, which is 95% of the total (the first quarter changes for the years following link years being non-comparable). Chain volume aggregates would provide 45 comparable quarterly changes, or 75% of the total. For monthly GDP series, only January monthly changes would be non-comparable, so comparable monthly changes would be 91.7% of the total.

And for that matter, if Edgeworth-Marshall volume aggregates were calculated, the only distortion in a fourth quarter to first quarter comparison would be in the replacement of one set of base prices by another, with both sets being very current and sharing half of their prices in common. In many cases the impact of the change in price structure would be negligible. This would also be true of four-quarter comparisons, which would have to contend with a single link at the year and not on four quarterly links as SNA93 postulates.

Users of SNA data want to have one official set of quarterly and annual estimates, and not go to one series for annual growth rates and another, possibly with quite different annual movements, for quarterly growth rates. Surely users should be provided with overlapping sets of direct volume aggregates that provide meaningful quarterly growth rates where the chain volume aggregates do not do so. In many cases, these alternative series would likely only provide assurance that the quarterly growth rates generated by the chain volume aggregates are not very different from those provided by measures of pure volume change. As was noted in the previous section fixed-price volume aggregates with base prices defined over two years even if finally defined for a five-year span could be initially calculated over a span of 10 to 11 years, so there would be a lot of overlap between fixed-price volume aggregates, ensuring some kind of a fixed-price measure for all quarterly and four-quarter comparisons.

The quarterly volume index estimates equivalent to the Fisher annual estimates would have the following formula:

$$(5\text{-}1)\quad Q^{F}_{1q/0} = \left[Q^{L}_{1q/0} \times Q^{P}_{1q/0}\right]^{(1/2)} = \left[\frac{\sum p_0 q_{1q}}{\sum p_0 q_0}\,\frac{\sum p_{1q} q_{1q}}{\sum p_{1q} q_0}\right]^{(1/2)}.$$

This is the same formula as (4-9) except that all period 1 quantities and the Paasche index's period 1 prices are now for a specific quarter rather than for a year. As far as this particular index comparison goes, proportionality is still satisfied, since what we have is still the geometric mean of two fixed-price volume indexes. Factor reversal is also satisfied since:

$$Q^F_{1q/0} \times P^F_{1q/0} = \left[\frac{\sum p_0 q_{1q}}{\sum p_0 q_0}\frac{\sum p_{1q} q_{1q}}{\sum p_{1q} q_0}\right]^{(1/2)}\left[\frac{\sum p_{1q} q_0}{\sum p_0 q_0}\frac{\sum p_{1q} q_{1q}}{\sum p_0 q_{1q}}\right]^{(1/2)} = \frac{\sum p_{1q} q_{1q}}{\sum p_0 q_0}$$

However, since there is also annual rather than quarterly linking, the quarterly growth ratios of this index do not satisfy proportionality. What we have is

$$Q^F_{1q/0}/Q^F_{1q-1/0} = \left[\frac{\sum p_0 q_{1q}}{\sum p_0 q_0}\frac{\sum p_{1q} q_{1q}}{\sum p_{1q} q_0}\right]^{(1/2)} \Big/ \left[\frac{\sum p_0 q_{1q-1}}{\sum p_0 q_0}\frac{\sum p_{1q-1} q_{1q-1}}{\sum p_{1q-1} q_0}\right]^{(1/2)}$$

$$= \left[\frac{\sum p_0 q_{1q}}{\sum p_0 q_{1q-1}}\frac{\sum p_{1q} q_{1q}}{\sum p_{1q} q_0} \Big/ \frac{\sum p_{1q-1} q_{1q-1}}{\sum p_{1q-1} q_0}\right]^{(1/2)},$$

and even in the absence of quarterly price change by any commodity, the growth rate will generally be different from one due to price movements between the base year and the quarters of the current year. The problem stems from the Paasche component of the Fisher index, and not from the Laspeyres component; a direct Paasche index, because its relative price structure changes every period, does not satisfy the proportionality axiom for multi-period comparisons; therefore, neither does the direct Fisher index.

Formula (5-1) can be simplified by replacing its Paasche component with a fixed-price index reflecting the price structure of year 1:

$$\text{(5-2)}\quad Q^{GMFP}_{1q/0} = \left[Q^L_{1q/0} \times Q^1_{1q/0}\right]^{(1/2)} = \left[Q^0_{1q/0} \times Q^1_{1q/0}\right]^{(1/2)} = \left[\frac{\sum p_0 q_{1q}}{\sum p_0 q_0}\frac{\sum p_1 q_{1q}}{\sum p_1 q_0}\right]^{(1/2)},$$

where the superscript GMFP indicates a geometric mean of fixed-price volume indexes. Following the second equality sign, the superscripts of the volume indexes indicate what year they take their fixed price structure from. Thus, $Q^0_{1q/0}$ is identical to $Q^L_{1q/0}$, the Laspeyres index. In some cases, in the absence of quarterly price data, such a formula might be used to represent a Fisher volume index, although strictly speaking it is not one. A GMFP index does satisfy proportionality for its quarterly growth rates:

$$Q^{GMFP}_{1q/0}/Q^{GMFP}_{1q-1/0} = \left[\frac{\sum p_0 q_q}{\sum p_0 q_0}\frac{\sum p_1 q_{1q}}{\sum p_1 q_0}\right]^{(1/2)} \Big/ \left[\frac{\sum p_0 q_{1q-1}}{\sum p_0 q_0}\frac{\sum p_1 q_{1q-1}}{\sum p_1 q_0}\right]^{(1/2)} = \left[\frac{\sum p_0 q_{1q}}{\sum p_0 q_{1q-1}}\frac{\sum p_1 q_{1q}}{\sum p_1 q_{1t-1}}\right]^{(1/2)}$$

as one would expect of the geometric mean of the growth rates of two fixed-price volume indexes. However, the GMFP index does not satisfy the factor reversal test when multiplied by its equivalent geometric mean fixed basket (GMFB) index:

$$Q^{GMFP}_{1q/0} \times P^{GMFB}_{1q/0} = \left[\frac{\sum p_0 q_{1q}}{\sum p_0 q_0}\frac{\sum p_1 q_{1q}}{\sum p_1 q_0}\right]^{(1/2)}\left[\frac{\sum p_{1q} q_0}{\sum p_0 q_0}\frac{\sum p_{1q} q_1}{\sum p_0 q_1}\right]^{(1/2)} \neq \frac{\sum p_{1q} q_{1q}}{\sum p_0 q_0}$$

These geometric mean indexes are the quarterly indexes that are closest to Fisher indexes while retaining the proportionality property. Rather than leaving it to the different national statistical agencies to decide what to do, this is what SNA 1993 should have prescribed for quarterly measures when it advised the adoption of the Fisher formula for annual measures. However, so far these measures have not been adopted by either the United States or Canada, the only countries, so far, that have adopted the Fisher formula for their chain volume measures.

Often there is a greater level of detail available for both price indexes and value series at the annual level than at the quarterly level, so there is a need to adjust a quarterly volume indicator to annual benchmarks. For a geometric mean volume index, it would be inappropriate to directly adjust it so that it averaged to a Fisher volume index. Instead, one would want to benchmark the quarterly chain Laspeyres volume index to its annual benchmarks, and the quarterly chain fixed-basket index compatible with a chain Paasche volume index to its annual chain Paasche benchmarks, and then calculate the geometric mean of the adjusted series.

Since the additivity problem is usually discussed in a general sense, many people may be unaware of the crucial distinction between additivity of quarters to years and other types of additivity (over commodities, industries or regions) in calculating annually-linked chain volume indexes. Generally speaking, chaining destroys all types of additivity except the adddivity of quarterly values to annuals, where that additivity exists to begin with. Therefore it is simply not true that there is not much difference, as far as additivity is concerned, between chain fixed-price volume measures such as the Edgeworth-Marshall series and other measures such as Fisher or Sato-Vartia that do not have this additivity property.

Unfortunately, the implementation of chain Fisher volume measures by both the U.S. Bureau of Economic Analysis (BEA) in the U.S. National Accounts and by Statistics Canada in the CSNA has muddied these distinctions. Both have imposed additivity on their quarterly chain Fisher measures, although it is illogical to do so. The BEA calculates quarterly-linked chain Fisher indexes and benchmarks them to annually-linked chain Fisher benchmarks. The CSNA has also calculated quarterly-linked chain Fisher indexes, but has not benchmarked these estimates to anything at all; the annual estimate is the arithmetic mean of the quarterly estimates.

Formula (5-1) is a better way to decompose an annually-linked index than using a quarterly-linked distributor, if deflation occurs at the same level of detail for the annual and the quarterly levels. If this is not the case, the appropriate thing to do would be to adjust a quarterly distributor of chain Laspeyres annual benchmarks and another distributor to chain Paasche annual benchmarks, and then month by month calculate the geometric mean of the two series. (Assuming that it were appropriate to have a quarterly-linked chain Fisher distributor, it should be adjusted to the chain Fisher benchmarks by using the chain Laspeyres quarterly series as the distributor for the chain Laspeyres benchmarks and the chain Paasche quarterly series for the chain Paasche benchmarks.) Whatever distributors were used, the quarterly index numbers would not average to the annual benchmarks.

As for the CSNA measure, given that the quarterly index numbers are based on quite different price structures, their arithmetic average is essentially meaningless. It would have been more appropriate to calculate their annuals as a geometric mean since the chain series is nothing but a strand of quarterly growth ratios linked together.

Both the BEA and Statistics Canada seem to have had misgivings about the consequences that adopting the Fisher formula would have for the additivity of their estimates, and this has kept both of them from calculating annuals and quarterlies in a way that is logical and consistent. This is especially surprising for the BEA because they have been publicly dismissive of the value of additivity in national accounting (see, for example, the 2000 paper by Ehemann et al.).

Why doesn't the BEA practice what it preaches? Or, to turn the question around, why doesn't it preach what it practices? Given that it is so unwilling to give up additivity of quarterly estimates to annuals that it will impose this property, against all logic, on its chain Fisher estimates, why doesn't the BEA advocate and implement chain fixed-price volume aggregates like the Edgeworth-Marshall measures that would legitimize this additivity? And the same goes for Statistics Canada.

The use of quarterly-linked chain estimates by both the United States and Canada has a serious potential for degrading the quality of growth estimates, so it merits further comment. As Hill remarks in SNA93:

"[A] chain index should be used when the relative prices in the first and last periods are very different from each other and chaining involves linking through intervening periods in which the relative prices and quantities are intermediate between those in the first and last periods" (SNA93, p.388).

If, for example, one wants to know the difference in output between the first quarter of 2001 and the first quarter of 2003, linking eight times through different quarters will hardly give us in each and every case a relative price structure that departs smoothly from that of the initial quarter in the direction of the terminal relative prices in the next quarter and that will inevitably be intermediate between those of the first and last quarters. Suppose, for example, one were measuring gross output of the air transport sector. Does it really make sense to link through the prices of third quarter and fourth quarter 2001, given the highly abnormal pricing situation in the wake of the September 11th terrorist atrocities? The consequences of linking where one shouldn't be are reduced because the Fisher formula has the time reversal property, but this in no way justifies linking inappropriately.

Some commodities are seasonally disappearing and this is especially a problem for northern countries like Canada. Prices may well be missing for one or both quarters of a quarterly comparison. More seriously if quantities go to zero, one must calculate output relatives with a zero base, which makes the index number undefined.[12]

This problem is only partially resolved by the seasonal adjustment of economic time series. First, even if a statistical agency only publishes GDP at constant prices as a seasonally adjusted series, it is sound statistical practice to calculate the same aggregate unadjusted for seasonal variation. Any chain linking procedure that makes the calculation of such raw estimates impossible, or requires so much tinkering to calculate them that their comparability with the official seasonal adjusted series is compromised, has little to recommend it.

---

[12] In principle, for a formula like the Fisher, if the volume relative of one of its components is undefined due to zero production in the base quarter, the calculation can be redefined as an aggregative formula in which the production value for that commodity simply disappears from the sum for the base quarter. This is the advantage of an aggregative formula like Fisher (or Edgeworth-Marshall) over a log-change formula like Törnqvist, since there is no way the latter can be defined, except as a function of volume relatives. However, in a production context, it might be inconvenient to calculate the estimates using an aggregative formula rather than a sum of weighted averages formula.

Second, one is necessarily resorting to highly artificial base prices. Certainly seasonal adjustment procedures can arrive at a first quarter price for field-grown corn one way or another, but it is not and can never be a solid number, unlike its annual unit price.

Although both BEA and Statistics Canada procedures involve quarterly linking, the BEA procedures are better, because at least the quarterly-linked estimates are adjusted to good annual benchmarks. The Canadian estimates are not, which leaves open the possibility of substantial chain index drift in one direction or another.

Another danger with the CSNA procedure is that more than anything else, the quality of output estimates at constant prices depends on the level of disaggregation at which the estimation takes place.[13] More disaggregated information on prices, revenues or production volumes is, and always will be available at the annual than at the quarterly level. Creating a methodology that requires quarterly estimates encourages the calculation of production estimates to occur at too gross a level of detail.

One of the properties of the Fisher formula is proportionality; i.e., if all quantities of all commodities increase by the same percentage, that will also be the rate of increase of the Fisher volume index:

$$\left[\frac{\sum p_0 \lambda q_1}{\sum p_0 q_0}\frac{\sum p_1 \lambda q_1}{\sum p_1 q_0}\right]^{(1/2)} = \left[\frac{\lambda \sum p_0 q_1}{\sum p_0 q_0}\frac{\lambda \sum p_1 q_1}{\sum p_1 q_0}\right]^{(1/2)} = \lambda\left[\frac{\sum p_0 q_1}{\sum p_0 q_0}\frac{\sum p_1 q_1}{\sum p_1 q_0}\right]^{(1/2)}$$

Note that the geometric mean index shown in (5-1) also has the proportionality property for quarterly changes. On the other hand, the BEA measures only approximately have this property for quarterly changes. The quarterly changes of their quarterly-linked series would have this property prior to benchmark adjustment, but not afterwards. In other words, the quarterly data may show no quantity change from one quarter to another in any commodity, but due to benchmark adjustment an increase or decrease in output will nonetheless be indicated. And this could happen even if the quarterly distributor and the annual benchmarks were based on the same data for the same commodities. The BEA documents on their chain measures have not paid any attention to this important caveat.

Nonetheless, the BEA measures do satisfy proportionality for annual changes. This is not true of the Statistics Canada measures. Calculated as the average of the quarterly Fisher estimates, different years are not compared based on the same sets of relative prices, so the annual estimates could show an increase or a decrease even if all outputs were unchanged. In other words, the BEA has chosen to give priority to their annual growth rates; Statistics Canada to their quarterly growth rates. Obviously, the BEA has made the better choice. The quality of quarterly estimates will never be up to the standard of the annual estimates.

However else the Statistics Canada changes its methodology for calculating chain volume estimates for the CSNA, the agency should switch to chaining annually regardless of the choice of formula. Chaining quarterly with no annual benchmarks is contrary to SNA93, contrary to BEA practice, contrary to Eurostat practice, and contrary to common sense.

[13] On this topic, see the paper by Horner (1971).

Quarterly- or monthly-linked indexes do have their uses. For example, they are a required adjunct if one is calculating seasonal-basket price indexes and wishes to make some sense of quarterly or monthly price movements. However, they are only useful as adjuncts to official series, rather than *as* official series.

Besides the Fisher formula, a number of log change formulae have been recommended for measuring volume indexes, including the Törnqvist, Montgomery-Vartia, and Vartia-Sato ones. All conform to the following general formula:

$$Q_{1/0}^{LC} = \prod (q_1 / q_0))^w = \sum w(\ln(q_1) - \ln(q_0)),$$

whence the name log-change indexes.

The Törnqvist index is mentioned as an alternative to the Fisher index in SNA93. The Montgomery-Vartia formula was recommended as the best technical formula by consultants to Eurostat for its good properties, despite the fact that it does not meet the proportionality test. By the way, this report dismissed the Fisher formula from consideration because it is not even weakly consistent in aggregation.[14] The closely related Sato-Vartia formula has also attracted considerable interest. Like the Fisher formula, it passes both the factor reversal and the time reversal test, and it is exact with respect to a CES aggregator function.[15]

However, the Törnqvist formula has a serious problem when production goes to zero for a commodity. Technically the index becomes undefined, since the logarithm of zero does not exist. This is a real problem for calculating quarterly and especially monthly GDP. Production of some commodities does go to zero for seasonal and other reasons. Vartia states in his paper that the Sato-Vartia formula will properly handle quantities or prices going to zero. However, this is only true if the index weights and component index numbers are changing at the same time. If one is linking annually but calculating quarterly or monthly index estimates, and output does not go to zero in all quarters of the year, the Sato-Vartia index will also be undefined. For calculating subannual series then, it is not more robust than the Törnqvist formula, since it is much more likely that production will drop to zero for a few months than for an entire year.

So the Sato-Vartia index is exact for the CES aggregator function yet becomes undefined for situations that frequently occur in calculating quarterly economic accounts. This is why one should put quotes around the word "superlative" when applied to an index that is exact for an aggregator function; it may be anything but superlative in terms of its index properties.

6. Analysis of Changes for Quarterly Chain Volume Aggregates

Any annually-linked chain volume aggregate will have a problem of non-comparability for quarterly changes for the first quarter due to the switch from one relative price structure to another. However, it is possible to precisely measure the distortion due to this switch. The quarterly percent change in the volume aggregate if there were no change in the relative price structure would be:

[14] See Al et al. (1986, p.354) for dismissal of the Fisher formula and p.355-56 in this same reference for their endorsement of the Montgomery-Vartia formula, which they call the Vartia-I formula.

[15] See the articles by Vartia (1976) and by Reinsdorf and Dorfman (1999) for more on this fascinating formula.

(6-1) $100 \times \sum \bar{p}_{t-2t-1}(q_{t,1} - q_{t-1,4}) / \sum \bar{p}_{t-2t-1} q_{t-1,4}$.

The difference between this quarterly percent change and the actual change in the official index is the measure of the interaction between the change in the relative price structure and output change. In most cases, this difference would not be great. Annual prices are less volatile than quarterly prices to begin with, and a two-year moving average of annual prices would help iron out the fluctuations in annual movements. However, where the difference was considerable for an official aggregate, a publication release could draw attention to the pure volume change measure, and deemphasize the official quarterly estimate of volume change.

The same principle would apply in the case of four-quarter percent changes. The percent change in the chain volume aggregate from the fourth quarter of year t-1 to the fourth quarter of year t, if there were no change in the relative price structure, would be:

(6-2) $100 \times \sum \bar{p}_{t-2t-1}(q_{t,4} - q_{t-1,4}) / \sum \bar{p}_{t-2t-1} q_{t-1,4}$,

and the difference between this percent change and the official estimate would show the distortion of the measured growth rates due to annual linking.

It should be noted that if the Edgeworth-Marshall aggregates were linked at the fourth quarter and not at the year, then the four-quarter percent change of the official estimates would be a measure of pure volume change:

(6-3) $100 \times \sum \bar{p}_{t-1t}(q_{t,4} - q_{t-1,4}) / \sum \bar{p}_{t-1t} q_{t-1,4}$,

and there would be no distortion due to changes in relative price structure. However in this case the annual price movements would be compromised.

In Statistics Canada, linking at the fourth quarter is the practice for some, but not all, price indexes whose baskets are updated once a year.[16] Regardless of whether this is the best practice for those price indexes, it should be observed that the context is different here. There are no annual benchmarks for the price indexes that are linked at the fourth quarter. Their annual data are derived from their quarterly data. For SNA volume aggregates, there are annual benchmark estimates for many series and in some cases sub-annual estimates are non-existent. Hence, linking at the fourth quarter would be inadvisable; it would be better to link at the year.

A couple of recent papers by Rossiter (2000) and Whelan (2000), American economists who work outside of the BEA have outlined quite arcane calculations to derive the contributions of components to growth for the US chained volume measures.[17] Neither seems to give sufficient attention to the fact that when comparing chained volume estimates across link periods, strictly speaking, no precise calculation of contribution shares to growth is possible. Rossiter does acknowledge a residual component, reflecting the difference between the sum of component contributions and the actual change in GDP. Over the 1991Q1 to 1998Q1 this residual, reflecting interaction between volume change and shifts in price structure accounts for 7.6% of the

---

[16] The non-residential building construction price index and the apartment building construction price index are linked at the fourth quarter; the air fares index is linked at the year.

[17] The Rossiter paper also shows contributions to change summing to 100, rather than to the percent change of total GDP over the period, a formulation that can break down completely if overall GDP growth is zero or nearly so.

measured growth in GDP. It seems to be an abuse of language to call such estimates contributions to change, when they are at best partial contributions to change.

For longer time periods, say the segment of 1991Q1 to 1998Q1 that Rossiter considers in his paper, output comparisons based on a single set of constant prices, while problematic, are possible. Indeed, it would seem from the discussion in section 4 that even a quarterly Laspeyres series at 1992 prices (1992 being a base year for the BEA and the CSNA both) would likely be calculated from 1990Q1 to 2000Q2, more than covering the segment at issue. Component contributions to the percent change in the aggregate could be simply calculated and would be true contributions, not having a residual component. Their principal drawback is that they relate to an analytical series and not to the official chain measure of volume change.

Such fixed-price series would also be useful for the dating of business cycles. This is a delicate task at best, and it would become largely impossible if one had only chained volume estimates to work with. The fixed-price series would be useful to monitor the changes in volume shares of components of GDP from one period to another where chain volume estimates are non-additive. (As discussed above, for the most recent year or years, the Edgeworth-Marshall estimates would be additive, so one could compare, say, the share of ICT products in current quarter GDP with the share in the previous quarter cleanly and correctly.) In his paper, Whelan acknowledges that chain measures are not particularly useful for this task and argues instead that one should base comparisons of component shares on expenditures at current prices, ignoring the inflationary distortions inevitable in such a procedure. This is simply ridiculous, and would mean a big step backward for analysis of economic statistics if it ever became commonplace.

Yet BEA economists Ehemann et al (2000) agree with Whelan and argue that shares of volume series are inherently meaningless because investment in computer equipment exceeds investment in software with a 1996 base but not with a 1992 base. I fail to see the point of this argument. Not all bases are created equal, which is precisely why there has been a move to annual chain measures. Anyone who wanted to know if software's share in the volume of investment between 1996 and 1999 was growing would prefer estimates at 1996 prices; estimates at 1992 prices would be rejected given a choice. The two base years are not on an equal footing. But estimates at one set of prices or the other would inevitably be preferred to comparing investment shares between the two years each at their own set of prices. What is to be gained by such an apples and oranges comparison?

7. An Aside on Price Indexes for GDP

The implicit price indexes for GDP that are derived from the Edgeworth-Marshall volume aggregates would not be the most suitable price measures for the components of GDP. In order to be consistent with the calculation of the volume measures, it would make sense to also calculate annually-linked chain Edgeworth-Marshall price indexes. The index would be calculated as:

$$(7\text{-}1)\quad P_{y/0}^{EM(Ch)} = \prod_{t=1}^{y} P_{t/t-1}^{EM}$$

where

$$P^{EM}_{1/0} = (\sum p_1(q_0 + q_1)/2)/\sum p_0(q_0 + q_1)/2 = (\sum p_1(q_0 + q_1))/\sum p_0(q_0 + q_1)$$

This may be contrasted with the similar formula for a Walsh chain price index:

$$\text{(7-2)} \quad P^{W(Ch)}_{y/0} = \prod_{t=1}^{y} P^{W}_{t/t-1}$$

where $P^{W}_{1/0} = (\sum p_1\sqrt{q_0 q_1} / \sum p_0\sqrt{q_0 q_1}$,

and where the prices are weighted by the geometric mean of the quantities in years 0 and 1.

Note that the calculation of average quantities over the two years for the Edgeworth-Marshall price index is based on a simple arithmetic mean whereas the calculation of average prices over the two years is based on a weighted harmonic mean. There is no inconsistency here. As can be seen, there is no difference in terms of result between weighting by the mean of quantities or the sum of quantities. The most natural way of combining the two periods' quantities is to add them together, just as the most natural way of calculating their average price for a homogeneous product is to take the unit value. It is not more natural to take the geometric mean of quantities in years 0 and 1-- that is, it is not more natural to calculate a Walsh price index -- than to take their sum. Moreover, the Walsh index will ignore any commodity that is available in only one of the two periods since the geometric mean of a positive value and a zero value is zero. (On the other hand, this does mean that a commodity will simply fall out of the index basket for a Walsh price index where an Edgeworth-Marshall index must impute for a missing price.)

In some cases, for commodities with highly volatile production profiles, a two-year basket may not be adequate to generate a stable weighting pattern.[18] For such commodity groups or industries, the chain Edgeworth-Marshall series could be replaced with similar indexes based on three- to five-year baskets. At higher levels of aggregation, the chain Edgeworth-Marshall formula could continue to be employed.

Such an adaptation of the Edgeworth-Marshall formula would not pass the time reversal test as defined above. However, that is not a big problem; it would still break the association between basket change and price change that makes the use of the Laspeyres formula a hazard in chain computations. Unlike the chain Laspeyres series, an Edgeworth-Marshall series would not be much subject to chain index drift.

Also, the Edgeworth-Marshall formula would have to be adapted to accommodate monthly baskets for seasonal commodity groups, using the Rothwell (1958) formula or the Balk (1980a) formula or both. These formulae will not be shown or discussed here beyond saying that there would be more reason to use the Balk formula the more irregular the seasonal pattern of the commodity group in question, since the Rothwell formula postulates a constant seasonal pattern. Also, while the long revision period required to properly calculate a Balk price index has kept it

---

[18] Within Statistics Canada, the new housing price index, non-residential building construction price index and apartment building construction price index all have three-year baskets; the farm product price index has a five-year basket.

from being employed in consumer price indexes, and for the most part in industry price indexes, the much greater tolerance of national accounts estimates for revisions should not keep it from being used in price indexes for national accounting aggregates.

Although there is a dichotomy between price and volume indexes with the same formulas being used for both, there is no reason to believe that the best price index formula for a commodity group is also necessarily the best volume index formula, and still less reason to believe that this formula will satisfy the strong factor reversal property.

Prices have their cyclical and irregular movements as do production flows, and this is one reason for favouring fixed-price series with a two-year base period, but it is less likely that a volume series will require a three- to five-year base period than it is that a price index will require a three- or five-year basket. As for seasonal commodities, the Rothwell and Balk formulas are strictly price index formulas; no-one has ever used them to measure the volume change for seasonal commodities and no-one ever will. There is really no place for special treatment of seasonal commodities in volume indexes, except in the special case where a good can be usefully considered to be a different commodity in every month or quarter of the year. Although such cases do arise, they are rare, and at the level of aggregation at which national accountants operate, probably non-existent.

Therefore, it is really quite immaterial that the Fisher formula satisfies the strong factor reversal test and the Edgeworth-Marshall doesn't, since if one wanted to calculate the best price index for national accounting aggregates, one would necessarily be adjusting the Fisher price index to handle cyclical or seasonal commodities in a special way, and factor reversal would no longer apply.

These chain Edgeworth-Marshall price series should have their fixed-basket counterpart in a price index defined as:

$$P_{y/0}^{EM} = \frac{\sum p_y(q_0 + q_1)}{\sum p_0(q_0 + q_1)}; y = -2, -1, 0, 1, 2, \ldots$$

For the five years previous it would be chained as follows:

$$\begin{aligned} P_{y/0}^{EM} &= f \times \frac{\sum p_y(q_{-5} + q_{-4})}{\sum p_{-5}(q_{-5} + q_{-4})} \\ &= \left(\frac{\sum p_{-2}(q_0 + q_1)}{\sum p_0(q_0 + q_1)} \Big/ \frac{\sum p_{-2}(q_{-5} + q_{-4})}{\sum p_{-5}(q_{-5} + q_{-4})} \right) \times \frac{\sum p_y(q_{-5} + q_{-4})}{\sum p_{-5}(q_{-5} + q_{-4})} \\ &= \frac{\sum p_{-2}(q_0 + q_1)}{\sum p_0(q_0 + q_1)} \times \frac{\sum p_y(q_{-5} + q_{-4})}{\sum p_{-2}(q_{-5} + q_{-4})}, \qquad \text{for } y = -7, -6, -5, -4, -3. \end{aligned}$$

Earlier spans would be linked along the same lines. Arguably, if the price index were quarterly or monthly in frequency, the chain price index might be linked at the terminal quarter or terminal month, rather than the terminal year.

These would not be chain Edgeworth-Marshall price indexes; they would be chain Lowe indexes, but they would be based on baskets used in the chain Edgeworth-Marshall price indexes, and they would benefit from the use of two-year baskets, which would tend to give them a smaller amplitude than their chain Laspeyres counterparts.

8. Examples of Volume Measures for Declining and Rapidly Expanding Industries

To get a feel for the importance of the transactions equality principle, it is useful to illustrate this with a pair of examples. Table 1 lists data for a declining industry with four goods. Output and prices are decreasing for all of the goods in this industry, and there is the expected negative correlation between price changes and output. As can be seen, the volume of production in year 0 is only about five eighths its level in base year 0, evaluated at base year prices. Particularly significant is the decline in output of good 3, accompanied by a doubling in its price.

Table 1. Hypothetical Prices and Quantities for a Declining Industry

	p_0	q_0	p_0q_0	p_1	q_1	$Q_{1/0}$	p_0q_1
Good 1	1.0	3,000	3,000	0.5	1,940	0.647	1,940
Good 2	1.0	2,000	2,000	0.4	1,600	0.800	1,600
Good 3	1.0	1,000	1,000	2.0	180	0.180	180
Good 4	1.0	1,000	1,000	0.5	650	0.650	650
All goods			7,000				4,370

Source: Ehemann et al. (2000, p.6).

Table 2 shows the relative shares of the four commodities for Laspeyres, Paasche, Edgeworth-Marshall and Fisher volume indexes.[19] Note particularly the much stronger relative share of good 3 for the Paasche index, a consequence of good 3 doubling in price. While good 3 (along with good 4) is the least important commodity for the Laspeyres index, it is the dominant commodity for its Paasche counterpart. The Fisher shares are a weighted average of the Laspeyres and Paasche shares, but they differ very little from a simple average of these shares. For good three, for example, there is a 28.9% share, which is slightly larger than the 28.0% share if one takes the mean of the Laspeyres and Paasche shares. In contrast, because the Edgeworth-Marshall shares are based on average prices for years 0 and 1 that are calculated as unit values, they give more importance to year 0 than year 1, and are much closer to the Laspeyres shares than the Paasche shares. The share for good 3 in particular is much lower, at 19.8%, which is only about three eighths more than the Laspeyres share.

---

[19] The relative shares for the Fisher index were calculated using the formula shown in Balk (2004; p.109) with the appropriate substitution of price indexes for volume indexes and vice versa.

Table 2. Relative Importance of Goods for Different Volume Indexes for the Declining Industry Example

	Laspeyres	Paasche	Edgeworth-Marshall	Fisher
Good 1	0.429	0.313	0.413	0.367
Good 2	0.286	0.167	0.251	0.222
Good 3	0.143	0.417	0.198	0.289
Good 4	0.143	0.104	0.138	0.122

Table 3 shows the volume indexes generated in terms of this example. Given the negative correlation between prices and quantities, the Paasche index is lowest and the Laspeyres index is the highest. Note that the Fisher index is only slightly less than the Bowley-Sidgwick one (as it must be, since the geometric mean of any two numbers will always be less than the arithmetic mean), but the Edgeworth-Marshall index is much greater than either, being considerably closer to the Laspeyres measure than the Paasche one. The Walsh index is also larger than either of the crosses of Laspeyres and Paasche indexes, but less than the Edgeworth-Marshall index. In relative terms, lying closer to the Fisher index than to the Edgeworth-Marshall one.

The Edgeworth-Marshall measure gives a fairer measure of the decline in output in year 1 for this declining industry. The Fisher measure gives excessive importance to the price structure of year 1, since that production is much lower by any measure for this declining industry in the second year. In particular, it gives too high a share to good 3, whose production in year 1 had essentially collapsed.

Table 3. Comparison of Volume Indexes for the Declining Industry Example

Paasche	0.478
Fisher	0.546
Bowley-Sidgwick	0.551
Walsh	0.562
Edgeworth-Marshall	0.593
Laspeyres	0.624

If one simply inverts the previous situation, so that the prices and quantities of period 0 are those of period 1 and vice-versa, one gets the case of an expanding industry. Now there is expansion for all four goods in the industry, but particularly for good 3 whose output more than quintuples going from year 0 to year 1. Again there is the expected negative correlation between price change and volume change: the good with the largest price increase, good 2, also has the smallest increase in output. Notice that at prices of base year 0, the output of the industry in year 1 is more than double what it was in the previous year 0.

Table 4. Hypothetical Prices and Quantities for a New Expanding Industry

	p_0	q_0	p_0q_0	p_1	q_1	$Q_{1/0}$	p_0q_1
Good 1	0.5	1,940	970	1.0	3,000	1.546	1,500
Good 2	0.4	1,600	640	1.0	2,000	1.250	800
Good 3	2.0	180	360	1.0	1,000	5.556	2,000
Good 4	0.5	650	325	1.0	1,000	1.538	500
			2,295				4,800

Table 5 shows the shares of the different goods using different index formulae. Again, the most important change is for good 3, which is much less important using the Paasche index due to the halving of its price in year 1. Once more the Fisher shares, although representing a weighted average of the Laspeyres and Paasche shares, differ little from their simple average. But the Edgeworth-Marshall index, given the much greater volume of activity in year 1, has shares that more nearly reflect those of the Paasche measure. Also note that its shares for goods 1 and 4 fall outside the bounds defined by the shares of the Laspeyres and Paasche indexes, being slightly higher than the Paasche shares in both cases. The hybrid expenditures on which these shares are based must always lie between the bounds defined by the actual expenditures that determine the Laspeyres shares and the hybrid expenditures that determine the Paasche shares, but this is not true of the expenditure shares themselves.

Table 5. Relative Importance of Goods for Different Volume Indexes for the New Expanding Industry Example

	Laspeyres	Paasche	Edgeworth-Marshall	Fisher
Good 1	0.423	0.444	0.450	0.434
Good 2	0.279	0.366	0.339	0.325
Good 3	0.157	0.041	0.060	0.095
Good 4	0.142	0.149	0.151	0.145

Table 6 shows the rankings of the volume indexes calculated for the expanding industry case. Again, given the negative correlation between prices and quantities the Laspeyres index shows the highest growth and the Paasche index the lowest. The Fisher index is right between them, showing only a little less growth than the Bowley-Sidgwick index (as it must, given that a geometric mean will always be less than an arithmetic mean). In this case, the Edgeworth-Marshall index is inferior to most of the other indexes, exceeding only the Paasche index. The Walsh index is greater than the Edgeworth-Marshall index but less than the Fisher index; in relative terms, it lies closer to the Fisher index.

Table 6. Comparison of Volume Indexes for the New Expanding Industry Example

Index	Value
Paasche	1.602
Edgeworth-Marshall	1.685
Walsh	1.778
Fisher	1.830
Bowley-Sidgwick	1.847
Laspeyres	2.092

More than the previous example, this one illustrates the dangers of employing the Fisher formula due to its failure to satisfy the property of transactions equality. Although the volume of output in the comparison (i.e., current) period is much more important than in the base period, the Fisher formula essentially treats the two periods on equal terms, and so assigns undue importance to good 3. The small share for good 3 in the Fisher volume index belies its important contribution to change. It alone accounts for 43% of the measured 83% growth for this industry, which is surely excessive given that its production really only took off when its prices were cut in half. In the Edgeworth-Marshall index, good 3 is still the most important contributor to growth, but it only accounts for 27% of aggregate industry growth, barely exceeding good 1 which is responsible for 25% of aggregate growth.

Much has been written in recent years about the new economy, and indeed annual chaining of volume measures was introduced in many countries in hopes of achieving more accurate measurement in the new economy. However, the use of the chain Fisher formula in measuring growth of output for the new economy only reduces rather than eliminates the possibility of upward bias in measured growth rates. For this sector, the replacement of chain Fisher measures by their Edgeworth-Marshall equivalents would likely give lower and more meaningful estimates of growth in output.

Besides the consideration of the transaction equality principle, there is also the consideration that in a rapidly growing industry, new products may be introduced at concessionary prices that are not true market prices. There is also the problem of introducing prices for new goods in price index programs, with prices of new goods often proxied rather than priced for some time after their introduction. (These problems are discussed in more detail in Baldwin et al (1997).) If these factors don't create an obvious upward or downward bias in measuring prices for new goods, they certainly reduce the reliability of such measures. This is another reason why, if the volume of activity in two consecutive years is much greater in the second year reflecting an increasing maturity in the industry, it makes more sense to give greater weight to the price structure of the second year (as the Edgeworth-Marshall formula does) than to treat the two years on an equal footing (as the Fisher formula or the Walsh formula does).

The author received comments on an earlier version of this paper concerning realistic situations in which a Fisher price or volume index would allegedly perform better than its Edgeworth-Marshall counterpart. One was when a small open economy suffered a major devaluation of its currency, precipitating a contraction. In this situation there would be a dramatic increase in the price of imported goods, and a big decline in their purchases. Here the Edgeworth-Marshall price index would allegedly be inferior to the Fisher price index because it would closely approximate a Laspeyres price index, its basket being much more like the basket of the base year than of the subsequent year.

Table 6. Comparison of Price Indexes for the Example of a Declining Industry / Open Economy in a Devaluation

Paasche	0.525
Walsh	0.584
Fisher	0.600
Bowley-Sidgwick	0.605
Edgeworth-Marshall	0.624
Laspeyres	0.686

In a sense the declining industry example shown earlier can be reinterpreted in this way, with good 3, whose prices double in a year, representing imported goods. And using its data to construct price indexes rather than volume indexes it can be seen that the Edgeworth-Marshall index does come closer to the Laspeyres index than do any of the others.(See Table 6 above.) Interestingly, the Walsh index, which in terms of its formula would seem to be so similar to the Edgeworth-Marshall index, actually comes the closest to the Paasche index; both the crosses of Laspeyres and Paasche indexes are closer to the Edgeworth-Marshall index than the Walsh index. In fact, it can be easily shown that if one assumes a doubling of prices is sufficient to choke off imports altogether so that good 3 disappears from the basket in year 1, the Walsh index would be virtually identical with the Paasche index, exceeding it by only 0.5%, since in this case good 3 would disappear from its basket just as it does from the year 1 basket.

Note that the Fisher index is only very slightly lower than the Bowley-Sidgwick index, which is just the mean of the Paasche and Laspeyres price indexes.

So which of these index numbers is more reasonable? At year 0 prices, good 3, the imported good has a 10.4% basket share for years 0 and 1 combined, a 14.3% basket share for year 0 only but only a 4.1% share for year 1. The Fisher and Bowley-Sidgwick indexes are lower than the Edgeworth-Marshall index in large part because they treat the two basket shares as being equally valid, which means that the doubling of prices for the import good does not have nearly the same impact on them that it does on the Edgeworth-Marshall index. But it is surely unreasonable to treat the two baskets as having equal validity when at year 0 prices the volume of expenditures in year 1 is only 60% of those of year 0. Thus the Edgeworth-Marshall index produces the most reasonable result.

Nor is there any reason to believe that the use of the Edgeworth-Marshall formula would seriously overweight imports were the year 1 situation to become the depressing new normal. What is being calculated is not a direct Lowe price index with a year 0 and year 1 basket, but a chain Edgeworth-Marshall price index with annual links. If year 2 saw no change in basket shares from year 1, all index links would show the same price increases, whatever their formulas.

The other situation mentioned was the case of high rates of inflation, which would tend to make the Marshall-Edgeworth volume measures more closely resemble Paasche measures, since the more highly inflated values in year 1 would, other things being equal, have a greater impact on the determination of base prices.

There are two points to make about this. First, the assumption that an Edgeworth-Marshall volume index would necessarily be closer to a Paasche volume index in a high inflationary situation needs to be greatly qualified. It can easily be shown that if one doubles every price in year 2 for the declining industry case shown in Table 1, the Edgeworth-Marshall index would still have the highest value except for the Laspeyres index and the Fisher index would still have the lowest value except for the Paasche index. When the relative importance of year 0 compared to year 1 in volume terms is such as to make the Edgeworth-Marshall base prices look more like Laspeyres base prices, even a very high rate of inflation isn't going to change this.

High rates of inflation combined with a sharply declining volume of output is by no means an unrealistic scenario. This was the situation in virtually every country in the former Soviet Union for several years or more after 1991.

Second, the Laspeyres and Paasche base prices from which the Fisher volume measures are built are constructed like the Edgeworth-Marshall base prices, only for a single year instead of two. So if a high inflation rate is deemed to distort the weighting pattern of an Edgeworth-Marshall volume aggregate in favour of year 1 over year 0, by the same token it distorts the weighting pattern away from commodities that are purchased more in the first quarter and in favour of commodities that are purchased more in the fourth quarter. Therefore, in a Fisher aggregate under high inflation, Christmas trees and turkeys will tend to be overweighted, package holiday trips to winter sun spots underweighted.

Logically, if the Edgeworth-Marshall formula is considered inferior to the Fisher formula on this basis, the Fisher formula would be inferior to the formula:

$$Q_{1/0}^{Fmod} = \left[\prod_{q=1}^{4} \left[\frac{\sum p_{0q} q_1}{\sum p_{0q} q_0} \frac{\sum p_{1q} q_1}{\sum p_{1q} q_0} \right]^{1/2} \right]^{1/4}$$

i.e. the geometric mean of the volume ratios for year 1 compared to base year 0 as weighted by each set of quarterly prices for the two year period. One could also envision a monthly version of the same formula.

However, it seems unproductive to let a high inflation rate dictate the choice of formula when Peter Hill (1996) has already proposed a workable solution in terms of constant price level (CPL) accounts, of dealing with the same problem, whatever index formula is used for volume series. It would involve the deflation of all value weights by the same general price index for the overall economy before being used in the index formula. Although the exact mechanics of his solution are open to debate, for certain some such method could be applied, and would be applicable to a volume index based on any formula.

It should be noted that where such a method was applied to a Fisher volume index, because it would use adjusted value weights, it would no longer satisfy the factor reversal property. Hill (1996; p.49) notes that "under high inflation, it is not possible to partition changes in the aggregate values in the current accounts into price and quantity changes both of which are acceptable as index numbers in their own right."

So while a high inflation environment would not strip the Edgeworth-Marshall formula of its superior representativeness compared to the Fisher formula, it would certainly strip the Fisher formula of its claim to satisfy the factor reversal property since with CPL accounts this would no longer be true.[20]

9. What Are the Remedies for Small or Developing Countries?

The SNA93 recommendations for price and volume measures do impose onerous statistical requirements on the agencies that would implement them, and the modifications to them suggested in this paper do not greatly reduce this burden. The SNA93 manual itself recognized that its preferred methodology, its A-level methodology, annual-link chain Fisher volume measures, was perhaps too costly to implement for many countries. It therefore also suggested a B-level methodology, annual-link chain Laspeyres volume measures, as an acceptable alternative.

The SNA93 A-level methodology has been poorly received by the international community; only the United States and Canada at the time of writing have implemented annual-link chain Fisher volume measures, and Canada only for its industry estimates. The SNA93 B-level methodology has been much better received. Eurostat has gone on to recommend annual-link chain Laspeyres countries for the European Community, and all its members have either

[20] The claim is inflated in any case, since due to the complications involved in deflating the value of physical change in inventories, factor reversal is not satisfied for such series in the Fisher world, nor for any aggregate containing VPC series, including total GDP itself.

converted to this methodology or are in the process of doing so. Other developed countries like Australia have also implemented SNA93's B-level methodology.

However, a number of countries, and not all of them in the developing world, essentially remain in the SNA68 universe, seeming to have neither the resources for chain Fisher or for chain Laspeyres estimates. I suspect they would not be persuaded to summon up the resources to calculate chain Edgeworth-Marshall estimates either.

For these countries there is probably no immediate escape from chain Laspeyres volume measures and their corresponding Paasche price indexes. But the SNA93 standards has left them with an all-or-nothing choice between annual chain linking and continuing as they are. So they will likely continue as they are, with Laspeyres volume series using constant prices for a base year 10 or 15 or more years in the past.

However, as discussed in section 4, such estimates could be greatly improved simply by replacing a ten-year rebasing cycle with a five-year rebasing cycle and making the base year the third or central year of the five-year span) rather than the initial year. In fact, in one important respect such estimates would be superior to those of many countries that have adopted annual-linked chain Laspeyres measures, since with less frequent links the series would be less prone to chain index drift.

And in addition to the corresponding Paasche price indexes, developing countries should be encouraged to calculate Laspeyres price indexes, which like the volume series would follow a five-year rebasing cycle with the basket reference year the central year of the five-year span.

While such a program would be considerably inferior to the system of annual-link chain Edgeworth-Marshall price and volume series outlined above, it would still mark a considerable advance over the SNA68 standards, and the index number procedures of most national accounting agencies in the developed world for most of the 20th century.

These volume measures might be comparable with direct Laspeyres volume aggregates calculated by developed countries, since according to SNA93 they are supposed to calculate these as analytical adjuncts to their annual-link chain measures.

10. Conclusion

The recommendations of this paper regarding chain indexes are fairly conventional as regards linking. I agree with the idea of chaining at the annual level and that is also what the SNA93 recommends and what most countries that calculate experimental or official chain volume series have done.

I also support the calculation of fixed-price volume aggregates rather than Fisher volume indexes. This conclusion, although at variance with SNA93 and with BEA and Statistics Canada practice, is in keeping with the decisions made by Eurostat and by the Australian Bureau of Statistics, and with the advice of a number of economists who have studied the subject.

However, most economists who have favoured chaining using fixed-price volume series have opted for Laspeyres aggregates, with only Erwin Diewert (1996), so far as I know, favouring the Walsh formula. No-one, to the best of my knowledge, has ever recommended the

Edgeworth-Marshall formula for use in the SNA. Statistics Sweden planned to revamp their consumer price index as a chain Edgeworth-Marshall index but finally they opted for the quite similar Walsh formula instead.

In recent years, the German economist Claude Hillinger has recommended using Edgeworth-Marshall price indexes as deflators to calculate volume aggregates.[21] It is not within the scope of this paper to comment on Professor Hillinger's work in detail, but it should be underlined that his proposal is quite different from the one in this paper. However, Professor Hillinger did a good thing at least in bringing renewed interest to the Edgeworth-Marshall formula.

This formula has always had its defenders, from Knibbs in the 1920's to Krtscha in the contemporary period, but it has never had as strong backing as other formulae. In my view this is due to an undue emphasis on whether formulae pass the factor reversal test and on whether they are exact for an aggregator function, neither of which the Edgeworth-Marshall formula does.[22] However, time reversal, matrix consistency (or additivity), the new good property and the property of transactions equality are important considerations too -- in my judgement, *more* important considerations -- for choosing a chain index formula, and the Edgeworth-Marshall formula is unique in possessing all of these properties.

The Walsh formula, which *is* exact for a utility function, is just as good with respect to time reversal, matrix consistency and the new good property, but fails the transactions equality property.

If I had only a 90-second TV slot to deliver my message, this would be it:

Chain price and volume aggregates with annual links hold the promise of improved measures of growth. It is most unfortunate that discussion has centred on two formulae, the Laspeyres and the Fisher, neither of which is well-suited for the calculation of chain aggregates. The Laspeyres formula doesn't pass the time reversal test, and a healthy fear of chain drift should lead us to reject it. The Fisher formula passes the time reversal test, but it fails the matrix consistency test, is not even weakly consistent in aggregation and fails the new good test, all of which make it an awkward and unsatisfying formula for both producers and consumers of National Accounts estimates. None of these criticisms hold for the Edgeworth-Marshall formula and only the Edgeworth-Marshall formula has the property of transactions equality that has very important implications for growth measurement in the new economy. So far as any one formula will be the formula for price and volume measurement in the National Accounts in the 21st century, it should be the Edgeworth-Marshall formula. However, we should cease to try to make all industries or commodities fit into the Procrustean bed of one formula and, where required, we should change

---

[21] See Hillinger (2000). A number of papers have been written that comment on his methodology, one of which -- Ehemann et al. (2000) -- is listed in the references to this paper.

[22] The true factorial price index that is consistent with a Leontief, fixed-coefficients utility function is the ratio of an expenditure index to an Edgeworth-Marshall quantity index as shown by Balk (1983). This is *not* the Edgeworth-Marshall implicit price index defined by (4.6): its formula would be:

$$(\Sigma p_1 q_1 / \Sigma p_0 q_0)/(\Sigma p_{01} q_1 / \Sigma p_{01} q_0).$$

But the Edgeworth-Marshall price index itself is not consistent with this or any other utility function, and in any case, a "superlative" index that is only consistent with a fixed-coefficients utility function is of very limited interest.

our formulae for price and volume measures to take account of cyclical and seasonal commodities. Finally, matrix consistency is dependent not only on formula choice but on linking policy. We must follow the good example of Australia and the United Kingdom, and change our reference year annually, linking our chain-volume estimates backward rather than forward.

Appendix: Weak, Specific and Strong Consistency in Aggregation

So far in the literature on index numbers, the discussion of consistency in aggregation has revolved around price rather than volume indexes. For now, let us then stick to definitions of consistency in aggregation in the domain of price indexes.

Balk (1996) [23]defines the following properties for an index to be consistent in aggregation:

1. the index for the aggregate, which is defined as a single-stage index, can also be computed in two stages, namely by first computing the indexes for the subaggregates and from these the index for the aggregate;
2. the indexes used in the single-stage computation and those used in the first stage computation have the same functional form,
3. the formula used in the second stage computation has the same functional form as the indexes used in the single and in the first stage after the following transformation has been applied: elemental indexes are replaced by subaggregate indexes and the values of the elemental indexes are replaced by subaggregate values.

Balk takes an all-or-nothing approach to consistency in aggregation, and would not consider a formula that satisfies the first two properties to be consistent in aggregation, although he notes that Blackorby and Primont (1980) ignored the third property altogether in their definition of consistency in aggregation. It probably makes better sense to consider an index formula that meets all three criteria as being strongly consistent in aggregation, and one that meets only the first two criteria as being weakly consistent in aggregation.

Balk notes that the Walsh formula, which is very similar to the Edgeworth-Marshall one, satisfies the first two criteria for a price index but not the third. This is also true of the Edgeworth-Marshall price index.

Auer (2004) writes of weak and specific consistency in aggregation; specific consistency in aggregation, as he defines it, is identical with Balk's criteria.[24] However, he notes that the Edgeworth-Marshall price index can be defined in terms of base and comparison period values, but also in two alternative ways involving values at constant prices, and for these definitions, single-stage and two-stage solutions are identical. It therefore passes the weak consistency test.

---

[23] See Balk (1990, p. 358-359). I have largely adopted Balk's phrasing.

[24] Auer (2004) also discusses strict consistency in aggregation, which would imply that consistency in aggregation holds whichever variant of the index formula is used to define it. Although the Stuvel and Montgomery-Vartia price formulae are specifically consistent in aggregation, neither is strictly consistent in aggregation.

Although there is a difference between weak consistency as defined by Balk's first two properties and weak consistency in Auer's sense, the Edgeworth-Marshall formula is weakly consistent by either definition, as is the Walsh formula.

The Fisher formula is not even weakly consistent in aggregation, and one cannot (or at least should not) calculate a Fisher of Fishers. At any stage of aggregation one must have a set of Laspeyres and Paasche indexes and the Fisher index should be calculated as their geometric mean. Auer also shows that if one erroneously does treat the Fisher formula as being consistent in aggregation, the empirical implications of the error can be far from trivial. In his example, calculating a Fisher of Fishers changes a correctly estimated 1.6% price increase into a misestimated price decrease of 0.5%.[25]

He is also surely right in believing that the important distinction is between formulae that are weakly consistent in aggregation (like Edgeworth-Marshall) and not consistent at all (like Fisher). Strong consistency (or specific consistency), by contrast, is not particularly important.

All of the formulae that are strongly consistent in aggregation without exception have one or more very bad properties that would seem to more than offset any advantage this might incur over their weakly consistent rivals. Neither the Laspeyres formula nor the Paasche formula satisfies the time reversal property; neither the Montgomery-Vartia nor the Stuvel formula satisfies proportionality.

Expressed in terms of value series and price deflators, the Edgeworth-Marshall volume index can be calculated as:

$$\text{(A1)}\quad \frac{\sum p_{01}q_1}{\sum p_{01}q_0} = \frac{\sum \frac{v_0+v_1}{q_0+q_1}q_1}{\sum \frac{v_0+v_1}{q_0+q_1}q_0} = \frac{\sum \frac{v_0+v_1}{p_0q_0+p_0q_1}p_0q_1}{\sum \frac{v_0+v_1}{p_0q_0+p_0q_1}p_0q_0} = \frac{\sum \frac{v_0+v_1}{v_0+v_1/P_{1/0}}v_1/P_{1/0}}{\sum \frac{v_0+v_1}{v_0+v_1/P_{1/0}}v_0}$$

or as

$$\text{(A2)}\quad \frac{\sum p_{01}q_1}{\sum p_{01}q_0} = \frac{\sum \frac{v_0+v_1}{q_0+q_1}q_1}{\sum \frac{v_0+v_1}{q_0+q_1}q_0} = \frac{\sum \frac{v_0+v_1}{p_1q_0+p_1q_1}p_1q_1}{\sum \frac{v_0+v_1}{p_1q_0+p_1q_1}p_1q_0} = \frac{\sum \frac{v_0+v_1}{v_0P_{1/0}+v_1}v_1}{\sum \frac{v_0+v_1}{v_0P_{1/0}+v_1}v_0P_{1/0}}$$

Using the formulation on the rightmost side of either (A1) or (A2), the Edgeworth-Marshall volume index gives the same result for Auer's example of a three-commodity economy whether calculated in two steps or in a single step.

For statistical agencies themselves, the failure of a formula to satisfy either weak or strong consistency in aggregation is probably more of a nuisance issue than a real issue. The problem is more what users who are not well-versed in index number properties will do with data series. In this respect, data users are more likely to go seriously wrong working with Fisher aggregates than they are with Edgeworth-Marshall ones.

[25] See Auer (2004), pp.385-386.

References

Al, P. G., B.M. Balk, S. de Boer and G.P. den Bakker (1986), "The Use of Chain Indices for Deflating the National Accounts," *Statistical Journal of the United Nations ECE* 4, 347-368.

Aspden, C. (2000), "Introduction of Chain Value and Price Measures – The Australian Approach", paper presented at the Jint APB/ESCAP Workshop on Rebasing and Linking of National Accounts Series", Bangkok, Thailand.

Baldwin, Andrew, Pierre Després, Alice Nakamura and Masao Nakamura (1997), "New Goods from the Perspective of Price Index Making in Canada and Japan", in Timothy F. Bresnahan and Robert J. Gordon (eds.), *The Economics of New Goods*, The University of Chicago Press, 437-476.

Balk, B.M. (1980), *Seasonal Products in Agriculture and Horticulture and Methods for Computing Price Indices*, Statistical Studies No. 24, The Hague: Netherlands Central Bureau of Statistics

Balk, B.M. (1983), "A Note on the True Factorial Price Index," *Statistische Hefte* 24, 69-72.

Balk, B.M. (1995), "Axiomatic Price Index Theory: A Survey," *International Statistical Review* 63, 1969-1993.

Balk, B.M. (1996), "Consistency-in-Aggregation and Stuvel Indices," *Review of Income and Wealth*, series 42, Number 3, 353-363.

Balk, B.M. (2004), "Decomposition of Fisher Indexes," *Economic Letters*, 82, 107-113

Blackorby, C. and D. Primont (1980), "Index Numbers and Consistency in Aggregation", *Journal of Economic Theory*, 22, 87-98

Bowley, A.L. (1923), review of *The Making of Index Numbers: A Study of Their Varieties*, Tests and Reliability, by Irving Fisher, *Economic Journal*, 33, 90-94.

Dalén, J. (1999), "A Proposal for a New System of Aggregation in the Swedish Consumer Price Index," a revised and extended version of paper presented at the fifth meeting of the International Working Group on Price Indices under the title "Some Issues in Index Construction," November.

Diewert, W.E. (1993), "The Early History of Price Index Research," in *Essays in Index Number Theory, Volume I,* Contributions to Economic Analysis 217, W.E. Diewert and A.O. Nakamura (eds.), Amsterdam: North Holland, 33-65.

Diewert, W.E. (1996), "Price and Volume Measures in the System of National Accounts," in J. Kendrick (ed.), *The New System of National Economic Accounts,* Norwell, Kluwer Academic Publishers, 237-285.

Diewert, W.E. (2001), "The Consumer Price Index and Index Number Purpose," *Journal of Economic and Social Measurement* 27, 167-248.

Dikhanov, Y. (1994), "Sensitivity of PPP-Based Income Estimates to Choice of Aggregation Procedures," paper presented at the Conference of the International Association for Research in Income and Wealth, St. Andrews, New Brunswick, August 21-27.

Edgeworth, F.Y. (1925), *Papers Relating to Political Economy*, Vol.1, Burt Franklin.

Ehemann, C., A.J. Katz, and B.R. Moulton (2000), "How the Chain Additivity Issue Is Treated in the U.S. Economic Accounts," paper presented at the OECD meeting of National Accounts Experts, 26-29 September.

Eurostat (2001), *Handbook on Price and Volume Measures in National Accounts*, Luxemburg.

Eurostat, IMF, OECD, UN and World Bank (1993), *System of National Accounts 1993,* Brussels, Luxemburg, New York and Washington, D.C.

Hill, P. (1996), *Inflation Accounting: A Manual on National Accounting Under Conditions of High Inflation*, Paris: OECD

Hillinger, C. (2000), "Consistent Aggregation and Chaining of Price and Quantity Measures," paper presented at the OECD meeting of National Accounts Experts, 26-29 September.

Horner, F.B. (1971), "Effect of Grouping of Data on the Divergence Between Laspeyres and Paasche Forms of Quantum Indexes," *Review of Income and Wealth*, series 17, number 3, 263-72.

Krtscha, M. (1984), "A Characterization of the Edgeworth-Marshall Index," *Methods in Operations Research*, 48, Königstein: Athenaüm/Hain/Hanstein.

Landefeld, J.S. and R.P.Parker (1995), "Preview of the Comprehensive Revision of the National Income and Product Accounts: BEA's New Featured Measures of Output and Prices," *Survey of Current Business*, July, 31-38.

Lynch, Robin (1996), "Measuring Real Growth – Index Numbers and Chain-Linking", *Economic Trends*, No. 512, June 1996, 31-37.

Moulton, B.R. and E.P. Seskin (1999), "A Preview of the 1999 Comprehensive Revision of the National Income and Product Accounts: Statistical Changes," *Survey of Current Business*, October , 6-17.

Reinsdorf, M.B. and A.H. Dorfman (1999), "The Sato-Vartia Index and the Monotonicity Axiom," *Journal of Econometrics*, 90, 45-61.

Rossiter, R.D. (2000) "Fisher Ideal Indexes in the National Income and Product Accounts," *Journal of Economic Education*, Fall, 363-373.

Rothwell, D.P. (1958), "Use of Varying Seasonal Weights in Price Index Construction", *Journal of the American Statistical Association*, XLIII, pp. 66-77

Szulc, B. (1998), "Effects of Using Various Macro-Index Formulae in Longitudinal Price and Volume Comparisons", Paper for the Fourth Meeting of the Ottawa Group on Price Indices, Washington, D.C., April 22-24, 1998.

Tuke, A. and J. Beadle (2003), "The Effect of Annual Chain-Linking on Blue Book 2002 Annual Growth Estimates", *Economic Trends*, No. 593, April 2003, 29-40.

United Nations (1968), *A System of National Accounts*, New York, Series F, no. 2, Revision 3.

Vartia, Y.O. (1976), "Ideal Log-Change Index Numbers," *Scandinavian Journal of Statistics* 3, 121-26.

von Auer, L. (2004), "Consistency in Aggregation," *Jahrbücher für Nationalökonomie und Statistik*, 224 (4), 383-398.

Whelan, K. (2000), "A Guide to the Use of Chain Aggregated NIPA Data," Federal Reserve Board.

Chapter 14

INEXACT INDEX NUMBERS AND ECONOMIC MONOTONICITY VIOLATIONS: THE GDP IMPLICIT PRICE DEFLATOR

Ulrich Kohli[1]

1. Introduction

Several countries have recently switched – or are about to do so – to chained price and quantity indexes in the framework for their national accounts. Thus, the United States and Canada have adopted the chained Fisher indexes, whereas the United Kingdom, Switzerland, Australia and New Zealand have opted for chained Laspeyres indexes for real GDP, and chained Paasche for the implicit price deflator. Nonetheless, the vast majority of countries, including most OECD members, have not yet embraced chaining. In these countries the GDP implicit price deflator is still computed as a *direct* (or fixed-base) Paasche price index. Time series data on the deflator are obtained by taking *runs* (or sequences) of these direct indexes. Changes in the price level over consecutive periods are measured by the change in the direct Paasche index, a use for which it is ill suited.

Indeed, using the economic approach to index numbers in the context of supply theory, we show that runs of direct Paasche indexes fail an economic monotonicity test if the number of periods exceeds two.[2] That is, the price index can register a drop between consecutive periods even though none of the disaggregate prices has fallen, and some have actually increased.

The purpose of this paper is thus to draw attention to some of the undesirable properties of the direct Paasche price index, and, more generally, to the problems that the absence of chaining can raise. Examples based on a constant elasticity of substitution or constant elasticity of transformation (*CES* or *CET*) aggregator function are provided. A similar result holds for runs of direct Fisher indexes. This provides a powerful argument in favor of chaining. It should also serve as a warning against the use of unit values as elementary price indexes at the most disaggregate level.

---

[1] When this paper was written, the author was the chief economist, Swiss National Bank. He is now with the University of Geneva and can be reached at Ulrich.Kohli@unige.ch. He is grateful to W. Erwin Diewert, Andreas Fischer, Kevin J. Fox, Alice Nakamura, and Ludwig von Auer for their comments on earlier drafts of this paper, but they are not responsible for any errors or omissions.

[2] This problem also arises in the context of demand theory; see Kohli (1986). However, Paasche index numbers are probably most prevalent in supply theory, since they are widely used in the national accounts.

Citation: **Ulrich Kohli (2011), "Inexact Index Numbers and Economic Monotonicity Violations: The GDP Implicit Price Deflator," chapter 14, pp. 317-328 in W.E. Diewert, B.M. Balk, D. Fixler, K.J. Fox and A.O. Nakamura, *PRICE AND PRODUCTIVITY MEASUREMENT: Volume 6 -- Index Number Theory.* Trafford Press.**

© Alice Nakamura, 2011. Permission to link to, or copy or reprint, these materials is granted without restriction, including for use in commercial textbooks, with due credit to the authors and editors.

Our analysis is based on the economic approach to index numbers. Much of this literature focuses on exact index numbers, to use the terminology introduced by Diewert (1976). That is, knowing the precise form of the aggregator function (e.g. the production possibilities frontier), one seeks to find an index number formula that is exact for it. Alternatively, starting from an arbitrary index number formula, one looks for the aggregator function for which this index number would be exact.[3] For instance, it turns out that the Paasche price index is exact as long as the transformation function is either linear or Leontief.

The strategy followed in this paper is somewhat different. We investigate the properties of a given, commonly used index number formula when we know in advance that this index is *not* exact for the underlying aggregator function, which itself is assumed to be fairly general and well behaved. Specifically, we will look at the direct Paasche price index (the Laspeyres and the Fisher indexes will be briefly examined as well), while assuming that the production possibilities frontier is strictly concave.

The case of the *CET* aggregator function can be thought of as an example of a well-behaved production possibilities frontier. Clearly, one could argue that if the aggregator function is *CET*, then it would be a simple matter to use a *CET* price index, which would then be exact. The point, though, is that analysts and commentators often have no choice in this matter, statistical agencies typically supplying Paasche, Laspeyres and Fisher indexes only. In any case, the selection of the *CET* is only meant as an illustration. Any other functional form that allows the production possibilities frontier to be strictly concave would yield similar results.

2. Runs of Direct Paasche Price Indexes

The *direct Paasche price index* ($P_{t,0}^P$) makes a direct comparison between the cost of a basket of goods in the current period (period *t*) and the cost of the same basket at base period (period 0) prices. Period *t* quantities are used for this comparison. Formally, the direct Paasche price index can be defined as follows:

$$(1) \qquad P_{t,0}^P \equiv \frac{\sum_i p_{i,t} q_{i,t}}{\sum_i p_{i,0} q_{i,t}},$$

where $p_{i,t}$ and $q_{i,t}$ denote the price and the quantity of good *i* at time *t*.

A *run* of direct Paasche price indexes is then given by the following sequence:

$$(2) \qquad 1, \frac{\sum_i p_{i,1} q_{i,1}}{\sum_i p_{i,0} q_{i,1}}, \frac{\sum_i p_{i,2} q_{i,2}}{\sum_i p_{i,0} q_{i,2}}, \ldots, \frac{\sum_i p_{i,t-1} q_{i,t-1}}{\sum_i p_{i,0} q_{i,t-1}}, \frac{\sum_i p_{i,t} q_{i,t}}{\sum_i p_{i,0} q_{i,t}},$$

[3] Much emphasis has been devoted to superlative indexes; i.e., index numbers that are exact for flexible functional forms. A functional form is flexible if it can provide a second-order approximation to an arbitrary aggregator function. The terms “flexible,” “superlative,” and “aggregator function” were coined by Diewert (1974, 1976).

or, in more compact form:

$$(3) \qquad 1,\ P^P_{1,0},\ P^P_{2,0},\ \ldots,\ P^P_{t-1,0},\ P^P_{t,0}\ .$$

It is common practice to use elements of this sequence to make comparisons between arbitrary pairs of periods. For instance, if one wanted to compare period t with period t-1, one would calculate $\Pi_{t,t-1}$ defined as follows:

$$(4) \qquad \Pi_{t,t-1} \equiv \frac{P^P_{t,0}}{P^P_{t-1,0}} = \frac{\sum_i p_{i,t}q_{i,t}}{\sum_i p_{i,0}q_{i,t}} \frac{\sum_i p_{i,0}q_{i,t-1}}{\sum_i p_{i,t-1}q_{i,t-1}}$$

It is important to note that, although $\Pi_{t,t-1}$ rests on the comparison between two Paasche indexes, it is not itself a Paasche index, unless period t-1 happens to be the base period.[4] Although its properties are little known, $\Pi_{t,t-1}$ is routinely used in economic analysis. Consecutive changes in the GDP price deflator, in particular, are often used as a broad measure of inflation. If $\Pi_{t,t-1}$ turns out to be greater than one, one might be inclined to conclude that, on average, prices have gone up between period t-1 and period t. As we shall see below, this conclusion could be diametrically wrong.

3. Profit Maximization and the Economic Approach to Index Numbers

The economic approach to index numbers assumes that the observed quantities ($q_{i,t}$) are not random, but rather that they are the outcome of economic decisions. In particular, they reflect prices, technology, and optimizing behavior.

Assume for simplicity that national production involves just one input (e.g., an aggregate of labor and capital), the quantity of which we denote by x_t, and two outputs (i = 1, 2). We assume constant returns to scale, nondecreasing marginal rates of transformation, and profit maximization. Let the country's production possibilities frontier be given by the following transformation (or factor requirements) function:

$$(5) \qquad x_t = h(q_{1,t}, q_{2,t})\ .$$

Constant returns to scale imply that $h(\cdot)$ is linearly homogeneous, and the assumption of nondecreasing marginal rates of transformation means that $h(\cdot)$ is convex. Profit maximization implies that the marginal rate of transformation is equal to the output price ratio:

---

[4] This is also pointed out by Afriat (1977). It is interesting to note that $\Pi_{t,t-1}$ can be viewed as the value index divided by a Lowe quantity index, and as such it could be termed an implicit Lowe price index; see Kohli (2004b). Moreover, as pointed out to me by Bert Balk, it can be seen from (4) that $\Pi_{t,t-1}$ violates the Proportionality and Identity tests, which bodes ill for its other properties.

$$(6) \qquad \frac{h_1(q_{1,t},q_{2,t})}{h_2(q_{1,t},q_{2,t})} = \frac{p_{1,t}}{p_{2,t}},$$

where $h_i(\cdot) \equiv \partial h(\cdot)/\partial q_{i,t}$, $i = 1, 2$. It is possible to solve (5) and (6) for $q_{i,t}$:

$$(7) \qquad q_{i,t} = q_i(p_{1,t}, p_{2,t}, x_t) = y_i(p_{1,t}, p_{2,t})x_t ,$$

where $y_i(\cdot) \equiv q_i(\cdot)/x_t$ can be interpreted as unit output (output per unit of input). The linear homogeneity of $q_i(\cdot)$ with respect to x_t results from the linear homogeneity of $h(\cdot)$. Moreover, the assumption of optimization and the convexity of $h(\cdot)$ (concavity of the production possibilities frontier) imply that $q_i(\cdot)$ – and $y_i(\cdot)$ for that matter – is homogeneous of degree zero in prices and nondecreasing in its own price:

$$(8) \qquad \frac{\partial q_i(\cdot)}{\partial p_{1,t}} p_{1,t} + \frac{\partial q_i(\cdot)}{\partial p_{2,t}} p_{2,t} = 0, \quad \frac{\partial q_i(\cdot)}{\partial p_{i,t}} \geq 0, \quad i = 1, 2.$$

The economic approach to index numbers then amounts to introducing expressions such as (7) into index number formulas such as (1). In the two-good case, the direct Paasche price index becomes:

$$(9) \qquad \begin{aligned} P_{t,0}^P &= \frac{p_{1,t}q_1(p_{1,t},p_{2,t},x_t) + p_{2,t}q_2(p_{1,t},p_{2,t},x_t)}{p_{1,0}q_1(p_{1,t},p_{2,t},x_t) + p_{2,0}q_2(p_{1,t},p_{2,t},x_t)} \\ &= \frac{p_{1,t}y_1(p_{1,t},p_{2,t}) + p_{2,t}y_2(p_{1,t},p_{2,t})}{p_{1,0}y_1(p_{1,t},p_{2,t}) + p_{2,0}y_2(p_{1,t},p_{2,t})} \end{aligned}.$$

It is customary to normalize base period (period 0) prices to unity ($p_{1,0} = p_{2,0} = 1$). Thus, expression (9) can be rewritten as:

$$(10) \qquad P_{t,0}^P = P_{t,0}^P(p_{1,t},p_{2,t}) = \frac{p_{1,t}y_1(p_{1,t},p_{2,t}) + p_{2,t}y_2(p_{1,t},p_{2,t})}{y_1(p_{1,t},p_{2,t}) + y_2(p_{1,t},p_{2,t})} .$$

4. Economic Monotonicity Test

It seems reasonable to expect a well-behaved measure of the general price level to be monotonically increasing – or at least nondecreasing – in its arguments.[5] That is, if one disaggregate price were to rise, while all other prices are held constant, one would like to see the aggregate price index increase, or at least not fall, *after having allowed for the endogenous adjustment in quantities.*

To investigate the slope properties of the direct Paasche price index, it suffices to differentiate (10) with respect to a disaggregate price, say the first one:

[5] See Kohli (1986) for an examination of the monotonicity properties of index numbers in the context of demand theory.

$$\frac{\partial P^P_{t,0}}{\partial p_{1,t}} = \frac{\left(y_{1,t} + p_{1,t}\frac{\partial y_{1,t}}{\partial p_{1,t}} + p_{2,t}\frac{\partial y_{2,t}}{\partial p_{1,t}}\right)(y_{1,t}+y_{2,t}) - (p_{1,t}y_{1,t}+p_{2,t}y_{2,t})\left(\frac{\partial y_{1,t}}{\partial p_{1,t}} + \frac{\partial y_{2,t}}{\partial p_{1,t}}\right)}{(y_{1,t}+y_{2,t})^2}$$

$$= \frac{y_{1,t}^2 + y_{1,t}y_{2,t} + y_{2,t}\frac{\partial y_{1,t}}{\partial p_{1,t}}(p_{1,t}-p_{2,t}) + y_{1,t}\frac{\partial y_{2,t}}{\partial p_{1,t}}(p_{2,t}-p_{1,t})}{(y_{1,t}+y_{2,t})^2}$$

(11)

$$= \frac{y_{1,t}^2 + y_{1,t}y_{2,t} + y_{1,t}y_{2,t}(\varepsilon_{11,t}-\varepsilon_{21,t})\left(1-\frac{p_{2,t}}{p_{1,t}}\right)}{(y_{1,t}+y_{2,t})^2}$$

$$= \frac{y_{1,t}^2 + y_{1,t}y_{2,t}\left[1-\theta_{12,t}\left(1-\frac{p_{2,t}}{p_{1,t}}\right)\right]}{(y_{1,t}+y_{2,t})^2} \gtrless 0$$

where $\varepsilon_{11,t} \equiv \partial \ln y_{1,t}/\partial \ln p_{1,t} \geq 0$ and $\varepsilon_{21,t} \equiv \partial \ln y_{2,t}/\partial \ln p_{1,t} \leq 0$ are the price elasticities of output supply with respect to $p_{1,t}$ at time t; and $\theta_{12,t} \equiv [h(\cdot)h_{12}(\cdot)/h_1(\cdot)h_2(\cdot)] \leq 0$, where $h_{12}(\cdot) \equiv \partial^2 h(\cdot)/(\partial q_{1,t}\partial q_{2,t})$, is the elasticity of transformation between the two outputs. Note that $\varepsilon_{11,t} = -\theta_{12,t}s_{2,t}$ and $\varepsilon_{21,t} = \theta_{12,t}s_{1,t}$, with $s_{i,t}$ being the revenue share of output i at time t,[6] so that $\varepsilon_{11,t} - \varepsilon_{21,t} = -\theta_{12,t} \geq 0$.[7]

It is apparent from the last line of (11) that $\partial P^P_{t,0}/\partial p_{1,t}$ can be negative if the ratio $p_{2,t}/p_{1,t}$ is sufficiently large, i.e. if $p_{1,t}$ is small enough relative to $p_{2,t}$, unless $\theta_{12,t}$ happens to be nil.[8] If the production possibilities frontier is strictly concave, on the other hand, and if production is diversified, $\theta_{12,t}$ is strictly negative. In that case, which can be viewed as the normal case, the Paasche price index (10) fails to be globally monotonically increasing in its components. That is, it may register a fall as $p_{1,t}$ increases and $p_{2,t}$ is held constant.

Since the price ratio is unity in the base period, economic monotonicity violations can only occur at a point away from the base period; that is, if one compares two situations that do not encompass the base period.

---

[6] See Kohli (1991), for instance.

[7] Note that it follows from (8) that $\varepsilon_{11,t} \geq 0$ and $\varepsilon_{21,t} = -\varepsilon_{22,t} \leq 0$.

[8] This would be the case if the factor requirements function were linear or Leontief, in which case the Paasche price index would be exact and thus necessarily well behaved.

5. Numerical Illustration

A simple numerical example might help to show how economic monotonicity violations might occur. Assume three periods: periods 0, 1, and 2. Table 1 shows the given values of p_1 and p_2 for the three periods, together with the optimizing values of q_1 and q_2, assuming that the factor requirements function is given by $2 = q_{1,t}^2 + q_{2,t}^2$, a quarter circle in the first quadrant.[9]

Table 1.
Economic monotonicity violations: Numerical illustration

t	$p_{1,t}$	$p_{2,t}$	$q_{1,t}$	$q_{2,t}$	$P_{t,0}^P$
0	1.0000	1.0000	1.0000	1.0000	1.0000
1	0.2000	1.0000	0.2774	1.3868	0.8667
2	0.4000	1.0000	0.5252	1.3131	0.8286

It is then straightforward to compute the direct Paasche price index. It is shown in the last column, and it can be seen that between periods *0* and 1, as p_1 falls from 1 to 0.2 while p_2 remains unchanged, P^P drops from 1 to 0.8667. Between periods 1 and 2, p_1 recovers and increases from 0.2 to 0.4, while p_2 is still being held constant, but P^P keeps dropping, from 0.8667 to 0.8286. That is, the GDP price deflator registers a fall, thus suggesting deflation (at a rate of 4.4%), even though one disaggregate price has doubled and the other one has remained unchanged.

6. The *CET* Aggregator Function

The behavior of the direct Paasche price index can be further investigated with the help of some simulations. Let the country's factor requirements function (5) have the following *CET* form:[10]

$$x_t = (q_{1,t}^{\rho} + q_{2,t}^{\rho})^{1/\rho}, \quad \rho > 1 . \tag{12}$$

[9] The supply of output *i* is then given by $q_{i,t} = p_{i,t}\sqrt{2/(p_{1,t}^2 + p_{2,t}^2)}$; see expression (13) below.

[10] The name *CET* stands for *constant elasticity of transformation.* The elasticity of transformation implied by (12) can be calculated as $\theta_{12} = 1/(1-\rho)$.

Under profit maximization, the output supply functions are:

$$(13) \qquad q_{i,t} = \frac{p_{i,t}^{1/(\rho-1)}}{\left[p_{1,t}^{\rho/(\rho-1)} + p_{2,t}^{\rho/(\rho-1)}\right]^{1/\rho}} x_t, \quad i = 1,2 .$$

The GDP function can then be written as:[11]

$$(14) \qquad \pi(p_{1,t}, p_{2,t}, x_t) = \left[p_{1,t}^{\rho/(\rho-1)} + p_{2,t}^{\rho/(\rho-1)}\right]^{(\rho-1)/\rho} x_t = r(p_{1,t}, p_{2,t})x_t ,$$

where

$$(15) \qquad r(p_{1,t}, p_{2,t}) \equiv \left[p_{1,t}^{\rho/(\rho-1)} + p_{2,t}^{\rho/(\rho-1)}\right]^{(\rho-1)/\rho}$$

is the unit revenue function. The following *CET* price index will then be *exact* in the sense of Diewert (1976):

$$(16) \qquad P_{t,0}(p_{1,t}, p_{2,t}) = \frac{r(p_{1,t}, p_{2,t})}{r(p_{1,0}, p_{2,0})} = \frac{\left[p_{1,t}^{\rho/(\rho-1)} + p_{2,t}^{\rho/(\rho-1)}\right]^{(\rho-1)/\rho}}{2^{(\rho-1)/\rho}} .$$

Given that $p_{1,0} = p_{2,0} = 1$, it follows from (13) that $q_{1,0} = q_{2,0}$. The direct Laspeyres price index can thus be written as:

$$(17) \qquad P_{t,0}^{L}(p_{1,t}, p_{2,t}) \equiv \frac{p_{1,t}q_{1,0} + p_{2,t}q_{2,0}}{q_{1,0} + q_{2,0}} = \frac{1}{2}(p_{1,t} + p_{2,t}) .$$

It is obvious from (17) that the direct Laspeyres price index is monotonically increasing in prices.

Next, making use of (13), we can derive the direct Paasche price index. It is as follows:

$$(18) \qquad P_{t,0}^{P}(p_{1,t}, p_{2,t}) \equiv \frac{p_{1,t}q_{1,t} + p_{2,t}q_{2,t}}{q_{1,t} + q_{2,t}} = \frac{p_{1,t}^{\rho/(\rho-1)} + p_{2,t}^{\rho/(\rho-1)}}{p_{1,t}^{1/(\rho-1)} + p_{2,t}^{1/(\rho-1)}} .$$

As indicated by (11), and given that θ_{12} is strictly negative in the *CET* case, the direct Paasche price index (18) is not globally monotonically increasing in prices.

The direct Fisher index, finally, can be obtained as:

$$(19) \qquad \begin{aligned} P_{t,0}^{F}(p_{1,t}, p_{2,t}) &\equiv \sqrt{P_{t,0}^{L}(p_{1,t}, p_{2,t}) P_{t,0}^{P}(p_{1,t}, p_{2,t})} \\ &= \sqrt{\frac{1}{2}(p_{1,t} + p_{2,t}) \frac{p_{1,t}^{\rho/(\rho-1)} + p_{2,t}^{\rho/(\rho-1)}}{p_{1,t}^{1/(\rho-1)} + p_{2,t}^{1/(\rho-1)}}} . \end{aligned}$$

[11] See Kohli (1978, 1991) and Woodland (1982) for details.

Note that when $\rho = 2$, $P^F_{t,0}(p_{1,t}, p_{2,t}) = P_{t,0}(p_{1,t}, p_{2,t})$; i.e., the direct Fisher index is exact for aggregator function (12). This is because in that case the *CET* factor requirements function becomes a special case of a quadratic mean of order 2 (the square rooted quadratic function), and, as shown by Diewert (1976), the Fisher index is exact for that functional form. In this case, the direct Fisher price index is necessarily monotonically increasing in prices. However, for other values of ρ this may no longer be true, since it might well be that the adverse behavior of the Paasche component dominates that of its Laspeyres counterpart.

Our results can easily be illustrated with the help of some simulations. We show in Figure 1 $P^P_{t,0}(p_1, p_2)$ as a function of p_1 for alternative values of ρ, after having set $p_2 = 1$. It is apparent that $P^P_{t,0}(p_1, p_2)$ is not monotonically increasing in p_1 for low values of p_1. That is, as p_1 increases, the GDP price deflator will actually fall, even though p_2 is held constant by assumption.

Figure 1

Direct Paasche price index for alternative values of ρ

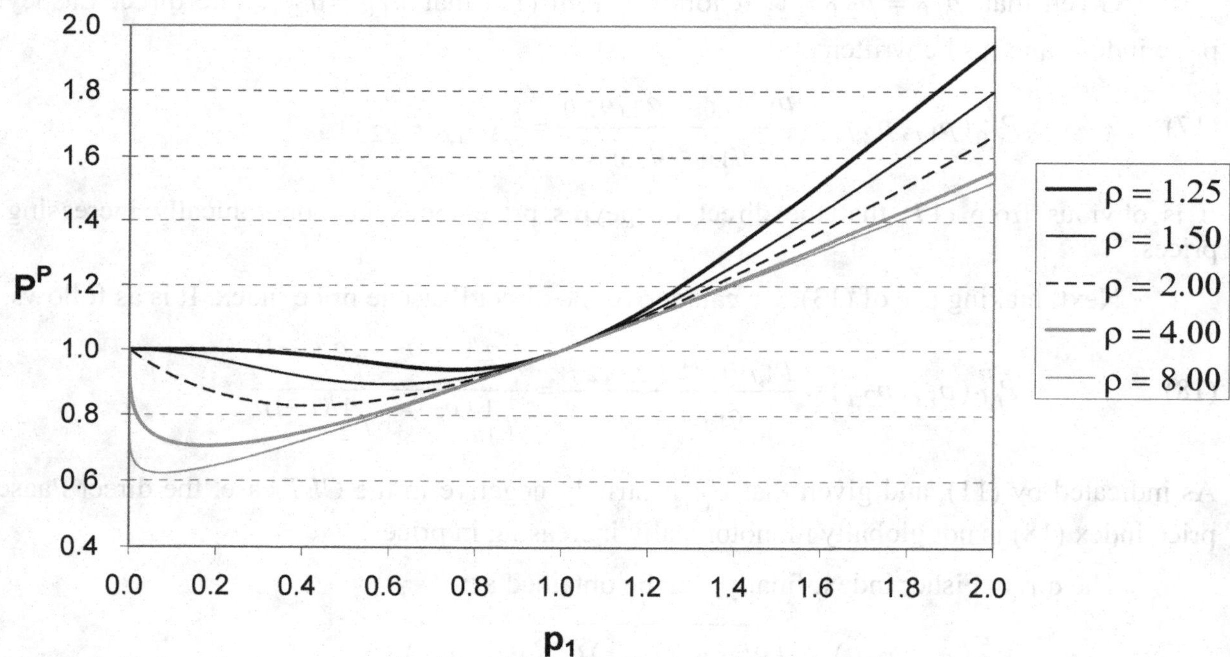

Next, in Figure 2, we show $P^P_{t,0}(p_1, p_2)$, $P^F_{t,0}(p_1, p_2)$, and $P^L_{t,0}(p_1, p_2)$ as functions of p_1 for $\rho = 4$. It can be seen that, although $P^P_{t,0}(p_1, p_2) \geq P^F_{t,0}(p_1, p_2) \geq P^L_{t,0}(p_1, p_2)$ as expected, there are ranges for p_1 where $\partial P^P_{t,0}(p_1, p_2)/\partial p_1 < \partial P^F_{t,0}(p_1, p_2)/\partial p_1 < \partial P^L_{t,0}(p_1, p_2)/\partial p_1$, and where, moreover, $P^P_{t,0}(p_1, p_2)$ and $P^F_{t,0}(p_1, p_2)$ are decreasing in p_1.

Figure 2
Direct Paasche, Fisher and Laspeyres indexes for ρ = 4

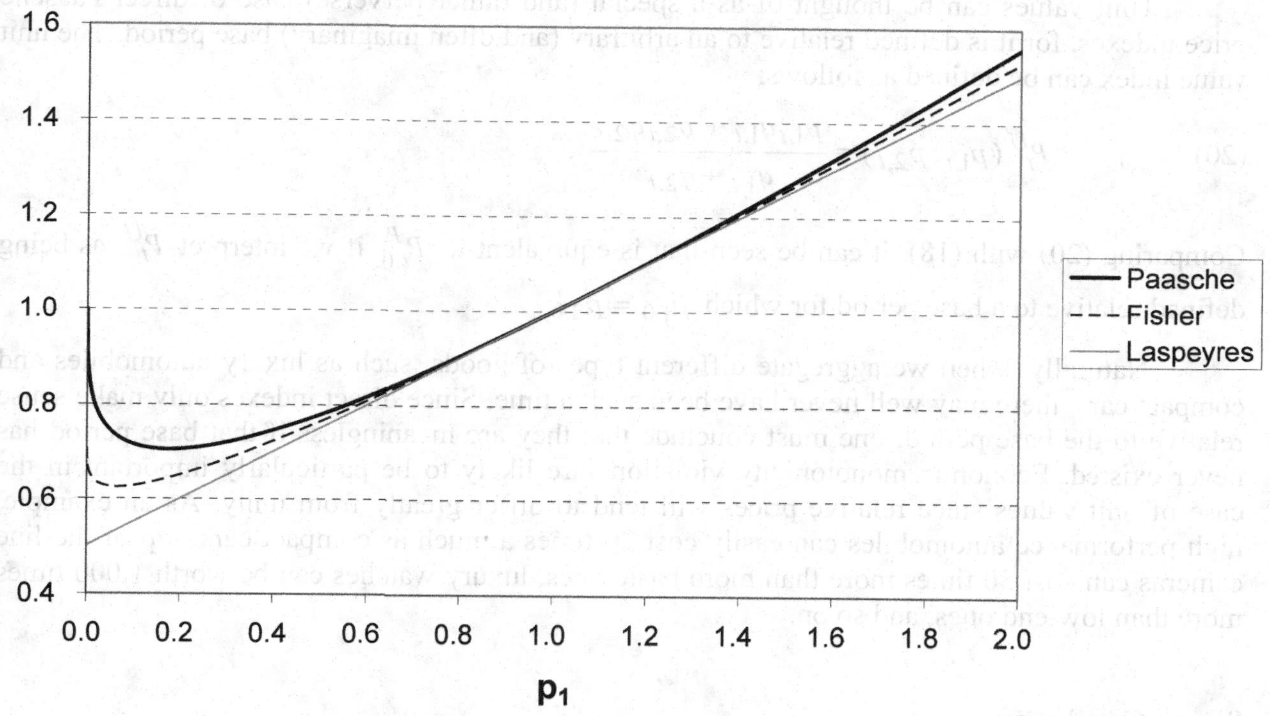

Finally, it can be seen from Figures 1 and 2 that for $p_1 > 0$, $P^P_{t,0}(p_1,1) \geq P^P_{t,0}(1,1)$ if and only if $p_1 \geq 1$. The same is true for the direct Fisher index. That is, *relative to the base period*, both indexes are monotonically increasing in prices. This provides a strong argument in favor of chaining.

7. Unit Values

Economic monotonicity violations are likely to plague unit values even more so than they do direct Paasche indexes. Yet unit values are routinely used at the elementary level to aggregate goods seemingly belonging to a same category. The average price of an apparently homogeneous product that is nevertheless sold at different times, different places, and under different conditions is often calculated by simply dividing total revenues by the number of items sold. The use of unit values is particularly prevalent in the area of foreign trade, where differences in quality and specification are not always taken into account when calculating the average price of exported cars, cameras, or watches. Thus, import and export price deflators are often computed on the basis of unit values.

Unit values can be thought of as a special (and rather perverse) case of direct Paasche price indexes, for it is defined relative to an arbitrary (and often imaginary) base period. The unit value index can be defined as follows:

$$(20) \qquad P_t^U(p_{1,t}, p_{2,t}) \equiv \frac{p_{1,t}q_{1,t} + p_{2,t}q_{2,t}}{q_{1,t} + q_{2,t}} .$$

Comparing (20) with (18), it can be seen that is equivalent to $P_{t,0}^P$ if we interpret P_t^U as being defined relative to a base period for which $p_{1,0} = p_{2,0}$.

Naturally, when we aggregate different types of goods, such as luxury automobiles and compact cars, there may well never have been such a time. Since direct indexes only make sense relative to the base period, one must conclude that they are meaningless if that base period has never existed. Economic monotonicity violations are likely to be particularly important in the case of unit values since relative prices will tend to differ greatly from unity. As an example, high performance automobiles can easily cost 20 times a much as compact cars, top-of-the-line cameras can cost 50 times more than more basic ones, luxury watches can be worth 1,000 times more than low-end ones, and so on.

8. Conclusions

It is well known that, in the context of supply theory, the Paasche price index tends to lie above the true price level, and the Laspeyres index underneath it. This is often understood to mean that the Paasche price index overstates price increases, and that the Laspeyres index underestimates them. This is clearly does not need to be true if the reference period is not the base period, i.e. the period for which the data are normalized. Note also that relative to the base period, the direct Paasche price index will understate price falls, whereas the Laspeyres index will exaggerate them. At a time when several countries have been flirting with deflation, this might be something to keep in mind.

The fact that the direct Paasche GDP deflator is not monotonically increasing in prices makes it a poor indicator of inflation, since it might point at a price increase when prices are actually falling, and vice-versa. Yet it is widely used in the literature, including in the areas of monetary economics and macroeconomics. For instance, Taylor (1993) has used it as a measure of inflation in his famous rule for monetary policy, and this well before chaining was introduced in the United States.

Naturally, the criticism applying to the GDP deflator can also be addressed to the other implicit price deflators in the context of the national accounts. These deflators typically have the direct Paasche form as well, and thus they fail to be globally monotonically increasing in their price components. Yet, some of these indexes are closely scrutinized. The deflator of consumption expenditures, for instance, is often used as a yardstick of inflation. In view of its failure of the economic monotonicity test, this would seem rather inappropriate.

There are other reasons why the use of the direct Paasche GDP deflator as a measure of the price level should be avoided, independently of whether chaining takes place or not. Thus, the Paasche functional form is unduly restrictive. As already noted, it is exact for very restrictive aggregator functions only (linear and Leontief). Superlative indexes, which are exact for flexible aggregator functions, are therefore to be preferred. Second, GDP price deflators incorporate terms-of-trade changes, which are fundamentally a real – not a price – phenomenon (this point also applies when the GDP deflator is measured by a superlative index and when it is chained). The problem with the standard procedure becomes apparent if import prices fall, for instance. This will increase the GDP price deflator (since import prices enter the calculation of the GDP deflator with a negative weight), even though this shock is clearly not inflationary, quite the contrary.[12]

References

Afriat, S.N. (1977), *The Price Index*, Cambridge University Press.

Diewert, W.E. (1974), "Applications of Duality Theory," in Michael D. Intriligator and David A. Kendrick (eds.) *Frontiers of Quantitative Economics* 2, North-Holland.

Diewert, W.E. (1976), "Exact and Superlative Index Numbers," *Journal of Econometrics* 4, 115-145.

Kohli, U. (1978), "A Gross National Product Function and the Derived Demand for Imports and Supply of Exports," *Canadian Journal of Economics* 11, 167-182.

Kohli, U. (1986), "Direct Index Numbers and Demand Theory," *Australian Economic Papers* 25, 17-32.

Kohli, U. (1991), *Technology, Duality, and Foreign Trade: The GNP Function Approach to Modeling Imports and Exports,* University of Michigan Press.

Kohli, U. (2004a), "Real GDP, Real Domestic Income, and Terms-of-Trade Changes," *Journal of International Economics* 62, 83-106.

Kohli, U. (2004b), "Basic Index Number Theory: Comments on W.E. Diewert," paper presented at the International Conference on the IMF Producer Price Index Manual, Helsinki, Finland, August 26-27, http://www.unige/ses/ecopo/kohli/Helsinki%202004N.pdf.

[12] See Kohli (2004a) for additional details.

Taylor, J.B. (1993), "Discretion versus Policy in Practice," *Carnegie-Rochester Conference Series on Public Policy* 39, 195-214.

Woodland, A.D. (1982), *International Trade and Resource Allocation*, North-Holland.

Chapter 15
Economic Monotonicity of Price Index Formulas

Ludwig von Auer[1]

1. Preliminary Remarks

The strict monotonicity test is probably one of the most widely accepted axioms in axiomatic index theory. In a paper included in this volume, Kohli (2011) implements the idea of monotonicity in an economic framework where quantities depend on prices. I show how the notion of strict monotonicity, as defined in the traditional axiomatic index theory approach, is somewhat different from Kohli's notion of economic monotonicity. Specifically, in the traditional approach, it is assumed that quantities and prices are independently determined.

Kohli convincingly demonstrates that, embedded in an economic framework, both the Paasche and Fisher index formulas violate monotonicity. Since the Fisher formula is often advocated as the most appropriate price index and the Paasche formula is widely used for the GDP implicit price deflator, Kohli's findings challenge the "general wisdom of index theory."

The present paper relates Kohli's approach to traditional axiomatic index theory. Building on the notion of monotonicity as defined in axiomatic index theory, I show how the notion of economic monotonicity can be defined in a precise manner.

2. Monotonicity in Axiomatic Index Theory

A price index formula P is a positive function that maps all of the prices and quantities in the base and comparison periods into a single positive number; i.e.,

$$P : R^{4n}_{++} \rightarrow R_{++}, \quad (\mathbf{p_0}, \mathbf{q_0}, \mathbf{p_1}, \mathbf{q_1}) \rightarrow P(\mathbf{p_0}, \mathbf{q_0}, \mathbf{p_1}, \mathbf{q_1})$$

where $\mathbf{p_t} = (p_{1,t}, ..., p_{N,t})^T$ and $p_{i,t} > 0$ denotes the unit price of commodity i $(i=1,2,...,N)$ in period t, $\mathbf{q_t} = (q_{1,t}, ..., q_{N,t})^T$ and $q_{i,t} > 0$ is the quantity of commodity i in period t, and where $t=0$ is the base period and $t=1$ is the comparison period.

The traditional axiomatic approach embodies the assumption that there is no causal relationship between prices and quantities. What follows are two monotonicity tests – a weak test and a strict test – set out in the usual context for the axiomatic approach regarding the independence of changes in prices and quantities.

---

[1] Contact information for the author: Universität Trier, Germany;e-mail: vonauer@uni - trier.de.

Citation: Ludwig von Auer (2011), "Economic Monotonicity of Price Index Formulas,"
chapter 15, pp. 329-332 in
W.E. Diewert, B.M. Balk, D. Fixler, K.J. Fox and A.O. Nakamura,
PRICE AND PRODUCTIVITY MEASUREMENT: Volume 6 -- Index Number Theory. **Trafford Press.**

© Alice Nakamura, 2011. Permission to link to, or copy or reprint, these materials is granted without restriction, including for use in commercial textbooks, with due credit to the authors and editors.

Weak Monotonicity Test (Olt, 1996): *Suppose that for all commodities we have* $p_{i,1} \geq p_{i,0}$ *and for at least one i the inequality is strict. Then*

$$P(\mathbf{p_0}, \mathbf{q_0}, \mathbf{p_1}, \mathbf{q_1}) > P(\mathbf{p_0}, \mathbf{q_0}, \mathbf{p_0}, \mathbf{q_1}).$$

Strict Monotonicity Test (Eichhorn and Voeller, 1976): *Consider two different scenarios for the comparison period (t =1 and t =1*) and the base period (t =0 and t =0*). Suppose that for all commodities we have* $p_{i,1^*} \geq p_{i,1}$, *and suppose that for at least one i the inequality is strict. Then*

(1) $$P(\mathbf{p_0}, \mathbf{q_0}, \mathbf{p_{1^*}}, \mathbf{q_1}) > P(\mathbf{p_0}, \mathbf{q_0}, \mathbf{p_1}, \mathbf{q_1}).$$

Or suppose for all commodities we have $p_{i,0^*} \geq p_{i,0}$, *and suppose that for at least one i this inequality is strict. Then*

(2) $$P(\mathbf{p_{0^*}}, \mathbf{q_0}, \mathbf{p_1}, \mathbf{q_1}) < P(\mathbf{p_0}, \mathbf{q_0}, \mathbf{p_1}, \mathbf{q_1}).$$

For the special case where $\mathbf{p_1} = \mathbf{p_0}$, inequality (1) simplifies to the weak monotonicity test case.

3. Monotonicity in Economic Approaches to Index Theory

Kohli's (2011) concept of *economic monotonicity* relates to the strict monotonicity test. Moreover, it relates only to postulate (1) of the strict monotonicity test and not to the postulate expressed by inequality (2). Postulate (1) considers alternative scenarios for the comparison period. In contrast, postulate (2) considers alternative scenarios for the base period. I recommend taking a more symmetric approach – that is, also considering postulate (2) as a necessary condition for monotonicity. I suggest this change as a "friendly" amendment to Kohli's concept of economic monotonicity; i.e., I suggest this is a change that is consistent with and would improve Kohli's contribution.

There is a second important difference between Kohli's notion of economic monotonicity and the strict monotonicity test. In Kohli's economic framework, quantities are functions of prices; i.e., we have $\mathbf{q_0} = \mathbf{q}(\mathbf{p_0})$ and $\mathbf{q_1} = \mathbf{q}(\mathbf{p_1})$. Thus we have $q_{i,t} = q_i(\mathbf{p_t})$ with either

(3a) $\partial q_{i,t} / \partial p_{i,t} \geq 0$ ($i = 1,2,...,N;\ t = 0, 1$), or

(3b) $\partial q_{i,t} / \partial p_{i,t} \leq 0$ ($i = 1,2,...,N;\ t = 0, 1$).

A formal definition of the economic monotonicity axiom (including the symmetric treatment of base and comparison period scenarios) can now be given:

Economic Monotonicity Test: *Let* $\mathbf{q_0} = \mathbf{q}(\mathbf{p_0})$ *and* $\mathbf{q_1} = \mathbf{q}(\mathbf{p_1})$. *Consider two different scenarios for the comparison period (t=1 and t=1*) and the base period (t=0 and t=0*). Suppose that for all commodities we have* $p_{i,1^*} \geq p_{i,1}$ *and for at least one i the inequality is strict. Then*

(4) $$P(\mathbf{p_0},\mathbf{q_0},\mathbf{p_{1^*}},\mathbf{q_{1^*}}) > P(\mathbf{p_0},\mathbf{q_0},\mathbf{p_1},\mathbf{q_1}).$$

Or suppose for all commodities we have $p_{i,0^*} \geq p_{i,0}$ *and for at least one i the inequality is strict. Then*

(5) $$P(p_{0*},q_{0*},p_1,q_1) < P(p_0,q_0,p_1,q_1)\,.$$

In (4), p_{1*} differs from p_1 and simultaneously q_{1*} is allowed to differ from q_1, whereas in (1) the quantity vector q_1 is kept fixed. Analogously, in (5) p_{0*} differs from p_0 and simultaneously q_{0*} is allowed to differ from q_0, whereas in (2) the quantity vector q_0 is kept fixed. This is the crucial difference between economic monotonicity and strict monotonicity.

4. Laspeyres and Paasche Index

Kohli (2011) has demonstrated that the Paasche and Fisher index formulas violate economic monotonicity. Taking the approach stated in (4) and (5), the Laspeyres index formula also violates economic monotonicity. In order to see *why* the Laspeyres formula violates economic monotonicity too, it is useful to reformulate this index as the weighted arithmetic mean of price ratios, where the weights are "expenditure shares" for the base period:

(6) $$P^L_{1,0} = \frac{\sum_i p_{i,1}q_{i,0}}{\sum_i p_{i,0}q_{i,0}} = \sum_i \frac{p_{i,0}q_{i,0}}{\sum_j p_{j,0}q_{j,0}}\frac{p_{i,1}}{p_{i,0}}$$

Formula (6) violates inequality (5) of economic monotonicity. Suppose, for example, that the price of only one good *i* differs between base period *t=0* and base period *t=0**. Inequality (5) postulates that if $p_{i,0} < p_{i,0*}$, then for the Laspeyres index we must have $P^L_{1,0} > P^L_{1,0*}$, which will not necessarily be true. Suppose, for example, that the case defined by relationship (3a) applies – that is, quantities are non-negatively related to prices – then $p_{i,0} < p_{i,0*}$ implies that $q_{i,0} \le q_{i,0*}$. As a consequence, the weight $p_{i,0}q_{i,0}/\sum_j p_{j,0}q_{j,0}$ may be much smaller than $p_{i,0*}q_{i,0*}/\sum_j p_{j,0*}q_{j,0*}$. In formula (6), the (larger) price increase $(p_{i,1}/p_{i,0})$ will receive a *smaller* weight than the (smaller) price increase $(p_{i,1}/p_{i,0*})$. In extreme cases, the changes in the weights will overcompensate the impact of the respective price changes, resulting in a violation of economic monotonicity.

The same line of reasoning can be applied to the Paasche index. This index formula can be reformulated as the weighted harmonic mean of price ratios, where the weights are "expenditure shares" of the comparison period:

(7) $$P^P_{1,0} = \frac{\sum_i p_{i,1}q_{i,1}}{\sum_i p_{i,0}q_{i,1}} = \left[\sum_i \frac{p_{i,1}q_{i,1}}{\sum_j p_{j,1}q_{j,1}}\left(\frac{p_{i,1}}{p_{i,0}}\right)^{-1}\right]^{-1}.$$

This formula violates inequality (4) of economic monotonicity. To see this, suppose, for example, that the price of only one good *i* differs between comparison period $t = 1$ and base period $t = 1^*$. Inequality (4) postulates that for $p_{i,1} < p_{i,1*}$, the Paasche index must produce $P^P_{1,0} < P^P_{1*,0}$. If quantity changes are non-negatively related to price changes, then $p_{i,1} < p_{i,1*} < p_{i,0}$ implies that

$q_{i,1} \leq q_{i,1*}$. As a consequence, the weight $p_{i,1}q_{i,1}/\sum_j p_{j,1}q_{j,1}$ could be much smaller than $p_{i,1*}q_{i,1*}/\sum_j p_{j,1*}q_{j,1*}$. In formula (7), the (larger) price decline $(p_{i,1}/p_{i,0})$ will receive a smaller weight than the (smaller) price decline $(p_{i,1*}/p_{i,0})$. In extreme cases, the difference in the weights will overcompensate the difference in the respective price changes, leading to $P^P_{1,0} > P^P_{1*,0}$.

Above, in demonstrating that the Laspeyres and the Paasche index violate the economic monotonicity test, it was assumed that quantities are positively related to prices. However, the case described by relationship (3b), where quantities are negatively related to prices, is standard in the context of the economic theory of consumer demand. In this case, the Laspeyres index still violates (5) and the Paasche index still violates (4).

5. Concluding Remarks

A primary concern of axiomatic index theory is the construction of tests that can provide insight into the properties of index formulas. Many price index formulas in common use violate some of the proposed axioms of index theory. Knowing which axioms are, and are not, satisfied is one important criteria for assessing the appropriateness of a formula for specific uses.

Among the axioms that have been proposed, the strict monotonicity test is one of the most widely accepted. Kohli (2011) has introduced the concept of index monotonicity in an economic framework. The present paper has shown that the notion of economic monotonicity can be formalized along the lines of the traditional strict monotonicity test of the axiomatic approach to index theory.

Kohli has demonstrated that the Paasche and Fisher index formulas violate economic monotonicity. This paper has shown that the same deficiency applies to the Laspeyres index.

References

Eichhorn, W. and J. Voeller (1976), *Theory of the Price Index, Lecture Notes in Economics and Mathematical Systems*, 140, Berlin: Springer.

Kohli, U. (2011), "Inexact Index Numbers and Economic Monotonicity Violations: The GDP Implicit Price Deflator," chapter 14 in W.E. Diewert, B.M. Balk, D. Fixler, K.J. Fox and A.O. Nakamura (eds.), *Price and Productivity Measurement,* Trafford Press, 301-312.

Olt, B. (1996), Axiom und Struktur in der statistischen Preisindextheorie, Frankfurt: Peter Lang.

Chapter 16
ON THE STOCHASTIC APPROACH TO INDEX NUMBERS

W. Erwin Diewert[1]

"In mathematics disputes must soon come to an end, when the one side is proved and the other disproved. And where mathematics enters into economics, it would seem that little room could be left for long-continued disputation. It is therefore somewhat surprising that one economist after another takes up the subject of index-numbers, potters over it for a while, differs from the rest if he can, and then drops it. And so nearly sixty years have gone by since Jevons first brought mathematics to bear upon this question, and still economists are at loggerheads over it. Yet index-numbers involve the use of means and averages, and these being a purely mathematical element, demonstration ought soon to be reached, and then agreement should speedily follow."

Walsh [1921; preface].

1. Introduction

The recent appearance of a book on the stochastic approach to index number theory by Selvanathan and Prasada Rao [1994] marks an appropriate occasion to provide a critical review of this approach. This is the primary purpose of the present paper.

The stochastic approach[2] to index number theory originated with Jevons [1863; 23-26] [1865; 121-122] [1869; 156-157], Edgeworth [1887; 245] [1888a] [1888b] [1889; 286-292] and Bowley [1901; 219] [1911] [1919; 346] [1926] [1928; 217]. Basically, this approach was driven by the quantity theory of money: as the quantity of gold or money is increased, all prices should increase approximately proportionally. Thus a measure of the general increase in prices going from period 0 to period t could be obtained by taking an appropriate average of price relatives, p_{it} / p_{i0}, where p_{it} denotes the price of commodity i in period t. This average of the price relatives can be regarded as an index number of price change going from period 0 to t. Selvanathan and Prasada Rao [1994; 5-6] express this ancient theory in more modern language as follows:

---

[1] W. Erwin Diewert is with the Department of Economics at the University of British Columbia and can be reached at diewert@econ.ubc.ca. This research was supported by a Strategic Grant from the Social Sciences and Humanities Research Council of Canada. Thanks are due to Louise Hebert and Keltie Stearman for typing a difficult manuscript.
[2] This term is due to Frisch [1936; 3-4].

Citation: **W. Erwin Diewert (2011), "On the Stochastic Approach to Index Numbers," chapter 16, pp. 333-360 in**
W.E. Diewert, B.M. Balk, D. Fixler, K.J. Fox and A.O. Nakamura,
***PRICE AND PRODUCTIVITY MEASUREMENT: Volume 6 -- Index Number Theory*. Trafford Press.**

© Alice Nakamura, 2011. Permission to link to, or copy or reprint, these materials is granted without restriction, including for use in commercial textbooks, with due credit to the authors and editors.

"The stochastic approach considers the index number problem as a signal extraction problem from the messages concerning price changes for different commodities. Obviously the strength of the signal extracted depends upon the messages received and the information context of the messages."

The recent resurrection of the stochastic approach to index number theory is due to Balk [1980], Clements and Izan [1981] [1987], Bryan and Cecchetti [1993] and Selvanathan and Prasada Rao [1994][3]. The main attraction of the approach over competing approaches to index number theory is its ability to provide confidence intervals for the estimated inflation rates:

"Accordingly, we obtain a point estimate of not only the rate of inflation, but also its sampling variance. The source of the sampling error is the dispersion of relative prices from their trend rates of change -- the sampling variance will be larger when the deviations of the relative prices from their trend rates of change are larger. This attractive result provides a formal link between the measurement of inflation and changes in relative prices."

Clements and Izan [1987; 339].

Selvanathan and Prasada Rao note the above advantage but go further and claim that the stochastic approach can be utilized to derive standard errors for many well known index number formulae:

"The attraction of this approach is that is provides an alternative interpretation to some of the well known index numbers as the estimators of parameters of specific regression models. For example, the Laspeyres, Paasche, Theil-Törnqvist and other index numbers can be derived from various regression models. Further this approach provides standard errors for these index numbers."

Selvanathan and Prasada Rao [1994; 6].

At this point, it should be mentioned that the two main competing approaches to index number theory are the test approach and the economic approach.

The test approach can apply to two periods (the bilateral case) or to many periods (the multilateral case). The bilateral test approach assumes that complete price and quantity information on the relevant set of commodities is available for the two periods under consideration, say periods s and t. Denote the price and quantity vectors for these two periods by p^s, p^t and q^s, q^t, where $p^s = [p_{1s}, \ldots, p_{Ns}]$, etc. A bilateral price index is defined as a function P of the four sets of variables, $P(p^s, p^t, q^s, q^t)$. The bilateral test approach attempts to determine the functional form for P by assuming that P satisfies certain plausible tests, axioms or mathematical properties. In the case of only one commodity in the set of commodities to be aggregated, the imposed tests generally cause the price index $P(p_{1s}, p_{1t}, q_{1s}, q_{1t})$ to collapse down to the single price ratio, p_{1t}/p_{1s}. There is an analogous bilateral test approach for the quantity index $Q(p^s, p^t, q^s, q^t)$. Fisher [1911; 403] observed that in the present context of complete information on prices and quantities, the price and quantity indexes, P and Q, should satisfy the following conservation of value equation:

[3] See Selvanathan and Prasada Rao [1994; 6] for an extensive list of their recent contributions.

(1) $P(p^s,p^t,q^s,q^t)Q(p^s,p^t,q^s,q^t) = p^t \cdot q^t / p^s \cdot q^s$

where $p^t \cdot q^t = \sum_{n=1}^{N} p_{nt} q_{nt}$. The importance of (1) is that once the functional form for P has been determined, then (1) automatically determines the functional form for Q. Moreover, tests for the quantity index Q can be translated into tests for the corresponding price index P defined via (1). Useful references for the test approach are Walsh [1901] [1921] [1924], Fisher [1911] [1921] [1922], and Diewert [1992a] [1993a; 6-10]. The early history of the test approach is reviewed by Frisch [1936; 5-7] and Diewert [1993b; 38-41].

In the test approach, the vectors of prices and quantities for the two periods are regarded as independent variables. In the economic approach, the two price vectors are regarded as independent variables but the quantity vectors are regarded as solutions to various economic maximization or minimization problems. In the consumer price context, it is assumed that the consumer has preferences over N commodities and these preferences can be represented by an aggregator or utility function $f(q_1,...,q_N) \equiv f(q)$. It is also assumed that in each period t, the consumer minimizes the cost $C[f(q^t),p^t]$ of achieving the utility level $f(q^t)$ when facing the period t vector of prices $p^t[p_{1t},p_{2t},...,p_{Nt}]$. The Konüs [1924] true cost of living index between periods s and t, using the reference utility level $f(q)$, is defined as the ratio of costs of achieving the reference utility level when facing the period s and t prices, $C[f(q),p^t]/C[f(q),p^s]$. If the consumer's utility function is linearly homogeneous, then the cost function $C[f(q),p]$ factors into two components, $f(q)c(p)$, where $c(p)$ is defined as the unit (utility level) cost function, $C[1,p]$. In this homogeneous case, the Konüs true cost of living index reduces to the unit cost ratio, $c(p^t)/c(p^s)$ and the corresponding quantity index is the utility ratio, $f(q^t)/f(q^s)$.

Finally, consider a given formula for the price index, say $P(p^s,p^t,q^s,q^t)$. We say that P is *exact* for the consumer preferences dual to the unit cost function c if under the assumption of cost minimizing behavior on the part of the consumer for periods s and t, we have

(2) $P(p^s,p^t,q^s,q^t) = c(p^t)/(c(p^t)$.

Similarly, a given functional form for the quantity index, $Q(p^s,p^t,q^s,q^t)$, is exact for the linearly homogeneous utility function f if, under the assumption of cost minimizing behavior for periods s and t, we have

(3) $Q(p^s,p^t,q^s,q^t) = f(q^t)/f(q^s)$.

The economic approach to index number theory concentrates on finding functional forms for price indexes P that are exact for flexible[4] unit cost functions c and on finding functional forms for quantity indexes Q that are exact for flexible linearly homogeneous utility functions f. Index number formulae that are exact for flexible functional forms are called superlative.[5] The theory

[4] A flexible functional form is one that has a second order approximation property; see Diewert [1974; 115].

[5] See Diewert [1976; 117].

of exact index numbers was developed by Konüs and Byushgens [1926], Afriat [1972; 44-47], Samuelson and Swamy [1974] and Pollak [1989; 15-32]. The early history of exact index numbers is reviewed in Diewert [1993b; 45-50]. For examples of superlative indexes, see Diewert [1976] [1978] [1992b; 576].

As can be seen from the above brief reviews of the test and economic approaches to index number theory,[6] these approaches are silent on the problem of providing an estimate of the reliability of the suggested bilateral index number formulae. Thus the new champions of the stochastic approach appear to have a strong a priori argument in favor of their approach.

In section 2 below, we review the original approaches of Jevons, Edgeworth and Bowley. In section 3, we review the initial new stochastic approaches of Clements and Izan [1981] and Selvanathan and Prasada Rao [1994; 51-61]. In section 4, we review the more sophisticated stochastic approaches of Balk [1980], Clements and Izan [1987] and Selvanathan and Prasada Rao [1994; 61-110]. The stochastic specifications that are utilized in the models presented in sections 3 and 4 are easily rejected from an empirical point of view. Thus in section 5, we present a new stochastic model that seems to be in the spirit of the type of model that Edgeworth had in mind but was never able to implement. In section 6, we present some practical criticisms of the new stochastic approaches to index number theory that will make it difficult for Statistical Agencies to embrace these approaches. Section 7 concludes by reconsidering the problems involved in providing measures of reliability for based on the test or economic approaches.

2. The Early Statistical Approaches to Index Number Theory

We assume that we are given price and quantity data, p_{it} and q_{it}, for periods t=0,1,...,T and for commodities i=1,2,...,N. The first stochastic index number model that Selvanathan and Prasada Rao [1994; 49-51] consider is given by the following equations for t=1,2,...T:

$$(4) \qquad p_{it}/p_{i0} = \alpha_t + \varepsilon_{it}; \; i=1,2,...,N;$$

where α_t represents the systematic part of the price change going from period 0 to t and the independently distributed random variables ε_{it} satisfy the following assumptions:

$$(5) \qquad E\varepsilon_{it} = 0; \; \mathrm{Var}\,\varepsilon_{it} = \sigma_t^2; \; i=1,2,...,N;$$

i.e., ε_{it} has mean 0 and variance $\sigma_t^2 > 0$. The least squares and maximum likelihood estimator for α_t in Model 1 defined by (4) and (5) is the Carli [1764] price index:

$$(6) \qquad \hat{\alpha}_t = \Sigma_{i=1}^{N} (1/N) p_{it}/p_{i0},$$

[6] Selvanathan and Prasada Rao [1994; 15-44] provide a rather inadequate review of the test and economic approaches. For example on page 17, they attribute Walsh's [1901] [1921; 97] price index to Drobisch, they misspell Marshall and they cite an incorrect reference to Marshall [1887], the cofounder of the Edgeworth-Marshall index.

which is the unweighted arithmetic mean of the period 0 to t price relatives, p_{it}/p_{i0}. The variance of $\hat{\alpha}_t$ is

$$(7) \quad \text{Var}\,\hat{\alpha}_t = (1/N)\sigma_t^2$$

and Selvanathan and Prasada Rao [1994; 51] note that an unbiased estimator for the variance is

$$(8) \quad \sigma_t^2 = [1/(N-1)]\Sigma_{i=1}^N [(p_{it}/p_{i0}) - \hat{\alpha}_t]^2 .$$

Using (7) and (8), a confidence interval for the Carli price index $\hat{\alpha}_t$ can be calculated under the assumption of normally distributed errors. As Selvanathan and Prasada Rao [1994; 51] note, if the dispersion of the price relatives p_{it}/p_{i0} increases, then the precision of our period t fixed base price index $\hat{\alpha}_t$ will decline.

Instead of assuming that the independent errors ε_{it} are additive, we could more plausibly assume that the errors are multiplicative.[7] This leads to Model 2, which is defined by the following equations for t=1,...,T:

$$(9) \quad \ell n[p_{it}/p_{i0}] = \pi_t + \varepsilon_{it}\,;\ i=1,...,N;$$

$$(10) \quad E\varepsilon_{it} = 0; \quad \text{Var}\,\varepsilon_{it} = \sigma_t^2;\ i=1,...,N.$$

The least squares and maximum likelihood estimator for π_t in Model 2 is

$$(11) \quad \hat{\pi}_t = [1/N]\Sigma_{i=1}^N\,\ell n[p_{it}/p_{i0}] .$$

A variance estimator for $\hat{\pi}_t$ can be constructed in a manner analogous to the use of (7) and (8) in Model 1. If we define α_t to be the exponential of π_t, we can exponentiate $\hat{\pi}_t$ to obtain the following estimator for α_t:

$$(12) \quad \exp[\hat{\pi}_t] = \Pi_{i=1}^N [p_{it}/p_{i0}]^{1/N} .$$

The right hand side of (12) is the Jevons [1863; 53] geometric mean price index. Jevons [1869; 157] later applied least squares theory to equation (9) and calculated a "probable error" (or confidence interval in modern terminology) for his estimator $\hat{\pi}_t$ defined by (11). This appears to be the first relatively complete exposition of the stochastic approach to index number theory.

Jevons [1865; 120-122] also used the arithmetic mean index number (6) in his empirical work but he did not report any confidence intervals for his Carli indexes. Edgeworth [1887; 226-246] considered both arithmetic and geometric mean (unweighted) index numbers and Edgeworth [1888a] was entirely devoted to the problems involved in constructing confidence intervals for these indexes. Bowley [1901; 203-229] [1919; 345-346] [1928; 216-222] was very

[7] Edgeworth [1887; 237-243] argued on empirical and logical grounds that Model 2 was more plausible than Model 1, assuming normally distributed errors. His logical argument was based on the positivity of prices; hence a price relative could have any upper bound but had a definite lower bound of zero, leading to an asymmetric distribution of price relatives. However, the logarithm of a price relative could be symmetrically distributed.

much concerned with the problems involved in determining the precision of index numbers.[8] Bowley [1911] was concerned with the precision of weighted index numbers while Bowley [1926] extended his earlier work to cover the case of correlated price relatives. Finally, Bowley was aware that precision in official indexes was rather important, since so many government expenditures were indexed to official price indexes. The following quotation refers to a potential upward bias of 18 percentage points in the Ministry of Labour index numbers for the UK over the years 1914-1918:

> "Every 4 points cost over a million pounds in the annual railway wage bill."
>
> Bowley [1919; 348]

We turn now to an exposition of the new stochastic models.

3. The New Stochastic Approach to Index Numbers

Model 3 consists of equations (4) again but our old assumptions (5) on the independently distributed errors ε_{it} are now replaced by the following assumptions:

$$(13)\quad E\varepsilon_{it} = 0; \quad \mathrm{Var}\,\varepsilon_{it} = \sigma_t^2 / w_i; \qquad i=1,\ldots,N$$

where the w_i are nonrandom fixed shares to be determined later; i.e. the w_i satisfy

$$(14)\quad w_i > 0 \text{ for } i=1,2,\ldots,N \text{ and } \Sigma_{i=1}^N w_i = 1.$$

Since the w_i are positive, we can multiply both sides of equation i in (4) by the square root of w_i, $w_i^{1/2}$, in order to obtain homoscedastic errors. The resulting least squares and maximum likelihood estimator for the period 0 to t inflation rate α_t is

$$(15)\quad \hat{\alpha}_1 = \Sigma_{i=1}^N w_i[p_{it}/p_{i0}] \big/ \Sigma_{n=1}^N w_n = \Sigma_{i=1}^N w_i[p_{it}/p_{i0}]$$

where the second equality follows using (14). Using (13), it can be seen that $\hat{\alpha}_t$ is an unbiased estimator for α_t and its variance is

$$(16)\quad \mathrm{Var}\ \hat{\alpha}_t = \Sigma_{i=1}^N w_i^2[\sigma_i^2/w_i] = \sigma_i^2$$

where the second equality follows using (14). An unbiased estimator for σ_t^2 is

$$(17)\quad \hat{\sigma}_t^2 \equiv [1/(N-1)]\Sigma_{i=1}^N w_i[(p_{it}/p_{i0}) - \hat{\alpha}]^2.$$

[8] Mills [1927; 240-247] succinctly reviewed the above literature and also computed standard errors for various index number formulae using BLS data on US wholesale prices.

Under the added assumption that the residuals ε_{it} are normally distributed, (16) and (17) may be used to obtain confidence intervals for the share weighted index numbers $\hat{\alpha}_t$ given by (15).

Selvanathan and Prasada Rao [1994; 51-55] consider the following special cases:

(18) $w_i \equiv p_{i0}q_{i0} / \sum_{n=1}^{N} p_{n0}q_{n0}$; i=1,...,N;

(19) $w_i \equiv p_{i0}q_{it} / \sum_{n=1}^{N} p_{n0}q_{nt}$; i=1,...,N.

In order to make the w_i fixed variables, we need to assume that base period prices and quantities, p_{i0} and q_{i0}, and current period quantities, q_{it}, are fixed. Thus in equations (4), the only random variables are the current period prices p_{it}.

Substituting (18) into (15) causes $\hat{\alpha}_t$ to become the fixed base Laspeyres price index, $p^t \cdot q^0 / p^0 \cdot q^0$, and substituting (19) into (15) leads to the Paasche price index, $p^t \cdot q^t / p^0 \cdot q^t$. Furthermore, substitution of (18) and (19) into (15)-(17) yields estimators for the variances of the fixed base Laspeyres and Paasche price indexes. Thus the new stochastic approach of Selvanathan and Prasada Rao does lead to estimates of the precision of these well known indexes (provided that their stochastic assumptions (13) are correct).

We turn now to the new stochastic approach of Clements and Izan [1981]. Consider two distinct periods s and t where $0 \le s < t \le T$. Let π_{st} be the logarithm of the price change going from period s to t. The equations that define Model 4 are:

(20) $\ell n[p_{it} / p_{is}] = \pi_{st} + \varepsilon_{ist}$; i=1,...,N;

(21) $E\varepsilon_{ist} = 0$; $\text{Var } \varepsilon_{ist} = \sigma_{st}^2 / w_i$; i=1,...,N

where the weights w_i again satisfy (14). Multiplying both sides of (20) through by $(w_i)^{1/2}$ leads to homoscedastic variances. The least squares and maximum likelihood estimator for π_{st} in this transformed model is

(22) $\hat{\pi}_{st} = \sum_{i=1}^{N} w_i \ell n[p_{it} / p_{is}]$.

Using (21), the variance of $\hat{\pi}_{st}$ is σ_{st}^2. An unbiased estimator for σ_{st}^2 is

(23) $\hat{\sigma}_{st}^2 \equiv [1/(N-1)] \sum_{i=1}^{N} w_i [\ell n(p_{it} / p_{is}) - \hat{\pi}_{st}]^2$.

Let $w_{it} \equiv p_{it}q_{it} / \sum_{n=1}^{N} p_{nt}q_{nt}$ be the expenditure share of commodity i in period t. Clements and Izan [1981; 745-746] and Selvanathan and Prasada Rao [1994; 76-77] choose the weights w_i that appear in (21) as follows:[9]

(24) $w_i \equiv (1/2)w_{is} + (1/2)w_{it}$; i=1,...,N;

[9] These authors choose period s to be period t-1 but this choice is not essential to their argument.

i.e., w_i is chosen to be the average expenditure share on commodity i over periods s and t. Substituting (24) into (22) yields

$$(25) \quad \exp[\hat{\pi}_{st}] = \Pi_{i=1}^{N}[p_{it}/p_{is}]^{(1/2)w_{is}+(1/2)w_{it}} .$$

The right hand side of (25) is known as the Törnqvist [1936] price index.[10]

Under the assumption of normally distributed errors, (23) can be used to form confidence intervals for $\hat{\pi}_{st}$, the logarithm of the Persons-Törnqvist price index. However, since the weights w_i defined by (24) depend on p_{is} and p_{it}, it will be necessary to assume that the conditional (on w_i) distribution of $\ell n(p_{it}/p_{is})$ is normal and satisfies assumptions (21). Thus the stochastic assumptions justifying Model 4 are more tenuous than those for Model 3 above.

The variance assumptions (13) and (21), $\mathrm{Var}\,\varepsilon_{it} = \sigma_t^2/w_i$ and $\mathrm{Var}\,\varepsilon_{ist} = \sigma_{st}^2/w_i$, require some justification.[11] The following quotation indicates how Clements and Izan justify their assumptions on the variances of the log price relatives:

> "If all goods were equally important, the assumption that var ε_i is the same for all i would be acceptable. However, this is not so, since the budget share $\overline{w}_i$ varies with i. If we think in terms of sampling the individual prices to form Dp_i for each commodity group, then it seems reasonable to postulate that the collection agency invests more resources in sampling the prices of those goods more important in the budget. This implies that var ε_i is inversely proportional to $\overline{w}_i$."
>
> Clements and Izan [1981; 745]

In contrast to the explicit sampling approach of Clements and Izan [1981], Selvanathan and Prasada Rao [1994] (with the exception of their section 7.4) regarded their prices as being accurately known, or in any case, they wanted their analysis to apply to this case.[12] They justify their variance assumptions in (13) and (18) as follows:[13]

---

[10] This index first appeared as formula 123 in Fisher [1922; 473]. Fisher [1922; 265] listed it as number 15 in his list of the 29 best formulae, but he did not otherwise distinguish it. Walsh [1921; 97] almost recommended (25), but he used the geometric average of the weight, $(w_{is}w_{it})^{1/2}$, in place of the arithmetic average. Finally, Persons [1928; 21-22] recommended (25), the Fisher ideal index, $(p^t \cdot q^t p^t \cdot q^s / p^s \cdot q^t p^s \cdot q^s)^{1/2}$ and seven other indexes as being the best from the viewpoint of his test approach. Thus (25) should perhaps be known as the Persons-Törnqvist formula.

[11] The first person to make a variance specification of this form appears to have been Edgeworth [1887; 247] as the following quotation indicates: "Each price which enters into our formula is to be regarded as the mean of several prices, which vary with the differences of time, of place, and of quality; by the mere friction of the market, and, in the case of 'declared values', through errors of estimation, it is reasonable to support that this heterogeneity is greater the larger the volume of transactions." Edgeworth did not make any formal use of these observations.

[12] "Even in the case where prices of all the commodities of relevance are measured, and measured without any errors, the question of reliability of a given index arises." (Selvanathan and Prasada Rao [1994; 4]).

[13] The reader will deduce that, in the interests of a homogeneous presentation, I have modified the original notation of Clements and Izan and Selvanathan and Prasada Rao.

> "Under this assumption we have that the variance of the price relative of i is λ_t^2 / w_{i0} and is inversely proportional to w_{i0}. This means that the variability of a price relative falls as the commodity becomes more important in the consumer's budget."
>
> Selvanathan and Prasada Rao [1994; 52]

In their more sophisticated stochastic model to be discussed in the next section, Clements and Izan [1987] no longer relied on their earlier sampling theory justification for their variance assumptions of the form (21). Instead, they provided the following justification:

> "As e_{it} is the change in the ith relative price, specification (7) implies that the variability of a relative price falls as the commodity becomes more important in the consumer's budget. Thus the variability of a relative price of a good having a large budget share, such as food, will be lower than that of a commodity with a smaller share, such as cigarettes. This is a plausible specification, since there is less scope for a relative price to change as the commodity in question grows in importance in the budget."
>
> Clements and Izan [1987; 341]

As can be seen from the above quotations, the justifications presented for the variance assumptions in the new stochastic approaches are rather weak.[14] We will return to this point in section 5 below.

Clements and Izan [1981; 747] and Selvanathan and Prasada Rao [1994; 89] point out a positive feature of the new stochastic models such as Model 3 or 4: the resulting index numbers such as (15) or (22) are invariant to the level of commodity aggregation, provided that the same shares w_i that appear in the variance specifications (13) or (21) are used to do the aggregation. To see this, consider Model 3 represented by (4) and (13) and suppose that commodities 1 and 2 are aggregated together. Let p_{At} be the price of the aggregate commodity in period t. The weights w_1 and w_2 are used to define the following aggregate period 0 to t price relative:

$$(26) \quad p_{At} / p_{A0} \equiv [w_1 / (w_1 + w_2)][p_{it} / p_{i0}] + [w_2 / (w_1 + w_2)][p_{2t} / p_{20}].$$

Replace the first two equations in (4) by the new aggregated equation $p_{At}/p_{A0} = \alpha_t + \varepsilon_{At}$. Using the first two equations in (4) as well as (26), it can be seen that the new aggregate error is equal to

$$(27) \quad \varepsilon_{At} = [w_1 / (w_1 + w_2)]\varepsilon_{it} + [w_2 / (w_1 + w_2)]\varepsilon_{2t}.$$

Using (13) and (27), the expectation of p_{At}/p_{A0} is equal to α_t, the expectation of ε_{At} is 0 and the variance of ε_{At} is

$$(28) \quad \text{Var}\, \varepsilon_{At} = [w_1 / (w_1 + w_2)]^2 [\sigma_t^2 / w_1] + [w_2 / (w_1 + w_2)]^2 [\sigma_t^2 / w_2] = [\sigma_t^2 / (w_1 + w_2)].$$

[14] In his new stochastic model, Balk [1980; 72] simply assumed a variance specification analogous to (13) or (21) without any justification other than mathematical convenience.

Thus the mean and variance of the aggregated error are of the same form as the means and variances of the original errors, ε_{it} and ε_{2t}, see (13). It is straightforward to show that the maximum likelihood estimator $\hat{\alpha}_1^*$ for α_t in the aggregated model is equal to the disaggregated estimator $\hat{\alpha}_t$ defined by (15).

We turn now to more sophisticated new stochastic approaches to price indexes.

4. A Specific Price Trends Stochastic Approach

The models presented in the previous section are similar to the classical stochastic models presented in section 2, except that the variance assumptions were different. These simple signal extraction models were effectively criticized by Keynes [1930; 58-84]. Clements and Izan summarize this Keynsian criticism as follows:

> "Thus the rate of inflation can be estimated by averaging over these n observations. This approach was correctly criticized by Keynes (1930, pp. 85-88) on the basis that it requires the systematic component of each price change to be identical. In other words, all prices must change equiproportionally so that there can be no changes in relative prices. The objective of this article is to rehabilitate the stochastic approach by answering Keynes's criticism by allowing for systematic changes in relative prices."
>
> Clements and Izan [1987; 339]

Selvanathan and Prasada Rao [1994; 61] also acknowledge that the Keynesian criticism applies to their Laspeyres and Paasche models (Model 3 with the w_i defined by (18) and (19) respectively). In order to rectify this deficiency in their Laspeyres model, Selvanathan and Prasada Rao [1994; 61-73] generalize their model as follows: assume that the period t over period 0 price ratios satisfy

$$(29)\quad p_{it}/p_{i0} = \alpha_t + \beta_i + \varepsilon_{it}\quad i=1,\ldots,N;\ t=1,\ldots,T$$

where the independently distributed residuals ε_{it} satisfy the following assumptions:

$$(30)\quad E\,\varepsilon_{it} = 0;\quad \mathrm{Var}\,\varepsilon_{it} = \sigma_t^2/w_i;\ i=1,\ldots,N;\ t=1,\ldots,T.$$

As usual, the positive variance weights w_i are assumed to be shares; i.e., the w_i satisfy (14). Selvanathan and Prasada Rao [1994; 62] interpret β_i as the expectation of the change in the ith relative price in addition to general inflation; i.e., it is the systematic part of commodity i price change in addition to the overall period 0 to t price change α_t[15] Selvanathan and Prasada Rao

[15] It is immediately evident that the specification (29) is not very satisfactory. As we go from period 0 to 1, it is reasonable to postulate that β_1 is the systematic part of the commodity 1 price change p_{11}/p_{10} in addition to the general period 0 to 1 price change α_1 but it is <u>not</u> reasonable to assume that this same β_1 will characterize the systematic part of the commodity 1 relative price changes p_{11}/p_{10} for later periods, t=2,3,...,T, since as t increases, these fixed base systematic trends will tend to increase in magnitude.

[1994; 62] note that the parameters α_t and β_i are not identified. Thus they add an identifying restriction of the following form:

$$(31) \quad \sum_{i=1}^{N} w_i\beta_i = 0.$$

The restriction (31) says that a share weighted average of the specific commodity price trends β_i sums to zero, a very reasonable assumption since the parameter α_t contains the general period t trend. What is not so reasonable, however, is the assumption that the w_i which appears in (31) is the <u>same</u> as the w_i which appear in (30).

Let us call the model that consists of (14) and (29)-(31) Model 5. Maximum likelihood estimators, $\hat{\alpha}_t, \hat{\beta}_i$, and $\hat{\sigma}_t^2$, for the parameters which appears in this model can be obtained in a manner analogous to the way Selvanathan and Prasada Rao [1994; 63-66] derived estimators for their specific version of this model. Define the maximum likelihood residuals $\hat{e}_{it}$ by:

$$(32) \quad \hat{e}_{it} \equiv \left(p_{it}/p_{i0}\right) - \hat{\alpha}_t - \hat{\beta}_i; \; i\text{-}1,...,N; \; t=1,...,T.$$

The maximum likelihood estimators for the parameters of Model 5 can be obtained by solving the following system of equations, along with equations (32):

$$(33) \quad \hat{\alpha}_t \equiv \sum_{i=1}^{N} w_i\, p_{it}/p_{i0}; \qquad t=1,...,T;$$

$$(34) \quad \sigma_t^2 = (1/N)\sum_{i=1}^{N} w_i \hat{e}_{it}^2; \qquad t=1,...,T;$$

$$(35) \quad \hat{\beta}_i = \sum_{i=1}^{T}[1/\hat{\sigma}_t^2][(p_{it}/p_{i0}) - \hat{\alpha}_t] / \sum_{i=1}^{T}[1/\hat{\sigma}_t^2] \qquad i=1,...,N.$$

Substitution of equations (33) into (35) shows that the $\hat{\beta}_i$ satisfy the restriction (31). Equations (34) show that the period t variance estimator $\hat{\sigma}_t^2$ is a weighted sum of the squares of the period t maximum likelihood residuals, $\hat{e}_{it}^2$. Equations (35) show that the ith commodity effect $\hat{\beta}_i$ is a weighted average over T periods of the deviations of the period 0 to t price relatives p_{11}/p_{10} from the period t general inflation rates α_t, where the weights are inversely proportional to the period t variance estimates, $\hat{\alpha}_t^2$. Equations (33) show that the estimator for the period 0 to t general inflation rate $\hat{\alpha}_t$ is a simple weighted average of the period 0 to t price relatives, p_{it}/p_{i0} -- an amazingly simple result!

If we let the weights w_i equal the base period expenditure shares w_{i0}, we obtain the specific price trends stochastic model of Selvanathan and Prasada Rao [1994; 61-67] and the period 0 to t inflation estimate $\hat{\alpha}_t$ defined by (33) collapses down to the fixed base Laspeyres price index, $p^t \cdot q^0 / p^0 \cdot q^0$. It is easy to show that $\hat{\alpha}_t$ is an unbiased estimator for α_t with the variance σ_t^2. Thus Selvanathan and Prasada Rao feel that they have justified the use of the fixed base Laspeyres price index (and provided measures of its variability) from the viewpoint of a sophisticated stochastic approach that blunts the force of the Keynesian objection to stochastic index number models.

However, a problem with Model 5 is that its specification for the specific commodity effects β_i in equations (29) is not very compelling. A more credible specific price trends stochastic model was developed by Clements and Izan [1987; 341-345] and repeated by Selvanathan and Prasada Rao [1994; 78-87]. The equations that characterize the model of these authors are:

$$(36)\quad \ell n[p_{it}/p_{it-1}] = \pi_t + \beta_i + \varepsilon_{it} \qquad i=1,\ldots,N;\ t=1,\ldots,T;$$

$$(37)\quad E\,\varepsilon_{it} = 0;\ \mathrm{Var}\,\varepsilon_{it} = \sigma_i^2/w_i; \qquad i=1,\ldots,N;\ t=1,\ldots,T;$$

As usual, the variance weights w_i that appear in (37) are assumed known and assumed to satisfy (14). As in the previous model, the π_t and β_i are not identified. Hence Clements and Izan [1987; 342] assume that the β_i satisfy the following restriction:

$$(38)\quad \Sigma_{i=1}^{N} w_i\beta_i = 0$$

where the w_i weights that appear in (38) are the same as those appearing in (37). It is this coincidence that leads to the following elegant formulae for the maximum likelihood estimators for the parameters of Model 6, consisting of (14) and (36)-(38):

$$(39)\quad \hat{c}_{it} \equiv \ell n[p_{it}/p_{it-1}] - \hat{\pi}_t - \hat{\beta}_i; \qquad i=1,\ldots N;\ t=1,\ldots,T;$$

$$(40)\quad \hat{\pi}_t = \Sigma_{i=1}^{N} w_i \ell n[p_{it}/p_{it-1}]; \qquad t=1,\ldots,T;$$

$$(41)\quad \hat{\sigma}_t^2 = (1/N)\Sigma_{i=1}^{N} w_i \hat{e}_{it}^2; \qquad t=1,\ldots,T;$$

$$(42)\quad \hat{\beta}_i = \Sigma_{i=1}^{T}[1/\sigma_s^2][\ell n(p_{it}/p_{it-1}) - \pi_t]/\sum_{i=1}^{T}[1/\sigma_s^2]; \qquad i=1,\ldots,N.$$

The interpretation of (40) to (42) is analogous to the earlier interpretation of (33)-(35). However, the interpretation of the specific commodity price trend parameters β_i is much more reasonable for Model 6 than for Model 5: the β_i in the ith equation of (36) can be thought of as an average (multiplicative) price trend in the commodity i chain price relatives p_{it}/p_{it-1} around the general period t-1 to t inflation rates, $\exp[\pi_t]$, over all T periods in the sample; i.e., exponentiating both sides on the equation in (36) that corresponds to commodity i and period t and dropping the error term yields p_{it}/p_{it-1} approximately equal to $\exp[\pi_t]$ times $\exp[\beta_i]$. Thus the specification (36) will capture constant commodity specific growth rates over the sample period in prices (in addition to the general growth in prices).

Note that the logarithm of the period t-1 to t inflation rate, π_t, is estimated by the right hand side of (40), which is identical to the right hand side of (22) if we set s=t-1 and use the same weights w_i in each formula.

Recall that $w_{it} \equiv p_{it}q_{it} / \sum_{n=1}^{N} p_{nt}q_{nt}$ is the ith expenditure share in period t. Clements and Izan [1987; 342] make the following specification for the w_i which appear in (37) and (38):

$$\text{(43)} \qquad w_i \equiv \Sigma_{i=0}^{T} w_{it} \big/ (T+1); \; i=1,...,N;$$

i.e., the w_i are the mean expenditure shares over the entire sample period.

Of course, since the w_i defined by (43)[16] are not generally equal to the w_i defined by (24) when s=t-1, the Model 6 period t-1 to t inflation estimates $\hat{\pi}_t$ defined by (40) will not coincide precisely with the Model 4 estimates $\hat{\pi}_{t-1,t}$ defined by (22) when s=t-1. Thus Model 6 does not lead to a precise justification for the Törnqvist price index of Model 4, but Clements and Izan [1987; 343] argue that since the shares defined by (43) will not differ much from the shares defined by (24) when s=t-1, their specific price trends model provides an approximate justification for the use of the Persons-Törnqvist price index.

Clements and Izan [1987; 344-350] go on to show how variance estimates for the price indexes $\hat{\pi}_t$ defined by (40) can be derived. However, as in Model 4, the w_i defined by (43) depend on the prices p_{it} and hence the "fixed" weights w_i which appear in (37) and (38) are not really independent of the price relatives p_{it}/p_{it-1}. Hence the applicability of Model 6 when the w_i are defined by (43) is in doubt.[17]

This completes our review of the new stochastic approaches to index number theory. In the following two sections, we subject these approaches to a critical appraisal.

5. A Formulation of Edgeworth's Stochastic Approach to Index Numbers

The new stochastic models presented in the previous two sections suffer from a rather major defect: the variance assumptions of the type $\operatorname{Var} \varepsilon_{it} = \sigma_t^2 / w_i$ where w_i is an observed expenditure share of some sort are simply not supported empirically. Clements and Izan [1987; 345] note explicitly that their variance assumptions (37) and (43) are not supported by their empirical example.[18] However, formal statistical tests are not required to support the common observation that the food and energy components of the consumer price index are more volatile

---

[16] It is interesting to note that Walsh [1901; 398] almost derived the transitive multilateral system of index numbers defined by (40) and (43): in place of the arithmetic means of the sample expenditure shares defined by (43), Walsh recommended the use of the corresponding geometric means. It should also be noted that Balk's [1980; 71] specialization of his seasonal model is a special case of Model 6 with w_i defined as $\Sigma_{t=0}^{T} p_{it}q_{it} \big/ \Sigma_{s=0}^{T} p_{js}q_{js}$.

[17] Note that Model 5 when $w_i \equiv w_{i0}$ does not suffer from this difficulty. However, the interpretation of the β_i in Model 5 is more problematic.

[18] "As can be seen, the variances are not inversely proportional to the budget shares as required by (16")." (Clements and Izan [1987; 345]).

than many of the remaining components. Food has a big share while energy has a small share -- volatility of price components is not highly correlated with the corresponding expenditure shares.

The observation that different price components have widely differing volatility dates back to the origins of index number theory. For example, Edgeworth [1887; 244] observed:

> "Cotton and Iron, for example, fluctuate in this sense much more than Pepper and Cloves."

Later, Edgeworth [1918; 186] commenting on Mitchell's work observed:

> "...that the fluctuation in price from year to year is much greater for some kinds of commodities than for others... Thus manufactured goods are steadier than raw materials. There are characteristic differences among the price fluctuations of the groups consisting of mineral products, forest products, animal products, and farm crops. Again, consumers' goods are steadier in price than producers' goods, the demand for the farmer being less influenced by vicissitudes in business conditions."

For a summary of Mitchell's evidence on the variability of different components of US wholesale prices over the years 1890-1913, see Mitchell [1921; 40-43]. Finally, Mills [1927; 46] summarizes his evidence on the monthly variability of commodity prices as follows:

> "It is clear from Table 4 that individual commodities differ materially in the matter of price variability and, also, that the variability of specific commodities has changed from period to period."

In the light of the above criticism of Models 3 through 6, let us reconsider the classical stochastic models presented in section 2. However, instead of assuming that the period 5 residuals have a common variance, we now assume that the log of each chain commodity price relative, $\ell n[p_{it}/p_{it-1}]$, after adjusting for a common period t inflation factor π_t has its own commodity specific variance σ_i^2. Thus Model 7 is defined by the following equations:

(44) $\quad \ell n[p_{it}/p_{it-1}] = \pi_i + \varepsilon_{it}; \qquad i=1,...,N;\ t=1,...,T;$

(45) $\quad E\,\varepsilon_{it} = 0; \quad \mathrm{Var}\,\varepsilon_{it} = \sigma_i^2; \qquad i=1,...,N;\ t=1,...,T.$

The parameter π_t is the logarithm of the period t-1 to t price index for t=1,...,T and for i=1,...,N. The parameter σ_i^2 is the variance of the inflation adjusted logarithmic price ratios $\ell n[p_{it}/p_{it-1}] - \pi_t$ for t=1,...,T.

It is interesting to note that a model similar to that defined by (44) and (45) was first vaguely suggested by Edgeworth as the following quotations indicate:

> "A third principle is that less weight should be attached to observations belonging to a class which are subject to a wider deviation from the mean."
>
> Edgeworth [1887; 224].

> "Or, if more weight attaches to a change of price in one article rather than another, it is not on account of the importance of that article to the consumer or to the

shopkeeper, but on account of its importance to the calculator of probabilities, as affording an observation which is peculiarly likely to be correct..."

Edgeworth [1889; 287].

"In combination of these values derived from observation, less weight should be attached to one belonging to a class which is subject to a wider deviation from the mean, for which the mean square of deviation is greater."

Edgeworth [1923; 574].

"The term may include weighting according to 'precision' in the sense in which that term is attributed to errors of observation; a sense in which the price of pepper might deserve more weight than that of cotton, as M. Lucien March has the courage to maintain."

Edgeworth [1925; 383].

In the last quotation, Edgeworth is referring to March [1921; 81] who endorsed Edgeworth.[19] Irving Fisher summarized Edgeworth's vague suggestions efficiently as follows:

"Professor Edgeworth has made somewhat analogous, though less definite, proposals. He suggests that any commodity belonging to a class that is subject to wide scattering is a less reliable indicator than one belonging to a class not so subject. To take account of such differences in reliability he suggests that weights be assigned to each commodity in inverse proportion to the square of some variability-measure of the class to which it belongs.

This idea is scarcely capable of specific application, partly because the classification of commodities is so arbitrary and multiform, partly because of the difficulty of calculating any useful variability-measure for each class when determined. I wish Professor Edgeworth would take my 36 commodities, assign each to what he believes is its proper class, estimate each class-variability-measure, and calculate an index number accordingly."

Fisher [1922; 380]

We now show how estimators for our neo-Edgeworthian model defined by (44) and (45) can be obtained. The log of the likelihood function corresponding to Model 7 is, apart from inessential constants,

$$(46)\quad L(\pi_1,\ldots,\pi_T;\sigma_i^2,\ldots,\sigma_N^2) \equiv -\sum_{i=1}^N T\ell n\sigma_i^2 - \sum_{i=1}^N \sum_{i=1}^T \sigma_i^2[\ell n(p_{it}/p_{it-1}) - \pi_t]^2 .$$

Differentiating (46) with respect to the parameters and setting the resulting partial derivatives equal to 0 leads to the following system of T+N simultaneous non linear equations to determine the maximum likelihood estimators for Model 7 (assuming that the $\hat{\sigma}_i^2$ are all strictly positive):

$$(47)\quad \hat{\pi}_t = \sum_{n=1}^N [1/\hat{\sigma}_n^2]\ell n(p_{it}/p_{it-1}) / \sum_{i=1}^N [1/\hat{\sigma}_i^2]; \qquad t=1,\ldots,T;$$

[19] March [1921; 81] observed that if the price of paper varied less than the price of wheat, then the former price should be given more weight in the index number formula.

(48) $\hat{\sigma}_i^2 = [1/T]\Sigma_{i=1}^T[\ell n(p_{it}/p_{it-1}) - \hat{\pi}_t]^2$ i=1,...,N.

The interpretation of the specific commodity price variance estimators $\hat{\sigma}_i^2$ defined by (48) is straightforward. Equation t in (47) says that the estimator for the logarithm of the period t-1 to t inflation rate, π_t, is a weighted average of the individual period t-1 to t log price changes, $\ell n[p_{it}/p_{it-1}]$, with the weight for the ith log price change being inversely proportional to its estimated variance, $\hat{\sigma}_i^2$. Thus Model 7 seems to capture the essence of Edgeworth's suggested stochastic approach to index number theory.

There can be at most one finite solution to equations (47) and (48) that has all $\hat{\sigma}_i^2$ strictly positive. A suggested algorithm for finding this solution if it exists is the following one. Begin iteration 1 by estimating $\hat{\pi}_t$ as the mean of the unweighted log price changes:

(49) $\hat{\pi}_t^{(1)} \equiv \Sigma_{i=1}^N(1/N)\ell n(p_{it}/p_{it-1})$; t=1,...,T.

Thus $\exp[\hat{\pi}^{(1)}]$ is the Jevons geometric mean price index for the t-1 to t price change. Once the $\hat{\pi}_t^{(1)}$ have been defined, define the iteration 1 variances $[\hat{\sigma}_i^{(1)}]^2$ by (48) replacing $\hat{\pi}_t$ by $\hat{\pi}_t^{(1)}$. At the first stage of iteration 2, define the $\hat{\pi}_t^{(2)}$ by (47) using the iteration 1 $[\hat{\sigma}_i^{(1)}]^2$ in the right hand sides of (47). At the second stage of iteration 2, define the $[\hat{\sigma}_i^{(2)}]^2$ by (48) using the $\hat{\pi}_t^{(1)}$ in the right hand sides of (48). Now carry on repeating these first and second stage iterations until the estimates converge. It can be shown that if the $\hat{\sigma}_i^{(k)}$ remain positive, then each stage of each iteration will lead to a strict increase in the log likelihood function (46) until convergence has been achieved.

Unfortunately, the above algorithm may not always work in degenerate cases. For example, consider the case where the period t prices are proportional to the base period prices for all t. In this case, the $\hat{\pi}_t$ are explicit functions of the proportionality factors and all of the commodity variances defined by (48) will be 0. There are other problems as well: if we pick any i and define $\hat{\pi}_t = \ell n[p_{it}/p_{it-1}]$ for t=1,...,T and let σ_i^2 tend to 0 (with the other σ_j^2 positive and finite), we find that the log likelihood function approaches plus infinity. To rule out degenerate solutions of this type, it may be necessary to add a positive lower bound to the admissible variances in our model; i.e., we may need to add to (44) and (45) the following restrictions:

(50) $\sigma_i^2 \geq \sigma^2 > 0$; i=1,...,N

for some σ^2 chosen a priori.

We now turn to a critical evaluation of these new stochastic models for price indexes.

6. A Critical Evaluation of the New Stochastic Approaches

Our first criticism of the new stochastic models presented in sections 3 and 4 has already been made: the variance assumptions made in these models are not consistent with the observed behavior of prices. This is a very fundamental criticism that has not been addressed by the proponents of these new models. The assertion of Selvanathan and Prasada Rao [1994; 6] that their stochastic approach has provided standard errors for several well known index number formulae is correct only if their stochastic assumptions are correct, which seems very unlikely!

Our second criticism is directed towards the specific price trend models of Balk [1980], Clements and Izan [1987] and Selvanathan and Prasada Rao [1994; 63-66]: these models force the same weights w_i to serve two distinct purposes and it is unlikely that their choice of weights could be correct for both purposes. In particular, their expenditure based weights are unlikely to be correct for the first purpose (which is criticism 1 again).

Our third criticism of the new stochastic approaches presented in sections 4 and 5 is that the resulting price indexes are not invariant to the number of periods T in the sample. Balk [1980; 72-73] was very concerned with this problem (since he works in a Statistical Agency and hence must suggest "practical" solutions to problems) and he presented some evidence on the stability of his estimated index numbers as T was increased. His evidence indicates that our third criticism is empirically important. Due to the fact that variances of price relatives can change considerably over time (recall Mills [1927; 46]), our neo-Edgeworthian Model 7 presented in the previous section will be particularly subject to this instability criticism.

The above invariance problem also occurs in the multilateral context and in the multiperiod time series context when we want our estimated index numbers to satisfy the circularity test; i.e., to be transitive. Walsh, after noting how multilateral transitivity can be achieved by using weights that pertain to all of the periods in the sample (e.g., recall equations (43) in Model 6), draws attention to the above invariance problem and also notes why the multilateral case is more difficult than the bilateral case:

> "In no case is this remedy satisfactory, for two principle reasons: (1) Because the present epoch is extending every year, requiring recalculations; and it does not appear that a later recalculation will be more correct than an earlier. Besides, how is a past variation between two years several years ago to be affected by present variations? (2) Because we really do not know how to calculate weights, or to determine equivalence of mass-units, or to average mass-quantities, over more than two periods, since the geometric average loses its virtue when applied to more than two figures."
>
> Walsh [1901; 399]

Our fourth criticism of the new stochastic approaches is simply a restatement of the fundamental objection of Keynes:

> "The hypothetical change in the price level, which would have occurred if there had been no changes in relative prices, is no longer relevant if relative prices have in fact changed -- for the change in relative prices has in itself affected the price level.

> I conclude, therefore, that the unweighted (or rather the randomly weighted) index number of prices -- Edgeworth's 'indefinite' index number -- ...has no place whatever in a rightly conceived discussion of the problems of price levels."
>
> Keynes [1930; 78]

Thus if price relatives are different, then an appropriate definition of average price change cannot be determined independently of the economic importance of the corresponding goods. What is an appropriate definition of aggregate price change? Earlier in his book, Keynes [1930; 59-61] indicated that the price relatives in a producer or consumer price index should be weighted according to their relative importance as indicated by a census of production or by a consumer budget study. Thus the best index number formula according to Keynes is an expenditure weighted sum of relative prices; i.e., the price relatives must be weighted according to their economic importance, not according to their statistical importance, a la Edgeworth.[20] Of course, in the approach advocated by Keynes, there is still the problem of choosing the "best" economic weights (base or current period expenditure shares or a mixture of them), but precise answers to this question simply lead back to the test or economic approaches to index number theory.

Criticism four can be restated as follows. The early statistical approaches of Jevons and Edgeworth (see section 2) treated each price relative as an equally valid signal of the general inflation rate: the price relative for pepper is given the same weight as the price relative for bread. This does not seem reasonable to "Keynesians" if the quantity of pepper consumed is negligible.

Another more technical way of restating the Keynesian objection to stochastic approaches can be accomplished by drawing on the models presented in section 5: if we make more reasonable variance assumptions, models of the form (36)-(38) are reasonable, except that the constant β_i's should be replaced by sets of period specific β_{it}'s. But then the resulting model has too many parameters to be identified.

Our conclusion at this stage is: in the present context where all prices and quantities are known without sampling error, signal extraction approaches to index number theory should be approached with some degree of caution.[21]

Of course, there is a huge role for statistical approaches when we change our terms of reference and assume that the given price and quantity data are samples. The founders of the test approach, Walsh [1924; 516-517] and Fisher [1922; 336-340], did not deny a strong role for statistical techniques in the sampling context. In addition to the work of Bowley [1901] [1911] [1919] [1926] [1928], more recent references on the sampling aspects of price indexes include Mudgett [1951; 51-54], Adelman [1958], McCarthy [1961], Kott [1984] and the BLS [1988].

---

[20] Keynes' belief in the importance of economic weighting (as opposed to Edgeworth [1901; 410] and Bowley [1901; 219] who at times believed that weighting was unimportant) dates back at least to Keynes [1911; 46].

[21] The dynamic factor index approach of Bryan and Cecchetti [1993; 19] is an example of a signal extraction approach to index numbers that we did not cover due to its complexity. Their approach is only subject to our criticisms 3 and 4. Their approach is also subject to a criticism that can be leveled against the specific price trend models of section 4: the nonstationary components of their specific price trends (their counterparts to the β_1 which appear in Models 5 and 6 above) are assumed to be constant over the sample period.

7. Other Approaches to the Determination of the Precision of an Index

Having rejected the new stochastic approaches to index number theory (when all prices and quantities are known with certainty over the sample period), we have to admit that the proponents of these new approaches have a point: if all of the price relatives pertaining to two periods are identical, it must be the case that the "precision" of the index number computation for those two periods is greater than when the price relatives are widely dispersed. On the other hand, the proponents of the test and economic approaches to index number theory use their favorite index number formula and thus provide a precise answer whether the price relatives are widely dispersed or not. Thus the test and economic approaches give a false sense of precision.

The early pioneers of the test approach addressed the above criticism. Their method works as follows: (i) decide on a list of desirable tests that an index number formula should satisfy; (ii) find some specific formulae that satisfy these tests (if possible); (iii) evaluate the chosen formulae with the data on hand and (iv) table some measure of the dispersion of the resulting index number computations (usually the range or standard deviation was chosen). The resulting measure of dispersion can be regarded as a measure of <u>functional form error</u>.

Fisher [1922; 226-229] applied the above method to address the charge that the test approach gave a false precision to index numbers. He found 13 index number formulae (including the ideal) that satisfied the commodity, time and factor reversal tests and were not "freakish"; i.e., descended from modes or medians (and hence discontinuous). Fisher [1922; 227] found that the standard deviations between his 13 best fixed base indexes increased as the two periods being compared grew further apart; his "probable error" reached a maximum of about .1% when his 13 indexes were compared between 1913 and 1918. Fisher called this functional form error, <u>instrumental error</u>. In response to outraged criticisms from Bowley, Fisher later summarized his results as follows:

> "What I do claim to have demonstrated is something quite different, namely, that the 'instrumental' error, i.e., that part of the total error which may be ascribed to any inaccuracy in the mathematical formula used, is, in the case of the ideal formula (and, in fact, in the case of a score of other formulae as well), usually less than one part in 1000."
>
> Fisher [1923; 248]

Warren Persons [1928; 19-23] also implemented the above test approach to the determination of functional form error. Persons looked for index number formulae that satisfied the time reversal test and his new test, the absence of weight correlation bias test. He found nine admissible index number formulae (including the Persons-Törnqvist and the Fisher ideal) and used Fisher's [1922] data to numerically evaluate these nine. Finally, Persons [1928; 23] tabled the range of the resulting indexes over the sample period; he found the range was a maximum in 1917 when it slightly exceeded 1%. It turned out that indexes satisfying Fisher's tests had a narrower range of dispersion than the indexes satisfying Persons' tests for the same data set.

Walsh [1921; 97-107] almost recommended the above approach to functional form error. He chose six index number formulae on the basis of how close they came empirically to satisfying his multiperiod identity test.[22] Walsh [1921; 106] used a small but somewhat extreme data set from Bowley [1901; 226] to evaluate his six index number formulae; he found that their range was about 2%. However, Walsh did not stop at this point; he went on to choose a single best index number formula:

> "To return to theory: would anything be gained by drawing an average of the results yielded by several methods? Hardly, as they have different merits. All that we can do is choose the best, after testing all the candidates; for to average the others with the best, would only vitiate the result."
>
> Walsh [1921; 106-107]

What was Walsh's [1921; 102] theoretically best index number formula? None other than Irving Fisher's [1922] ideal index![23]

It is clear that there are some problems in implementing the above test approach to the determination of functional form error; i.e., what tests should we use and how many index number formulae should be evaluated in order to calculate the measure of dispersion? However, it is interesting to note that virtually all of the above index number formulae suggested by Fisher, Persons and Walsh approximate each other to the second order around an equal price and quantity point.[24]

The above approach may be used to estimate the functional form error that arises from choosing an index number formula that is based on the economic approach. The economic approach recommends the use of a superlative index number formula, such as the Fisher-Walsh ideal formula[25] or the Persons-Törnqvist formula[26] or the direct and implicit quadratic mean of order r families of price indexes that include two indexes recommended by Walsh [1901; 105].[27] Many of these superlative indexes appear in the list of best test approach index number formulae recommended by Fisher, Persons and Walsh.[28] As was done for the test approach, the functional form error involved in using any specific superlative index could be approximated by evaluating a number of superlative indexes and then tabling a measure of their dispersion.

---

[22] Walsh [1921; 104] called his test the circular test but it is slightly different from the Westergaard-Fisher [1922; 413] circular test; see Diewert [1993b; 39]

[23] Walsh [1901] [1921] was an originator of the test approach to index number theory and he also proposed the use of the ideal index either before Fisher [1921] or coincidentally. Perhaps the reason why Walsh has been forgotten but Fisher lives on is due to the rather opaque writing style of Walsh whereas Fisher wrote in a very clear style.

[24] Thus these indexes are either superlative or pseudo-superlative; i.e., they approximate superlative indexes to the second order around an equal price and quantity point; see Diewert [1978; 896-898].

[25] See Diewert [1976; 134].

[26] See Diewert [1976; 121].

[27] See Diewert [1976; 134-135]. The two Walsh indexes are obtained when we set r=1. Walsh [1921; 97] listed his two recommended indexes as formulae (5) and (6). The right hand side of (5) needs to be multiplied by the expenditure ratio for the two periods under consideration, since on the previous page, Walsh [1921; 96] assumed that these expenditures were equal.

[28] On the basis of its consistency with revealed preference theory and its consistency with linear and Leontief aggregator functions, Diewert [1976; 137-138] recommended the Fisher-Walsh ideal index as the best superlative index number formula. Allen and Diewert [1981; 435] also endorse this index number formula as being the best superlative one since it is consistent with both Hicks' [1946; 312-313] Composite Commodity Theorem and Leontief's [1936; 54-57] Aggregation Theorem.

A specific proposal to measure the dispersion of superlative indexes is the following one. Choose the following members of Diewert's [1976; 131] quadratic mean of order r price indexes $P_r : P_2$ (the Fisher-Walsh ideal price index), P_1 (Walsh), P_0 (Persons-Törnqvist), and P_{-2}. Choose the following members from Diewert's [1976; 132] implicit quadratic mean of order r prices indexes $\widetilde{P}_r : \widetilde{P}_2$ (implicit Walsh), $\widetilde{P}_0$ (implicit Törnqvist) and $\widetilde{P}_{-2}$.[29] These formulae include the most frequently used superlative indexes. To measure the dispersion of these indexes, consider the following dispersion measure D, which is the range of the seven indexes divided by the minimum index:

$$(51) \quad D(p^s,p^t,q^s,q^t) \equiv [\max\{P_2,P_1,P_0,P_{-2},\widetilde{P}_1,\widetilde{P}_0,\widetilde{P}_{-2}\}/\min\{P_2,P_1,P_0,P_{-2},\widetilde{P}_1,\widetilde{P}_0,\widetilde{P}_{-2}\}]^{-1}$$

where $P_i \equiv P_i\left(p^s,p^t,q^s,q^t\right)$ and $\widetilde{P}_j \equiv \widetilde{P}_j\left(p^s,p^t,q^s,q^t\right)$ D can be interpreted as the percentage difference between the highest and lowest price indexes in the set of admissible indexes.

Note that $D(p^s,p^t,q^s,q^t) \geq 0$. Moreover, since each of the seven indexes that appear on the right hand side of (1) satisfy the Fisher [1911; 534] [1922; 64]-Walsh [1901; 368] time reversal test:

$$(52) \quad P(p^s,p^t,q^s,q^t) = 1/(p^s,p^t,q^s,q^t),$$

it can be verified that the dispersion measures defined by (51) will satisfy the following base period invariance property:

$$(53) \quad D(p^s,p^t,q^s,q^t) = D(p^t,p^s,q^t,q^s);$$

i.e., if we interchange periods, the dispersion remains unchanged.

The dispersion measure defined by (51) can be adapted to the test approach: the set of index number formulae that would appear in (51) would be restricted to formulae that satisfied the appropriate set of tests. In particular, assume that the admissible P satisfy the time reversal test (52) and Walsh's [1901; 385] strong proportionality test:

$$(54) \quad P(p^s,\lambda p^s,q^s,q^t) = \lambda \text{ for } \lambda > 0;$$

i.e., if the period t price vector p^t is proportional to the period s price vector p^s, then the index equals the common proportional factor. Under these hypotheses on the class of admissible price indexes in (51), the dispersion measure defined by the appropriate version of (51) would satisfy the base period invariance test (53) and would equal 0 if all the price relatives were identical.

Returning to the economic approach to index numbers and the specific measure of formula error defined by (51), it can be verified that if both prices and quantities are proportional during the two periods under consideration, so that $p^t = \alpha p^s$ and $q^t = \beta q^s$ for some $\alpha > 0, \beta > 0$, then each of the seven indexes which appears in the right hand side of (51) is equal

[29] Fisher's [1922; 461-487] identification numbers for these formulae are: 353, 1153, 123, the geometric mean of 13 and 19, 1154, 124, and the geometric mean of 14 and 20.

to α and hence the dispersion measure $D(p^s,\alpha p^s,q^s,\beta q^s)$ will attain its lower bound of 0. However, if only prices are proportional, then $D(p^s,\alpha p^s,q^s,q^t)$ will not necessarily equal 0. If we want a measure of dispersion that will equal zero when only prices are proportional, a different approach is required, which we now turn to.

A more direct approach to the reliability of a price index, $P(p^s,p^t,q^s,q^t)$, is to simply look at the variability of the individual price relatives, p_{it}/p_{is}, around the index number "average" value, $P(p^s,p^t,q^s,q^t)$. In order to implement this approach, define the ith absolute deviation by

$$(55)\quad d_i(p^s,p^t,q^s,q^t) \equiv \left|(p_{it}/p_{is}) - P(p^s,p^t,q^s,q^t)\right| \quad i=1,\ldots,N.$$

A <u>measure of relative price variability</u>, V, could be defined as an appropriate function of the deviations d_i defined by (55), say:

$$(56)\quad V(p^s,p^t,q^s,q^t) \equiv M[d_1(p^s,p^t,q^s,q^t),\ldots,d_N(p^s,p^t,q^s,q^t)]$$

where M is a linearly homogeneous symmetric mean.[30]

A desirable property for a price variability measure V is that it satisfy the base period invariance property (53) (where we replace D by V). Unfortunately, the V defined by (56) and (55) will not generally have this property.

In order to obtain a base period invariant measure of price variability between two periods, define the ith absolute logarithmic deviation e_i by

$$(57)\quad e_i(p^s,p^t,q^s,q^t) \equiv \left|\ell n(p_{it}/p_{is}) - \ell nP(p^s,p^t,q^s,q^t)\right|, \quad i=1,\ldots,N.$$

Define a <u>logarithmic price variability measure</u> V by

$$(58)\quad V(p^s,p^t,q^s,q^t) \equiv M[e_1(p^s,p^t,q^s,q^t),\ldots,e_N(p^s,p^t,q^s,q^t)]$$

where again M is a homogeneous symmetric mean. If the index number formula P satisfies the time reversal test (52), then it can be verified that $e_i(p^s,p^t,q^s,q^t) = e_i(p^t,p^s,q^t,q^s)$ and hence the V defined by (58) satisfies the base period invariance property (53) (with V replacing D).

Define the mean of order r of N positive numbers $x_1,\ldots,x_N$ for $r \neq 0$ by[31]

$$(59)\quad M_r(x_1,\ldots,x_N) \equiv [\Sigma_{i=1}^N (1/N)x_i^r]^{1/r}.$$

---

[30] A symmetric mean $M(x_1,\ldots,x_N)$ is defined to be a continuous, symmetric increasing function of N real variables that has the mean value property, $M(\lambda_1,\ldots,\lambda_N) = \lambda$. $M(x_1,\ldots,x_N)$ will also satisfy the following min-max property: $\min_i\{x_i\} \leq M(x_1,\ldots,x_N) \leq \max_i\{x_i\}$ This last property and (55) imply that V will be nonnegative.

[31] See Hardy, Littlewood and Polya [1934; 12].

The means of order r, M_r, are homogeneous symmetric means and hence can be used as M's in (58). For example, if we choose r=2 and substitute M_2 into (58), we obtain the following logarithmic price variability measure:

$$(60) \quad V_2(p^s,p^t,q^s,q^t) \equiv [(1/N)\sum_{i=1}^{N}\{\ell n(p_{it}/p_{is}) - \ell nP(p^s,p^t,q^s,q^t)\}^2]^{1/2}.$$

Note that (60) bears some resemblance to the earlier stochastic measure of reliability, $\hat{\sigma}_{st}$ defined by the square root of (23). It should also be noted that a monotonic transformation of the measure of relative price variability defined by (60), $N[V_2(p^s,p^t,q^s,q^t)]^2$, was suggested as a measure of the nonproportionality of prices by Allen and Diewert [1981; 433]: the price index P that they used in (60) was the Jevons equally weighted geometric mean defined by the right hand side of (12) (with p^s replacing p^0).

Unfortunately, the measures of price variability defined by (58) or (60) are still not satisfactory in the present context. The problem is that some price relatives are completely unimportant and hence should not be given the same weight as items that are important in the budgets of the consumer or producer for the two periods under consideration: recall Edgeworth and March's discussion about the relative importance of pepper versus wheat or cotton. We could use the budget shares of period s, w_{is}, or the budget shares of period t, w_{it}, as weights, but it seems less arbitrary to use an even handed average of these two sets of weights.[32] Thus we will weight the ith absolute logarithmic price deviation e_i defined by (57) by $m(w_{is}, w_{it})$, where m is a linearly homogeneous symmetric mean of two variables. Note that the symmetry property of m implies that

$$(61) \quad m(w_{is}, w_{it}) = m(w_{it}, w_{is}),\ i=1,...,N.$$

Thus our final class of price variability measures is defined as follows:

$$(62) \quad V(p^s,p^t,q^s,q^t) \equiv M[m(w_{1s},w_{1t})e_1(p^s,p^t,q^s,q^t),\ldots,m(w_{Ns},w_{Nt})e_N(p^s,p^t,q^s,q^t)]$$

where the e_i are defined by (57) and M is again a homogeneous symmetric mean. If the price index P satisfies the time reversal test (52) and the share aggregator function m satisfies (61), then it can be verified that the V defined by (62) satisfies the base period invariance test (53).

[32] Our reasoning is similar to that of Walsh [1921; 90], who made the case for the use of average weights in a price index as follows: "Commodities are to be weighted according to their importance, or their full values. But the problem of axiometry always involves at least two periods. There is a first period, and there is a second period that is compared with it. Price-variations have taken place between the two, and these are to be averaged to get the amount of their variation as a whole. But the weights of the commodities at the second period are apt to be different from their weights at the first period. Which weights, then, are the right ones -- those of the first period? or those of the second? or should there be a combination of the two sets? There is no reason for preferring either the first or the second. Then the combination of both would seem to be the proper answer. And this combination itself involves an averaging of the weights of the two periods."

This V will also be nonnegative.[33] Moreover, if the price index P satisfies the strong proportionality test (54), then V will equal 0 if prices are proportional so $V(p^s, \lambda p^t, q^s, q^t) = 0$.

The most straightforward special case of (62) is obtained if we let M and m be means of order 1; i.e., arithmetic means. In this case, V becomes

$$(63) \quad V_1(p^s, p^t, q^s, q^t) \equiv \Sigma_{i=1}^{N} (1/N)\overline{w}_{ist} \left| \ell n(p_{it}/p_{is}) - \ell nP(p^s, p^t, q^s, q^t) \right|$$

where $\overline{w}_{ist} \equiv (1/2)(w_{is} + w_{it})$ is the average expenditure share on commodity i during periods s and t. The measure (63) is simply the arithmetic average of the weighted absolute logarithmic deviations, $\overline{w}_{ist} e_i(p^s, \lambda p^t, q^s, q^t)$. The only disadvantage of this measure is that it is not differentiable. A differentiable special case of (62) is obtained if we set $M = M_2$ and still let m be the arithmetic mean:

$$(64) \quad V_2(p^s, p^t, q^s, q^t) \equiv \{\textstyle\sum_{i=1}^{N} (1/N) \Sigma_{i=1}^{N} (1/N) w_{ist} [\ell n(p_{it}/p_{is}) - \ell nP(p^s, p^t, q^s, q^t)]^2\}^{1/2}.$$

Note the resemblance of (64) to the square root of (23). Comparing (64) to (63), V_2 gives larger weight to the larger weighted absolute logarithmic deviations, $\overline{w}_{ist} e_i(p^s, \lambda p^t, q^s, q^t)$. Both of the measures V_1 and V_2 will serve as satisfactory measures of variability or degree of nonproportionality of relative prices relative to the index number formula $P(p^s, p^t, q^s, q^t)$.

There is another approach to the measurement of relative price variability that has the advantage that it is simultaneously a measure of relative quantity variability. Consider the following variability measure due to Robert Hill [1995; 81][34]:

$$(65) \quad V_H(p^s, p^t, q^s, q^t) = \ell n(p^s \cdot q^t \; p^t \cdot q^s / p^t \cdot q^t \; p^s \cdot q^s)] \geq 0$$

$$(66) \quad \equiv [\ell n(P_L / P_P)]$$

$$(67) \quad \equiv [\ell n(Q_L / Q_P)]$$

where $P_L \equiv p^t \cdot q^s / p^s \cdot q^s$ and $P_P \equiv p^t \cdot q^t / p^s \cdot q^t$ are the Laspeyres and Paasche price indexes and $Q_L \equiv p^s \cdot q^t / p^s \cdot q^s$ and $Q_P \equiv p^t \cdot q^t / p^t \cdot q^s$ are the Laspeyres and Paasche quantity indexes. Equation (66) shows that the variability measure defined by (65) can be written as the absolute value of the log of the ratio of the Laspeyres and Paasche price indexes while (67) shows a similar equality involving the ratio of the Laspeyres and Paasche quantity indexes. Thus if prices in the two periods are proportional (so that $p^t = \alpha p^s$), then $P_L = P_P = \alpha$ and using (66), $V_H = 0$. Similarly, if quantities in the two periods are proportional (so that $q^t = \beta q^s$), then

[33] If P satisfies the usual homogeneity properties with respect to prices and quantities (e.g., see tests PT5-PT8 in Diewert [1992a; 215-216]), then it can be shown that $V(p^s, p^t, q^s, q^t)$ will be homogeneous of degree zero in each of its four sets of variables.

[34] Hill defined $V_H \equiv \ell n[\max\{Q_L, Q_P\}] / \min\{Q_L, Q_P\}$. It can be shown that this definition is equivalent to (67).

$Q_L = Q_P = \beta$ and using (67), $V_H = 0$. Hence as Hill [1995; 81] observed, if either prices are proportional (recall Hicks' [1946; 312-313] Aggregation Theorem) or quantities are proportional (recall Leontief's [1936; 54-57] Aggregation Theorem), then the variability measure V_H defined by (65) attains its lower bound of 0. Note also that if we interchange periods, V_H remains unchanged; i.e., it satisfies the base period invariance property (53).

If x is close to 1, then $\ln x$ can be closely approximated by the first order approximation, $x-1$. Hence the Hill variability measure V_H can be approximated by the following measure:

$$(68) \quad \overline{V}(p^s,p^t,q^s,q^t) \equiv [(P_L/P_P)-1] = [(Q_L/Q_P)-1].$$

This variability measure has the same mathematical properties that were noted for V_H. Both measures are base period invariant measures of the spread between the Paasche and Laspeyres price (or quantity) indexes; both measures are approximately equal to the absolute value of the percentage difference between the Paasche and Laspeyres indexes. From the viewpoint of the test approach to index numbers, Bowley [1901; 227], Fisher [1922; 403] and Diewert [1992a; 219-220] proposed that the price index P should be between the Paasche and Laspeyres price indexes. These bounds are also valid from the economic point of view if we have a homothetic or linearly homogeneous aggregator function. Thus the variability measures defined by (65) and (68) provide convenient methods of describing the width of these index number bounds.

Note that the variability or nonproportionality measures V_H and V do not depend on a particular index number formula P. However, if the index number formula P is a symmetric mean of the Paasche and Laspeyres indexes (e.g., $P = (P_L P_P)^{1/2}$, the Fisher Walsh ideal index), then P will lie between P_L and P_P and V_H or $\overline{V}$ may be used as reliability measures for P.

We have presented three classes of dispersion measures (see (51), (62) and (65) or (68) above) that could be used to measure the reliability of an index number formula. The use of (62), (65) or (68) as measures of dispersion would meet some of the criticisms of the test and economic approaches that have been made by the proponents of the stochastic approach. If all of the relative prices were identical, the above dispersion measures would attain their lower bounds of zero, but if the price relatives were dispersed, nonzero measures of dispersion or variability would be obtained if (51) or (62) were used.

It is now almost 75 years after Walsh [1921] made his comments on the diversity of approaches to index number theory and economists are still "at loggerheads." However, perhaps this diversity is a good thing. The new stochastic approach to index numbers has at least caused this proponent of the test and economic approaches to think more deeply about the foundations of the subject.

References

Adelman, I. [1958], "A New Approach to the Construction of Index Numbers," *Review of Economics and Statistics* 40, 240-249.

Afriat, S.N. [1972], "The Theory of International Comparisons of Real Income and Prices," pp. 13-69 in D.J. Daly (ed.), *International Comparisons of Prices and Outputs*, New York: Columbia University Press.

Allen, R.C. and W.E. Diewert [1981], "Direct versus Implicit Superlative Index Number Formulae," *The Review of Economics and Statistics* 63, 430-435.

Balk, B.M. [1980], "A Method for Constructing Price Indices for Seasonal Commodities," *Journal of the Royal Statistical Society* A, 143, 68-75.

Bowley, A.L. [1901], *Elements of Statistics*, Westminster England: P.S. King and Son.

Bowley, A.L. [1911], "The Measurement of the Accuracy of an Average," *Journal of the Royal Statistical Society* 75, 77-88.

Bowley, A.L. [1919], "The Measurement of Changes in the Cost of Living," *Journal of the Royal Statistical Society* 82, 343-372.

Bowley, A.L. [1926], "The Influence on the Precision of Index-Numbers of Correlation between the Prices of Commodities," *Journal of the Royal Statistical Society* 89, 300-319.

Bowley, A.L. [1928], "Notes on Index Numbers," *The Economic Journal* 38, 216-237.

Bryan, M.F. and S.G. Cecchetti [1993], "The Consumer Price Index as a Measure of Inflation," *Economic Review, Federal Reserve Bank of Cleveland* 29, 15-24.

Bureau of Labor Statistics [1988], *BLS Handbook of Methods*, Bulletin 2285, Washington: U.S. Government Printing Office.

Carli, Gian-Rinaldo [1764], "Del valore e della proporzione de'metalli monetati," reprinted in pp. 297-336 in *Scrittori classici italiani di economia politica*, Volume 13, Milano: G.G. Destefanis, 1804.

Clements, K.W. and H.Y. Izan [1981], "A Note on Estimating Divisia Index Numbers," *International Economics Review* 22, 745-747.

Clements, K.W. and H.Y. Izan [1987], "The Measurement of Inflation: A Stochastic Approach," *Journal of Business and Economic Statistics* 5, 339-350.

Diewert, W.E. [1974], "Applications of Duality Theory," pp. 106-171 in M.D. Intriligator and D.A. Kendrick (eds.), *Frontiers of Quantitative Economics*, Vol. II, Amsterdam: North-Holland.

Diewert, W.E. [1976], "Exact and Superlative Index Numbers," *Journal of Econometrics* 4, 115-145.

Diewert, W.E. [1978], "Superlative Index Numbers and Consistency in Aggregation," *Econometrica* 46, 883-900.

Diewert, W.E. [1992a], "Fisher Ideal Output, Input and Productivity Indexes Revisited," *The Journal of Productivity Analysis* 3, 211-248.

Diewert, W.E. [1992b], "Exact and Superlative Welfare Change Indicators," *Economic Inquiry* 30, 565-582.

Diewert, W.E. [1993a], "Overview of Volume 1," pp. 1-31 in *Essays in Index Number Theory*, Vol. 1, W.E. Diewert and A.O. Nakamura (eds.). Amsterdam: North-Holland.

Diewert, W.E. [1993b], "The Early History of Price Index Research," pp. 33-65 in *Essays in Index Number Theory*, Vol. 1, W.E. Diewert and A.O. Nakamura (eds.), Amsterdam: North-Holland.

Diewert, W.E. [1993c], "Symmetric Means and Choice Under Uncertainty," pp. 355-433 in *Essays in Index Number Theory*, Vol. 1, W.E. Diewert and A.O. Nakamura (eds.), Amsterdam: North-Holland.

Edgeworth, F.Y. [1887], *Measurement of Change in Value of Money I*, the first Memorandum presented to the British Association for the Advancement of Science; reprinted as pp. 198-259 in *Papers Relating to Political Economy*, Vol. 1, New York: Burt Franklin, 1925.

Edgeworth, F.Y. [1888a], *Tests of Accurate Measurement*, the second Memorandum presented to the British Association for the Advancement of Science; reprinted as pp. 304-343 in *Papers Relating to Political Economy*, Vol. 1, New York: Burt Franklin, 1925.

Edgeworth, F.Y. [1888b], "Some New Methods of Measuring Variation in General Prices," *Journal of the Royal Statistical Society* 51, 346-368.

Edgeworth, F.Y. [1889], *Measurement of Change in Value of Money*, the third Memorandum presented to the British Association for the Advancement of Science; reprinted as pp. 259-297 in *Papers Relating to Political Economy*, Vol. 1, New York: Burt Franklin, 1925.

Edgeworth, F.Y. [1901], "Mr. Walsh on the Measurement of General Exchange Value," *The Economic Journal* 11, 404-416.

Edgeworth, F.Y. [1918], "The Doctrine of Index-Numbers according to Professor Wesley Mitchell," *The Economic Journal* 28, 176-197.

Edgeworth, F.Y. [1923], "Mr. Correa Walsh on the Calculation of Index-Numbers," *Journal of the Royal Statistical Society* 86, 570-590.

Edgeworth, F.Y. [1925], "The Plurality of Index-Numbers," *The Economic Journal* 35, 379-388.

Eichhorn, W. [1978], *Functional Equations in Economics*, Reading, Massachusetts: Addison-Wesley.

Eichhorn, W. and J. Voeller [1976], *Theory of the Price Index*, Berlin: Springer-Verlag.

Fisher, I. [1911], *The Purchasing Power of Money*, London: Macmillan.

Fisher, I. [1921], "The Best Form of Index Number," *Journal of the American Statistical Association* 17, 533-537.

Fisher, I. [1922], *The Making of Index Numbers*, Boston: Houghton Mifflen.

Fisher, I. [1923], "Professor Bowley on Index-Numbers" (with a comment by Bowley), *The Economic Journal* 33, 246-252.

Frisch, R. [1936], "Annual Survey of General Economic Theory: The Problem of Index Numbers," *Econometrica* 4, 1-39.

Hardy, G.H., J.E. Littlewood and E. Polya [1934], *Inequalities*, London: Cambridge University Press.

Hicks, J.R. [1946], *Value and Capital*, Second Edition, Oxford: Clarendon Press.

Hill, R.J. [1995], "Purchasing Power Parity Methods of Making International Comparisons," Ph.D. Thesis, Economics Department, University of British Columbia, Vancouver, Canada.

Jevons, W.S. [1863], "A Serious Fall in the Value of Gold Ascertained and its Social Effects Set Forth," reprinted as pp. 13-118 in *Investigations in Currency and Finance*, London: Macmillan and Co., 1884.

Jevons, W.S. [1865], "The Variation of Prices and the Value of the Currency since 1782," *Journal of the Statistical Society of London* 28, 294-320; reprinted as pp. 119-150, *Investigations in Currency and Finance*, Macmillan and Co., 1884.

Jevons, W.S. [1869], "The Depreciation of Gold," *Journal of the Statistical Society of London* 32, 445-449; reprinted as pp. 151-159 in *Investigations in Currency and Finance*, London: Macmillan and Co., 1884.

Konüs, A.A. [1924], "The Problem of the True Index of the Cost of Living," translated in *Econometrica* 7, (1939), 10-29.

Konüs, A.A. and S.S. Byushgens [1926], "K. Probleme Pokupatelnoi Cili Deneg," *Voprosi Konyunkturi* II:1, 151-172.

Keynes, J.M. [1911], "Comment on the Course of Prices at Home and Abroad, 1890-1910," *Journal of the Royal Statistical Society* 75, 45-47.

Keynes, J.M. [1930], *A Treatise on Money* Vol. 1, New York: Harcourt, Brace and Company.

Kott, P.S. [1984], "A Superpopulation Theory Approach to the Design of Price Index Estimators with Small Sampling Biases," *Journal of Business and Economic Statistics* 2, 83-90.

Leontief, W. [1936], "Composite Commodities and the Problem of Index Numbers," *Econometrica* 4, 39-59.

March, L. [1921], "Les modes de mesure du mouvement général des prix," Metron 1, 57-91.

Marshall, A. [1887], "Remedies for Fluctuations of General Prices," *Contemporary Review* 51, 355-375.

McCarthy, P.J. [1961], "Sampling Considerations in the Construction of Price Indexes with particular Reference to the United States Consumer Price Index," pp. 197-232 in *The Price Statistics of the Federal Government*, George J. Stigler, chairman of commission and editor, New York: National Bureau of Economic Research.

Mills, F.C. [1927], *The Behavior of Prices*, New York: The National Bureau of Economic Research.

Mitchell, W.C. [1921], "The Making and Using of Index Numbers," pp. 7-114 in *Index Numbers of Wholesale Prices in the United States and Foreign Countries*, Revision of Bulletin 173, Bureau of Labor Statistics, Washington D.C.: Government Printing Office.

Mudgett, B.D. [1951], *Index Numbers*, New York: John Wiley and Sons.

Persons, W.M. [1928], *The Construction of Index Numbers*, Cambridge, Massachusetts: The Riverside Press.

Pollak, R.A. [1989], *The Theory of the Cost-of-Living Index*, Oxford: Oxford University Press.

Samuelson, P.A. and S. Swamy [1974], "Invariant Economic Index Numbers and Canonical Duality: Survey and Synthesis," *American Economic Review*, 24, 566-597.

Selvanathan, E.A. and D.S. Prasada Rao [1994], *Index Numbers: A Stochastic Approach*, University of Michigan Press.

Törnqvist, L. [1936], "The Bank of Finland's Consumption Price Index," *Bank of Finland Monthly Bulletin* 10, 1-8.

Walsh, C.M. [1901], *The Measurement of General Exchange Value*, New York: Macmillan and Co.

Walsh, C.M. [1921], *The Problem of Estimation*, London: P.S. King and Son.

Walsh, C.M. [1924], "Professor Edgeworth's Views on Index-Numbers," *Quarterly Journal of Economics* 38, 500-519.

Westergaard, H. [1890], *Die Grundzüge der Theorie der Statistik*, Jena: Gustav Fischer.